Redefining American Literary History

Edited by

A. LaVonne Brown Ruoff and
Jerry W. Ward, Jr.

The Modern Language Association of America
New York   1990

Library of Congress Cataloging-in-Publication Data

Redefining American literary history / edited by A. LaVonne Brown Ruoff and Jerry W. Ward, Jr.

     p.   cm.
    Includes bibliographical references and index.
    ISBN 0-87352-187-0 — ISBN 0-87352-188-9 (pbk.)
      1. American literature—Minority authors—History and criticism. 2. Ethnic groups in literature. 3. Minorities in literature. 4. Ethnicity in literature. 5. America—Literatures. 6. Canon (Literature) I. Ruoff, A. LaVonne Brown. II. Ward, Jerry Washington.
    PS153.M56R4 1990
    810.9'920693—dc20   90-6530

Edna Acosta-Belén, "Puerto Rican Literature in the United States," is reprinted with revisions from *ADE Bulletin* (1988): 56–62. Houston A. Baker, Jr., "Figurations for a New American Literary History: Archaeology, Ideology, and Afro-American Discourse," is reprinted with revisions from *Blues, Ideology, and Afro-American Literature* by permission of the University of Chicago Press. Juan Bruce-Novoa, "Canonical and Noncanonical Texts: A Chicano Case Study," is reprinted with revisions from *Americas* 14.3–4 (1986): 119–35; a portion of the article also appeared in *Council of National Literature Quarterly* 6.1–2 (1983): 13–18. Juan Flores, "Puerto Rican Literature in the United States: Stages and Perspectives," is reprinted with revisions from *ADE Bulletin* 91 (1988): 39–44. Robert Hemenway, "In the American Canon," is a revised version of "The Sacred Canon and Brazzle's Mule," *ADE Bulletin* 73 (1982): 26–32.

Published by The Modern Language Association of America
10 Astor Place, New York, New York 10003-6981

Contents

Introduction

Anyone teaching American literature must at some point confront the issue of a canon. Not surprisingly, growing numbers of teachers have begun to question the works to be included in a literary history of America, the place of works in languages other than English, and the intellectual, cultural, and political implications of selecting certain works and rejecting or ignoring others. Such questions suggest that the study of American literature, the inquiries made about it, and the methods of teaching it warrant thorough reconsideration. In fact, many literature teachers and American writers believe that the history of American literature must be reconstructed. The Committee on the Literatures and Languages of America of the Modern Language Association shares this belief.

Since its inception, this committee, formerly the Commission on Minority Literature, has developed programs and projects that emphasize the need to reconsider the existing canon. Through its 1977 seminars in Native American and African American literatures, co-sponsored with the National Endowment for Humanities, its programs at annual conventions, and volumes of critical essays and course designs published under its sponsorship, the committee has urged that the literary history buttressing a canon of American literature be reconceptualized. These seminars and programs have resulted in the publication of four volumes by the Modern Language Association: *Minority Language and Literature*, edited by Dexter Fisher; *Afro-American Literature: The Reconstruction of Instruction*, edited by Dexter Fisher and Robert B. Stepto; *Three American Literatures*, edited by Houston A. Baker, Jr.; and *Studies in American Indian Literature*, edited by Paula Gunn Allen.

The present volume grew out of the committee's 1981 convention forum The New American Literary History and its allied workshops, which stressed the critical approaches and scholarship necessary to rethinking America's literary history. To be sure, some issues of concern to forum participants had been addressed in *Toward a New American Literary History*. In his essay for that book, "The Cycle and the Roots: National Identity in American Literature," Robert E. Spiller discusses "a cultural model which could be useful in all phases and stages of our effort to understand not only the early but perhaps even the more complex later American identity in literature" (6). However, Spiller's cultural model of the westward frontier movement is predominantly an Anglo-American conception, which, as Spiller himself admits, excludes blacks, Jews, and immigrant groups coming late to this country (15). His conception, which also excludes American Indians, Hispanics, and Asian Americans, still prevails to a large degree among American literary historians and is transmitted to those who will educate future generations.

The committee is convinced that an adequate American literary history requires a model based on a multiethnic and multiracial, rather than a European, theory of culture. Creating a framework for a new American literary history, and for a new pedagogy, requires radical inquiries about the relations between literature and national identity. A redefinition of literary history means expanding canon, forging new critical perspectives, and scrutinizing underlying cultural and ideological assumptions. Above all, it calls for an understanding that American literature is a patchwork quilt created by many hands.

Redefining American Literary History, which includes invited essays as well as papers from the committee's 1981 MLA forum and workshops, emphasizes African American, American Indian, Asian American, Chicano, and Puerto Rican literatures. The first section considers various ways of redefining the American literary canon and its relation to the literatures of minorities and white women. In "The Literatures of America: A Comparative Discipline," Paul Lauter suggests that a comparative approach to American studies will lead us out of the distortions and misunderstandings produced by the traditional view that divides American literature into mainstream and tributary. Harold H. Kolb, Jr., concludes, in "Defining the Canon," that expanding the canon is not a viable solution: choice is mandatory, and "a canon of American literature, however difficult to define, is necessary." It is preferable, Kolb suggests, that we think of the literary canon as a "tiered set of options, relatively stable at one end, relatively open at the other, joined by the possibility of change."

Jarold Ramsey and Robert Hemenway emphasize the need to expand the canon to incorporate minority literatures. In "Thoreau's Last Words—and America's First Literatures," Ramsey reminds us how much American literature has reflected images of American Indians and how little this literature has been influenced by native imaginative traditions. Hemenway's "In the American Canon" proposes that instead of retreating from the gains of the 1960s and 1970s, we must work even harder to include minority writers in the canon of American literature. Hemenway also questions the desirability of a more inclusive but merit-structured canon.

The second section is devoted to the dimensions of orality in American literature. The essays, which examine the traditions and influence of American Indian, Hispanic, and Asian American oral literature, include "The Oral Tradition and the Study of American Literature," by Theresa Meléndez; "His Life in His Tail: The Native American Trickster and the Literature of Possibility," by Andrew Wiget; "The African American Animal Trickster as Hero," by John W. Roberts; "Orality and Hispanic Literature of the United States," by Nicolás Kanellos; "Oral Tradition and Poetic Influence: Two Poets from Greater Mexico," by José E. Limón; and "Oral Tradition in Kingston's *China Men,*" by Linda Ching Sledge. As these essays make clear, oral literatures remain a vibrant force. They continue to be created and performed; in their traditional and contemporary forms, they also influence ethnic writers.

Critical and historical perspectives are the focus of the third section. In "Archaeology, Ideology, and African American Discourse," Houston A. Baker, Jr., discusses how criticism furthers the process of reconceptualization by applying the principles of archaeology of knowledge and rhetorical analysis to African American discourse. Baker examines African American slave narratives for a "fit ideological perspective" on African American literary history, seeking to expose the subtextual dimensions of black discourse. Two essays deal with critical and historical aspects of Hispanic literature. Juan Bruce-Novoa, in "Canonical and Noncanonical Texts: A Chicano Case Study," emphasizes that the current pressure to include Hispanic literature in the American literary canon has caused the mainstream society to expect Hispanic writers and critics to establish their own canon. Bruce-Novoa examines the critical issues, authors, and works involved in setting forth a Chicano canon. Juan Flores provides a historical overview in his essay "Puerto Rican Literature in the United States: Stages and Perspectives."

The other essays in this section consider how writers combine in their works the conventions of American literature and the traditions and themes from their ethnic backgrounds. Amy Ling, in "Chinese American Women Writers: The Tradition behind Maxine Hong Kingston," and Shirley Geok-lin Lim, in "Twelve Asian American Writers: In Search of Self-Definition," survey the themes and genres of major Asian American authors. Two essays—"Three Nineteenth-Century American Indian Autobiographers," by A. LaVonne Brown Ruoff, and "African American Progress-Report Autobiographies," by Frances Smith Foster—examine the development of forms of autobiographies written by American Indians and African Americans in the nineteenth and twentieth centuries, demonstrating the influence of the literary traditions of the spiritual confession, slave narrative, and progress autobiography.

The volume concludes with information helpful for teachers wishing to establish courses or for librarians building library collections. The fourth section contains selected bibliographies of multiethnic (including Hispanic), African American, American Indian, Asian American, Chicano, and Puerto Rican literatures. These bibliographies include works selected by the compilers as well as those cited by the authors of essays. Each bibliography is divided into primary categories such as Bibliographies and Aids to Research, Anthologies and Collections, Primary Works, and Secondary Works. Additional subdivisions are used where relevant. The African American, American Indian, and Chicano bibliographies of anthologies and collections include a subsection on oral literatures. The African American and American Indian bibliographies also include a subsection on autobiographical works. Where sufficient scholarship exists, the sections on secondary works are divided into (1) general works and (2) individual authors. Because of the great amount of scholarship on African American literature, secondary works in that bibliography are primarily limited to books. Though selected, these bibliographies are extensive and are up to date as of 1989. The final two sections list journals and presses that publish works by and about the authors and literatures represented in the volume.

Spellings of the names of American Indian tribes in this volume are those either used in the most recent editions of the *Handbook of North American Indians* or adopted by tribes and linguistic organizations: for example, *Athapaskan* rather than *Athabaskan*,

Algonquian rather than *Algonkian*, *Mashpee* rather than *Marshpee*, *Navajo* rather than *Navaho*, *Nez Perce* rather than *Nez Percé*, *Paiute* rather than *Piute*, *Sauk* rather than *Sac*.

The essays collected here provide starting points for a redefinition of American literary history, especially to the extent that they challenge teachers to probe fundamental questions: What is American? What is literature? What is history? Is one ideology of canon formation better than another? The approaches, of course, are as diverse as the cultures and literary perspectives the writers represent. What links the writers is a commitment to deal with history and attributes of literature in ways that have been slighted in the making of previous literary histories of the United States. The writers urge us to transform our habitual ways of thinking about history, culture, and literature. Nevertheless, the diverse viewpoints can only illustrate how problematic and political the redefinition of American literary history is, shed light on crucial disagreements, and set us off in new directions.

The task of rethinking American literary history by necessity involves an expansion of the canon and a deliberate revision of traditional perspectives. Including what has been excluded by oversight or by design in the American canon is praiseworthy. So too are attempts to eradicate Eurocentric, male biases and to show that all literary histories are social constructions. In practice, the redefinition destroys what Kolb calls "traditional harmonies." It seeks to decenter existing authority and to locate its own authenticity in providing a more judicious description of what is American literature. Its choices are never innocent.

In drawing our attention to the opposing views of E. D. Hirsch and Richard Ohmann on the "difficult political decision of choosing," Kolb identifies what is central in the transformation of our literary thinking: How is the cultural thought of literate Americans to be channeled? Who shall choose for whom? Are teachers of American literature content to be what Ohmann calls "a subordinate but influential class" that might "in a nonrevolutionary period end up conforming root elements of the dominant ideology" (219)? The issue is illuminated, to some degree by what Hirsch proposed in *Cultural Literacy: What Every American Needs to Know*. He recommends that American schools abandon both the "content-neutral ideas of Rousseau and Dewey" and experiments in multicultural education and get on with the business of ensuring "our children's mastery of American literate culture" (18–19). He is convinced that "the connection between mainstream culture and the national written language justifies calling mainstream culture *the* culture of the nation" and assumes that "the traditional forms of literate culture are precisely the most effective instruments of political and social change" (22). So conceived, cultural literacy serves a normalizing function, ensuring a common body of content, information, knowledge, and values.

Concerned with the kinds of cultural literacy transmitted by the study and teaching of American literatures, *Redefining American Literary History* begins to sketch out oppositions to Hirsch's ideas. The redefining project eschews traditional, patriarchal thought about culture and literature, seeking instead explanatory models that account for the multiple voices and experiences that constitute the literature and literary history of the United States. In contrast to Hirsch, and to the traditional Americanists for whom he could be a spokesman, those committed to a redefinition emphasize the idea that American literature is not mainstream, that what everyone needs to know about it may be quite beyond the creation of a canon.

A modification of how we think about and teach American literatures, or some combination we provisionally call American literature, has important consequences for the present and future of the profession, and of literate culture in the United States. Unless we pose fundamental questions about why certain theoretical models of American literary history are accepted as dominant and how we can evolve more effective ones, it is unlikely we will progress toward new knowledge. The editors and the essayists hope that this volume will stimulate serious discussion of these questions among teachers of American literature and be a resource for the new American literary history.

A. LaVonne Brown Ruoff and Jerry W. Ward, Jr.

Works Cited

Hirsch, E. D., Jr. *Cultural Literacy: What Every American Needs to Know.* Boston: Houghton, 1987.

Ohmann, Richard. "The Shaping of a Canon: U.S. Fiction, 1960–75." *Critical Inquiry* 10 (1983): 199–223.

Spiller, Robert E. "The Cycle and the Roots: National Identity in American Literature." *Toward a New American Literary History.* Ed. Louis J. Budd, Edwin H. Cady, and Carol L. Anderson. Durham: Duke UP, 1980. 3–18.

I

Redefining the American Literary Canon

The Literatures of America: A Comparative Discipline

Paul Lauter

An image has long haunted the study of American culture. It limits our thought, shapes our values. We speak of the "mainstream," implying the existence of other work, minor rills and branches. In prose, the writing of men like Emerson, Thoreau, Hawthorne, Melville, James, Eliot, Hemingway, Faulkner, and Bellow constitute the mainstream. Others—writers of color, most women writers, "regional" or "ethnic" writers—might, we said, be assimilated into the mainstream, though probably they would continue to serve as tributaries, interesting and often sparkling but, finally, less important. They would, we assumed, be judged by the standards and aesthetic categories we had developed for the canonical writers. We acknowledged that including in the canon writers like Wharton, Cather, Chopin, and Ralph Ellison might, at best, change somewhat our definition of the mainstream, but the intellectual model based on the Great River theory of American letters has persisted even among mildly revisionist critics (see, e.g., Bercovitch, *Reconstructing*). Such critics have continued to focus on a severely limited canon of "major" writers based on historical and aesthetic categories from this slightly augmented mainstream.

The problem we face is that the model is itself fundamentally misleading. The United States is a heterogeneous society whose cultures, while they overlap in significant respects, also differ in critical ways. A normative model presents variations from the mainstream as abnormal, deviant, lesser, perhaps ultimately unimportant. That kind of standard is no more helpful in the study of culture than is a model, in the study of gender differences, in which the male is considered the norm, or than paradigms, in the study of minority or ethnic social organization and behavior, based on Anglo-American society. What we need, rather, is to pose a comparative model for the study of American literature. That may seem like an odd concept, especially coming from a North American academic. Few branches of academe in the United States have been so self-consciously indifferent to comparative study as has been the field we call "American literature." While we have, for example, studied Spanish or French influences on American writing, and vice versa, we have seldom been trained in any truly comparative discipline, and the academic journals that serve the American literature professoriat certainly offer no comparative perspective. Nevertheless, only what we might call "comparative American studies" will lead us out of the distortions and misunderstandings produced by the mainstream and tributary framework.

This essay presents a strategy for approaching the many and varied literatures of the United States. It is not conceived as an overview of "marginalized" literatures, except to the extent that it underlines certain areas of critical practice that, I think, we must reexamine if we are to contemplate these literatures with accuracy, let alone respond to them with verve. In this sense, what I am presenting may be thought of more as counsel to explorers than as a map of the territory. While parts of the territory are well known, and others are coming into view, what is being found has not yet fully been absorbed or shared. By "marginalized" I designate those writings that, by virtue of their subject matter (e.g., menstruation rather than learning to hunt), function (propagandistic, ceremonial rather than belletristic), formal elements and conventions (improvisational, epistolary rather than organic, dramatic), audience (women, Spanish speakers rather than white men), or other factors, have been esteemed relatively less significant to, not at the center of, the definition of a nation's culture. Marginalized works are, largely, the products of groups who have relatively less access to political, economic, or social power. To say it another way, the works generally considered central to a culture are those composed and promoted by persons from groups holding power within it. Thus, as my definition and my examples suggest, we are concerned with the work of women as well as that of minority men—for while there are profound differences between a culture defined significantly in terms of gender and one defined significantly in terms of race or national origin, nevertheless the burdens and opportunities posed by marginality generate unusually significant parallels. And thus, finally, we are discussing the writing of a *majority* of the people of this nation, a majority whose cultures, I would argue, continue to be less than fully understood or appreciated by virtue of the factors I examine here.

I want to look, first, at conceptions of literary history and the ideas of significance in subject that inform historical constructs. Subsequently, I shall discuss the functions of imaginative writing, and then the problem of evaluating differing forms and conventions. Finally, I shall turn to questions of characteristic patterns of imagery and language, and to audience as a problematic. Of course, I can hardly scratch the surface of these issues, central to critical discourse. My intent, rather, is to illustrate how a comparative approach to the literatures of America can help recast our assumptions about these matters.

An advantage of a comparative model is that it allows us to discard the notion that all literatures produced in this country must be viewed through the critical lenses shaped to examine mainstream—that is, largely white and male—culture. We can then begin to see that, for example, subjects and forms invoked by African American writers are influenced not only by the traditions of Anglo-European literature but by indigenous folk and formal cultures of black communities in the United States and elsewhere. We can note that for many "hyphenated" Americans, the tension between assimilation in and separation from the majority helps define theme and plot—exemplified by the frequent concern with the mulatto, half-breed, greenhorn—a phenomenon largely absent from the work of majority writers. Stepping outside mainstream assumptions, we can ask not whether or how any work fits an established cultural pattern or given formal structure, but rather how it is that people within a particular social group or class—

including white men—speak, sing, write to one another (and perhaps to others) and what are, for them, significant concerns, appropriate forms, desirable artistic goals. Beyond that, the comparative study of American literatures allows us to reexamine traditionally established works from fresh perspectives provided by minority and white female texts. Frederick Douglass's use of books illuminates in quite new ways Emerson's ideas of the value of letters; Harriet Jacobs's [Linda Brent's] years in an attic cast an oblique light on Thoreau's more comfortable notions of simplification, of where one lives and what one lives for; the radically similar cultural origins of works by Stowe and Hawthorne force on us a certain decentering of the latter, a necessary reconstruction of how we understand antebellum fiction. Most of all, a comparative strategy allows us to see Anglo-European, male writing as but one voice, albeit loud and various, in the chorus of "American" culture.

Of course, a comparative study brings its own problems. Indeed, one particular difficulty rises as a main bar to this approach: the limitation of our own training and knowledge. Marge Piercy offers a cautionary portrait of the blinders often imposed by graduate training:

> . . . English is a hierarchical department. . . . We are taught the narrowly defined Tradition, we are taught Structure, we are taught levels of Ambiguity. We are taught that works of art refer exclusively to other works of art and exist in Platonic space. Emotion before art is dirty. We are taught to explicate poems and analyze novels and locate Christ figures and creation myths and Fisher Kings and imagery of the Mass. Sometimes I look up and expect to see stained-glass windows on our classroom. Somewhere over our heads like a grail vision lurks a correct interpretation and a correct style to couch it in. We pick up the irony in the air before we comprehend what there is to be ironic about. (274–75)

In these familiar precincts, where the ironic stance precedes the emotional response and art works are held up for arm's-length scrutiny, what can become of the Toni Morrison's *Bluest Eye* or James Welch's *Winter in the Blood*?

A second set of difficulties arises from the uneven development of the cultures of the United States. "Uneven development" suggests more than the obvious fact that different groups established themselves in this land at quite different times. The term implies, first, a point about chronology: the relationship between the arrival of an immigrant group on these shores and the emergence of a literary (i.e., written) culture (or the beginning of the written articulation of an oral culture) is quite irregular. A literary culture requires, obviously enough, literacy. Only some of the groups that came to this country, or were here, were literate—in their own languages, much less in English. Many immigrants were rural peoples, like this land's original inhabitants, with strongly established but not literary cultures. At the turn of the century, Jewish—at least male— garment workers in New York (as well as Welsh miners in Colorado) were among the most "literary" of immigrant workers. That might help to explain the relatively rapid and widespread emergence of a significantly Jewish, as distinct from a Polish or Italian, literary culture.

Then, too, development of a literary culture requires the diffusion through a group of a set of ideas, particularly the notion that it is possible or valid for a person to devote time to the wonderfully arrogant act of artistic composition. Hawthorne had a good deal to say about that in the "Custom House," though his reflections, particular to his male,

New England, Puritan immigrant heritage, differ strikingly from those, on the one hand, of mid-nineteenth-century women writers, like Caroline Kirkland or Fanny Fern, who felt forced by possible social disapproval to discount their own "scribblings," and, on the other, of Anzia Yezierska in *Red Ribbon on a White Horse*, Tillie Olsen in *Silences*, or Maxine Hong Kingston in *The Woman Warrior*. Finally, a literary culture requires the existence of an audience, a reading public that resonates to the beat of the writers' language and concerns. An audience imbued with ideas about the value of producing literary art *may* provide institutional means for supporting artists, including publishing outlets, networks for distribution, opportunities for artists to concentrate on creation. The importance of such material supports to the evolution of a literary culture can hardly be overestimated (see Madhubuti). Differences in literacy, diffusion of ideas, and means of support help explain why the establishment of literary culture in one group does not predict its development in another.

We can identify a second critical point about "uneven development": literary culture emerges in a minority or marginalized group in part independently of, in part in response to, developments in the majority culture. This comes as no surprise: linguistic traditions differ; concerns and subjects differ; popular oral expressions differ from written; audiences differ; institutions extend their support unevenly. Finally, the functions of culture in the life of a group of people change significantly over time, as social realities and evolving consciousness about them change. For all these reasons, the literary history of the dominant white and male culture will only in a limited degree be a useful account of the development of the varied literary cultures of the United States. A full literary history of this country requires both parallel and integrated accounts of differing literary traditions and thus of differing (and changing) social realities.[1] We are only at the beginning of the creation of such a complex history.

II

The structures of literary study are based, as Geoffrey Hartman has acknowledged, on limited "text milieux" (299). That is, we derive aesthetic and historical theories from a selection of works, often lifted from their historical contexts and quite limited in outlook and even form. In general our choice of these texts is rooted in assumptions based on the particular characteristics of our class, race, and sex, reshaped, to be sure, by the powerful influence exerted—especially over those of us from minority or ethnic origins—by the professors of the dominant culture. From this limited set of texts we project standards of aesthetic excellence as well as the intellectual constructs we call "literary history." And once we have developed such constructs, we view other works in their terms, whether the works originate from that initial "text milieu" or from outside it.[2] That commonplace and hardly conscious procedure helps explain the apparently self-evident character of the canon. It also produces serious distortions in value judgments (as I shall suggest below) as well as in historical accounts of literary development.

Consider, as an example of faulty literary history, what was until the late 1970s the usual portrait of the evolution of fiction in North America (a portrait that still shapes curricular choices). Writers like Charles Brockden Brown, Washington Irving, and James Fenimore Cooper, it was said, were forerunners, who cleared and plowed the colonial cultural wilderness so that, in the "American Renaissance," the first generation of major writers—Poe, Hawthorne, Melville—could flourish. They were succeeded by three generations of fiction writers: Twain and James, who elaborated alternative west-ward-looking and eastward-looking subjects and styles; realists and naturalists, like Howells, Crane, and Dreiser; and finally, in the 1920s, a new, modernist renaissance, exemplified by the work of Faulkner, Hemingway, Fitzgerald, Dos Passos, and a host of others.

If this chronology were a broadly useful historical account, it should illuminate the texts of writers other than those whose work forms its basis. What then might it tell us of the first group of black novelists? William Wells Brown's *Clotel* (1853), Frank Webb's *Garies and Their Friends* (1857), Martin Delany's *Blake* (1859), and Harriet Wilson's *Our Nig* (1859) are roughly contemporaries of *The Scarlet Letter* (1850) and *Moby-Dick* (1851). Read in terms of Hawthorne's and Melville's works, they seem painfully under-developed, in places even crude and propagandistic. But to view them in such a perspec-tive would, I think, be unhelpful and an error in historical understanding. In one sense the novelists are more the contemporaries of a writer like Cooper and share many of his shortcomings—and virtues. For these black writers are only beginning the process of establishing a novelistic style for their culture and of elaborating, in that style, fictional material of consequence to the audience to which they aspire. In another, metaphoric, sense their texts reach back to the semiautobiographical fictions of Elizabethan and Jacobean writers.

But the comparisons with *The Last of the Mohicans* or *The Unfortunate Traveler* are in other respects equally misleading, since they would obscure what were undoubtedly the major cultural influences on these books: the well-established tradition of black slave narratives, the African American oral tradition of tales and legends, and the publi-cation of *Uncle Tom's Cabin* (1852). The narratives and Stowe's novel helped establish and broaden an audience for which reading and writing was integrated with social activism; an audience that responded to images of heroic and adventurous black men and women and was willing to confront the complex realities of the oppression, particu-larly sexual, of black women; that also accepted the very idea of a black *writer*—a problematic conception for many people, even some blacks, in antebellum America. Further, a historical account to which the slave narratives, Stowe, and the black oral tradition are integral helps us understand how, as Richard Yarborough has suggested, black writers sought, during the nineteenth century, to assert through fiction the poten-tial of black people in America and, at the same time, to document and preserve their history.

As the older accounts of American fictional history left us asking, "Where were the blacks?" so they provoked the parallel question "Where were the women?" The work of critics like Elizabeth Ammons, Nina Baym, Hazel Carby, Cathy Davidson, Josephine Donovan, Judith Fetterley, Annette Kolodny, Jane Tompkins, and Mary Helen Wash-ington have begun to answer that question. It poses Stowe as a key figure,[3] in a sense a bridge between the earlier female writers both of realistic and romantic narratives—Susanna Rowson, Catharine Maria Sedgwick, Caroline Kirkland, Fanny Fern, Susan Warner, E. D. E. N. Southworth—and the next generation of realistic writers, women like Rebecca Harding Davis, Elizabeth Stuart Phelps, Rose Terry Cooke, Sarah Orne Jewett, and Mary Wilkins Freeman. These authors turned neither east nor west but, at their finest, focused eyes keen for detail on the constricting material, and often domi-nantly female, worlds they inhabited in New England, New York, and the South. In turn, building consciously on the accomplishments of that previous generation, the women writers of the early twentieth century—Chopin, Wharton, Mary Austin, Glasgow, Cather—produced the most significant novels of the period by engaging the most burning questions of the time—at least for many white women—concerning social, political, and sexual equality for females.

In fact, an account of changing patterns of nineteenth-century women's—and some men's—fiction can be constructed around questions of gender, race, creativity, and power. The novelists of the earlier generation—the subjects of Nina Baym's *Woman's Fiction*—wrote success tales, in which virtue, in the form of constancy, often self-denial, and sometimes devotion to craft generally brought happy endings for the heroines and those who, in effect, they had gathered around themselves. Alcott and Stowe continued to present domestic values as key to ethical life, to public virtue, and, in a story like Alcott's "Psyche's Art," to valid creation. Although women's and men's spheres are separate, the subordination of hearth to countinghouse has not yet, fictionally at least, taken place; indeed, Stowe offers both fictive and theoretical validations of the kitchen as value center. In Jacobs, while the form of self-denial is even more profound, both the meanings of "constancy" and the happiness of the ending are made problematic by virtue of how American culture construes race. In Phelps, the contradictions between countinghouse and the sphere of women become harsher, for in *The Silent Partner* the women are excluded from the sources of economic power, and while Sip and Perley, the two heroines, continue to try to improve the lives of workers, it is not clear whether that project can reach beyond the consolations of Christian charity. In Phelps's later work, like *The Story of Avis* and *Dr. Zay*, the conflicts between domesticity and a woman's art or work heighten; such conflicts remain but are less central to the instructional program of Frances Ellen Watkins Harper's *Iola Leroy*. Jewett sustains the values of an elaborated, extended domestic sphere; indeed, *The Country of the Pointed Firs* emerges as a kind of mythic center of family strength, to which an urban inhabitant may travel for renewal, though she cannot stay. Freeman is even less optimistic, for while many of her women are strong and independent, they are so in a narrowing world, at its bleakest in a story like "Old Woman Magoun," but constricting even in the triumphant "The Revolt of 'Mother.'" The arc of this fictional history can thus be tracked, as it were, from the successes of *Ruth Hall* and Capitola in *The Hidden Hand* to the contrasting fates of the heroines in *The Awakening* and *The House of Mirth*.

Obviously, this account of fictional history is radically at variance with conventional versions. The differences arise, I want to suggest in a moment, from fundamentally divergent understandings of what was, and is, historically significant. But first we need to observe that such differing accounts of literary history are deeply embedded in critical terminology and historical categories. For example, the expression "regionalist" or "local colorist" continues to be applied to Jewett, Freeman, Chopin, Paul Laurence Dunbar, Charles Chesnutt. I think that term marks them as peripheral to the development of a national culture, supposedly one of the major accomplishments of nineteenth-century American letters. But a critical category like "regionalism" is about as useful—and as accurate—in describing these writers as a phrase like "escapist fiction" would be if applied to Poe, Melville, and Twain.[4] Categories like "regionalist"—and, I suspect, "ethnic" or even "minority"—encapsulate particular accounts of literary development; they also embody judgments of the value of writers and works based on assumptions about the importance of particular subjects and certain forms, as well as on differing conceptions of the functions of art and the role of artists.

A similar set of problems arises when we examine the use of a category like "realism." In our culture, the term and its cognates, including "realistic," imply positive, perhaps even weighty, judgments. The older account of white male fictional history that I sketched above suggested that realism somehow arose as a later nineteenth-century dialectical corrective to the romance or fantasy tradition self-consciously developed by Poe, Hawthorne, and Melville. In fact, however, literary historians have demonstrated that the roots of fictional realism can be found in earlier nineteenth-century women writers like Kirkland, Alice Cary, and Susan Warner (Fetterley; Tompkins; Donovan). Kirkland described her book *A New Home . . . Who'll Follow* (1839) as a "rough picture . . . pentagraphed from the life," dealing with "common-place occurrences—mere gossip about every-day people." Fetterley points out that Kirkland specifically dissociated herself from the dominantly male tradition of adventure, mystery, and romance because she chose to tell the story of the frontier from the diurnal perspective of a woman plunged into its not very glamorous woods and fields—or, rather, its mudholes and hovels. Similarly, Alfred Habegger has traced some of the ways in which the dominantly female practice of realism in mid-nineteenth-century America shaped the fictional strategy of the later male writers that critics have traditionally described as "realists."

What is at stake here is not simply a revisionist claim to prior occupation of valued turf—however significant that might be. The stakes emerge if we begin from Toni Morrison's proposition that narrative is "the principal way in which human knowledge is made accessible." The issue is, then, what of human knowledge a particular set of narratives—a canon or a historical construct—encodes, makes accessible—or obscures. In a certain sense, the effect if not the design of literary history is to make it seem self-evident that the kinds of problems worked out in the texts it considers constitute the universe of significant issues. The "territory ahead"—at least as it came to be defined as the grounds for the encounter of lone individuals with nature—was for clear material reasons far more of a presence in white male imagination during the middle and late nineteenth century—and for ideological reasons again in the 1920s. Before the Civil War, Horace Greeley's injunction to "Go west, young *man*" simply voiced what had become a commonplace of action among many men. With the decline of farming, fishing, and trade in much of New England after the war, with the increased mobility and entrepreneurial opportunities stimulated by the war, the railroads, and that westering ideology, many Yankee men struck out for new frontiers or imagined what it meant to do so. It would not therefore be surprising if images encoding that theme characterized the work of white male writers, like Poe, Melville, Twain, Harte, Crane, Norris, London, Richard Harding Davis—or reengaged the interests of male intellectuals, professors, and critics after the First World War, when a definition of a "masculine" role on the world stage for the United States was being created.

American Indians, like William Apes, Elias Boudinot, Black Hawk, shared a vision of the importance of the frontier, but in their experience it was often represented as the intrusion of the boots of a giant into the grounds of their hunt and the graves of their people. For antebellum black writers, the frontier was located as much at the Mason-Dixon Line as anywhere else, and the perilous journey from slavery to selfhood the major concern. In time, to be sure, it became clear that the psychological boundaries presented by color prejudice were more difficult to surmount than the geographical divide between North and South. In such contexts, individual confrontations with whales or wars were never central, for the issue was neither metaphysics nor nature but the social constructions called "prejudice," and the problem was not soluble by or for individuals (except the very few who could and wished to "pass"), but only through a process of *social* change.

For women, the great question of life might be that addressed by Jewett in "Aunt Cynthy Dallett" or in "The Foreigner": that is, how to build and sustain a largely female community in the face of poverty, narrowness, even pride. Or it might be the problem, addressed by Freeman in "A Church Mouse" or "The Revolt of 'Mother,'" or, very differently, by Jacobs in *Incidents in the Life of a Slave Girl*, of how the weak achieve through disobedience a modicum of power. Such concerns after a half-century in which they were taken to be trivial, have, as I need hardly say, returned to prominence, and with them works that encode and interpret them. I don't want to belabor the obvious, but the canon is, after all, a construct, like a history text, expressing what a society reads back into the past as important to its future.

My intent is not to deny the significance of defining an isolated, heroic self against the forces of nature—a theme, as we all know, peculiarly persistent in the Romantic fictions of American white males that have constituted the received canon. That problem was, no doubt, of both real and symbolic consequence to American entrepreneurs well into the twentieth century. And the ideological manifestations of Romantic individualism remain so. But equally substantial and interesting are the social issues: the prices paid, often by women, for men's upward, or outward, mobility, the sacrifices of community to self, the difficulties of sustaining community. Moreover, the conceptions of self and the processes of definition as they emerge for Deerslayer, Ishmael, Huck, Nick Adams, Ike McCaslin differ sharply from those we encounter in the work of many minority writers, where the problematic of self consists more often of its emergence within conflicting definitions of community and continuity, as is the case in Zora Neale Hurston's *Their Eyes Were Watching God*, Kingston's *Woman Warrior*, Rudolfo Anaya's *Bless Me, Ultima*, or John Joseph Mathews's *Sundown*.

What is at stake here can, I think, be apprehended in two related passages, the first from the introductory material of Leslie Marmon Silko's *Ceremony*, the second from Meridel Le Sueur's *Girl*:

> You don't have anything
> if you don't have the stories.

> Their evil is mighty
> but it can't stand up to our stories.
> So they try to destroy the stories
> let the stories be confused or forgotten.
> They would like that
> They would be happy
> Because we would be defenseless then. (2; 1978)

And from *The Girl*:

> Memory is all we got, I cried, we got to remember. We got to remember everything. It is
> the glory, Amelia said, the glory. We got to remember to be able to fight. Got to write
> down the names. Make a list. Nobody can be forgotten. They know if we don't remember
> we can't point them out. They got their guilt wiped out. The last thing they take is
> memory. (142)

From this perspective, what is involved in literary history is survival.[5] If that seems an
aggrandizement of what writers and critics do, consider at the simplest level the history
in this century of works like Frederick Douglass's *Narrative*, Rebecca Harding Davis's
Life in the Iron Mills, or Charlotte Perkins Gilman's "The Yellow Wallpaper." In 1965
they were virtually extinct as literary works; they addressed concerns remote from those
at the core of the cultural mainstream. That they are now enshrined in American
literature anthologies testifies to the force exerted on literary history by political movements. Indeed, when I speak of "survival" here, I refer not so much to these works in
themselves as to the knowledge they make accessible, the experiences to which they
give expression and shape—experiences that enable new generations to comprehend
themselves and their world.

What I have thus far said suggests a view of the function of art, indeed a functional
perspective *on* art, perhaps uncongenial to those of us brought up on formalist paradigms. I wish now to turn directly to that concern, for it is indeed true that conceiving
American literature as a comparative discipline implies some differing perspectives on
what it is that literary works attempt to do in our world.

III

Like many minority writers, Charles Chesnutt was extraordinarily sensitive to questions
of the functions of art as well as to the status of artists from marginalized groups. For
many years, he was regarded as a local colorist, a writer of humorous dialect tales, and,
because of his focus on the "tragic mulatto" in his supposedly more serious work, a
writer central to neither black nor white fictional concerns. In *The Conjure Woman*
Chesnutt himself compares versions of the roles of a literary artist and poses a distinctive role for the African American writer. The narrator of that book is a liberal white
Northerner, John, who has moved to North Carolina in part for the sake of his wife's
health and in part to try his hand at making money through grape cultivation. Resident
on the land John buys and deeply knowledgeable about it is Uncle Julius, an elderly
black man, former slave, teller of tales, and sometime coachman for John and his wife,
Annie. John views Julius with something of the well-meaning condescension of a turn-
of-the-century white literary critic toward a black artist. On the one hand, Julius's
stories serve to while away the long southern hours, and in particular to distract Annie
from the meaninglessness of her life. On the other hand, as John sees it, Julius's stories
are a means by which the old man, generally by winning Annie's response, is able to
extract from John a living or some kind of concession for himself or his relatives. For
John, Julius's art is a kind of minstrelsy, an amusement for his hearers and a source of
income, or at least livelihood, for himself. Serious art is the kind of novel John reads to

Annie—in the vain hope of rousing her from the depression into which she increasingly and fearfully sinks as the book progresses.

In certain respects, the key story in the structure of *The Conjure Woman* is "Sis' Becky's Pickaninny," a tale in which the conjurer uses a hummingbird and a hornet, among other creatures, to reunite Sis' Becky with her child and thus restore her to health. In the course of the narration, Annie—like Sis' Becky in Julius's tale—is moved from a threatening illness toward recovery. The vital ingredient in that cure is the magic *of* Julius's story, clearly presented by Chesnutt as parallel to the conjurer's magic *in* Julius's story and symbolized by the rabbit's foot Julius carries. To John, the rabbit's foot represents merely the superstition of a race barely emerging from primitive backwardness:

> "Julius," I observed, half to him and half to my wife, "your people will never rise in the world until they throw off these childish superstitions and learn to live by the light of reason and common sense. How absurd to imagine that the forefoot of a poor dead rabbit, with which he timorously felt his way along through a life surrounded by snares and pitfalls, beset by enemies on every hand, can promote happiness or success, or ward off failure or misfortune!" (135)

Similarly, while John perceives the invigorating impact of Julius's tale upon Annie, he cannot understand the source of its power for her, much less the significance of the rabbit's foot itself.

> My wife had listened to this story with greater interest than she had manifested in any subject for several days. I had watched her furtively from time to time during the recital, and had observed the play of her countenance. It had expressed in turn sympathy, indignation, pity, and at the end lively satisfaction.
>
> "That is a very ingenious fairy tale, Julius," I said, "and we are much obliged to you."
>
> "Why, John!" said my wife severely, "the story bears the stamp of truth, if ever a story did."
>
> "Yes," I replied, "especially the humming-bird episode, and the mocking-bird digression, to say nothing of the doings of the hornet and the sparrow."
>
> "Oh, well, I don't care," she rejoined, with delightful animation; "those are mere ornamental details and not all essential. The story is true to nature, and might have happened half a hundred times, and no doubt did happen, in those horrid days before the war."
>
> "By the way, Julius," I remarked, "your story doesn't establish what you started out to prove,—that a rabbit's foot brings good luck."
>
> "Hit's plain 'nuff ter me, suh," replied Julius. "I bet young missis dere kin 'splain it herse'f."
>
> "I rather suspect," replied my wife promptly, "that Sis' Becky had no rabbit's foot."
>
> "You is hit de bull's eye de fus' fire, ma'm," assented Julius. (158–60)

Annie responds to the feelings communicated by the tale, rather than to its "mere ornamental details"; in the same spirit, she accepts the rabbit's foot from Julius and proceeds in the book's final story to make common cause with him—thus establishing, as it were, a community of feeling to which John is largely marginal. It seems clear to me that Chesnutt is proposing the conjurer/Uncle Julius as a model for the work of the African American creative artist.[6] Yes, an entertainer, and yes, of necessity concerned with survival, the artist is in this vision most fundamentally committed to creating health, and especially "right feeling" (to use Stowe's phrase) about race and history, in the audience through the magic of art. "Right feeling" lies at the root of "right actions," and it is right actions in the world to which those who emphasize the social functions of art are committed. The careers, as well as the writings, of Chesnutt's contemporaries Frances Harper and W. E. B. Du Bois embody similar conceptions of prose driven by the engine of social reform—though they were, of course, more activists than Chesnutt. This basic understanding of artistic function has, I think, been asserted, contested, transformed throughout the history of African American letters—and of other minority communities as well. Such ideas played a critical role in the Black Arts movement and in the emergence of Chicano and Puertorriqueño literature in the 1960s. They reemerge, as Alice Walker's "faith in the power of the written word to reach, to teach, to empower and encourage—to change and save lives" (*New York Times Book Review*).

My point here is less to argue the validity of such conceptions of the social functions of the writer than to pose them against the more generally accepted view of artistic achievement, and to suggest the implications of this distinction for the development of aesthetic theory and artistic practice among marginalized writers in the United States. In "The Art of Fiction," published just as Chesnutt began to reach his stride as a writer, Henry James states as succinctly as anyone has a contrasting view of art—especially of fiction, but of painting and history quite as well. James's fundamental assertion is that fiction, like history, is an attempt "to represent and illustrate the past, the actions of men. . . . " He has little patience with a moral view of the purpose of fiction. "What is the meaning," he asks,

> of your mortality and your conscious moral purpose? Will you not define your terms and explain how (a novel being a picture) a picture can be either moral or immoral? You wish to paint a moral picture or carve a moral statue: will you not tell us how you would set about it? We are discussing the Art of Fiction; questions of art are questions (in the widest sense) of execution; questions of morality are quite another affair, and will you not let us see how it is that you find it so easy to mix them up? (94–95)

Chesnutt had some answers to James's questions. In an often-cited passage in his journal, he posed the aspirations he had set for himself as a literary artist:

> The object of my writings would not be so much the elevation of the colored people as the elevation of the white—for I consider the unjust spirit of caste which is so insidious as to pervade a whole nation, and so powerful as to subject a whole race and all connected with it to scorn and social ostracism—I consider this a barrier to the moral progress of the American people; and I would be one of the first to head a determined, organized crusade against it. Not a fierce indiscriminate onset, not an appeal to force, for this is something that force can but slightly affect, but a moral revolution which must be brought about in a different manner. . . .
>
> This work is of a two-fold character. The negro's part is to prepare himself for recognition and equality, and it is the province of literature to open the way for him to get it—to accustom the public mind to the idea; to lead people on, imperceptibly, unconsciously, step by step, to the desired state of feeling. If I can do anything to further this work, and can see any likelihood of obtaining success in it, I would gladly devote my life to it. (8)

Chesnutt sustained this sense of vocation—together with the desire to become rich and famous by writing—throughout his career, even as he perforce observed the failure of prose to contain the rising tide of turn-of-the-century racism.

It should come as no surprise that from the perspective of minority or marginalized groups, art should have a more clearly social, perhaps utilitarian, function. In one of his letters Bartolomeo Vanzetti writes, "[O]ur friends must speak loudly to be heard by our murderers, our enemies have only to whisper or even be silent to be understood" (Sacco and Vanzetti 277). Vanzetti is explaining how the imbalance of social and political power requires demonstrative behavior if a group of Italian anarchists is ever to be noticed, much less responded to, in Yankee New England, but what he says is suggestive about marginality more generally. The struggle for survival, for space and hope, commands all the limited resources available to a marginalized people. Art cannot stand outside that struggle; on the contrary, it must play an important role in it.[7]

It will be instructive in elaborating a comparative study of literary culture to examine how art has functioned in the sustenance of marginalized communities. In "Poetry of the Colorado Miners, 1903–1906," Dan Tannacito has, for example, examined the role of poetry and song in the organization of western miners during the early years of this century. In *Black Culture and Black Consciousness* Lawrence Levine discusses the varied ways in which song has been used in black communities during and after slavery. A different set of instances is provided by the development in the 1960s of newspapers like *El Malcriado* and *El Grito del Norte*, of El Teatro Campesino, and of a variety of other community-based institutions of Chicano culture. Commenting on the poetry published in *El Malcriado*, Tomás Ybarra-Frausto has written that its primary "function was to sustain the spirit of struggle while simultaneously evoking aesthetic response" (85). Similarly, Luis Valdez, the founder of El Teatro Campesino, saw specifically social functions for the work of the troupe. The Actos, he wrote, "(1) inspire the audience to social action, (2) illuminate specific points about social problems, (3) show or hint at a solution, and (4) express what people are thinking" (qtd. by Ybarra-Frausto from *Actos* 87). Cultural activity thus becomes part of a process for transforming people from passive sufferers into activists in struggle.

This is, however, only one of the roles art may play in a community. Artistic function must be considered within a historical context, as well as in terms of the specific audience to which a work is directed. I shall have more to say about audience later. As to history, it is plain that if art performs social functions, those functions may change as a society or a community within it changes. One need only lay side by side Wigglesworth's "Day of Doom," Whitman's "Song of Myself," and Eliot's "Wasteland" to observe profound alterations in poetic function—as well, of course, as in form. One cannot, then, simply say that "art functions in thus and such a fashion for minority communities." One needs, rather, to say that in certain periods art may help unify and stir a people; in others it may express sustaining beliefs; in still others it may help arouse the awareness of those outside a group; in yet others it may come to be a mode primarily of individual expression and self-actualization. In some periods art may serve all these purposes. My point, then, is the need to be aware not only of the varieties of artistic function but of its changing character over time.

In a certain sense, the issue posed between Chesnutt and Valdez, on the one hand, and James, on the other, is less a conflict over hostile theories of art than a difference over what one looks at in the process of creating and experiencing art. James focuses attention on the polishing of technique, the shaping of the forms by which a work achieves the "solidity of specification" he regards as the truest measure of artistic achievement. Lying behind his point of view is the assumption that artists are people much like himself and that they address people much like himself, that art emerges from fineness of sensibility and intelligence and helps hone a like refinement in its audience. The poets and painters of the ethnic cultural movements of the 1960s and 1970s, like their predecessors, were by no means indifferent to form; on the contrary, in meetings and in print they discussed formal issues, the elaboration of technique, and the need to balance the demands of social activism and those of aesthetic excellence. But the primary concern was, in the first instance, how the *creation* of art helps its creators emerge from passivity and indifference before the world—and then, on the other side of the creative work, so to speak, the *impact* of the work on the consciousness of those who experience it. Creator and audience—James speaks little of them except to urge the young novelist to "catch the color of life," and to shrug, regarding the reader, that there's no disputing taste. But for most people, and especially those from poor and minority communities, art cannot be contemplated, as it were, only from within.[8]

From another point of view, however, we are facing quite distinct artistic theories. That becomes clear when we realize that the usual standards of aesthetic merit are, as James proposes, the form and language of a text. "Truth of detail," James says, "the air of reality (solidity of specification)" constitute "the supreme virtue of a novel—the merit on which all its other merits (including that conscious moral purpose of which Mr. Besant speaks) helplessly and submissively depend. . . . The cultivation of this success, the study of this exquisite process, form, to my taste, the beginning and the end of the art of the novelist" (85).[9]

"To what end," Chesnutt might have responded, "should a writer 'catch the color . . . the substance of the human spectacle'? Is not merit determined by the capacity of a work to engage genuine feelings and thus to open us to others' lives, and worlds, and needs? Even to prod us to action *in* the world?"

With that idea, James would show little patience. Speaking in what emerges as his own voice, he writes:

> I needn't remind you that there are all sorts of tastes: who can know it better? Some people, for excellent reasons, don't like to read about carpenters; others, for reasons even better, don't like to read about courtesans. Many object to Americans. Others (I believe they are mainly editors and publishers) won't look at Italians. . . . [Readers] choose their novels accordingly, and if they don't care about your idea they won't, a fortiori, care about your treatment.
>
> So that it comes back very quickly, as I have said, to the liking: in spite of M. Zola . . . who will not reconcile himself to this absoluteness of taste, thinking that there are certain things that people ought to like, and that they can be made to like. . . . Selection will be sure to take care of itself, for it has a constant motive behind it. That motive is simply experience. As people feel life, so they will feel the art that is most closely related to it. (89–90)

James speaks with the ease of one whose subjects, at least many of them, will suit the interest and taste, will register the experience of his audience. But that presumption is not universally shared. The artist from a marginal group can by no means rely on readers feeling the life that throbs in the world of the carpenter or the Italian. Indeed, the very first battle this artist must fight is precisely that defined by Zola: making readers like or, more to the point, find interest in, matters and people quite outside their experience.[10]

There are different ways in which you can respond to the perception that your audience may find your subject not to its taste: you *can* try to persuade your readers, by novelty, expostulation, or seduction, to take an interest in the case; you can set fresh banners snapping in the wind; you can extend a calming hand, leading quietly down the unfamiliar, rutted path. It may all come to nothing. Your choice may be to settle upon a circle of devotees, running the risk of becoming merely precious to them—and yourself. Or you may lapse, in Tillie Olsen's apt word, into "silences."

The question of function is thus critically related, on the one hand, to subject and, on the other, to audience. The emphasis on form, which has dominated criticism and teaching since the 1920s, obscures these connections. Formalist critics concentrate on tracing the lineaments and dimensions of a book's structure, and they judge a work as a more or less fully realized aesthetic object, as a picture that "renders the look of things" (James 85), a world in itself. The alternative we have been tracing asks whether the work acts effectively *in* the world, of which it and we constitute parts, by touching human feeling and shaping consciousness. Recent reader-response criticism has, once again, begun to examine the experience of literature in terms of its power to influence consciousness and shape concepts of self (see, e.g., Alcorn and Bracher). It seems to me likely that such a trend will be enhanced by the need to reconstruct the role of criticism implicit in a comparative approach to the literatures of the United States.

In thus balancing the emphasis on form and structure with a concern for subject, feeling, audience, and impact, I would not wish to be taken as suggesting an indifference to form on the part of marginalized writers. On the contrary, as I wish now to propose, formal questions are critical to a comparative study. At issue are the forms and structures organic to the work of marginalized writers and the way elements may differ from those in the literary tradition represented by Henry James and his successors.

IV

Few elements of human creativity are as hierarchically organized as presentational language. We have, implicitly or explicitly, a Received Standard form of speech and dialects, which mark lower class or provinciality. Certain languages—French, for example—have carried more status for English speakers than others—Spanish, for example. In prosody, we value complexity, ambiguity, irony over simplicity, directness, transparency; written, fixed forms over oral, improvisational; the formal genres we call "fine arts" over the "practical" we call "crafts" or "fragmentary genres," like letters. Thus we learn to place epic poetry at the apogee of forms. Below it, ranging down a great chain of types, we find dramatic and lyric poetry, the novel, short fiction; and then, as if crossing into suspect territory, genres like autobiography, journals, letters, transcriptions. The status of genres in some degree informs the status of their professors. In the study of marginalized literatures, however, we need to reexamine—even suspend—our assumptions about formal hierarchy and concentrate on discovering the formal conventions that emerge from those literatures themselves rather than from our training as literary practitioners.

Conventions of composition and language are, after all, largely culture-specific as well as hierarchic. One of the most persistent and dominant patterns in English poetry, for example, is the iambic pentameter line, which may be rooted in stress patterns in the declarative sentence characteristic of Received Standard English. Poetic structures built on this iambic line, like blank verse and the sonnet, exercise a compelling influence on writers, perhaps because authors simply learn to use patterns they hear, read, and study. By contrast, West African–based cultures, including those of black Americans, reflect the importance of a call-and-response pattern of verse construction—as in work songs, the blues, and many hymns. Similarly, code switching (the shifting within a line or sentence from English to Spanish, or the reverse) is important in some Chicano and Puerto Rican poetry—as it can be in street-corner conversation, verbal play, and the creole called Spanglish. Likewise, repetitive forms are vital in American Indian chants and in many poems. Further, the rhythms of black folk English differ from those of Received Standard; obviously, the cadences of non-English primary speakers differ still more.

This is by no means to say that African American writers invariably display the influence of call-and-response patterns, that bilingual poets inevitably switch codes,[11] and that Indian writers must use repetitive forms. No more do they necessarily use folk speech or remain free of the influence of forms like the sonnet. On the contrary, the pulls of traditional English forms and upper-class white standards of speech have been very strong on minority writers, perhaps because such forms implicitly embody the English tradition they often wish to possess. Indeed, the history of each minority culture shows a period in which the artists are influenced deeply by the practice of earlier generations of British or British-actuated authors. Thus most American Indian and African American poetry of the nineteenth and early twentieth centuries imitates Scott, Byron, and Longfellow to excess, and the early black novel sometimes shows the stifling hand of sentimental fictional conventions.

Differences in formal conventions come into particular prominence when we confront those derived from oral and from written traditions. Written literary traditions tend to impose a sacredness on texts that, in turn, produces two primary techniques of literary study: historical and textual analysis, designed initially to establish "true" texts, and *explication de texte*, designed to tease out its many potential meanings. Underlying this view of the sanctity of the written text is a romantic understanding of a literary work as the artist's private product, emerging from the power of his or her genius to express in a distinctive voice responses to a uniquely experienced world. The function of literary study, from this perspective, is to focus the reader's attention on the literary work itself because of its inherent value as an aesthetic structure. Further, change within the frameworks of a written literary culture is often wrenching and violent, as if the new poet had to explode out of the gravity pull of established conventions. Pound's injunction to "make it new" was only, as it were, a codification of what American predecessors like Whitman and Dickinson had practiced, but their difficulties in establishing the value of what they created illustrate my point. Further, the "anxiety of influence" about which Harold Bloom has written may well be a distinctive feature only of dominant written traditions.

By contrast, oral traditions are less obsessed with the sacredness *of* a text, more with its functions, sometimes including its sacred functions, sometimes its functions in sustaining popular resistance to ideological domination. The precise reproduction of a song, poem, or story is probably of less moment than, on the one hand, the maintenance of its basic qualities and, on the other, its vivid re-creation in a new context for a new time and a new need. Improvisation is a major virtue of oral tradition, but it is important to recognize that improvisation is based on known and shared materials. Pound's sense of "make it new"—that is, dispensing with what exists and evoking wholly different texts from differing materials—would probably offend people whose culture is distinctly oral. In *Mules and Men* a woman in one of Zora Neale Hurston's "lieing" contests tells a story to explain why Negroes are black. One of the men, offended by her success, accuses her of inventing the "lie": "'Tain't no such story nowhere. She jus' made dat one up herself." Her friend responds, "Naw, she didn't. I been knowin' dat ole tale"—that is, the story is well established, traditional, and therefore worthy of repeating and staking a claim to.[12] Oral forms also depend on apparent simplicity of structure; on oral-formulaic devices, including repetition of words, phrases, and lines; often on certain stock characters, situations, phrases well known to the original audience. These qualities obviously suggest the needs of performance and of reception by a listening audience, but they are at least in some respects carried over into written genres that continue to reflect oral traditions.

It would be a mistake, however, to suppose that the problem with which we are dealing concerns simply the difference between established written and oral cultures. In the first place, virtually all ethnic and minority literatures in the United States are by now in written form. But more to the point: *all* written cultures represent the transformation and codification of earlier oral cultures; once writing is developed among a people, oral cultures gradually unfold themselves into written form. That is as true of the traditions of British literature as it is of Navajo. Thus, as Ann Fitzgerald has suggested to me, what we are comparing are cultures at different stages in the process of transformation from oral to written. Part of the difference is simply chronological: writing came to Britain twelve to fifteen hundred years ago, but to American Indian tribes as well as to most African Americans, within the last century. But perhaps more important, the processes through which oral forms pass into written forms differ substantially from culture to culture. They invariably involve performance, but the concept of performance that informs Shakespearean drama—still close to British oral traditions—is far different from that which underlies Hurston's *Their Eyes Were Watching God* or N. Scott Momaday's *Way to Rainy Mountain*. The medieval trope and the Elizabethan stage may be cousins, but distant ones, of the AME testimony and preaching and the street-corner theatrics Hurston displays in *Mules and Men*. And these, in turn, only remotely resemble the ceremonies and myths that inform Momaday's narrative.

Still, it is instructive to remember that Shakespeare composed at the nether end of a process of oral-to-written transformation. In their brawling, topical quality, their changeableness from performance to performance, their dependence on traditional subjects and themes, their function in reinforcing recently established social and political norms, in the manner in which their language forever plays against the edges of meaning, his dramas reflect how open they were to the still generative orality of British common culture. These are, many of them, qualities we might expect—indeed will find—in works with which we are concerned here, like those of Hurston, for example, or Morrison and John Wideman. Such writers use, of course, today's most popular genre, the novel, which offers a different set of opportunities and constraints from Elizabethan drama. Within that genre, however, they self-consciously strive to sustain a *voice*, at once elevated and commonplace, serious and linguistically playful. As in oral cultures, success in verbal play confirms artistic power, serves to provide a certain breathing space within the dense and often dark fabric of plot, and registers a kind of ascendancy in the continuing struggle of marginalized cultures to emerge from the shadows. But there is a cost to what Wideman calls "bi-lingual fluency"; he writes in "The Black Writer and the Magic of the Word":

> Afro-Americans must communicate in a written language which in varying degrees is foreign to our oral traditions. You learn the language of power, learn it well enough to read and write but its forms and logic cut you off, separate you from the primal authenticity of your experience, experience whose meaning resides in the first language you speak, the language not only of words but gestures, movements, rules of silence and expressive possibilities, of facial and tactile understanding, a language of immediate, sensual, intimate reciprocity, of communal and self-definition. (28)

In studying texts still tuned to oral cadences, we need to bring back into question some generally unexamined critical assumptions and touchstones. One of these is the idea that a literary work should, so far as possible, be complete in itself, should not have to depend for fulfillment of its intentions on knowledge, ideas, images that the text does not provide. The best fiction, Henry James proposes, "renders" (85) the world it pictures; it is not up to the reader to supply what the text omits. But in many traditional cultures—those of American Indians, for example—the audience for a tale or ritual presentation would a priori be familiar with characters or situations. It would be superfluous, indeed meaningless, for the artists to introduce, describe, and elaborate on what is known and shared, like Coyote and his machinations or the role of the storyteller. Indeed, works like Leslie Marmon Silko's "Storyteller" or "Yellow Woman" vibrate with echoes of such traditional figures. Thus a tale may not be "complete" precisely because the expectation is that the audience will bring to it whatever is left unstated. In fact, when we look closely, we find that the notion of a work of art as self-contained, complete in itself, is a chimera. Any art work plays upon, sometimes against, the expectations, the patterns of knowledge, the assumptions about form and content—not to speak of the conventions of language—an audience brings to it. Thus, whether we are talking about a Henry James novel or a Harlequin romance, the issue is not in this respect whether a work is "fully realized" or not, but what it anticipates an audience will bring to it and what purposes are served by thus depending on what the reader furnishes for the book. That leads to a new set of questions—such as, for example, whether Ellison in *Invisible Man* draws on certain folk traditions of the trickster to differentiate the responses of black and white readers to scenes like those involving Clifton, whether there are in effect "inside" and "outside" readings of his book.

A second set of issues involves how we evaluate texture. As critics of written literature, we have largely ascribed value to organic complexity in structure, ambiguity, and tension in language—each line crafted new, each situation fresh. In "The Metaphysical Poets" T. S. Eliot argues that "poets in our civilization, as it exists at present, must be *difficult.* . . . The poet must become more and more comprehensive, more allusive, more indirect, in order to force, to dislocate if necessary, language into his meaning" (248). Reading such preferences back into the past, Eliot and his successors extolled the virtues of the metaphysical poets; suiting practice to theory (or, perhaps, vice versa), they developed the complex modernist style exemplified by *The Four Quartets*, Pound's *Cantos*, or Hart Crane's "Bridge."

I would not deny the virtues of complex poetic structures, or of the dense, allusive modernist line—in their place. But these are not the only virtues in poetry, nor are they the only means for representing the modern world, much less "our civilization." Indeed, the phrase "our civilization" is itself problematic. Obviously, not all inhabitants of a given space participate in what is defined as "civilization" or, for that matter, have real access to its privileges. "Complexity" in language can be, in fact, a mask for privilege, a screen behind which power sustains itself—in criticism as in poetry. Gwendolyn Brooks had no need for obscurity of language when she sent her poetic sensibility to observe the ordinariness of hate in Little Rock. What image better catches our "civilization" than Langston Hughes's ordinary "raisin in the sun"? Indirection is not at a premium when Judy Grahn writes of the "common woman," or Susan Griffin thinks of Harriet Tubman and the problem of feeding children, or Denise Levertov writes of what the Vietnamese were like. To what extent is the manner in which one uses language dependent upon where one is placed in "our" civilization, or upon one's audience, one's conception of the functions of art?

An artist's outlook on the culture underlies the conventions he or she adopts. Eliot saw his civilization in decline and from its shards and fragments erected a Great Allusive Wall against the impending ruin. In a sense his poems, like Pound's, constitute certain kinds of humanities curricula, "The Rise and Decline of Christian Civilization." That may help to explain the great popularity of their poetry with an earlier generation of academics, as well as the faintly musty quality some of today's critics detect. But there are other assumptions about American culture and thus other ways even of "assembling fragments of experience" from the past—indeed, other conceptions of the fragments suitable for preservation.[13] In studying "women's work" like quilts and blankets, Shiela de Brettville has proposed that their "assemblage of fragments pieced together whenever there is time" has often been organized into a "complex matrix [that] suggests depth and intensity as an alternative to progress (117–18). Vera Norwood has examined the efforts of a number of southwestern women artists to utilize in their contemporary work fragments of the ordinary lives of their foremothers—stitching, pieces of lace, botanical drawings, snatches of letters, diaries, conversations. Rolando Hinojosa's Klail City Death Trip series assembles fragments of imagined south Texas experience, often widely separated in time—newspaper reports, diary entries, narrative accounts—precisely to contest the definition of what constitutes "our civilization" and who will have power within it. Similarly, books as diverse as Momaday's *Way to Rainy Mountain*, Anaya's *Bless Me, Ultima*, and Kingston's *Woman Warrior* are, among other things, efforts to preserve as well as to utilize anew elements of their diverse cultural traditions.

I am not proposing that works by marginalized writers are necessarily simple in language or in structure, or that they inevitably ignore Euro-American traditions. On the contrary, books like Morrison's *Sula*, Walker's *Meridian*, and Silko's *Ceremony*—and, indeed, *Invisible Man*—are structurally rich, and there are dozens of minority poets whose language and imagery operate fully within the modernist mode. Still, we need to understand certain artifacts of critical response: for example, Thomas Pynchon has published three novels, and there are at least a dozen books and untold articles out explaining them. About the group of black women novelists—Gwendolyn Brooks, Paule Marshall, Toni Morrison, Toni Cade Bambara, Alice Walker, Gayl Jones, Gloria Naylor—writing perhaps the most compelling fiction today, there are few works (Christian, *Black Women Novelists* and *Black Feminist Criticism*; Evans, *Black Women Writers*; Pryse and Spillers, *Conjuring*). To be sure, some of the work of these writers is more recent, and the disproportion will no doubt change over time. But to an extent, as critics we have been taught and have learned to "valorize" the pleasures of the epistemological games constructed by writers like Pynchon, Nabokov, and Barth. Let us leave apart the question of whether promoting the virtues of complexity, denseness, and even obscurity, and maintaining an outlook of genteel pessimism, are in some degree functions of sustaining the roles—and jobs—of literary interpreters. We still need to ask whether the expectation, the demand for denseness and speculative play in a work does not disable critics from apprehending other virtues, of transparency in structure, of immediacy in language, of feelings deeply engaged by symbol.

Further, few minority writers can evade the tension imposed by the implicit demand that they appeal to quite differing language and cultural communities. A writer for the *New York Review of Books* can, perhaps, sneer at oral traditions in literature, but minority writers do so, or otherwise detach themselves from the linguistic contexts of their own communities, at peril of drying up the sources of creativity and also validation. Art works can be ranged along a wide spectrum, from those that are most dense, elaborated, to those that are most transparent, straightforward. It seems to me that writers from marginalized groups make use of more bands on this spectrum than those whose reference group is in significant measure academic intellectuals. In reading work produced by writers from marginalized groups, in developing a comparative approach to American literature, we must ourselves widen our perception and appreciation of formal features often different from those we have been trained to acknowledge.

We are only at the beginning of understanding and explaining the pervasive influence of non-European traditions in the forms and conventions developed by minority writers. A number of critics, most notably Sherley Williams and Houston Baker, have examined the interaction of song styles like the blues with the more formal productions of black writers. More recently, the understanding of the impact of call-and-response patterns has been extended to fiction. In "Untroubled Voice" Barbara E. Bowen has convincingly analyzed the structure and development of Jean Toomer's *Cane* in such terms, arguing that the work is most successful "when Toomer opens up for us what it means to turn the call-and-response pattern into a literary form."

Similarly, the subject and aims of Silko's novel *Ceremony* emerge from patterns of repetition with variation. The story of its hero, Tayo, reproduces, albeit with the differences necessary to new times and the remixing of cultures, the "mythic" purification ceremony carried forward by Hummingbird and Fly on behalf of the people, who have strayed after strange and dangerous magic. The language of the mythic and traditional and of post–Second World War ceremonies interpenetrates, especially in seemingly casual phrases—like "it wasn't easy," "it won't be easy," "it isn't easy"— which migrate from the mythic passages of the novel into descriptions of the experiences of Tayo and his aunt. What we discover with Tayo is the commonality of that experience, through time:

The anticipation of what he might find was strung tight in his belly; suddenly the tension snapped and hurled him into the empty room where the ticking of the clock behind the curtains had ceased. He stopped the mare. The silence was inside, in his belly; there was no longer any hurry. The ride into the mountain had branched into all directions of time. He knew then why the oldtimers could only speak of yesterday and tomorrow in terms of the present moment: the only certainty; and this present sense of being was qualified with bare hints of yesterday or tomorrow, by saying, "I go up to the mountain tomorrow." The ck'o'yo Kaup'a'ta somewhere is stacking his gambling sticks and waiting for a visitor; Rocky and I are walking across the ridge in the moonlight; Josiah and Robert are waiting for us. This night is a single night; and there has never been any other. (201)

The book's heuristic objective repeats that of the traditional storyteller: "to fight off / illness and death" (2) by regenerating awareness of pattern and order through the language of ceremonies (cf. Toelken and Scott 88). Repetition, to say it another way, is here not merely a convention of composition but the fundamental principle of psychological and social order, and the book takes on ever-deeper echoes for those familiar with the repetitive patterns of traditional Indian narratives. Thus traditional forms become in more than a metaphorical sense the lifeblood of minority artists.

But the problem of identifying and validating differing forms and conventions extends to the work of white women as well. Elizabeth Ammons, for example, has contrasted the organizing principles of Jewett's *Country of the Pointed Firs* with the "hierarchical mode" of conventional narrative as created by men. Jewett does not use a linear structure, with its built-toward climax coming near the end, but rather what Ammons describes as a "webbed, net-worked" organization, in which the "most highly charged experience of the book . . . comes at the center (85, 89). Further, Ammons argues, "psychically, the aggregative structure of Jewett's narrative reproduces female relational reality" in the process of constructing a female-oriented community. I do not wish here to enter the vexed and problematic issue of the existence of a distinctly female structure or style. What might help illuminate Jewett could obscure her contemporary, Freeman, for she organizes her stories along much more traditional patterns of creating and quickly resolving conflict, even though the concerns of women, mostly poor, are at the center of almost all of the stories. My point is narrower: critics have often asked of Jewett's stories questions drawn from other literary contexts and have thus missed the distinctive organizational strategy with which Jewett was working. Thus she was portrayed as engaging despite her presumed formal shortcomings, rather than seen as important because of her formal innovations.

The issue here is not only differences in the forms and conventions marginalized writers use but the uses to which they put traditional conventions. Point of view is a technical device often employed by Henry James, for example—to produce psychological verisimilitude and intimacy of narrative; Chesnutt uses it in "The Passing of Grandison," however, to raise political consciousness. The story is told from the point of view of a white character *in* it, which necessarily places the predominantly white readership *of* the story outside the head and experiences of the black slave, Grandison. The story seems to be constructed to produce an O. Henry–style surprise ending, in which the slave masters initially celebrate Grandison's unexpected return from Canada. But the ending is less a surprise than a political lesson, for, like the whites in the tale, readers tend to impose their versions of reality on events. Grandison has his own, which emerges only at the story's conclusion, when we find that he had returned only long enough to spirit his whole family off to freedom. If that ending is a surprise—and in the classroom I have found that it almost always is, even for black students—it confirms that the audience knows as little of Grandison as his slave master, a matter for some embarrassed reflections. "The Passing of Grandison" uses the device of point of view and the conventions of the "puttin' on ol' massa" tale to pursue certain social objectives. Alice Walker's *Meridian* offers a more complex instance of how point of view and sliding time frames are used to move readers from detached amusement to informed malaise, and to point outward from the fiction to the world it encourages us to transform. Thus a reconception of forms entails a comparable rethinking of function.

Formal analysis is, and is likely to remain, the meat and potatoes of the literary profession, at least in the classroom. A comparativist strategy compels us to appreciate a broader range of conventions, to set form more fully into historical and functional context, and to comprehend how audience expectation and assumption mandate formal priorities. It is to this last problem, audience, that I now wish briefly to turn.

V

Twenty-five years ago, audience was seldom a problematic in literary study. To be sure, it was important for historians of the drama and for medievalists to establish what kinds of people saw or participated in a performance. And the starting point for work like Ian Watt's on the development of the novel was the recognition of its primarily bourgeois audience. But on the whole, and certainly in the classroom, the responding reader was conceived to be as universal as the work itself. The wide differences in background, assumption, and perception among readers are now a commonplace of literary instruction—or at least of comment about literature, for it is not at all clear how the commonplace translates into changed classroom practice. However that might be, a new style of literary criticism emerged in the 1980s, focused on the implications of reader response to texts. While this criticism may have had its origins in psycholinguistic concerns, it seems to me to have evolved precisely because it registers a central reality that is also vital to the comparative study of American literatures: the diversity of audience response to literature in late twentieth-century America.

That diversity, as I have suggested elsewhere in this paper, arises from the disparity in cultural histories and needs of the heterogeneous population of this country. Increasingly since the 1970s, that heterogeneity has been reflected in college and university classrooms and, in some degree, in changing American literature curricula (see Lauter, *Reconstructing*). Most instructors, however, continue to regard the classroom as a neutral ground for literary study, within which differing works can, whatever the context of their original articulation, be studied with equal success and without a great deal of attention to differences among students apart from the levels of their literacy. In fact, however, the classroom is hardly neutral territory for literary study, since its character privileges certain kinds of texts—particularly those that offer rich and ambiguous possibilities for interpretation—and strips others of their functional qualities—like those that are parts of rituals and performances, or those with heavily defined historical missions and contexts. Equally to our point here: while it would be foolish to deny the literary handicaps many of our students face, it would be equally dangerous not to see that they have substantially different cultural outlooks and diverse expectations—however unarticulated—about art. To say this another way: the recognition of how audiences for art differ in assumptions and desires has been pressed upon many literary practitioners by the fact of classroom diversity.

In confronting audience diversity, teachers and critics of literature are in a sense departing down a road long traveled by marginalized writers. Both for practical and for ideological reasons, minority writers have, since the earliest colonies, had to contend with—even if they finally chose to ignore—disparities between readers from the majority culture and those from their own cultures. Until the turn of the twentieth century, and probably into the 1920s, few minority writers—mainly journalists and pamphleteers—could afford to confine themselves to readers from their own group. Black readership, for example, was too limited to provide practical vocations for artists like Chesnutt, Dunbar (who turned to musical theater), Frances Harper (who earned a living as organizer and educator), or even Pauline Hopkins, though she published with a black-run press. Only in the 1920s, with the increasing concentration, in northern urban centers, of blacks who were at least modestly affluent, and with the self-conscious efforts of men like Charles S. Johnson to interest white publishers in black writers, was it possible for black authors to begin to depend on—and thus be able to speak primarily to—a black constituency. Further, earlier black writers—as we have seen in the case of Chesnutt—*wished* to address a white audience as part of a campaign to establish the personhood of blacks in white consciousness. Thus, in some sense like slang or other verbal games, writing both revealed to and hid from the majority audience qualities of the minority writer's society and experience. As a spiritual might signal "happy darkies" to whites and "prepare for flight" to blacks, so a poem or play could figure both play and rage.

Such generalizations do not, of course, hold for American Indian tribal art forms, whose audiences were groups within the tribe and which, indeed, varied in performance depending upon audience factors—like the age and sex of listeners. Nor are such generalizations applicable to Mexican American writing in the nineteenth and early twentieth centuries. Many authors writing in Spanish in the southwestern United States had their work printed in Spanish-language newspapers whose constituencies identified themselves as Mexican, or at least as "borderers." For such authors, of course, the tensions of addressing a dual audience did not exist, or duality emerged as a function of subject, and perhaps of style. It is thus clearly the case that, in regard to audience, the evolutions of minority literatures are even more different one from another than in other respects and that generalizations are here even more fragile than elsewhere. For minority writers, the major problem of audience appears—at least after some degree of literacy obtains within the group—whenever they choose to speak to those outside the group. But at what point historically that choice becomes important—and, indeed, at what point it seems again to be irrelevant—differs from group to group.

These considerations also apply to the history of white women and white men writers in the United States, though the problems that emerge are clearly distinct. For men like Hawthorne and Melville, as is well known, the difficulty was that many of their potential readers were female and thus, in certain ways like minority writers, they had to address an audience whose culture and expectations partly differed from their own. The resulting tensions seem to have been the source of considerable rage and perhaps a certain duplicity, especially in Melville's stories. For white women there have been other anxieties. In the 1850s and 1860s, writers like Stowe and Alice Cary could converse quite comfortably in their prose with their dominantly female audience. But later, the practice of writing to a definitively female audience, as "lady novelists" were "expected" to do, might ensure the trivialization of one's work, especially in the hands of male critics. Cather seems to have imagined a significantly male audience, whereas at least some of the women modernists may have self-consciously spoken differently to male and to female readers.

For after all, the existence of a dual audience cannot be seen simply as a problem; it is also an opportunity, in at least two respects. First, in ideological terms, it allows an important community role to marginalized writers, as interpreters (even apologists) for their community to the "outside"—the "straight," the "vanilla"—world, even while becoming a source of instruction, delight, and power within. One thinks of writers like Langston Hughes and Adrienne Rich; indeed, this duality of audience helps explain some basic features of, and shifts in, their poetry and prose. The second opportunity is perhaps best suggested by a comment made in "Cultural Mis-readings by American Reviewers" by Maxine Hong Kingston apropos many of the misguided reviews of her first novel:

> The audience of *The Woman Warrior* is also very specific. For example, I address Chinese Americans twice, once at the beginning of the book and once at the end. I ask some questions about what life is like for you, and, happily, you answer. Chinese Americans have written that I explain customs they had not understood. . . . There are puns for Chinese speakers only, and I do not point them out for non-Chinese speakers. There are some visual puns best appreciated by those who write Chinese. I've written jokes in that book so private, only I can get them; I hope I sneaked them in unobtrusively so nobody feels left out. I hope my writing has many layers, as human beings have layers. (65)

The writer, thus addressing multiple audiences, emerges as trickster and clown, deferential and sweet even as she spins away with a grotesque gesture of . . . is it triumph? defiance? invitation? Survival is serious business that, it may be, cannot be taken all too seriously.

In a certain sense, citing Hughes and Kingston in the same paragraph suggests something about the related masks—of simplicity, invisibility, incapacity—minority writers have often chosen to present to at least part of their audience. But the two raise a profoundly contrasting question about audience as well. Hughes wrote regularly in the *Chicago Defender* and in books like *Simple Speaks His Mind* for an extensive black audience. It is not clear, as yet, how widely a writer like Kingston is heard within the Chinese American community. To be sure, the issue of who reads, who listens is not peculiar to marginalized writers. What is distinctive is the question of how, indeed whether, one can aspire to speak, at once, to generalized human concerns and for the particular experiences of a people defined in the world by caste and class and gender. At what, if any, historical moment is Invisible Man's assertion that perhaps "on the lower frequencies, I speak for you" true, or does Rich's "*dream* of a common language" become a reality? Can marginalized writers in practical ways speak both to the communities that nurtured them and to the majority audience that is part of the social and cultural fabric of oppression? When does aspiring toward the latter audience cut one off from the former?

I do not think there are easily generalizable answers to these questions, and the answers change over time. But if the comparative strategy I have been proposing is a sensible approach to marginalized writing in the United States, then surely the problem of audience will be one of its critical foci.

A comparative approach to the literatures of the United States imposes serious scholarly and pedagogical responsibilities upon us. We need to learn about, study, be sensitive to a far broader range of audiences, conventions, functions, histories and subjects than has in general been the case in literary analysis.[14] And while I have touched on such issues here, I have not really addressed the large question of whether there are qualities of language and patterns of imagery distinctive to particular marginalized groups, concerns of consequence to some of our most notable critics today.

In pursuing such tasks, I think we should acknowledge the limitations of our own training. For example, relatively few students of American literature are acquainted with the way oral cultures have influenced writing. But rare indeed are those thoroughly familiar with more than one of the oral traditions of the United States, like those of American Indians and African Americans. Some scholars of Emerson, Thoreau, and Whitman have shown how their work rings of platform and pulpit, but few are also knowledgeable about working-class or minority oral traditions. In fact, a comparative approach could not have been proposed before 1975, because the detailed study of minority, ethnic, or even female cultures had not then sufficiently advanced: too many texts were unavailable or unexamined; little had been done to pose comprehensive theories about African American literary traditions, the "female imagination," the evolution of Chicano literature, and like subjects.

But such work has moved forward rapidly, and while it is not yet adequately reflected in undergraduate, much less in graduate school, curricula, the changes are notable. Further, we can learn from our colleagues in other fields. For example, in approaching literary works still partly moving within the orbit of one or another oral tradition, we can benefit from the modes of studying early English texts. They remind us of how much work in linguistics and cultural and social history we must do in order to encounter the literary works. Beyond that, many feminist and minority critics have perforce trained themselves as comparativists; their work exists as both challenge and lesson for the profession at large. I do not wish to exaggerate the difficulties of this task: if we are, as I suggested at the beginning, not very far advanced in the processes of collective exploration, with commitment we may more rapidly than has seemed possible fill in the map and provide richer understanding of all the literatures of the United States.[15]

Notes

[1] Cf. Sommers; Sommers and Ybarra-Frausto, 37–38; for example, "Logically, then, the trajectory of Chicano literature differs crucially from the mainstream models both of Mexico and the United States."

[2] Thus the objection to most of the narrow graduate and undergraduate reading lists that have characterized the academic study of literature, and to the overemphasis on a limited set of paradigmatic critical texts—for instance, those of Derrida or Barthes. To sharpen the point of this objection, compare the indexes in books of almost any male theoretical critic—structuralist or poststructuralist—with those in any of the recent collections of feminist and African American

critics. The worlds of experience represented by these sets of references differ profoundly, and in some cases absolutely.

[3] For example, Ammons writes: "My thesis throughout is that Stowe's manipulation of maternal ideology is adapted and remodeled in illuminating ways in the work of American women writing before the 1920s and that, taken together, this body of fiction from Stowe forward constitutes a rich female tradition in American literature that challenges the dominant, twentieth-century, academic construction of the canon in terms of the adventure tale and the antisocial, which is to say antifeminine, escape narrative" ("Stowe's Dream" 156).

[4] Donovan has taken a somewhat different tack, attempting to rehabilitate such terms, as the title of one of her books illustrates: *New England Local Color Literature: A Women's Tradition*.

[5] Cf. Toelken and Scott 80. Toelken asks the storyteller, Yellowman, why he narrates the tales. "'If my children hear the stories, they will grow up to be good people; if they don't hear them, they will turn out to be bad.' Why tell them to adults? 'Through the stories everything is made possible.'" Later Toelken and Scott examine the role of ritual (the stories) in establishing health through ordering "an otherwise chaotic scene" (88).

[6] It may be interesting to compare this view of the African American creative artist with Houston Baker's appropriation of Trueblood, in Ellison's *Invisible Man*, to that role, in "To Move."

[7] One can observe this phenomenon even in the most pastoral paintings created by the peasant artists of Solentiname, in Nicaragua. The *subjects* are seldom even remotely political, but the *process* of creating the paintings was a major factor in energizing and mobilizing the people to emerge from their sense of "marginalization" (the term is one they use) and enter the struggle against the Somoza dictatorship. That they could create art meant that they could create change.

[8] Cf. Ybarra-Frausto: "Although the artist was free to experiment with form and content, the 'Plan de Aztlán' called for an art that was functional in extending the political consciousness of its audience. . . . The function of art is to extend and heighten our cognition of the world, its limitations and its potentialities for action. It is not an autonomous, internal mode of individual realization" (94).

[9] A loving but critical comment by Edith Wharton helps underline certain of the limitations of James's outlook: "I sent the book [Proust's *Du côté de chez Swann*] immediately to James, and his letter to me shows how deeply it impressed him. James, at that time, was already an old man and, as I have said, his literary judgments had long been hampered by his increasing preoccupation with the structure of the novel, and his unwillingness to concede that the vital centre (when there was any) could lie elsewhere. Even when I first knew him he read contemporary novels (except Wells's and a few of Conrad's) rarely, and with ill-concealed impatience; and as time passed, and intricate problems of form and structure engrossed him more deeply, it became almost impossible to persuade him that there might be merit in the work of writers apparently insensible to these sterner demands of the art" (*Backward Glance* 323). Cf. her comment on James's own late fiction on p. 190.

[10] In general, many readers are willing enough to become engaged with people of higher status, with more money and power, than they. The problem Zola identifies is, we may say, to engage readers without condescension in a "downward" view.

[11] In fact, as the Chicana poet Lorna Dee Cervantes has pointed out, code switching and other forms of verbal play are rather more characteristic of male Latino poetry than of female.

[12] Cf. Toelken and Scott: "When I asked him if he told the tale exactly the same way each time, he at first answered yes; but when evidence from compared tapes was brought into the discussion, it became clear that he had understood me to be asking him if he changed the nature of the prototype tale of his own volition; the wording was different each time because he recomposes with each performance, simply working from his knowledge of what ought to happen in the story and from his facility with traditional words and phrases connected, in his view, with the business of narrating Ma'i stories. He did not mention it, but it is quite obvious from the tapes

made of his stories when no children were present that the audience plays a central role in the narrative style" (79–80).

[13] Obviously, the debate over the canon, over books like E. D. Hirsch's *Cultural Literacy*, and over former education secretary William Bennett's curricular priorities involves precisely these issues.

[14] Karl Kroeber writes: "In constructing hypothetical relations between their texture, text, and context, we can only *improve* and *extend* our appreciation of the art of the writers and enrich our understanding of the cultures from which their works emerged. Exactly the same exploring processes are appropriate and rewarding for Indian literatures, although often we must start from more basic elements because Indian literatures lack the wealth of earlier studies with which Western works are surrounded. It is our scholarship, not Indian literature, which is 'primitive' or undeveloped" ("An Introduction" 9).

[15] I wish to thank both the Soviet and American participants in the Symposium on Literatures of American Ethnic Groups, Philadelphia, July 1985, for which this paper was originally prepared; Joel Conarroe, president of the Guggenheim Foundation; Andrew Wiget and Elizabeth Ammons for extremely helpful suggestions; and Ann Fitzgerald, without whose persistence and support it would not have been done. A longer and more detailed version of this article appears in my *Canons and Contexts* (Oxford).

Defining the Canon

Harold H. Kolb, Jr.

———

The art of free society consists first in the maintenance of the symbolic code; and secondly in fearlessness of revision, to secure that the code serves . . . an enlightened reason. Those societies which cannot combine reverence to their symbols with freedom of revision must ultimately decay.

A. N. Whitehead

The word *canon*, through its Greek root *kanōn* (rule, rod), is cousin to *cannon* (Greek *kanna*, reed), an appropriate relationship given the battle-scarred history of the concept. For many centuries church scholars debated, as Thomas Norton put it, "what bookes are to be reckened in the canon" of holy Scripture. Secularization of the word *canon* has not diminished the debate. The question of what books are to be required in our schools is, with the exception of salaries, the chief topic of concern among teachers, administrators, and school boards. In colleges and universities, discussions about humanities courses, major programs, and degree requirements often center on the issue of what texts make up the content of apparently protean fields of studies. In the publishing world, pockets are being filled left and right: Norton boasts that its anthology of American literature redresses "the long neglect of women and black writers"; Van Nostrand reports that the company sold over 100,000 copies of McGuffey's *Readers* in a single year.

What is the canon of American literature? And what is the canon of literature from all countries for Americans? What authors and books constitute our cultural heritage? Should Shakespeare be required for all students or only, or even, for all English majors? Has *Paradise Lost* been replaced by *One Flew over the Cuckoo's Nest*? Are great books really timeless, or do civilizations create monuments of aging intellect? Should Richard Wright be included in major-author sections of PhD examinations? Can folklore—especially when understood as performance—be considered part of literature? Is Spanish an American language? Who makes these judgments, and by what criteria? How does change come about?

The difficulty in answering these questions expands in a huge, populous, diverse country whose place names chart a complex history of amalgamation: New England, New Amsterdam, New Orleans, New Madrid, New Berlin, New Mexico. America's strength is a curious mixture of assimilation and diversity—united states—and most discussions of canon lean to one of these poles or the other, to a desire for unity or a celebration of difference. Two important essays illustrate these tendencies, as well as the difficulty of resolution.

In the first of his studies of cultural literacy, E. D. Hirsch reports how his investigation of formal writing skills led him unexpectedly to a new appreciation of content, an appreciation in accord with current psycholinguistic theory which holds that reading is based on prediction and that prediction is organized by everything we know, by what Frank Smith calls "the theory of the world in our heads" (54). Hirsch argues that there is a literacy of content as well as a literacy of skills and that the decline measured by SAT scores results from a "decline in . . . commonly shared knowledge." He advocates the formation of a National Board of Education, which might present lists of literary works, and warns that America "is perhaps getting fragmented enough to lose its coherence as a culture." Hirsch may go too far in recanting his earlier formalist views: "We English teachers tend to believe that a good style is all the more helpful when the content is difficult, but it turns out we are wrong" (160, 163, 167). Many English teachers, I suspect, are not ready to give up that belief, and there is evidence to support them. A study of instructions from judges demonstrates that jurors find bad style the most problematic part of difficult legal content (Charrow and Charrow).[1] But surely Hirsch is correct in focusing our attention on the importance of content in our definitions of literacy and on the "difficult political decision of choosing" the texts that represent our national culture.

Richard Ohmann, in "The Shaping of a Canon," agrees that the selection of texts is a political act, one that embodies "complex social relations and a continuing historical process" (199). But there the agreement stops, for his study suggests conclusions directly opposed to Hirsch's. Ohmann's thesis is that literature in a society controlled by monopoly capitalism is a marketplace commodity "saturated with class values and interests." He claims that a number of successful novels, candidates for eventual inclusion in the canon, were selected, advertised, reviewed—and, for that matter, written—by a small group of business executives and intellectuals, "the Professional-Managerial class," whose values the novels dramatize. While Hirsch advocates standards, Ohmann criticizes the narrow standardization imposed by gate-keeping intellectuals who "went to the same colleges, married one another, lived in the same neighborhoods, talked about the same movies . . . and earned pretty good incomes" (200, 209). Hirsch locates the problem of cultural illiteracy in the "diversity and pluralism now reign[ing] without challenge"; Ohmann argues for greater diversity and more pluralism.

The fact that students of literary and cultural definition differ so widely illustrates the difficulty of defining the literary canon. And, if anything, the task is becoming thornier. The ethnic base that underlies our culture continues to broaden, with recent dramatic increases in the Hispanic, Native American, and Asian American populations and a steady percentage gain in the number of black citizens. In the decade from 1970 to 1980, population increases were markedly unequal: whites, 9.4%; blacks, 17.9%; Hispanics, 61.0%; American Indians, 79.2%; Asian Americans 133.3% (US Bureau of the Census, *Statistical Abstract: 1972* 29; *1982–83* 15; *Historical Statistics* 14; *1970 Census* I-262). The general leveling of population growth that has followed the boom of the late 1940s and 1950s has been greatest among white middle- and upper-middle class families, a fact that will have continuing repercussions in our schools and in our literary curricula.

Hirsch notes somewhat wistfully that in the decade of the 1890s, a large number of our schools taught a common core of literary texts: *Julius Caesar, Hamlet, Macbeth, Ivanhoe, The Sketch-Book, Silas Marner, Evangeline, David Copperfield,* Gray's "Elegy," "The Deserted Village," "Thanatopsis," "Snow-Bound." But we need to remember that in 1900, only 94,883 students graduated from high school, not only a very small number but a very small percentage of the age group (6.4%), and probably one that was relatively homogeneous. In 1980, 3,630,000 students, 73.6% of the age group, graduated from high school (National Center, *Digest: 1982* 65). The population increased about three-fold during the eighty-year period; the number of high school graduates increased thirty-eight-fold. Moreover, some of the 1980 graduates came from homes where competency in English cannot be assumed. There are now 23 million Americans over the age of five who speak a language other than English at home, apparently a larger number than at any time in the nation's history.[2]

The impact of this diversity has been multiplied in the last three decades by political forces. We are not only an increasingly pluralistic society; we are increasingly conscious of that pluralism, as can be seen in governmental statistics on minority hiring and in publishers' advertisements for new or newly discovered works by black, Hispanic, Asian American, Native American, and female authors. Many of the publications of the Modern Language Association now concern what we call "historically underrepresented minorities" and women, who, at 51.4% of the population, constitute a historically underrepresented majority. For a generation, eloquent voices have insisted that "American literature includes a body of diversified writings previously unacknowledged by most literary scholars and critics, and that these writings are expressions of vital but neglected cultures within our society" (Fisher, *Minority Language* 7).

The traditional American response to the pressures of real and felt pluralism has been simple: expansion. The American way has been to swallow the whole. This process is not as rapid, amiable, or complete as many would like, but, for the most part, we have responded to the pressure of strangers at the gate by opening the door. The tendency is at work in educational enrollments as well as in revised curricula.

Since the mid-1970s, the issues of coeducation and minority recruiting have dominated many colleges and university campuses. My undergraduate college and my present university are representative. Amherst College long believed that quality in education was enhanced by a relatively small community of teachers and students, and the size of the student body was carefully limited. The number of men enrolled at Amherst in the fall of 1968 was 1,224. After seven turbulent years of war and protest and social change, the number of men enrolled at Amherst in the fall of 1975 was 1,223. But that was the year coeducation began; after a good deal of agonizing, the college decided that this new policy could take place only by increasing the enrollment to 1,600 students, men and women.

At the University of Virginia, the statistics are even more dramatic. In 1969 the enrollment in the College of Arts and Sciences totaled 3,915, made up almost entirely of white males. Fourteen years later, after the dual revolutions of race and gender, the white male enrollment was roughly the same, 3,884, though the total college student body had doubled, to 8,048 in order to accommodate 3,089 female, 766 black, and several hundred other minority students.[3]

The powerful tendency toward inclusion, rooted in American democracy, has also been felt in textbooks, syllabi, and curricula, which simultaneously reflect and create the cultural attitudes that govern education. One of the most influential American literature texts, the Norton anthology, mirrors the expansion in the society at large. The first edition of Norton's *American Tradition in Literature* was published in 1957, the year that Martin Luther King, Jr., organized the Southern Christian Leadership Conference. This two-volume, 2,584-page collection presented the writings of eighty-nine tradition-al American authors, including nine women. No black writers were represented; in-stead, the *American Tradition* printed five pages of "Negro Songs," including "Go Down, Moses," "Swing Low, Sweet Chariot," and "All God's Chillun Got Shoes." The editors, Sculley Bradley, Richmond Croom Beatty, and E. Hudson Long, spoke confidently in the preface about the task of selecting from a "national inheritance the works that would best represent its nature and its values." Making "literary merit [the] final criterion for selection," they assured their readers that "masterpieces endure." Later editions increased the page count (to 3,137 in 1962 and 3,484 in 1967) and added a few more authors, mainly twentieth-century poets, but the tradition, as Norton defined it, endured unchanged.

There was, however, a hint of something new in the preface of the third edition. By that time Richmond Beatty was dead and Martin Luther King, Jr., had won the Nobel Peace Prize. Bradley and Long, in making minor adjustments and adding one black and four female poets, also added a qualifying adjective, speaking for the first time of "the ever-evolving American tradition in literature." They observed that "time has brought changes in the prevailing evaluation of American literature."

A dozen years later, time had brought so many changes that Norton abandoned *The American Tradition in Literature* and issued a new anthology "devised to close the ever-widening gap between the current conception and appraisal of the American liter-ary heritage and the way in which American literature is represented in existing anthologies"—including, of course, their own. In 1979, less certain about defining the American tradition, the publisher chose a neutral title, *The Norton Anthology of Ameri-can Literature*, and boasted that the work was "entirely new." Its newness, however, is very much in the American grain. Almost all of the material in the original *Tradition* is still present. The newness stems not from reconsideration or selectivity but from addi-tion, for the *Anthology* has expanded to an extraordinary 4,951 pages, twice the size of the 1957 *Tradition*, thus making room for twenty-nine female and fourteen black authors.[4] Whatever the tradition may be, these square volumes seem to say, we've got it in here somewhere. Teachers and students are admonished to create their own anthologies inside the *Anthology*: "Teachers are offered . . . more selections than, in all probability, they will have time to assign or teach. This principle of copiousness in selection is designed to allow teachers to set up their own reading lists." And yet in all five thousand pages there are no Hispanic, Asian American, or Native American authors. Unlike surfers, anthology makers prefer to ride behind the crest of the wave. (See Hemenway, in this volume, for additional discussion of the Norton works.)

Looking westward in 1801, Thomas Jefferson said there would be land to the thousandth generation. According to the superintendent of the 1890 census, Jefferson was wrong by 996 generations, for by the 1880s the land had been filled in and the frontier was gone. Expansion is not an infinite process, even in America. If we are to have a national culture, there must be consensus about its makeup. If we are to educate our young people, there must be agreement about what they are to learn. If we are to talk with one another, we must have common points of reference. Even if we disagree about our history and our values, we still must have a framework for discussion. Choice is mandatory, for "copiousness in selection" is virtually no selection at all, and a citizen cannot read a thousand books any more than he or she can wear a thousand shirts. All our writers are important, but some—at any given moment—are more important than others. A canon of American literature, however difficult to define, is necessary.

And it may be that at the present moment a canon is more necessary than ever, for the literary curriculum is under attack from inside and out. Inside departments of English, the number of graduating majors has dropped precipitously, from 57,026 in 1971 to 30,794 in 1988, and the focus on skills has diminished literary content. The ADE reports "that the nature of English departments is changing [because] there is an increasing emphasis on writing courses and a decreasing emphasis on literature." Almost two-thirds of the English courses now taught at the college level are writing courses, and at many schools the basic composition course teaches writing skills exclusively rather than the old-fashioned mixture of composition and literature. Outside departments of English, students faced with vocational neuroses and expanding universes of knowledge, especially in the sciences, are electing fewer courses in literary and humanistic studies.[5]

If there is less room for literature in our schools and in the lives of students after they graduate—half of them don't read at all and the other half have turned increasingly to nonliterary works—it becomes even more important to choose, and to choose well. Thus contemporary America presents a barbed challenge to its educators: it is more difficult than ever to define our literary canon, and at the same time it is more essential. As democrats we must be inclusive and pluralistic, yet as humanists we must have the courage to be selective, for making judgments about value is at the center of the humanities. Let us approach this challenge by considering first the nature of a canon, and then how one might be constructed.

II

Two essential points must be kept in mind about the nature of a canon. The first is that a list of great books cannot exist by itself, separate from convictions about greatness. A canon is a cultural mirror, imaging our notions of who we are. It is a national repository of historical and social values, of pedagogical notions, of ideas about the purpose of literature. Since individuals have different values and ideas, they will disagree about books. Those who find economics the basis of society are likely to admire the marketplace struggles of *The Octopus* and *The Grapes of Wrath* more than the inward moral dramas of *The Scarlet Letter* and *The Wings of the Dove*. A list of books drawn up by a teacher whose chief concern is to introduce students to the enjoyment of reading may not have much in common with the list compiled by a teacher who uses literary texts to instruct students about history. Literature can be thought of as the embodiment of the great ideas of human civilization, or as the voice of social protest; as a manifestation of a specific society in a specific time and place, or as the product of an individual artistic consciousness; as a blend of narrative, character, language, and idea, or as a demonstration of rhetorical forms, genres, or linguistic changes. Literature can be understood as a confirmation of the reader's experience, an explanation of that experience, or an enlargement of experience. The values and emphases selected by any one reader constitute an individual decision; those chosen by a nation represent a political decision. The wave of interest in American literature in the last three decades in Japan, with new studies of Faulkner crowding out traditional studies of Shakespeare, proves less about Oxford, Mississippi, or Stratford-upon-Avon than it does about Hiroshima. In the United States, the fact that black writers have had greater success than Hispanic writers in being accepted into the canon measures, among other things, the greater population and political power of the black community.

Second, a canon is never fixed, except in homogeneous, hierarchical communities. In 1584 the Council of Trent resolved the issue of the biblical canon, at least for the Roman church. Four centuries later, the resolution of canons seems charmingly naive, culturally impossible. In a democratic, pluralistic society the canon is ever-changing, both for the nation as a whole and within individual communities. In the middle of the nineteenth century, poetry represented our public voice, and Americans stood in line to buy copies of *The Courtship of Miles Standish*. One hundred years later, poetry had gone underground and Americans lined up again at the bookstores, this time for *Franny and Zooey*.[6] Today we seem to find Salinger almost as archaic as Longfellow.

Even a book that has lasted, like *Adventures of Huckleberry Finn*, is read differently in different American communities. When school administrator John H. Wallace had Huck thrown out of the Mark Twain Intermediate School in Fairfax County, Virginia, in 1982, editorial writers throughout the country massaged the irony of the school's name and the fact that Wallace was black, and they went on to explain that Mark Twain's book was our classic satire on slavery, our eloquent treatise on interracial brotherhood. And so it has been for generations of white teachers, but not, apparently, for contemporary black students, many of whom find something deeply disturbing about what Ralph Ellison has called "a white man's inadequate portrait of a slave" (*Shadow and Act* 72; NAL, 1964). If a canon is a national repository, it is one in which our citizens are constantly making deposits and withdrawals.

Still, as individuals and as a nation, we must choose. How can we construct a canon that provides a measure of stability and cultural communication, and yet at the same time takes into account our pluralism and our shifting values? My suggestion is that we think of the literary canon not as a single authoritarian list and not as a pluralistic cacophony of innumerable voices but as a tiered set of options, relatively stable at one end, relatively open at the other, joined by the possibility of change. We might start with a first level of authors whose acquaintance we find necessary for educated Americans in our society at this time, no matter what their ethnic or religious or gender identification. The membership in this pantheon would be small, restricted to those authors who profoundly represent their times and yet whose vision, amaranthine, seems to transcend time; authors whose popularity is long-standing with both general and specialist readers; authors whose style is so memorable that it has changed the language in form and expression, whether it is Dante's terza rima, Homer's epic simile, the citations from Shakespeare that take up sixty-three double-columned pages of the *Oxford Dictionary of Quotations*, or the many biblical expressions, whose name is legion, embedded in our language. Here, then, is one definition of the literary summit, using Western European literature as an illustration:

First Level (Western European literature): The Bible, Homer, Chaucer, Dante, Shakespeare, Cervantes

We could construct a first level for literature in English, or separately for British literature, or for American literature, though, aided less by the winnowing of time, these categories become more controversial. Here is one possible top level for a canon of American literature:

First Level (American literature): Hawthorne, Emerson, Thoreau, Melville, Whitman, Dickinson, Twain, Henry James, T. S. Eliot, Richard Wright, Faulkner

Then we might construct a second tier in our canon, consisting of those authors who, while not as predominant as the first group, have made a significant contribution to our culture. An educated American should be generally acquainted with all of these writers, specifically familiar with some:

Second level (American literature): Franklin, Irving, Cooper, Poe, Douglass, Howells, Stephen Crane, Henry Adams, Dreiser, Cather, Chopin, Frost, Fitzgerald, Hemingway, Jewett, O'Neill, Pound, Stevens, Ellison, William Carlos Williams, James Baldwin, Momaday

Finally, we can add a third level, which combines two groups: older writers whose work continues to be of interest; and newcomers, massed like the Boston Marathon runners at Hopkinton, in the race but with endurance yet to be tested. Our hypothetical educated American should know some of these writers, a sampling based on interest, community, happenstance. Here is a representative selection of a small fraction of this large group:

Third Level (American literature A–C): Oscar Zeta Acosta, Andy Adams, George Ade, James Agee, Conrad Aiken, Edward Albee, Louisa May Alcott, Thomas Bailey Aldrich, Miguel Algarín, Horatio Alger, Nelson Algren, James Lane Allen, Paula Gunn Allen, Alurista, A. R. Ammons, Rudolfo Anaya, Maxwell Anderson, Sherwood Anderson, Maya Angelou, William Apes, Sholem Asch, John Ashbery, Isaac Asimov, Gertrude Atherton, Louis Auchincloss, Joseph G. Baldwin, Toni C. Bambara, George Bancroft, Imamu Amiri Baraka, Joel Barlow, Djuna Barnes, Helen Barolini, Raymond Barrio, Philip Barry, John Barth, Donald Barthelme, William Bartram, L. Frank Baum, Ann Beattie, S. N. Behrman, David Belasco, Edward Bellamy, Saul Bellow, Ludwig Bemelmans, Robert Benchley, Stephen V. Benét, Thomas Berger, John Berryman, Robert Beverley, Ambrose Bierce, Robert M. Bird, Elizabeth Bishop, John Peale Bishop, Robert Bly, Louise Bogan, Arna Bontemps, Kay Boyle, Hugh H. Brackenridge, Ray Bradbury, William Bradford, Anne Bradstreet, Jorge Brandon, Richard Brautigan, Gwendolyn Brooks, Van Wyck Brooks, Charles Brockden Brown, Rosellen Brown, Sterling Brown, William Wells Brown, Charles Farrar Browne, William Cullen Bryant, Pearl Buck, John Burroughs, William Burroughs, William Byrd, James B. Cabell, George W. Cable, Abraham Cahan, James N. Cain, Erskine Caldwell, Hortense Calisher, Truman Capote, Rachel Carson, Raymond Carver, R. V. Cassill, Raymond Chandler, William E. Channing, Jerome Charyn, Fray Angélico Chávez, Paddy Chayefsky, John Cheever, Mary Chesnut, Charles W. Chesnutt, Frank Chin, Winston Churchill, John Ciardi, Walter Van Tilburg Clark, Eldridge Cleaver, Cyrus Colter, Laurie Colwin, Marc Connelly, Jack Conroy, Ebenezer Cook, John Esten Cooke, Rose Terry Cooke, Robert Coover, George Copway, John Cotton, James G. Cozzens, Hart Crane, F. Marion Crawford, Robert Creeley, Michel-G. de Crèvecoeur, Harry Crews, Countee Cullen, E. E. Cummings, J. V. Cunningham

Immediately, disclaimers must be made. We might, for some purposes, wish to suggest individual works rather than writers. Perhaps we should include categories for literatures, like that of the American Indian, not organized by authors. We might separate a popular canon from a professional canon, and note that three generations ago American literature itself lay outside the confines of official study; two generations ago living authors were seen as too young for canonization. And, with a list now in front of us, we can see clearly the specific ramifications of the two general points made earlier. With canons, as with computers, input determines output. A list with a historical basis might elevate Franklin and Jefferson to more prominent positions. One that included nonfictional prose as an essential part of literature would perhaps include Parkman and William James. One whose explicit purpose was ethnic representation might promote Ellison, Baldwin, and Momaday to the first rank, and Baraka and Maxine Hong Kingston to the second.

And, to clarify the second general point, even if we could agree for the moment on both the premises of a canon and on individual authors, our choices would change over time, slowly at the first level, more rapidly at the second and third. T. S. Eliot seems more dated than we would have thought possible two decades ago, a modern who is no longer a contemporary. He may gradually be losing his hold on the highest tier. Thoreau has been an effective philosophical outsider for so long that he is now inside the first rank of American writers, having climbed the platform to take his place beside his Concord neighbors. Emily Dickinson's success is counting sweeter every year; she is closing on Walt Whitman for the title of America's finest poet, a race that would astonish our great-grandparents, who thrived on Bryant, Whittier, Holmes, Lowell, and Longfellow.

In the middle section of our triple-tiered canon, a more rapid turnover can be seen. Cather, no longer merely a female writer and no longer trapped in the limbo between traditional literary periods, is rapidly rising out of the pack, as are Chopin, Wharton, Sarah Orne Jewett, and Maxine Hong Kingston. Douglass, Ralph Ellison, James Baldwin, and Momaday have established their importance beyond question for all American readers, and in doing so have altered our definitions of literary significance. Other authors are dropping behind. Thomas Wolfe seems to be disappearing. Artemus Ward, O. Henry, Vachel Lindsay, Stephen Vincent Benét, and Ring Lardner were omitted from the third edition of *The American Tradition in Literature*. Mary Wilkins Freeman, interestingly, was also omitted from the third *Tradition*, apparently to make room for Sarah Orne Jewett, and then resurrected in the fifth edition and the *Anthology*, which not only kept Jewett but increased her page count and added Stowe and Margaret Fuller as well.

Most important, a disclaimer must be made about audience. Like any act of communication, a canon must take into account the members of the audience for whom it is intended—not only their premises and cultural biases but their ages, levels of sophistication, and educational aspirations as well. Here the tiered concept of canon becomes especially useful, for we can distinguish different goals for different groups. One possible set of goals for the American literature canon sketched above could be made as in fig. 1.

Diagrams and charts, though they have their uses, need to be taken with a grain of salt and an ounce of vinegar. A military instructor once explained to me that "if you have read the text or were present for the lecture, you get credit for knowing the lesson." No wonder battles are lost. We all know too many students who manage to

Figure 1

	High school students; college students	College English majors; secondary school English teachers	Graduate students in English and college English teachers specializing in American literature
First Level: Hawthorne, etc.	Reading of major texts	Mastery of major texts	Mastery of major and minor texts and secondary sources
Second Level: Franklin, etc.	Some knowledge	Extensive knowledge	Mastery of major texts, acquaintance with minor texts and secondary sources
Third Level: Acosta, etc.	Sampling	Substantial sampling	Extensive knowledge

read assignments without learning, and there are a few who seem to learn without reading. Most of us know a good deal about certain books we have never actually read; all of us have forgotten more than we care to admit. The processes of learning and retaining are complex, and researchers stand only at the thresholds of enlightenment. Perhaps future research will substantiate our intuition that learning is often indirect, diagonal, circuitous.

The circuitous quality of learning presents an opportunity to connect the canon with pedagogy and to provide the rationale for a recommendation that our teachers be better taught. Many instructors complain that they cannot make allusions to Greek mythology in today's classrooms, but one reason students do not pick up literary references to classical texts is that they are not exposed to them enough. A good deal of canonical knowledge could be conveyed implicitly by informed teachers. The simple fact about American education is that our teachers need to know more, at all levels. Many high school teachers are trapped in jobs that provide neither the time nor the opportunity nor the resources to increase their mastery of content. The burnout that we hear so much about may be partially rustout. A number of education schools and boards seem more concerned with requirements in public health, classroom procedures, and pupil adjustment than in English, history, and mathematics. And too many college and university teachers of literature, seduced by a false analogy to the sciences, have narrowed and overspecialized their instruction.

Good teaching in the humanities is richly referential, a fact that I first thought about explicitly while sitting in a first-year graduate course taught by the late Joe Lee Davis. The syllabus would show a standard course in fin de siècle American literature, but what amazed me was its range. A class on Dreiser might include remarks about Keats's letters, "A High-Toned Old Christian Woman," *The Oresteia*, Woolman's *Journal*, *The Day of the Locust*, Douglass's *Narrative*, "The Second Coming," *The Damnation of Theron Ware*, "The Dynamo and the Virgin," and, always, Shakespeare's plays by the handful. Professor Davis once told me that every Americanist ought to read through Shakespeare every year. These classes forced me to invent a new system of note taking: right-hand page for the text for the day, left-hand page for everything else. The right-hand pages helped me pass the course examination; the left-hand pages gave me an education. To be meaningful, a canon must be alive in our schools. Only a knowledgeable teacher can make it live.

What, then, is the relation of the traditional canon of American literature to the essays in this volume, which seek as a group to overturn that tradition? These are essays on the attack, ranging along a broad popular front. At one extreme Theresa Meléndez consigns much previous literary study to the "dustwebs of the nineteenth century." More temperately, Linda Ching Sledge argues that "Americanists like Spiller are only now addressing [the] . . . rich, as yet unmined vein of ethnic writing," and José Limón states that "we can confidently begin to speak of a [Hispanic] literary history . . . [that] should inevitably also become part of the literary history of the United States." Houston Baker maintains that these changes have already occurred, that minority writers and scholars have "revealed the limiting boundaries of traditional American historical discourse."

Whether contumacious or confident, these essays make large demands. Ramsey, Meléndez, Wiget, Kanellos, Limón, and Sledge all argue that folklore should be "seen as sharing the full thematic and artistic weight of written productions" (Limón), although the current emphasis on "cultural and performance contexts" (Meléndez) makes it more difficult than ever to incorporate folklore into the canon of letters. Sledge challenges us to "listen for the living word behind the narrow letter," and Limón, reversing folklore's "traditional role as handmaiden to literature," sees it instead as a "powerful, disturbing, and dominating influence on a written poem." Jarold Ramsey claims that these new directions must be solidly buttressed by scholarship. He makes a breathtaking proposition, advocating "the systematic preparation and publication of a 'standard' dual-language edition of the surviving Native American repertories—proceeding tribe by tribe, with full textual apparatus as needed."

In the course of their discussions, the authors of these essays present a collective list of authors whose names would make a difficult examination for traditional scholars. Among the writers discussed in detail are Jorge Brandon, Tato Laviera, Miguel Algarín, Rolando Hinojosa, Américo Paredes, Maxine Kingston, William Apes, George Copway, Sarah Winnemucca, Jade Snow Wong, Lin Yutang, Virginia Lee, Monica Sone, John Okada, Jeanne and James Houston, Louis Chu, Jeffery Chan, Frank Chin, Toshio Mori, Diana Chang, George Henry, Jane Edna Hunter, and Harry Edwards. Substantial as this list is, the new voices recommended to us in this volume represent a selection, a small fraction of a much larger possible list. Most of the authors anthologized by Gerald Haslam in his *Forgotten Pages of American Literature* are still forgotten in *Redefining American Literary History*, as are the minority literatures of European origin: Greek American, Jewish American, South Slavic American, Scandinavian American, and many others.

When looked at closely, the category terms of "Hispanic," "black," "Asian American," and "Native American" explode into diverse cultures and languages and literatures. Hispania, after all, is not a country but a vague concept, loosely linking Americans of Colombian, Cuban, Dominican, Mexican, Puerto Rican, and other ancestries. "Asian American" refers to over a dozen language groups, from Korean to Tagalog. There are hundreds of mutually unintelligible American Indian languages and dialects. The writers discussed in these essays, introduced to put pressure on the traditional canon, themselves represent a canon, a small percentage of the many voices in America's minority communities.

The question remains: How will these voices, and the others they symbolize, affect the traditional study of American literature? At the community level these authors have an immediate value for readers of similar heritage, whether the readers represent a community that is local (a Mexican American school in west San Antonio) or extended (native speakers of Spanish throughout the country). The intensity and the duration of this special link will depend on the future integration of these groups into the cultural mainstream. Americans of Italian descent, who move easily between assimilation and ethnic preservation, seem not to have a particular need for courses in the Italian American novel.

At the national level, the impact of these minority writers will be felt more slowly. Like most human ideas, from the economic theory of history to the concept of the quark, a literary canon is a momentary stay against confusion. The phrase is Robert Frost's, and it succinctly summarizes recent work in cognitive psychology. In order to function, the mind must select, focus, exclude; but at the same time it must remain open to aspects that don't fit, to dissonances hovering at the edges of a momentarily fixed concept. Thinking, like writing, is a continuous process of thesis formulation and revision. At the present time, these new American authors are at the perimeter of our traditional ideas, making raids on the standard canon, forcing us to debate our history, define our values, reconsider our notions of literature. They oblige us continually to relearn the American lesson that minority cultures enrich and transform the dominant culture by bringing to it the freshness of differing perspectives as well as a deeper understanding of our common humanity—"expressions," as Eunice Faber puts it, of "our sameness, our dreams, and our suffering" (114). The new writers represent dissonances at the edge of our traditional harmonies, but as we begin to listen, we will find that the music is changing, that present confusion is becoming part of future stay. Which writers, which books, which ideas will ultimately become incorporated into the higher levels of the canon remain to be seen. *Redefining American Literary History* is an important start toward collection, sifting, evaluation, inclusion. The essays gathered here help make these new writers accessible. It is now the responsibility of knowledgeable teachers and fair-minded scholars to further the effort, to bring this literature to the attention of American students and the public at large, to take an active part in the ongoing process of defining, and redefining, the canon.

Appendix: Writers included in *The American Tradition in Literature* and *The Norton Anthology of American Literature*, 1957–81

ATL (Norton) 1st ed. 1957 2,584 pp.	ATL (Norton) 2nd ed. 1962 3,137 pp.	ATL (Norton) 3rd ed. 1967 3,484 pp.	ATL (Random House) 5th ed. 1981 4,221 pp.	NAAL (Norton) 1st ed. 1979 4,951 pp.
Bradford	Bradford	Bradford	Bradford	Bradford
Bradstreet	Bradstreet	Bradstreet	Bradstreet	Bradstreet
Sewall	Sewall	Sewall	Sewall	
Taylor	Taylor	Taylor	Taylor	Taylor

ATL 1st ed.	ATL 2nd ed.	ATL 3rd ed.	ATL 5th ed.	NAAL 1st ed.
C. Mather	C. Mather	C. Mather	C. Mather	C. Mather
Edwards	Edwards	Edwards	Edwards	Edwards
Knight	Knight	Knight	Knight	Knight
Byrd	Byrd	Byrd	Byrd	Byrd
Woolman	Woolman	Woolman	Woolman	Woolman
Crèvecoeur	Crèvecoeur	Crèvecoeur	Crèvecoeur	Crèvecoeur
Franklin	Franklin	Franklin	Franklin	Franklin
Paine	Paine	Paine	Paine	Paine
Jefferson	Jefferson	Jefferson	Jefferson	Jefferson
Federalist	*Federalist*	*Federalist*		*Federalist*
Freneau	Freneau	Freneau	Freneau	Freneau
Irving	Irving	Irving	Irving	Irving
Cooper	Cooper	Cooper	Cooper	Cooper
Bryant	Bryant	Bryant	Bryant	Bryant
Hawthorne	Hawthorne	Hawthorne	Hawthorne	Hawthorne
Poe	Poe	Poe	Poe	Poe
Melville	Melville	Melville	Melville	Melville
Emerson	Emerson	Emerson	Emerson	Emerson
Thoreau	Thoreau	Thoreau	Thoreau	Thoreau
S. Smith	S. Smith			
Longstreet	Longstreet		Longstreet	
Hooper	Hooper		Hooper	
G. W. Harris	G. W. Harris		G. W. Harris	G. W. Harris
Longfellow	Longfellow	Longfellow	Longfellow	Longfellow
Whittier	Whittier	Whittier	Whittier	Whittier
Holmes	Holmes	Holmes	Holmes	Holmes
J. R. Lowell	J. R. Lowell	J. R. Lowell	J. R. Lowell	J. R. Lowell
Timrod	Timrod	Timrod		
Lincoln	Lincoln	Lincoln	Lincoln	Lincoln
Whitman	Whitman	Whitman	Whitman	Whitman
Lanier	Lanier	Lanier	Lanier	
Dickinson	Dickinson	Dickinson	Dickinson	Dickinson
Negro Songs	Negro Songs			
Cowboy Ballads	Cowboy Ballads			
Billings	Billings			
J. Phoenix	J. Phoenix			
A. Ward	A. Ward			
Clemens	Clemens	Clemens	Clemens	Clemens
Harte	Harte	Harte	Harte	Harte
Cable	Cable	Cable	Cable	
J. C. Harris	J. C. Harris	J. C. Harris	J. C. Harris	J. C. Harris
Freeman	Freeman		Freeman	Freeman
Howells	Howells	Howells	Howells	Howells
H. James	H. James	H. James	H. James	H. James
H. Adams	H. Adams	H. Adams	H. Adams	H. Adams
W. James	W. James	W. James		
Moody	Moody	Moody	Moody	
Wharton	Wharton	Wharton	Wharton	Wharton

ATL 1st ed.	ATL 2nd ed.	ATL 3rd ed.	ATL 5th ed.	NAAL 1st ed.
O. Henry	O. Henry			
Garland	Garland	Garland	Garland	Garland
S. Crane	S. Crane	S. Crane	S. Crane	S. Crane
Dreiser	Dreiser	Dreiser	Dreiser	Dreiser
Robinson	Robinson	Robinson	Robinson	Robinson
Frost	Frost	Frost	Frost	Frost
Sandburg	Sandburg	Sandburg	Sandburg	Sandburg
Lindsay	Lindsay			
Cather	Cather	Cather	Cather	Cather
Glasgow	Glasgow	Glasgow	Glasgow	
S. Benét	S. Benét			
Mencken	Mencken	Mencken	Mencken	
S. Anderson	S. Anderson	S. Anderson	S. Anderson	S. Anderson
Lardner	Lardner			
S. Lewis	S. Lewis	S. Lewis		
Fitzgerald	Fitzgerald	Fitzgerald	Fitzgerald	Fitzgerald
Millay	Millay	Millay	Millay	Millay
O'Neill	O'Neill	O'Neill	O'Neill	
Pound	Pound	Pound	Pound	Pound
Eliot	Eliot	Eliot	Eliot	Eliot
Jeffers	Jeffers	Jeffers	Jeffers	
MacLeish	MacLeish	MacLeish	MacLeish	MacLeish
H. Crane	H. Crane	H. Crane	H. Crane	H. Crane
Porter	Porter	Porter	Porter	Porter
Faulkner	Faulkner	Faulkner	Faulkner	Faulkner
Hemingway	Hemingway	Hemingway	Hemingway	Hemingway
T. Wolfe	T. Wolfe	T. Wolfe	T. Wolfe	
Steinbeck	Steinbeck	Steinbeck	Steinbeck	Steinbeck
Warren	Warren		Warren	
Stevens	Stevens	Stevens	Stevens	Stevens
W. C. Williams	W. C. Williams	W. C. Williams	W. C. Williams	W. C. Williams
Ransom	Ransom	Ransom	Ransom	Ransom
Cummings	Cummings	Cummings	Cummings	Cummings
Tate	Tate		Tate	Tate
Dos Passos	Dos Passos	Dos Passos	Dos Passos	Dos Passos
Farrell	Farrell	Farrell	Farrell	
Thurber	Thurber	Thurber		
	M. Moore	M. Moore	M. Moore	M. Moore
	Eberhart	Eberhart	Eberhart	
	Rukeyser	Rukeyser		
	R. Lowell	R. Lowell	R. Lowell	R. Lowell
	Wilbur	Wilbur	Wilbur	Wilbur
		Jewett	Jewett	Jewett
		Roethke	Roethke	Roethke
		Malamud	Malamud	
		O'Connor	O'Connor	O'Connor
		Updike	Updike	Updike
		Ferlinghetti	Ferlinghetti	

ATL 1st ed.	*ATL* 2nd ed.	*ATL* 3rd ed.	*ATL* 5th ed.	*NAAL* 1st ed.
		Nemerov	Nemerov	
		Levertov	Levertov	Levertov
		Snodgrass	Snodgrass	
		J. Wright	J. Wright	J. Wright
		Merwin	Merwin	Merwin
		Sexton	Sexton	Sexton
		Rich	Rich	Rich
		Plath	Plath	Plath
		L. Jones	I. A. Baraka	I. A. Baraka
			Winthrop	Winthrop
			Rowlandson	Rowlandson
			P. Wheatley	P. Wheatley
			Barlow	Barlow
			Tyler	
			C. B. Brown	
			Songs of the folk	
			M. Lewis	
			Indian heritage	
			Prescott	
			Parkman	
			Stowe	Stowe
			Douglass	Douglass
			Bierce	Bierce
			Chopin	Chopin
			Chesnutt	Chesnutt
			Masters	
			Dunbar	
			Stein	Stein
			Aiken	
			E. Wylie	E. Wylie
			Bogan	
			C. Cullen	C. Cullen
			Wilder	
			A. Lowell	
			H. Doolittle	H. Doolittle
			Hughes	Hughes
			R. Wright	R. Wright
			Welty	Welty
			T. Williams	
			A. Miller	
			E. Bishop	E. Bishop
			J. Cunningham	
			D. Schwartz	
			Jarrell	Jarrell
			Nabokov	Nabokov
			Singer	
			Cheever	
			Ellison	Ellison

ATL 1st ed.	*ATL* 2nd ed.	*ATL* 3rd ed.	*ATL* 5th ed.	*NAAL* 1st ed.
			Bellow	Bellow
			Mailer	Mailer
			Baldwin	Baldwin
			Berryman	Berryman
			W. Stafford	
			Dickey	Dickey
			Ammons	Ammons
			Bly	
			Ginsberg	Ginsberg
			J. Merrill	J. Merrill
			Ashbery	Ashbery
			G. Kinnell	
			G. Snyder	G. Snyder
			Gass	
			Barth	Barth
			Oates	
				E. Cooke
				W. Bartram
				M. Fuller
				T. B. Thorpe
				B. T. Washington
				Du Bois
				E. Goldman
				Norris
				J. London
				Toomer
				N. West
				E. Wilson
				W. Morris
				M. McCarthy
				Kerouac
				Malcolm X
				P. Roth
				Sontag
				C. Olson
				G. Brooks
				R. Duncan
				Creeley
				F. O'Hara

Notes

[1] The Charrows concluded that "grammatical constructions and discourse structures . . . rather than the legal complexity of the jury instructions, were responsible for comprehension problems." This study does not necessarily refute Hirsch's claim that "good style contributes little to our reading of unfamiliar material." At the extreme, when the topic is incomprehensible, style makes no difference. And it may be that at the opposite extreme, when the topic is completely familiar to the audience, style is also unimportant. But for the middle ground of writing—prose of some

difficulty (perhaps with a cloze score of 40 to 70)—I continue to believe that good style will help. Hirsch's readers may be tempted to average *The Philosophy of Composition* and *Cultural Literacy*, concluding that form and content are both essential and that the decline in SAT scores may measure a combined deterioration of formal and of cultural literacy.

[2] See US Bureau of the Census, *Statistical Abstract: 1982–83* 38; *Ancestry and Language*. I am grateful to Edith K. McArthur, of the Population Division of the Bureau of the Census, for sending me a copy of her unpublished "Language Information from Censuses and Surveys" and for valuable advice in dealing with the shifting sands of population statistics. The "apparently" in the text is a qualification necessary because different sampling techniques, differently worded questions ("native language," "mother tongue," "language spoken at home"), and changing attitudes toward ethnicity make comparisons across censuses difficult.

[3] These statistics were kindly supplied by Robert F. Grose, Director of Institutional Research at Amherst College; and Christine L. Wiedman, Senior Programmer and Analyst at the University of Virginia, Office of Institutional Planning and Studies.

[4] In a curious turn of publishing history, the rights to *The American Tradition in Literature* were passed from Norton to Grosset & Dunlap, who brought out a fourth edition in 1974. Then Random House took over the project and published the fifth edition, edited by Bradley, Beatty, Long, and George Perkins, in 1981. The fifth edition of *ATL*, like the Norton *Anthology*, is a much-expanded version of the 1957 *ATL*, although the expansion is based on a different principle. While the fifth *ATL* contains a number of new authors, much of the increased page count is a result of adding what might be called standard minor authors—Winthrop, Barlow, C. B. Brown, Parkman, Bierce, Masters, Wilder, Arthur Miller—and extending the coverage of major authors, including, for example, the complete text of *As I Lay Dying*. See the Appendix for a comparison of five editions of *ATL* and *NAAL*.

In 1985, each publisher brought out a new edition. The Random House *ATL* boasts of "more readable volumes," which means a larger page and thus more selections, both traditional (Roger Williams, *The Bay Psalm Book*, Ebenezer Cook, T. B. Thorpe, Jack London, Jean Toomer) and new (Toni Morrison, Thomas Pynchon, Bobbie Ann Mason, Anne Tyler, Tim O'Brien). The principle of inclusion and expansion governs even the preface, which maintains on the first page that "the aims remain essentially what they have always been. . . . Literary merit remains the most important criterion for selection." Four paragraphs later, the editor states that "a major effort has been directed toward bringing the contents fully in line with current critical opinion." Not to be outdone, Norton broke the 5,000-page barrier in 1985 with its 5,187-page *Anthology of American Literature*, second edition. This expansion also contains more of both the old and the new, and boasts of the inclusion of 16 black writers and "nearly 800 pages [devoted] to the work of 35 women."

[5] The information on English majors comes from the National Center, *Digest: 1989* 259 and *1990* (in ms.). The number of majors hit a low in 1983 (25,632 BAs in English were awarded); the succeeding five years thus demonstrate a modest recovery. The ADE study, by Margaret Gorman, Michael Gorman, and Arthur P. Young, is entitled "The 1982–83 Writing and Litera- ture Survey" and can be obtained from the ADE at MLA headquarters in New York. I am grateful to Jayme Sokolow, of the NEH, for discussion of these matters. Sokolow passes along a depressing statistic: 87% of college students who take humanities courses do so to fulfill require- ments. Henry Louis Gates, Jr., summarizes the dilemma in his contradictory response to the interim recommendations of the MLA's Commission on the Future of the Profession:

> Nor would I want the study of Greek and Latin diminished for the study of Yoruba and Swahili. Rather, in what is already a scaled-down profession facing reduced demand, we must teach well more of the world's languages and literatures, even if offering less instruction in the "traditional" courses of "the canon." (6).

What is the place of literature in the composition classroom? The earlier tendency to teach literature in lieu of composition was obviously an error, as is the current trend of focusing solely on writing skills. Literature has a legitimate role in the teaching of composition, for it provides excellent material for students to think and write about, and avoids such canned topics as summer vacations, abortion, dorm rooms, and drugs. The trick is for the instructor to use literature in the teaching of composition and to refrain from lectures on literary history and extensive *explications de texte*.

[6] A classic work on this subject is Hubbell's *Who Are the Major American Writers?* which concludes that "my survey of changing American literary fashions indicates that in the nature of things critical estimates can be only relative" (xvii).

Thoreau's Last Words—
and America's First Literatures

Jarold Ramsey

The last intelligible words spoken by Henry David Thoreau in this life were, according to his friend William Ellery Channing, the Algonquian term *moose* and that epic misnomer of misnomers, *Indian* (319). Now these details are hardly surprising, given Thoreau's lifelong interest in Native American lore in general, and in particular his deathbed editing of his book *The Maine Woods*, with its evocations of Indian guides like Joe Polis and Joe Aitteon, and of what the author called "the moosey woods." It has long been assumed that Thoreau intended, in fact, to write an ethnological treatise on the American Indians; Robert Sayre has cast some doubt on the reality of such a purpose per se, but it still seems likely that, had Thoreau lived, he would have attempted some sort of concentrated treatment of his Indian researches (163).

The task of trying to redefine the origins of American literature in terms of the American Indian traditional literatures has drawn me, inevitably, to this conjectural aspect of Thoreau's career. No disputing that, of our classic writers, his work owes as much as anybody's to an intense awareness of the native cultures—but what if he had been given another ten or fifteen years to write? The question is unanswerable, irresistible, and instructive, because it suggests a whole series of "what if" conjectures about American writers who might have been profoundly influenced by the aboriginal lore of their country, but in fact weren't.

What if, for example, Longfellow had somehow gone into Indian Territory with his early idol, Washington Irving, in 1832, or preceded Thoreau by seeking out the Abenakis of his own state? Or what if he had at least read, along with the works of Schoolcraft and Heckewelder, Lewis Henry Morgan's masterly 1851 story of the Iroquoian peoples in *The League of the Iroquois*, including accounts of the historical hero named Hiawatha? What if Morgan himself, whose interest in Iroquoian myths and legends is well documented in his books, had been a poet or novelist as well as an ethnographer? What if Edgar Allan Poe had somehow happened upon the great Iroquois Condolence Ritual, with its gothic interplay of light and shadow? What if Prince Maximilian had somehow taken James Fenimore Cooper along on his expedition into the Great Plains, in company with the painter Karl Bodmer? What if Herman Melville had gone among the Cheyennes or the Kiowas rather than to the Marquesas? What if Whitman, or William Carlos Williams, had managed to hear a performance of the Navajo Night Chant? What if Ezra Pound had stayed home (at least for a few years) and set his mind to translating Ojibwa or Papago lyrics?[1]

In such conjectures about individual writers, we begin to see, I think, that instead of talking about the "Indian origins" of American literature, we would do better to acknowledge that such origins are mostly hypothetical and to inquire why, after four centuries of contact, America's first traditional literatures have had so little influence on our literary heritage. We would also have to acknowledge, I think, the Anglo-American imperviousness to the literary traditions of other ethnic groups among us—most notably, of course, those of black Americans. But the case of the Indians, and what might have been our literary legacy from them, is special, because of the sheer length of time involved in our associations and because of the simple but crucial fact that the Indian peoples were *native* to the American land and in full verbal and imaginative possession of its features before the rest of us came over. From the beginning, how little we have taken in of names and languages, myths and tales! The open-minded curiosity about such matters that animates the first book to refer in detail to native narratives, Roger Williams's *Key into the Language of America* (1643), has proved to be the exception in our literary history rather than the rule.[2]

Certainly, from the beginning, the gross fact of the native presence has been indelibly stamped on American writings as subject matter and image. From John Smith's narratives on through Cooper's romances and into the heyday of Hollywood, we have had no lack of stylized Indian images to conjure with: noble savages and savage brutes, natural gentlemen and redskinned devils. Scholars like Roy Harvey Pearce (*Savages*), Richard Slotkin, and Robert Berkhofer have shown in detail how arbitrary, absolute, and self-perpetuating these images have tended to be—how *mythic*, in fact, as refractions of reality having the power to alter reality, and revealing more about the image makers and their aggressive or guilty preoccupations than about their subjects (see also Bataille and Silet, *The Pretend Indians*). As Berkhofer observes:

> For most Whites throughout the past five centuries, the Indian of imagination and ideology has been as real [as], perhaps more real, than the Native American of actual existence and contact. As preconception became conception and conception became fact, the Indian was used for the ends of argument, art, and entertainment by White painters, philosophers, poets, novelists, and moviemakers among many. (71)

But literary imaging of native life, of which there has been so much, must not be confused with literary assimilation of native imaginative traditions, of which there has been so little. The disparity between the persistent popularity of the first and the utter neglect of the second is certainly striking. Perhaps the very strength of the fixation of our writers on *images* of "the Indian" largely accounts for their indifference to the existence of tribal literatures. Why take the trouble to find out how Native Americans picture themselves imaginatively, when you and your readers already *know* their official Anglo literary iconography?

At least Longfellow actually saw fit to interest himself in an authentic native narrative, the Ojibwa Manabozho cycle he found in Schoolcraft: the interest itself, so rare in its century, reflects more credit on Longfellow from a literary and historical standpoint than he has received as the author of the much-ridiculed *Song of Hiawatha*. But the poem is, alas, shaped through and through by Anglo prejudices and stereotypes. Despite the abundant evidence provided by Schoolcraft that the Manabozho cycle was in fact part of another, distinctive literary tradition—one largely incompatible, formally, with our own—Longfellow appropriated the Ojibwa material instead of assimilating and re-creating it with anything like fidelity to the original. The episodes of Nokomis's story-telling, for example, owe virtually nothing to Schoolcraft's accounts of Ojibwa recitations; these episodes are charming—but according to Western ideas of "children's liter-ature." And if Longfellow did read George Catlin's *Letters and Notes on the Manners, Customs, and Conditions of the North American Indians*, its wild and vivid descriptions of native fertility ceremonies among the Mandans and other groups seem to have borne no fruit in his imagination, judging from the pallid episode he makes of Minnehaha bless-ing the maize at night.[3]

One might object on behalf of a writer like Longfellow, and others in the nineteenth century who were even less concerned with Indian languages and oral traditions, that these materials were largely untranscribed and unpublished until the last decades of the century, when the Bureau of American Ethnology began to release its texts. But the lack of conveniently available texts does not explain the kind of neglect we are consider-ing: it seems to be deeply ingrained, not just a matter of scholarly work lagging behind literary interests. When the native linguistic and literary texts did become available, there was hardly a surge of attention to them on the part of our writers. The literary interest was, in the main, simply not there. The sad fact is that American literature has never really enjoyed that literary and philological zeal, essentially Romantic, for redis-covering and assimilating folk art and aboriginal literatures that sent Goethe, Schiller, Herder, and others out to transcribe boatmen, farmers, and peasant grandmothers in the cause of extending German literature; that sent Lönnrot out through back-country Finland in quest of the performed tales that he would eventually shape into the *Kaleva-la*; and that made Bartók turn ethnomusicologist for the enrichment of Hungarian music, first of all his own. Nor have many American writers expressed the kind of interest in the unwritten native traditional art of their land that Sir Philip Sidney admits to in a famous passage in *A Defense of Poesy*:

> I have never heard the old song of Percy and Douglas that I found not my heart moved more than with a trumpet. And yet it is sung but by some blind crowder, with no rougher voice than rude style; what being so evil apparalled in the dust and cobwebs of that uncivil age, what would it work, trimmed in the gorgeous eloquence of Pindar? (29)

(It is part of the pathos of Sidney's early death that he was never able to pursue this nativistic impulse himself and perhaps reconcile it with his classical biases; but in surviv-ing contemporaries—Spenser and Shakespeare preeminently, and secondary figures like Samuel Daniel—it soon became an important motive in the Elizabethan literary spirit.) I don't know that William Faulkner ever read Sidney's *Defense*; I'd like to think that he did, and found in the Elizabethan culture hero an imaginative forebear. For Faulkner did hearken deeply to the rude song of the blind crowder, or rather to its American folk equivalent in the stories and oral traditions of the whites and blacks of Mississippi—and the Indians. It is revealing that, instead of looking for possible sources of the Indian episodes in *Go Down, Moses* and other works in Choctaw and Chickasaw folklore, Faulkner's critics have mostly been content to accept the spirit of the author's off-putting remark that he just "made them up" (qtd. in Dabney 11). It is also revealing that, even in a fine study that conclusively shows the ethnographic accuracy and penetration of Faulkner's knowledge of these tribes, Lewis Dabney does not take the final step and adduce the Choctaw and Chickasaw myth texts that might prove the authentic Indian origins of the tragic story of the hunters and the Bear.[4]

To sum up this rather dismal survey: we cannot really claim an Indian origin for American literature, if by that we mean—as we should—a significant and persistent origin in the native repertories themselves. Sympathetic writers like Thoreau and Faulkner and scholars like Morgan, Adolf Bandelier, Daniel Brinton, Charles Leland, Washington Matthews, George B. Grinnell, Mary Austin, Paul Radin notwithstanding, the failure to engage the native legacy would constitute a long chapter in our history of missed chances, well into the middle of the twentieth century.

If it is too late for origins, it is never too late for discoveries, and I think that within the current trendiness of Indian studies, "getting into Indians," and so on, there really are the makings of a genuine American literary engagement with the first literatures of the country. To a considerable extent it is imaginative writers—poets and novelists—who are leading the way. Where in the last century, Philip Freneau, Thomas Cooper, and William Cullen Bryant were fond of writing sympathetic poems about native characters and situations, irrespective of ethnological distinctions, we now have poets like Gary Snyder, who writes with an ethnographer's knowledge of western Indian folkways; David Wagoner, whose collection *Who Shall Be the Sun* is based on scholarly transcriptions of Northwest Indian myths; and W. S. Merwin, whose adaptation of Crow songs and of narratives and songs from other North and South American native peoples is linguistically and ethnologically scrupulous. Remarks by Snyder typify, I think, the interest such artists feel in getting past Anglo conceptions of Indian life, to native literary images in, for example, stories about trickster heroes like Coyote. "[The] first thing that excited me about Coyote tales," Snyder has written, "was the delightful Dadaistic energy, leaping somehow into a modern frame of reference" (81). And, as a more general comment, he notes:

> So, why do modern writers and some young people today look for native American lore? Well, the first answer [is], there is something to be learned from the native American people about where we are. It can't be learned from anybody else. We have a western white history of a hundred and fifty years; but the native American history (the datings are always being pushed back) was first ten thousand years, then it was sixteen thousand years, then people started talking about twenty-five thousand years, and now . . . fifty thousand years. So, when we look at a little bit of American Indian folklore, myth, read a tale, we're catching just the tip of an iceberg of forty or fifty thousand years of human experience, on this continent, in this place. It takes a great effort of imagination to enter into that, to draw from it, but there is something powerfully there. (79–80)

These interests and undertakings represent something new, at least for Anglo writers of such stature. Although there have been more Native American writers in our history than most of us have realized—as important bibliographic and text-recovery work by A. LaVonne Brown Ruoff and others is revealing—there is also something auspicious about the rise to prominence, since the late 1960s, of so many gifted younger native authors. The novels and short stories of N. Scott Momaday, Leslie Marmon Silko, Simon Ortiz, James Welch, and Louise Erdrich; the plays of Hanay Geigogamah; the poetry of Silko, Ortiz, Duane Niatum, Ray Young Bear, and others; and the proliferation of anthologies of Indian writing all testify to the arrival of a genuine Native American current in contemporary writing, comparable to the breakthrough into publication and critical self-awareness of black writers a generation before. Much of this work— Silko's extraordinary first novel, *Ceremony*, for example, and Niatum's volumes of poetry—is explicitly and self-consciously grounded in tribal mythology, ritual, and song.[5]

How does the discovery of the traditional verbal arts of the tribes bear on the work of scholars and teachers in the field of American literature and, beyond that, on literary studies generally? First of all, the creative ferment has been matched in the scholarly domain, not coincidentally, by the appearance of a new field of literary study, *ethnopoetics*. Deriving its methods and principles from cultural anthropology, literary formalism, structuralism, semiotics, and contemporary linguistics, the ethnopoetic movement has extended our grasp of oral and traditional literature *as* literature. In the work of two of its most distinguished scholars, Dennis Tedlock and Dell Hymes, there is promise of new literary perceptions that will carry far beyond the native repertories. Hymes's *"In Vain I Tried to Tell You,"* the first of a series, is the benchmark in the field so far; to read this brilliant, difficult book is to see the western Chinookan narratives come alive under Hymes's scrutiny as sophisticated art—and also to feel an enhancement of one's sense of what literature is and what it does. The same can be said of Tedlock's *Spoken Word and the Work of Interpretation.*

In a response to the "Working Papers" of MLA's Commission on the Future of the Profession, Henry Louis Gates, Jr., has argued cogently that the incorporation of new literary texts—black, Chicano, Native American—must include new methods, fresh ideas about literature, or else the widening of the canon is merely appropriation, or "token integration," as we used to say. In Gates's phrase: "Method arises from text, and critical method *must* change" (6). A book like Hymes's is certainly aimed at expanding our notions of literary texts; its critical methodology—especially its combinations of methods—will, I predict, influence the study of more conventional forms of narrative:

> There are linguistics in this book, and that will put some people off. "Too technical," they will say. Perhaps such people would be amused to know that many linguists will not regard the work as linguistics. "Not theoretical," they will say, meaning not a part of a certain school of grammar. And many folklorists and anthropologists are likely to say, "too linguistic" and "too literary" both, whereas professors of literature are likely to say, "anthropological" or "folklore," not "literature" at all. But there is no help for it. As with *Beowulf* and *The Tale of Genji*, the material requires some understanding of a way of life. Within that way of life, it has in part a role that in English can only be called that of "literature." Within that way of life, and now, I hope, within others, it offers some of the rewards and joys of literature. And if linguistics is the study of language, not grammar alone, then the study of these materials adds to what is known about language. . . . The joy, the understanding, the language are all of a piece. (Hymes 5)

In terms of academic politics, the appearance of an MLA session or two on Indian writers and on traditional native material does not a new field or discipline make; it should count for something, however, that at both the annual convention and at the several western regional meetings, such sessions have been held for a number of years now, well attended and lively. As for professional societies beyond the MLA, there are at least three: the Society for American Indian Studies and Research, the Society for the Study of the Multi-Ethnic Literatures of the United States, and the Association for the Study of American Indian Literatures. The first two groups support publication of *American Indian Quarterly* and *MELUS*, respectively. ASAIL publishes its *Studies in American Indian Literature*, edited by Helen Jaskoski and featuring articles, reviews, symposia on new work by Indian writers, and a continuing series of Indian studies bibliographies; the association has launched *ASAIL Notes*, a newsletter covering activities and opportunities in the field of Native American studies. On the West Coast, a group of scholars at the University of California, Los Angeles, produces a quarterly review with similar aims: *American Indian Culture and Research Journal*. Other periodicals, too, have recognized the growing academic interest in Native American work by publishing articles on the subject—*College English*, *Book Forum*, *Georgia Review*, *Genre*, *Western American Literature*, *American Quarterly*, *Parnassus*, *New Literary History*, *Poetics*, *Boundary II*, *PMLA*.

What about a journal like *American Literature*? The question is not meant maliciously. For all I know, *AL* has not been regularly receiving manuscripts on native literature (in 1979 it did publish Vernon E. Lattin's "Quest for Mythic Vision in Contemporary Native American and Chicano Fiction," and in 1981 it printed Arnold Krupat's "Indian Autobiography: Origins, Type, and Function"). But it would be nice if Americanist journals like *AL* actively undertook to help our field define and locate itself academically. Until we find a way to see our subject as a special but legitimate zone of American literary studies, the field is in danger, I fear, of flying apart under the stress of so much hyphenation: ethnopoetical-anthropological-folkloristic-sociolinguistical. . . . If *Hiawatha* is an official canonical piece of American literature, why isn't the great Ojibwa Manabozho trickster cycle on which it is uncertainly based, and likewise the magnificent Iroquois Condolence Ritual, which memorializes the real Hiawatha? Why, in terms of academic policies and politics, are there no designated chairs of Native American literatures and languages in this country?

If perceived within the Academy as a branch of American literary scholarship, newfangled but devoted to our oldest literary traditions, Indian studies could, I think, make up for lost time and get on better with its proper pursuits. Foremost among these is the kind of intensive work on native languages, tribe by tribe, that heretofore has been carried on almost exclusively for linguistic and anthropological ends: here, on a basic philological level, is where the major literary discoveries are going to be made, and in fact are already being made by ethnopoetic scholars (see esp. Hymes, "Discovering"; Tedlock, *Finding the Center*). Perhaps it is not too farfetched to imagine a time when students of American literature will learn Indian languages so as to engage their oral literatures—and, equally desirable, Native Americans will formally prepare to edit, interpret, and teach the repertories of their own cultures.

Along with the learning of languages, and consequent upon it, much work needs to be done in retranslating and reediting the older texts, those that appeared, for example, under the auspices of the Bureau of American Ethnology. The possibilities of making transcriptions from performances even at this late date are not to be neglected, as the work of Dennis Tedlock, Larry Evers, J. Barre Toelken, William Bright, David McAllester, Richard and Nora Dauenhauer, and the transcribing and translating team connected with the British Columbia Indian Language Project makes clear.[6] In addition, of course, scholars should make systematic attempts to record native literary concepts and attitudes, both conventional and idiosyncratic. The fact that such crucial information was rarely solicited in the past is a severe handicap to our work with the older texts (see Toelken and Scott 72–73, 78).

In terms of literary works by Indian writers, efforts are under way on the rediscovery, reassessment, and republication of "lost" texts: Dexter Fisher's edition of *Co-ge-we-a*, a novel (possibly the first by an Indian woman) by the neglected Okanagan writer Mourning Dove; A. LaVonne Brown Ruoff's edition of *The Moccasin Maker*, by E. Pauline Johnson; and a reissue of Sarah Winnemucca's important *Life among the Piutes* (1883), with an introduction by Russ and Anne Johnson. However, much reclamation work remains to be done.

More generally, there is much to do in what might be called "literary ethnography"—that is, the systematic study of tribal and intertribal history and customs in relation to the traditional and modern literatures. What's necessary now is not so much new field work, as a specifically linguistic and literary recovery of the enormous amount of ethnological information collected and filed between 1880 and 1920 and mostly neglected. For example, one of the stories I discussed in my 1977 *PMLA* article on two Oregon myth narratives ends with the promise that the heroes of the piece will eventually turn into woodpeckers. I had to resolve this odd detail rather dubiously in contextual terms and only later discovered, in some old ethnographic notes, that in fact woodpeckers' scalps and feathers were highly prized among West Coast tribes as symbols of status and authority—so the transformation is auspicious indeed, and fully in keeping with its heroic tone (*Reading the Fire* 92). We take such illuminations for granted in the study of *Beowulf*, or Ben Jonson's plays; and the serious study of the native repertories will require a philological base no less meticulous. In Dell Hymes's words: "With texts, as sometimes with the myths themselves, what is dead can be revived. We cannot bring texts to life by stepping over them five times, but we can by scholarship. There is much to do and few to do it" ("*In Vain*" 14).

On more narrow literary grounds, other challenges present themselves. One is to develop a systematic classification of the features—I mean the characters, the motifs, the plot configurations—of the native repertories by tribe and region, so that typological fields and the primary storytelling permutations within them can be identified. It is typical of the spasmodic history of Indian studies that such knowledge was once in view, if not in hand, in the comprehensive myth studies of Boas and his protégés, around 1910. In a famous essay refuting the solar-myth theories of Paul Ehrenreich, for example, T. T. Waterman adduced featural details from no fewer than fifty-eight tribal repertories! It is humbling to think that nobody commands such a range today.

Another pressing interpretive need is for comparative studies—that is, between the narrative and poetic art of the Indian repertories and that of our own. What, to take two obvious examples, do *Beowulf* and the *Odyssey* have to do with some of our Indian hero cycles? The mysterious figure of the trickster is prominent in both the Indian and Western literatures—what of it? Such questions represent an area in which conventional literary scholarship is capable, even though not founded on the native languages, of making important contributions to the understanding of Indian texts. Conventional American literary scholarship also has the opportunity, and I think the obligation as well, to help bring about the formal recognition of the native literatures in our schools—through a careful review of American literature curricula, through insistence that classroom anthologies include significant and authentic native texts, through closer attention to the literary training of teachers, through the purchase by libraries of modern translations of traditional texts, new studies of native languages and oral literatures, and new books by American Indian writers.

Returning to more purely critical work: we speak confidently of the Indian literatures as "traditional" and "anonymous," but as we perceive them more clearly as art, the possibility of there being a personal element of creativity in some texts becomes more distinct, expressing itself not in our authorial terms but rather in subtle transformations of traditional elements. Hymes has suggested, conclusively I think, that the nineteenth-century Chinookan storyteller Charles Cultee was a bona fide literary artist in this sense, not just a terminal vehicle for Chinookan lore ("Folklore's Nature). Perhaps in such work, looking for the ghostly nuances of individual artists within what Hymes has called the "imperturbable self-transmogrifications of myth"—perhaps in such difficult work we stand to learn a great deal about myth, about our concepts of authorship, and about the very origins of literature.

In somewhat the same vein, we have almost everything to learn about the element of *adaptation* in American Indian texts—specifically adaptation and incorporation of Anglo literary materials, and for that matter those of blacks and Hispanics. If one set of biases led many nineteenth-century writers to deny that Indians had literary traditions worth mentioning at all—

> I am far from believing the many long and strange traditions with which we are often entertained. It is more than probable, that they are in most instances the gratuitous offerings of designing and artful traders and hunters to that curiosity which is ever awake and attentive to subjects of this description. . . . (Parker 235)

—then another set of biases has led to a rigid "classicism" whereby most scholars have avoided transcribing narratives in which Caucasian influences are at work, such as native incorporations of Bible stories and French folktales. Works interweaving the two cultures were and in many regions still are popular in Indian communities; it is regrettable, in terms of what they can reveal about the continuities of native values and imaginative forms, that so few texts have been collected and that the topic has been virtually ignored.[7]

This worksheet for the study of native literatures could go on and on—and should and will go on, I hope, elsewhere and in other hands. I will leave off with one final project, the undertaking of which would signal more clearly than anything else I can think of that the American literary establishment had actually accepted, belatedly, its intellectual and artistic obligations to America's first literatures. Nothing less than a native counterpart to the monumental collaboration that has produced the Center for Editions of American Authors series, it would call for the systematic preparation and publication of a "standard" dual-language edition of the surviving Native American repertories—proceeding tribe by tribe, with full textual apparatus as needed. The task I propose is formidable, and no doubt at present far beyond either our scholarly or our financial capabilities, but in the light of historical barriers between Anglo and native literatures, the missed chances and literary rootlessness of Americans writing in the

European tradition, the continuing loss among the Indians of stories and storytellers and the continued inaccessibility to them of scholarly texts, can we afford to do anything less now?

One of those Anglo authors whom we have fittingly standardized is, of course, Thoreau. In the handsome Princeton edition of *The Maine Woods*, I found two passages that somehow evoke both a poignant sense of how much we literary people—even men like Thoreau—have ignored, neglected, or misunderstood in the Native American cultures, and a thrilling sense of the crucial value of the native imaginative heritage in American life, if we could only understand that heritage. In the first passage, Thoreau offers—the only time he does so in the book—a summary of an Abenaki myth, about how Gluskap the Transformer foiled a giant female moose and turned her carcass into Mt. Kineo. Now, as Robert Sayre observes, Thoreau was "a poet and traveler" in his interest in Indians, not an anthropologist (or student of ethnopoetics)—but it *is* disappointing to find him following the myth summary with this glibly scornful observation, worthy of a Parkman or a Twain perhaps but not of someone so capable of imaginatively escaping his own ethnocentrism:

> An Indian tells such a story as if he thought it deserved to have a great deal said about it, only he has not got it to say and so he makes up for the deficiency by a drawling tone, long-windedness, and a dumb wonder which he hopes will be contagious. (172)[8]

The second passage describes what Thoreau heard one night while bedded down in the "Moose Camp" with Joe Aitteon and some Abenaki guides; it has a very different resonance:

> While lying there listening to the Indians, I amused myself with trying to guess at their subject by their gestures, or some proper name introduced. There can be no more startling evidence of their being a distinct and comparatively aboriginal race, than to hear this unaltered Indian language, which the white man cannot speak or understand. We may suspect change and deterioration in almost every other particular, but the language which is so wholly unintelligible to us. It took me by surprise, though I had found so many arrowheads, and convinced me that the Indian was not the invention of historians and poets. It was a purely wild and primitive sound, as much as the barking of a *chickaree*, and I could not understand a syllable of it. . . . These Abenakis gossiped, laughed, and jested, in the language in which Eliot's Indian Bible is written, the language which has been spoken in New England who shall say how long? These were the sounds that issued from the wigwams of this country before Columbus was born; they have not yet died away, and with remarkably few exceptions, the language of their forefathers is still copious enough for them. I felt that I stood, or rather lay, as near to the primitive man of America, that night, as any of its discoverers ever did. (212)[9]

So near, one is tempted to say on Thoreau's behalf; so near and yet so far off. It is not just a boyish exultation over his close encounter with aboriginal life that Thoreau is expressing here; it is also his dilated awareness in such company of being an American himself, an American writer, but lacking the imagination of native origins and incapable of speaking or comprehending the first languages of the land. How to understand one's own American identity in relation to Abenaki words from Maine, or the myths of the Wasco Chinookans of the Northwest, or the fiction of Momaday—that is part of the challenge in the serious study of native oral traditions and writing. Those of us who are now engaged in this study ask not for an Indian redefinition of the origins of American literature but rather for recognition of Native American literature as one of its essential categories.

Notes

[1] Early in his career Pound wrote a brief and apparently unironic *Hiawatha* imitation titled "Legend of the Chippewa Spring and Minnehaha, the Indian Maiden." See King 280–81.

[2] Typical of Williams's brief but appreciative summaries of Narragansett and other myths is his note on the natives' reverence for crows: ". . . they have a tradition, that the Crow brought them at first an *Indian* Graine of Corne in one Eare, and an *Indian* or *French* Beane in the other, from the Great God Kautantouwits field in the Southwest from whence they hold came all their Corne and Beanes" (96–97).

[3] See Schoolcraft, *Indian* and *Schoolcraft's Indian Legends*. On Longfellow's debt to the *Kalevala*, see Keiser 192. Keiser himself does not acknowledge the existence of Native American traditional literature per se; he makes no reference to the contemporary work of Franz Boas, A. L. Kroeber, Robert Lowie, Paul Radin, and other transcribers and commentators.

[4] Dabney is not far off the mark in asserting that Faulkner is "the one fiction writer of consequence since before the Civil War to make substantial use of the Indian subject" (4); but he does not consider actual myth texts about totemic bears from southern tribes, like those in Mooney, *Myths of the Cherokees* (see esp. "Bear Man" 325). Similarly, in *Bear, Man, and God*, Utley, Bloom, and Kinney ignore specific myth analogues and offer only a selection from A. Irving Hallowell's "Bear Ceremonialism in the Northern Hemisphere" (187–89) and a *Delaware* text about a woman's bear dream (185–86).

[5] For a discussion of Silko's and Niatum's use of native traditions and the obligations of the critic in dealing with adaptations by Native American writers, see Ramsey, "Teacher." See also the symposium issue of *American Indian Quarterly* on Silko's *Ceremony*, and Niatum, "On Stereotypes" (160–66).

[6] Representative works are Tedlock, *Finding the Center*; Toelken and Scott; Evers and Molina; and Bouchard and Kennedy.

[7] See Ramsey, "Bible." In *The Golden Woman*, Mattina offers a remarkable instance of native adaptation of a European folktale.

[8] In his neglected *Algonquin Legends of New England*, Leland gives another version of the story and takes sharp issue with Thoreau's remark. "This concluding criticism is indeed singularly characteristic of Mr. Thoreau's own nasal stories about Nature, but it is as utterly untrue as ridiculous when applied to any Indian story-telling to which I have ever listened . . . " (65–66). An authentic dual-language text of Thoreau's garbled Mt. Kineo myth is given by Speck in "Penobscot Transformer Tales" (204).

[9] Philip F. Gura has illuminated the whole subject of Thoreau's mixed feelings about the Native Americans he encountered in Maine in "Thoreau's Maine Woods Indians."

In the American Canon

Robert Hemenway

Once upon a time I was asked to speak at a summer meeting of English department chairpersons. I accepted the invitation with solemn allopathic purpose, sure that I could offer restorative therapy to this honorable group of ex-idealists, these staff officers regularly battered by occupational hazards. I planned to energize those slipping toward ennui and levitate those seeking higher ground amidst that alligator-infested swamp known as "The Department."

Then a funny thing happened on the way to therapy. In what was viewed by some as co-option, by others as the university's death wish, I was ambushed into a chairmanship before I could begin ministrations.

Today, after five years as a department chair, three years as a dean, and one year as a chancellor, I find that although my own idealism may have begun a long, slow slide toward that dismal slough known as "administrative responsibility," the perspective of administration has helped me understand better than ever before the importance of a literary canon. I find that I have lost none of my idealism about what should constitute that canon, and I have become even more convinced that a rethinking of the canon is essential for the health of our discipline.

Instead of retreating from the gains of the 1960s and 1970s, we must continue to evaluate our canon; and we must work even harder to include minority writers in it. In what follows, I wish to bring into question, as the theorists say, some of our ideas about that canon and challenge some of the reactionary self-congratulation (a kind of collective sigh of relief) that has greeted the move toward a return to the traditional library of English and American texts.

Because African American literature is my specialty, my thesis will concentrate on black authors, but much of what I say can apply equally to other ethnic literatures. Chicano, Puerto Rican, Asian American, Native American, and African American writers have been excluded from our classrooms, often by English professors standing in the doorway, waving copies of a mystical writ called the standard canon.

Although it sounds immodest to say so, English professors largely define the literary canon by choosing to teach certain works. The individual professor may respond, consciously or unconsciously, to subtle pressures from other domains of the literary world—the *New York Times Book Review*, the economics of hardcover publishing, the snob appeal of the Great Tradition—but no writer, no book, is likely to be accepted into the canon without the sanction of the university curriculum.

The modern idea of a literary canon originates in ancient ecclesiastical scholarship, where the sacred canon consisted of the books accepted as genuine and inspired holy scriptures. Eventually, any collection of sacred books was called a canon. The word carries a strong sense of authority and has the effect of validating certain works as the most respected and profound writing in the language. Just as the church canonizes saints, scholars and teachers elevate texts to the canon. Having a canon means that you divide the best from the rest. We have always considered canon central to our authority. Murray Krieger has, playfully but seriously, called our respect for the canon a form of "fetishization." He says that "the ground for our primal reading experience" as scholars and teachers "is the elite body of works made sacred by the special attention we grant them" (29).

My very practical purpose is to urge that we press forward in our efforts to expand the canon, that we open the door even wider than before by including black writers in our standard English curriculum at every level and in every way—not just in the obligatory black literature class created during the late 1960s to purchase peace and keep the students from occupying the faculty club, but in all our American literature classes, all our genre courses, all our composition courses.

Even more practically, I want to urge chairpersons to support and encourage scholars engaged in research on African American literary issues, indeed to urge them to protect such scholars—who are almost always young—from hoary mugwumps who advise them to work with "a major author," or who call their areas of specialization "peripheral" to the grand march of Western civilization.

I want to argue for the restructuring of the graduate curriculum so that our departments do not train students ignorant of black literature. Training in black literature will soon become as useful to graduates seeking jobs as training in rhetoric is now. Finally, I advocate a program of faculty development that will help remedy the ignorance of the current professoriate about black literature. There is a body of African American texts, authenticated by scholarly research, that should be a part of every literature teacher's repertoire. In sum, I want the intellectual borders of the English department to expand so that it is not, as it is now, simply the North Atlantic division of the ethnic studies curriculum.

I firmly believe that these actions are essential to the English department of the future, not only because they have distinct pedagogical benefits for a rapidly changing student population but also because an enlarged canon signals health and intellectual vigor for the profession of English studies, just as the promulgation of that canon in the literature classroom contributes directly to health and humanism in the society at large. Although it is now fashionable to congratulate the profession for returning from the streets, for adopting an attitude of aloofness from social issues, such a retreat may also be dangerous to our professional well-being.

We have a president who played on racial fears in his election campaign, suggesting that black rapists were being sponsored by his opponent. Our former president told a national television audience that there was "no racial problem" in his youth. Sociologists see what they call a new "meanness" characterizing our racial interactions. Black students are beaten on campus, and black youths are killed for eating at the wrong pizza joint or for trying to buy a used car in the wrong neighborhood. Crosses burn in the Ivy League. High school seniors in Concord, Massachusetts—the hometown of Ralph Waldo Emerson and Henry David Thoreau, a town whose citizens harbored fugitive slaves on their flight to Canada—list membership in the Ku Klux Klan as one of their yearbook activities, just after the glee club, just before the lacrosse team: "KKK, 3, 4."

Yet at this time our profession seems to be withdrawing from the tentative steps toward democratizing literary study that were taken in the 1960s and 1970s. During those decades, did we really alter our ideas of what constitutes the departmental canon? Many fear that we did. I wish I had more confidence in their anxiety.

As the politics of the country become more conservative, as we begin to feel the effects of a federal judiciary that has passed a litmus test of neoconservative ideology, as the average age of the professoriate approaches fifty, as departments at major universities (all of which are not just predominantly white but white beyond the racial demographics of the society) become gridlocked with tenure, as a secretary of education, in the late 1980s, asked us to compare the value of the literary experience we offer with the pleasure of owning a small business—as these events occur, there will be less and less room for the black author in the modern classroom.

In a speech given in the late 1970s, J. Hillis Miller frankly admitted what he called his "preservative and conservative instincts." Using a linguistic structure whose paradigm is the Apostles' Creed, Miller said, "I believe in the established canon of English and American literature and in the validity of the concept of privileged texts." [I believe in God the Father Almighty, Maker of heaven and earth: and in Jesus Christ his only Son our Lord. . . .] "I think it is more important to read Spenser, Shakespeare, or Milton than to read Borges in translation or even, to say the truth, to read Virginia Woolf."

As we all know, the concept of "privileged" texts is central to modern critical theory. Although my argument is not new, it is, I believe, still valid: the political and class assumptions in the metaphor of privilege all too often reflect the political and class assumptions of the academic study of literature. In fact, by collapsing the idea of the privileged nature of literature in Western culture into the idea of privilege for a class of superior texts (and, incidentally, for those who teach them), Miller provides an unintentional gloss on one of Dennis Brutus's remarks about South Africa. The problem of South Africa, Brutus says, may be less the question of who has the power than a question of the surrender of privilege (12). The protection for privilege has, of course, been carried to Olympian heights by Allan Bloom in *The Closing of the American Mind.*

Miller's essay appears in an ADE special issue published in 1979 and entitled *The State of the Discipline: 1970s–1980s.* The issue accurately reports on what has crossed the borders into this state named "discipline." It clearly indicates that curricular innovation characterized the 1970s and will continue to be a dominant influence in the future. Paul Hunter sees one of the "healthiest" curricular developments of the 1970s to be the "addition of new literary and quasi-literary areas, such as film, to the canons of our domain." Jonathan Culler urges English department graduate programs to teach psychoanalytic and philosophical texts as literature. Carolyn Heilbrun argues that new courses in feminist criticism will invigorate the department. Nowhere does this special

ADE issue mention a black writer or a black critic. In fact, Murray Krieger, one of the contributors, ties the tin can of ethnic studies courses to the anthropological tail of structuralist and poststructuralist poetics, which he sees as an

> enemy to the assumptions on which the definition of the functions of a department of English literature is based. Chief among these assumptions . . . is the claim to the elite nature of literary works, or at least of those works that constitute the canon out of which our department curriculum and the syllabi of the individual courses within it are constructed. (28)

The "political arm of structuralism," Krieger goes on to say, "in its attack on literary privilege, is also—in the name of the third world—attacking the exclusivistic concern with the Western literary tradition, as characterized by the production of its high (as opposed to its popular) culture."

I am not suggesting that the contributors to *The State of the Discipline* are guilty of serious omissions. They accurately surveyed the field of literature in colleges and universities, and black writers were not part of the topography.

What is interesting is that black writers should continue to be absent—what we used to call invisible—from the curriculum even though most major university English departments offer black literature courses and even though standard anthologies include black writers. Obviously, there is nothing wrong with African American literature courses. Many of us have earned a reasonable living teaching them, a living much better, in fact, than most of the authors taught in them ever earned by their writing. But having one or two black literature courses, taught by the department's black lit man or woman, is a form of ghettoization. The response elicited is, black writing does not have to be taught in other courses because that is Hemenway's thing, his area of expertise. Time after time, when Frederick Douglass and W. E. B. Du Bois are suggested for the nineteenth-century course, the reply is, "But don't you teach them in the black lit course? I don't know anything about them. That's why we have you here." Perversely, one effect of opening up the curriculum to black authors has been to preserve the traditional canon. We are now in the peculiar position where the "Americanists" know virtually nothing about African American literature, while the "African Americanists" know nearly everything about the so-called American literature. In effect, our "Americanists" are incompletely trained in their area of specialization, and their students emerge culturally deprived.

Nor does the appearance of black writers in the standard anthologies translate into a meaningful appearance by black writers in the classroom or the canon. True, the anthologies have improved. The one-volume Norton anthology of American literature in wide use throughout the 1970s—edited by Bradley, Beatty, and Long—included one black writer, LeRoi Jones, who occupied the last 2 of the book's 1,906 pages. The reader was told that "race is not often an issue in Jones's poetry and does not restrict its appeal." Yet a new Norton anthology, published in 1979 under the general editorship of Ronald Gottesman, includes seven black writers among its eighty-seven authors and gives 70 of its 1,925 pages over to black writings. The quality of editorial comment has improved somewhat, but not overwhelmingly. The last sentence of the commentary on Langston Hughes, for example, raises the non sequitur to the level of cultural politics: "While Hughes never militantly repudiated cooperation with the white community, the poems which protest against white racism are bold and direct." The remark leaves me at a loss about how to interpret such poets as Robert Frost, who "militantly repudiated cooperation with the white community." (See Kolb, in this volume, for additional discussion of the Norton editions.)

With Nina Baym's editing of the most recent Norton anthology, the situation is further improved. Baym's two-volume edition of 1989 devotes 310 of its 5,242 pages to the works of twenty-one black writers.

Superficially, the numbers are encouraging. You might conclude from the 1979 edition that the black part of the American literature canon had increased thirty-five-fold, and from the 1989 edition that it had more than quadrupled in a decade—even though the pages devoted to black writings constitute only 3.6% of Gottesman's anthology and 5.9% of Baym's. But the more relevant questions are: Do the black selections get taught? Do they get taught sensitively and well? And does their inclusion in the anthology, given our notions of a sacred canon, mean that they have now been accepted? I rather suspect not. What may happen in the anthologies of the 1990s is that black writers will slowly begin to fade from the tables of contents, just as black writers began to disappear from publishers' lists in the 1980s and just as works by black authors now go rapidly out of print. It is an instructive sign of the times that when Toni Morrison appeared on the cover of *Newsweek*, two of her four books were out of print and unavailable for classroom use.

But if departments have survived the decades since the 1960s without really incorporating black writing into the canon, why should they do so now, when the heat's off? (Of course, the heat is not entirely off. Advocates of cultural and gender studies are keeping the heat on.) One answer is that the acceptance of black works is morally right; another is that it would reflect our commitment to egalitarian principles, democratic education, and academic humanism. But I would like to suggest two quite practical reasons. First, black literature can release the literary classroom from its aura of privilege—no small benefit for a student population that from now to the end of the century will be increasingly from the working class and increasingly black. Second, black literature, as predominantly a literature based on folklore, can help to liberate our theories of narrative, trope, and aesthetic performance, concerns that frequently are a part of the latest critical theory.

The Carnegie Commission Report on the next twenty years for higher education, *Three Thousand Futures*, published in 1981, was cautious in many of its projections, but about one prediction it was dead certain: many more black students would be entering colleges and universities in the next twenty to thirty years. By the year 2000, the report stated, minority students will constitute 25% of the total student body.

Although the Carnegie projections have proved incorrect in the short run—black undergraduate enrollments, for example, have actually declined since the mid-1980s, the result of cutbacks in student aid and attacks on affirmative action—the long-range projections will, I believe, be on target. Particularly at state universities, where tuition is lower, black enrollments will be substantially higher by the end of the century.

I see no reason why the many additional black students entering college will not appear in our literature classes. In an era of declining English majors and poor economic opportunities for humanities graduates, these students may not specialize in English, but they are certainly going to be a presence, particularly in lower-division courses.

These black students will not necessarily demand black literature—as students did in the 1960s—but *we* should demand it in order to promulgate the values of serious art to a student population increasingly suspicious of our product. This does not mean that we should teach what we think the students want or what they read last week. Curricular populism was one of the worst mistakes of the 1960s, reflecting the idea that we could win converts by offering courses in the dormitory's latest, drug-inspired library list. (Remember *Steppenwolf*?) Black students will not enter the classroom panting to read Ralph Ellison. They must be taught why his writing is important to their lives.

Let no one misunderstand. It is racism to suggest that without African American literature English teachers cannot reach black students. Almost four hundred years of evidence proves that Spenser, Shakespeare, and Milton—to accept Miller's triune god—have been important to young black readers. But black students will be more receptive to such a profound trinity if they do not feel that men and women of color have been excluded, a priori, from the literature classroom.

We must be more honest about what that classroom represents to many students. One of the dangers in the concept of canonization, the theory of texts with privilege, is that the literary classroom can become, literally, what Victor Doyno of the State University of New York, Buffalo, has called a CLASS-ROOM—in other words, an arena for reinforcing the professor's class prejudices (and for hiding his or her insecurities) by putting down the students' proletarian instincts. Too often the traditional classroom and the traditional canon become a bludgeon in the cause of high culture. We must admit that in the classroom, literature becomes an institution primarily maintained by its teachers; limiting the canon becomes a political act in the politics of culture. As Leslie Fiedler remarks in his preface to the 1979 English Institute essays, *Opening Up the Canon*, "The contributors to this volume raise critical questions about the study of literature in the university, limited as it is by unconscious assumptions of the teachers, rooted in race, class and gender. Merely to recognize the problem is to begin solving it" (viii).

But is Fiedler correct, that recognition leads to remedy? The assumptions he refers to did not notably diminish during the 1970s, despite all the decade's upheavals. One reason may be the kind of fundamental threat that black literature poses for professional preconceptions.

As the pop psychologists say, the problem is one of value clarification. How do we determine what we value as a culture? If we value literature, how do we determine what literature we value most? As professional academics, we presume to be able to answer such questions, and we have traditionally prided ourselves on being able to make such determinations, usually on aesthetic grounds, under the label of "universality."

As the criteria for determining value has begun to deconstruct (universality is largely a discredited critical concept) and as the assault on the canon has continued, many sensitive and decent scholars have responded by arguing for a more inclusive but merit-structured canon.

Possibly drawing a parallel with the academic rank structure, where the work of full professors is assumed by definition to be of greater value than that of assistant professors, these scholars have suggested a ranked canon in which some authors are more important than others. All qualified applicants, regardless of race, enter the canon, but most minorities cluster at the lowest levels, while the upper ranks remain predominantly white, male, and relatively free of the coming and going of literary reputations. In the lower ranks, meanwhile, because they are more inclusive, a good deal of substitution occurs—a situation analogous to the coming and going of assistant professors in the search for tenure. Under the merit-system canon, Melville's place is secure, Hemingway is good but not of the first rank (an associate professor, presumably), and Langston Hughes has a precarious hold. (This ranking system ignores, of course, the fact that Melville's canonization is a historically recent phenomenon reflecting the changing values that accompanied the rise of modernism.)

While such efforts may be well-meaning, and while they do have an effect on the classroom—since black writers are more likely to be taught under an inclusionary rule than not—the ranked canon seems an attempt to preserve the power of traditional value determination without confronting the fundamental interrelationship between social class and aesthetic value. Although no one has ever accused him of understatement, Bruce Franklin focused on this issue when he said:

> The fundamental definition of American literature remains what it was before 1964, with Afro-American literature safely ghettoized within the curriculum and represented by tokens in the anthologies. Certainly since 1964, those professors who edit the anthologies, survey the literary history, and decide the curriculum, have been actively searching for black authors who fit their notion of excellence. That is precisely the point, for the criteria they apply are determined by their own people and social class, and most Afro-American literature conforms to criteria determined by a different people and a different social class. And, thus, any large-scale inclusion of Afro-American literature within what we call American literature forces a fundamental redefinition and a complex process of revaluation. (xxi)

No one has yet redefined or revalued American literature in Franklin's sense, but the process has begun and will gain strength in the next twenty years. All the elements are in place. There is now an established body of African American literary scholarship, and more is added each day. The dross of the 1960s, the rhetoric without substance, has dropped away, leaving a core of profound explorations of African American texts. The work of Robert Stepto, Houston Baker, Henry Louis Gates, Arnold Rampersad, Sherley Williams, George Kent, Stephen Henderson, Werner Sollors, Mary Helen Washington, and many others has helped to sharpen the theoretical tools for understanding black writers. There is a renewed effort to liberate African American texts from the sociological straitjacket that meant that each black poem had to serve as an anecdote about school busing. The racist texts in the field have been largely discredited. White critics who could not separate African American writing from their own pathological fantasies of what it must mean to be black are no longer taken seriously.

Moreover, changes that have occurred in the discipline of history suggest that many more breakthroughs will be forthcoming. Indeed, as Robert Stepto has suggested, the way our historians have truly made African American history a part of United States history might well serve as a model for American literary scholarship. An impressive group of white and black scholars—led by John Blassingame, Nell Painter, Nathan Huggins, and Lawrence Levine, among others—has revolutionized American historical study by accepting radically new kinds of testimony into the canon of historical evidence.

Black texts challenge traditional literary ideas. That the slave narrative is unquestionably the first indigenous written literary genre America offered the world places a whole literary tradition in a new perspective and helps us understand both generic properties and the European influence on American literature. Gates has suggested that black texts predict their opposites, that slave narratives provide a kind of perverse literary foregrounding, virtually ensuring the creation of the plantation novel as a reversed image of the slave narrative's indictment. Such a theory begins to assess the dialectic between white aesthetics and black aesthetics.

Earlier I mentioned that black literature can have positive effects on the literature classroom and on our notions of a literary canon because of black literature's folkloric content. As a body of works that has developed out of an oral narrative tradition, black literature is much like Native American literature. (At one of the first conferences in the United States on ethnic contributions to American literature, at the University of Oklahoma in the 1930s, the Native American representative rose and announced that the Indians' contribution to American literature was nothing—Indians never put it on paper. Then he sat down.)

There is a long history of written African American narrative, but the chief form of art making during slavery and reconstruction was folklore. Black people created a special narrative tradition that provided unique forms and unique subjects for the act and art of storytelling. Embodied in the spirituals, heroic legends, proverbs, and traditional jokes, but especially in folktales, this tradition eventually became a reservoir of stylized expression that helped black people survive and affirm themselves as a culturally unique group. When black people began to publish in fairly significant numbers during the last half of the nineteenth century, the tradition crossed over into written literature, where its positive, heuristic, group-affirming function has continued to be displayed.

A literature assumes patterns and replicates forms, because these patterns and forms communicate a shared understanding of the world. The most viable aesthetic forms of African American writing arise from the traditional poetic performances of black people, those acts of creative communication within small groups called folklore. Ralph Ellison has said, "Negro folklore, evolving within a larger culture which regarded it as inferior, was an especially courageous expression. It announced the Negro's willingness to trust his own experience, his own sensibilities as to the definition of reality, rather than allow his masters to define these crucial matters for him." The understanding of African American art, whether in the classroom or in written discourse, must be founded on folk expression. Folklore was what "black people had before they knew there was such a thing as art." (*Shadow and Act* 173; NAL, 1964).

The role of folklore in black literature is so widespread, and so integral to formal properties such as genre and trope, that the literature itself challenges our preconceptions—many of which derive from our faith in the canon—about the function and nature of art.

An instructive folktale told by black people during reconstruction illustrates my point. An illiterate young black man, reared in the North, came South to seek employment. He was filled with stories about the ways of white Southerners, and he expected hostility. But surprisingly, the first man he encountered, a rich farmer, was extremely polite. The planter explained that he had no work now, but maybe Colonel Jones, down the lane, did. The farmer gave the man a note of introduction, and the worker took it to Colonel Jones. No, Jones didn't have work, but why not take the note to Cap'n Smith, a mile across the pasture? Cap'n Smith didn't have work either; why not try Widow Breckinridge, on the river road? After a long day of this kind of traveling, the tired young man found himself a considerable distance from his starting point. Trudging along, he met a brother passing the other way and told him of his troubles. The man looked at the note and read: "The bearer of this paper is a trouble maker. Do not give him work. Keep him moving."

Anyone who has read Ralph Ellison's *Invisible Man* identifies the story immediately as the source for a major structuring device in that novel. Ellison's book is organized around a series of incidents, each introduced by the narrator's receiving a piece of paper. Once he receives a letter of recommendation he is not to open; another time a scholarship to a Tuskegee-like institution; a third time a slip of paper giving him a new identity. In each of their forms, the papers say essentially the same thing: in Ellison's words, "Keep this nigger boy running."

The American literary canon must not be interpreted as pieces of paper containing messages coded to say, keep this boy moving. Yet I fear that the idea of a privileged canon may very well make some of our students feel that way. Our celebration of the properties of art must be less supremacist, less didactic, less dependent on the class assumptions built into the idea of a canon. In fact, we would do well to consider the teaching strategy of the folktale just cited.

On a superficial level, the tale's meaning is political. Passed from one generation to another around a campfire, after Sunday school, in a barbershop, on a street corner, the tale teaches that whites cannot be trusted, that The Man will do you wrong. Beware of white folks bearing gifts. One can laugh at the young man's naiveté and resolve not to commit the same mistake. In this sense the story is a protest tale and could be dismissed as such—just as other black writings have been categorized as protest literature and denied access to the established canon.

But at a deeper cultural level, the tale serves as a heuristic instrument demonstrating the importance of education. The young man is duped because he cannot read. The tale teaches that illiteracy enslaves. If you cannot read, you are vulnerable, as the youth was vulnerable, to manipulation by forces that control the word.

The "words" of black narrative tradition have often originated in speech, not on paper. And, unfortunately, they gained stature as literature only after they were put into children's books. Priests of the written canon have often considered black folklore the primitive art of a limited race, childlike tales with obvious meanings. To a great extent, the person responsible for this view is Joel Chandler Harris, the creator of Uncle Remus.

Harris's career becomes a parable for my subject. His literary genius was to know that Br'er Rabbit—the revolutionary trickster, created by black storytellers to transmit a culture of resistance and self-affirmation amid the darkest despair of slavery—would never be accepted by whites unless his outlaw antics, his demonstrations of the weak triumphing over the strong, were defused, juvenilized, by being put into the mouth of an old-time darky named "Uncle" Remus. Uncle Remus tells Br'er Rabbit's stories to a young white boy, who thinks of the animal in the same way he thinks of his teddy bear. Yet these tales, every one of which was created by black storytellers long before Harris ever heard of them, were accepted by black people as adult entertainments, art forms of enormous subtlety and profound purpose. Br'er Rabbit's stories became part of the canon of American literature because a white voice came forth to authenticate their right to a literary audience. And because the source was folklore, the stories entered that canon through the back door of children's literature.

We, as a profession, must reject paternal primitivism—the idea that a few, but only a few, talented black writers have evolved beyond the crude forms of oral expression, have mastered our written traditions, and can now receive club privileges. Much more viable is a communal sense of creation—the individual storyteller merely being the latest manifestation of the narrative art that has enabled the group to survive, the individual story a culmination of linguistic possibilities, both written and oral, perpetuated by the community.

It is this sense of literary creation that black literature offers to our semiological, structuralist, and deconstructionist theoreticians, as well as to our traditionalists. Krieger and others are worried that if all discourse is brought to the same level of significance, there will be no way to distinguish between privileged literary texts and scientific reports, between James Joyce and your neighborhood barber's conversation. But this fear seems to me to ignore the lessons of Brazzle's mule.

Brazzle's mule is a cantankerous yellow animal owned by Matthew Brazzle, a man so cheap he buys side meat by the slice. The mule serves as the constant source of inspiration for a group of storytellers who inhabit the front porch of the general store in the all-black village of Eatonville, Florida, in Zora Neale Hurston's novel *Their Eyes Were Watching God* and in a play entitled "Mule Bone" coauthored by Hurston and Langston Hughes.

The mule is "so skinny that the women use his rib bones for a rub board and hang clothes on his hock bones to dry." He's so mean he refuses to get fat, staying poor and rawbony just for spite. He is the kind of mule who sticks his head in the Pearsons' window while the family is at the dinner table, and Mrs. Pearson mistakes him for the Reverend and hands him a plate. He is the kind of mule who sleeps in the kitchen one night and fights until he gets a cup of coffee for his breakfast the next morning.

When Brazzle's mule eventually dies, he is buried in a town ceremony that "mocked everything human in death." Six months later, two men near the grave begin arguing over a girl. During the dispute, one man gropes for a weapon and comes up with the hock bone of Brazzle's mule, which just happens to be lying nearby. He knocks out his opponent with a well-placed blow.

In a subsequent trial for assault and battery, the assailant admits to hitting his adversary but argues that a common brawl does not constitute a criminal act. His ingenious defense is shattered by a shrewd villager, a keeper of the sacred canon perhaps, who points out, with impeccable logic, that anyone who has ever been kicked by a mule knows that the closer one gets to the mule's rear, the more dangerous the animal becomes. Thus if Samson could slay a thousand Philistines with the jawbone of an ass, just think what a hock bone could do.

Clearly, the storytelling canon of Eatonville recognized no special privileges. The most sacred text of all, the Bible, can easily cross borders between written and oral art. The town's storytellers did not worry about whether they were in the schoolroom or the barbershop. Creative inspiration comes in both divine and secular forms, to saints and sinners alike. The classroom was one with the literature itself, not set apart as a special cultural institution.

I think Eatonville has much to teach us about what constitutes literature and the art-making intelligence, just as Hurston has much to offer us as we step into the classroom of the future.

II

Oral Dimensions of American Literature

The Oral Tradition and the Study of American Literature

Theresa Meléndez

The problems encountered in attempting to institute oral literature into American literary canons are as complex as the study of oral literature itself. Most literary critics and literary historians have ignored or underestimated the oral tradition as a flourishing and vital literature. The reasons for its exclusion in the study of literature rest on the conventional definitions of what literature is and who creates it and participates in it.

The problem largely began with the metaphor of the "Book" in the history of Western European thought—a metaphor that has exerted a powerful influence on the assumption of what constitutes literature. Ernst Curtius, in his *European Literature and the Latin Middle Ages*, explains that in early cultures in which a priestly caste preserved religious teachings, writing had a sacred character. In other societies, in which there were no privileged scribes, such as ancient Greece, the Book did not have figurative meaning. It was speech, not written records, that imparted wisdom. When a literature had to be recorded in order to be preserved (as in the Hellenistic period), the "Book" as metaphor gained ascension. The metaphor was enhanced by the separation of literary activity from everyday pursuits: literature became an acquired product of an individual's official (institutional) education, instead of an integral part of the society's culture. In the definition of literature, the document, the recorded text, took the place of the aesthetic acts of composing, performing, and responding. The earlier term *poesy* or *poetry* meant simply a creation, a making, while the word *literature* took on a meaning not necessarily related to creative activity. When literature as document became equivalent to higher learning, it imbued its creators with like value. Literature came to be associated with the erudite, the educated, the person of letters, as distinct from the unlearned, the unlettered. The idea of the Book made possible the division of verbal expressive systems into prejudged ranks.

The further distinction between the learned and the unlearned occurred with the spread of Christianity and the monastic tradition, when the Book was equated with the sacred or revealed truth, accessible only to a chosen few. According to this concept, "text" included not only written works but also the experience of living in the world itself, as suggested in the figures of speech "book of the heart" and the "book of nature." Curtius says "a comprehension of the world was not regarded as a creative function but as an assimilation of given facts; the symbolic expression of this being reading" (326; see also Needler). Accordingly, reading in the Middle Ages became synonymous with interpretation by authorities. Thus, who composed, read, and interpreted—artist, audience, and critic—was for the most part dictated by ecclesiastical officials.

In the nineteenth century, similar consequences arose as the result of the ethnocentricity of the social Darwinists, who neatly categorized the world and its literary productions into hierarchical classifications of cultures: savagery, barbarism, civilization. Primitives had myth; peasants had folklore; the more civilized, of course, had literature. Myth and folklore were fascinating creations of simpler people but were not to be compared with the complex artistry of civilization. If they were studied, it was as part of the new discipline of anthropology; scholars sought to glean from these texts cultural or linguistic evidence of earlier societies. Such distinctions continue to exist implicitly in the literary academy, as is apparent to anyone who examines university curricula and textbooks. The oral tradition rarely forms a serious part of a literature student's field of inquiry. (And the study of oral traditions is further hampered by the politics of mainstream aesthetics, which relegates art and artists to commodities and defines art as what is palpable and therefore marketable; for a discussion of the role of art in the Western world, see Maquet.)

A correlate problem to consider is the definition of *folklore*. Who the *folk* are and what the *lore* consists of have been debated by scholars since the term was coined by William Thoms in 1846. The twenty-one definitions of *folklore* in the *Standard Dictionary of Folklore, Mythology, and Legend* (Leach) indicate that the question remains unresolved. The issue is not so much who creates folklore as what materials are to be studied *as* folklore.[1] In addition, the study of oral literature is divided into what Alan Dundes has called the "scientific" and the "aesthetic" or literary sides of the discipline of folklore ("American Concept" 229). This division of labor further complicates the view of folklore as a coherent entity. But there is one important difference between the seemingly parallel problems of defining literature and of defining folklore: in academia it is the study of written literature, and not that of folk literature, that determines the direction of literary scholarship. The exponents of the oral tradition remain on the periphery of academic and publishing interests.

Most literary folklorists have approached the issue of oral literature by examining how folklore is utilized in literature. In 1957, the *Journal of American Folklore* published a series of articles stemming from a joint meeting of the American Folklore Society and the Modern Language Association.[2] This brief and somewhat oblique series, which examined the common interests of scholars in the two disciplines, concentrated on the identification and classification of folklore elements in literary works. It was a basic step but one that can lead, later scholarship would agree, to an unproductive study of isolated folklore genres or motifs for their own sake. Commenting on the limitations of this approach and reflecting the more recent perspective of folklorists, Dundes stresses that the proper interpretation of folklore in literature must include the concept of folklore within a specific context ("Study").[3]

When the next major journal of folklore took up the problem, some twenty years later, the subject was framed as "Folklore *and* Literature," and care was taken not to subsume either. Most contributors to that issue of the *Journal of the Folklore Institute* (1976) explored the deep levels of interpretation revealed by the study of folklore as process, involving the cultural and performance contexts of the text. The redirection of the discipline of oral literature was promoted in part by the earlier Parry-Lord study of a living oral tradition, meant to illuminate Homeric poetics (Lord, *Singer*).[4] The scholarship focused on the composition of epic poetry in a cultural context and resulted in the oral formulaic theory, a still debated but highly influential construct. In another format, studies such as *Traditional Literatures of the American Indian: Texts and Interpretations*, edited by Karl Kroeber, consider the inadequacies of traditional views of oral literature—shortcomings that arise in great part from oral literature's transformation from one medium to another, the accuracy of its translation or the representation of sounds, and its abstraction out of its sociocultural continuity.[5] These critical works demonstrate the major concerns of folklore and literature studies: the relevance of folklore to literary criticism and the application of the principles of literary criticism to folklore.

More recent folklore studies, however, distinguish between literature in its written form and literature as an oral process, because of the recognition that analyzing oral works as only literary products can distort their interpretation. The fact that oral literature operates in a different mode from that of written literature is what informs performance theory in folklore. Drawing its models from communication theory, this approach emphasizes the view of verbal art as performance, a "species of situated human communication" within an interpretative frame (Bauman, *Verbal Art* 8; cf. Lomax; Abrahams, "Folklore"; Ben-Amos and Goldstein). In anthropology, the approaches to the lore of the people depend, as in any discipline, on the prevalent theories, but those who specifically address the issue study verbal art either in terms of its functions (Bascom), as cognitive models of reality (Lévi-Strauss, "Structural Study"), or as symbolic arenas of social processes (Turner, *Ritual Process*).

However, these and other scholars do not discuss the central question of the representation of oral literature in conventional literary histories. Daniel Hoffman, the moderator of that earlier symposium in the *Journal of American Folklore*, phrased the point thus: "How can folklore be otherwise than marginal and atavistic to the scholar concerned with centrality in the development of culture?" (17). Underlining this issue is Hoffman's belief that folk cultures provide us with "traditional shared symbols, important—at the least—to our understanding of the cultures from which they derive." He answers the question he raises by citing George R. Foster's theory on the dynamic nature of social and creative development in which folk traditions are seen as a significant tributary to the mainstream culture.[6] Although Hoffman's self-named "functional symbolism," demonstrated in his *Form and Fable in American Fiction*, remains on the theoretical level of the use of folklore *in* literature, the question he posed has valuable implications for our study.

For in spite of the relative success of folklore as a discipline, folklore scholarship itself continues to be "marginal and atavistic" to the central concerns of literary critics. Few major literary journals publish studies of folk literature,[7] while studies such as Wayne Shumaker's *Literature and the Irrational* point out the similarities between folklore and literature by informing us that we all have a bit of the "primitive" in us. Major anthologies cite most oral literature as either antecedents of or sources for written literature, denying oral genres literary merits of their own. This stance is an inherited one, stemming from the concerns of the Romantic nationalists of the nineteenth century, who sought to revitalize the literary traditions from the natural fonts of the common folk, and the cultural evolutionists, who believed that the study of less civilized peoples would benefit the examination of their own higher, more complex social organizations (I leave to the reader's discretion the use of the appropriate quotation marks). Thus oral literature came to be seen as the spontaneous outgrowth of unlettered, ignorant, more primitive societies in which tradition served as the artless muse, the collective creative force. In this light also, oral literature was not considered worthy of serious study for its own sake, and those who pursued such an endeavor suffered a similar neglect. The lore of the folk was interesting primarily because of its historical value as "relics" of a richer era.

These assumptions, which affected literary critics and folklorists alike, have been extremely influential in the contemporary view of oral literature. In an informal and brief survey, I examined six general American literature anthologies and one in American poetry. Three of them do not mention oral literatures: *The Norton Anthology of American Literature* (Baym et al., 2nd ed., 1985); *American Poetry* (Allen et al.); and *Anthology of American Literature* (McMichael). Three include a few folk songs and some oral works by Native Americans: *The American Tradition in Literature* (Bradley et al., 6th ed., 1985); *Literature of the United States* (Blair et al.); *The Harper American Literature* (McQuade et al.).[8] Only one—*American Literature* (Brooks, Lewis, and Warren)—makes a heroic attempt to represent folk literature accurately, citing white and black folk songs, Indian oratory and poetry, and blues lyrics. (*The Norton Anthology* and *The American Tradition in Literature* are also discussed in Kolb and in Hemenway, in this volume.) I also reviewed *Literary History of the United States*, by Robert E. Spiller and others,[9] and two general histories, *Main Currents in American Thought*, by Vernon Louis Parrington, and *Backgrounds of American Literary Thought*, by Rod W. Horton and Herbert W. Edwards. (The latter two have no reference to oral traditions.) Unlike *American Literature*, the two anthologies that include the oral tradition generally follow Spiller's lead in defining their values and attitudes toward it.

I have examined Spiller's work in some detail, even though it is seemingly outdated, because it demonstrates clearly some of the attitudes that still prevail in academia. Spiller's perspective of what constitutes American literature is clear from the outset. The "Address to the Reader" starts with the observation that "the literary history of this nation began when the first settler from abroad of sensitive mind paused in his adventure long enough to feel that he was under a different sky. . . ." Spiller goes on to explain that the roots of our literary culture extend into British literature and defines literature, "a record of our experience," as "any writing in which aesthetic, emotional, or intellectual values are made articulate by excellent expression . . . by the right words in the right order" (xv–xviii). This insistence on the written, on the male settler, and on the British leaves little room for the discussion of oral works, American Indian literature, or for any examination of stray roots from other literary traditions. The primacy of British literature in the development of American letters is not what is involved here, but rather the attitude toward other cultures and other forms of literature embedded in these statements. Such a perspective is especially in evidence in the section "Expansion," referring to nineteenth-century European settlement.

The attitude is reflected in other essays in *Literary History of the United States*. In "The Widening of Horizons," for example, Henry Nash Smith writes disparagingly of the immigrants who brought with them "an invisible baggage of cultural tradition: folklore, crafts, religions . . ." and of the decline of the emigrant heritage: "Much of this cultural baggage disappeared in the process of Americanization, but much of it was absorbed into the American way of life" (644)—hardly much of a distinction, I would say. Nevertheless, Smith admits that this "cultural baggage" played an important role in the arts and that the growing interest in folklore (Indian, southern Appalachian, southern black) "enriched man's understanding" of the New World.

This understanding apparently did not apply to the vast open lands of the West: Frederick J. Turner's thesis of the frontier as "the meeting point between savagery and civilization" (200) colors Dixon Wecter's essay in Spiller's work. Turner's legacy is especially noticeable when Wecter looks (briefly, in four sentences) at the influence of Mexican culture in the West and Southwest. Wecter begins inauspiciously: "The Spanish civilization of the Pacific coast was too thin in population, too indolent, to make a concerted stand against the Anglo-Saxon" (659). But he cites the evidence of some literary effort in this "indolent" group by way of Spanish-language newspapers, sermons, and "a few quaint remains of liturgical drama." Mexican culture fares better in Henry A. Pochmann's "Mingling of Tongues," in the same volume. Pochmann reports the existence of "an oral literature of plays, songs, ballads, and folk tales" among the descendants of Spanish colonists. However, he assigns the works solely to "old Spain," ignoring the influence of indigenous materials (687–88).[10]

The presence of the separate sections "The Indian Heritage" and "Folklore" in Spiller's work reflects the prevailing conflict in the 1950s in the study of folklore: the distinction between the lore of the primitives and the lore of the peasants. But in "The Indian Heritage" essay, Stith Thompson, discussing the oral traditions of the American Indian, describes their works as "literary forms" (699). Another folklorist, Arthur Palmer Hudson, who wrote the section "Folklore," perpetuates the simplistic view of folklore as "the spontaneous play of naive imaginations upon common human experience" (703) and the "possession of the ignorant and the illiterate," although "many of the best texts have come from educated and locally prominent people . . ." (706). He also reinforces the primacy of British materials: "These old [Child] ballads . . . are the bluebloods of folk song in the United States" (705). Ballads from cultures other than British, such as the Spanish *romance*, are "foreign" (706). Of the other genres that Hudson studies, the majority of the examples are nonethnic, except when he discusses the spirituals, the blues, and the African American origin of the minstrel show. He concludes by citing a quotation from Thomas Mann on the two sources of poetry: "folk-simplicity" and "the literary gift." While the latter is "undoubtedly the higher form . . . it cannot flourish cut off from the other, needing it as a plant needs soil" (727).[11] Thus, Hudson equates folk literature with improvisation and ignorance and erects a hierarchy of class and culture. At the same time, he removes folk materials from the realm of literature by relegating them to a subliterary ground.

The view of folklore as "relics" or "survivals" also constricts the definition of both oral literature and its artists to "folk-simplicity." The opening remarks of William Wells Newell, editor of the first issue of the *Journal of American Folklore*, in 1888, reflected this view. Newell's avowal to collect the "fast-vanishing remains of Folk-Lore in America," the "relics of old English Folk-Lore" and the lore of blacks in the South, of American Indians, and of immigrant groups gives us his definition of both the lore and the folk (cf. Bell). That is, the lore consists of remnants of a dying form and is the exclusive possession of nonintegrated groups in the United States. And, of course, Francis J. Child's collection of *The English and Scottish Popular Ballads* (1882–98) established an authoritative canon of its own in balladry, outside of which few native ballads could be considered. A review of folklore journals far into the twentieth century would show the enduring influence of these precepts.[12]

Remedying the problem, then, entails redefining the goals of traditional literary criticism and of folklore scholarship as well. In his survey of the theoretical assumptions underlying the American concept of folklore, Dundes states that folklore was conceived as a "historical science whose primary aim was the reconstruction of the past ("American Concept" 240).[13] In some cases, such as ethnic literature (which has suffered a similar neglect as oral literature), the use of folklore as a valid tool to explore the past has concrete objectives: to explain the symbolic and structural elements in literature derived from folk cultures and to correct the distortions and to fill the lacunae of otherwise disregarded civilizations. As revealed in the development of their folkloric or verbal art forms, these cultures can now be seen as evolutionary and dynamic, not static and homogeneous. But in mainstream American literature, the oral heritage of Native and ethnic peoples merits recognition not only as a primary historical and literary resource but also as documentation of the unofficial traditions, for its artistic expressiveness, and for its distinctive form.

Discussing the relation between literature and myth, Northrop Frye underlines his stance on myth criticism—(which calls for an understanding of oral tradition in general—as the basis for the study of the "structural principles of literature itself" and as "essential to the study of the structure of society" (40–41).[14] He states that the "essential link" between literature and myth (and other oral narratives) "is indicated by the Greek word *mythos*, which means the plot or narrative of a story" (34). By this Frye is referring to certain storytelling elements, like characterization, that myth and literature have in common, as well as superstructures of belief that enclose narrative, such as the establishment of a canon or authorized versions. Both myth and literature inherit a corpus of stories whose significance is determined by convention. Both are communicative, aware of an audience, and set within a historic and cultural context. Thus, according to Frye, the oral tradition is "already literature: it is not something else that develops into literature" (33). More important for Frye, the social function of both bodies of narrative is to provide a society "with an imaginative vision of the human situation," for literature "expresses not so much the world that man lives in as the world that he builds" (41)—a definition of literature that is comprehensive and humane.

This idea is nowhere so self-evident as in oral literature, for it enacts its own poetics in the continual "building" of its vision in the creative process. In this tradition the question of textual study, for instance, differs from that in standard criticism when one considers the variety of forms in which the text exists: collected and published versions; irretrievable versions in the past; potential versions in the future; and versions to which analysts do not have access because they exist in the minds and performances of undocumented artisans. Analysis must be culture-specific when theories, construed from the study of a particular tradition, simply do not meet the formal and contextual needs of a different tradition.

Any definition of literature cannot be considered adequate or complete if it excludes the expressive systems of the majority of its people. For literature, in its written and oral forms, remains a participatory act that derives its meaning from the cooperative effort of creator and audience, each reading or "lecture" becoming a re-creative act that insists on its relevance to the referent, the "real" world, the experience of individuals in their culture, history, and society. This re-creative act is the basis for the continuity of any literature; without it, the literary works of past ages or peoples would have little meaning or interest for any of us. And it is in this re-creative act that the oral tradition is differentiated from the written tradition.

For in the process of composition, transmission, selection, and performance that makes up oral literature, the re-creative act is itself the basic form of composition, which includes interpretation and the production of meaning. Only in oral literature is the perceiver of a work a potential author of that work, at least in cultures that have no professional singer or teller of tales. Thus the communication of oral literature is an open system at the level not only of interpretation (which may be true for written texts) but also of generation within the social group in which it is reproduced.[15] The creative process elicits and demonstrates its aesthetic principles through the collaboration of the individual in response to tradition, each exerting its force through variation in time and space. Not only does performance create an aesthetic product but the aesthetics of its public are shaped and formed through the "textualization." As anyone who has collected folklore in performance knows, the audience may not be able to verbalize its poetic principles, but it recognizes and appreciates them. Studying oral literature as an open system would entail the examination of its mode of existence, its strategies as symbolic acts, and its "aesthetics of reception" as a fictional mode of discourse, but only in an integrated methodology.

Most contemporary folklorists have given up reconstruction of the past for the advancement of theories of verbal art as communicative process and aesthetic system, while their literary colleagues remain in the dustwebs of the nineteenth century. In the study of the oral tradition as artistic creation, as a literary effort in its own right, however, several issues emerge as problematic for its inclusion in American literature: classification (in analytical terms or in ethnic terms [Ben-Amos, "Analytical Categories"; see also Ben-Amos, *Folklore Genres*]); context (performance-centered, tradition-centered); existence in print (accuracy of the rendering in prose, poetry, translations); and the appropriate selection from over 250 Native American cultures, for example, or the different Hispanic traditions: Puerto Rican, Chicano, and so on. The establishment of an oral-literature canon must not be subject to the same weaknesses that contributed to the apotheosis of the literary canon. Furthermore, the current inadequate availability of texts is a major obstacle that must be overcome by encouraging publishers and compilers to include oral literatures in their anthologies. And certainly the texts must be supplemented by a concise list of bibliographic materials that would allow the scholar, both professor and student, to place the work within a cultural and historical context. Most important, oral literature, like written literature, should be seen as part of the social process, encompassing individual experience in a dialectical encounter with the immediate community and the larger society.

Notes

[1] See also Utley; note the popular conception of folklore as meaning "untruth," a connotation Utley uses in his article.

[2] For a bibliography on folklore in literature, see Hoffman, "Notes" 21–24. See also Dorson, *American Folklore*, and Rosenberg.

[3] Cf. Dundes, "Text." Jansen is credited as being one of the earliest to consider performance as a necessary factor in the study of folklore (see his "Classifying Performance"). Malinowski had called for the study of performance context in folklore (104). Abrahams studies varying levels of performance in relation to genres ("Complex Relations").

[4] See, among others, Holoka. For an overview of criticism and a recent appraisal, see C. L. Edwards.

[5] For further examples of the problems encountered in translation, see Hymes, "Discovering," and Tedlock, "On the Translation."

[6] See also Paredes, "Tributaries." The concept of the "Great Tradition" and the "Little Tradition," in Robert Redfield's terminology, at least recognizes the contributions of nonmainstream cultures, while in literature we have the establishment of canons, such as Frank R. Leavis's *Great Tradition*, with no parallel work on the development of "little" traditions.

[7] For one of the few examples, see Opland.

[8] The preface of *Literature of the United States* stresses that "much of the material, of course, is just plain general American."

[9] All references to Spiller are to the revised edition, 1953.

[10] For a discussion of views toward Mexican folklore, see Paredes, "The Folk Base." For a description of early Spanish and Mexican literature, see Leal, "Mexican American Literature."

[11] For Hudson's elaboration on the theme, see Flanagan and Hudson.

[12] Dorson alludes to Newell's list when he asks, "But what are the common traditions of Yankee and immigrant, of Negro and Indian?" in his *American Folklore* 28.

[13] See Dorson, "Theory." For his view of using history to explain folklore and for his own reappraisal, see *American Folklore and the Historian* and "American Folklore vs. Folklore in America." Bauman, Abrahams, and Kalcik give a broader discussion in "American Folklore and American Studies."

[14] For a comprehensive, brief critical view, see Denham.

[15] For an example in Spanish balladry, see Catalán and Catarella.

His Life in His Tail:
The Native American Trickster
and the Literature of Possibility

Andrew Wiget

"The literature of this nation began," the lofty prose of Robert Spiller informs us, "when the first settler from abroad of sensitive mind paused in his adventure long enough to feel that he was under a different sky, breathing a new air, and that a New World was all before him with only strength and Providence for guides" (xvii; 3rd ed., 1963). Though Spiller and the other authors of *Literary History of the United States* argue that the Anglo-Saxon roots of American literature have been transformed as a consequence of the process that "made a nation from a complex of peoples" (xix), the imposition of a nationalistic model on an ethnocentric one further narrows an already limited vision.[1] In particular, it means the canon of American literature will accommodate immigrant literatures—Asian, East European, Mexican—only to the degree that they can be hyphenated into the dominant aesthetic, become "melting pot" literatures.

Not a few instances of Native American literature have found their way into conventional American literary history in this manner. When Jefferson quoted Logan's speech in its entirety and praised native oratory extensively, he did so primarily to refute Buffon's argument that the climate of America was deleterious to the intellect and so to the production of art or science. When America needed a native epic equivalent to those cresting the Continent's wave of Romantic nationalism, Longfellow adopted Algonquian myths, intruding into them Iroquoian characters and willfully altering their sense as freely as he distorted their style with his tripping Finnish tetrameter. Following the Great War, the decadence of New York salons gave birth to a cultivated exoticism that rediscovered Native American literature—this time disguised as Imagist poetry—sparking a wave of imitators like Lew Sarrett and Mary Austin and sending D. H. Lawrence packing to Taos. Native American literary tradition reemerged in the 1960s when discontent with the wars in Vietnam, Chicago, and Detroit became articulate. Then Coyote was made to dance through the pages of Gary Snyder, James Koller, William Stafford, and others, as the emblem of our national flight from responsibility toward some imagined primordial wisdom and innocence.

But this is not the Native American literature of which I write. The adoption of native themes, images, and literary forms to alien purposes, even of scholarship—establishing as it does through an expropriative act some extrinsic measure of the art—does not acknowledge the intrinsic merit of the literature. In the end it puts us in the historically unconscionable and critically awkward position of identifying Native American literatures as foreign. In the first decades of the nineteenth century, American literature constituted itself in a reflexive act by which displaced Europeans measured their alienation from their origins. At that same moment, Native American literatures were being sustained in a centuries-old vital relationship to their communities of origin. Figures like Trickster and story types like the Earth-Diver engaged the most creative minds of every generation in a continuous tradition stretching back thirty thousand years. Before there was even the eighteenth-century political dream of a single "nation from a complex of peoples," there was the land, sustaining several hundred native nations with distinctive languages and cultures. Unlike race, language, religion, or polity, the land alone provides a basis for a definition of America through time, sufficiently liberated from the vagaries of history but well schooled in its hazards. It is the common stage of those acculturative processes, at times violent and at other times peaceful, by which a pluralistic America is coming to be. It is, as well, the first and finally the best basis for a definition of American literature: the voices of the people of this land, all of them.

But expanding the academically restricted sense of American literature to include Native American traditional literatures presents problems for the conventional scholar. There are the expected difficulties of translation and transcription,[2] and the not infrequent encounters with those lapses of integrity known as "reworkings," wherein mediocre Anglo poets reduce native images to their own purpose. (I have in mind here not only the entire range of poets mentioned at the end of the second paragraph but the "ethnopoetry" rage led by Jerome Rothenberg—*Technicians, Shaking the Pumpkin*.) More critical than translation is the issue of meaning to which it points. Anglo-American readers cannot simply assume that the English word's limited and familiar definition adequately corresponds to that part of the native word's meaning that is essential for apprehending the story in anything like an original sense. Consequently, an informed reading requires much more information than one customarily expects, and texts that suggest—through lack of notes, introductions, and other material, or through overt appeals to supposedly universal features of human nature—that naked, naive readings can be deeply satisfying are misleading. Images of sun, moon, and water, for instance, recur throughout any literature, but they become more than mere phenomena—become involving objects of contemplation—only when they are invested with culturally specific meaning. In even more fundamental ways, this is true of any determination we might wish to make of motive, character, and theme.[3]

There is the issue, finally, of orality, which for some unaccountable reason has become a stumbling block to people who have unhesitatingly accepted *Beowulf* and the *Iliad*. To be sure, etymologically the word *literature* means "made of letters" and clearly points to a graphological model of text. But criticism is beginning to understand how complicated that model is, that far from fixing the meaning of the text in some public, mutually agreeable way, print does the opposite, conjuring a visual sense of the text that, however deliberately created, can never wholly determine the sense of the text as read or, more deeply, as heard. The graphic text is the preserved tracings of the communicative act, an inscribed utterance echoing through history. Then, too, the honorific sense of the term *literature* is clearly distinct from the etymological sense, addressing not the mode of presentation but the skillfulness, power, and beauty of the word-wrought vision. No great critical insight is required for understanding how deeply embedded in a metaphysics and an ethics any aesthetic must be, although pained response to much deconstructionist criticism suggests that we have invested a great deal of our communal ego in the belief that the Western sense of what is good, true, and beautiful is universal.

The matter of artful verbal form is the common concern of literary criticism, but the determination of form in an oral literature involves more than merely linguistic and paralinguistic elements.[4] Consequently, we need to acknowledge that there are limitations to adopting an exclusively linguistic sense of form, however familiar it might seem. For the moment, however, it is a useful point of entry into the forest of sound and silence that is the spoken world. One can distinguish three types of verbal expression: speech, chant, and song, each of which is increasingly structured in terms of rhythm and other prosodic features.[5] Our concern is with the first—speech—which encompasses a range of verbal forms from conversation and gossip to myth narration. Each of these forms is governed by rules that shape the form as it emerges in situated communication.[6] Being correct, however, is not necessarily the same as being artful. Verbal art is a matter of skillful performance. Performance transforms an unreflexive communicative situation into an intentionally evaluated one, in which the performer tacitly agrees to display storytelling skills, as something beyond the mere act of communicating information or story. The audience in turn consciously prepares itself to evaluate not only what is told but how it is told.[7] Such an approach, of course, implies native aesthetic criteria for evaluating the artfulness of a performance and a distinctly cultural, honorific sense of literature as verbal art. In Native American oral literatures, successful performance often entails not only skillful characterization and significant thematic interest but also an elaborate stylistic manipulation of pauses and pitch, as well as a patterned use of important linguistic features such as discourse markers to create in sound what readers perceive in print.[8]

The stories in which these skills are displayed reflect conventional genres based on a conceptualization of narrative time that distinguishes the mythic era from the historical. Though it is by no means universal throughout Native America, groups as diverse as the Hopi, the Inuit, the Seneca, the Dakota, and the Zuni make such a distinction.[9] The conception of history is also independent of other factors such as credibility. The present and recent past might be called the Historical Period, in which narratives feature known personages in identifiable settings. These oral histories, often extending beyond "grandfather's time," are distinguished from stories of the Legendary Period, in which legendary personages engage in fantastic actions against an ethnographically familiar background. Unlike the historical period, the mythic era is divided into two periods. The Origin Period gave rise to stories like the Earth-Diver and the Emergence, which tell how the present people came to be in a raw world of the Origin Period. During the subsequent Transformation Period, the newly created world was altered by culture heroes who established the present social and physical order of things.

This essay focuses on a single figure from the enormous wealth of Native American traditional literatures, drawn from more than 350 linguistically distinct tribal communities, the compelling image of the trickster.[10] Space compels me to generalize while suggesting a basic approach to understanding his durability. Unlike culture heroes or legendary or historical figures, the trickster is not confined to any one of the narrative periods but lurks on the margins of history, carefully evading mortality. Many Native American peoples, such as the southwestern Navajo, the Crow and the Cheyenne of the Plains, and the California Maidu, count him among the first, uncreated beings. There is a fittingness to this, for tricksters seem to be an ancient and universal phenomenon, however uniquely realized and valued from one culture to the next. Part human, part animal, capable of presenting himself as one or the other at any moment, a creature of vision dominated by appetites, he stares out at us from the dripping limestone walls of Trois Frères, a Paleolithic image of ourselves. That cave painting may be the closest anyone has come to trapping him in time and space. He lives best in the ephemeral world of words. There, though some of his exploits assume familiar patterns, he survives clothed in culture-specific features, running under a number of aliases: Hermes, Prometheus, Lazarillo de Tormes, Gil Blas, Melville's confidence men, Mann's Felix Krull, Ellison's Rinehart, Bellow's Augie March.

II

"Coyote was going along," the stories usually begin, casually taking for granted the elaborate structure of metaphysical concepts, ethical principles, and social customs that a complex tribal mythology has labored for centuries to articulate. Enter Trickster. Overwhelmed by his own appetites, preoccupied with the orifices of his own and everyone else's bodies, suffering from such severe dissociation that his right hand often indeed does not know what his left hand is doing, proclaiming his irresponsibility in word and deed and relishing it despite all costs, here is a fool fit to discombobulate the self-important servants of status and the status quo. Trotting, skulking, whining, lurking, ranting, leering, laughing, always hungry, never satisfied, he is an animate principle of disruption, about to precipitate chaos and humor through sacrilege, self-indulgence, and scatology. He wanders through the dark field of the liminal imagination until he arrives to summon into play the forces at work in some dimly lit social scene. There for a few moments he exercises his trickery, displays his foolishness, sparks some sure flash of imagination and insight. Then he departs the circled light into the surrounding darkness almost as suddenly as he arrived, still oversexed, underfed, dissatisfied, and on the move.

Once, in the beginning of things, before the world came to be quite the way the Navajo know it to be today, Coyote was trotting across the redrock toward the mountains. As he climbed, the thought chanced to cross his mind that a beautiful woman lived in this area. It was well known that she was more than a little bit arrogant, having turned down proposals of marriage from the Sun and other powerful beings. Rightly or wrongly, Coyote felt that such a woman would be a fair prize for a handsome fellow like himself, and so, head down and tail tucked between his legs, he shuffled over to her hogan. There he proposed. She countered by laying down a small condition: he had only to slay one of the monsters that roamed the earth in those days, ferocious giants, famed for their massive weapons, unrelieved ugliness, and tantalizing golden hair. In the darkness of a sweatlodge he succeeded in tricking one of these giants into breaking his leg, immobilizing himself so that Coyote could finish him off.

He returned to the woman, freighted with the golden scalp and the massive weapons, but she was not impressed. Instead she imposed a further condition, requiring him to permit himself to be killed and then bring himself back to life. No one had ever done this before, of course, not even once—death customarily being a final condition—but she demanded that he perform the deed not once but four times. Gamely he accepted, so she led him some distance from the hogan and began to pound him to death, pulverizing every bone in his body. Then she hurried back to the hogan and to her work, for she was a busy woman. To her astonishment, he returned in but a few minutes, whole and well. "Here I am," he said, "one down, and three times to go." Again she took him out and crushed him utterly; again he returned. This happened a third time, too. The fourth time, she even ground his flesh into the sand and scattered the resulting powdered bits into the wind; yet he returned. She could not refuse the proposal now, but she was desperate to learn his recuperative strategy. "My life principle," he said, the grin slowly easing over his face, "I pushed into my tail. So busy were you assaulting the better part of me, you overlooked this, time after time, so I keep coming back." This was only the beginning of many adventures for Coyote. Eventually he lost his glossy coat for a scruffy one and gained a reputation as persistent as his smell. But he has never lost his life (paraphrased from Matthews, *Navajo Legends* 92–95).

In Native American oral literatures, Trickster is not always Coyote, of course. As a result of historical interaction among communities, he appears in a variety of animal guises that developed as regional variations. Among Northwest Coast peoples like the Kwakiutl and Tlingit, he frequently appears as Raven; among the subarctic Athapaskan forest tribes, as Canada Jay or Wolverine; among the Algonquian speakers of the eastern Woodlands and Great Lakes, as Hare; on the northern Plains he appears sometimes as Spider or Old Man; and throughout the Great Basin, the Southwest, and the southern Plains most often as Coyote. Regardless of his name and apart from his distinctive physical features, such as paws, tail, scent, and so on, he is understood as a human character. And while it is important to know that he can change his external appearance at will and manipulate his body in marvelous ways, it is more important to know that the name and the visage mask several personae. He may appear, in one instance, to be an absolute fool, bumbling into social situations from which his disposition or ignorance makes it impossible to escape without punishment. In another story, the same name and mask may be endowed with a high sense of mission and tremendous powers in order to accomplish tasks beneficial to humankind. And in yet another tale, he will appear deceitful, vain, and selfish, and bend all his talents toward the satisfaction of his own desires. This ambiguity at once horrifies and fascinates us. It also creates real problems of interpretation, often exacerbated by the sketchiness with which some of the stories are told.

Folklorists point out that the main lines of certain trickster stories have been widely disseminated throughout Native America. The Eye Juggler, for example, is told by the Nez Perce of the Columbia River Plateau, the Ute of the Intermountain and the Plains regions, the Apache and Zuni of the Southwest, the Montagnais of the St. Lawrence, and the Seneca of the Northeast, each of whom come not only from different regions but from entirely distinct language families, and by many other tribes as well. The discovery of the structural similarities among these classic stories, called *tale types* by folklorists, can serve as a guide to interpretation. In tale types like the Eye Juggler, the Sharpened Leg, the Offended Rolling Stone, the Dancing Ducks, the Reflected Fruit, the Skull Trap, the Laxative Bulb, and others, a basic pattern emerges around which the action is organized. Prompted by his appetites, Trickster the Overreacher fixes his mind on a single goal, but the means required to achieve this goal will effect a radical transformation of his personal identity or of society's norms. He attempts several times to accomplish his aim but meets with failure, expressed either as revenge by the abused power, as in the Offended Rolling Stone, or by an incongruous physical change that can only be called disfigurement, or even by death. These consequences are only temporary, of course; he lives to strive and fail again.

It is precisely because he fails to obtain any prerogative or status in his own community (though he may when operating on foreign turf, as among white people), because he ultimately takes punishment, that these tales can be held up as eminently moral. This is true in spite of the fact that Trickster seems inclined to engage in activities only insofar as they are forbidden.

The stories themselves are marked by recurrent formal features, which provide a background of expectations even if their appearance is not necessary in each telling. Three require some comment. The first is that most tales are genuinely ahistorical. When they are set in a particular locale, which is not often, the location does not bear any inevitable connection to the plot but is used for verisimilitude (see Tedlock, "Pueblo Literature"); it is always a known place.

Second, Trickster frequently initiates action by addressing the antagonist with some kinship term. Since kinship provides everyone with a social identity in most Native American communities, entitling them to certain prerogatives and at the same time imposing certain restraints, Trickster's address can be construed as the opening gambit toward compelled status negotiation. Such a move challenges the other's sense of how the encounter ought to proceed. Should one respond to the character of Trickster as learned only too well from past experience or to the relationship Trickster is entitling himself to? The first route is the safer, of course, but invariably the opponent responds with a kinship term, thus acknowledging Trickster's claim and ensuring a humorous entanglement of their fates. Not infrequently, the term is the kind reserved for the formalized joking relationship between relatives like siblings-in-law or uncles.[11]

Finally, many stories conclude with an explanatory element that appears to transform the tale into an ethnoscientific elucidation of physical phenomena—for instance, why weasels change color in winter. The statements may or may not express the beliefs of the individual storytellers, but Waterman has demonstrated that, as textual features, they do not bear any necessary relation to the story, the same explanation often being found in several different tales, and a single tale providing the opportunity for several different explanations. More than science or religion, a perception of homologies of form is at work in these instances, as when the felling of a tree produces a river system: the ponds replace leaves, rivulets the stems, rivers the branches, and so on.

Trickster narratives may be presented as brief anecdotes that compress encounters with burlesque simplicity, as developed tales with exchanges of dialogue and scene shifts, or as cycles that weave together many tales into a narrative lasting an hour or so. The tales themselves can be divided into two types on the basis of subject matter. The first is focused on a discrete cultural event or scene—hosting customs or religious rituals, for example. A story of this type offers explicit criticisms of the social structure but also implicitly suggests that humans may be unable to bear the weight of their public role and status even under the best conditions. The attack then comes home, sharpening its point in the second kind of story, in which the weakness is attributed to human nature itself.

A good example of the first type of tale, the barely disguised satire of social structures, is the widespread story in which Trickster masks himself as a beautiful woman in order to marry the chief's son, who is a good hunter, and so obtain without labor all the food he desires. The Winnebago version opens with the disguised Trickster inducing an old lady at the edge of the village to announce his entry into the village as the bride-to-be of the chief's son. The chief leaps up to embrace Trickster, encourages his daughters to address him as "sister-in-law," and hurriedly assembles a wedding party. At the feast Trickster devours his food with such rapidity and ill manners that he makes a public spectacle of himself. Trickster later bears several sons—all things are possible in fiction, of course—the youngest of whom is inconsolable until he is brought the four seasons as a plaything. One day, in the course of joking with his mother-in-law, Trickster is discovered, his disguise abandoned, and his true identity revealed, much to everyone's horror.

Before tales like this can be discussed fruitfully, some comment on Trickster's gender is required. That Trickster has been customarily represented in the ethnographic literature as a Priapean male, dominated by his sexual appetites, may be the result of a peculiar bias in the collection of these stories. Male ethnographers of the Boasian school expected elder males to be the repository of traditional knowledge and seldom sought out women storytellers. If, one argues, tricksters are collective representations, their particular manifestations in a community of males or in situations for which social custom requires a male role would be male. Female trickster figures are known in Native American traditional literatures, however, and their occurrence does not seem to depend on the sex of storyteller or audience or even particular contexts. Thus, at least in some societies, a female trickster was a commonly understood, unexceptional figure, whose character is contrasted with that of the male. Among the Arizona Tewa, for instance, Coyote Woman is all treachery and malevolence and lacks the pathetic qualities of the male figure that ameliorate our judgment of him. Why this is so, one can only speculate. In other cases, however—a Hopi story comes to mind—the female sex of the trickster seems only a contrivance to initiate the action, an element of setting, and is not integral to the central action. Both the Tewa and the Hopi tales are discussed by Martha Kendall.

The existence of stories featuring both male and female tricksters suggests that, considered simply as a calculus of motives, Trickster can be imagined as either sex. Of course, once we begin to talk about the figure, to involve it in a story, we must engender "him" or "her." Throughout the stories in this particular Winnebago cycle, the figure is understood as male. It is true, as a story we will shortly discuss illustrates, that he carries his detached penis in a box, but it is identified as his own, and as a natural, if unusually long, penis, in contrast to the artificial female genitals made of deer liver that he uses to disguise himself in this episode.

A version of this story told by the Algonquian-speaking Plains Cree of Manitoba (narrated in Bloomfield, *Plains Cree Texts*) contrasts with the tale prevalent among the Siouan-speaking Winnebago from Wisconsin. As in the Winnebago tale, the Cree trickster transforms himself, marries, and has animal offspring from extramarital intercourse (with his sled dogs). The birth of these unusual children heightens the central point of the story, the foolishness of a conceited young man who had disdained all legitimate marriage proposals while waiting for the girl of his dreams. When the projection of his fantasy materializes and is revealed to be Trickster, he is humiliated and flees into the arms of another, considerably more average woman. He soon grows ashamed of his wife, whom he considers to be dumpy; sensing his dissatisfaction, she reveals herself to be Trickster. In traditional Plains Cree societies, marriages were often arranged by parents who knew the distribution of kin among the different social groups, and from an early age women were educated to be working partners in the economic life of the family. In the Manitoba story Trickster's transformation of sex is the means by which the foolhardiness of marriages contracted on less than practical terms is expressed.

Winnebago society, divided into patrilineal clans, is more highly structured than that of the Plains Crees. Status and prerogatives accrued to male elders, particularly to the chief and his sons. In the Winnebago version of the story, Trickster's transformation of sex is only a vehicle for exposing the perils of institutionalized power. The chief's behavior is more horrific than Trickster's precisely because we do not expect it of him. In a foolish, even dangerous way, he has given his son's hand and his tribe's future to a woman he does not know, who is in fact without "place," without kin of any kind in the village. He has done so on the recognizance of "an old woman living on the outskirts of the village," a conventional Winnebago character type the audience would understand as untrustworthy. Rashly encouraging his daughters to acknowledge the relationship and hastily gathering a wedding party, he puts the satisfaction of having his son marry a beautiful woman ahead of the prudence and judgment required by his position (Radin, *Winnebago* 22–24). If, in the exercise of authority, passion and self-interest can override the demands of tradition and responsibility for the common good, then no one is safe. Such a story reminds us of the danger of confusing the person and the role. It can only do so, however, if we know that such behavior, however justified in our post-Romantic culture, is subject to criticism among the Winnebago. Radin's notes make the point clearly and, together with Babcock-Abrahams's culturally contextualized discussion of the Medicine Bundle Ceremony in the same narrative, illustrate the impossibility of understanding the ramifications of satire apart from a knowledge of the society's values.[12]

The effectiveness of Trickster in disclosing the potential for abuse inherent in social structures of any kind also makes him a useful medium for attacking the institutions of invading peoples. The Plains Cree tell the story of how Wisahketchak the Trickster buys some goods at the trading post on credit. Unable to pay for them and being an inept trapper, he decides to use poison to ensure his success. Returning home from the post, he has his wife mix the poison into little round cakes that he sets to harden. When they are hardened, he packs up and sets out to the woods, where, after a good deal of pleading, he convinces a wolf to gather all the other wolves and foxes to hear some "good tidings." When he has seated them in a semicircle in front of him, he begins to speak and places the cakes "in their mouth one by one, round the circle," all the while assuring them that if they eat the cakes and accept religion, they will live a long time. They die before he finishes their first, fatal homily, and with their skins he settles his debt (adapted from Bloomfield, *Sacred Stories*).

This tale is a stinging attack on the relation between organized religion and the fur trade, well documented historically as a matter of French national policy, a conspiracy that bound the trappers' bodies and their labors to the post credit system, and their souls and spiritual longings to a postponed reward beyond the grave. As such, it is an explicit warning to Native Americans of the duplicity of whites and of the willingness of some of their own people, once having been duped as Wisahketchak is, to betray the "wild ones" as a means of increasing their wealth. Other tale types, like the Money Tree or the Excrement Gold, make Trickster a deceiver and make white people, by virtue of their own appetites, the butt of his jokes.

Many stories suggest that the very attempt to impose order and structure on human experience is laughably presumptuous. In one such tale, again from the Winnebago, Trickster awakes to find his enormous, erect penis—one must imagine it several yards long—raising like a flag the blanket that had been covering him. Loudly he announces that this must be his "chief's banner," which is flown on special occasions among the Winnebago before the door of the chief's lodge as a sign of his authority; in this way Trickster sheds new light on what it might mean to be a "big man." He then hauls the penis down, hand over hand as if it were a long rope, coils it carefully in a box, which he closes and packs on his back, and then sets off. This momentary glimpse of man's vanity—this briefest scene (not even yet a story) which exists only to suggest that a man can have an enormous sexual appetite and yet keep it under control—this illusion is destroyed utterly in the subsequent scene. Trickster's walk brings him to the edge of a lake, on the opposite side of which he observes the chief's daughter and some friends bathing. Overcome with lust, he removes the box from his back, opens it, and releases his penis, commanding it to have intercourse with the daughter. Like some huge water serpent it slithers down the grassy bank, swims across the lake, and lodges itself in her. A full-scale tug of war follows, the woman's attendants and even the strongest men in the village trying in vain to pull the Penis Snake out. Finally an old woman, recognizing that the perpetrator could only be Trickster, compels him to withdraw by straddling the penis and stabbing it repeatedly with an awl (Radin, *Trickster* 18–20).

In its distorted scale and boisterous humor, this is at once a brutal and comic tale. The fact that Trickster keeps his penis in a box has suggested to some a psychological dissociation of consciousness and body; in this Winnebago cycle, Trickster does seem to suffer this disorder—in another his right hand attacks his left. But that incident, or the episode in which Trickster orders his anus (endowed with consciousness and voice) to guard his meal while he sleeps, differs from the present tale in one important respect. The Penis Snake obeys Trickster's command. It is—one can hardly say "merely"—an extension of his will; the origin of the action is shifted from the organ itself to the will, and the burden of responsibility from the instrument to the agent. The tale then becomes a pointedly moral one concerned with motive and intent; it cannot support any final justification for Trickster's behavior, including a physiological one. For all its bawdiness, it remains a telling satire on the great lengths to which some men will go to satisfy an enormous sexual desire to which they have surrendered themselves and yet over which they pretend to maintain absolute control. It is Trickster in epitome, the life principle in a box.

Such tales illuminate one of the highest values of comedy, its ability to instruct. As fictions, framed and set apart from ordinary life, they display to the audience situations in which two spheres of experience, one conceptual and the other existential, are conjoined in an apparently paradoxical relationship that leaves the reader and the central agent in a dilemma in which will must be betrayed for wish, or vice versa. The very absurdity of the situation highlights cultural categories we all use for ordering experience but which we have so successfully internalized that we never perceive them as social phenomena; they seem merely the way things are. Trickster's foolishness unhinges such assumptions, displacing the ordinary from the realm of commonality and making it available for contemplation. (See Babcock-Abrahams's "Tolerated Margin" and her introduction to *Reversible World*; see also Douglas, *Purity* and *Natural Symbols*.)

The Bungling Host type tale provides a clear instance of this. Trickster is invited to share a meal on separate occasions with four different animals. Each time he reciprocates, and when the guest arrives at Trickster's house, the fool tries to provide food by the same means with which the guest had previously supplied him. Trickster must go through a great deal of trouble to imitate the animals, provoking much laughter in the process. Trying to imitate Black Bear's ability to produce fat from his paws, in a version told by Thompson River Indians, he too holds his hand over a fire and burns himself severely. The repetition of four similarly structured incidents frames the conflict between form and function, raising issues of identity as well as hospitality. In the end, the tale suggests, the most generous and least painful reciprocity is not to flatter but to give what is truly yours. Other type tales highlight the potential conflicts between public role and private personality (Big Turtle's War Party), belief and practice (religious satires like the Dancing Ducks or the Skull Trap), and will and appetite (the Laxative Bulb and similar tales).

As Judy Trejo points out, the trickster stories provide the occasion for an elder's entertaining reaffirmation of the social order. But it is also true that in any storytelling situation the audience and the storyteller do not always form a homogeneous group; their interests may vary according to age, sex, kinship, degree of acculturation, and so on. One of the functions of storytelling is to bring to light what Richard Bauman, in his essay of the same title, has called "differential identity." (See also Bascom; how differential identity might affect performances is illustrated in Sherzer, "Strategies.") Too little is known about this phenomenon in Native American literature, because of the predisposition of early ethnographers to interview only older men who had the most to gain from affirming the status quo and interpreting Trickster as a negative model. But in another part of the world, Bruce Grindal interviewed members of the Sisala tribe from Ghana on this issue, because he observed that older people and younger people laughed at different times when listening to trickster stories. The older people laughed more often at the end of the tale, when Trickster got his comeuppance, while the juvenile audience tended to laugh during the story. Grindal found that the youngsters focused on the character's deceptions and ignored the outcome (probably because it is conventionalized and thus foreordained); their interest was in Trickster's skill in evading adult social responsibilities. And marginal members of the community, when confronted by authority figures, could cite Trickster as a sanction for idiosyncratic behavior (see esp. Stevens; Native American examples include T. Lewis; Makarius; Hieb).

Such ambiguity of interpretation does not result from Trickster's marginality. Marginality produces what Victor Turner calls *communitas*, a state independent of roles prescribed by the social structure.[13] On the contrary, it is the misfortune of Trickster to embody two or more social and ethical domains (that is, he has a liminal rather than a marginal status) that creates his dilemma and our crisis of interpretation. Because what we know is rooted in what we believe, Trickster tales, as Beidelman has noted, shift the burden of meaning from the cognitive sphere to the moral one. When the crux of interpretation is recognized as a dilemma, the interpretative stance toward the situation changes. Instead of asking, What is Truth in the matter?—an unanswerable question in a dilemma in which both horns can claim legitimacy—one must ask, What is right? and assess the tale on the basis of the Good.

Nowhere is this more clearly the issue than in stories featuring two trickster figures. The most widely known example is Trickster's Race, a Blackfeet version of which is particularly pointed. One character, known as Old Man (a familiar Plains persona), tricks first a herd of elk and then a herd of deer into jumping off a cliff to their deaths; only pregnant does are spared. After he butchers the animals and hangs their meat to dry, Coyote (another familiar persona) approaches camp with a badly bandaged leg and a shell hung around his neck. When Coyote asks for something to eat, Old Man demands the shell so he can skim the fat off his soup. Coyote refuses, claiming the shell is his medicine; Old Man challenges him to a race for his supper, figuring that he can easily beat a cripple. Old Man soon builds a big lead, but at the halfway point, Coyote casts off his bandages and races past him. Reaching camp far ahead of his rival, Coyote calls all the animals together to help him finish off Old Man's hoard of food, much to the latter's dismay (Thompson, *Tales* 61–62). Here the trickery of both is plain, but the issue is not means but motive. Old Man is at once lazy and gluttonous. Staging a jump is an inordinately wasteful way of procuring food for one mouth. He is also stingy in refusing to share food with a guest—an unconscionable act of inhospitality—even demanding that the guest pay some price for the meal. His lack of generosity is highlighted by his challenging what he believes to be a cripple to a race. In hindsight, Coyote's deception is viewed not only as a means of securing food without labor (in itself a scurrilous activity) but as an effective punishment for a prairie Scrooge. Similar revenge stories involving acts of duplicity by two characters occur throughout the Trickster corpus.

The issue of interpretation can be elevated from the individual to the communal level. Such a case occurred during Paul Radin's stay among the Winnebago when younger members of the tribe attempted to introduce the peyote religion (*Winnebago* 424–25). They used trickster stories, but not, as one might think, to provide themselves with a model for change. Instead Trickster was invoked to question the implicit rightness of the traditionalists' settled view of human—that is, Winnebago—nature. In this way they attacked the elders' justification for social order and the authority of tradition. After telling the story in which Trickster dances with reeds thinking they are Indians, the peyoteist commented: "So do we Winnebago act. We dance and make a lot of noise, but in the end we accomplish nothing." After Trickster mistakes a stump for a man and is led into a foolish imitation, the peyoteist observed: "So are we Winnebago. We never look before we act. We do everything without thinking. We think we know all about it." In the same vein, the Dancing Ducks story illustrates that the Winnebagos "like all that is forbidden . . . but are afraid to speak of it. We, the Winnebagos, are the birds, and the Trickster is Satan." Similarly, the Laxative Bulb story demonstrates that though "we travel on this earth all our lives, . . . when one of us tastes something that makes him unconscious, we look upon this thing with suspicion when he regains consciousness." In these statements, Trickster remains a model for negative behavior, even for the reformers. The application of the model is other- rather than self-directed and is used to undermine the conservatives' reluctance to admit the peyote religion. Through his inversion of the norms, Trickster provides both a reflex image of what is probable, preferred, and considered absolute, and a direct image of what is possible.

III

In situations such as these, Trickster functions not so much to call cultural categories into question as to demonstrate the artificiality of culture itself. Thus he makes available for discussion the very basis of social order, individual and communal identity. Barre Toelken has called him the "exponent of all possibilities," a neat summation of what Yellowman, the Navajo storyteller with whom he worked, told him. "Through the stories," Yellowman said, "everything is made possible. . . . If [Coyote] didn't do all those things, then those things would not be possible in the world." For this reason, Yellowman adds, though people laugh at the way Coyote does things and the manner in which the story is told, the story itself is not funny (" 'Pretty Languages' "; see also Toelken and Scott for a revised and expanded version).

It is the humor of the telling, nevertheless, that delivers us the truth. When a trickster tale opens, it immediately mobilizes the audience's sense of the cognitive system and the ethical system that supports it. Because the story is told through the eyes of Trickster, whom we recognize, however guiltily, as a potential image of ourselves and with whom we are compelled to identify by the narrator's adoption of his point of view, we are brought to consider the possibility of altering or abolishing the categorical restraints that govern our behavior. In the end, by manipulating us into laughing at a figure with whom we have just identified, the tale forces us to reaffirm the beliefs we have been momentarily permitted to question. It is not at all clear, however, that the last laugh is the most significant one. Differential focusing on the theme—as a result either of diverging interests (as in the case of the Sisala children) or of a subsequent interpretation (as among the Winnebago peyoteists)—suggests that the earlier, critical laugh that implicates the audience and sustains the trickster may be the most consequential.

Johan Huizinga has suggested that "play is older than culture," that culture, considered as ordered behavior, always emerges from play, insofar as play, occurring in a time and place and rule system apart from ordinary life, necessarily evaluates life. Because it has rules and limitations in time and space, play can be "played out," run its course, from inception to consequence, and so create meaning.[14] Literature is just such a kind of play, and Trickster a marvelous instance of player. But in one sense, and an important one, Trickster is larger than the literature in which he lives and the opponent he plays. Though he is dominated by the excess of appetites each of us shares in lesser degree, and is driven by them to desperation, he eludes final defeat by his trickery. It keeps him in the game. "In his meaning one thing," Karl Kroeber writes, "the power to mean another is implicated" ("Deconstructionist Criticism" 78).

From this perspective Trickster is far from being a picture of abased humanity, an image of failure, of the collapse into bestiality that those who want to improve us would have us believe. We keep telling the stories because we know better, see differently: a ragged and road-weary witness to the resilience and indestructibility of the human spirit, which may finally be more a matter of instinct than intellect. When the weight of culture is felt as a crushing burden on the self, when our heroic sense of all that we ought to be has beaten down our common sense of what we more frequently are, when we feel imprisoned by our own designs, having provided a place for everything in our world except passion, risk, and, yes, failure, then at the edge of the imagination, where the all too brightly illuminated present merges into the dark overdetermined future, life twitches in his scruffy tail, and Trickster speaks from some unbeaten part of us, for change and the possibility of a good laugh.

Notes

[1] This is the context for Hubbell, *Who Are the Major American Writers?* (288, 308–09), but numerous similar examples can be found in any study of the development of the American canon; cf. Baym, "Melodramas"; Kolodny. Believing that the interests of an introductory essay are best served by leaving as broad a bibliographic wake as possible, I have expanded many of the notes, trusting their usefulness to justify their length.

[2] Bevis's useful introduction to this problem has been reprinted in Chapman, *Literature*. See also Tedlock's "On the Translation" and Witherspoon.

[3] Readers interested in a rich and contemporary understanding of culture might look at Geertz and at E. Leach.

[4] A good discussion of how oral events are formalized is found in Irvine, but the key essay for literary forms is Ben-Amos, "Analytical Categories." The principal demonstration is Gossen. A contemporary literary critic's assessment of fundamental problems in working with oral literature can be found in Krupat, *An Approach.* Both the Krupat essay and the relevant chapter of Gossen's book are reprinted in Wiget, *Critical Essays.*

[5] An argument over whether one can distinguish between poetry and prose in an oral culture is here momentarily circumvented for the more tangible distinction between speech and song. Those having difficulty with that distinction are referred to List.

[6] This is the domain of sociolinguistics and of the ethnography of speaking. Many of the essential articles in this field can be found in Hymes, *Foundations*; Gumperz and Hymes, *Directions*; and Giglioli. Useful case studies can be found in Bauman and Sherzer. The current utility of this field derives from the conception of language not merely as sign but as act; see the work of J. L. Austin and of Searle. What the application of this perspective to Native American literature can mean is indicated by Gill; Sherzer, *Kuna*; and Sherzer and Woodbury. What it means for the study of more familiar literature is suggested by Pratt, *Toward a Speech Act Theory*, and Smith, *On the Margins.*

[7] Performance theory emerged from speech act theory and sociolinguistics. Central works here are Ben-Amos and Goldstein, and Bauman, *Verbal Art.* Performances of Native American trickster tales have been recorded on videotape and are available from Clearwater Publishing, with an excellent commentary, produced by Larry Evers of the University of Arizona. Good analyses of performances, illustrating how form emerges in the situation, include Wiget, "Telling the Tale," and Darnell. What a text might look like that took these factors into consideration is demonstrated by Tedlock, *Finding the Center*, and Evers and Molina.

[8] Especially identified with this literary, textural perspective is Hymes, whose *"In Vain I Tried to Tell You"* includes more than a half-dozen landmark essays. See also Tedlock's "On the Translation," included in Tedlock, *The Spoken Word*, and Jacobs's classic *Content and Style.* Especially valuable collections of criticism are Kroeber, *Traditional Literatures*; Swann, *Smoothing the Ground*; Swann and Krupat; and Wiget, *Critical Essays.*

[9] Over a dozen widely dispersed Native American communities distinguish stories according to these conceptions of time, in a manner similar to that noted by Deloria (*Dakota Texts*). For a discussion of narrative-time categories, see Wiget, *Native American Literature*, ch. 1.

[10] Native American trickster tales first became available to the general public through the Annual Reports and Bulletins of the Bureau of American Ethnology, which was founded in 1879 and incorporated into the Smithsonian Institution in 1964. Despite the frequency of stilted translations, these are useful volumes, especially *Tsimshian Mythology* and *Kutenai Tales*, both by Franz Boas, whose notes of cross-cultural comparison are invaluable. A folkloric introduction to the

stories is provided by Stith Thompson's *Folktale* and *Tales*. Paul Radin's *Trickster* enjoys wide distribution, and the Winnebago trickster cycle therein has provided grist for many a critical mill; it is an anomalous text, however, and Radin's Jungian psychodevelopmental characterization of the trickster is no longer favored. Handled with care, however, it remains a useful text and a good place to begin, if not end, any exploration of the figure. Other good collections are Jarold Ramsey's *Coyote Was Going There* and Roger Welsch's *Omaha Tribal Myths*. A popular treatment is Barry Holstun Lopez's *Giving Birth to Thunder, Sleeping with His Daughter*.

[11] The notion of "entitlement" here is derived from Kenneth Burke, and its implications are traced by Crocker, "The Social Function." The role of Trickster in social behavior like institutionalized joking is well established, especially for African communities. Useful articles are Douglas, "Social Control"; Kennedy; and Bricker. Basso's is an important performance study of Native American humor.

[12] Babcock-Abrahams's "Tolerated Margin" remains the best introductory essay on Trickster, although it relies too heavily on Radin in places. Another useful essay, especially for surveying the different historical responses to the figure, is that of Mac Linscott Ricketts, whose suggestion that Trickster is a critical representation of the shaman is consonant with my point of view, though too restricted to one social role to provide a generally useful focus of interpretation.

[13] Turner's suggestive, if nebulous, sense of *communitas* can be examined in his *Ritual Process* and *Dramas*.

[14] *Homo Ludens*. This quotation is from page 1, but the entire first chapter is especially insightful, except for Huizinga's remark that "the savage knows nothing of the conceptual distinction between 'being' and 'playing'" (25). The language and the historical ignorance are distressing, but nevertheless the statement touches only the application and not the essence of Huizinga's insight.

The African American Animal Trickster as Hero

John W. Roberts

Trickster-tale traditions, especially those in which clever animals act as humans, were ubiquitous in the cultures from which Africans enslaved in the United States had come. Therefore, it is not surprising that tales of trickery that were developed around the exploits of anthropomorphized animals occupied a central position in the oral narrative performances of the enslaved Africans. Although the existence of animal trickster tales was seldom noted during slavery, folktale collectors in the late nineteenth and early twentieth centuries amassed hundreds of them and expressed amazement at the size, distribution and coherence of the black trickster-tale repertoire. For example, in 1892, Octave Thanet, whose experiences echoed those of other collectors, declared that "all over the South the stories of Br'er Rabbit are told. Everywhere not only ideas and plots are repeated, but the very words often are the same; one gets a new vision of the power of oral tradition" (121). The trickster tales of enslaved Africans not only proved to be remarkably similar to one another throughout the South, but they also exhibited a close kinship to trickster tales in African oral tradition. Shortly after the appearance in print of the first animal trickster tales found among African Americans, scholars began publishing tales from African tradition demonstrating that, in some instances, the trickster tales of black Americans were developed around the same plots and situations as those in the African tales.

Folktale collectors in the late nineteenth century expressed little doubt that black animal trickster tales, which revolved primarily around the exploits of Br'er Rabbit, constituted a heroic tradition. Joel Chandler Harris, the foremost popularizer of the tales in the late nineteenth century, declared emphatically that "it takes no scientific investigation to show why he [the African American] selects as his hero the weakest and most harmless of all animals, and brings him out victorious in contests with the bear, the wolf, and the fox" (Harris, *Uncle Remus, His Songs* 57; 1982). While study of the animal trickster tales as a heroic tradition has remained constant in the literature, the reasons for the trickster's heroism have been the subject of endless discussion, focusing primarily on the source of black identification with the trickster. More precisely, as Bill R. Hampton notes, "Much of the discussion has been a controversy over whether there has been any identification at all" between African Americans and the trickster in folklore (57). The debate that has arisen over the issue of identification results chiefly from the lack of a culture-specific model for study of the hero in American folk tradition.

In the investigation of American folklore, the most consistent approach assumes the existence of a normative model of heroic action. This model is based on the assumption that, at some point in the past, there existed a "heroic age" in which a tradition of heroic creation was established. Roger Abrahams summarizes this view when he notes that "the actions that we recognize as heroic are based on contest values and a model of a male-centered family. A hero is a man whose deeds epitomize the masculine attributes most highly valued within a society." The normative function of hero stories, according to Abrahams, is to project values in story form that serve as a "guide for future action in real life" in "a warlike age where heroic values are operative." Hero stories serve simultaneously as "an expression of dream-life, of wishfulfillment," a function that comes to the fore when a heroic age or, in Abrahams's term, a "heroic culture" disappears and "the war and resultant context values" may become embodied in figures identified with other activities in a society. The stories that result from the transfer of heroic values to other endeavors, however, cannot serve a normative function, since "to encourage such actions would be to place the existence of the group in jeopardy" ("Some Varieties" 341–42). Therefore, hero stories created and/or performed in such a sociocultural milieu serve only the vicarious needs of the performers and audience in defining masculinity; they cannot offer a model of behavior for real-life situations.

The requirement that normative heroic action be conceptualized as reflecting the values of a heroic age has been extremely influential in the study of folk literature in American culture. Richard M. Dorson, for example, argues that "heroic literature not only portrays an heroic age; it must date from that age" ("Davy Crockett" 104). While folklorists generally point to the Western folktale and epic traditions that emphasize warlike values and physical confrontation as the prototypical heroic age, they also recognize that conditions can create a sociocultural environment in which the values of the earlier age again become operative. Abrahams contends that "there was much in the early national experience in the United States which was conducive to thinking and acting in heroic terms." ("Some Varieties" 353). At the same time, folklorists realize that not all heroic literature portrays or dates from a heroic age as it is generally conceptualized; however, they simply do not view these expressions of heroic values as functioning normatively.

The conceptual model for the study of folk heroic literature that has emerged from an emphasis on the normative role of the Western folktale and epic traditions highlights the need for the development of culture-specific models in the study of American oral traditions. The normative model that envisions the values of Western European culture as transformed in America as an objective, if not universal, basis for evaluating the aesthetic and cultural values on which the oral literature of diverse groups rests is ethnocentric, to say the least. Because folklore exists as a reflection of the cultural experiences of those who create it, we are forced to consider oral traditions that do not reflect Western values to be the product of a distorted cultural experience at best and subterfuge at worst. In many ways, this approach reflects the intimate relationship between folklore and culture building—an activity by which groups create and maintain an image of themselves as different from others. Folklore creation should contribute to culture building by serving as a means of transmitting the values on which a group's ideal image of itself is based.

Culture building and folklore creation, however, constitute ongoing activities with historical and emergent dimensions. In both cases, the historical dimension is implicit in the notion of traditionality as defining characteristics, while the emergent quality derives from transformational properties that make both folklore and culture dynamic. In other words, folklore creation as supportive of culture building is wedded to the history and traditions of a particular group. Therefore, in developing culture-specific models in American folklore study, we must recognize that groups who do not have roots in Western tradition engage in folklore creation and culture building that do not necessarily reflect values of mainstream culture but represent neither deviance nor subterfuge. Moreover, if we evaluate such traditions from the vantage of American cultural values, we distort not only the aesthetic principles within the folk group but also the multicultural basis of American literature.

The study of African American animal trickster tales as a heroic tradition is a case in point. Though one of the most extensively studied oral literary traditions in black culture, the trickster tale created by enslaved Africans has not been discussed as a normative model of heroic action. More often than not, folklorists have suggested that the African American trickster tale is a primary example of how heroic fiction can serve the needs of a people in creating a dream life rather than offering an expressive mechanism for transmitting a conception of emulative cultural behaviors. This view of African American trickster tales derives from the scholarly perspective that, in order to be considered normative, folklore should enhance American culture building. Although folklorists supposedly operate under the assumption that American society is composed of diverse cultures, they have not studied folklore creation as a reflection of the norms and values of these varied groups.

The African American trickster tale, however, can be discussed as a normative model only when conceptualized against the backdrop of black culture building in America. More important, black culture building must be recognized as an extension of African culture building rather than European, as it has so often been envisioned. The tendency to evaluate the African American trickster tale from the vantage of Euro-American cultural values is deeply rooted in folkloristic thinking. From the beginning, this approach has represented a denial of the importance of the African heritage to an understanding of black folk tradition. Adrienne Lanier Seward, for instance, observes that

> when Afro-American folk culture has been examined in terms of its African antecedents, the results have been predictably, if not inherently, controversial. Resistance to so-called Africanist's views have rested less . . . on the overwhelming weight of scholarly evidence than on a conceptual framework influenced by long and deeply held notions about the aberrant nature of black cultural development under slavery in the United States. (49)

Lanier Seward concludes that "Afro-American folk culture has been seen as self-evident and capable of being understood solely within the context of conventional wisdom about slavery in the antebellum South" (50). The "conventional wisdom" is based on a view of slavery as an experience that left African people in the United States culturally bankrupt and dependent on the European cultural coffers for capital as they began life in the New World.[1] From this perspective, black culture building has necessarily been viewed as an extension of European culture building.

Although early discussions of the trickster tale portrayed the issues of African origins and the trickster as hero as interrelated, this approach rested on the denial of any profound relationship between African and African American tradition. On the one hand, this approach was influenced by the popular nineteenth-century conception of folklore as a survival from humankind's savage past, existing in the present as a kind of mental relic among peoples closest to that earlier stage of cultural development. Throughout the period of slavery, Europeans propagated the idea that African cultures were arrested in a savage state of progress by the innate inferiority of African people. On the other hand, also during the period of slavery, white Americans had promulgated the notion that, though blacks were innately inferior to whites, their acculturation under the discipline of slavery had served to eradicate the more savage aspects of the African character, an effect reflected in their docile and childlike behavior as slaves. Therefore, when confronted with the animal trickster tale, which portrayed the hero as a small animal whose cunning and wit could explode into acts of brutality and violence, scholars evaluated the tradition in terms of the duality that governed their own thinking about African people.[2] Most could readily equate the character and actions of the animal trickster with those of Africans on the continent; however, they could not so easily accept them as an accurate reflection of black identity or behavior, actual or potential, in America. Consequently, early scholars clung tenaciously to the African-origins thesis and suggested that animal trickster tales in their more brutal aspects reflected their development in Africa. Nevertheless, Africans enslaved in America continued to perform trickster tales because they could identify with the witty creature to whom nature had assigned an inferior position in the animal kingdom, a position not unlike that of African people in the human order.

Throughout the late nineteenth and early twentieth centuries, folklorists collected hundreds of animal trickster tales from African Americans and found little reason to question the basic thesis of African origins or the trickster as a harmless heroic symbol. However, Richard Dorson, who collected some thousand African American folktales in the early 1950s, a small number of which were animal trickster tales, challenged the African-origins thesis in the introduction to his collection *American Negro Folktales*. He noted in particular that "many of the fictions, notably the animal tales, are of demonstrably European origin. Others have entered the Negro repertoire from England, from the West Indies, from American white tradition, and from the social and historical experiences of colored people in the South" (15–16; Fawcett, 1967). He concludes that "only a few plots and incidents can be distinguished as West African." Dorson utilized motif and tale-type analysis to demonstrate the dominance of European influence on African American folktales.

In the wake of Dorson's contention, few African American folktale scholars who were interested in the question of origins retreated from the African-origins thesis but rather followed his lead and turned to motif and tale-type analysis to support their conclusions, exclaiming at the same time that indices for such analyses were unreliable in dealing with African-derived tales (see, e.g., Crowley). However, these scholars generally based their conclusions on a small corpus of tales and, as Dorson repeatedly stated in defense of his thesis, failed to establish that more than a handful of African American trickster tales could be traced to Africa. Since midcentury, the debate over the origins of the trickster tale has occupied students of the tradition, but those interested in the trickster as hero have demonstrated at least an indirect influence of the origins controversy. After midcentury, scholars who have discussed the animal trickster as hero have tended to ignore the question of origins altogether or to suggest that it is unimportant to an understanding of the tradition. Lawrence W. Levine, for instance, has offered an extensive treatment of the early manifestation of the tradition. In *Black Culture and Black Consciousness,* Levine acknowledges the possibility of African influence but suggests that "regardless of where the tales came from, the essential point is that . . . slaves quickly made them their own and through them revealed much about themselves and their world" (82).

With the shift in emphasis from African origins as an explanation for black identification with the trickster as hero, scholars turned to the slave experience and the repressive social climate of post-Emancipation America to account for black trickster-tale creation. In these discussions, the trickster tale continues to be seen as the embodiment of an ambiguous view of existence occasioned by sociopolitical conditions that force blacks to identify with white values and cultural goals. However, because whites have vigorously denied blacks the ability to participate equally in the society, blacks cannot live according to these values.[3] From this perspective, the trickster's manifestation as a small animal reflects the retarded social development of black Americans under white oppression, while the character's actions reveal black feelings of rebelliousness against their position in the society. The animal trickster, in his rebelliousness, characteristically indulges in actions that are not only socially unacceptable but also morally tainted. Therefore, the trickster tale, though psychologically fulfilling as a compensatory expressive vehicle, cannot function as a normative model of heroic behavior. If blacks were to emulate the behavior of the animal tricksters, their actions would jeopardize the American value system with which they identify, presumably simply because they live in American society.

However, neither was the African American animal trickster tale created in America nor can the values reflected in the tales be understood solely by reference to conditions faced by blacks in the United States. To understand the trickster tale as a normative model of heroic action, it is essential to recognize the African roots of the tradition from the vantage of African culture building as a continuous process that has served as a source of black identity and heroic values. In *The Afro-American Trickster Tale,* Jay D. Edwards offers a model for examining African American trickster tales that links them to the African tradition at the deepest level. He argues convincingly that folklorists, Dorson included, concerned with the extent to which Africans in the New World retained their trickster-tale traditions have erred by focusing on surface elements such as plots, motifs, and tale types—elements that "are sufficiently broad that they may easily be interpreted as including, and thereby falsely uniting, historically unrelated tales" (5–6). Edwards further suggests that evidence for either African or European origin based on an examination of these elements is unlikely to give either side an advantage, since they are mutable narrative elements with little influence on the deep structure of folktales.

Instead, Edwards demonstrates, on the basis of a deep-structural analysis that attempts to establish a "systematic grammar for the types of the folktale," that both Africans on the continent and people of African descent throughout the New World show a marked tendency toward a tale type he calls the "Anansi Frame," or "Class I"

(36). He bolsters his argument by examining the deep structure of the European animal trickster cycle of Reynard the Fox, a tradition often noted as a source of African American tales. From this analysis, he concludes that

> because of their special appeal, Afro-Americans preserved African trickster tales, shared them, and borrowed new Class I tales wherever they found them. This may explain why a relatively minor theme in the oral heritage of Europe (i.e., the dozen or so Class I tales associated with Reynard the Fox) is so well represented in the oral heritage of Afro-America, while many genres of European oral literature are represented poorly or not all. (77)

While a recognition of deep-structural similarities between African and African American trickster tales does not conclusively settle the question of plot or motif origin, it does suggest that the relation between African and African American tales resides in cognitive orientations different from those of Europeans.

Edwards also indicates a possible direction for analysis of other aspects of the tales when he observes early in his discussion of the structure of African American trickster tales that "the central ethnological problem is whether a knowledge of the principles of organization of African culture is prerequisite to an understanding of the deeper patterns of Afro-American folklore and folk life" (6). In the past, folklorists, even those who have advocated a strong African influence on African American trickster tales, have emphasized the expressive links between African and African American tales and have shown little interest in deep-structural similarities between African and African American cultures that may have influenced the transformation of African trickster tales in America. The similarities between trickster traditions throughout Africa and those among peoples of African descent throughout the New World, even on a surface level, would suggest that similar concerns very likely played a role in the perpetuation of trickster tales among African people, even those geographically removed from the continent. It is also probable that the common concerns of African people were the primary reason for the creation of the trickster, concerns that can be uncovered only through an examination of the role of trickster tales in African culture.

The African Trickster-Tale Tradition

In African cultures, trickster-tale traditions were not only ubiquitous but were remarkably similar in various ways. The trickster tale, though frequently associated with specific African religions, was extremely adaptable; stories with similar plots but different characters appeared in the oral traditions of diverse cultural groups. Although the principal actors tended to be animals, they usually acted as humans and sometimes appeared in human or divine forms. In many African cultures, the animal trickster was believed to have once been either a man or a god. Moreover, the characteristic attitude and behaviors of African tricksters exhibited enough similarities to allow for an assessment of them as a type. Susan Feldmann, for instance, suggests that African tricksters, like those in other cultures, have as their principal trait "superior cleverness"; however, she further observes that African tricksters exhibited some qualities that were not characteristic, for example, of tricksters in the folk traditions of American Indians:

Unlike the New World trickster he [the African trickster] is represented by the underdog rather than the chief. His amorality is not that of the anomic, presocialized individual, who has not yet matured to a sense of responsibility. Suave, urbane and calculating, the African trickster acts with premeditation, always in control of the situation; though self-seeking, his social sense is sufficiently developed to enable him to manipulate others to his advantage. He is mercenary rather than promiscuous. . . . On the whole, he shows a singular indifference to sex in favor of food or the sheer enjoyment of making a dupe of others. (15)

Feldmann offers a similar composite sketch of the African trickster's dupe:

Though in a given cycle trickster will victimize any of his fellow creatures, he usually concentrates on a particular prey. Trickster's favorite foils and dupes are Lion, Elephant and Hyena. The victim is always larger and therefore stronger; inevitably slow and dull-witted, often hard-working and honest. (15–16)

Of course, Feldmann's assessment of the behavior and relationship of African tricksters and their dupes should be viewed as only a basic characterization of the African trickster tale. However, she does capture the essential attributes of the tradition as it appears in numerous African cultures.

Throughout sub-Sahara Africa, diverse groups embodied in their trickster tales not only similar character types but also remarkably similar situations. Edwards notes, for instance, that "a distinctly African emphasis" in trickster tales is the "focus on the seeming inevitability of making and then terminating social ties in order to gain material (or other) goals. An assumption underlying the tales seems to be that material (or other) rewards are strictly limited, and that actors tend to be greedy" (3). In addition, Feldmann and others have pointed out that the material reward that most frequently motivates the African trickster, and his African American descendant, is food, a not-so-curious concern on the African continent. The emphasis on material acquisition, especially food, through the breaking of social ties suggests that the distribution and coherence of trickster traditions across sub-Sahara Africa were related to social conditions shared by Africans of diverse cultural backgrounds.

First of all, Africans have historically endured a subsistence-level existence as well as chronic shortages of material necessities because of various factors peculiar to the continent. Dependent on agriculture and hunting for their diet, Africans have faced numerous hazards in attempting to maintain a stable food supply. The favorable environmental conditions and stable work force necessary for successful agricultural production have been unpredictable or difficult to maintain. Among many groups, agriculture has been the province of women, while hunting has fallen to the men. Throughout much of black Africa the technology of farming, as well as the environment, has not been conducive to the production of large-scale crops or the accumulation and storage of significant reserves. On the one hand, climatic and soil conditions have favored the growing of tubers and shoot plants such as plantain and yams, which can be stored for only short periods of time. On the other hand, fluctuations in weather conditions—from excessive rain to prolonged droughts—have frequently led to severe shortfalls. The result all too often has been famine and other human misfortunes, such as dislocations.

Many of the same factors that had a negative impact on agricultural production have also interfered with the success of the hunter. Although most African communities raise domestic animals for food, hunting has traditionally served as the primary source of meat among many groups. For these societies, hunting has constituted a full-time activity, a risky enterprise at best. Its success has depended not only on the skill of the hunters but also on favorable environmental conditions that determine the availability of game. In addition, because of the indistinguishability of the techniques and weapons for hunting and those for war, hunters have had to be concerned with territorial violations, since encroachment could easily culminate in armed conflict with other groups. Furthermore, when environmental conditions have produced a shortfall in the game supply, the domestic animal populations have dwindled quickly as Africans have sought to supplement their diets with the only meat available.

In African trickster tales, the trickster's need to compensate for shortages in the food supply, often under faminelike conditions, is mentioned often enough to be considered a formulaic opening sequence. In tale after tale and among various groups, African raconteurs introduce their audiences to the adventures of tricksters in the midst of conditions such as the following:

There was great lack of meat in the country and people's mouths were sour from eating leaves of manioc and of sweet potatoes. . . .

They say that once upon a time a great famine came, and that Father Ananse the spider, and his wife Aso, and his children . . . built a little settlement and lived in it.

There was once a famine in the country, a terrible famine. Nobody had enough to eat. People and animals and plants were all dying, so the animals of the forest called a meeting.

The African world was an unsettled one in which chronic shortages of material necessities constantly threatened survival as well as individual and group autonomy. When faced with food or other shortages, whether caused by natural disasters or human catastrophes such as war, members of a particular group had to compete with one another as well as with neighboring groups for the same scarce resources. In such situations, which tended to occur frequently in sub-Sahara Africa, both intra- and intergroup alliances and friendships became tenuous as individuals were forced to secure the means of physical survival as best they could—often at each other's expense.

Trickster tales characteristically portray situations in which the principal actors create alliances that they inevitably break, or break long-standing ones in pursuit of their own apparently egocentric goals. The prevalence of false friendship, in which contracts are made and violated, has been noted by several scholars as a peculiarly African trickster-tales pattern (Edwards 10). In a social and natural environment in which individuals must struggle for their physical survival, harmony, friendship, and trust become ideals difficult to sustain, while deception, greed, and cleverness emerge as valuable behavioral traits. The African conception of the trickster as a figure particularly adept at securing the material means of survival, especially food, through deception and false friendship is aptly captured in the following tale from the Azande. Ture, the sacred spider trickster, emerges as a culture hero who is credited with having brought food to earth.

How Ture Got Food from the Sky God

Once there was no food on the earth. There was only one man who had food, and he had come down from the sky. When people began to die of hunger they went to that man so that he might give them food, but he chased them away. So, many people died of hunger. They told this affair to Ture, saying, "There is a man here with food, beside which he gets very angry." Ture said "You be silent, I am certainly going after that man."

Ture went to that man's house and deceived him, saying "Let us make blood-brotherhood, master." It pleased this man very much. He and Ture made blood-brotherhood. Shortly afterwards Ture went to this man and said "O my blood-brother, please give me some food, my children are dying of hunger." Ture's blood-brother bent and said "My blood-brother Ture, put your head between my legs." Then this man flew with Ture to the sky. When they arrived there this man spoke to Ture thus: "My blood-brother, collect some eleusine and some manioc and dig up twelve rats, and then come and we will leave." Ture did this completely. So once again this man bent and Ture put his head between his legs and he descended with Ture to this world here.

Ture returned to his home and gave the food to his wives. As they were eating this food Ture began to abuse this man, saying "The man to whose home I went is bad. He told me to put my head between his legs before he would fly me to get food." This man heard what Ture said about him and he was very annoyed by it.

Afterwards, when the food Ture had brought was finished, hunger tightened on Ture and his wives. So he went to his blood-brother again and he flew with Ture to the sky. Ture collected every kind of food there is in the world and put them into his big bag. But Ture's blood-brother went away from him and descended to earth here. Rain caught Ture in the sky and rained upon him till he was soaked. Ture then began to look for the way by which they had come. Ture found a very narrow path descending to the earth. Ture walked for some distance and when he arrived at a bare stone-flat he tapped on a drum, and people came from all over the world. Ture distributed every kind of food to them and he returned home with his. Because of Ture people eat today. (Feldmann 93)

The African's conception of the trickster as a sacred being, usually a god, undoubtedly influenced their attitude toward the adaptability of behaviors embodied in trickster tales. The actions of sacred tricksters, as gods or god-like figures, conveyed the idea that material shortage was an aspect of the natural order and that behaviors which involved trickery were appropriate under such conditions.

The Africans' attitude toward tricksters was related to their religious beliefs in a more profound way than is indicated by the appearance of the trickster in divine form. Feldmann observes, for instance, that "what is striking . . . is that unlike the fairy tale hero, trickster accomplishes the seemingly impossible by trickery rather than by supernatural aid. Trickster operates in a real world where the hero cannot count on supernatural helpers, and clever cheating replaces magic" (17). The African conception of the trickster as a hero who succeeds without the aid of magic must be viewed within the context of African religious beliefs as they revolved around the use of magic in human interaction. In the African religious worldview, the manipulation of the mystical forces in nature or magic created a greater threat to the Africans' values and the integrity of social life than the actions associated with Africans.[4] This view of magic derived from the socioreligious conception of human beings as intricately linked to one another by a mystical force in the universe that also connected them to nature and the supernatural in a hierarchical and interdependent relationship. Any attempt to manipulate or subvert the force in nature through magic for individual gain (a behavioral option available to all individuals) threatened not merely the object of such action but the well-being of the entire community and, by extension, the natural order of the universe itself.

At the level of community, African social structure existed as a microcosm of the larger universal order that, in turn, influenced a view of social life in which strong communal bond, respect for a hierarchy of social and religious powers, and harmony in social relationships were emphasized. Africans viewed allegiance to the community not merely as a social obligation but as a religious necessity. Therefore, regardless of the circumstances, the individual was expected to value behaviors that promoted communal welfare and preserved communal harmony above those that provided personal gain. In essence, individuals should accept their place in the social order and respect that of others by submitting to the hierarchy of powers, which extended upward from the social world to the supernatural realm. In this vision of society, individuals did not exist outside of participation in communal life. Those who violated the laws and customs that defined the appropriate forms of behavior subjected themselves to severe communal sanctions. However, because this vision of the individual's proper role in the social and natural order was essentially religious, violations of law and custom were defined in religious terms. To act in disharmony with one's community by seeking private gain through magic was considered one of the worst moral evils that a person could commit.

The African conception of the trickster, however, recognized that the rigid hierarchical social structure repressed individuals, especially those at the bottom. In times of material shortage, those at the lower end of the hierarchy were more likely not only to experience the greatest misery but also to have the fewest options to compensate for it. Feldmann argues, for instance, that African trickster tales often "illustrate the traditional right of the individual to contest irrational authority" (17). In this regard, African socioreligious structure influenced the conception of the trickster as a small animal pitted against larger ones in a struggle for material or other rewards. The portrayal of trickster and dupe offered both a conception of behaviors and a relation in which the trickster's characteristic actions represented the most advantageous way of securing individual interests without disrupting the social order. The value of using native intelligence in dealing with social superiors was enhanced by the socioreligious belief that magic against those in positions of authority, whether human or divine, was ineffective in directly achieving results. At the same time, those in positions of authority—whether defined by age, status, rank of spiritual existence—possessed a kind of divine right to use their superior power to accomplish their ends at the expense of inferior beings.

The Africans' view of a hierarchy in both social and religious terms was important in their ability to accept the trickster's actions as beneficial adaptive behavior under certain conditions. In a harsh natural environment and a rigid hierarchical social structure, the trickster offered Africans a model of behavior that facilitated both individual and communal well-being without violating their identity or values. While those at the top of the hierarchy could rely on their inherent power—defined in religious and social terms— those at the bottom demonstrated worth and ability to survive through wit. This natural state of affairs was reinforced through the trickster's interaction with antagonists in the natural world as well as in the supernatural. For example, in numerous West African tales, the trickster wages an ongoing battle of wits with the Sky God. Through sheer cunning and wit, the spider trickster, sometimes conceptualized as a demigod, manages to obtain from the all-powerful Sky God his food, thoughts, and stories. In these tales, the trickster's actions not only win the Sky God's respect but also benefit the community. Such tales obviously offered more than a behavioral strategy; they infused the trickster's actions with a kind of moral integrity not readily apparent on the surface.

In essence, Africans enslaved in America had cultural roots in societies that had historically faced chronic food shortages and a rigid hierarchical social structure. The rigidity of African social structure, however, fostered individual well-being in a harsh natural environment. In this environment, those behaviors that reflected and facilitated harmonious relationships and a cooperative atmosphere gained a level of social acceptability denied those that would disrupt the harmony of the natural order. Therefore, the tricksters' treatment of their dupes, familiar to Africans in both religious and social terms, could serve as a model of behavior for individuals. Furthermore, the frequent association of the African trickster with religion infused the tricksters' behavior with a sense of moral and cultural significance even when the actions involved the most outrageous behaviors.

The African American Trickster-Tale Tradition

I have been so pinched with hunger that I have fought with the dog . . . for the smallest crumbs that fell from the kitchen table. . . . Many times have I followed, with eager step, the waiting girl when she went out to shake the table cloth, to get the crumbs and small bones flung out for the cats.

Frederick Douglass, *My Bondage and My Freedom*

The life-style of Africans on the continent and those enslaved in America, though different in many ways, both revolved around behaviors designed to compensate for chronic shortages of material necessities and existence in a rigid social hierarchy. The plight of Africans in America, however, was obscured by the fact that they had been incorporated into an economic system in which they planted and harvested basic agricultural products, often in abundance. Nevertheless, they realized minimal benefits from the enormous energy they expended. Rather, their productivity served their slave masters, who used their control over Africans to deny them access to the rewards of their labor. While the masters made an effort to provide for the basic needs of Africans, they determined what the slaves would receive. As William D. Postell concludes from his examination of slaveowner records of the physical care of Africans, masters placed an emphasis "on quantity and not quality," an emphasis that threatened the Africans' survival as a people (26).

The slaveholders' attention to the physical needs of Africans was indifferent at best, dehumanizing in almost every respect, and ultimately devastating to their well-being. The most serious effects of the masters' control over their lives were to their health—especially the diseases created by the inadequate and nutritionally deficient food supply. John W. Blassingame notes that most slave masters based their food allotment on their perception of an "average" amount (158). As he further notes, an amount that proved "sufficient for one man was not necessarily enough for another." The Africans themselves also expressed the opinion that the food was seldom adequate. For example, William Brooks, who spent his days of bondage in Virginia, described the slaves' weekly food allotment in the following terms: 'Dey use to gib de slaves bout 6 pounds meat an' 5 pounds o' flour a week effen you ain' got chillun. If you got chillun, you git a little mo'. Well dat ain' 'nough lasten a dog a day" (from an interview in Purdue, Burden, and Phillip [57]). While the quantities may have varied according to the miserliness or generosity of the master, they never reached the proportions that an enslaved African was "ever likely to suffer from gout superinduced by excessive high living," to quote Solomon Northup in his slave narrative (169; Dover).

The physical conditions imposed on enslaved Africans was made all the more difficult to negotiate by the rigidity of the socioeconomic system into which they were forcefully placed. Despite their complete control over the distribution of goods produced under slavery, masters attempted to foist on Africans an illusion of the system as a cooperative enterprise in whose success both master and slave had a significant stake. The Africans, however, recognized that such a claim was illusory and its propagation ultimately in the interest of slave masters, who contributed little if anything to the functioning of the system. What Africans saw was that they were forced to work endlessly to make the system productive while the masters went to great lengths to limit their autonomy. Basically, Africans began work at sunup and often did not finish until well into the night, leaving little time for family and leisure activities. Although the nature of work varied from plantation to plantation and from season to season, it required long hours under the watchful eye of master, mistress, or overseer. The Africans were governed by rigid rules devised and enforced by the masters and were subjected to floggings for the least (real or supposed) transgressions, at the masters' discretion. When they were not at work, their movements were regulated by masters and overseers as well as by patrols that restricted their comings and goings. In addition, they were expected to be deferential in the presence of whites and punished with verbal and physical attacks when they were not (Blassingame, *Slave Community* 154–83). They were, in essence, treated like the other domestic animals the masters owned.

Not surprisingly, enslaved Africans came to view their world as one in which they were literally in a struggle for their survival. Opportunistically, however, as they pooled their individual memories and rivaled one another as raconteurs in the telling of animal trickster tales in the course of evening entertainments, they realized that the stories represented situations with which they could identify. The animal trickster's actions could serve as focus for transmitting a conception of behaviors they had traditionally accepted as the most advantageous to their survival. However, the differences, both sociocultural and practical, in the life-style of Africans on the continent and those enslaved in America led to a transformation in the African animal trickster. First of all, on the continent, Africans had viewed the animal trickster's characteristic exploits as adaptive behaviors in the struggle to survive in a harsh natural environment and rigid socioreligious hierarchy. In America, it was the artificially created conditions of material shortages imposed by the slave masters that threatened their lives. Second, Africans on the continent had infused the animal trickster's behavior with moral and even cosmic significance through the frequent association of tricksters with the gods. However, in America, their enslavers' efforts to control them by suppressing African religious expression had a profound influence on how they were to conceptualize and justify behaviors adapted from the animal trickster.

In America, the suppression of a religion that had informed the African conception of the trickster as a folk hero whose deeds involved manipulative actions against others did not seriously inhibit the ability of the slaves to transform the animal trickster tale to reflect their own situation. They found in their treatment by the slave masters sufficient justification for transmitting an oral expressive tradition in which the animal trickster's behavior was regarded as adaptive. The conspicuous disparity between the material and physical conditions under which they and the masters lived did not offer them a reason to envision their situation as a result of the natural order of things, a worldview implied by the African animal trickster's divine association. Their situation was perceived, however, as one for which there were clear analogues in nature, in which those possessing physical power and those not possessing it were equally endowed with mechanisms for survival. Furthermore, theirs was a world, not unlike that inhabited by the animal trickster, in which harmony was an illusion created by a natural balance between those forced to rely on keen survival instincts and those who could rely on physical power.

In essence, the animal trickster-tale tradition of enslaved Africans, as a model of heroic action, emerged as they sought to develop and transmit a conception of the types of behaviors that would compensate for the material and physical conditions imposed by the slave masters. They embodied their view of the trickster primarily in tales of Br'er Rabbit and other animals who, in the wild, would have been considered prey for those animals most often acting as dupes. They portrayed the animal trickster as smaller in stature than the dupes against whose physical power the trickster had to match wits for survival. This social and physical relationship in slave animal trickster tales, though not the only possible one between trickster and dupe, predominated and allowed the Africans to depict a type of confrontation within which the animal trickster's behavior was socially justifiable. Although the relationship between trickster and dupe enabled them to be placed in situations that were perfect metaphors for the Africans' own situation as the dehumanized, exploited, and preyed-upon victims of the slave masters, it also infused the trickster tale with a social ethos important to the building of their community. For instance, the animal trickster fails to achieve his goal most often when he attempts to victimize an animal not considered his natural enemy.

Not surprisingly, the African animal trickster's superior abilities in acquiring food through wit, guile, and deception became primary topics of slave trickster tales.

> Once upon a time Brother Rabbit and Brother Wolf decided to buy a cow together. And they bought the cow. So Ber Rabbit tell Ber Wolf that he must go and fetch a knife to butcher the cow with. After Ber Wolf was gone, Ber Rabbit kill the cow, and stuck the tail and horns and feet up in the mud. And begin to cry, "O Ber Wolf! the cow gone down in de mud!" And Ber Wolf run in. And he begin to pull on the cow's horn, and the horn fling him yonder. He pull on the tail, but the tail fling him yonder. And poor Ber Wolf look so pitiful! And Brother Rabbit said the cow gone down in the mud fast as he pull. (Parsons 31)

In his quest to obtain food and other material rewards, however, the animal trickster based his actions on the demands of living in a world not unlike that inhabited by enslaved Africans. Famine is seldom mentioned as a motivation for Br'er Rabbit's deeds, a situation that often caused his manipulation of his dupes to appear simply gratuitous or malicious. Noting the apparent lack of specific motivation in many of the tales, Levine concluded that "it was primarily advancement and not preservation that led to the trickster's manipulation. . . . Among a slave population whose daily rations were at best stark fare and quite often a barely minimal diet, it is not surprising that food proved to be the most common symbol of enhanced status and power. In his never-ending quest for food the trickster was not content with mere acquisition which he was perfectly capable of on his own; he needed to procure the food through guile from some stronger animal" (108). Levine's view of the function and nature of the animal trickster's characteristic behavior represents a misreading both of the symbolism of the relationship between trickster and dupe and of the situation of enslaved Africans as they perceived it, which made the trickster's approach to material acquisition a model of emulative behavior.

The Africans viewed access to the material rewards of the slave system as both their right as producers and as essential to their physical well-being. However, slaves, like the animal trickster whose world represented a thinly disguised version of their own, could not simply reach out and take what they wanted. Consequently, "Of course they'd steal. Had to steal. That the best way to git what they wanted." Of course, "when dey steal dey git caught, an' when you git caught you git beat. I seen 'em take 'em in-a-de barn an' jes tie 'em over lak dis an' den beat 'em 'twell de blood run down" (Yetman 116). Inasmuch as enslaved Africans were not "perfectly capable of" acquiring sufficient amounts of food or other necessities on their own without incurring great risks, they utilized animal trickster tales as an expressive mechanism for transmitting a conception of behaviors that, from their perspective, offered the greatest advantages in compensating for the shortages they faced.

The animal trickster of enslaved Africa was portrayed not as one obsessed with status but rather as a thief and malicious liar adept at manipulating others to achieve the material rewards that he sought without upsetting the order of things. No matter how many times the trickster secured the makings of a meal from his dupes or how clever his ruse, he remained cognizant of the fact that he was their prey and, therefore, justified in acting in any way that accomplished his ends. One of the most popular trickster tales finds Br'er Rabbit in a food-sharing scheme with another animal. Although the two presumably have equal access to the food, Br'er Rabbit invariably concocts a ruse that allows him to slip away from his partner to steal the food. When the theft is discovered, Br'er Rabbit boldly lies and then devises a plan to locate the culprit and thus place blame on another animal. There is no apparent moral or social justification for Br'er Rabbit's duplicity in the situation pictured in the tales. However, when viewed from the vantage of enslaved blacks—who were consistently short-portioned at the communal dinner table on the plantation—the actions of the trickster reflect a situational moral code for survival.

In addition, animal trickster tales were not intended to provide a literal guide for actions in everyday life but rather to promote cleverness, guile, and wit as the most advantageous behavioral options for dealing with the slave masters in certain generic situations. Therefore, in many tales the trickster's skillful use of wit to achieve a goal was simply played off against the stupidity and ineptness of the dupe in dealing with the same situation.

Oncet Ber Rabbit know where some heagle-eggs is. An' he wen' back an' tol' Ber Wolf. An' he wen' back de nex' day an' get some mo' eggs. An' tol' Ber Wolf when go dere he mus' say "Veel," and' when he wan' to come out mus' say "Val," and de do' open. An' instead he say "Ber Val," he say "Ber Veel," an' de do' close dat much tighter. An' when

Ber Eagle come in, he tol' his daughter to get some flour to bakin' some bread. An' de girl tol' her fader some one in de flour. An' when Ber Eagle wen' dere, dere was Ber Wolf in de flour. An' he kill him. An' dat was de las' of Ber Wolf. (Parsons 36)

Not uncommonly in such tales, the dupe's fate is a severe beating and, sometimes, death, consequences of ineptness not unknown to enslaved Africans: "I never whip a nigger for stealing, but I'll lick him half to death for being found out," declared a nineteenth-century slaveholder. "They will steal; all nigs will, but if they aren't smart enough to hide it, they deserve to be thrashed, and I tell my niggers so" (qtd. in Genovese, *Roll, Jordan* 604). In some instances, animal trickster tales served to remind enslaved Africans not only of the importance of acting like the trickster but also of the consequences of being like the dupe.

In creating animal trickster tales, blacks constantly sought to portray situations familiar to them and for which the trickster's characteristic actions could serve as a model. Like their animal trickster, they were in a contest of indeterminate duration for their survival with a limited number of ways for securing it. Therefore, they had to rely to a great extent on their ingenuity to develop endless variations on a single theme: the transcendent power of wit. They realized, however, that though susceptible to subversive behaviors that undermined their control, the slave masters were usually not stupid. Thus, their animal trickster tales emphasized the importance of creativity and inventiveness in dealing with situations peculiar to the slave-master relationship. In various tales, the trickster preys on the gullibility of his dupe to reveal that behaviors that proved successful in a particular situation, no matter how clever, were unlikely to work again.

Man comin' along de road with a kyartload o' fish. Ber Rabbit lay down alongside de road like he dead. De man saw him lay down. De man jump out his kyar' an' pick him up an' t'row him right on de kyartload o' fish. While Ber Rabbit layin' on de kyartload o' fish, he t'rowed enough for 'e to tote. After he t'row enough, den 'e jump off de kyart. An' de man didn' know. After he jump off, den he picked up dose fish. So while he pick up de fish now, he have a chance now to meet Ber Fox. After meet Ber Fox, Ber Fox say, "Ber Rabbit, where you get all dem fish?" He said, "O man! you kyan do like mo." Say, "Man, I lay 'longside de road, an' a man comin' wid' kyartload fish. Man pick me up, 'e t'row me on de kyart. An' I t'row as much as I want. Man, I took dem fish, I gone home." He said, "Man, you do jus' like you see me do. Yo go 'longside de road an' lay down, an' dey pick you up an' t'row you on de kyart. Den, man, you will get de fish how I do it." So Ber Wolf [Fox] done de same trick. After he done de trick so, de man come along an' see Ber Wolf lay down 'longside de road. Jump off de kyart, ketch him by de two hin' foot, raise him up. An lick him on de two hin' wheel, knock him on de wheel-tire. Man said, "You wouldn' done me like Ber Rabbit." He kill Ber Wolf. (Parsons 39)

Enslaved Africans were not totally dependent on their own devices in minimizing the risks of adapting tricksterlike behaviors against the masters. Like the dupes, the masters blinded themselves, by their own view of the slaves as grateful partners in the system, to the potential for blacks to act in their own best interests:

I cannot bear the thought that I have among my servants a wretch so depraved of every sense of gratitude to his mistress and myself as to break open the garden fence in order to rob my small patch of ten or fifteen small watermelons for to eat or sell in Town, when the price it would bring could not be more than perhaps a dollar or a dollar and a half. (Qtd. in Genovese, *Roll, Jordan* 604)

While the masters' paternalism supported their illusion of the slave system as a cooperative enterprise accepted as legitimate by the Africans, the masters left themselves open to manipulation that allowed slaves to gain an advantage in negotiating some of its harsher realities. "I knew that the best way to get around master was to be very humble," wrote Israel Campbell in his autobiography. "I set my wits to work to find out something that would please him" (62). Enslaved Africans permeated the animal trickster tales with the cajoling and flattering that made the masters susceptible to manipulation. In the world of the animal trickster, these insights were nowhere better revealed than in the animals' decorum toward each other. Decorously, they addressed each other as "Br'er" and "Sis" as they victimized and plotted against each other.

In many ways, the perspective from which enslaved Africans' found in the animal trickster a focus for the creation of a folk hero derives meaning from the workings of the slave system from their point of view. Unless we take their worldview into account, their appreciation of the trickster's exploits appears problematic, indeed. For example, collecting animal trickster tales in the late nineteenth century, A. H. M. Christensen noted of her informant that "he regards the rabbit stories with much respect, evidently considering them types of human experience, his own in particular. . . . He praises the Rabbit when successful in spite of his treachery" (1–5). Christensen was repulsed by the enthusiasm and delight expressed by her informant for what she viewed as the immoral antics of the wily trickster and warned her readers that "we of the New South cannot wish our children to pose long over these pages. . . ." From the point of view of enslaved Africans, who created and derived pleasure and meaning from the tales, treachery was not a behavior from which they could protect their children. Slavery itself was a treacherous system in which illusions paraded as reality; it was for its victims the ultimate trick—a trick with words that turned a human being into a piece of property. In the world of enslaved blacks, the ways of the treacherous had to be learned, mastered, and dealt with on a daily basis.

Now I tell yer a riddle 'bout Ber Rabbit. In dat part of country he used to dig well. So man wen' aroun' to all de animals, 'cause de animal couldn' get no water, an' ax dem to he'p an' dig de well. So all 'gree, all but Ber Rabbit. Ber Rabbit he refuse. Say he could get water, jew [dew], off de grass an' t'ings. So, after de well done dig, all de animals get water dere, an' de man fo'bid Ber Rabbit to get no water to his well. So de man wen' after him, an' tell him to keep away from his well. Rabbit say he don' go dere. So de man wen' home an' make a tar baby, an' set him to de well. So 'fo' day he wen' to get his water. He see dis tar baby standin' up right side de well. So he went wid his jug to de well, an' say, "Who you? Who you? You bes' talk. Ef you don' talk, I'll slap you." An' slap him wid one hand', an' dat one fasten on him. "Le' me loose! I'll slap you wid de oder one." Slap him wid de oder one, an' dat one fasten. Said, "Min', I got two mo' laig." Slap him, dat one fasten. Ain't had power to raise de oder one at all.

Day clean. So de fahmer walk down to his well, an' saw Ber Rabbit hangin' on to de tar baby. "Hellow, Ber Rabbit! what you doin'?"—"I come down, suh, an' I see dis t'ing, an' I try to run him f'om yer well, an' he fasten me dere." De man say, "Dis day, Ber Rabbit, I'll t'row you dat briar, cockspu', t'ick' [thicket], together." Rabbit say, "Do, for Gwad's

sake, t'row me in de riber! Don' t'row me in de brair patch!" De man loosen f'om de tar
baby an' star' to t'row him in de riber. "Do, fo' Gawd's sake, t'row me in de riber! Don'
t'row me in de briar patch!" De man pick 'em up an' t'row him in de briar patch. Rabbit
say, "Keeng! Keeng! Man, I was born in de briar patch." (Parsons 27–28)

Compared with the deeds of folk heroes in other contexts, the animal trickster's
cleverness, guile, and wit hardly seem like heroic behaviors. However, to display the
ability to think and act on one's own was an attribute that carried dire physical consequences, especially if perceived as serving the interests of the slave rather than that of
the masters. It is certainly not accidental that the denouement in many tales revolved as
much around how the trickster was going to get the makings of his next meal from his
dupes as how he was going to escape being their meal. The animal trickster's world,
like that inhabited by enslaved Africans, was one fraught with hidden dangers to survival—was one in which the appearance of harmony and cooperation masked an incredible
and often vicious struggle for survival. In this world, no deed against the enemy was too
outrageous.

One day the wolf said, "Brother Rabbit, I am going to eat you up."—"No," said Brother
Rabbit, "don't eat me! I know where some fine geese is. If you let me tie you here, I will
go and get them for you."—"All right," said the wolf. So the rabbit tied the wolf. Then
the rabbit went on his way until he came to a farmyard. Then he said, "Farmer, give me
trouble." So the farmer went into the yard and get a hound-dog and two hound-puppies
and put them in a bag, and said, "When you get out in the field, you must open the bag,
and you will have all the trouble you want."—"All right," said the rabbit. So the rabbit
went back to the wolf. He waited until he came near the wolf, then he loose the bag and
ran the dogs behind him. He ran right straight for the wolf. Wolf said, "Bear off, Rabbit,
bear off!" So he saw the rabbit was close upon him, he called out harder, "Bear off,
Rabbit, bear off!" The rabbit said, "Not a bit. I am running in straight deal this morning." So the dogs killed the wolf and eat him up. The story is end. (Parsons 67)

While the survival of the slaves was protected up to a point by the masters' interests in
their physical well-being as property, they faced the ever-present danger of an even
worse form of death—the total surrender of their humanity to the slave system.

The animal trickster tale reveals that what constitutes normative heroic action depends both on the tradition of heroic creation historically embraced by a group and on
the obstacles that the hero's actions are designed to overcome. Therefore, the normative
function of heroic literature must be conceptualized not only from a culture-specific
perspective but also from a situational one. Actions recognized as heroic in one cultural
context and by one group of people may be viewed as ordinary or even criminal in
another context or by another group, or even by the same group at different times. For
slaves, the animal trickster's characteristic actions, which involved the manipulation of
others to achieve material rewards, represented a normative model of heroic behavior in
their situation. By the same token, the trickster's actions when viewed from the perspective of the slave masters was a form of subterfuge and, therefore, a threat to their
values and culture building. However, enslaved blacks, whose culture was rooted in their
African heritage, in which respect for wit and ingenuity had historically served as a
means of protecting their values, discovered in the trickster's actions a model of behav-

ior for coping with devastating circumstances and attempting to maintain dignity and self-respect.

Notes

[1] Seward offers an informative summary of the role that theories of black acculturation have played in the study of African American folklore.

[2] Frederickson. He offers extended analysis of the dualism that characterized white thinking about blacks, particularly in the late nineteenth century.

[3] This approach to the African American trickster tale is most clearly revealed in Weldon and in Abrahams, *Deep Down in the Jungle* (62–66).

[4] Numerous scholars have written about the African view of magic and its relationship to sociocultural values. See, for example, John S. Mbiti; E. A. Ruch and K. C. Anyanwu; and E. J. Marias.

Orality and Hispanic Literature of the United States

Nicolás Kanellos

Since the breakthrough work done by Milman Parry and Albert B. Lord on epic poetry, the study of orality and oral literature has drawn increasing attention from scholars. Work by structuralists like Claude Lévi-Strauss (*Savage Mind*) and theorists of ethnopoetics like Jerome Rothenberg (*Pre-Faces*) and Michel Benamou has brought attention to ethnic minority literature in the United States, notable examples of which are jazz and blues poetry, Native American chants, and performances by street poets in Hispanic barrios.

One of the most accomplished and respected students of orality, Walter J. Ong, has distanced himself somewhat from the Parry-Lord assumption that the oral and literary modes cannot mix, that the worldviews, mind-sets, and formulaic techniques of preliterate society are incompatible with the literate. He has indeed created a middle ground for mixed oral-written literature by identifying a "primary orality," as in tribal songs, a "secondary orality," in the primarily nonliterate world, and a "residual orality," in writers who depend on formulas, rhetorical structures, and speech patterns inherited from the folktales, epics, and songs of their people (*Orality and Literacy* 5–156). But Ong continues the Parry-Lord insistence on segregating what is supposedly oral in composition and worldview from what is literate. Stating that oral literature, along with the culture that it represents, "fosters personality structures that in certain ways are more communal and externalized, and less introspective, than those common among literates" (24), he categorizes orally based thought (and expression) as follows (37–57): (1) additive rather than disjunctive, (2) aggregative rather than analytic, (3) redundant, (4) conservative, (5) close to the "human life world," in Ong's terminology, (6) agonistically toned, (7) emphatic and distanced, (8) homeostatic, and (9) situational rather than abstract. The impact of Ong's work on minority literature in the United States would thus be to lead us to the study of residual orality and the identification of the formulas and characteristics he has outlined. But the overriding problem with this approach for minority literature is that the traits were, for the most part, derived from linguistic and anthropological studies of so-called primitive peoples around the world—including ancient and medieval Europeans—in states of primary or secondary orality. And all the biases of technological civilization against such societies would only further impede an appreciation of the already maligned and marginalized minority literature.

What is worse, various mainstream literary theorists have championed orality as a means of stemming the loss of audience by "American" poetry, which is seen as too Eurocentric (Rothenberg, *Pre-Faces* 39–47) and, I would add, academic. Inspired in part by the work of Lévi-Strauss and Mircea Eliade, Rothenberg—with his Romanticism in full bloom!—calls for a "retribalization" of poetry (39), for Indians to teach whites to sing (75), for a return to the wilderness (176), for the adoption of an Indian poesis (32), and for the incorporation into poetry of the dynamics of actual speech, of orality. As in "primitive" tribes, poets would function as the shamans, the visionaries; they would become, in the words of one of Rothenberg's titles, "technicians of the sacred," directly serving the community by acting as its mouthpiece, exorcist, and exegete.

While Rothenberg's understanding of orality may be too Romantic and reminiscent of nineteenth-century attitudes toward the noble savage, Ong's analysis also tends to exaggerate the difference between orality and literacy. In a more realistic analysis of orality and oral literature in various African societies, as well as in societies ranging from the South Pacific to the Asian, Ruth Finnegan found no real evidence of a specifically "oral" tradition that can be definitively distinguished from the "written" or "literate" as it affects mental patterns, literary forms, and/or culture (243). She acknowledges, however, that the major difference is that oral literature is performed (244) but notes that from Tibet to Ireland, there are varying degrees of interdependence of oral and written literature, even in performance. She further points to the centuries of written tradition in Africa, the interchange between the written and the oral, and the continuation of the latter even on radio and television through the use of technology. There is, in addition, evidence from Tibet and Mongolia, as well as from Chinese medieval ballads, Anglo-American ballads, and Irish street songs—and, of course, European medieval and classical texts—of reliance on oral delivery of literature initially composed in writing. But most important for our study, Finnegan examines the work of a literate, college-trained Limba poet, as well as others, who composes in the oral mode and shows no essential difference, in style, presentation, and use of traditional elements, from Limba poets who are illiterate (245). She concludes her study by citing numerous examples of writers around the world who compose (either in written or oral form) and memorize their work before performing it (248–49): there is no clear-cut distinction between the oral and written literatures.

A number of writers of Hispanic literature in the United States—perhaps the majority of poets and, to a lesser degree, the prose writers—compose their work for oral performance. In one of the cases to be studied, the intention of the literature is exclusively oral; in the others, publication and distribution to a primarily reading audience is also the aim. Although Ong's nine characteristics are derived principally from oral cultures, they help us identify a commonality that Hispanic writers have with poets and storytellers from primary, secondary, and residual oral cultures around the world. But, as in Finnegan, the common denominator for their orality may not be a worldview but the need to perform and the physical and social exigencies of performance itself. Furthermore, the need to perform may be determined more by Hispanics' marginal or minority status in the United States than by any other cultural factors, as shall be illustrated below.

In order to understand the phenomena of orality and performance, I introduce four examples of writers, who run the gamut from the street-corner poet to the novelist who creates in a secluded studio. Regardless of the physical distance of their intended audiences, the oral performance is central to each of these writers. No matter how educated or integrated any of them may be into the society, their need to interact with their audience and community and to keep close to the "human life world" irrevocably forces them to rely on oral modes of presentation.

The first of these is a street bard whom many would immediately identify as a folk poet, a minstrel. Now in his late seventies, Jorge Brandon is a Puerto Rican poet who spent much of his life performing in the public plazas of Puerto Rico, Venezuela, Colombia, Central America, and Mexico, before settling in New York's Lower East Side. His proud calling has always been to be a poet; for him there is no greater rank or position in society. The only function of the poet that he can conceive of is to communicate directly, orally, to a public audience. He is perhaps one of the few left in a long line of _declamadores_—performers of their own compositions and those of other writers, both oral and literate, both famous and unknown. In fact, part of his repertoire features the works of poets who exist only in the oral tradition, poets he places alongside Cervantes and Rubén Darío. Brandon, who does not allow anyone to see his work written or to publish any of his poems, performs his poems, nothing else; he gestures, acts out the passages, and projects his trained voice, reliving the emotional nuances so deeply that he is sometimes thought to be eccentric. In this he represents an example of Ong's traits of the emphatic and participatory, as well as of the agonistically toned. Moreover, his epic poem "El Masacre de Ponce" ("The Ponce Massacre"), composed from firsthand observation, is one of the unknown masterpieces of Puerto Rican literature, in which virtually all the formulas and characteristics identified by Ong are displayed. Up to this point I have described the oral poet of any nineteenth-century Spanish American country, roaming the countryside, gracing town plazas during festivals and feast days, eulogizing heroes, mourning the dead.

Brandon is distrustful of Broadway, Wall Street, and Madison Avenue—the world of entertainment, finance, and publishing. He performs his works for money but, fearful that recording and publishing companies may pirate his works, transcribes his poems in mnemonic patterns. He continually goes over these in memorizing and planning his performances. I have seen his book of codes and I have personally observed him while rehearsing. The poet uses a tape recorder to listen to himself and analyze his delivery. He stands on street corners wearing a World War I army helmet with a sign stating in English and Spanish that he recites the one hundred best poems of the Spanish language. As a gimmick to attract an audience, he places a small speaker inside a coconut with a face painted on it and recites his poems into a microphone so that the head appears to be performing (_coconut_ is figuratively used to mean _head_ in Spanish). His pitch is "el coco que habla," the "talking coconut."

Brandon's astonishing memory, his performance style, his commitment to poetry and Art with a capital _A_ inspire the most sophisticated writers. He considers himself to be an artist in the highest sense of the word. His language and diction are impeccable; at the same time, he is a linguistic innovator and creator of neologisms. Although Brandon's English is as elegant as his Spanish, he never mixes the two languages. His favorite poet in English is Edgar Allan Poe, probably because of the oral qualities of Poe's work. What most characterizes Brandon's performances, however, is the delight of the public and of other poets as well. No festival or public celebration in the Puerto Rican community of the Lower East Side is complete without him.

Tato Laviera, author of several books of poetry and several produced plays, composer and lyricist of commercially recorded songs, is an important Hispanic writer in the United States. As Brandon's apprentice, he committed to memory much of that poet's (as well as his own) work and adopted some of Brandon's performance styles. He too considers poetry to be essentially an oral art, one that must be shared in performance with a group or a community—a commitment that comes from his observation of the power of oral poetry to move the listener. In order to overcome the distance between the individual performer and the group, Laviera believes, the poet must master certain physical and emotional postures and declamatory techniques. As a writer who also depends on published works to reach an unseen audience, he is wary of the physical and intellectual demands of the written tradition in both English and Spanish. But, in Laviera, even the written word is the product of an effort to re-create the oral performance. The process is so evident in his published poems that, without the gestures, the enunciation, the physical and oral nuances, and the music that are an integral part of their performance, many of them lose their essence and their power.

Laviera writes in English, Spanish, and what he calls "Spanglish"—the blending of two European tongues by a poet with roots in the African and American continents. His work is emphatic, situational, and homeostatic, feeding from the "human life world." Contentious, proud, and often "agonistic," as Ong would put it, Laviera is by any account a virtuoso in his use of language. Perhaps relying on the Puerto Rican oral tradition of the *bomba* and *décima* debates, he is ready to engage anyone in contests of improvisation or presentation. His second work, *Enclave*, is the other side of the agonistic, however; it celebrates such imaginary personalities as Tito Madera Smith, half Southern black and half Puerto Rican, and the barrio gossip Juana Bochisme; he also sings the praise of such real culture heroes as John Lennon, Miriam Makeba, the Cuban dancer Alicia Alonso, Suni Paz, and the writer Louis Palés Matos. One of the poems in this work, "Jesus Papote," is a modern epic, a long monologue sung by a fetus struggling to be born, on Christmas Day, from the womb of a dying drug addict (*Enclave* 12–21). The fetus personifies the future of Laviera's people in the United States.

A black Puerto Rican living in New York's Lower East Side, Laviera incorporates themes from several cultures but remains marginalized, like his own community. His poems may speak to his native Santurce, Puerto Rico; to Spanish Harlem, black Harlem, Africa; and to white America and Europe, but always from his particular racial, political, and cultural perspective. Laviera's bilingual poems, like those of Chicano writers Abelardo, Alurista, Ricardo Sánchez, and Evangelina Vigil-Piñón, are obviously aimed at a specialized audience. For the most part, they use the language of a people whose daily lives are articulated through a continuous exchange of English and Spanish. But like Alurista, Sánchez, and Vigil, Laviera goes beyond the simple reproduction of recognizable speech patterns to explore the aesthetic possibilities of contrasting and mixing the sound and sense of the two languages, even stretching both linguistic systems and virtually creating a new one. An example of Laviera's blending of popular and standard dialect levels of both languages and his creating a new poetic experience is his poem "velluda: alliterated y eslembao," in which he demonstrates his alliterative vir-

tuosity while acting out one of the most sensual, but nonoffensive, works in his repertoire:

velluda: alliterated y eslembao

it was all about my fingers, each one of them:
el meñique se figuraba fuerte
fabulosamente fermentando figuras
fraternales en el rocío de tu boca.

it was all about my fingers, each one of them:
el anular circulando cuadros
concéntricos cariñosamente
caminando por el pecho en tus
montañas.

it was all about my fingers, each one of them:
el del corazón suavizando sensualmente
sobos sexuales suspirando
en las venas de tu vientre.

it was all about my fingers, each one of them:
el indice lubricando lazos lucientes
en las ramas de tus piernas.

and finally, mi negra,

it was all about my fingers, each one of them:
el pulgar hincándose íntimamente
ilustrándose en las bases de
tus raíces.

i came down, all the way down,
completing nurture
then you, mulata, you gave
birth to my hands, which
you caressed until the
touches tinkled stars of
delight as you introduced
me to your universe:
velluda: alliterated y eslembao,
i got lost inside your rain forest. (*Enclave* 49)

Like many black poets whose works incorporate musical structures such as the blues,
Laviera has written poems to be sung in part or in full. His inspiration comes from the
native *plena* lyric and rhythmic structures of Puerto Rico, both of which rely on rhymed
couplets improvised by a leader and repeated by a chorus or counterpointed by a choral
refrain. His purpose is not to discover roots; rather, the *plena* represents a pattern of
expression that he has heard in popular music his whole life. The dividing line between
song and poetry is elusive to Laviera and, I would think, should be so for poets of
residual orality. An example of his sung poetry is "Unemployment Line" (*Enclave* 29),

in which phrases are repeated as many as seven times and sung with slightly varying melodic lines.

Miguel Algarín, a poet, playwright, prose writer, professor of English at Rutgers University, links the worlds of avant-garde American writing and grass-roots folklore. He goes from the halls of academia, where he teaches Shakespeare, to poetry festivals in Amsterdam and Rome, to the streets of the Lower East Side, where he lives and where he runs the Nuyorican Poets Cafe, a center for the performance of literature. In New York, Algarín is intimate with Imamu Amiri Baraka, Allen Ginsberg, William Burroughs, and Joseph Papp. He has written for the PBS series *Realidades* and rewritten Hollywood films in production in New York; translated Neruda's poems in a book entitled *Song of Protest*; and compiled the anthology *Nuyorican Poetry*, the first of its kind. Algarín acknowledges the imperative of orality and performance in poetry in his article "Volume and Value of the Breath in Poetry." If it were not that Algarín creates from within his own community, in some aspects his efforts would resemble Rothenberg's attempt to revitalize American poetry.

Algarín is the consummate performer, the master of diction, the creator of musical verse, the exposer of the most intimate and shameful corners of the psyche—the exorcist in the Rothenberg sense. For all his sophistication, his graduate studies at Princeton, his work at the Jack Kerouac School of Disembodied Poetics of the Naropa Institute, Algarín is an oral poet. As a writer, his task is to create in his poetry the emotional impact of his oral performance. The way that poetry is understood and taught in English in this country presents an obstacle that Algarín's writing must overcome; he has to sensitize the English reader to the re-creation of the oral performance of the poem. His poetry is alive, primarily in performance, as is Laviera's and Brandon's. Algarín's poetic bilingualism is not as extensive as Laviera's, however, partly, I believe, because of his need to address the American literati. His bilingual poems generally use a more standardized language, and they are not as situational as Laviera's, but every bit as agonistic in tone and content.

Algarín's first book, *Mongo Affair*, follows up its bilingual title with a text that creates a linguistic, emotional, and philosophical tension between English and Spanish usage. *On Call*, his second work, is aimed at a national English-speaking and bilingual audience; the last section of the book emerges from his travels in the Southwest. His third book, *Body Bee Calling from the Twenty-first Century*, is Algarín's interstellar exploration of existence in a bionic future; the book, written entirely in a bare-bones English, is the furthest removed from the communal, oral mode, which is partially regained in *Time's Now*.

The stories and novels of Rolando Hinojosa, celebrated prose writer in Spanish and English, consist predominantly of monologues, dialogues, and first-person narratives, all of which suggest verbal performance by the individual characters. The novels and stories are part of a continuing, complex mosaic of life in a mythical south Texas town, Klail City. Written in Spanish, English, and bilingual text, the hundreds of portraits in the novels are created through the characters' ideolect (personal dialect) in talking about themselves and others. Many of the portraits are, in fact, dramatic monologues similar to the poetic monologues of Tato Laviera's characters in *Enclave* and *AmeRican*. Hinojosa's *Mi querido Rafa*, departs in structure from the three previous books in that the first half is epistolary and experiments with the graphic representations of speech by the two main characters. But the second part of the novel uses techniques similar to those in his other books: testimony, interviews, storytelling in bars, gossip—the types of speech of small-town social settings, in which people can paint individually inaccurate pictures of characters and events. *Rites and Witnesses*, published in 1982, was his first novel written totally in English. The choice of language was determined by the work's focus on the Anglo-American landowners, the big ranchers, and much of the text is articulated in a dialogue style that approaches drama. Following *Rites and Witnesses*, Hinojosa published a re-creation in English of *Mi querido Rafa*, entitled *Dear Rafe*, and of his prize-winning *Klail City y sus alrededores*, entitled *Klail City*. His only other English-only book is *Partners in Crime*, an experimental detective novel. In 1986 he returned to the bilingual format of his first works with the publication of *Claros varones de Belken /* *Fair Gentlemen of Belken*. At least one scholar considers the long narrative poem *Korean Love Songs* to be part of the tradition of border balladry in south Texas (Saldívar).

Klail City, the pivotal book in Hinojosa's generational series, best exhibits the orality of culture in Hinojosa's novelistic world as well as the orality of Hinojosa (see Broyles). The work itself is a mosaic of oral performance styles, including everything from Protestant sermons and hymns to pitches by traveling salesmen, jokes, tales, and *corridos*, or folk ballads. The central performance piece, however, is a speech by an aging patriarch of the Rio Grande Valley that underscores the ideology of Hinojosa's orality and, perhaps, provides insight into that of Hispanic literature in the United States. In the monologue entitled "Echevarría tiene la palabra," Yolanda Broyles sees the act of speech granted the status almost of a hallowed rite, comparable in English to the respect shown to the Gospel according to St. John (115). She further states that Echevarría

is the voice of collective memory. Historical memory is transmitted through verbal performance, not through written materials. Events of significance in the Mexicano community are the guideposts of Echevarría's narrative. His dramatic and emotive narrative in the bar El Oasis recounts the violence perpetrated by the rinches (Texas Rangers) and the gullibility of *raza* [Mexican Americans]. It is a subversive history for it contradicts the official Anglo record upheld by the courts, and disseminated in history books. (114–15)

This particular monologue is one of the most popular selections requested of Hinojosa, the performer, the reader of his works in public. Through inflection, subtle facial expressions, and gestures, Hinojosa adopts the character of Echevarría and becomes the official purveyor of that alternative history and worldview that his community embodies.

Unlike Brandon and Laviera, Hinojosa is an academically trained intellectual, with a PhD in literature and experience as a professor in both the Spanish and English departments of major universities. Despite the orality of his works, they are clearly anchored in the Hispanic and Anglo-American written traditions. Ong would probably recognize a residual orality in the works derived from Hinojosa's socialization in the bilingual communities of the Rio Grande Valley, where secondary and residual orality shape popular culture. What Ong would, perhaps, be unfamiliar with is the region's combative folktale and balladry tradition, in which intense feelings of Mexican and Anglo nationalism clash and are often articulated in the dialectic of Spanish versus English, literate versus oral, social institution versus popular culture, Anglo official history and authority versus collective memory and resistance by the Mexican dispossessed. Thus for Hinojosa—despite his academic training and employment—and the other writers studied here, the oral mode is more than just a style, a conditioning of their backgrounds, a romantic attitude, a search for roots. It is the only authentic and, to a great degree, unself-conscious posture for them as creators of the literature of their community.

Were the Hispanic community in the United States to possess the means of production, promotion, and distribution of its literature in printed form, were it to control its history and image in print, then Hinojosa's and the other writers' works might be more print-bound and less performance-oriented. It is the very marginality of Hispanic communities in the United States, their lack of political and economic power, that determines the need for and popularity of orality and performance. Hinojosa, Laviera, and Algarín reach more people through the spoken word than through their books, which are published exclusively by small, noncommercial presses. And their published materials in Spanish are even more marginalized in the United States, where Spanish-language and literature teachers and the book industry snub them in favor of the official Hispanic culture products from abroad. As is clearly demonstrated by Jorge Brandon, orality and performance are conscious choices, determined by the economics, politics, and culture of the community and the individual artist. All four of these writers are highly literate; most of their audiences are literate. The currency of their exchange, however, is neither the printed page nor the book. It is the spoken word, alive and painfully throbbing as an expression of communitas, commonality, communion.

Orality and performance are conscious technical and ideological choices. The writers we have examined are not limited by these modalities but are liberated by them. They are freer to communicate directly with a known audience, to control the destiny and impact of their works. Even prose writers like Hinojosa are consummate readers and performers of their material. Hinojosa sees the effects of his works, sees the audience react and recognize themselves in his literature, sees it reenter popular culture in a thousand ways.

It is hard for me, as the largest publisher of Hispanic literature in the United States, to admit to the low sales volume of our books and to the fact that our small presses are the only printed outlet for our major writers, that not one commercial publishing house is issuing their works. But as a coordinator of tours, readings, and performances for these writers, I am well aware of the number of people they reach through performance. If there were a distribution and promotion system for us, as there is for mainstream literature, perhaps the numbers represented in our audiences would translate into sales.

The complexities of orality and performance are numerous. I have not mentioned the poets of *salsa* verse, like Héctor Lavoy, whose commercial recordings reach millions throughout the Spanish-speaking world, or Rubén Blades, also a recording star, who has composed two albums of narration in song that deal with three generations of a family, in an attempt to do in music what Gabriel García Márquez has done in *Cien años de soledad* (*One Hundred Years of Solitude*). I have not analyzed poetic works that are recited on commercial recordings between cuts of music, or the continuation of the *corrido* tradition on disks and tapes mainly heard on early morning Spanish-language radio broadcasts. The study of prison writers is a task unto itself: the genres and styles, the commitment of large audiences of prisoners to poetry, and the poets, like the late Miguel Piñero and Ricardo Sánchez, who emerged from that oral tradition. There are also the street theaters and farm workers' theaters; the jazz poetry of Victor Hernández

Cruz, Ana Castillo, and David Hernández; and many other writers and forms that depend on orality and performance.

Hispanic writers have various alternative forms through which to distribute their works: recordings, radio, community newspapers, performances. The newspaper has for more than a century served as the major vehicle for Hispanic writers in the United States. Hundreds of newspapers have been published and continue to publish throughout the country. Since 1823 in New York alone, there have been more than fifty Spanish-language newspapers, most of them providing ample space for poetry, short stories, essays, and even serialized novels. Before World War II, newspapers from New York and the Southwest also published novels, books of poetry, and nonfiction, ran their own bookstores, and took mail orders for their publications. The Hispanic tradition in the United States has never been an illiterate one. The orality and performance of today's writers come from the writers' upbringing in popular culture, conscious working-class orientation, and purposeful merging of the oral and written traditions. In fact, this merging represents a revolution in written literature, a renewal, a rebirth . . . but one quite different from what Rothenberg hoped to inspire among white poets.

Oral Tradition and Poetic Influence: Two Poets from Greater Mexico

José E. Limón

It's a wise child that knows its own father.

The Odyssey

Man is in love and loves what vanishes, What more is there to say?

Yeats

The development of a literary history may involve a combination of strategies, including the rediscovery of forgotten texts, the reevaluation of writers and traditions slighted by mainstream scholarship, and the criticism of criticism in order to open up new conceptual windows onto the literary landscape. This essay proceeds along each of these revisionist lines, and it does so with respect to the literary history of Mexicans in the United States.[1] It may seem premature to speak of *revision* for a literary history still in its infancy, but perhaps emergent histories should be revised from the outset, lest they ossify into undesirable patterns. That some ossification is already occurring will be one point of departure for these remarks. In addition, I will address a more general issue in the construction of any literary history—namely, the relation of folklore, especially oral tradition, to written literature.

I will address these issues by examining one concrete instance in the relation of oral tradition to written literature in Texas-Mexican cultural history. My analysis focuses on the influential relationship between the Mexican ballad, or *corrido*, and one example of the relatively unknown poetic work of an otherwise prominent Texas-Mexican intellectual—the distinguished folklorist, anthropologist, and cultural historian Américo Paredes (see Limón, "Américo Paredes").

I submit that this instance, and perhaps many others that are cross-cultural, cannot be adequately understood through the dominant conceptualizations of the folklore-literature relation. After acknowledging these structures and discussing their limitations, I shall offer Harold Bloom's theory of poetic influence as a more powerful approach for grasping the meaning of this instance.[2] Yet I shall also point to the ultimate inadequacy of Bloom's ideas, inattentive as they are to literature as socially symbolic acts embedded in historical process. By expanding the range of Bloom's interpretive framework, I will make an initial anthropological statement on intergenerational cultural change in Texas-Mexican society.

Folklore and Literature: Dominant Conceptualizations

My reading of the conceptual scholarship on the folklore-literature relation indicates three general tendencies. The first, oldest, and increasingly more marginal of these might be called the *precursory* position. This approach, never quite made explicit but still most evident in literary anthologies, understands folklore primarily as oral tradition that constitutes a kind of ill-formed and ill-informed "literature." The preliterature slowly gives way to well-formed and learned written productions. This position is, as I say, becoming much less prevalent in comparison to the second, which continues to dominate the subject; it is practiced by those whom Roger D. Abrahams has labeled the "lore-in-lit people" ("Folklore" 77). They are fundamentally concerned with folklore as it is found embedded in literary texts. Within this camp, however, we can make a further distinction between those who seemingly rest content with the formal iden-tification of folklore in literature and those, like Alan Dundes, who advocate not only identification but also interpretation, to set out the stylistic and thematic significance of the folklore item for the literary text ("Study").

Before moving to the third position, we might note the influence of the first two on the emergent literary history of Mexicans in the United States, a late product of what has been called the "Chicano literary Renaissance." Since the 1960s, young writers of Mexican descent in the United States have produced a veritable outpouring of literature in all its modern genres, with poetry, perhaps, taking a leading role. The literary flower-ing occurred in the context of a militant redefinition of the political and cultural rela-tions between the dominant society and a still subordinated Mexican American commu-nity. Led principally by a university-based cadre and resting on a generally ethnic na-tionalist ideology, the Chicano movement sought to better the social conditions of Mexicans in the United States. It also inspired and created the new Chicano literature.[3]

This literature has been accompanied by a scholarship that seeks the critical under-standing of the new artistic production as well as its historical enlargement; the latter, which is proceeding largely through efforts to identify undiscovered texts, has an inter-esting paradoxical character (see, e.g., R. Paredes, "The Evolution"). While such a literary past may be discovered and historically reconstructed, it seems clear that it cannot be an informing tradition, in Eliot's sense, at least not for the Chicano literature produced up to the present. Chicano writers have simply not had the time to digest the recently discovered texts. Indeed, one may wonder whether the quality of the latter is such that they will ever become truly influential.

Chicano literature is indebted, however, to two other traditions—one, Western liter-ary culture, especially North American and Latin American writers; the other, Mexican folk culture, particularly verbal art. Yet while scholarly criticism has paid some attention to the former relation, the literary connection to folk culture has remained almost wholly unexplored. Thus, Juan Rodriguez, an important critic of Chicano letters, can tell us in "El desarollo del cuento Chicano: Del folklore al tenebroso mundo del yo" that the Chicano novelist Tomás Rivera has as his masters "Sherwood Anderson, Wil-liam Faulkner and Juan Rulfo," but we learn little of folklore in relation to Rivera's fiction (164). The "folklore" in Rodriguez's title refers to what he sees as a local color style in some early, premovement Chicano writers, and it would appear that this critic views folklore as a limiting historical factor in the development of Chicano literature, as the "progressive" movement of his subtitle suggests. Although Rodriguez clearly objects to "folkloristic" writing, it is not clear what his critical views are of folklore in its own right and in relationship to written literature.

To the limited extent that other critics address this relation, they seem to be guided—or misguided—by the two major prejudices inherited from mainstream criticism. One—and there is a hint of this in Rodriguez—is, as noted earlier, to think of folklore as a precursory and secondary form of literature, before the culture develops a "mature" written literature. The powerful, if unconscious, influence of this bias is illustrated in the organization of an important volume devoted to Chicano literature (Sommers and Ybarra-Frausto), which opens with a reprinted article on the "folk base" of the literature, while the rest of the largely original seventeen articles are devoted to written literature. Individual critics as well as editors can demonstrate this prejudice. In a comment that directly applies to the present case, Raymund Paredes tells us that "the *corridos* of border conflict and other types of folk song may be regarded as an *incipient* form of Chicano literature" in which one may find "the components of a *nascent* Chicano sensibility: ethnic pride and strong belief in the group's durability" ("The Evolution of Chicano Literature" 39; emphasis mine). Still another influential critic, Felipe de Ortego y Gasca, acknowledges, in "An Introduction to Chicano Poetry," that at the onset of the Chicano literary Renaissance "the old and traditional forms of Chicano poetry were still vital: *corridos, coplas, redondillas,* all artfully wrought in the tradition of Hispanic poetry" (113). Yet this is the first and last we hear of the "artfully wrought" poetry, because Ortego y Gasca devotes the rest of his essay to the explication of written literature.

Other critics take the lore-in-lit perspective noted earlier. While acknowledging the contemporary presence of folklore, they confine their scholarly task to the textual identification of folklore items in literature, or, at best, they try to demonstrate the stylistic and thematic contributions made by the folklore item to the literary text as a whole. What few appraisals have been made along these lines take the second perspective. Jane Rogers, for example, tells us of the function of *la llorona* in Rudolfo Anaya's fiction, and a few critics have focused on folk speech in Chicano literature.[4]

Nevertheless, the criticism and history of Chicano literature have given minimal attention to its relation to Mexican folklore, even while it is commonly asserted that, somehow, the literature is indebted to such folklore. To the extent that it deals with the relation, however, it does so according to the two dominant models I have outlined, and it necessarily reflects certain limitations in these approaches. In the first position, folklore takes an artistic and thematic backseat role to written literature in a chronological sense, an attitude unacceptable to scholars who still find much folkloric creativity today. And it is precisely this contemporary recognition of folklore's artistic vitality that makes some folklorists uncomfortable with the lore-in-lit perspective, for, in its own way, it too assigns folklore to a secondary role. While the presence of folklore *in* literature may enhance the latter's value, it is clear that the critical focus remains on the written text.

To be sure, Mary Ellen B. Lewis has argued for an expanded view of the folklore-literature relation. Influenced by the folklore-as-performance school, she regards folklore not solely as a text embedded in literature but as a full performance involving text, stylistics, and context, all of which the writer brings to the written literary creation and which the scholar needs to account for in any critical interpretation:

With reference to literature then, I am suggesting that a creative writer may use folklore on several levels: that is, folklore may enter a work of literature on the *situation, medium,* or *product* level. I think future scholars must not limit their identification and analysis of folklore to *product*; but this will necessitate a well developed understanding of the multi-faceted nature of literature. (345–46)

While certainly an improvement over strictly textualist approaches, this view nonetheless appears to be still fundamentally a lore-in-lit approach, albeit a more sophisticated one. We now have the writer appropriating a full folkloric performance rather than a simple text; the task of the critic is made more interesting and more complex, but the secondary role of folklore still lingers.

I believe that both in general and in Chicano criticism we should reconceptualize the folklore and literature relation to avoid the historically and artistically unwarranted relegation of folklore to a secondary position. The models of folklore as "incipient" literature or as lesser items functioning *in* literature do not do justice to the thematic and artistic complexity of verbal art suggested by the best current work in contemporary folkloristics, particularly performance-oriented folkloristics.

Folklore as Literature

We can, however, identify the third general perspective on this issue, one that essentially abandons the folklore as *pre-* or *in* literature in emphatic favor of a folklore *as* literature approach. Adherents of this viewpoint see folklore as sharing the full thematic and artistic weight of written productions. Like Lewis, these theorists depart from a concept of folklore as performance, although it is more accurate to say that they *directly* represent this school of folkloristic thought. Since this approach recognizes the full artistic potential of folklore as performance, it seems only natural that we should find here a symmetrical view of the folklore and literature relation.

We find an early statement of this model in Américo Paredes's 1964 essay "Some Aspects of Folk Poetry," in which he explicitly evokes the concept of performance to point to the range of folk poetry, different from but artistically equal to written forms. In a more recent essay, "Folklore and Literature as Performance," Abrahams invites us to consider both folklore and literature as performances with the parallel artistic power to enlist the attention and sympathy of their audiences. Finally, Susan Stewart, in *Nonsense,* points to the shared, profound ways in which folklore and written literature make sense and nonsense of experience.

Upholding the equality of folklore and literature, however, does not necessarily bring the two domains into a dynamic relationship. While important, this perspective says only that they are equal but essentially separate ways to achieve the artistic experience, sharing the resources of language and human aesthetic consciousness. To the folklore *pre-* and *in* models we can now add folklore *as* equal to but essentially separate from written literature. We need a perspective that brings the two artistically equal domains into a reciprocal relation, for only then can we be cognizant of both the continuity and the diversity of literary endeavor.

In a review of Russian and Prague School semiotics and their connection to folklore, Richard Bauman points to such a necessary relation ("Conceptions"). Along with the other folklore-as-performance theorists, he does not settle for an expanded view of folklore *in* literature but forcefully argues for an understanding of folkloric performance as a full and important artistic elaboration in its own right. Thus he writes that "the folklorist, no less than the scholar of written literature, confronts individual folk poets and unique works of literary creation, worthy of critical attention as such, as artists and works of art" (15). Yet, as noted, one can advocate folklore's equality without asserting a reciprocal bond between the two forms. Those interested in this link cannot settle for separate but equal, and neither does Bauman. Drawing on Mikhail Bakhtin, he notes that both folklore and written literature are dialectically akin to tradition and therefore to each other:

> [Of] course, neither the artists who produce these works of oral literature nor the folklorists who record them are oblivious to their traditionality, to the relationships between these particular texts and others that preceded them, in their own performances and those of others. So too must Milton have been aware of other texts of his tale of *Paradise Lost*, or Goethe of other texts of *Faust*, or Joyce of *Ulysses*. But as Bakhtin has shown us, all texts, oral or written, within a given field of expression or meaning, are part of a chain or network of texts in dialogue with each other. To identify a particular oral text as traditional is to highlight its place in a web of intertextuality that, far from placing it on the opposite side of a boundary that sets it apart from written literature, unites it with written literature still more firmly. (15)

With the performance theorists, I accord full importance to folklore in relation to written literature. Like Bauman who follows Bakhtin, I am interested in exploring the intertextual connections of these domains, each as a full and significant literary production. However, in developing my particular cultural case, I take perhaps a more radical position that incorporates but also breaks with the others. In a sense I too will speak of folklore as precursory, although not as inferior; I will analyze a performance of folklore as it appears *in* written literature, yet I will posit the independent existence of an influential folklore outside and prior to the written text. Finally, and most important, I will demonstrate the intertextual relation of folklore and literature but not as fully literary equals. Rather, reversing its traditional role as handmaiden to literature, I shall speak of folklore as a powerful, disturbing, and dominating influence on a written poem. If, as Bauman says, Milton, Goethe, and Joyce were aware of other and presumably prior texts of their tales and if at least some of these were folkloric in character, there is no reason to assume that they were artistically inferior versions—indeed, they may have been superior.

I will argue for such a relationship of influential superiority in the particular cultural case at hand. A folkloric performance—the Mexican ballad—is taken as a dominating mode of artistic expression by a later nonfolk poet "within a given field of expression or meaning"—namely, the cultural history of Mexicans in the United States. Before moving to a close examination of this poetic-cultural relation, let us review the character of the Mexican ballad.

The Mexican *Corrido*

The ballad, or *corrido*, has a prominent place in the folklore and cultural history of the Mexican people on both sides of the border. As formally and thematically defined by its leading students, the *corrido* is a folk narrative composed in octosyllabic quatrains and sung to a tune typically in ternary rhythm and in 3/4 or 6/8 meter. The quatrains are usually structured in an *a b c b* rhyme pattern, and the entire narrative may be framed by formulaic openings and closings. Its most general function is to record those events that have significantly affected the sensibilities of the Mexican masses, including social conflict, natural calamities, political changes, and interpersonal crisis (Mendoza; A. Paredes, "Mexican Corrido").

While distantly related to Spanish medieval *romance* introduced into the New World during the Conquest, the *corrido* as a distinctive form did not fully crystallize until the second half of the nineteenth century; it seems to have done so not in Mexico per se but among the people of Mexican descent who found themselves suddenly living in a subordinated condition in the "United States" after the annexation of 1848. Or so the leading contemporary scholar of the genre suggests, as he goes on to argue that the *corrido* may actually have been a creation of the Mexican community in the United States and later diffused southward as the events of the Mexican Revolution of 1910 provided new narrative themes. While *corridos* of the Mexican Revolution are much better known throughout the greater Mexican folk world, the oldest-known *corrido* tells of competition and conflict between Mexican and Anglo cowboys in south Texas in the 1860s. And some years before the ballad heroes of the revolution seized the Mexican folk imagination, the Mexican-descent community of south Texas was composing songs about local heroes like Gregorio Cortez, who resisted Anglo-Texan persecution "with his pistol in his hand" (see the work, of the same title, by Américo Paredes). Paredes is not dogmatic on this question. "That the Mexican *corrido* went through its first stages on the Lower Rio Grande Border—under the impulse of border conflict—is a thesis that could never be definitely proven" ("Mexican Corrido" 104). But, he maintains, no one as yet has identified any older *corridos* in internal Mexico.

In one sense the issue is of considerable importance, for it identifies this genre as a native Mexican American folk poetry born of social conflict with the dominant society. Thus one has a viable candidate for the beginnings of a Mexican American literary history. In another sense, however, the issue loses some of its significance, if one keeps in mind that most Mexican Americans are actually immigrants or descendants of immigrant/refugees leaving Mexico following the social upheaval of the revolution of 1910 and its aftermath. These people carried their own, similar folk poetry with them, speaking to that social experience. Eventually as natives and immigrants became one people, the two repertoires became as one, at least in the folk mind.

Whatever its origins, the Mexican *corrido* became a major folk poetry; while somewhat diminished today, it is still heard within the greater Mexican community in oral, though more often in popular recorded, form. In its epic character and even in its reduced form, the *corrido* stands as a poetic creation of its community. In addition to Américo Paredes's analysis, John H. McDowell demonstrates the social poetics of the *corrido*, leaving little doubt that this is a complex, socially engaged form.

The appreciation that contemporary Chicano critics and writers felt for the poetic and cultural power of this folk creation first led me to think of it as a dominating influence on subsequent poetry in the same tradition. I have already noted Raymund Paredes's and Ortego y Gasca's somewhat skewed recognition of the *corrido* as the beginning of Chicano literature. We can also note that the prominent Chicano writer Tomás Rivera has acknowledged its powerful influence (Bruce-Novoa, *Chicano Authors* 73, 150), while the noted poet-critic Alurista has demonstrated the clear moral-aesthetic superiority of one ballad hero over a Chicano novel and its hero ("From Tragedy"). Similarly, in the ballad of Gregorio Cortez, Guillermo Hernández finds "the most powerful and symbolic characterization" of the Chicano social experience ("On the Theoretical Bases"). Finally, Erlinda Gonzales Berry accounts for the popularity of poetry among Chicano writers by recognizing that "many of today's poets were undoubtedly nourished on *corridos* and popular verse forms which abound in the oral tradition" (45)—a judgment supported by Sergio Elizondo when, speaking of the *corrido*'s influence, he tells us that in the Chicano poetry of "Alurista, Abelardo, and Ricardo Sánchez, among the best known, one observes it" (73). It remains to be specified how this influence actually works in contemporary Chicano poetry.[5]

If, as the evidence seems to indicate, a bond exists between the Mexican *corrido* and the work of today's Chicano writers, the link was surely more powerful for a poet who knew the *corrido* intimately and was historically and geographically closer to the epic period of the genre, at the turn of the century, in south Texas and northern Mexico. Later I will describe how a writer of the 1930s responded to the ballad's dominating presence with the poetic attitude that Harold Bloom has called the "anxiety of influence." Before proceeding to this close reading, let us examine Bloom's ideas.

On Anxiety and Poetic Influence

I shall summarize and, I hope, in the best sense simplify Bloom's position, as expressed in a number of allusive, elusive, terminologically burdened statements and restatements. Great or "strong" poems are produced largely through the influence of stronger precursory poems. (What constitutes strength is unclear, or Bloom may think it self-evident.) Yet the relation between poems and their makers is not a happy one. The genesis of a later poem lies in the poet's act of rebellion against the precursory work, which must be overcome even as the poet senses a deep indebtedness to it. It is the anxiety of influence that underlies the struggle.

Freud informs Bloom's analysis throughout. Indeed, at times Bloom broadly hints that his own critical writing is the result of creative struggle with Freud; the anxiety of influence is not limited to poets and can structure the relation of all manner of discourse (conversely, the concept suggests that all discourse is fundamentally poetic, a point I will exploit later). The earlier poet/poem is *as* parent who dominates the child and stands in the way of the latter's own creativity, dialectically inhibiting and stimulating it. Yet the poetic child, or *ephebe*, to use Bloom's term, knows that originality is impossible, that to a fundamental extent creativity necessarily and paradoxically entails borrowing from that which one is trying to overcome. Poetic life is the continuous rebellion against the poetic parent; poetry, the result of the effort to produce a different and better poem, with the largely unconscious understanding that "different" and "better" are relational terms that imply the superior *other*.

In an effort to escape, the ephebe engages in what Bloom sees as a flexible sequence of defensive strategies. Bloom identifies six such strategies; I shall deal specifically with some of them later. Initially they help the ephebe avoid the precursor's influence but later lead to an acknowledgment of the precursor's influence without wholly negating the ephebe's own poetic existence. These strategies—what Bloom calls "revisionary ratios"—find their analogues in Freudian defense mechanisms, although, as David Gordon has noted, Bloom parts company with Freud at a critical point. For Freud these defenses against the parent usually result in a well-adjusted personality and thus are valuable and necessary. For Bloom, however, the strategies seem ultimately to end in defeat for the ephebe and, paradoxically to result in poems that are strong but always weaker than those of the master of the poetic household.

Nevertheless, the defenses against the precursor are interpretively found in the complex of images that together yield a poem. Any substantial poem and its distinctive images can, in principle, be analyzed as a variety of defensive revisions of a precursory poem within the same linguistic and cultural tradition. For Bloom, the history of Anglo-American poetry represents a series of major revisions, always in rebellion against a past and ultimately leading back to a dominant master poet—Milton. Since *Paradise Lost*, this tradition consists of artistically profitable but nevertheless weakened attempts to deal with stronger percursory poets like Milton. And indeed, Bloom's applications have been largely confined to the Anglo-American heritage and to relations between written poems. In the next section I shall test his notions of the bond between folklore and literature within the greater Mexican tradition.

The Mexican Ballad and "Guitarreros"

In 1935 Américo Paredes, a twenty-year-old Texas–Mexican poet, wrote the following poem, published thirty years later.

Guitarreros (Guitarists)

Bajaron el toro prieto
que nunca lo habían bajado

(They brought the black bull down,
Never before brought down.)

Black against twisted black
The old mesquite
Rears up against the stars
Branch bridle hanging,
While the bull comes down from the mountain
Driven along by your fingers,
Twenty nimble stallions prancing up and down the *redil* of the guitars.
One leaning on the trunk, one facing—
Now the song:
Not cleanly flanked, not pacing,

But in a stubborn yielding that unshapes
And shapes itself again,
Hard-mouthed, zigzagged, thrusting,
Thrown not sung
One to the other.
The old man listens in his cloud
Of white tobacco smoke.
"It was so," he says,
"In the old days it was so."

We could easily analyze this poem using the lore-in-lit approach; even to someone not versed in greater Mexican culture, it is fairly evident that the poem incorporates folkloric elements. As its central image the poem features two guitarists singing in a rural setting, perhaps on a rural theme, although this last point requires the not-too-difficult understanding of bull either as the subject of the song or as a metaphor for song.

Our knowledge of the Mexican *corrido* tradition, however, permits us to identify the folklore in the poem. To begin with, the epigraph the poet provides consists of two lines from the traditional Mexican *corrido* "El Hijo Desobediente" ("The Disobedient Son").[6] I offer a Spanish-language text furnished by Américo Paredes and my own translation:

El Hijo Desobediente	*The Disobedient Son*
Un domingo estando herrando	On a Sunday during branding
se encontraron dos mancebos,	Two young cowboys did meet,
echando mano a los fierros	Each going for their steel
como queriendo pelear;	Each looking to fight;
cuando se estaban peleando	As they were fighting
pues llegó su padre du uno:	The father of one arrived:
—Hijo de me corazón,	—My beloved son,
ya no pelees con ninguno.—	Do not fight with anyone.—
—Quítese de aquí me padre	—Get away from here my father
que estoy mas bravo que un leon,	I feel more fierce than a lion,
no vaya a sacar la espada	I do not want my knife
y la parta el corazón.—	To split your heart in two.—
—Hijo de mi corazón,	—My beloved son
por lo que acabas de hablar	Because of what you have said
antes de que raye el sol	Before the next sunrise
la vida te han de quitar.—	Your life will be taken away.—
—Lo que le pido a mi padre,	—I only ask of my father
que no me entierre en sagrado,	Do not bury me in sacred ground,
que me entierre en tierra bruta	Bury me in plain earth
donde me trille el ganado,	Where the stock may keep me company.
con una mano de fuera	With one hand out of the grave
y un papel sobre-dorado,	And a gilded paper.
con un letrero que diga,	With an epitaph that reads
"Felipe fue desdichado."	"Felipe was disgraced."

—La vaquilla colorada,	—The red yearling
hace un año que nació.	Born a year ago,
ahi se la dejó a mi padre,	I leave to my father
por la crianza que me dió;	My upbringing to him I owe;
los tres caballos que tengo,	My three stallions
ahi se los dejó a los pobres	I leave to the poor
para que digan en vida,	So that they may say
"Felipe, Diós te perdone."—	"May God forgive Felipe."—
Barjaron el toro prieto,	They brought the black bull down,
que nunca lo habían bajado,	Never before brought down,
pero ora sí ya bajó	But now the bull has come down
revuelto con el ganado;	With the rest of the stock;
ya con esta me despido	Now with this I say farewell
por la estrella del oriente,	Guided by the eastern star
y aquí se acaba el corrido	This ends the ballad
de El Hijo Desobediente.	Of the disobedient son.

We also realize that the guitarists are singing this particular song in the poem; indeed, even without the epigraph we can identify the song based on internal evidence. However, having made this identification, what can we say interpretively from the lore-in-literature perspective?

Clearly the occasion for the song is a folkloric performance and not merely the incorporation of a text. As such, it seems a ready-made example of Lewis's recognition that writers may use folklore events and not just texts. We still have to ask, however, what the thematic and artistic purpose of the event is and how it serves the purposes of the poet. We might call the work an exercise in nostalgia. With consummate detail Paredes presents a description of the guitarreros playing a traditional song—a description taking up the bulk of the poem. Indeed, it is one continuous complex sentence ending with the lines "Thrown not sung / One to the other." Another scene, in which an old man says simply, but perhaps nostalgically, "It was so / In the old days it was so," closes the poem. Folklore serves as a symbol of the past in a poem crafted in the present. This is, again, from the lore-in-literature perspective.

However, we can make a more interesting case for this otherwise limited poem if we approach it with Bauman's notion of intertextuality between folklore and literature and Bloom's theory of poetic influence. I suggest that the *corrido* and its anonymous folk poet(s) have a precursor relation to "Guitarreros" and conversely that the ephebe maker of this poem is a latecomer struggling against the dominating achievement of the folk poem.

We should note first that this is a poem about singing, about poetic performance. Writing in the 1930s, the ephebe did not have a printed text of the ballad before him as we do; rather, he had seen many *corrido* performances in his native border country of south Texas. The poem is fashioned in response not to what he read but to what he heard and felt. We might assume that Paredes, as he wrote, remembered the performance of the composition. The presence of the *corrido* is manifest in the epigraph, which, like the title, is in the original Spanish. And, of course, the title and opening scene speak explicitly of singing.

For Bloom, no strong latecomer wholly accepts the precursor; in a creative struggle in which defensive strategies are cast as poetic images, the ephebe achieves an artistic work even if it necessarily falls short of complete victory. The six strategies tend to appear in matched pairs. Bloom calls them *clinamen–tessera, kenosis–daemonization,* and *askesis–apophrades* and finds them operating in the poetry of Western culture.

Having established in the epigraph the presence of the poetic forebear, Paredes the ephebe opens his poem with an eight-line section that, in my estimation, constitutes one of Bloom's primary revisionary ratios. The lines execute a *clinamen,* or poetic swerve, with respect to the ballad. In *The Anxiety of Influence,* Bloom tells us that a *clinamen* appears as a corrective move in the ephebe's poem "which implies that the precursor poem went accurately up to a certain point, but then should have swerved, precisely in the direction that the new poem moves" (97). In a later statement Bloom explains that a poem's opening *clinamen*

> . . . is marked by dialectical images of absence and presence, images that rhetorically are conveyed by the trope of simple irony . . . and that as psychic defense assume the shape of what Freud called reaction-formation. . . . Just as rhetorical irony . . . says one thing and means another, even the opposite thing, so a reaction-formation opposes itself to a re- pressed desire by manifesting the opposite of the desire. (97)

Implied error and asserted correction. Absence and presence. Irony and the literal. Desire and repression. These are the dialectical meanings of the first eight lines; it is important to note that the manifest content may be only a secondary key and that we must also be aware of the role of form (a concern that receives Bloom's less-than-ade- quate attention). Even as the *corrido*'s presence is established through the epigraph, it is quickly removed, at least formally. Having just read (and "heard") two lines from pre- cursory tradition, we immediately find ourselves in a different poem. Spanish gives way to English; the regular meter and rhyme of folk poetry is replaced by a written form that has varying meter and little rhyme. Most important, in contrast to the conventional diction of folk song, Paredes's creation draws on a constellation of modernist imagery— "Black against twisted black"; a mesquite like a stallion; fingers, also like stallions, that drive along a bull as they play a song. These formal choices, the essence of the ephebe's poetic swerve, implicitly and initially say that the poem is different from and better than its precursors.

Yet this new formal presence is necessarily caught in an irony conditioned, paradoxi- cally, by the appearance of tradition. For even as the "correction" of implied error is made, the formal declaration of poetic independence is thematically dominated by the *corrido.* What appears to be an autonomous poem in lines one through five reacknow- ledges tradition in lines five through eight as two folk singers slowly emerge in the long poetic clause

> While the bull comes down from the mountain
> Driven along by your fingers,
> Twenty nimble stallions prancing up and down the *redil* of the guitars.

The ephebe is addressing his precursory poets—"*your* fingers"—as it becomes clear that they are playing their guitars and singing the ballad alluded to in the epigraph. The portrait becomes even clearer with the line "One leaning on the trunk, one facing—."

In explicitly recognizing his precursors, the ephebe is engaging in the revisionary movement Bloom calls the *tessera*, in which the formal swerve of the *clinamen* falters or at least gives way to the emerging presence of tradition in the images of the poem. The *tessera* is an expression of truce between ephebe and precursor. The ephebe talks to and talks only about the earlier poets as they begin to craft their song; the imagery of fingers like "Twenty nimble stallions" reveals the ephebe's admiration for his precursors. In this sense we can say that the precursor exerts control over the ephebe. However, the folk poets are at the same time within the control of the ephebe, for their singing can be "heard" only through his poetic skill. Only, the ephebe seems to say, through his more modern verse can one make sense of the precursory power. In the movement of *tessera*, Bloom tells us,

> . . . the later poet provides what his imagination tells him would complete the otherwise "truncated" precursor poem or poet. . . . In this sense of a completing link, the *tessera* represents any later poet's attempt to persuade himself (and us) that the precursor's Word would be worn out if not redeemed as a newly fulfilled and enlarged Word of the ephebe. (*Anxiety* 67)

Having made this temporary adjustment—this compromise—between self and tradition, the ephebe continues the poem by seemingly negating his own poetic presence. In this final negotiation with the precursor—the *kenosis*—the ephebe submits to the authority of tradition while yet exacting a price from the precursor. Although "apparently emptying himself of his own afflatus, his imaginative godhood," the later poet

> . . . seems to humble himself as though he were ceasing to be a poet, but this ebbing is so performed . . . that the precursor is emptied out also, and so the later poem of deflation is not as absolute as it seems. (14–15)

The *kenosis* begins with the line "Now the song," as the ephebe engages in direct evaluatory encounter with the precursor poem. What does he think of it and, by implication, how does it compare to his own song before us? His description betrays too much, for clearly the young ephebe is overwhelmed and his poem is suffused by the powerful poem from the past, which like a strong bull or cow pony (the metaphor is slightly but perhaps profitably confused here) is

> Not cleanly flanked, not pacing,
> But in a stubborn yielding that unshapes
> And shapes itself again,
> Hard-mouthed, zigzagged, thrusting,
> Thrown not sung
> One to the other.

The reader shares the admiration of the ephebe for his precursor song, but the other effect of the passage is to vitiate the ephebe's own poetic effort. It is still the ephebe, of course, who is in some degree of control as the *tessera* lingers, but it is now quite a shaky truce as the precursor takes over the ephebe and his poem.

Nevertheless, in the revisionary ratio of *kenosis*, the ephebe's voice remains, muted as it may be. In its final poetic analysis, the work empties itself in a way "that the precursor is emptied out also." The ephebe accomplishes the dual movement by the ingenious introduction of an old man in the last four lines:

> The old man listens in his cloud
> Of white tobacco smoke.
> "It was so," he says,
> "In the old days it was so."

What are we to make of this conclusion?

First, we must take the old man as what he most probably is—namely, an elder; and, as Paredes the cultural historian has noted, in the greater Mexican culture of early southern Texas, "decisions were made, arguments were settled, and sanctions were decided upon by the old men of the group, with the leader usually being the patriarch" (*"With His Pistol"* 12). In effect, the elder settles the struggle between the ephebe and tradition but does so in the manner of *kenosis*. That is, although in one sense he represents tradition, he is also speaking for the ephebe, and in the dual role of traditional image and poetic voice, he limits both tradition and the ephebe, "emptying" them out in relation to each other.

The limitation is carried primarily by the old man's "It was so." What "was so"? At one level, the old man is commenting on the powerful singing. As an essentially historical artistic performance, it *was* so, but by clear implication, it is not now. We are left with a different style of singing that is not singing at all—namely, the ephebe's poem. If it is less impressive than the "hard-mouthed, zigzagged, thrusting" song, then we are the poorer for it; yet at the same time, folk tradition has also reached its performative limits. It can no longer speak to us directly; the precursor's voice is muted; and only the ephebe's poem *is so*, for all its inferiority to the powerful song of the past.

At another level of meaning we need to recall the ballad itself—a ballad about sons, fathers, disobedience, and dire consequences, which up to now we have largely neglected. A miscreant son violates the moral hierarchy of his society and meets his fate in a world in which, according to Paredes, "the representative of God on earth was the father" and his "curse was thought to be the most terrible thing on earth" (*"With His Pistol"* 11). Symbolically, moral order is restored at two levels in the ballad. Even as he calmly accepts his fate, the young *vaquero* affirms the natural order of things by distributing his goods, especially his stock, a prized possession, and by asking to be buried in a secular setting. Second, the *corrido* ends as, presumably, other *vaqueros* establish control over a paradoxical power. Like the *vaquero*, the black bull is strong but potentially dangerous and perhaps, as his color connotes, even evil; therefore society must reestablish the moral order. To this control of potential disorder symbolized by the black bull, the old man, appropriately in a cloud of white smoke, tends his approving but limiting "It was so."

Once again, like the singing, we can understand this moral world only secondhand. For us it is a world no longer possible, and with the ephebe we stand empty before it, knowing that we have to construct our own moral existence. The normative impact of the past has been blunted, and only the ephebe's desire can give us imaginative access to it. It was so.

Both the moral and artistic dimensions of the *corrido* world are captured through the single metaphor of the *guitarreros* driving the song, as the *vaqueros* control the black bull. The *vaqueros* and the singers, of course, must exercise an intermediary control over their "stallions," one group literally, the other through the ability of their fingers to produce a finely crafted artistic whole. This is a world in which moral and artistic disorder is not permitted. Potential disorder must be controlled by human beings lest they suffer the degradation of their kind; but, again, it was so.

We cannot help sensing the ephebe's desire for the world of the *corrido*; after all, he writes of nothing else in this poem. Yet of course he writes about it; it does not come to us in an unmediated form. It is his generosity to tradition in his art that makes it possible to us. Even as he formally violates tradition in the ways noted earlier, he ultimately affirms it. While lending final assent to this dominant influence, he nevertheless implicitly and explicitly demonstrates its historicity, and thus, in Bloom's terms, "the precursor is emptied out also" in relation to the ephebe even as he is being overwhelmed by the precursor.

Perhaps the most poetic evidence of the paradoxical is the existence of the *two* ephebes. Like Felipe, the young hero of the *corrido*, our ephebe has swerved in *clinamen*; he has readjusted in *tessera*, as does the son when he willingly acknowledges his moral error; finally, in *kenosis*, both young men affirm tradition to the point of self-negation. As a poet our ephebe must die under the influence of the powerful moral-artistic order that is his inheritance. For such an order to live in our consciousness, there must be a rebellion, but one that in this instance can end only in the ephebe's willing assent to the superiority of the parent, even while the parent incurs a debt to the child.

In principle the poem need not end here, and we could have a paradise regained. With more time, experience, learning, and self-confidence there should follow the dialectical, antithetical completion of *kenosis* in what Bloom calls *daemonization*, in which the ephebe begins "a movement towards a personalized Counter-Sublime, in reaction to the precursor's Sublime" (*Anxiety* 15) as the "later poet opens himself to what he believes to be a power in the parent poem that does not belong to the parent proper, but to a range of being just beyond that precursor." The ephebe seeks an autonomous voice, and "turning against the precursor's Sublime, the newly strong poet undergoes *daemonization*, a Counter-Sublime whose function suggests *the precursor's relative weakness*" (120).

Our ephebe's poem ends short of this revision. There is no strong counterassertion, no attempt to articulate a distinctive poem that implicitly denies the adequacy of the precursor. In this poem at least, our later poet cannot find—perhaps chooses not to find—his own distinctive voice. The poem ends with an implicit recognition of the power of tradition made explicit in the dedication of Paredes's other major dialogue with the *corrido* heritage:

To the memory of my father,
who rode a raid or two with
Catarino Garza;
and to all those old men
who sat around on summer nights,
in the days when there was

a chaparral, smoking their
cornhusk cigarettes and talking
in low, gentle voices about
violent things;
while I listened.[7]

In the days of Catarino Garza when there *was* a chaparral and when men talked of violent things—here we find our ephebe as a poet with a sense of social history; I turn now to this relationship.

Texas-Mexican Poetry and History

I have argued for an intertextual relation between a folk poem from oral tradition and a later poem by a Texas-Mexican intellectual. Drawing on Harold Bloom, I have suggested that the written poem is an artistic manifestation of the "anxiety of influence" as the poet engages in a creative struggle with his strong precursor.

While I obviously find Bloom's ideas useful for the explication of at least some intertextual relations, I have a sense of unease concerning the ahistorical and asocial character of Bloom's argument. For while Bloom implicitly appeals to history by way of tradition and chronology when he speaks of "precursor" and "later," there is another, social, sense of history that he almost wholly ignores. In his interpretive world poets deal with each other as pure poets divorced from sociohistorical contexts and constraints. In the *Anxiety of Influence*, he is quite candid on this point: "That even the strongest poets are subject to influences not poetical is obvious even to me, but again my concern is only with *the poet in a poet*, or the aboriginal poetic self" (11). Bloom simply chooses not to consider that his poets and possibly their anxieties are products and producers of the social consensus and contradictions of their historical movement. His wisest critic shares my unease. Frank Lentricchia finds Bloom's idea of "the poet in a poet"

> shrewd, disarming, and also question begging and evasive. What about those "influences not poetical"? And what is the poet in a poet? Something isolate and impregnable to all externally originating influences except those literary in character? The unspoken assumption is that poetic identity is somehow a wholly intraliterary process in no contact with the larger extraliterary processes that shape human identity. (326)

Bloom does not deal with the ways a particular poem may be read simultaneously as a manifestation of the "anxiety of influence" *and* the effects of social change. Permit me to argue this expanded view of influence through the case at hand.

Clearly, the *corrido* of the lower Texas-Mexican border was an expressive product of a culturally homogenous and socially stable folk society that prevailed in this region from its founding in the mid-eighteenth century to the latter half of the nineteenth. As a fundamentally precapitalist society with certain semifeudal characteristics, it was not yet caught up in the transition to agrarian capitalism and the process of cultural change that descended on the area in 1848 and accelerated greatly between 1890 and 1930. This period of intense change was accompanied by physical and psychological violence against those recalcitrant Mexicans who resisted the new social order (see A. Paredes, *"With His Pistol"*; see also Montejano).

The *corrido* as an epic with the symbolic hero "with his pistol in his hand" became one form of folk resistance against the imposition of the new order. The epitome of the ballad of resistance is "El Corrido de Gregorio Cortez," as Américo Paredes has shown us. Such ballads contain the symbolic representations of the new social contradiction and express a manifest ideological content of resistance. There can, however, also be what Fredric Jameson, in *The Political Unconscious*, calls an "ideology of form," in which form itself captures consensus and contradiction (98–102). By this line of analysis we might put forth the speculative notion that at the moment of greatest social contradiction, between 1890 and 1930, the *corrido* as a formal process, and regardless of its particular symbolic content, articulated the principles of social hierarchy, moral order, collectivity, and a rhythmic life process threatened by oppressive and fragmenting social relations. However, as Paredes has also noted, by the 1930s the *corrido* itself entered a period of decline, a process I have elsewhere interpreted as the incorporation of the folk tradition into the hegemonic order and the dissolution of its organic folk base in south Texas (see A. Paredes, "Mexican Corrido," and Limón, "Rise").

As someone who witnessed the end of the *corrido* period in his adolescence, our ephebe experienced two anxieties of influence; one, toward the power of the *corrido* as I have demonstrated it, and, another—not accounted for in Bloom's ahistorical scheme— toward the influence of social change. If there is an ideology of form as well as of symbolic content, we might say that formally and linguistically our ephebe is attempting to swerve away from a tradition no longer serviceable, but is doing so in the direction of a style and language representing the cultural level of the new social order. Whatever its content at a formal level, "Guitarreros" is a profoundly modern American poem. Responding to the anxiety of influence fostered by the new order, the ephebe opens himself up almost wholly to it, in the manner of a *kenosis*, and in effect writes a poem for *them* (now really all of us). At the same time, he develops a poetic content that demonstrates an anxiety of influence toward the *corrido* and the traditional past. In 1935, Paredes also wrote "Flute Song":

Why was I ever born
Heir to a people's sorrow,
Wishing this day were done
And yet fearful for the morrow.

In that year Texas-Mexicans were already experiencing the dilemma and, as a generation, were responding in a variety of ways to the anxiety of influence they felt toward the past and the present. Our ephebe's formal and thematic poetic solution is a particularly fine manifestation of the social contradiction that will continue to haunt the poetry of Mexicans in the United States.

With the increasing production of literature by Mexicans in the United States and the growth of an accompanying scholarship, we can confidently begin to speak of a literary history for this population. Representing the second largest minority group in this country, such a history should inevitably also become part of the literary history of the United States.

My principal concern in this essay has been to contribute to this process in at least three distinctive ways. First, I have presented the work of relatively unknown and largely undiscovered poets—the anonymous folk poet(s) of "El Hijo Desobediente" and the distinguished Texas-Mexican intellectual Américo Paredes. Second, I have offered a critique of the prevalent and limited ways of treating the relations of folklore and written literature, objecting to these approaches both in general and to the degree to which they have dominated the literary history of Mexicans in the United States. Finally, I have argued for an alternative conceptualization of this relation by drawing on the Bakhtin-Bauman notion of intertextuality and, more significantly, on Bloom's theory of poetic influence. Any future intellectually defensible history of literature cannot in principle reject the equal status of folklore and written literature and should be able to accept instances in which the folklore emerges as a dominant influence on written literature and not merely as something that is *in* the literature. This final point has also involved a revision of Bloom's theory. For as Lentricchia has critically noted, Bloom argues that the "psychic and social life of the poet as a man in the world counts for nothing; history in a big, inclusive sense cannot touch the sacred being of intrapoetic relations," which "constitute an elite and inviolably autonomous body of discourse" (331). Lentricchia correctly observes that, as it stands, Bloom's theory is really the reappearance of the asocial New Criticism in a fresh guise. While I believe that Bloom's ideas offer a useful way to unite literary history, for Mexicans in the United States at least, a history of literary relations cannot ignore their obvious immersion in social process. To this end, I have offered an amplification of his thought. To the degree that I have succeeded I hope to have made a contribution to a new American literary history.

Notes

[1] I use the word *Mexican* as a simple translation of *mexicano*, the preferred Spanish-language term of self-reference for the Mexican-descent population of the United States, although I am not insensitive to the pejorative misuses of this term by the Anglo-Saxon tongue. This choice also takes into account the genesis of the Mexican ballad, or *corrido*, which is not uniquely the property of those on this side of the border. *Chicano* I shall reserve to designate the political and cultural persons and processes of social activism since the 1960s. For my elaborated views on the always controversial question, see "The Folk Performance of *Chicano* and the Cultural Limits of Political Ideology." Following Américo Paredes, I shall also use the term *greater Mexico* to refer to the movement of people and culture across a political boundary. I read versions of this essay at the 1980 meetings of the Modern Language Association and at the 1983 Symposium on Chicano Popular Art and Literature, University of California, Santa Barbara. I am grateful to Luis Leal and members of the audience for a helpful critical discussion. My particular thanks go to Teresa McKenna and Tomás Ybarra-Frausto.

[2] Bloom, *Anxiety*, *Map*, *Poetry*, and *Breaking*. My special thanks to Ramon Saldívar for leading me to Bloom's work.

[3] Ybarra-Frausto, "Chicano Movement." For a comprehensive treatment of this poetry—or at least the major figures—see Juan Bruce-Novoa, *Chicano Poetry*. This unabashedly "textualist" critic says relatively little about my central concerns—folklore, influence, history, and social changes. His concern is the "chicano" poetry "text"; the rest he leaves to "social scientists." I accept.

[4] Rogers. Studies of folk speech in Chicano literature include Mario Garza and Guadalupe Valdes-Fallis.

[5] The present essay is a version of one chapter of a study in press on this influence. Subsequent chapters include analyses of Rodolfo "Corky" Gonzalez, José Montoya, and Juan Gomez-Q.

[6] According to Paredes, this is the version he learned as a young man from the *corridistas* of the lower border. It is quite literally his direct influence. For another version, see Mendoza 266–68.

[7] Dedication *"With His Pistol."* Catarino Garza was a late nineteenth-century south Texas newspaper editor who led an armed resistance movement against both the dictatorship of Porfirio Díaz in Mexico and the Texas rangers on this side of the border.

Oral Tradition in
Kingston's *China Men*

Linda Ching Sledge

The young discipline of ethnic literary criticism has been lent welcome authority by Robert Spiller's influential proposal for a revised American literary history reflecting the "heterogenous and multi-ethnic components of American culture" ("Cycle" 5). Ethnic scholars have good reason to rejoice, for most have been aware for some time of what Americanists like Spiller are only now addressing: the bypassing of a rich, as yet unmined, vein of ethnic writing on the supposition that such works (particularly those deriving from non-Western minorities like the Chinese) lie outside our prevailing Anglo-American literary heritage. Spiller's paradigm for a multiethnic literary history is thus an admirable attempt to correct the cultural myopia of previous literary histories by replacing conventional notions of American culture as static and ethnically uniform with a notion of that culture as dynamic and ethnically polymorphous.

Within a pluralistic nation, Spiller argues, advancement in art is governed by the ordered, predictable processes of social history. His four-stage organicist model therefore draws a neat equation between the dialectical forces of cultural assimilation and the evolution of any regional or ethnic constituency's corpus of written texts.[1] If we apply Spiller's paradigm to the writings of Chinese in America, then, it would appear that this yet-unassimilated American people are at a second, provisional stage of literary development ("Instruments and Ideas") when a "settlement" first becomes culturally self-conscious and begins to discover via a growing body of polemical writing the "shape and power of its own mind" ("Cycle" 9).[2] One can cite as possible proof the small circle of activist-writers that constituted until the 1980s the community's most visible literary practitioners (Chin et al.). Their dominance of the Chinese American literary scene lends some credence to Spiller's organicist theory, for none of these writers has yet discovered "an educated and receptive audience" beyond the ethnic community's horizons or embodied in writing the conciliatory themes, the syncretic method, the expansive national "temper" that Spiller finds characteristic of the writings of wholly assimilated or "rooted" regions and peoples in America ("Cycle" 9).

Yet it occurs to me that Spiller's paradigm tells us more about the dynamics of history and society than of literature. It lacks sufficient systematic aesthetic criteria by which to explain perennial, thorny issues in Asian American literary criticism—namely, how to interpret the language, forms, and organic principles of an ethnocentric, non-Western minority literature for an American audience with little access to that heritage. Nor can a deterministic model like Spiller's provide an accurate overview of the historical evolution of Chinese letters in America, especially in the light of Maxine Hong Kingston's startling appearance on the national literary scene. The relation of *The Woman Warrior* and *China Men* to the slim corpus of published works by Chinese Americans is crucial to a responsible analysis of this constituency's evolving literary heritage; however, this relationship has been misunderstood and misrepresented by critics seeking, like Spiller, to use literature to document encompassing sociohistorical schema. Kingston's works simply elude extrinsic categories of this type. The fact that such syncretic, sophisticated writing can emerge from an unassimilated American people lacking what Spiller calls "preparatory expression [appropriate to the] appearance of a major writer" belies his central analogy of art ("Cycle" 8). Does the dearth of recorded belles lettres among the Chinese in America before Kingston really mean that her antecedents were caught in a protracted, apprentice stage of literary development and thus devoid of a mature literary tradition throughout the 150 years of their sojourn in America? Can a writer of Kingston's stature spring into literary history *ex nihilo?*

In considering Kingston's place in the evolution of American letters, many critics, like Spiller, keep an eye on the development of written texts, the visible signs of a culture's achievement over time. Kingston thus appears to be the single significant Chinese voice, heard by a wider American public, to shatter an immigrant people's long silence. Chinese themselves, however, realize that the case is not so simple: Kingston is the most recent artist in a long folk tradition of song and story conventionally called "talk-story" (*gong gu tsai*) in immigrant circles. The tradition, dating from Sung dynasty storytellers in China proper and continually revitalized by Chinese arrivals in America, is maintained within the confines of the family and rarely surfaces into print.[3] Talk-story is by my definition a conservative, communal folk art by and for the common people, performed in the various dialects of diverse ethnic enclaves and never intended for the ears of non-Chinese. Because it served to redefine an embattled immigrant culture by providing its members immediate, ceremonial access to ancient lore, talk-story retained the structures of Chinese oral wisdom (parables, proverbs, formulaic description, heroic biography, casuistical dialogue) long after other old-country traditions had died.

Deterministic theories such as Spiller's, which define literary history as diachronic aspects of the written word, do a disservice to "residually oral cultures" (like the Chinese in America) by seeing them via a "cultural squint."[4] These theories may not adequately consider the fact that oral forms are highly organized, structurally stable products of sophisticated cultures, as Milman Parry and Albert Lord proved decades ago about the Homeric epics. As Parry and Lord's numerous descendants in critical theory maintain, oral forms are an entirely different language from the written one, and therefore demand different assumptions and perspectives.[5] Thus Spiller's contention that an ethnic or regional literature is born anew on American soil can have little bearing for Chinese Americans, for their oral culture was fully established, already ancient and capable of producing masterpieces, by the time the first immigrants arrived in America in the early nineteenth century. This transplanted oral heritage simply embraced new subject matter or new forms of Western discourse, as evidenced by the immigrant versions of ancient song or story now being unearthed by Asian American ethnicists[6] and by Kingston's own written adaptations in English of that tradition.

I am convinced that the evolution of this tradition moves along a vastly different historical axis from the prototypical scriptographic and multiethnic one charted by Spiller. As scholars of oral cultures argue, all oral texts are foreseeable entities that are structurally and iconographically stable over time (Lord 120). Rather than a dialectical struggle toward a national literary ideal, as Spiller describes the evolution of written texts in America, there is, in my view, a haphazard pattern of the resurgence and decline of a fixed core of oral forms, the result of the uneven, often unwilling, contact, on the part of immigrants from China, with Western modes of thinking and writing. (In the case of Chinese immigrant oral culture, the community printing press was not the crucial spark of literature, as Spiller maintains about ethnic and regional American literature, but its greatest foe.) The characteristic autonomy of overseas Chinese—indeed, their very resistance to grafting their oral culture on the written one of their host society—has allowed their oral heritage to flourish unabated if unrecognized outside Chinese circles. Spiller's notion of literary assimilationism, therefore, cannot take into account how deeply Kingston and other contemporary Chinese American writers, like David Henry Hwang, draw from this ancient well.

The task of assessing a little-known oral tradition like that of Chinese in America is far more complex than seeking out new sociohistorical paradigms or arcane *materia historica*, as ethnicists are now attempting to do. It is complicated by the debate over the proper study of literary history itself. Definitions for writing literary history have been called into question by a new generation of critics looking to Frye, Derrida, or Hartman as its mentors. Subjectivist philosophies have exploded the nineteenth-century positivistic notion of literary history as "fixed empirical data (meanings, works, kinds) followed by successive interpretations" (A. Fowler 39–56). Any prospective literary historian must confront the fact that formalist critics, structuralists, and their descendants in the various contemporary schools of functionalism and communication have revised the foundations of literary history to encompass, as Paul de Man suggests, not the objective movement of time, which is another story, but the essence of literary interpretation itself.[7]

A multiethnic American literary history purified of extrinsic, nonliterary assumptions is an ambitious enterprise far exceeding the scope of this essay. I would suggest, rather, a possible direction for such a project, based less on sociohistorical definitions of culture and more on the idea of culture as synchronous layers of structuring forms persisting over time. If, as Edward Sapir, the founder of structural linguistics, maintains, the "shape of a culture" is determined by the shape of its language (qtd. in Hawkes 31), then an elucidation of the conservative root or trunk of Chinese American oral culture will enable scholars to see how a minority people under perpetual social transformation preserved its traditional wisdom so well. The issue is not necessarily how much a culture changes but why it remains so stable. A study of oral forms need not limit critics to ahistorical judgments but allows them to view immigrant literature and history in a new light, as the evolution of a mode of consciousness. Oral forms, after all, are tangible evidence of *noesis*, a culture's way of mentally storing and retrieving traditional knowledge (*noema*) (see Ong, *Presence* and "African Talking Drums"). A study of the noetic mechanism underlying talk-story can be the basis for a fruitful historical discussion of the particular contexts in which that traditional wisdom thrived or perished. By briefly describing some of the oral forms in Kingston's *China Men*, I will show how a prospective literary historian might investigate the oral noetic process. I hope to demonstrate how deeply oral forms have penetrated westernized ethnic writing; for not only is *China Men* a startlingly accurate throwback to that oral tradition, it is also a highly original work changing the direction of American letters by teaching the oral traditions of a tiny minority to a large audience of print-oriented non-Chinese.

II

Kingston's models in *China Men* are the professional storytellers of her community and the storytelling members of her own family. She also looks to the "quasi-literary" tradition[8] of Chinese vernacular fiction (passed orally within the family circle), which the sinologist Patrick Hanan maintains was a direct descendant of ancient oral tradition, "the only true mass literature of premodern times [in China]."[9] Even in this popular written form, oral tradition continued because of the persistence of oral mnemonic structures and stylistic features in the written fiction and of the unique nature of the Chinese language. Written Chinese is pictographic and homonymic, a language of visual symbols and aural puns continually pointing away from the visible surface of linguistic signs to meanings lying deeper than the signs themselves. Then, too, written Chinese, classical and vernacular, has never lost language's primordial connection with speech. Classical and popular vernacular writing was generally intended for verbal performance, to be chanted or declaimed on a particular occasion to an audience, whether festive gathering, scholarly jury, a body of naive, potentially errant folk, or the inner ear of the writer.[10] Kingston's ability to invest idiomatic English with the allusive texture and oral-aural qualities of Chinese thus distinguishes her from a dialect writer like Louis Chu, who creates a purely literary ethnic discourse through literal English translations of Cantonese stock phrases.

China Men looks back to oral noetic processes in form and function as well as style, as I hope to illustrate. Kingston consciously assumes the role of tribal bard in the guise of various storytelling personae. She spoke often in *The Woman Warrior* through the medium of the mother, the family teller of tales. In *China Men*, the narratorial voice has become more abstract and elevated, identifiable less with a specific woman than with a storytelling people. Commentators who recognize her unique style simply do not understand the centrality of the storytelling personae to that style. Thus they view the author through a "circumambient literacy" (Ong, "Oral Culture" 145), praising or faulting her language for its ambiguity, elusiveness, and suggestiveness, noting the tendency of her words to wander from fixed meanings, her tales from "definitive" sources or fixed endings, and attributing these distinctive features to the hybrid nature of her works or to her allegedly inaccurate knowledge of Chinese literature or immigrant history (Homsher). Yet these are typical features of heroic narrative and can be found in works as ancient as *Beowulf* and as modern as M. Scott Momaday's *Names*.

Kingston herself is well aware of the sources of her writing, for embedded in *China Men* are striking references to the oral noetic processes that govern her craft. For Kingston, talk-story provides an acceptable, formalized discourse through which the narrator, in the persona of an immigrant daughter, can communicate with the emotionally constrained father, who has hidden his history from his children under layers of rage and silence. That storytelling occasion becomes, in turn, the raison d'être of the work itself, an imaginative, epic reconstruction in talk-story form of the lives of male forebears (see Sledge).

> You fix yourself in the present, but I want to hear the stories about your life, the Chinese stories. I want to know what makes you scream and curse, and what you're thinking when you say nothing, and why when you talk, you talk differently from Mother. . . . I'll tell you what I suppose from your silences and few words, and you can tell me that I'm mistaken. You'll just have to speak up with the real stories if I've got you wrong. (*China Men* 13).

Talk-stories reshape real-life experiences into cautionary and heroic tales for the young, and through them silent men like the father can speak indirectly of their deepest sorrows and joys without relinquishing their authority within the family.[11] The father's sufferings and small final triumph in America, for example, receive their fullest elaboration in the corollary talk-story tale "The Li Sao: An Elegy," a recounting of the tragic fate of the statesman Ch'u Yuan, with whose struggles the father identifies closely (Birch 49–62). The juxtaposition of biography and myth lends verisimilitude and pathos to the ideal world of Ch'u Yuan while elevating the parallel story of the "American father" to the timeless, stylized realm of heroic history. So close, in fact, is the juncture between the mythical world of Ch'u Yuan and the father's own workaday one that the father becomes a pivotal though offstage character in the myth, serving as secondary protagonist and tale teller in the drama of Ch'u Yuan's banishment, degradation, and vindication.

By interweaving the experiences and perspectives of male family members with their deepest dreams as expressed in heroic talk-story, Kingston succeeds in duplicating the double vision of Chinese immigrants, for whom words have both a real-life referent and an allegorical one rooted in traditional wisdom. So inextricably bound to the family's life is oral tradition[12] that its mythic content and heroic forms are passed along unconsciously from parent to child, performer to listener, for talk-story is above all the language of common people in its most eloquent form: " 'All Chinese know this story,' says my father; if you are an authentic Chinese, you know the language and the stories without being taught, born knowing them" (256).

In personal interviews and correspondence, Kingston elaborates on her notion of the ethnic literary artist as one in a long line of performers shaping a recalcitrant history into talk-story form. She distinguishes between the "thematic" memory processes of a self-proclaimed storyteller like herself and the "verbatim" memory processes of a print-oriented culture (Ong, *Presence* 26) whose analytical and documentary method she forswears:

> I don't take notes and I don't use tape recorders. Some of the stories that I've heard, I've heard like 30 years ago, maybe. Maybe I heard them once 30 years ago; some are that old. Of course, at that time I didn't think about taking notes and I never take notes about anything. I trust memory as a technique and I believe that the memory sifts out so that the very important things remain. . . . Because they're so important to me, [those words] resurface. I'd write an incident again and sometimes I'd find the first note and it's told in

the same words. It's impossible to forget because it was that important. If it wasn't important, then let it be forgotten. I'm sure memory does distort but maybe that's all right too. For some good reason it's distorted. Maybe we shouldn't call it distortion; maybe we can just call that my style or my viewpoint or my imagination. (Hilgers and Molloy 1, 6)

Nor does the entry of print into storytelling substantially change her notion of the character of oral tradition. For Kingston, "writer" is synonymous with "singer" or "performer" in the ancient sense of privileged keeper, transmitter, and creator of stories now lost or left behind with the successive publication of "definitive" texts (H. C. Chang 12–13):

The way I see it, there has been continuous talk-story for over 4,000 years and it spans China and America. Once in a long while during these millennia, somebody writes things down; writing "freezes" things for a bit, like a rock, but the talk-story goes on around and from this rock. . . . There was no gap between Sui Sin Far and Jade Snow Wong, two pebbles like me. (Kingston to Sledge, 23 July 1981)[13]

To what extent does *China Men* validate its author's perception of the work as oral performance? If we search the work internally for what the structuralist critic M. Ngal calls the "fixed storehouse" of oral forms that provide a people with their "source of creative emotion" or their "sense of belonging to a common history" (342), we find that the oral tradition underlying the work is far broader than the specifically ethnic one Kingston herself has cited. *China Men*, to my mind, reveals those persistent, unchangeable forms common to all oral cultures: formulaic diction; a fixed "grammar" of repetitive themes, or topoi; a spectrum of stock characters; ceremonial and heroic reappropriation of history; symmetrical structures, including balanced oppositions (verbal or physical contests, antithetical characters, dialectical or casuistical discourse such as question-answer forms, riddles, and so on); copia and repetition (see Ong, "African Talking Drums").

These structures seem to me to permeate *China Men*, particularly the twelve short parables or "pure" talk-story sections (their titles are italicized in the table of contents) retelling folk legends, Chinese *hua-pen*, or vernacular short fiction or episodes from ethnic history, and alternating with the lengthier, less structurally uniform chapters on the experiences of Kingston's male relatives. Critical attention has focused on the latter sections because of their accessibility to non-Chinese readers unaccustomed to the metaphorical niceties, the didacticism and circumlocution of Chinese storytelling. Yet I would contend that the retold legends are far more important than the biographical sketches in defining Kingston's method: they delineate *China Men*'s essentially oral form and provide the scaffolding on which the eclectic, open-ended, true-to-life sections fit. In short, the legends are more than heroic analogues to the chapters on family history: they are paradigms of the storyteller's art, sanctioned and enriched by repetition within an immigrant community and family, and giving order, purpose, and historical authority to the roughly drawn biographies of family patriarchs.

The talk-story sections derive from diverse sources—Chinese literature and folklore, Hawaiian mythology, events in the author's life, even in one case a Western literary work, Defoe's *Robinson Crusoe*. Each tale re-creates a context felicitous to and identifiable with oral performance through the author's oral style, her direct address of the reader, the division of subject matter into exempla, her frequently (often satirically) expressed intent to impart a lesson ("Fancy lovers never last"). Even in those stories that cite written texts as sources, the author makes clear that the literary original has been transformed into a talk-story occasion. "The Li Sao: An Elegy," for example, is not a summary of the archaic Chou dynasty poem attributed to Ch'u Yuan but a remembered version recited by Kingston's poet-laundryman father during family storyfests. Similarly, the "Adventures of Lo Bun Sun" is not simply a Chinese translation of *Crusoe* but the spoken version the author recalls her mother reading her as a child.

The retold legends are clearly influenced by the demands of storytelling, for the tales reveal the spontaneity of oral performance and the prototypical forms of oral narrative. Storytellers conventionally consult no text but depend on the capacity to recall traditional themes, episodes, and plots and to tailor these chunks of remembered detail to their own bent for improvisation and to the tastes of their audience (Lord 4–5, 137–38, chs. 3, 4, 5). Thus the two opening talk-story sections, "On Discovery" and "Ghostmate," differ substantially in form and material from their literary antecedents in Chinese prose fiction. Neither story is especially faithful to the earlier texts. "Ghostmate" may look to the *hua-pen* genre of handsome youths tragically enamored of spectral ladies or fox-spirits; nevertheless, the author refuses to particularize events or characters and presents her tale as a compendium of conventions and devices from ghost-lover tales in general. Similarly, "On Discovery" diverges in several crucial instances from Li Ju-Chen's Ching dynasty novel (*Ching hua yuan*, or *Flowers in the Mirror*) of a wanderer named Tang Ao.[14] Li's novel is a long, heavy-handed satire of contemporary mores; the chapter from which "On Discovery" is drawn ("In the Country of Women") is an attack on women's customs and fashions using sexual role reversal. The unfortunate protagonist of Li's chapter is Lin, a "greedy old coxswain" who is unmanned by the very people he intends to bilk, whereas Tang Ao is a bumbling naif who rescues Lin after the women have already transformed him into their sexual plaything. "On Discovery" makes the impressionable Tang Ao the captive hero in the land of amazons and treats his adventure not as satire in the manner of *Candide* or *Gulliver's Travels* but as a tragic parable of a Chinese Everyman, told from the young man's point of view. The result is that Tang Ao the traditional gull becomes Tang Ao the patient hero, biding his time among female enemies as did Odysseus in the land of Circe. The discrepancy between Kingston's version and Li Ju-Chen's does not necessarily mean that "On Discovery" is a less definitive rendering of the ancient tale but that textual decorum simply does not apply to orally based literary composition. Oral "texts," being composed of memory patterns and sound, lack the obvious fixity of print. What matters most is the storyteller's ability to move an audience, to elicit its assent to the values or code of behavior expressed in the narrative. "On Discovery" and "Ghostmate," like the ten other talk-story sections, consequently strive less for verbatim reproduction of a remembered story than fidelity to a core of symbols and events sanctioned by frequent repetition. This core is the basis for Kingston's highly elastic method, for the talk-stories are fashioned by Kingston's trimming, extending, embroidering on the familiar themes and plots.

A close reading of the two stories reveals significant structures common to all oral narratives. Both stories open formulaically with a compressed summary of the plot. This device is an important mnemonic element in storytelling: a prologue in Chinese oral tradition fixed the tale's genre for the audience, announced the major themes (Liu,

Chinese Theories 64–65), and prepared the listeners to react appropriately to the tale; for the teller, it was a dress rehearsal for the composition to follow, as in the introduction to "On Discovery": "Once upon a time, a man, named Tang Ao, looking for the Gold Mountain, crossed an ocean, and came upon the Land of Women. The women immediately captured him, not on guard against ladies" (*China Men* 3).

Other formal elements remind the reader of the oral sources of Kingston's method. The author, for example, is explicitly characterized in the work as narrator and guide for readers. Her onstage persona is announced by parenthetical asides, literary quotations, and commentary that occasionally play in ironic counterpoint to the storytelling context. These features directly reflect the rhetoric of Chinese vernacular (as opposed to classical) fiction because of the former's source in oral tradition. Kingston may also abandon the syntax of written prose for the more elliptical, repetitive, or rhythmic phrasing of poetry or song (Lord 21). Sometimes the poetic forms take on the identity of the action described. For example, in "On Discovery," the narrator's language suggests the back-and-forth movement of Chinese maidservants' hands cinching Tang Ao's feet as they sing a footbinding song ("They gathered his toes, toes over and under one another like a knot of ginger root"). In another section, the maids' quick, jabbing gestures as they pierce Tang Ao's ears are rendered by short phrases, monosyllables, and alliteration for metrical emphasis ("They had to poke and probe before puncturing the layers of skin correctly, the hole in the front of the lobe in line with the one in back, the layers of skin sliding about so"). The rhythmic units function as a bard's body movements or props; like a storyteller's staff beating back imaginary waves with an oar, Kingston's words punctuate, outline important moments in the action. They can even be considered *gestes*, or narrative events, since they resemble the balanced dramatic gestures found in *verbomoteur* cultures, where thought is perceived, depicted, and stored "economically" in appropriately concrete human action (Ong, *Presence* 34).

Events in the tales are arranged in similar symmetrical metrical units, to build a story as a bricklayer lays down a wall. Catalogs organize details or events according to type, time, or cause-and-effect sequence. Characters themselves are drawn in bold strokes and are typically grouped in opposing pairs (man, woman; strong, weak; old, young; passive, active). Physical description has a head-to-toe or around-the-room ("banquet") logic (H. C. Chang 19), enabling the reader to visualize the persons or objects described and the author to assemble the themes and episodes of a remembered story. The description of the feminized Tang Ao is appropriately composed from top to bottom, in the manner of storytellers' blazons of famous beauties of yore:

> They plucked out each hair on [Tang Ao's] face, powdered him white, painted his eyebrows like moth's wings, painted his cheeks and lips red. He served a meal at the queen's court. His hips swayed and his shoulders swiveled because of his shaped feet. "She's pretty, don't you agree?" the diners said, smacking their lips at his dainty feet as he bent to put dishes before them. (4–5)

In "Ghostmate," oral formulas and mnemonic units of description are woven with notable skill into the fabric of the narrative. The polemical structures conventionally found in oral poetry appear as the anguished *flyting* of two unhappy lovers bitterly taking leave of each other:

"Stay with me today."

"I'll be gone for just a few hours." Or "I'll be back in just a few days."

"I love this scroll. Let me have it. Don't sell it."

"And these shoes." She says, "I love this cup, its lines, its design, its handle. Let me keep it," pulling things out of his pack.

"But I've already given you the best pieces. These are for market."

"But you don't need to go to market anymore," she says. (79–80)

Kingston's depiction of the husband's journey to and from his home in "Ghostmate" is a storytelling tour de force, showing how inventive a formulaic composition can be. The path he takes to his fateful encounter with his spirit-mistress becomes a figurative map of a harmonious universe by means of Kingston's manipulation of oral conventions and mnemonic forms. The youth sketches in song the sights he sees along the way from village to mountain, using sounds as a Chinese painter uses black ink and white space, to summon into being a natural world charged with sublimity. The man is small, yet reverent in the face of nature's immensity, like the tiny human figures in a Chinese landscape gazing up at an unpainted expanse of sky. This benevolent cosmos is shaped by Kingston's vivid depiction of scenery passing before the youth's eyes. The lush language may obscure the formulaic method Kingston employs: descriptions of objects are based not only on geographic position but on an increasingly complex level of abstraction. The reader and the youth move from the literal realm—that is, from the simple "cotton and silk" fabrics the youth holds to his back—to a glimpse of the ineffable, an ascending ridge of mountain peaks disappearing into the heavens:

. . . he carries a satisfying bunch of cotton and silk on his back and is heading into town. On the nooning day, sun and leaves dapple his face with shadows and golden coins. The fine road opens before him coming around turns and over rises. Grass and water above and below him, he glimpses the road ahead threading the mountains. Some of the one hundred kinds of birds that fly the sky and nest the earth let him see them, and even the phoenix seems to hover near. A music accompanies him. Released for this day from his past and future, the young traveler feels his freedom. His walk is loose. He cocks his head; the music is real. He laughs at its cacophony, which blasts any worries out of his head. He sings melodies that wind like ribbons into the vistas. His conducting hands lift notes out of the air, stroke them, and let them go. Long streams drop down mountains. Beyond mountains, still higher mountains rise until the peaks fade from human sight. . . . (74–75)

The passage is a daring reinterpretation of the traditional "banquet" formula of Chinese vernacular fiction. Instead of describing objects in circular fashion, Kingston turns the formula on its head and describes objects as they align themselves in vertical space. Thus the focus shifts from the earthly-horizontal plane to a vertical-cosmic one in keeping with the metaphysical musings of the young hero.

To convey the enormous changes in personality and perception the man undergoes, Kingston again uses the vertical descriptive formula, but now the intent and direction are reversed. The man's return from the enchantress's hideaway is a descent through the terrain he ascended earlier and so lightheartedly; it is also a rapid flight through time. Years have vanished during the man's idyll with the spirit-lover. The second journey is a downhill slide from heaven to earth, from bliss to suffering, from dream to reality, accomplished in the wink of an eye. The man is left, like Rip van Winkle, instantly old, dazed, estranged from family, victim rather than conqueror of time and space. No longer does nature unfold itself benevolently before him. Now the universe is menacing, claustrophobic and he a mere "bug" in an impenetrable landscape viewed by an uncaring, omniscient eye:

> His friend guides him along the mountain road toward the home village. They are like two bugs in the landscape. The nearby oaks are gnarling and the far pines standing straight. The trees hold gray antlers high, already budded with leaves. Midway home, the young man stops. He seems to hear something, and though he stares straight ahead, the whites under his irises show. Marionette strings pull him into the tall grass. He remembers a beautiful lady he met in a previous incarnation or a dream last night. (81)

It remains now to examine the overall form of *China Men*. Although the twelve talk-story sections share many of the forms of oral narrative in general, as I have tried to show in the analysis of "On Discovery" and "Ghostmate," I am also convinced that Chinese oral culture stamps the larger design of the work in a distinctive way. It is responsible for one of the chief features of the work, its apparent lack of "plot" in the Western sense. *China Men* may indeed look back to the Western epic in certain characteristics: a narrator "sings" of the *gestes*, or deeds of heroes; like the *Aeneid*, the work rehearses the epic theme of wandering and nation building. However, *China Men* in my view lacks the "simple unity" of the Western heroic plot as provided by a hero who "connects the events chronologically . . . and thematically by the continuous elements in his character" (Scholes and Kellogg 208–09). Kingston creates instead a gallery of diverse heroes drawn from different periods and literary or historical contexts. The structure of the narrative is serial, for one scene or story leads to another, without logical transitions or narrative bridges. *China Men*'s structure thus consists of incremental repetitions of a single lesson: that hard work, loyalty to the family, and endurance of family dislocation and harsh living conditions are heroic attributes enabling one to prevail in a barbarian wilderness (Eoyang 47).[15] The reader gains pleasure and understanding through the accumulation of parallel exempla—that is, through the reiteration of the narrator's lesson—and not, as in Western plots, through the resolution of a set of dramatic tensions.

The formal model for Kingston's work seems to be the pragmatic Chinese people's literary equivalent of the Western epic, the recitations of popularized history (the best example is the *San-kuo yen-yi*, or *Romance of the Three Kingdoms*, compiled by Lo Kuan-chung in the fourteenth century) and particularly the "romances of success," or *fa-chi pen-tai*, didactic biographies of swashbuckling men of destiny drawing from oral Sung tradition (Hanan 50, 111; H. C. Chang 6–8). Both types of fictionalized history display a proliferation of parallel heroic types with little regard for continuity of narrative or character, the rapid accretion of episodes that can be cut off at any point without harming the meaning or design of the work, and the mixture of fantasy and history found in *China Men*. The influence of the open-ended, didactic plots of Chinese pseudohistorical writings on Kingston is clear to me even in the problematic section entitled "The Laws." This chapter may at first glance appear to be a historical digression because of its departure, in method and material, from the other, more mythical and biographical sections. Yet it ought not to be read as a separate entity but in conjunction with the talk-story sections with which it seems formally allied. (Its title is italicized on the contents page; it, too, is sandwiched between chapters on male forebears.) Because of its talk-story context and its symbolic position at the midpoint of the work, "The Laws" seems less a textbook enumeration of ethnic history than the essence of immigrant history transformed into heroic lore.

The biographical sections should be considered part of the structural scheme as defined by the talk-story sections. Because the biographies are woven into the fabric of heroic history, the reader understands that the accounts of father, grandfathers, great-grandfathers, uncles, and brother are a ceremonial appropriation of one family's experiences in the old country and the new, in the manner of oral tradition. Lives are redefined by the community's artist in accordance with certain traditional heroic forms. One can easily glimpse the outline of Kingston's notion of heroic plot in stories like that of the father as he moves from many defeats in China and America to a final apotheosis as an old man tending his abundant garden, a Candide grown wise. Kingston has arranged the complicated history of the father into successive stages of heroic development, treating each stage in nondevelopmental Chinese fashion, as a separate parable with a different protagonist and a different accompanying talk-story analogue.

In general, however, the relation of biography to talk-story form is not as apparent as in the chapters on the father, since Kingston does not shape true-to-life sections into clear-cut exempla, perhaps because of her proximity to the material as narrator and participant in the events. The heroism of the brother, the grandfather of the Sierra Nevada, or "Mad" Uncle Sao may be less prototypical than that of the long-suffering Li Sao or the stoic Hundred-year-old man; the style of the biographies may be more mixed, the forms less polished and symmetrical than those in the talk-story chapters mainly because the material is still contemporary to both teller and audience. Yet in these chapters on her family, Kingston provides a fascinating glimpse of the process by which a "residual oral" culture, in Ong's term, can create art out of chaotic history. These sections on family patriarchs represent heroic narrative in the throes of creation by an innovative composer before it has received the refinement of repetition by generations of family bards. The singer is, in effect, composing a new song.

This brief treatment of Kingston as contemporary exponent of the Chinese storyteller's art will, I hope, counter prevailing extraliterary assumptions regarding the development of ethnic American literatures and suggest an intrinsic, formal model of interpretation more appropriate to a conservative culture like that of Chinese in America. The core of this transplanted folk culture is oral, not written; the complexity and influence of talk-story, or *gong gu tsai*, have not yet been adequately assessed; that tradition is far broader than the immediate ethnic American one that circumscribes a writer like Kingston, as my elucidation of oral narrative forms in *China Men* has tried to show. The ethnocentric definitions of culture devised by a current crop of ethnicists are called into question by *China Men*'s forms and structures, which demonstrate that immigrant culture is a continuation of the ancient oral tradition of the home. That culture, moreover, shares the primordial formulas and mnemonic structures of oral cultures past and present, East and West, as my comparison of *China Men*'s forms with the paradigmatic forms of heroic narrative cited by Parry and Lord, Scholes, Kellogg, and Ong have attempted to show. Finally, the sophisticated, synchronous character of Chinese American oral culture prompts a reconsideration of Spiller's sociohistorical and scriptographic model for multiethnic literary history by challenging the prospective literary historian to listen for the living word behind the narrow letter.

Notes

[1] Spiller's theory of literary cyclism is strikingly similar to Park's well-known theory of racial assimilationism, outlined in *Race and Culture*. Park's theory was adopted by Rose Hum Lee in *The Chinese in the United States of America*.

[2] In *Chinese Americans*, Stanford Lyman points out that "cultural and institutional intraterritoriality" is a predominant characteristic of overseas Chinese as a whole (6–7).

[3] There is a startling resemblance between the immigrant colloquial terms for oral storytelling ("talk-story," *gong gu tsai*) and the formal literary term for one of the three main types of oral storytelling in China, *hsiao-shuo*, or "small talk" (recitations of purely fictional stories). The two others are *chiang shih*, or historical recitations in debased classical dialect, and *shuo ching*, or Buddhist tales. See H. C. Chang 6–7; Liu, *Essentials* 58–59. Lu Hsun, however, argues that *hsiao-shuo* was an "all-embracing" term often encroaching upon the genres of history and biography (1–9). Two good discussions using western literary criteria are Eoyang and Wivell. The best treatment of the oral source of the *hua-pen*, or short story, is Hanan 20–27.

[4] Walter J. Ong distinguishes between "primary" oral cultures, which know no writing, and "secondary" ones, which are writing-oriented and know "orality" through electronic means. "Residual orality" refers to those "literate" cultures that retain the characteristics of primary orality, like the Irish. For a full discussion of these terms, see *The Presence of the Word*; for the term "cultural squint," see p. 21 in that work. Ong gives an abbreviated discussion of the concepts in the context of minority and non-Western literature in "Oral Culture and the Literate Mind."

[5] See Lord; Scholes and Kellogg 17–56; and Stolz and Shannon. In addition to *The Presence of the Word*, see Ong's essays on oral critical theory in *Interfaces of the Word*.

[6] See Lai et al., *Island*, a remarkable collection of original poems by immigrants, written on the walls of the San Francisco detainment center. See also Chin et al., "Resources for Chinese and Japanese American Literary Traditions," in *AIIIEEEEE!*; Mei et al., "The Bitter Society."

[7] The problem is summarized by Wellek and Warren (264–68); see also White, "Literary History." I have used Wolfgang Iser's broad categories for contemporary literary theory in his "Current Situation of Literary Theory."

[8] Scholes and Kellogg use the term "quasi-literary" to denote the stage at which oral performance is transcribed in writing, although the oral tradition remains paramount. See *The Nature of Narrative* 30.

[9] Hanan 13, 55. Hanan says that the connection between oral tradition and vernacular literature is "impossible to determine." See also Idema.

[10] The distinction between literary language (*yen*) and speech (*yen*) was often unclear, as the following discourse by the Ching scholar Juan Yüan demonstrates:

> Confucius himself gave the title "Embellished Words" to his commentary on the hexagrams Ch'en and K'un (in the Book of Changes): this is the ancestor of the literary compositions (*wen-chang*) of all ages. Those engaged in literary composition, who do not concern themselves with harmonizing sounds to form rhymes or polishing words and phrases to make them go far so that what they write should be easy to recite and easy to remember, but merely use single sentences and write in such wild abandon that, as soon as they begin, they will not stop until they have reached thousands of words, do not realize that what they write is what the ancients call "speech" (*yen*) which means "straightforward speech" or "talk" (*yü*), which means "argument," but not language (*yen*) that has embellishments (*wen*), not what Confucious called "wen" (embellished words/literature). (Qtd. in Liu, *Chinese Theories* 105).

[11] Lin Yutang, 6. Although Confucius did not elaborate on the relationship of father to children, one can surmise his attitudes on the basis of influential quotes like these: "Ch'an K'ang . . . quite delighted, said, . . . 'I have also heard that the superior man maintains a distant reserve toward his son.'"

[12] On the "participatory" nature of living oral traditions, see Tedlock, "Toward an Oral Poetics."

[13] Sui Sin Far is the pen name of Edith Eaton, Eurasian author of a collection of short stories, *Mrs. Spring Fragrance*; Jade Snow Wong wrote *Fifth Chinese Daughter*, a popular work of the 1950s, and *No Chinese Stranger*. For further discussion of these works see Amy Ling's article, "Chinese American Women Writers," in this volume.

[14] See "Eternal Prisoner under the Thunder Peak Pagoda," "Red Jade," and "Scholar T'an" in Ma and Lau.

[15] For a discussion of the structures of early Chinese historical novels as a "joining" of discrete "unitary plots," see Hanan 22–23.

III

Critical and Historical Perspectives on American Literature

Archaeology, Ideology, and African American Discourse

Houston A. Baker, Jr.

The old formulas had failed, and a new one had to be made, but, after all, the object was not extravagant or eccentric. One sought no absolute truth. One sought only a spool on which to wind the thread of history without breaking it.

Henry Adams, *The Education*

Relics of by-gone instruments of labour possess the same importance for the investigation of extinct economic forms of society as do fossil bones for the determination of extinct species of animals.

Karl Marx, *Capital*

(The bluesman Big Bill Broonzy sings:

I worked on a levee camp and the extra gangs too
Black man is a boy, I don't care what he can do.
I wonder when—I wonder when—I wonder when will
I get to be called a man.

Big Bill's stanza signifies American meaning embedded in rocky places. Archaeology employs tropological energy to decode such meaning. It foregrounds voices raised at the margin of civilization, at the very edge of the New World wilderness:

The first time I met the blues, mama, they came walking
through the woods,
The first time I met the blues, baby, they came walking
through the woods,
They stopped at my house first, mama, and done me all
the harm they could.

Little Brother Montgomery's stanza implies harm's unequivocal conquest by a blues voice rising. From piney woods, sagging cabins, and settling levees vernacular tones rise, singing a different America. Archaeology foregrounds and deciphers this song, and when its work is finished what remains is not history as such, but a refigured knowledge. Louis Althusser makes explicit the distinction between history as such *and* historical knowledge:

We should have no illusions as to the incredible force of that prejudice, which still dominates us all, which is the very essence of contemporary historicity, and which attempts to make us confuse the object of knowledge with the real object, by affecting the object of knowledge with the very "qualities" of the real object of which it is knowledge. The knowledge of history is no more historical than the knowledge of sugar is sweet.

The result of archaeology's endeavors is: "A mood blared by trumpets, trombones, saxophones and drums, a song with turgid, inadequate words." The song is a sign of an Afro-American discourse that strikingly refigures life on American shores.)

In 1822, Gideon Mantell, an English physician with a consuming interest in geology and paleontology, made a routine house call in Sussex.[1] On the visit, he discovered a fossilized tooth that seemed to be a vestige of a giant, herbivorous reptile. Since he had nothing in his own collection that was like his find, he traveled to the Hunterian Collection of the Royal College of Surgeons in London and spent hours searching drawers of fossil teeth attempting to find a comparable specimen. When he had nearly exhausted the possibilities, a young man who was also working at the Hunterian and who had heard of the Sussex physician's quest, presented him with the tooth of an iguana. The match was nearly perfect. On the basis of the similarity between the tooth of the living iguana and his own fossil discovery, Mantell named the bearer of the older tooth *Iguanodon* ("iguana tooth"). In 1825, his paper "Notice on the *Iguanodon*, a Newly-Discovered Fossil Reptile from the Sandstone of Tilgate Forest, in Sussex" appeared in the *Philosophical Transactions* of the Royal Society in London.

As the nineteenth century progressed and the fossil record expanded, it became apparent that Iguanodon was but one member of a family of reptiles that, in 1841, received the name "dinosaur" from Sir Richard Owen. By midcentury, it was possible to construct a feasible model of Iguanodon. Available evidence (including assumed homologies with living animals) indicated that the prehistoric creature was a giant, quadripedal reptile with a small triangular spike on his nose. The concrete and plaster model that was built on this plan in 1854 can be seen in England today.

The story of Iguanodon does not conclude at midcentury, however. The fossil record was substantially augmented later in the century by a splendid find of Iguanodon fossils at Bernissart, Belgium. Louis Dollo, the French paleontologist who oversaw the Bernissart site, was able to revise all existing models. Through cross-skeletal comparison and ethological inference, he concluded that Iguanodon was, in fact, bipedal. Moreover, he persuasively demonstrated that the triangular bone that had been taken for a nose spike was actually a horny thumb spike peculiar to dinosaurs.

The mode of thought implied by the Iguanodon example is similar to the mode of descriptive analysis Michel Foucault has designated the "archaeology of knowledge." Foucault writes of his project that the archaeology of knowledge "does not imply the search for a beginning; it does not relate analysis to geological excavation. It designates the general theme of a description that questions the already-said [i.e., a family of concepts] at the level of its existence" (131). He defines a family of concepts as a *discourse* (56). To analyze the mode of existence of a discourse (e.g., medicine, natural history, economics) is to engage in archaeological description.

The aim of Foucault's analysis is to accomplish in relationship to *families of concepts* what Dollo and others accomplished in relationship to Iguanodon. Beginning with limited fossil evidence, nineteenth-century investigators eventually arrived at an informed model of Iguanodon that contextualized the prehistoric reptile and rendered a descriptively adequate image of its living presence. The process through which this model was achieved is known to anthropologists as "descriptive integration" (see Tax et al. 229). It stands in contrast to archaeological excavation designed to unearth the remains of ancient life.

A more explicit definition of Foucault's project enables us to grasp its usefulness and effects in the study of American literary history. As a method of analysis, the archaeology of knowledge assumes that knowledge exists in discursive formations whose lineage can be traced and whose regularities are discoverable. Hence the mystery and sacrosanctness that often surround "bodies of knowledge" or "disciplines" are replaced, under the prospect of the archaeology of knowledge, by an acknowledgment of such bodies as linguistic constructs.

Rather than attempt to determine the nature of the human subject's access to, or generation of, knowledge, analyses conducted under the prospect of Foucault's project are designed to plot the line of a family of concepts from its origin in the statement to its full-blown manifestation within a constellation of families. In the analysis that follows, for example, the movement is from American historical statements such as "religious man," "wilderness," and "migratory errand" to a consideration of "American history" as a discourse situated among kindred families such as "natural history" and "economics." The goal of the archaeology of knowledge as project is to advance the human sciences beyond a traditional humanism, focusing scholarly attention on the discursive constitution and arbitrary figurations of bodies of knowledge rather than on the constitution and situation of human subjects (traditional concerns of humanism). The analytical work begins with the minimal, meaningful unit of discourse—that is, the statement.

II

For Foucault, the "statement" is the fundamental unit of discourse. He defines the statement as a materially repeatable (i.e., recorded) linguistic function. A chart, graph, exclamation, table, sentence, or logical proposition may serve as a statement (79–87). Statement thus seems to occupy the status of those linguistic gestures (even ones so minimal as letters or sounds of the alphabet) to which we refer when we say, "That makes a statement." Moreover, statement seems to imply a variety of enunciative positions rather than a unique utterance by a determinate speaker. The distribution and combination of statements in a discourse are regulated, according to Foucault, by discoverable principles or laws (56). These laws of formation are referred to as a "discursive formation" (38). They make possible the emergence of the notions and themes of a discourse.

Foucault's concern to set his archaeology in nonsubjective terms leads him to talk of statements and laws rather than of, say, speakers and intentions. His method is thus opposed to explanatory accounts that regard human knowledge as the "majestically unfolding manifestation of a thinking, knowing, speaking subject" (55). He insists, instead, that the locations and authorities for discourse are more productive analytical considerations than the motives, intentions, or transcendent subjectivity of individual speakers. In medicine, for example, doctors, researchers, and clinicians are authorities. But they must speak from institutional sites such as hospitals, laboratories, medical schools, and clinics if their statements are to count as official. Moreover, they are confined to a particular succession of statements and a particular group of objects if their statements are to count as medical discourse. Hence, discourse—its sites, objects, and enunciative positions—conditions the speaking subject rather than vice versa. Foucault's archaeology is statement-centered: "We must grasp the statement in the exact specificity of its occurrence; determine its conditions of existence, fix at least its limits, establish its correlations with other statements that may be connected with it, and show what other forms of statement it excludes" (28).

In his attempt to address such matters, Foucault insists that an explanatory model for any family of concepts must be based on a penetrating analysis of the primary conceptual structures of a discourse and the "discursive constellation" (i.e., the group of contemporary or related discourses) of which it forms a part (66). He writes:

> Archaeology, may . . . constitute the tree of derivation of a discourse. It will place a root, as *governing statements*, those that concern the definition of observable structures and the field of possible objects, those that prescribe the forms of description and the perceptual codes that it can use, those that reveal the most general possibilities of characterization, and thus open up a whole domain of concepts to be constructed, and, lastly, those that, while constituting a strategic choice, leave room for the greatest number of subsequent options. (147)

To survey the discursive family of "American history" from the perspective of the archaeology of knowledge is to discover certain primary linguistic functions that serve as governing statements. "Religious man," "wilderness," "migratory errand," "increase in store," and "New Jerusalem" are, in my estimation, essential governing structures of a traditional American history.[2] The first—"religious man"—signals a devout believer in God for whom matters of economics is a minimal consideration. "Wilderness" refers to a savage territory devoid of human beings and institutions. "Migratory errand" connotes a singular mission bestowed by God on "religious man," prompting him to sail the Atlantic and settle the wilderness. The "New Jerusalem" is the promised end of the errand; it is the prospective city of God on earth. It represents the transformation of the wilderness into a community of believers who interpret an "increase in store" as secular evidence of an abiding spiritual faithfulness.

The graphics of most school history texts—with their portrayals of bleak and barren Pilgrims' landings on New World shores and a subsequent "increase in store" and Thanksgiving—offer ample representations of these primary conceptual structures. The mode of dress, physiognomy, and bearing of the foregrounded figures in such graphics normally suggests seventeenth-century European man as the epitome of "religious man." Generally in such pictures non-Europeans are savagely clad, merging with the wilderness. In their proximity to the wilderness, non-Europeans are justifiably interpreted as less than human. The written accounts from which such graphics derive establish quite explicit boundaries of what might be called ethnic exclusion. Describing the Pilgrims' arrival in the wilderness, William Bradford, in "Of Plymouth Plantation," writes: "It is recorded in Scripture as a mercy to the Apostle and his shipwrecked company, that the barbarians [Native Americans] showed them no small kindness in refreshing them, but these savage barbarians when they met them . . . were readier to fill their sides full of arrows than otherwise" (qtd. in Foerster 20–21).

Traditional American literary history is a branch of American history. As a kindred body of concepts, it reflects its parentage with rigorously derivative logic, reading the key statements of the larger discourse onto the ancestry of literary works of art. The literary texts included in Robert Spiller's influential model of American literary history, for example, are arranged and explained in terms of an immigration-and-development pattern of events (*Literary History*, 4th rev. ed.). And in a more recent essay, Spiller clearly implies that his literary-historical model, like the discursive family of which it forms a branch, is characterized by boundaries of ethnic exclusion:

> We can . . . distinguish three kinds of ethnic groups which were not parts of the main frontier movement. These are the immigrant groups which came to this country compara-tively late; the blacks who were brought to this country under special circumstances; and the Jews who in all their history have mingled with, but rarely become totally absorbed into, any alien culture. All three are of great importance to the American identity today as expressed in its ever-changing literature, but only immigrations from European countries other than Great Britain followed a course close enough to our model to suggest inclusion here, even though the remarkable achievements of the Jews and the blacks in contempo-rary American literature suggest that—given a slightly different model—their contribu-tions to our culture would lend themselves to similar analyses. ("Cycle" 15)

If one were to produce graphics for the history implied by Spiller, they would consist of a foregrounded European author (or a succession of such authors) turning out ever more sophisticated literary works of art. Spiller's notion of a "basic evolutionary devel-opment" of American literature ("Cycle" 15) is equivalent to the larger historical dis-course's notion of European, or Euro-American, progress toward the "New Jerusalem." Within the larger discourse, God's divine plan is assumed to reveal (and, ultimately, to fulfill) itself only through the endeavors of religious, European men.[3] And just as such men are considered sole builders of the New Jerusalem, so, too, they are considered exclusive chroniclers of their achievements in the evolutionary phases of an American national literature.

A secularized Hegelian version of the framework implied by traditional American history would claim that the American *Volkgeist* represents the final form of absolute Spirit on its path through history. The millennium, the self-awareness of Spirit, the prophetically augured "fullness of time" are all embodied, in other words, in that pri-mary conceptual structure of American historical discourse—the New Jerusalem. Simi-larly, the world triumph of an absolute literary creativity finds its ground properly pre-pared in the evolutionary labors of American writers.[4] In his brilliant study *American Jeremiad*, Sacvan Bercovitch demonstrates that American authors repeatedly conflated New World literary and spiritual missions by adopting the prototypical, scriptural form of rhetoric known as the *jeremiad*. According to Bercovitch, such authors not only spoke of a divine destiny in America but also employed a divine form modified spe-cifically for American ears.

Given the providential framework of American history and literary history, it is not surprising that the authorities for the enunciation of historical statements have been ministers and college professors. The institutional sites guaranteeing the official status of such statements have been pulpits and academic classrooms.[5] From the seventeenth century to the twentieth, ministerial and lay professors of the white American academy have been official advocates, working as teachers, scholars, critics, editors, and so on. Their ranks have been confined, for the most part, to European or Euro-American males. The early providential aura of their instruction has been secularized through time, but one still receives the impression on reading their works that lay ministers are at work, taking account of and perpetuating literary workers and works of art that manifest adherence to the original errand—securing a New Jerusalem.

The exclusionist tendencies of Spiller, for example, are amply reinforced by the work of Cleanth Brooks, R. W. B. Lewis, and Robert Penn Warren in their giant anthology *American Literature: The Makers and the Making*. In an introductory "Letter to the Reader," the editors write:

> Since this book is, among other things, a history, it is only natural that its organization should be, in the main, chronological. But it is not strictly so; other considerations inevitably cross-hatch pure chronology. We have mentioned the two sections on southern writing, which overlap periods treated elsewhere. Similarly, the two sections on black literature together span many decades, for like Faulkner and other white southern writers, black writers in America, whether of the North or the South, have worked in terms of a special condition and cultural context. (xix)

Although the prose is slightly less penetrable than Spiller's, it is reasonably easy to see that Brooks, Lewis, and Warren are postulating that verbal creativity which lies outside traditional, orthodox patterns of a spiritually evolving American literature is merely a shadow ("crosshatch") on national history and literary history conceived as rigidly determinate chronologies. The telos of such chronologies is, presumably, the New Jerusalem—a recaptured Eden in America.

The "special condition and cultural context" of the editors' introductory "Letter" are identical to Spiller's "special circumstances." And like Spiller, Brooks, Lewis, and Warren begin with the Puritans and trace an evolutionary progression. Unlike their predecessor, however, they find it necessary—presumably for axiological reasons—to ensure that shadows on an exalted past are not mistaken for acts of authentic literary creativity. "Literature of the Nonliterary World" is the title they provide for the concluding section of the first volume of their anthology. The section includes David Walker, Frederick Douglass, Frederick Law Olmstead, "Folk Songs of the White People," Indian oratory, "Folk Songs of the Black People," non-Puritan historians, southwestern humorists, Abraham Lincoln, Davy Crockett, and so on. On the basis of definitions supplied by the editors, we must suppose that inclusions in this *category of the excluded* exist somewhere between secondary and *non*-literature (xii). The editors' definitions obviously conserve a Spillerian orthodoxy.

III

The archaeology of knowledge serves not only to isolate the governing statements of American history and literary history but also to focus attention on such formations as discourse. An emphasis on history and literary history as discourse compels us to think in symbolic, linguistic terms. In his essay "Historical Discourse," the French semiotician Roland Barthes writes that "the only feature which distinguishes historical discourse from other kinds is a paradox: the 'fact' can only exist linguistically, as a term in a discourse, yet we behave as if it were a simple reproduction of something on another plane of existence altogether, some extra-structural 'reality' " (153).[6]

Barthes's formulation enables us to conceive of the governing statements of American history and the evolutionary stages of American literary history as materially repeatable entities that assume the status of facts only because they are inscribed in historical discourse. On first view, this formulation seems to imply the presence of a human recorder, or noter, and thus to run counter to Foucault's decentering of the subject. But a further consideration indicates that the semiotician, like the archaeologist, is more concerned with the constraints of discourse than with a constraining subjectivity. Barthes says of historical facts, for example, that they "can only be defined tautologically; we take note of what is notable; but the notable . . . is nothing more than the noteworthy [i.e., that which has been 'already-said']" (153).

This tautology is clarified by an analogy between the fact linguistically conceived and the photograph of a scene. We say that a fact, like a scene, represents a bedrock reality. But since our sole access to the fact is through language, we are ever aware of an intervening presence—that of the noted, the recorded, the already said. Similarly, our access to a scene by means of a photograph makes us aware of an intervening process, with its "arranged" objects, croppings, burning, enlargements, and so on. Reality becomes an elusive matter.

Where historical facts are concerned, the implications of the analogy lead us to concur with Barthes that historical discourse "does not follow reality, it only signifies it" (154). What derives from linguistic, historical facts, therefore, is not reality but *meaning*. And meaning is always contingent upon the figurative, semantic resources available to us as readers, viewers, or auditors.

If we recur for a moment to the paleontological example with which the essay began, we might equate Mantell's fossilized tooth with a potential signifier, dependent for its meanings on a host of factors. After the initial model of Iguanodon had been constructed, it was soon apparent that meanings quite different from those conceived by early modelers could be derived from Mantell's discovery. (The Sussex physician would doubtless have accepted such meanings. American literary historians, by contrast, constrained by a quasi-religious orthodoxy, stand always opposed to new evidentiary considerations.) While the fossil signified dentition homologous to the iguana's, it did not signify quadripedalism. What occurred in the case of the tooth was a further accumulation of evidence that made it possible to provide an enlarged context of meaning. A substantially expanded perspective resulted in a descriptively integrated set of meanings.

Just as an enlarged context altered the conception of Iguanodon, so a consideration of the discursive constellation can alter our view of historical discourse. When the discourses and practices contemporary with American history are brought to bear, its religious orientation, site, and authorities are subject to radical reinterpretation. The barbarians of William Bradford's account manifest themselves, in the light of a contemporary seventeenth-century natural history, not as scriptural reprobates but as negative functions of a philosophical-scientific practice that classified European man as the acme of being.

Both "religious man" and "increase in store" are subject to similar revisions if one considers them from the perspective of economics. Euro-Americans who engaged in the transatlantic slave trade maintained a favorable balance of trade (both economic and spiritual) by defining Africans whom they loaded into ships' holds not only as heathens to be transported to occidental salvation, but as property, bullion, or real wealth. In an act of bizarre Western logic, Africans forcefully deported from their homeland to the New World became spiritual revenue.[7] The African American poet Robert Hayden succinctly captures this spiritually aberrant mercantilism in the following lines from "Middle Passage":

> Deep in the festering hold thy father lies,
> of his bones New England pews are made,
> those are altar lights that were his eyes. (*Selected Poems* 65; 1966).

If we consider historical discourse a family of concepts, we might say that the secular-economic perspective implied by a larger interpretive context signals the possibility of new governing statements from which a new genealogical line may be derived. (We might say, indeed, that the prospect of "standing Hegel on his feet" becomes imminent.) In the novel *Season of Adventure*, by the West Indian writer George Lamming, the protagonist reflects:

> The Americans took pleasure in their past because they were descended from men whose migration was a freely chosen act. They were descended from a history that was recorded, a history which was wholly contained in their own way of looking at the world . . . [but the history of African-descended black people] was a commercial deportation. (93)

As a new governing structure, "commercial deportation" dramatically alters the construction of traditional American historical discourse. The statement first signifies an involuntary transport of *human beings* as opposed to the export or import of will-less merchandise. And instead of bleak and barren beginnings on New World shores yet to be civilized, the history signified by "commercial deportation" implies European man as slave trader, divider of established civilizations, dealer in "hides of Fellatah/Mandingo, Ibo, Kru" (Hayden, *Selected Poems* 67). The transportable stock on American vessels is no longer figured as a body of courageous Pilgrims but as "black gold." And a providential American history reveals itself as a spiritual discourse coextensive with the non-discursive, economic practices of men who turned the middle passage to profit.

The graphics accompanying a historical formation derived from "commercial deportation" are strikingly different from those accompanying the accounts of a traditional American history. They evoke Armageddon rather than the New Jerusalem. And the shift effected in the larger historical perspective by the governing structure "commercial deportation" opens the way for a corollary shift in perspective on "American literary history." What comes starkly to the foreground are the conditions of a uniquely African American historical and literary historical discourse.

The emergence of conditions for African American literary history is a function not only of an enlarged perspective but also of the "method" of history itself. Moving beyond the explicit levels of discourse, the archaeology of knowledge seeks to discover organizing or formative principles of discourses that it evaluates. Such principles seem aptly conveyed for history by the observation that "history is tied neither to man nor to any particular object. It consists wholly in its method, which experience proves to be indispensable for cataloguing the elements of any structure whatever, human or non-human, in their entirety" (Lévi-Strauss, "History" 228).

If historical method consists in cataloging elements, then all histories are, at least theoretically, open-ended—the possible inclusions, limitless. In practice, histories are always limited by ideology. Catalogs are not merely constituted. They are instituted on the basis of principles of selection—on the basis of ideologies. In the essay cited earlier, Barthes writes: "historical discourse is essentially a product of ideology, or rather imagination if we accept the view that it is via the language of imagination that responsibility for an utterance passes from a purely linguistic entity to a psychological or ideological one" (153). A history may be conceptualized as an ideologically or imaginatively governed catalog of figurative elements. The catalog is inconceivable in the absence of ideology, and a shift, or rupture, in ideological premises promotes strikingly new figurations.

The ideological orientation foregrounded for "African American literary history" under the prospect of the archaeology of knowledge is not a vulgar Marxism, or an idealistically polemical black nationalism. The most appropriate ideological principles of formation, that is, do not suggest an outlook Fredric Jameson ascribes to a "familiar Western critique of *ideology*":

> the concept of ideology [in a "familiar" critique] already implies mystification, and conveys the notion of a kind of floating and psychological world view, a kind of subjective picture of things already by definition unrelated to the external world itself. The consequence is that even a proletarian world view is relativized, and felt to be ideological, while the ultimate standard of truth becomes the positivistic one of some "end of ideology" which would leave us in the presence of the facts themselves, without any subjective distortions. (*Marxism* 182–83)

Rather than an ideological model yielding a new "positivism," what interests me is a form of thought that grounds African American discourse in concrete, material situations. Where African American narratives are concerned, the most suitable analytical model is not only an economic one but also one based on a literary-critical frame of reference. The type of ideological model I have in mind is suggested by the scholarly reflections both of Jameson and of Hayden White, another well-known critic of dialectical thought.

White insists that a literary work of art can be evaluated as a discretely "social" action only if its commodity status in a society's exchange system is acknowledged. In "Literature and Social Action," White tells us that "the solution to the problem of the social status of 'literature' in the modern age, insofar as such a solution can be hoped for in the application of the Marxist method to its study, must consist of the explication of the different statuses that 'literature' has enjoyed or suffered in the hierarchy of value which assesses the worth of everything in terms of its exchange value for money or gold" (377). Jameson argues, in turn, that the relationship between a literary text and its social ground is the relationship that is "reinvented" by ideological analysis. In "The Symbolic Inference," Jameson writes: "The term 'ideology' stands as the sign for a problem yet to be solved, a mental operation which remains to be executed. It does not presuppose cut-and-dried sociological stereotypes like the notion of the 'bourgeois' or the 'petty bourgeois' but is rather a mediatory concept: that is, it is an imperative to reinvent a relationship between the linguistic or aesthetic or conceptual fact in question and its social ground" (510). The "social ground" can be identified as the *economics* or the *modes of production* characterizing the milieu in which an expressive work emerges.

To bring White and Jameson together in an analysis of African American narratives—an analysis designed to provide a fit ideological perspective on "African American literary history"—is to gain a view of subtextual dimensions of African American discourse that have never been effectively evaluated. The efficacious results for practical criticism that derive from what might be called the "ideology of form" should be apparent in critical analyses that follow.

IV

In African American literary study, a shift from a traditional to an economic perspective, from a humanistic to an ideologically oriented frame of reference, evokes what might be called the "economics of slavery." The phrase, like "commercial deportation," stands as a governing statement in African American discourse. In specifically African American terms, the "economics of slavery" signifies the social system of the Old South that determined what, how, and for whom goods were produced to satisfy human wants. As a function of the European slave trade, the economy of the Old South was an exploitative mode of production embodied in the plantation system and spirited by a myth of aristocratic patriarchalism. The formative relationship of the plantation system, as Eugene Genovese argues in *The Political Economy of Slavery* and *The World the Slaveholders Made*, was that between master and slave, lord and bondsman.[8]

At the level of economic production, the slave's labor was brutally exploited to maximize the master's profit. The slave existed exclusively for the master's greater gain. Genovese argues, however, that the more profoundly grotesque features of "Mr. Moneybags" (Marx's prototypical entrepreneur in *Capital*) are inappropriate for a representation of the planters of the American South. While the economics of slavery promoted the dehumanizing plunder of African labor, it also produced a corollary southern mythology of the ruling class. The primary features of this mythology were "patriarchy" and "economic paternalism" (*World* 24).

The southern planters, unlike their absentee counterparts in the Caribbean, were full-fledged, resident members of their own plantation. They conceived of themselves as beneficent patriarchs responsible to the full population of their estate. This populace, in fact, was deemed an "extended family" toward which slaveholders were obligated to display courtesy and concern. The second feature of Old South mythology, however, cast a bizarre shadow on the face of this assumed patriarchy.

"Economic paternalism" signified the masters as the owners of all stock in their "children-as-slaves." Contrary to the free-market economics of an expanding European capitalism, the southern master was not forced to negotiate with a laborer who was, in Marx's words, "the untrammelled owner of his capacity for labour, i.e., of his person" (*Capital*). The southern master, therefore, was always a functionary of an economics predicated on the cash nexus—always posing, paradoxically, as a stern adversary to capitalism.

No sharply qualifying mythology such as that of the Old South—Genovese and others have argued—stood in the way of the West Indian absentee planter's quest for profit. Indeed, the quest for profit proceeded in its own right, far from the (absentee) master's day-to-day concern (see E. Williams). Slavery in the Caribbean was a purely capitalistic matter, an investment expected to yield return. As a form of commercial gain, it could conveniently be replaced by alternative economic forms. Genovese writes: "The planters of the British Caribbean argued their case in London for years and finally, faced with defeat, roared their protests, accepted monetary compensation, transferred investments, and made the best of it. For a capitalist an investment in black bodies could be transformed into an investment in cotton textile machinery anytime, for the transformation was a matter of business" (*World* 122).

The consequences of the differing views of slavery in the West Indies and in the Old South are reflected in the possible degrees of freedom available to the enterprising West Indian and African American slave. The necessity to negotiate an "economics of slavery" was always present for the slave, whether in the Old South or in the Caribbean. But the degree of the masters' intransigence and resistance varied. West Indian slavery was more inclined than that of the Old South to permit the substitution of one form of capital for another. Southerners fought a civil war to avoid abolition. British planters accepted government compensation and altered their investment portfolios.

Both West Indian and African American slavery resulted in the creation of an excluded group of black men and women subjugated by violence and deprived of the fruits of their labor. The condition of existence of this caste (and its descendants) is sometimes extrapolated by historians from birthrate data. Because, for example, the United States slave population grew by reproducing itself rather than by fresh deportations from Africa, southern patriarchalism is assumed to have been less harsh than slave treatment in, say, the Caribbean. But as anyone familiar with the spiraling rates of teenage pregnancies in today's bleak inner cities can appreciate, an increase in population is not necessarily a reliable index of a tolerable life. It is not birthrates, one might suggest, but buildings that best signify the existence of Africans in America.

A *metaphorical* extension of the economics of slavery seems to verify W. E. B. Du Bois's claim that the size and arrangements of a people's homes are a fair index of their condition (*Souls* 304; 1965). While monographic histories of slavery describe important dimensions of the economics of slavery, it is possible to telescope many dimensions of such economics by means of a vertical, associative, metaphorical decoding. The diachrony of traditional historiography can be productively complemented, I think, by a nonsuccessive, synchronic prospect. The employment of such a prospect amounts to the introduction of what Hayden White defines as "tropological" thought (*Tropics* 5).

Tropological thought is a discursive mode that employs unfamiliar (or exotic) figures to qualify what is deemed "traditional" in a given discourse. To extrapolate from White, we might assert that attempts to signify the force of meaning of the economics of slavery by invoking buildings *and blues* (as I shall do forthwith) constitute an analytical move designed to incorporate into reality phenomena to which traditional historiography generally denies the status "real." The end of a tropological enterprise is the alteration of reality itself.

In White's account, a tropological approach constitutes a metalogical operation that turns logic against itself. Its conscious employment of metaphor releases us from what Hegel conceived as a tyranny of conceptual overdeterminations (*Tropics* 10). The process of tropological understanding is coextensive with dialectical thought. It, too, is designed to achieve an enlarged, altered, more adequate discursive rendering of the object of knowledge. A survey of images of African American dwellings demonstrates the effect of tropological thought in defining the economics of slavery.

In *The Slave Community*, the historian John Blassingame writes: "The slaves often complained bitterly about what their masters describe as 'adequate' housing. Most of the [slave] autobiographers reported that they lived in crudely built one-room log cabins with dirt floors and too many cracks in them to permit much comfort during the winter months" (159). After his own observation on the "size and arrangements" of a people's dwellings in *The Souls of Black Folk*, Du Bois goes on to describe homes in the black belt of Georgia at the turn of the century: "All over the face of the land is the one-room cabin,—now standing in the shadow of the Big House, now staring at the dusty road, now rising dark and sombre amid the green of the cotton-fields. It is nearly always old and bare, built of rough boards and neither plastered nor ceiled" (159). In a report on American working conditions in the late 1920s prepared for the Labor Research Organization, Charlotte Todes wrote of a logging camp owned by the Great Southern Railroad and worked by blacks: "Across the railroad track from the depot and company store were about one-hundred shacks for Negro workers. These are one room with a window at one end—not always glass but with a wood flap to let down." (qtd. in Oliver 79).

The scant diachronic modification in "size and arrangements" of black dwellings allows them, I suggest, to stand as *signs* for the continuing impoverishment of blacks in the United States. The places where Africans in America have lived (and continue to live) signify the economics of slavery. An "army-style barracks" formed the home of Horace Taft of Philadelphia, for example, while he was in North Carolina engaged in an experience that he describes as follows:

> It was real slavery-time work I did down there. My first week's salary was $3. That was a week's pay. They kept all the rest. It was just horrible, the things I seen at those camps. I seen men beat with rubber hoses. I seen a woman beat. There was always someone guarding and watching you. You couldn't get away because they were sitting out there with guns.

Taft was kidnapped into slave labor in 1979. His story appeared as "Slavery in a 'Migrant Stream'" in the *Philadelphia Inquirer* for 17 January 1982.

Yet if the profile of the masters cannot be confined to capitalist grotesquerie, neither can the dwellings of Africans in America be confined to an economic signification. The nonmonetary, "mythical" dimensions that arise from the size and arrangements of black homes are supplied by an African American expressiveness that can be succinctly denoted as "blues." Samuel Charters offers the following bleak description of a dwelling on the outskirts of Brownsville, Tennessee:

> About a mile and a half from the turnoff into Brownsville there is a sagging red cabin, the bare patch of ground in front is littered with bits of clothing, dirty dishes, a broken chair. . . . The cabin has two rooms; one of them empty except for a few rags that lie in the filth of the floor. . . . In the other room is a chair, a rusted wood stove, and two dirty, unmade beds. In the heat of a summer afternoon it looks like the other empty buildings scattered along Winfield Lane. (57)

But while the sagging cabin is like all such African American dwellings in its dilapidation and overcrowding (a man, his wife, and five children inhabit it), it presents identity with a difference. For the sagging red cabin outside Brownsville is the home of Sleepy John Estes, one of the greatest traditional blues singers to take guitar in hand. His brilliant expressiveness modifies, ameliorates, orders, and sharply qualifies the bleakness of a sagging cabin's size and arrangements. His song rises from a "slave community" and is fittingly designated by the single world *blues*.

The expressiveness represented by Sleepy John is as much a feature of the economics of slavery as deprivations of material resources that have characterized African life in the New World. It is not, however, the field, country, or classic blues that provide a *first* occasion for examining the operation of economics of slavery and commercial deportation as governing statements in African American discourse. A first view is provided, instead, by African slave narratives. When such narratives are analyzed in ideological terms, they reveal subtextual contours rich in "blues resources"—abundantly characterized, that is, by aspects of meaning that reveal brilliant economic and expressive strategies designed by Africans in the New World and the Old to negotiate the dwarfing spaces and paternally aberrant arrangements of Western slavery.

V

The locus classicus of African American literary discourse is the slave narrative. Appearing in England and America during the eighteenth and nineteenth centuries, the thousands of narratives produced by Africans in England and by fugitive slaves and freed black men and women in America constitute the first, literate manifestations of a tragic disruption in African cultural homogeneity. When the author of *The Interesting Narrative of the Life of Olaudah Equiano, or Gustavus Vassa, the African. Written by Himself* (1789) arrived at the African coast in the hands of his kidnappers, he had left behind the communal, familial way of life of his native village of Essaka in the province of Benin (now part of Nigeria). The family member whom he has a final opportunity to embrace is a sister kidnapped in the same slave-trading raid. His sibling serves as sign and source of familial, female love. And the nature of the final meeting is emblematic of the separations that "commercial deportation" effected in the lives of Africans: "When these people [Africans carrying Vassa and his sister to the coast] knew we were brother and sister, they indulged us to be together; and the man, to whom I supposed we belonged, lay with us, he in the middle, while she and I held one another by the hands across his breast all night; and thus for a while we forgot our misfortunes, in the joy of being together" (24; Bontemps, Beacon, 1969). The phrase "the man, to whom I supposed we belonged" signals a loss of self-possession. The man's position "in the middle" signals a corollary loss of familial (and, by implication, conjugal) relations. The narrator introduces a sentimental apostrophe to represent his emotional response to loss:

Yes, thou dear partner of all my childish sport! thou sharer of my joys and sorrows! happy should I have ever esteemed myself to encounter every misery for you and to procure your freedom by the sacrifice of my own. Though you were early forced from my arms, your image has been always riveted in my heart, from which neither time nor fortune have been able to remove it. (24)

But the import of loss is felt less in sentiment than in terror. Having arrived at the coast, Vassa encounters the full, objective reality of his commercially deportable status:

> The first object which saluted my eyes when I arrived on the coast, was the sea, and a *slave* ship, which was then riding at anchor, and waiting for its *cargo*. These filled me with astonishment, which was soon converted into terror, when I was carried on board. I was immediately handled, and tossed up to see if I were sound, by some of the crew; and I was not persuaded that I had gotten into a world of bad spirits, and that they were going to kill me. . . . When I looked round the ship too, and saw a large furnace of copper *boiling*, and a multitude of *black people* of every description *chained* together, every one of their countenances expressing dejection and sorrow, I no longer doubted of my fate; and, quite overpowered with horror and anguish, I fell motionless on the deck and fainted. (27; my emphasis)

The quotation captures, in graphic detail, the peremptory consignment of Africans—body and soul—to a chained and boiling economic hell. They will be forced to extract relief and release through whatever instruments present themselves.

At one interpretive level, the remainder of *The Life of Olaudah Equiano* is the story of a Christian convert who finds solace from bondage in the ministerings of a kind Providence. The Christian-missionary and civilizing effects of the slave trade that were vaunted by Europeans find an exemplary instance in the narrator's portrait of himself after a short sojourn in England: "I could not speak English tolerably well, and I perfectly understood everything that was said. . . . I no longer looked upon . . . [Englishmen] as spirits, but as men superior to us [Africans]; and therefore I had the stronger desire to resemble them, to imbibe their spirit, and imitate their manners" (48). Through the kindly instructions of "the Miss Guerins," Englishwomen who are friends of his master, the young Vassa learns to read and write. He is also baptized and received into St. Margaret's Church, Westminster, in February 1759 (49). As a civilized, Christian subject, he is able to survive with equanimity the vagaries of servitude, the whims of fortune, and the cruelties of fate. After his manumission, he searches earnestly for the true, guiding light of salvation and achieves (in chapter 10) confirmation of his personal salvation in a vision of the crucified Christ:

> On the morning of the 6th October . . . [1774], all that day, I thought I should either see or hear something supernatural. I had a secret impulse on my mind of something that was to take place. . . . In the evening of the same day . . . the Lord was pleased to break in upon my soul with his bright beams of heavenly light; and in that instant, as it were, removing the veil, and letting light into a dark place, I saw clearly with an eye of faith, the crucified Saviour bleeding on the cross on Mount Calvary; the scriptures became an unsealed book. . . . Now every leading providential circumstance that happened to me, from the day I was taken from my parents to that hour, was then in my view, as if it had just then occurred. I was sensible of the invisible hand of God, which guided and protected me, when in truth I knew it not. (149–50)

This passage from *The Life* represents what might be termed the African's providential awakening and ascent from the motionlessness that accompanied a coerced entrance into the mercantile inferno of slavery. To the extent that the narrative reinforces a providential interpretation, the work seems coextensive with an "old" literary history that claims Africans as spiritual cargo delivered (under "special circumstances") unto God Himself.

If, however, we return for a moment to the conditions of disruption that begin the narrator's passage into slavery and consider the truly "commercial" aspects of his deportation, a perspective quite different from that of the old history emerges. Further, by summoning an ideological analysis grounded in the genuine economics (as opposed to the European-derived "ethics") of slavery, we perceive quite a different *awakening* on the part of the African.

To bring together perspectives of Jameson and White in a discussion of *The Life of Olaudah Equiano* is scarcely to designate "the African" of the narrative's title an exclusively religious product of a transatlantic trade's providential mission. For Vassa's status as transportable property is finally ameliorated as much by his canny mercantilism as by his pious toiling in the vineyards of Anglicanism. *The Life of Olaudah Equiano* can be ideologically considered as a work whose protagonist masters the rudiments of economics that condition his very life. It can also be interpreted as a narrative whose author creates a text that inscribes these economics as a sign of its "social grounding."

The Life, therefore, is less a passive "mirroring" of providential ascent than a summoning "into being [by a narrative of] that situation to which it is also, at one and the same time, a reaction" (Jameson, "Symbolic Inference"). If there is a new, or different, historical subtext distinguishing Vassa's narrative from traditional, historical, and literary historical discourse, that subtext is, at least in part, a symbolic "invention" of the narrative itself. This subtext becomes discernible only under an analysis that explores a determinate relationship between *The Life* and the economics of slavery.

"Now the Ethiopian," writes Vassa, "was willing to be saved by Jesus Christ, the sinner's only surety, and also to rely on none other person or thing for salvation" (150). The religious "voice" and conversion narrative form implied by this statement stand in marked contrast to the voice and formal implications characterizing *The Life*'s representations of West Indian bondage. In the "West India climate," according to Vassa, the cruelest barbarities of the trade manifest themselves, resulting in the catalog of horrors that appears in chapter 5. The savage tides of the Caribbean are to the calm harbors of England as the gross deceptions and brutalizations of Montserrat are to the kind attentions of the Guerins and others in London. It would surely seem, therefore, that if "the Ethiopian" were anywhere "willing to be saved by Jesus Christ . . . and to rely *on none other person or thing*" (my emphasis), a "West India climate" would be the place for such reliance. Yet when the narrator enters the West Indies, in chapter 5, the voice dominating the narrative is hardly one of pious long-suffering.

After a year's labor for Mr. Robert King, his new owner, Vassa writes, "I became very useful to my master, and saved him, as he used to acknowledge, above a hundred pounds a year" (73). Thus begins a process of self-conscious, mercantile self-evaluation—a meditation on the economics of African, or New World, black selfhood—that continues for the next two chapters of *The Life.* "I have sometimes heard it asserted," Vassa continues, "that a negro cannot earn his master the first cost; but nothing can be further from the truth. . . . I have known many slaves whose masters would not take a thousand pounds current for them. . . . My master was several times offered, by different gentlemen, one hundred guineas for me, but he always told them he would not sell me, to my great joy" (73). These assertions of chapter 5 seem far more appropriate for a trader's secular diary than a devout acolyte's conversion journal.

Having gained the post of shipboard assistant, or "mate," to Captain Thomas Farmer, an Englishman who sails a Bermuda sloop for his new master, Vassa immediately thinks in secular terms that he "might in time stand some chance by being on board to get a little money, or possibly make my escape if I should be used ill" (83). The conflagration of getting "a little money" and freedom conditions the narrative experiences leading from the slave's first trading venture (chapter 6) to his receipt of a certificate of manumission, in chapter 7. Describing his initial attempts at mercantilism, the narrator writes in ledger-like detail:

> After I had been sailing for some time with this captain [Mr. Farmer], at length I endeavored to try my luck, and commence merchant. I had but a very small capital to begin with; for one single half bit, which is equal to three pence in England, made up my whole stock. However, I trusted to the Lord to be with me; and at one of our trips to St. Eustatius, a Dutch island, I bought a glass tumbler with my half bit, and when I came to Montserrat, I sold it for a bit, or sixpence. Luckily we made several successive trips to St. Eustatius (which was a general mart for the West Indies, about twenty leagues from Montserrat), and in our next, finding my tumbler so profitable, with this one bit I bought two tumblers more; and when I came back, I sold them for two bits equal to a shilling sterling. When we went again, I bought with these two bits four more of these glasses, which I sold for four bits on our return to Montserrat. And in our next voyage to St. Eustatius, I bought two glasses with one bit, and with the other three I bought a jug of Geneva, nearly about three pints in measure. When we came to Montserrat, I sold the gin for eight bits, and the tumblers for two, so that my capital now amounted in all to a dollar, well husbanded and acquired in space of a month or six weeks, when I blessed the Lord that I was so rich. (84)

Manifold ironies mark the foregoing account of the slave's transactions. Instead of taking the form of a spiritual multiplication of "talents" in providential terms, shipboard transactions are transcribed as a chronicle of mercantile adventure. The pure product of trade (i.e., transportable "property" or chattel) becomes a trader, turning from spiritual meditations to canny speculations on the increase of a well-acquired and husbanded store! The swiftness of this transformation is apparent when, amid the lawless savagery visited on blacks in the West Indies, Vassa calmly resolves to earn his freedom "by honest and honorable [read: mercantile] means" (87). In order to achieve this end, he redoubles his commercial efforts.

Eventually *The Life*, in its middle portion, almost entirely brackets the fact that a mercantile self's trans-Caribbean profit making is a function of an egregious trade in slaves plied between the West Indies and the southeastern coast of the United States. We find, for example, the following statement by the narrator: "About the latter end of the year 1764, my master bought a larger sloop, called the *Prudence*, about seventy or eighty tons, of which my captain had the command. I went with him in this vessel, and we took a load of new slaves for Georgia and Charleston. . . . I got ready all the little venture I could; and, when the vessel was ready, we sailed, to my great joy. When we got to our destined places . . . I expected I should have an opportunity of selling my little property to advantage" (91). One explanation for the bracketing of slavery that marks this passage is that the narrator, having been reduced to property by "commercial deportation," decides during his West Indian captivity that neither sentiment nor spiritual sympathies can earn his liberation. He realizes, in effect, that only the acquisition of property will enable him to alter his designated status *as property*. He thus formulates a plan of freedom constrained by the mercantile boundaries of a Caribbean situation.

With the blessings of a master who credits him with "half a puncheon of rum and half a hogshead of sugar," Vassa sets out to make "money enough . . . to *purchase my freedom* . . . for forty pounds sterling money, which was only the same price he [Mr. King] gave for me" (93–94; my emphasis). By chapter 7 the slave's commercial venture is complete. Having entered the "West India trade," he has obtained "about forty-seven pounds." He offers the entire sum to Mr. King, who "said he would not be worse than his promise; and taking the money, told me to go to the Secretary at the Register Office, and get my manumission drawn up" (101–02). In the act of exchange between lord and bondsman, there appears a clear instance of the West Indian slaveholder's willingness to substitute one form of capital for another. Mr. King's initial reluctance to honor his promise is overcome by a realization that his investment in black bodies can be transformed easily enough into other forms of enterprise.

The most striking linguistic occurrence in the process that commences with Vassa's shift of voice in chapter 5 is the transcription of his certificate of manumission in chapter 7. The certificate is, in effect, an economic sign that competes with and radically qualifies the ethical piousness of its enfolding text. The inscribed document is a token of mastery, signifying its recipient's successful negotiation of a deplorable system of exchange. The narrator of *The Life* (as distinguished from the author) is aware of both positive and negative implications of his certificate, and he self-consciously prevents his audience from bracketing his achievement of manumission as merely an act of virtuous perseverance in the face of adversity. "As the form of my manumission has something peculiar in it, and expresses the absolute power and dominion one man claims over his fellow, I shall beg leave to present it before my readers at full length" (103).

The document—which gives, grants, and releases to "the said Gustavus Vassa, all right, title, dominion, sovereignty, and property" that his "lord and master" Mr. King holds over him—signals the ironic transformation of property by property into humanity. Chattel has transformed itself into freeman through the exchange of forty pounds sterling. The slave equates his elation on receiving freedom to the joys of conquering heroes, or to the contentment of mothers who have regained a "long lost infant," or to the gladness of the lover who once again embraces the mistress "ravished from his arms" or the "weary hungry mariner at the sight of the desired friendly port" (103).

Two frames of mind are implied by the transcription of the manumission certificate and the response of the freeman. First, the narrator recognizes that the journey's end (i.e., the mariner's achievement of port) signaled by manumission provides enabling conditions for the kind of happy relations that seemed irrevocably lost when he departed his sister (i.e., familial relations like those implied by "mother-infant" and conjugal ones suggested by "lover-mistress"). At the same time, he is unequivocally aware that the terribleness of the economics he has "navigated" separated him from such relationships in the first instance. There seems no ambivalence, or split opinion, however, on the part of the *author* of *The Life of Olaudah Equiano*.

The structure of the text of the narrative seems to reflect the author's conviction that it is absolutely necessary for slaves to negotiate the economics of slavery if they would be free. The mercantile endeavors of the autobiographical self in *The Life* occupy the very center of the narrative. Chapters 5, 6, and 7 mark an economic middle passage in a twelve-chapter account.

The work's middle section represents an active, inversive, ironically mercantile ascent by the propertied self from the hell of "commercial deportation." It offers a graphic "reinvention" of the social grounding of the African American symbolic act par excellence. It vividly delineates the true character of African America's historical origins in a slave economics and implicitly acknowledges that such economics *must be mastered* before liberation can be achieved.

Vassa's hardships do not end with the purchase of freedom. Subsequent episodes make it clear that life for a free black in eighteenth-century England was neither simple nor easy. Nonetheless, the impact of the text following chapter 7 is qualitatively less than that of preceding chapters. The reduction in dramatic effect is at least in part a function of the predictability of the narrator's course once he has undergone economic awakening in the West Indies. The possibility of amorous heterosexual relationships, for example, is introduced immediately after manumission, with the narrator's tongue-in-cheek comment on the community's response (especially that of black women) to his liberation: "The fair as well as the black people immediately styled me by a new appellation, to me the most desirable in the world, which was freeman. . . . Some of the sable females, who formerly stood aloof, now began to relax and appear less coy . . ." (104). Vassa knows that it is scarcely "coyness" that has distanced him from "sable females" during his servitude. The impediment to union has always been the commercial "man in the middle," first encountered on his departure from his sister.

The economics of slavery reduced the African man to laboring chattel; it also reduced African women to sexual objects. After his description of separation from his sister, Vassa concludes the apostrophe cited earlier with the fear that she may have fallen victim to "the lash and lust of a brutal and unrelenting overseer" (24). The probability of such a fate for a young African girl is implicitly heightened in *The Life* by the narrator's own later account of the behavior of his shipmates on a trading sloop:

> It was almost a constant practice with our clerks, and other whites, to commit violent depredations on the chastity of the female slaves; and these I was, though with reluctance, obliged to submit to at all times, being unable to help them. When we have had some of these slaves on board my master's vessels, to carry them to other islands, I have known our mates to commit these acts most shamefully, to the disgrace, not of Christians only, but of men. I have even known them to gratify their brutal passion with females not ten years old. (73–74)

Not "coyness," then, but a disruptive economics that sanctions rape and precludes African male intervention causes sable females to stand aloof. Yet the successful negotiation of such economics is, paradoxically, the *only* course that provides conditions for a reunification of woman and sable man.

It is, ultimately, Vassa's adept mercantilism that produces the conflation of a "theory" of trade, an abolitionist appeal, and a report of African conjugal union that conclude *The Life of Olaudah Equiano*. After attesting that "the manufactures of this country [England] must and will, in the nature and reason of things, have a full and constant employ, by supplying the African markets" (190), the narrator depicts the commercial utopia that will result when the slave trade is abolished and free commerce is established between Africa and Britain. The abolitionist intent of his utopian commercial theory is obvious. If British manufacturers become convinced of the profitability of ending the slave trade, then it must of necessity come to an end for lack of economic and political support. The Africans who successfully negotiate their way through the dread exchanges of bondage to the type of expressive posture characterizing *The Life*'s conclusion are surely those who have repossessed themselves and, thus, achieved the ability to reunite a severed African humanity.

The conflation of economics and conjugal union is strikingly captured by the last sentence of the penultimate paragraph of Vassa's work. The narrator says: "I remained in London till I heard the debate in the House of Commons on the slave trade, April the 2nd and 3rd. I then went to Soham in Cambridgeshire, and was married on the 7th of April to Miss Cullen, daughter of James and Ann Cullen, late of Ely" (192). A signal image, indeed, is constituted by the free, public African man, aware of and adept at the economics of his era, participating creatively in the liberation of his people and joined, with self-possessed calmness, in marriage. It is an image unique to a discourse that originates in "commercial deportation" and recounts with shrewd adeptness the myriad incumbencies of the economics of slavery.

The ideological analysis of discursive structure that yields the foregoing interpretation of *The Life of Olaudah Equiano* is invaluable for practical criticism. It discovers the social grounding—the basic subtext, as it were—that necessarily informs any genuinely African American narrative text. What I want explicitly to claim here is that all African American creativity is conditioned by (and constitutes a component of) a historical discourse that privileges certain economic terms. The creative individual (the *black subject*) must, therefore, whether deliberately or not, come to terms with "commercial deportation" and the economics of slavery. The subject's very inclusion in an *African American* traditional discourse is, in fact, contingent on an encounter with such privileged economic signs of African American discourse. The "already-said," so to speak, contains unavoidable preconditions for the practice of African American narrative.

However, a randomly chosen black narrative will not automatically confirm—on the basis of its author's life situation and the "content" of the text—traditional adages about a determinant relationship between means of production and general cultural consciousness (i.e., commerce does not determine consciousness). What seems to hold, instead, is that under ideological analysis certain recurrent, discursive patterns suggest a unified economic grounding for African American narratives. In the nineteenth century, for example, the *Narrative of the Life of Frederick Douglass, an American Slave* (1845) reads, in ideologically analytical terms, like a palimpsest of Vassa's "traditional" account. To the properly adapted eye, Douglass's work comprises a manuscript in which the "already-said" is unequivocally visible. And the palimpsestic character of his narrative predicts that its superimposition on Vassa's work will reveal a tracing of the eighteenth-century African's economic topography in all major details. A view of episodes in the *Narrative* foregrounded by the ideological notion of the palimpsest serves to illustrate.

"My mother and I were separated when I was but an infant—before I knew her as my mother," asserts the narrator of *Narrative of the Life of Frederick Douglass* (48;

Penguin, 1982). "It is a common custom," he continues, "in the part of Maryland from which I ran away, to part children from their mothers at an early age. . . . I do not recollect of ever seeing my mother by the light of day. She was with me in the night. She would lie down with me, and get me to sleep, but long before I waked she was gone." The disruption of black familial relations signaled by the narrator's separation from his mother is equivalent to Vassa's kidnapping and severance from his sister. Douglass's narrator further announces that "it was rumored that my master [Captain Anthony] was my father," and he goes on to condemn unequivocally the "wicked desires," "lust," and "cunning" of slaveholders, traits that enable them to sustain a "double relation of master and father" to their mulatto children (49).

These assertions of the *Narrative* offer a recapitulation of the "man in the middle" first encountered in Vassa's account. The effect of "owners" destroying African American familial bonds (mother-infant, lover-beloved) is forcefully represented in both the *Narrative* and in *The Life of Olaudah Equiano*. The very possibility of black conjugal or familial bonds (legally sustained) is as anomalous within the slave geography of Douglass's *Narrative* as in the West India climate of *The Life of Olaudah Equiano*. In chapter 6 of Vassa's work, for example, the narrator tells of a "very clever and decent free young mulatto man, who . . . had a free woman for his wife, by whom he had a child" (89). A Bermuda captain boards the vessel on which this free man works, lays "violent hands on him," and carries him into slavery where he is "doomed never more in this world to see [his wife or child]" (89). Similarly, in the *Narrative*, Sandy Jenkins's status as slave prevents his living with his free wife in a sustained, day-to-day relationship. His free wife, in fact, lives "about four miles from Mr. Covey's" and can be visited only on Saturday night (80). In a world in which men are property and women victims of the owner's lust, separation and a blunting or eradication of affection are normal. The cruel lengths to which the "man in the middle" will go to reinforce and preserve such norms are indicated not only by Vassa's account of the treatment of African women on trading sloops but also by Douglass's description of his Aunt Hester's fate:

> Aunt Hester went out one night—where or for what I do not know—and happened to be absent when my master desired her presence. He had ordered her not to go out evenings, and warned her that she must never let him catch her in company with a young man, who was paying attention to her belonging to Colonel Lloyd. The young man's name was Ned Roberts, generally called Lloyd's Ned. Why master was so careful of her, may be safely left to conjecture. (51)

Discovering that Hester has, indeed, been in the company of Ned during her absence, the white owner strips her to the waist, binds her to a hook in the joist of the house, and flogs her until she is bloody. Douglass reports: "I was so terrified and horror-stricken at the sight, that I hid myself in a closet, and dared not venture out" (52). Vassa's words—"I was . . . obliged to submit . . . at all times, being unable to help" African women sexually assaulted by white ship's hands—echo through Douglass's report. The only relationship approximating traditional familial or conjugal ones is Douglass's temporary stay with his grandmother. This—like Vassa's brief moments of comfort among those who take him in as youthful servant on his way to the African coast—is a situation that soon ends when Douglass is delivered, as slave property, to the "home plantation of Colonel Edward Lloyd" (53).

The most decisive delivery of the African American slave into labor takes place, however—like Vassa's own transport—by water. The "commercial deportation" of Douglass occurs when the young boy travels on the trading sloop *Sally Lloyd* to Baltimore to serve in the household of Mr. Hugh Auld. On the day that he is transported, the sloop, which normally holds tobacco, corn, and wheat (53), carries "a large flock of sheep" bound for "the slaughterhouse of Mr. Curtis on Louden Slater's Hill" (74). An inland trading vessel and sheep on their way to slaughter are significantly milder features in the representation of deportation than the "*slave* ship . . . riding at anchor" and the "multitude of *black people* of every description *chained* together" encountered in *The Life of Olaudah Equiano.* Nonetheless, the irrevocable break with beginnings, the helplessness of the young boy to determine his own destiny, the cargo status that marks his passage, and his immediately favorable response to the wonders of an alien world of experience are aspects of the voyage from St. Michael's to "the metropole" that cause the *Narrative's* account to accord with Vassa's work.

A few pages after his report of his terrified response to ships and the sea, Vassa describes the treatment that he and his fellow Africans received on their arrival at Barbados: "We were conducted immediately to the merchant's yard, where we were all pent together, like so many sheep in a fold, without regard to sex or age. As every object was new to me, everything I saw filled me with surprise" (32). The conflation of an explicitly powerless situation and an awed and inquisitive response to novelty in *The Life* precedes by more than fifty years Douglass's record of his reaction to Annapolis on his journey to Baltimore: "It was the first large town that I had ever seen, and though it would look small compared with some of our New England factory villages, I thought it a wonderful place for its size—more imposing even than the Great House Farm!" (74). The passage not only signals wonder in the face of chatteldom but also introduces (through a striking temporal juxtaposition) a contrast between agrarian and industrial modes of existence. The capital of an industrially primitive, southern slave state is less impressive than (in words that could only belong to a traveled narrator) some of "our" New England factory villages. Vassa leaves an agrarian life devoid of "mechanics" (27) only to encounter on shipboard the wonders of the quadrant, a world of "mechanical" invention at the farm of his first Virginia master, and, finally, the captains of industry of his day, to whom the concluding remarks of his narrative are directed. Similarly, Douglass moves progressively beyond an agricultural landscape, where slavery is omnipotent, to the freedom of the "New England factory village." Urban experience mediates the progress of both narrators toward the economic sophistication implied by their privileging of industrial norms.

London, for Vassa, represents the most desirable mode of existence imaginable. The residents of the English metropole and the spiritual and secular possibilities it embodies represent for the African occasions for understanding and self-improvement that he feels are available nowhere else. He even rejects, for example, an opportunity while at Guadeloupe to escape slavery because the fleet in which he would have served as a seaman is bound not for England but for "old France" (90–91). It is in London and among Englishmen that Vassa comes to realize the "superiority" of Europeans to Africans and receives the kindly instructions of the Misses Guerin. Douglass's feelings toward Baltimore are scarcely as warmly affectionate as those of Vassa toward London. Still, the nineteenth-century author writes: "Going to live at Baltimore laid the foundation, and opened the gateway, to all my subsequent prosperity" (75). And it is in

Baltimore that Douglass (like Vassa in the English city) discovers the "displaced" maternity of a kindly white womanhood. The familial affections blunted by the "man in the middle" in the feudal regions of slavery find their rejuvenation in the ministrations of white women in the city. The Misses Guerin and Mrs. Hugh Auld offer relationships for Vassa and Douglass that satisfy the slaves' needs for emotional affiliation and intellectual advancement.

The women in the *Narrative* and *The Life of Olaudah Equiano* are represented as examples of the best evangelical-missionary impulses of their day. They are servants and fit disciples of a kind "Providence." Hence, there is a convergence in both Vassa and Douglass of a literacy that accrues from white women's instructions and a Christianity that governs the women's desire to render such instruction. An early result of Vassa's interaction with the Guerins is his baptism. Douglass ascribes his interactions with Sophia Auld to the "interposition of divine Providence in my favor" and also structures his representation of these interactions in implicitly Old Testament terms (75).

Reflecting the slave's literate mastery of Christian instruction and his comprehension of the ironies of his enslaved situation, Douglass's relationship with Sophia Auld is represented in the *Narrative* as a symbolically inverted account of the Fall of Man. On first view, the Edenic calm of the Auld household—a serenity that is emblemized by "a white face beaming with the most kindly emotions"—is seemingly disrupted by the entry of the slave (as serpent?) into the household. The bondsman's presence seems to transform the calm Auld habitat into a domain of "tiger-like fierceness" and calculated deception. Discovering that his wife, Sophia, has begun to instruct Douglass, Hugh Auld severely reprimands her, prohibits future instructions, and delivers a curt lecture on slaves and education. "She [Mrs. Auld] was an apt woman; and a little experience soon demonstrated, to her satisfaction, that education and slavery were incompatible with each other" (82). She becomes a person of "tiger-like fierceness."

One interpretation of Douglass's first educational encounter suggests that it is scarcely the entry of the bondsman that precipitates Mrs. Auld's transformation to tempestuous ire. If, in fact, Mrs. Auld stands in the role of Eve, it is *the slave* who must be figured as her ironical Adam. For he is the subject of providentially ordained instruction and, finally, a partaker of the Tree of Life. The true serpent in the *Narrative*'s short educational drama is Mr. Auld. He storms about in the rhetorically deceptive guise of a father (a patriarch) chastising the sinful intercourse between his "children." But Hugh Auld is far from a chastising Providence. He is much more akin to the legendary serpent, playing in fact the "Antichrist" by successfully tempting Eve (Sophia) to regard the Tree of Life—the bestowal of a *humanizing* instruction—as an interdicted Tree of Knowledge. He insists that the Tree of Knowledge *must* be denied the slave at all costs.

Douglass listens with fascination. The *Narrative* portrays him in this educational scene "in the garden" as a pristine Adam ignorant of the devious ways of the world the slaveholders made. The words of Auld-as-serpent, however, become for the narrator—in an ironic series of inversions—a "new and special revelation" of the source of slaveholders' power. Auld's words paradoxically take on the character of providential wisdom.

His master's injunctions to his wife lead the slave to realize that he is not a dweller in an Eden of urban benevolence but a subjugated victim in an inverted paradise of white denial. Primed by this realization, he sets out from a "false Eden" to discover the *true* path to freedom. Like an allegorical pilgrim or knight, he rejects the bower of soul-destroying ignorance and proceeds "with high hope, and a fixed purpose, at whatever cost of trouble, to learn how to read" (79).

The symbolically inversive account of the Fall of Man that the narrator employs to represent his educational encounter signals the slave's mastery as a "reader." He refuses the role of hapless victim of texts (the slave master's "false" moral rhetoric) and becomes, instead, an astute interpreter and creator of texts of his own. Hence, though Baltimore, like Vassa's London, bestows a traditional literacy and Christianity, Douglass's acquired skills *as reader* enable him to provide his own interpretations for received texts. His ability ultimately results in a tension between two voices in the *Narrative*. The tones of a providentially oriented moral suasion eventually compete with the cadences of a secularly oriented economic voice.

This bifurcation of voices parallels the earlier noted duality in *The Life of Olaudah Equiano*. One autobiographical self in the *Narrative* follows a developmental history that leads from Christian enlightenment to the establishment of Sabbath schools for fellow slaves to a career of messianic service on behalf of abolitionism. Of his address to a predominantly white audience at an abolitionist convention in Nantucket, Douglass says: "It was a *severe cross*, and I took it up reluctantly" (151; my emphasis). A self in contrast to this cross-bearing figure in the *Narrative* follows a course dictated by the economics of slavery.

This other self is a function of the slave's ability "to read." It is a self—or *voice*, if you will—that is *sotto voce*, subtextual, and, in a sense, "after the fact." It provides economic coding for what, on casual first view, appear to be simple descriptions in the service of moral suasion.

Returning for a moment to the first three chapters of the *Narrative*, we recognize that one of the most striking manifestations of the work's economic voice is the description of the wealthy slaveowner Colonel Lloyd's "finely cultivated garden, which afforded almost constant employment for four men, besides the chief gardener, (Mr. M'Durmond)" (59). This garden, which is found at the outset of chapter 3, prefigures the "false" Eden of the Auld encounter in chapter 6. Its description is coded in a manner that makes it the most significant economic sign in the initial chapters of the *Narrative*. The entire store of the slaveholder's "Job-like" (61) riches is imaged by the garden, which was "probably the greatest attraction of the place [the Lloyd estate]" (59). Abounding in "fruit of every description," the garden is "quite a temptation to the hungry swarms of boys, as well as the older slaves . . . few of whom had the virtue or the vice to resist it" (59). While a garden and its attendant temptations comprise a familiar Christian topos, a garden that images *all* the wealth of the "man in the middle" serves Douglass as a secular sign of surplus value.

Surplus value is the created exchange value that accrues to the owner after the subsistence costs of the laborer have been deducted from the price of a consumption good. The classical economist David Ricardo (1772–1823) floundered when he sought to push through his argument for a rigorous labor theory of value. If the value of the "constant capital," or objective factors of production, and the price of labor are perfectly mirrored in the cost of the resultant commodity, wherein, queried Ricardo, lies the profit for the entrepreneur? Marx resolved this dilemma in *Capital* by making a distinction between *labor power* (i.e., the capacity for labor) and actual labor. Of the former, Marx writes, "the minimum value of labour power is determined by the value of the commodities without the daily supply of which the labourer cannot renew his vital energy" (82).

The value of labor power, therefore, is equivalent to a subsistence wage. If such a value can be realized in six hours (i.e., if a commodity can be *produced* in this time, yielding the amount paid by the entrepreneur for labor power), then workers can sustain themselves with what, in Marx's day, amounted to a half-day's labor. But then comes the rub:

> The fact that half a day's labour is necessary to keep the labourer alive during 24 hours, does not in any way prevent him from working a whole day. Therefore, the value of labour power, and the value which that labour power creates in the labour process, are two entirely different magnitudes; and this difference of the two values was what the capitalist had in view when he was purchasing the labour power. . . . The owner of the money has paid the value of a day's labour power; his, therefore, is the use of it for a day; a day's labour belongs to him. The circumstance that on the one hand the daily sustenance of labour power costs only half a day's labour, while on the other hand the very same labour power can work during a whole day, that consequently the value which its use during one day creates is double what he pays for that use, this circumstance is, without a doubt, a piece of good luck for the buyer. (93)

Marx's model of surplus value as one resolution for Ricardo's dilemma and an explanation for the conversion of entrepreneurship into profit begins with free exchange in the market place between laborer and entrepreneur. But since the analysis in *Capital* is grounded in the assumption that "the value of each commodity is determined by the quantity of labor expended on and materialized in it" (89–90), Marx also assumed that the condition of freedom for the laborer was not determinant where surplus value was concerned. "The essential difference between the various economic forms of society, between, for instance, a society based on slave labour and one based on wage labour, lies only in the mode in which . . . surplus labour is in each case extracted from the actual producer, the labourer" (105). Given the scant rations of southern slaves and their daybreak-to-first-dark regimen, the amount of surplus value resulting from plantation production was substantial.

In the case of Colonel Lloyd's garden, the fruits of slave labor are *all* retained by the master. And any attempts by slaves to share such fruits are not only dubbed stealing but are severely punished. Even so, "the colonel had to resort to all kinds of stratagems [beyond mere flogging] to keep his slaves out of the garden" (59).

The image of vast abundance produced by slaves but denied them through the brutality of the owner of the means of production (i.e., the land) suggests a purely economic transformation of a traditional image of the biblical garden and its temptations. Douglass heightens the importance of this economic coding through implicit and ironic detailings of the determination of general cultural consciousness *by commerce*. The folkloric aphorism that a single touch of the "tar brush" defiles the whole is invoked in the *Narrative* as a humorous analogue for Colonel Lloyd's ideological and mystifying designation of those who are denied the fruits of the garden as *unworthy*. The colonel *tars* the fence around his garden, and any slave "caught with tar upon his person . . . was severely whipped by the chief gardener" (59).

The promotion of *tar* (of a *blackness* so sticky and entangling for American conscience that the Tar Baby, from a story of African provenance, has been an enduring cultural transplant) to a mark of low status, deprivation, and unworthiness is commented on by the narrator as follows: "The slaves became as fearful of tar as of the lash. They seemed to realize the impossibility of touching *tar* without being defiled" (59). Blacks, through the *genetic* touch of the tar brush that makes them people of color, are automatically guilty of the paradoxically labeled "crime" of seeking to enjoy the fruits of their own labor.

The "increase in store" of a traditional American history takes on quite other dimensions in light of Douglass's account of the garden in chapter 3. Later in the *Narrative*, he writes of the life of slaves on Thomas Auld's farm: "A great many times have we poor creatures been nearly perishing with hunger, when food in abundance lay mouldering in the safe and smoke-house, and our pious mistress was aware of the fact; and yet mistress and her husband would kneel every morning, and pray that God would bless them in basket and store!" (96). The keenly literate and secular autobiographical self that so capably figures the economics of Lloyd's garden—summing in the process both the nil financial gain of blacks, and their placement in the left-hand, or debit, column of the ledgers of American status—is the same self encountered when the narrator returns as a teenager to southern, agrarian slavery.

At the farm of Mr. Edward Covey, where he has been hired out for "breaking," the *Narrative* pictures four enslaved black men fanning wheat. Douglass comprises one of their number, "carrying wheat to the fan" (107). The sun proves too much for the unacclimatized Douglass, and he collapses, only to be beaten by Mr. Covey for his failure to serve effectively as a mindless ("the work was simple requiring strength rather than intellect") cog in the machine of slave production. Seeking redress from his master (Mr. Thomas Auld), who hired him to Covey, Douglass finds that the profit motive drives all before it: "Master Thomas . . . said . . . that he could not think of taking me from . . . [Mr. Covey]; that should he do so, he would lose the whole year's wages" (110).

The most bizarre profit accruing to the owners in the Covey episode, however, is not slave wages but slave offspring. If Colonel Lloyd would take the fruit of the slave's labor, Mr. Covey would take the fruit of the slave's womb. He puts a black man "to stud" with one of his slave women and proclaims the children of this compelled union his property. This is a confiscation of surplus value with a vengeance. It manifests the supreme aberrancy of relationships conditioned by the southern traffic in human chattel. At Covey's farm, produce, labor, wages, and profit create a crisis that Douglass must negotiate in the best available fashion. He resolves physically to combat Mr. Covey, the "man in the middle."

In contrast to a resolved young Douglass in chapter 10 of the *Narrative* stands Sandy Jenkins, the slave mentioned earlier in this discussion who has a free wife. Sandy offers Douglass a folk means of negotiating his crisis at Covey's, providing him with "a certain *root*," which, carried "*always on* . . . [the] *right side*, would render it impossible for Mr. Covey or any other white man" to whip the slave (111). What is represented by the introduction of Sandy Jenkins is a displacement of Christian metaphysics by African American "superstition." Ultimately, this displacement reveals the inefficacy of trusting solely to any form of extrasecular aid for relief (or release) from slavery.

The root does not work. The physical confrontation does. Through physical battle, Douglass gains a measure of relief from Covey's harassments. Jenkins's mode of negotiating the economics of slavery, the *Narrative* implies, is not *a man's way*, since the narrator claims that his combat with Covey converted him, ipso facto, into *a man*. In the same chapter in which the inefficacy of Jenkins's way is implied, the text also suggests that Jenkins is the traitor who reveals the planned escape of Douglass and fellow slaves to their master Mr. Freeland. Sandy seems to represent the inescapable limiting conditions of African American slavery in the South; he is the pure, negative product of an economics of slavery. Standing in clear and monumentally *present* (even to the extent of a foregrounding footnote) contrast to the Douglass of chapter 10, Sandy represents the virtual impossibility of an escape from bondage on the terms implied by the attempted escape from Freeland's.

At its most developed, *southern* extension, the literate abolitionist self of the *Narrative* engages in an act of physical revolt, forms a Christian brotherhood of fellow slaves through a Sabbath school, and formulates a plan for a *collective* escape from bondage. But this progress toward liberation in the agrarian South is foiled by one whose mind is so "tarred" by the economics of slavery that he betrays the collective. The possibility of collective freedom is thus foreclosed by treachery within the slave community. A communally dedicated Douglass ("The work of instructing my dear fellow-slaves was the sweetest engagement with which I was ever blessed" [120]) finds that revolt, religion, and literacy *all* fail. The slave does, indeed, *write* his "own pass" and the passes of his fellows, but the Sabbath school assembled group is no match for the enemy within.

What recourse, then, is available for the black man of talent who would be free? The *Narrative* answers in an economic voice similar to that found in *The Life of Olaudah Equiano*. Returned to Baltimore and the home of Mr. Hugh Auld after a three-year absence, the teenage slave is hired out to "Mr. William Gardner, an extensive shipbuilder in Fell's Point. I was put there to learn how to calk" (130). In short space, Douglass is able "to command the highest wages given to the most experienced calkers" (134). In lines that echo Vassa with resonant effect, he writes: "I was now of some importance to my master. I was bringing him from six to seven dollars per week. I sometimes brought him nine dollars per week: my wages were a dollar and a half a day" (134). Having entered a world of real *wages*, Douglass is equivalent to the Vassa who realized what a small "venture" could produce. And like Vassa, the nineteenth-century slave recognizes that the surplus value his master receives is but stolen profit: "I was compelled to deliver every cent of that [money contracted for, earned, and paid for calking] to Master Auld. And why? Not because he earned it . . . but solely because he had the power to compel me to give it up" (135).

Like Vassa, Douglass has arrived at a fully commercial view of his situation. He, too, enters an agreement with his master that results in freedom. Having gained the right to hire his own time and to keep a portion of his wages, Douglass eventually converts property, through property, into humanity. Impelled by his commercial endeavors and the opportunities resulting from his free commerce, he takes leave of Mr. Auld. He thus removes (in his own person) the master's property and places it in the ranks of a northern humanity. "According to my resolution, on the third day of September, 1838, I left my chains and succeeded in reaching New York" (143). By "stealing away," Douglass not only steals the fruits of his own labor (not unlike the produce of Colonel Lloyd's garden) but also liberates the laborer—the chattel who works profitlessly in the garden.

The necessity for Douglass to effect his liberation through flight results from the complete intransigence to change of southern patriarchs. Mr. Auld, as the young slave knows all to well, cannot possibly conceive of the child of his "family," of the "nigger" fitted out to work only for his profit, as simply an economic investment. Instead of exchanging capital, therefore, Douglass appropriates his own labor and flees to the camp of those who will ultimately be Auld's adversaries in civil war.

The inscribed document that effectively marks Douglass's liberation in the *Narrative* is, I think, no less an economic sign than Vassa's certificate of manumission:

This may certify, that I joined together in holy matrimony Frederick Johnson and Anna Murray, as man and wife, in the presence of Mr. David Ruggles and Mrs. Michaels.

James W. C. Pennington
New York, Sept. 15, 1938.

What Douglass's certificate of marriage, which is transcribed in full in chapter 11, signifies is that the black man has *repossessed* himself in a manner that enables him to enter the kind of relationship disrupted, or foreclosed, by the economics of slavery.

Unlike Sandy Jenkins—doomed forever to passive acquiescence and weekend visitation—Douglass enters a productive relationship promising a new bonding of African American humanity. As a married man, who understands the necessity for *individual* wage earning (i.e., a mastery of the incumbencies of the economics of slavery), Douglass makes his way in the company of his wife to a "New England factory village" where he quickly becomes a laborer at "the first work, the reward of which was to be entirely my own" (150).

The representation of New Bedford that the *Narrative* provides—with Douglass as wage-earning laborer—seems closely akin to the economic, utopian vision that closes Vassa's account: "Everything looked clean, new, and beautiful. I saw few or no dilapidated houses, with poverty-stricken inmates, no half-naked children and bare-footed women, such as I had been accustomed to see in . . . [Maryland]" (148). Ships of the best order and finest size, warehouses stowed to their utmost capacity, and ex-slaves "living in finer houses, and evidently enjoying more of the comforts of life, than the average slaveholders in Maryland" complete the splendid panorama. Such a landscape is gained by free, dignified, and individualistic labor—the New England ideal so frequently appearing in African American narratives. (One thinks, for example, of the Du Boisian vision in *The Souls of Black Folk* or of Ralph Ellison's Mr. Norton.) The equivalent vision for Vassa is, of course, composed of ships of the finest size and best order plying their transatlantic trade between Africa and England. And presiding over the concluding vision in both narratives is the figure of the black abolitionist spokesman—the man who has arisen, found his "voice," and secured the confidence to address a "general public."

What we experience in the conclusions of Vassa's and Douglass's narratives, however, is identity with a difference. For the expressive, married, economically astute self at the close of Douglass's work represents a convergence of the voices that mark the various autobiographical postures of the *Narrative* as a whole. The orator whom we see standing at a Nantucket convention at the close of Douglass's work is immediately to become a *salaried* spokesman, combining literacy, Christianity, and revolutionary zeal in an individual and economically profitable job of work. Douglass's authorship, oratory, and economics converge in the history of the *Narrative*'s publication and the course of action its appearance mandated in the life of the author.

Since his identity and place of residence were revealed in the *Narrative*, Douglass, who was still a fugitive when his work appeared, was forced to flee to England. In the United Kingdom, he sold copies of his book for profit, earned lecture fees, and aroused sufficient sympathy and financial support to purchase his freedom with solid currency. While his Garrisonian, abolitionist contemporaries were displeased by Douglass's commercial traffic with slaveholders, the act of purchase was simply the logical (and "traditionally" predictable) end of his negotiation of the economics of slavery.

What is intriguing for a present-day reading of the *Narrative*'s history is the manner in which ideological analysis reveals the black spokesperson's economic conditioning—that is, his necessary encounter with economics signaled by a commercial voice and the implications of this encounter in the domain of narrative transaction. The nineteenth-century slave, in effect, *publicly* sells his voice in order to secure *private* ownership of his voice-person. The ultimate convergence of the *Narrative*'s history is between money and the narrative sign. Exchanging words becomes both a function of commerce and a commercial function. Ideological analysis made available by the archaeology of knowledge thus reveals the commercial dimensions of African American discourse.

VI

The commercial dimensions of male narratives such as Vassa's and Douglass's do not exhaust the subtextual possibilities of African American literary discourse. An analysis of an account by a nineteenth-century black woman demonstrates that gender produces striking modifications in the African American discursive subtext. This gender difference does not eradicate the primacy of such governing statements as "commercial deportation" and the "economics of slavery," but it does alter and expand their scope. A view of Harriet Brent Jacobs's *Incidents in the Life of a Slave Girl* (1861) serves to illustrate.

As we read the initial chapters of the account of Linda Brent (the name borne by the narrator of *Incidents*), the word that comes to mind is *abandonment*. The slave girl's father and mother die when she is young, and she passes only a short time under the tutelage of a "kind" mistress. At twelve years of age, she enters the service of Dr. and Mrs. Flint, whose fictitious surname aptly captures the obdurate character of the sister and brother-in-law of her recently deceased mistress. Though she is actually "bequeathed . . . [to Mrs. Flint's daughter], a child of five years old," the slave girl effectively belongs to the elder Flints. The differences between the works of Vassa and Douglass and Brent's *Incidents in the Life of a Slave Girl* almost immediately manifest themselves in the relatively confined space of movement and absence of adventure characterizing the black woman's account. A world of mistresses and slaves-in-waiting emerges from the first chapters of Brent's narrative as an essentially domestic arena in which the female slave will confront her destiny.

But the domestic world of *Incidents* is far removed from the settled, genteel domesticity found in American sentimental novels. Brent's world is one of sudden transitions and violent disruptions, as chapter 2, "The Slaves' New Year's Day," makes clear. The chapter recounts the effects of "commercial deportation" on the life of the slave community. Noting that "hiring-day" in the South is the first day of January, the narrator asserts: "On the 2nd, . . . slaves are expected to go to their new masters" (25; AMS, 1973). Slaves, of course, have no voice in deciding their new location; they are transportable property. The plight of the slave mother under such a system is captured as follows:

> To the slave mother New Year's day comes laden with peculiar sorrows. She sits on her cold cabin floor, watching the children who may all be torn from her the next morning; and often does she wish that she and they might die before day dawns. She may be an ignorant creature, degraded by the system that has brutalized her from childhood; but she has a mother's instincts, and is capable of feeling a mother's agonies. (26)

Commercial deportation has its most profound effects in Brent's narrative on the slave woman's issue, disrupting black familial relations at the level of mother-and-infant.

Douglass's and Vassa's recognition of their own worth within the economic system of slavery prompts them to words of condemnation and acts of liberating mercantilism. In *The Life of Olaudah Equiano* and the *Narrative*, the fact that slave skills and labor yield surplus value is a spur to individualistic economic enterprise. In *Incidents in the Life of a Slave Girl*, by contrast, it is not the value of the female slave's works of hand that is emphasized. Rather, the narrative calls attention time and again to the surplus value deriving from the fruit of the slave woman's womb.

Brent's account explicitly suggests that within the economic system of slavery, the black woman's value is a function of her womb: "Women are considered of no value unless they continually increase their owner's stock. They are put on a par with animals" (76). The narrator does not confine her indictment of this perverse scheme of value to men; she also notes the complicity of southern white women.

> Southern women often marry a man knowing that he is the father of many little slaves. They do not trouble themselves about it. They regard such children as property, as marketable as the pigs on the plantation; and it is seldom that they do not make them aware of this by passing them into the slavetrader's hands as soon as possible, and thus getting them out of sight. (57)

Surely Douglass was aware of the bizarre mores described by Brent; his sketch of life at Edward Covey's demonstrates his awareness. But neither his own life nor his *Narrative* was radically determined by such aberrant mores.

Mulatto children in *Incidents* signify the master's successful sexual aggression; such offspring both increase his stock and mark his domination. The central relationship in Brent's narrative is, in fact, between an implacable male sexual aggression (Dr. Flint as master) and a strategically effective female resistance and retreat (Linda Brent as slave). The appearance of the indefinite article "a" in the title of the narrative implies that this relationship is defining in the life of *any* slave girl.

At age fourteen, after two years in the Flints' service, Brent becomes the beleaguered object of her master's verbal sexual abuse. Flint, who has already fathered eleven mulatto children, becomes the clear antagonist. The black slave girl knows that the battle commenced for her is the general lot of black female adolescents:

She [the black adolescent girl] will become prematurely knowing in evil things. Soon she will learn to tremble when she hears her master's footfall. She will be compelled to realize that she is no longer a child. If God has bestowed beauty upon her, it will prove her greatest curse. That which commands admiration in the white woman only hastens the degradation of the female slave. (45–46)

One of the signal ironies in *Incidents in the Life of a Slave Girl* is that the means adopted by Brent to avoid *conquest* is a willing liaison with yet another white southern man.

Mr. Sands, an educated southerner, becomes the father of the slave girl's children. Though she does increase her master's stock through this transaction, the slave girl is quick to point out the psychological advantage the act brings in her war with Flint:

It seems less degrading to give one's self, than to submit to compulsion. There is something akin to freedom in having a lover who has no control over you, except that which he gains by kindness and attachment. A master may treat you as rudely as he pleases, and you dare not speak; moreover, the wrong does not seem so great with an unmarried man, as with one who has a wife to be made unhappy. There may be sophistry in all this; but the condition of a slave confuses all principles of morality, and, in fact, renders the practice of them impossible. (84–85)

What emerges from the "crisis of . . . fate" that leads Brent to a sexual relationship with Sands is a new morality. This new code of ethics emphasizes a woman's prerogative to control her own sexuality—to govern the integrity of her body. Articulating such a code in a violently patriarchal system is a monumental and dangerous accomplishment. For "fatherhood," under the aspect of slavery, assumed all the connotations of "rape." The "*patriarchal* institution" (288) appears in the eyes of the black adolescent slave as a vast arena of coerced sexual coupling, a prodigal *fathering* of "stock" by the patriarch-as-rapist. Economics and power conflate in the physical and psychological violations of black victims by white masters.

Linda Brent successfully neutralizes this bizarre equation of dominance and gain. Although she has no power to discount his economic gains ("Dr. Flint did not fail to remind me that my child was an addition to his stock of slaves" [94]), she does thwart Flint's power of violation by choosing, on her own initiative, the man who will actually father her child.

The economics of the slave girl's situation finally translates in power terms. Submission to the master's will becomes the only act of value the slave woman can perform in a violent patriarchy. Mr. Sands seeks to purchase the freedom of Brent and her children, but his willingness, as the narrator makes clear in chapter 15, is of little consequence: "The money for the freedom of myself and my children could be obtained; but I derived no advantage from that circumstance. Dr. Flint loved money, *but he loved power more*" (122; my emphasis). It would be tedious to enumerate the multiple instances of Flint's violence in *Incidents*—the blows struck and verbal abuse received. It is sufficient, I think, to note that the only stratagem that serves to obviate his power of abuse is the slave girl's total retreat from scenes of daily life, the interiorization and enclosure that are equivalent to burial alive.

At the beginning of chapter 21, the following description of a southern building appears:

> A small shed had been added to my grandmother's house years ago. Some boards were laid across the joists at the top, and between these boards and the roof was a very small garret, never occupied by anything but rats and mice. It was a pent roof, covered with nothing but shingles, according to the southern custom for such building. The garret was only nine feet long and seven wide. The highest part was three feet high, and sloped down abruptly to the loose board floor. There was no admission for either light or air. (173)

For seven years, this garret (which is certainly more akin to a grave than a garret) serves as Brent's habitat. She takes refuge in it after fleeing the plantation of Dr. Flint. The chapter in which this habitat is described is entitled "The Loophole of Retreat," a phrase rich in connotation. For although the slave girl chooses "retreat" as a strategy, the new position that she occupies is very much a "loophole"—a hole in the wall from which she wages effective combat. Her battle plan results, finally, in the significant transformation of her children's status.

The implacable Dr. Flint, who on several occasions has taken a razor to her throat in attempts to make her submit, eventually comes to regard possession and domination as all-subsuming ends in themselves. "You are mine," he raves after the birth of her first child, "and you shall be mine for life. There lives no human being that can take you out of slavery" (123). The slave's children become, for Flint, means toward his goal of domination. The power he possesses as master of her children compels the slave girl to bear his furious abuse. Brent eventually realizes, however, that if she puts herself beyond his range, Flint will be forced to alter his conception of her children. He will come to perceive them as commercial ends rather than empowering means. "Dr. Flint, would soon get discouraged, and would be willing to sell my children, when he lost all hopes of making them a means of my discovery" (159).

The slave, therefore, creates commodifying conditions for her children's disposition. In a tactically brilliant act of withdrawal, she converts the fruit of her womb (rather than the skill of her hand or the capital of a husbanded store) to merchandise. Her retreat culminates in the children's sale to Mr. Sands. Thus she not only chooses her children's father but also controls, in the final analysis, that second aspect of what Douglass described as the "double relation of master and father." She provides conditions for Mr. Sands to become both father *and* master.

While the commercial, autobiographical selves in Douglass's and Vassa's narratives achieve advantage through derring-do and shrewd financial arrangements with masters, the slave girl in Brent's account secures commercial success by retreat, by nullification of the conditions of the master's implacable force. Fleeing the patriarch-as-rapist, she maintains a physical and psychological integrity that bring the fruits of her labor nearer her own possessing. If in the act of withdrawal she does not achieve immediate conversion of property through property into humanity, she at least provides necessary conditions for such a conversion to occur.

Mr. Sands eventually manumits Brent's children and sends them north. The mother soon follows, making her escape on board a ship to Philadelphia. She moves to New York and enters the service of a white family named Bruce. The second Mrs. Bruce purchases the slave's freedom from Dr. Flint's son-in-law for three hundred dollars.

Hence the garreted withdrawal of chapter 21 commences a commercially successful course of events whose rewards finally include the liberation of Brent and her children.

With the foregoing analysis in mind, it is possible to assert that gender does not alter a fundamentally commercial set of negotiations represented as liberating in the black narrative. The gender of Brent and her narrator does, however, immeasurably broaden the descriptive scope of "commercial deportation" and the economics of slavery. The implied domain of sexual victimization (so briefly represented in male narratives) becomes the dramatically foregrounded topos of the woman's account. And the subtextual dimensions of African American narrative that receive full voice *only* in the work of the black woman include representations of the psychologically perverse motivations of the patriarch-as-rapist, the female slave's manipulation of a sexual and financial partnership outside the boundaries of the master's power, and the strategy of retreat that leads to commercial advantage and physical freedom.

In a sense, the world of the slave woman represented in *Incidents in the Life of a Slave Girl* constitutes "an idea in fiction." Ultimately, Brent is but one figure in what Nina Auerbach calls a "community of women," a sisterhood of slavery that possesses "no majestic titles . . . but must create . . . [its] own, somewhat quirky and grotesque authority" (8). The "grotesqueness" of the authority that accrues to the female slave community (or to any of its individual sisters) is a function of southern patriarchal economics. This system granted such bizarre power to white males that it might well have been designated an "economics of rape."

Linda Brent, her grandmother, mother, fellow slaves including Betty and Fanny, her daughter and countless others implied by the indefinite article of the narrative's title share a collective identity that makes them, in a final phrase from Auerbach's searching study, "a furtive, unofficial . . . underground entity" (11). This entity has its being in seclusion but achieves its expressive effects in the generic expansions that it entails for African American discourse.

A community of women, as represented by Linda Brent, controls its own sexuality, successfully negotiates (in explicitly commercial terms) its liberation from a crude patriarchy, and achieves expressive fullness through the literate voice of the black, female author. *Incidents in the Life of a Slave Girl* is intended, we are told in the work's preface, to make manifest to "the women of the North" the "condition of two million woman at the South, still in bondage, suffering what I suffered, and most of them far worse" (6). Unlike the narratives of Vassa and Douglass, Brent's work gives a sense of *collective*, rather than individualistic, black identity. Nurtured and supported by a sisterhood yoked by common oppression, Brent does not seek the relationship of marriage that signals a repossession of self and the possibility of black reunification in male narratives. True to a governing condition of her communal status, Brent's account concludes with a vision that stands in dramatically marked contrast to the image of a black woman miserably awaiting the "commercial deportation" of her children:

Reader, my story ends with freedom; not in the usual [read: male] way, with marriage. I and my children are now free! We are as free from the power of slaveholders as are the white people of the north; and though that, according to my ideas, is not saying a great deal, it is a vast improvement in *my* condition. (302)

A new bonding of African American humanity consists, for Brent, in the reunion of mother and child in freedom.

Brent's narrative was edited by Lydia Maria Child, the white abolitionist noted for her *Appeal in Favor of That Class of Americans Called Africans* (1833). And *Incidents* contains an appendix by another nineteenth-century white woman by the name of Amy Post. The laudatory testimony to Brent's character and achievement provided by both white women—in "introduction" and "appendix" respectively—suggests that the author's expressive goal of arousing "women of the North" was admirably accomplished. That we recognize, in a present-day reading, the strong contours of a "community" of black women joined by common economics and capable of stunning negotiations of a mercantile oppression testifies to the nineteenth-century black woman's enduring success.

In *Archetypal Patterns in Women's Fiction*, Annis Pratt decodes the image of Apollo's rape of Daphne as a "displacement." The warlike male, according to Pratt, attempts to rape the nymph-goddess and institute his authority in her dominions by controlling "logos," or the word. Daphne's alternative is biological change: she transforms herself into a laurel. There is a striking difference between Pratt's decoding of a traditional archetype and the explanation we might offer of Linda Brent's figuration of a community of female slaves. In Brent's account, women must indeed *transform* themselves in order to avoid the implacable, warlike aggression of masters. But unlike Daphne, they retain both human form and a quintessentially human power of the word. Transforming herself into a withdrawn celibate, the slave woman issues, even from her gravelike garret, letters to Dr. Flint that foil his schemes of possession and domination. Once she is in the North, her power of the word is transmuted to public abolitionism and the communally oriented ends of sisterly liberation. By successfully negotiating the economic domain traditionally marked and controlled by a male exteriority, Brent achieves an effective expressive posture. She attains a voice that can both arouse public sympathy and invoke sisterly communion by imaging a quite remarkable community of black women. Under the aegis of ideological analysis, this community reveals itself as a striking expansion of the subtextual dimensions of traditional African American discourse.

VII

The subtext that emerges from ideological analyses of male and female slave narratives reveals the "traditional" dimensions of such narratives. The commercial subtextual contours of eighteenth- and nineteenth-century black narratives find their twentieth-century instantiations in works that are frequently called "classic" but that are seldom decoded in the ideological terms of a traditional discourse. It is vital, however—if we are to derive full value from the archaeology of knowledge in discovering a uniquely African American discourse—to recognize the subtextual bonding between a novel such as, say, Zora Neale Hurston's *Their Eyes Were Watching God* and its *African American* narrative antecedents.

An ideological analysis of *Their Eyes Were Watching God* reveals the endurance and continuity of a discourse that finds its earliest literate manifestations in slave narratives. By revealing the effects of "commercial deportation" and the economics of slavery in Hurston's work, ideological analysis makes available, from the standpoint of practical criticism, new meanings. At a more general level of the archaeology of knowledge, the analysis moves us closer to the realization that a Foucaultian "rupture" exists between traditional American history and literary history and an alternative African American discourse. The relationship between Hurston's subtext and that of narratives discussed so far provides adequate grounds for postulating a literary history quite different from a traditional "American literary history." An examination of *Their Eyes Were Watching God* serves to clarify.

The property designation of an "economics of slavery," as Linda Brent's narrative makes abundantly clear, meant that the owner's sexual gratification (forcefully achieved) was also his profit. The children resulting from such a violation followed the enslaved condition of their mother, becoming property. "Succeeding generations," as we have seen in the previous discussion, translated as "added commodities" for a master's store. The Civil War putatively ended such a commercial lineage.

Zora Neale Hurston's *Their Eyes Were Watching God* traces a fictive history that begins with the concubinage of Nanny to her white owner. The relationship results in the birth of the protagonist's mother. Nanny's experiences have endowed her with what she describes as "a great sermon about colored women sittin' on high" (32). There are, however, no observable phenomena—either in her own progress from day to day or in the surrounding world—to lend credibility to her unarticulated text. She feels that the achievement of a "pulpit" from which to deliver such a sermon is coextensive with the would-be preacher's obtaining actual status on high. In a sense, Nanny conflates the securing of property with effective expression. Having been denied a say in her own fate because she was *property*, she assumes that *only* property enables expression. *Their Eyes Were Watching God* implies that she is unequivocally correct in her judgment and possesses a lucid understanding of the economics of slavery.

The pear tree metaphor—the protagonist's organic fantasy of herself as an orgasmic tree fertilized by careless bees—is a deceptively prominent construct in *Their Eyes Were Watching God*; it leads away from the more significant economic dimensions of the novel so resonantly summed up by Nanny. This romantic construct is, in fact, introduced and maintained in the work by a nostalgic, omnipresent narrator. For Janie's true (authorial?) grounding is in the parodic economics of black middle-class respectability marked by Logan Killicks and Joe Starks.

These two black men are hardly "careless" bees. Rather, they possess the busyness characteristic of the proverbial bee in another of his manifestations—the "industrious bee." Joe Starks is so intent on imitating the economics of Anglo-American owners that he, paradoxically, manages to obtain a fair abundance of goods; he becomes wealthy, that is to say, by African American standards. It is finally Starks's property, gained through industriousness, that brings about Janie's "freedom."

When Starks dies, the protagonist discovers that she is left with both "her widow-hood and property" (139). One might suggest that Vergible Woods, or "Tea Cake," the young man who appears to fill the bee's slot in Janie's fantasy, is less a "cause" of freedom than a derivative benefit. Janie confidently asserts of her relationship with Tea Cake: "Dis ain't no business proposition, and no race after property and titles." But she is able to make this claim because she sells Starks's store to finance the relationship (171). The attentions of a young man, after all, do not in themselves guarantee that a relationship will be a "love game," as the dreadful example of a deceived and stranded Mrs. Annie Tyler proves (177–79). It is important to note, however, that the term "Starks's store" disguises, at least in part, the fact that a share of the store as a commodity is surely a function of the protagonist's labor. Janie works for years in the store without receiving more than subsistence provisions. The "surplus value" that accrues from her labor as equity is rightfully hers to dispose of as she chooses.

Their Eyes Were Watching God is, ultimately, a novel that inscribes, in its very form, the mercantile economics that conditioned a "commercial deportation." If Janie is, in the last analysis, a person who delivers a text about "colored women sittin' on high," she is one who delivers this text from a position on high. Her position derives from the petit bourgeois enterprises she has shared with her deceased husband.

To say this is not to minimize the force of Janie's lyrical, autobiographical recall. She can, indeed, be interpreted as a singer who (ontogenetically) recapitulates the blues experience of all black women treated as "mules of the world." She is, indeed, a member of a community of black women. And the expressiveness that she provides in her bleak situation in a racist South is equivalent to the song of Sleepy John Estes that qualifies the bleakness of Winfield Lane.

The descent to the "muck" that provides Janie's artistic apprenticeship among the "common folk" is, nonetheless, unequivocally a function of entrepreneurial, capitalist economic exchange. (Zora Hurston's own trip to the South to collect her people's lore was financed by a rich white patron, Mrs. Rufus Osgood Mason.) The duality suggested by Janie's blues song and its capitalist enabling conditions is simply one manifestation, finally, of the general dilemma of the African American artist born from an economics of slavery.

The protagonist of *Their Eyes Were Watching God* is known to her childhood cohorts as "Alphabet" because she has been given so many "different names" (21). Likewise, the African American artist has been marginally situated in American culture, without a single, definite name, but embodying within herself the possibility of all names—the alphabet. The only way to shape a *profitable*, expressive identity in such a situation is to play on possibilities—to divide one's self, as Janie does, into "public" and "private" personalities.

In the example of the African American artist, this has meant shaping an expression to fit the marketplace—an act akin to Janie's voluntary silences and seeming complicity in the public, commercial world of her husband's store. Once adequate finances are secured, however, the alphabet can be transformed (as Vassa, Douglass, and Jacobs all demonstrate) into the manifold combinations that make for expressive authenticity. Janie, for example, goes south, gains experience, and returns to the communal landscape of Etonville as a storyteller and blues singer par excellence.

Her striking expressiveness within the confines of Etonville, however, is framed, or bracketed, by the bourgeois economics of Anglo-America. The terrible close of her arcadian sojourn on the "muck" is a return, in the company of a rabidly infected Tea Cake, to a viciously segregated world. A sign of the type of relationships sanctioned by such a world is the mad (male) dog atop the back of a terrified female cow (245). (The patriarchal economics of Brent's work come forcefully to mind.) Given a world implied by such a sign and by the Jim Crow ethics of the urban environs that Janie and Tea Cake enter, where can the protagonist sing her newly found song of the folk? Having discovered the terrible boundaries on her freedom and its expressive potentialities, she returns to sing to an exclusively black audience.

An ideological reading of *Their Eyes Were Watching God* thus claims that the novel inscribes not only the economics signaled by "commercial deportation" but also the economic contours of the African American artist's dilemma. Nanny, Janie's grandmother, is resoundingly correct in her conclusion that the pulpit (a propertied position on high ground) is a prerequisite for a stirring sermon. From an ideological perspective, Hurston's novel is a commentary on the continuing necessity for African Americans to observe property relationships and to negotiate the restrictions sanctioned by the economics of slavery if they would achieve expressive wholeness.

Janie does not *transcend* the conditions occasioned by commercial deportation; she, like the narrative protagonists of her discursive predecessors, adapts profitably to them. And like many thousands gone before, she sings resonantly about the bleak fate and narrow straits that such an adaptation mandates. Her song is not identical to the unmediated folk expression of those many thousands gone before. Despite its authentic dialectal transcription, her blues for the townfolks' consumption are made possible— financed, as it were—by a bourgeois economics. They are, in this respect, allied to entertainment. The full contours of the expressive dilemma she so successfully negotiates become even clearer in the analysis of such succeeding examples of African American narrative as Ralph Ellison's *Invisible Man*.

If my judgment of Hurston's work fails to accord with more romantic readings of *Their Eyes Were Watching God*, at least it possesses the virtue of introducing essential, traditional, subtextual dimensions of African American discourse into the universe surrounding the novel. It is difficult to see how economic and expressive-artistic considerations can be ignored in treating a narrative that signals its own origination in a "commercial deportation." Surely *economics*, conceived in terms of an ideology of narrative form like that represented in the foregoing analyses, has much to contribute to an understanding of the classic works of an expressive tradition grounded in the economics of slavery.

The value of the archaeology of knowledge and the ideological perspective it occasions does not lie exclusively in an expanded, practical criticism of African American narratives, however. The specific governing statements I have introduced could be replaced (and an entirely different discursive structure constituted) by alternative governing statements. "Territorial invasion," for instance, might serve especially well to structure a Chicano or Native American literary history. The archaeology of knowledge vis-à-vis American literary history need not be confined to a single expressive frame of reference.

The greater utility of archaeology consists in the fact that it asks questions about *the nature and method of history and literary history in themselves*, bringing into question the role of ideology in literary history and literary study in general. The mode of thought occasioned by Foucault's project, therefore, might well be employed to substitute other American constructs for "African American history" and "African American literary history." But such displacements could not occur without further raising the kinds of questions and motivating the type of analyses that have characterized the foregoing discussion.

VIII

In recent years there have been dramatic shifts in both the elements and ideological ordering principles deemed essential for American historical and American literary historical discourse. At the level of practical criticism, such shifts have offered conditions for revised readings of traditional texts. At a more global level, however, reconceptualizations of historical discourse have led to the laying bare, the surfacing and re-cognition, of myriad unofficial American histories. I believe that these seismic shifts in the universe of American historical discourse are precisely the types of upheavals that Foucault has in mind when he speaks of "ruptures."

Epistemological cataclysms in historical discourse being to view dimensions of experience excluded from extant accounts. And in the reordering effected by such ruptures (i.e., their constitution of revised models), one discovers not only new historical terms but also the variant historicity of the statements and terms of a traditional discourse. In *The Archaeology of Knowledge,* Foucault explains that a rupture is not a "great drift that carries with it all discursive formations at once"; instead, it is a "discontinuity specified by a number of distinct transformations, between two particular positives" (175).

One would not, by any stretch of the archaeological imagination, expect a resolute totality such as "American history" to disappear without a trace in the transformation that marks the emergence of new positivities. Foucault writes:

> To say that one discursive formation is substituted for another is not to say that a whole world of absolutely new objects, enunciations, concepts, and theoretical choices emerges fully armed and fully organized in a text that will place that world once and for all; it is to say that a general transformation of relations has occurred, but that it does not necessarily alter all the elements; it is to say that statements are governed by new rules of formation; it is not to say that all objects or concepts, all enunciations or all theoretical choices disappear. (173)

The content of ideologically oriented analyses like those above is a sign of the rupture effected when traditional American history and literary history are subjected to epistemological shift. They suggest a different *America,* without totally discounting the terms of a dated perspective.

A less diachronically analytical view of the epistemological rupture is offered by an example drawn from the very African American literary discourse that stems from commercial deportation. The illustrative, figurative example that I have in mind appears in Ralph Ellison's *Invisible Man* at the point in that narrative where the protagonist wanders into a New York subway station (and, hence, beneath the official surface of things). Underground, the invisible man studies "three boys . . . tall and slender, walking stiffly with swinging shoulders in their well-pressed, too-hot-for-summer suits, their collars high and tight about their necks, their identical hats of black cheap felt set upon the crowns of their heads with severe formality about the hard conked hair" (429–30; Random, 1972). The boys seem to him "outside . . . historical time." Yet they are undeniably *present* in the fastidiousness of their style. The protagonist is thus compelled to alter both his historical catalog and his tacitly held ideology of history. His observations occasion an epistemological shift—an enlargement of perspective that alters his notions of historicity altogether.

Ascending into Harlem, he surveys an urban scene full of black men and women who share the boys' unique style. He reflects in shock and amazement: "They'd been there all along, but somehow I'd missed them. I'd missed them even when my work had been most successful. They were outside the groove [record, phonograph disk] of history, and it was my job to get them in, all of them" (432–33).

The experience of *Invisible Man*'s protagonist is like that of a number of "minority" (i.e., those who have little *power* in the academy) literary scholars in recent years. As such spokespersons—in the roles of activist, critic, teacher, scholar, and so on—have pursued what has been specified in this essay as the archaeology of knowledge, they have revealed the limiting boundaries of traditional American historical discourse. They have also discovered, in the process, new elements and governing statements that they have framed according to specific ideological principles. In brief, such scholars have demonstrated through a form of dialectical (and, at times, extraordinarily "tropological") thought that their literary histories have been present all along but somehow "missed" by the official historians.

One reason that official historians have missed dimensions of experience currently surfacing is that they have refused to grant due attention to what I have referred to as synchronic and metaphoric signs of unofficial histories. The metaphoric dimensions that arise in African American discourse from sagging cabins, felt blues, and fastidious style must be apprehended in their vertical (or synchronic) completeness if one wishes to elaborate exacting accounts of African American history and African American literary history.

Ellison seems patently aware of this stipulation. In the moment of epistemological rupture and historical renewal in *Invisible Man*, his protagonist slowly becomes aware of "the growing sound of a record shop loudspeaker blaring a languid blues. I stopped. Was this all that would be recorded? Was this the only true history of the times, a mood blared by trumpets, trombones, saxophones and drums, a song with turgid, inadequate words" (433)? Indeed, the very fact that the protagonist hears a *recorded* blues (one designed for commercial duplication and sale) speaks to the historical and literary historical possibilities of the single, imagistic figure, or trope. For if the blues heard by the invisible man *are* history, they are not constituted as such in any simple sense. The economics that these recorded blues signal in an era of multinational corporations, mass markets, and advertised commodities recapitulates, in striking ways, the black artist's dilemma depicted in *Their Eyes Were Watching God*. What is one's true history? How can its presentation be *financed*? And for whom can one sing of blues and "the man"? In brief, Ellison's blues of historical renewal may well signify (like the expressiveness of those gone before) the scarcity and brutalization of an economics of slavery. But they also reveal an economic complexity that implies black men and women negotiating slavery's tight spaces in movingly expressive ways. The blues, considered as an economically determined and uniquely black "already-said," are both inscribing and formally inscribed in an African American discourse whose very *presence* demands their comprehension.

(And so . . . we are left with the song known at the outset. A traditional American history and literary history give way before the blues artist's restless troping mind:

You know I laid down last night,
You know I laid down last night, and tried to take
*   me some rest,*
But my mind got to ramblin' like wild geese
*   from the west.*
                                    Skip James

The "rambling" is meaning embedded in rocky places. Its discovery creates a vastly enlarged perspective. Indeed, if one were to put forward a model of American literary history to represent present knowledge, it would be far more akin to Louis Dollo's accounts than to the prosaic quadripedalism of Gideon Mantell's England of the 1850s.)

Notes

[1] The story of Gideon Mantell and Iguanodon is captivatingly recorded in Edwin H. Colbert's *Men and Dinosaurs*. I want to thank Alan Mann for introducing me to both the story and the reference.

[2] The classic statement of this construction of American history is, of course, Perry Miller's *Errand into the Wilderness.*

[3] In *Literature and the American Tradition*, Leon Howard details the conviction held by Puritans and Pilgrims alike that their signal task was to establish New World communities that would facilitate God's plan to constitute the earthly paradise in America.

[4] I am indebted to E. H. Gombrich's "In Search of Cultural History," in his *Ideals and Idols*, for its insights on providential and cultural history.

[5] The convergence of ministers and professors, classrooms and pulpits, is a function of American higher education's beginnings and primary associations. Carved on the gates of Harvard College are the following words:

> After God had carried us safe to *New-England*, and we had builded our houses, provided necessaries for our liveli-hood, rear'd convenient places for Gods worship and settled the Civill Government; One of the next things we longed for, and looked after was to advance *Learning* and perpetuate it to Posterity; dreading to leave an illiterate Ministry to the Churches, when our present Ministers shall lie in the Dust.

Learning and religious learning, in the quoted passage, stand in a relationship of identity. The contours of providential immigration and development that characterize the discourses Harvard was established to teach mark that institution's own statement of mission. Ministers at the "seminary in the wilderness" are thus capable of teaching American history and literary history because they, too, are part of the civilizing "errand." In order to fulfill their role, they are required to bring to notice and perpetuate those historical accounts and literary works of art that reveal God's divine plan for the world working itself out in his dealings with New England.

[6] I am aware of Foucault's disagreements with the structuralist project. But I am also aware that he (and his hypothetical questioner in the conclusion to *The Archaeology of Knowledge*) concede certain analytical successes to that project (201). Further, I am certain that Barthes's analysis of historical discourse is far less concerned with what Foucault disparages as notions of a "constituent consciousness" (302) than with the "discursive formation" of historical discourse examined in its "dispersed" totality. Looking ahead, we can say much the same of Lévi-Strauss's essay "History and Dialectic," which I refer to later in the discussion.

[7] One suspects that it was this type of "spiritual revenue" that D. H. Lawrence had in mind when he described the God of eighteenth-century America as "the supreme servant of men who want to get on, to *produce*. Providence. The provider. The heavenly store-keeper. The everlasting Wanamaker. And this is all the God the grandsons of the Pilgrim Fathers had left. Aloft on a pillar of dollars . . . He is head of nothing except a vast heavenly store that keeps every imaginable line of goods, from victrolas to cat-o-nine tails" (15, 27).

[8] I have relied heavily on the works of Genovese for my claims about slavery in the Old South.

Canonical and Noncanonical Texts: A Chicano Case Study

Juan Bruce-Novoa

for Emir Rodríguez Monegal
In memoriam

Canon, we are reminded repeatedly by those who study the topic, derives from the Greek *kanōn,* meaning rod, measuring line, standard; the word passed through the Latin *canon,* with the definition model or standard, then to assume its ecclesiastical character in the Middle Ages as part of the Catholic church's terminology: law, rule, doctrine; the unchangeable, central part of the mass ritual; and, finally, the list of sacred books. From here, the application to literature is clear. Yet contemplating the history of national literary canons, I constantly am tempted to check whether the subject might not also appear under *cannon,* a word with a clearly distinct etymology but synecdochically relevant for our etiology: a weapon consisting of a tube for focusing power in a small area in order to project an object great distances, either for the defense of strategically important places or for an assault on enemy fortifications; a weapon built up through a series of forgings, often with overlays and reinforcing coils; a weapon of such great weight that it requires the support of a mount or carriage. In the wake of popular revolutions that threatened absolutism—in the English American colonies and France—the cannon was applied to crowd control by that defender of the people's revolution turned empire builder, Napoleon. The cannon was capable of projecting almost anything, even human beings, as long as they were stuffed down on top of a charge fitting the caliber and design of the piece. Until the advent of the airplane, cannon power was virtually synonymous with national power, yet another synecdochical link with its false cognate. Unfortunately, however, no similar technology has appeared to displace the other canon from its synonymic relationship with centralized nationalism.

Nationhood and literature have found themselves closely allied, particularly in the Occident since the invention of print. Walter J. Ong points out that certain regional dialects invested heavily in writing, eventually developing chirographically beyond neighboring tongues until they assumed the status of national languages (*Orality* 106–07). Once this hegemony was achieved, the state invested even more in maintaining and even exporting its language and written products as part and parcel of the political and economic national program. The utilization of writing in the building of nation-states has long been recognized. While George Steiner rightfully credits the German Romantics with setting the precedent, in the West, for the creation of national identity through the teaching of one's literary heritage (78–82), he fails to note that nationalistic politicos in Spain had waged literary warfare against the Franks and Moors centuries before Romanticism. After the Moors were expelled, in 1492, the Catholic kings set about institutionalizing their new bicephalous state through, among other centralizing vehicles, a grammar and dictionary of Castellano. It is no coincidence that shortly after 1492, Spanish literature began its Golden Age, one that roughly corresponds to the apex of the Spanish world empire and the invincibility of the Spanish infantry. And when the Spanish conquered their most spectacular colony, New Spain, they had no way of knowing that Tlacaelel, the mastermind behind Aztec ascendancy in the century preceding the Spanish invasion, had demonstrated a keen understanding of the significance of written texts when he ordered the Indian codices burned and rewritten in terms more favorable to his own tribe. Nor could Tlacaelel have foreseen that the Spaniards would ignite their own fires, repeat the burning to clear the way for the imposition of a European rewriting of American history, the first in a long series of colonial impositions on our continent.

National literatures and national histories go hand in hand, as chauvinistic, rhetorical weapons—selective representations designed to produce a coherent past and a flattering self-portrait. These textual axis-mundi inform succeeding generations of citizens and can expand to colonize foreigners, as the Aztecs and Spaniards proved even before the United States existed. In the process, enemies are defined, territories drawn, suffrage granted or denied, and the fundamental national definition of good and evil established.

The United States, born into the age of print, did not avoid the nationalistic pattern. Despite the efforts to jettison Old World prejudice, the founders of American literature displayed an intolerance equal to that of European critics who scorned the upstart writers across the ocean. While we must acknowledge the great variety of opinions constituting the country's heritage as usually studied, from an outsider's point of view, Timothy Dwight characterized the chauvinism of the literary canon rather well in 1776: it would reflect a "people, who have the same religion, the same manners, the same interests, the same language, and the same essential forms and principles of civil government. . . . A people, in all respects one . . . indeed a novelty on earth" (qtd. in Spencer 3). This arrogant and highly political statement demonstrates well the close ties of literary canonists and nation builders. That it came from Yale (the valedictory address in the year of independence), one of the traditional seats of canonizing activity, is of no small consequence. Nations and canons were built simultaneously, not on the playing fields of West Point but in the classrooms of our major universities.

From the start, then, whether looking into the past to salvage texts, or creating new ones, the guardians of the literary canon have excluded other major language groups within or bordering on its national territory. That canon has been the servant, or progenitor, to historiography's paradigm of British stock, the melting pot, and westward expansion. Students are not taught to conceive of the United States as the product of multiple and simultaneous national colonization that ruthlessly displaced Native American peoples. Nor could students find, until recently, literary anthologies that juxtaposed to Cotton Mather samples of Native American oral tradition. For that matter, one is still never told that Mather was so obsessed with Latin America that he learned Spanish and wrote the first book in that language by an English-speaking resident in what is now the United States. A similar attitude can be found in Samuel Sewall, Benjamin Franklin, and Thomas Jefferson, to mention often anthologized names. It seems that the "founding fathers" of our literary-national state had a broader picture of the country's international and intertextual status than those who, over the years, have been in charge of trimming the canon to more isolationist proportions. What can we expect students to say of the dynamic field of early American history and literature if no writings from French explorers or missionaries, or their Spanish counterparts, are included in anthologies? Is Mather's narrow "American pen" vision more basic to our present understanding than the journal of Cabeza de Vaca's wandering from Florida to Texas (1555) or Villagrá's poem on the settlement of New Mexico (1610)? Their mere existence debunks paradigms of cultural exclusivity or priority on this continent. Which seems the more appropriate foundation for the expansiveness of the spirit of mobility, the Puritans' limited vision of the house on the hill or the Spaniards' will to venture far beyond the limits? Would the national self-image not be better balanced and more realistic if these, and other experiences from the past and present, were included in the active dialogue of literature? At least it should be understood that the literary and historical canon has been forged at the expense of a pluralistic perspective more genuinely reflective of the country's development.

In 1883, after a century of anti-British rhetoric that established an independent canon, Whitman, the apotheosis of that process, recognized the danger of its incestuousness. "Impress'd by New England writers and schoolmasters, we Americans tacitly abandon ourselves to the notion that our United States have been fashion'd from the British Islands only . . . which is a very great mistake," Whitman wrote, and then went on to decry the materialism of British and German stock, predicting that balance would come from the Spanish and Native American characters (224). His was still the melting-pot ideal, and every element available had to be added to the mixture to ensure total representation. It is doubtful that even Whitman envisioned a polyglot canon, however; the forging process was aimed at burning out impurities, such as foreign languages, and demanding that all expression be in English. While it is true that the canon has been forced to expand, that expansion has rejected the tendencies of Mather, Jefferson, or Franklin toward at least bilingualism, in favor of Dwight's monolingual-monocultural nationalism. So while it cannot be denied that the New England literary predominance has been eroded by a series of minority writers—southern, Jewish, black, and women— the all-embracing code remains American English, with its inherent biases.

Two of the essential biases of culture in the United States are a general anti-Hispanism and a specific anti-Mexicanism. Thus the recent emergence of a multifaceted cultural identity—which bespeaks an American experience, but speaks sometimes in Spanish and at other times with a Hispanic accent—has been received with nothing short of alarm. The new literary expression represents itself as a legitimate product of this country and, as such, demands a place in the canon. This literature apparently also demands, or at least implies, a radical change in the ideal of one common language and culture. While it is still relatively small in the number of texts it has produced, the literature constitutes the most significant challenge to Anglo-American chauvinism to date. The repressed pluralism lamented by Whitman has begun to surface as a threat to the very material of the canon, language. Language is not ahistorical, however, and the Hispanic challenge affects thematic content as well as form.

I need not repeat Paul Lauter's well-wrought denunciations of the literary canon's class, gender, and racial biases in "Caste, Class, and Canon." I would only emphasize that in the United States, class must always be cross-checked on the grids of language and Hispanophobia. When contextualized this way, what Hispanic literature and history infuse into the canon is radical dialectics. It could be argued, of course, that black, Jewish, feminist, and even mainstream American writers challenge the paradigms of identity, but it is the language difference—a difference present even in Hispanic texts written in English—that makes Hispanic literature a more general threat to the canon. Nationalism has been associated with monolingualism; now the question arises of a polyglot state, which implies a pluralistic alternative to the monism of Timothy Dwight's homogeneous society. By forcing itself onto the nation's consciousness, this historically old, but only recently recognized, ethnic presence demonstrates the truth of a statement made by Fredric Jameson: "American literature has therefore become problematical, not to say impossible, because if it limits itself to the traditional language and form of a national literature it misses the basic truth about itself, while if it attempts to tell those truths it abolishes itself as literature" (*Marxism* 399–400). Ironically, Hispanic literature infuses a negative dialectic even into Jameson's declaration—he came to the conclusion after myopically repeating the ideologeme that capitalism has eliminated the economic lower class from United States territory. A cursory study of Chicano literature proves him wrong, revealing the nationalistic trap into which even our foremost Marxist critic can fall when he reads only canonically.

The pressure to revise the concept of American literature and culture is undeniable. Recent studies and new anthologies attempt to open the canon, while denouncing elitist manipulations of it. Hispanics in the United States continue to publish, and the communities they emerge from and write about and for attract attention as economic and political pressure groups to be courted by the mainstream. The literary canon and its academic-commercial support are faced with a dilemma. It is no longer a matter of absorbing "foreign" expressions within a national literature but of heeding an insistent, multivoiced call for the restructuring of the canon into a polyglot, pluralistic expression of the many nations within a common frontier. The canon is under egalitarian pressure to melt itself down and include more in the next recasting. As that process begins, the mainstream looks to the Hispanic community for guidance, shifting the burden of selection and justification to Hispanic critics, who once thought of themselves free of such consideration. It is to the question of canon and canonizing in one of these groups, Chicanos, that I now turn.

At the beginning of the contemporary Chicano literary movement, 1965–75, any mention of a canon was clearly understood as a reference to mainstream literature, one that conveyed, to those of us involved in the somewhat romantic idealism of what seemed a revolutionary struggle, the image of the elitist Other, the body of works created by Anglo-American or European authors and sanctified by critics of the same class and cultural background. To state that we were excluded from the canon was to utter the obvious. Moreover, there was an ironic feeling of worth associated with being outside the canon, a sense almost of purity, because beyond the exclusionary ethnocentrism implied by the canon, Chicanos infused the term with a criticism of the very existence of a privileged body of texts. The process of selecting and eliminating works to create a superior core of definitive texts seemed less than egalitarian in a movement professing egalitarian ideals. Also, to those of us who were searching for any text we could call Chicano, the idea of excluding some appeared to be a luxury far down the road. And now, after having traveled what in terms of literary history is a short distance down any road, I presume to speak about the canon of the Chicano novel.

The fact is, however, that from the start, Chicano literature has been subjected to a canonizing process, in the basic denotations of the term. Chicanos have been a party to that process, most likely the primary molders of it. First and foremost was the need to find works by Chicanos, materials we could read, discuss, and—a matter of no little concern—compare with the works of other minority groups undertaking similar projects. The attempt at comparison explains, in part, why, at a time when the number of works listed in a Chicano bibliography was minuscule, our then leading critic coined the expression *Chicano Renaissance* (Ortego). Not only was this an obvious imitation of *Harlem Renaissance* but through it a reference to a line of supposed renaissances extending back to the elite category beginning in fourteen-century Europe. I do not mean to open up yet again the fruitless discussion of the virtues and vices of Ortego's term but only to show that we ourselves were involved early on in the canon game, even to the extent of hyberbolizing the small amount of writing we actually had.

That the emphasis, during the first years of the Chicano movement, was on finding any text that could be utilized in literature classes, as well as in political consciousness-raising efforts, might lead one to expect that the earliest canons would have been all-inclusive. If one wanted to teach the Chicano novel in 1970, the choice of titles seemed to be dictated by scarcity: José Antonio Villarreal's *Pocho*, Raymond Barrio's *Plum Plum Pickers*, and Richard Vásquez's *Chicano*. Yet things were not as they seemed, and what appeared a matter of necessity was actually one of choice. Even in that time of need, few critics or teachers included in their bibliographies Floyd Salas's *Tattoo the Wicked Cross* or *What Now My Love*, or Fray Angélico Chávez's *Conquistadora*, and probably only Raymund Paredes would have insisted on one or both of Josephina Niggli's novels. Another Chicano, John Rechy, had published three novels by 1970, two of which (*City of Night* and *Numbers*) had attracted international notoriety among readers and reviewers, yet his works were not taught in Chicano courses then, and, for the most part, they are still excluded. While in the case of Salas and Chávez one could have justified their exclusion because their work lacked literary merit, such an argument would have been more difficult to make in regard to Niggli and Rechy. As for the question of literary merit, we should keep in mind the date, 1970, and those canonized texts that set the standard of the day. In the context of *Pocho*, *Chicano*, and *The Plum Plum Pickers*, the exclusion of Niggli or Rechy on grounds of bad writing was hardly defensible. No, the canon of the Chicano novel from the beginning, like all canons, has been as much a result—if not more so—of implicitly or explicitly expressed needs and ideologies as of formal excellence.

The pressing need at the start of the movement was one of identity, which has since become the favorite topic of Chicano criticism. But the question of identity was not to be resolved through a call of the roll. Political identity could not be the sum of all possible parts of the community but was granted to those who fit into the ideological program. Identity was seen as a process of historical review carried out through an ideology of nation building that stressed several key points: retrieval of family and ethnic tradition, solidarity with the working class, struggle against assimilation, and the dire consequences of not pursuing those goals. Identity was not simply to be found but had to be forged, with attention to history and ideology. In some cases, as in much of the movement poetry, this plan was obvious. The novelist seemed to have been less affected by the ideological consideration. Canons are not the product of authors, however—although they supply the necessary raw material—but rather of readers, critics, and teachers, and in this case the interests of those groups coincided in large part with those of politically involved Chicanos, especially in the educational system, for to teach Chicano literature in 1970 was a political act. The texts chosen by those first teachers lent themselves to allegorical readings of society that the movement desired.

It is no coincidence that *Pocho*, the first of those three novels that formed the core of the Chicano curriculum in 1970, and even beyond, centered on the question of identity as played out in the development of a boy and his immigrant father. *Chicano* expanded that plot to describe the hardships facing the children and grandchildren of another immigrant. Both were family histories of a struggle to define oneself in the environment of the United States and survive with some sense of the old ethnicity. And *The Plum Plum Pickers*, although we can certainly justify it as the clearest of the three in the expression of the ideology of class struggle, can also be seen as the rendering in novel form of what had by 1969 become almost synonymous with the new Chicano identity: Cesar Chavez's United Farm Workers struggle. All three works certainly were taken as metaphors of movement concerns, despite their troublesome contradictions and negative outcome.

Rechy's *City of Night*, however, was another matter altogether. Although this work had sold more copies than the three novels mentioned above put together, few Chicano critics were in a rush to claim it as a success story. The greatest stumbling block was the blatant homosexuality of its characters. Yet sexual preference aside, Rechy had written the most searing denunciation of United States society of any of the Chicano novels. We cannot dismiss the novel for its negative message, for *Pocho* (as usually read) and *Chicano* are no less pessimistic in their portrayal of the disintegration of the Chicano family. Nor is it acceptable to claim that Rechy's characters are too individualistic and thus lacking in communal sensitivity, because the same accusation can be leveled at Villarreal's and Vásquez's characters. What superficially distinguishes *City of Night* from the novels chosen for the canon is the lack of a narrow focus on ethnicity. Rechy does not convert ethnicity into a problem, nor even a necessary context. He neither asserts it nor denies it, but rather lets it exist as one element in the protagonist's background. More significant, however, is another, essential difference: Rechy's novels deny the social values of stability, order, security, and monogamy. His characters reject those familial values that Chicanos, especially in the early movement, considered paramount. At the same time, Rechy revealed the irony of homosexuality's close link with machismo, undermining the chauvinistic stalwart of the male-dominated movement. Rechy's ideology was diametrically opposed to that of the movement and that of the community. At that time—and perhaps it is still true—Rechy's extreme antisocial position could not be appreciated as a metaphor or allegory of liberation. His novels were simply ignored in favor of aesthetically inferior texts that, even though they did not bespeak the movement ideology of triumphant victory over the enemies of the Chicano community, at least stated the problems in the rhetorical terms that the movement wished to employ.

In 1970 there came into existence an effort to create a series of canonized texts: El Premio Quinto Sol. As part of an overall project to foster a Chicano consciousness, if not a Chicano culture itself, the Quinto Sol publishers had taken on the task of stimulating the production of a Chicano literature. It was they who published the first

anthology of Chicano creative writing at a time when there was almost no such literature to be had. (As Tomás Rivera remarked to me years ago, Chicanos were the first
people to have an anthology—*El espejo / The Mirror*, edited by Octavio Romano-V.
and Herminio Rios-C.—before they had a literature.) With the prize awarded for best
work of literature, Quinto Sol intended to repeat the achievement with the novel, and
the success of the venture is unquestionable. No one need be reminded that during the
1970s the three Quinto Sol prizewinners became the most studied and, probably, the
most read Chicano authors. To the satisfaction of some and the continual frustration of
others, Rivera, Anaya, and Hinojosa became the Chicano Big Three. Almost two decades after the last Quinto Sol prize was awarded, and despite the publication of novels
that have tripled the number available, most of the critical attention is still dedicated to
these authors; they are the subjects of more essays and presentations at conferences than
any others.

Do not misunderstand me. I in no way deny the merit of the Big Three, nor take
anyone—editors or conference organizers—to task for what has happened, but simply
observe that this situation was the result, at least in part, of the planned creation of a
canon, a plan that selected and, therefore, also excluded. Everyone in the field knows by
now that Rivera's "Pete Fonseca" story (Valdez and Steiner 146–54) was turned down
by the same Quinto Sol editors who had awarded him the prize, not because it was any
less skillfully written—some consider it his best story—but because it supposedly did
not convey a positive image of Chicanos. The question was one of identity, but the
canonizers had a predetermined image of what that identity was to be. Those canonizers who gave us what many regard as the first truly Chicano novels also assumed the
power to deprive us of other material they deemed unfit. We know they practiced
exclusion in the case of that story by Rivera, but what we do not know is which novels,
if any, were rejected by the Quinto Sol prize committee. We would have to read the
manuscripts to know what was excluded from the canon. As a matter of fact, it would
be interesting to know how many losers competed against the prizewinners, to assess
the state of the field at that time. And if there were any other novels in the running,
what became of them? In this regard the canon has dropped a veil of silence.

It should come as no surprise that two of the three novels awarded the prize focused,
once again, on the search for identity by a young boy. The difference is that Tomás
Rivera's . . . *y no se lo tragó la tierra* and Rudolfo Anaya's *Bless Me, Ultima* end in
positive affirmations of the Chicano community and its creative process, whereas their
earlier counterparts were perceived as moving in the opposite direction. It is also no
surprise that, like *The Plum Plum Pickers*, *Tierra* has as its protagonist what then
seemed the epitome of the Chicano, the farmer-worker. And once again the texts lent
themselves to the allegorical reading of the development of the community, although
now it was through stages of growth to a point at which a healthy and positive maturity
could be projected into the future. Both novels mirrored the ideology of the movement:
find out who you are by learning your history and the lessons inherent in the communal
heritage. Those lessons, and the very process of search and retrieval, would teach survival techniques and sustain life. Although Rolando Hinojosa's *Estampas del valle* did not
seem to fit this mold, it, too, was structured around the need for discovering the oral
tradition, the values, and vital processes of survival of the older generations. And, of
course, *Estampas* was only the first installment in the now multivolumed life, from
childhood to maturity and who knows how much further, of the boys Hinojosa intro-

duced there. In short, Hinojosa too was giving us the image we wanted of ourselves, an affirmation of the process of our communal selves.

Another advantage in these three novels over the previous ones is the apparent separatism. In all of them, despite the constant contact with Anglo-American culture, the characters seem to exist in a separate space. All three novels implicitly posit the possibility of an alternative other space of Chicano existence in which the family and individual can survive as an ethnic entity. All three are rural and as such distance themselves from the contemporary urban setting of the majority of Chicano readers and the United States reading public in general. In addition, they seem distant in a temporal sense: the action appears to take place some decades in the past. None of the works deals with the contemporary urban malaise, and thus they permit, even foster, a nostalgic view of culture.

This period also produced its troublesome novelist: Oscar Zeta Acosta, whose two works coincided with the Quinto Sol prize project (*The Autobiography of a Brown Buffalo*, 1972, and *The Revolt of the Cockroach People*, 1973). There are those who would rather not include Acosta in the canon. His intimate contact with the mainstream counterculture produced the opposite sensation to that discussed in the previous paragraph. In Acosta's works the interaction between Chicano and the great mixture of other groups that make up the United States is too close and ultimately unavoidable. Certainly my Chicano students from Colorado, Texas, Arizona, and New Mexico over the years have consistently expressed the view that Acosta's characters are less than entirely Chicano. And at least one critic, our friend Raymund Paredes, has echoed this sentiment in print. "Acosta wants so desperately to retrieve his ethnic heritage. But the reader is struck by the superficiality of his quest and the flimsiness of the foundation on which he hopes to build his ethnic identity. In the end, Acosta's books seem indistinguishable from numerous other works that lament the destruction of ethnicity in America" ("Evolution" 74). In other words, Acosta's novels should be set afloat in the mainstream where, it is hoped, they will drift off to somewhere well outside the Chicano canon. In the same article Paredes states that "Chicano literature is that body of works produced by United States citizens and residents of Mexican descent for whom a sense of ethnicity is a critical part of their literary sensibilities and for whom the portrayal of their ethnic experience is a major concern" (74). The definition is general enough to be entertained at least, yet Paredes's exclusion of Acosta seems to imply a further criterion. Acosta's concern for his ethnic experience was so important to him that he devoted two books to exploring the traumas it had caused him. Apparently Paredes's added criterion is that one's experience may question ethnicity but in the end must affirm it. This view, of course, would eliminate the protagonists of *Pocho* and *Chicano* as well.

I suspect that, more than the flimsiness of Acosta's ethnic foundation, what bothers some Chicano readers is that Acosta calls into question the insubstantiality of a movement based on ethnicity in the context of a mobile and highly versatile society like that of the United States. His first novel ends with a statement in which the narrator distinguishes between ethnicity as an accident of birth and political commitment as a product of choice. "I am a Chicano by ancestry and a Brown Buffalo by choice" (*Autobiography* 199). Brown Buffalo, as Acosta explains in the acknowledgment to the book, was a political party. Acosta had prefaced this distinction with an even more direct attack on the primacy of ethnic identity as a basis for healthy motivation in life: "My single mistake has been to seek an identity with any one person or nation or with any part of history." In *The Revolt of the Cockroach People*, Acosta portrays the result of his efforts to identify with the Chicano ethnic movement as, first, his being cut off from non-Chicanos by the separatist (read: racist) restrictions placed on him by his fellow Chicanos—he is not allowed near a "Gabacha" who wants to congratulate him (230). Second, while he is forced into strictly Chicano relationships, the story culminates in a fratricidal court battle among Chicanos of different levels and persuasion: "Chicano defendants and defense attorney and prosecution. And there on the bench is good old Chicano lackey, Superior Judge Alfred Alacran" (202). He could have added that the case included Chicano witnesses for both sides and the matter of the death of a Chicano reporter. Into this microcosm of Chicano conflict, Acosta introduces Cesar Chavez and Rodolfo "Corky" Gonzales as representatives of pacificism and militant violence, and he places himself between the two alternatives, as the link that holds them together— the source of a rhetoric that might lend order to chaos and fragmentation. But in the end, Acosta is forced to flee after attempting to bomb the Chicano judge's chambers, an attempt that apparently kills a Chicano. This was not the picture of ethnic unity Chicanos wanted to see.

As the German critic Horst Tonn has noted, as early as 1972 Acosta was debunking the self-image of the Chicano movement. Perhaps what makes Acosta questionable in the eyes of some canonizers is his recognition that, in spite of a desperately sought-after bond of ethnicity, significant ideological concerns fragmented the community whenever the realities of political action demanded confrontation with the dominant society. Unity was approximated only during cultural celebrations within a segregated space, such as the rally in chapter 13 (168–75) of *The Revolt*. That event could be a metaphor of what the canonizers at Quinto Sol wanted to achieve with their publications: a bringing together of the Chicano community to celebrate the best of itself without concern for political differences and the emphasis on ethnicity. Yet even in that moment Acosta managed to infuse conflict barely suppressed below the surface. And the conflict centered on the use of the term *Chicano*. It is seen as a dangerous term that, when finally uttered, releases tension and carries the people to an "orgy of nationalism . . . [through which] the crowd melts into one consciousness and no man is alone in that madness any longer" (175) As the rest of the novel demonstrates, however, that kind of unity is untenable under the pressures from both exterior and interior forces.

Like Rechy, Acosta chose to plumb deeper than ethnicity. Unlike Rechy, though, his novels treat readily identifiable Chicano subjects and figures, even to the extent that Chavez and Gonzales appear as characters in his second novel. In addition, he gives both of his books the facade of documentary reportage by presenting them in the form of the autobiography of a veteran militant—himself—of the Chicano movement's most renowned urban struggle, that of Los Angeles at the end of the 1960s and start of the 1970s. So he cannot be excluded as easily as Rechy, who seems marginal to Chicano political activism. Yet another consideration we must entertain with respect to the canon is that, with the presence of works, like Acosta's, that foreground "undesirable traits," readers find traces of those same traits in the canonized texts. Acosta's novels force us to reread those of Anaya, Rivera, and Hinojosa in a different light and observe in them the same seeds of interior division. After Acosta stated openly what others had revealed more subtly, ethnicity can never again be, if it ever was, the monological absolute that some canonizers may have desired. He remains a thorny presence for many, and a liberating one for others.

In 1974, when that interior tension surfaced among the Quinto Sol editors themselves, putting an end to the short-lived prize series, Miguel Méndez published what could be considered the successor to the canonized Big Three. Méndez had appeared in the original *El espejo / The Mirror* with the short story "Tata Casehua," generally considered one of the best pieces in the anthology. So it was almost natural that he should join the Big Three as a novelist. *Peregrinos de Aztlán*, like Acosta's novels, treats the urban malaise. It also focuses unmercifully on the divisions in the ethnic community. However, its saving grace for many critics who preferred to ignore Acosta and Rechy was that its protagonist is one of the underprivileged, the forgotten, with whom the movement wanted to associate itself. Also Méndez ends his text with an affirmation of unity through ethnic heritage—the harsh divisions in society can be transcended by a return to pre-Columbian tradition. In other words, Méndez's text was more acceptable because, although it highlights the urban malaise and interior conflicts, it supports the movement ideal of a utopian future through the recuperation of ethnic heritage. Acosta utilizes similar elements to attack that ideal.

As the differences in ideologies began to make themselves more and more obvious, the criteria for the canon were debated. Critics used their publications to persuade us to apply different standards from those that had been used to establish the first canon. For instance, *Bless Me, Ultima*'s success has ired more than one leftist critic. Joseph Sommers would have liked to dismiss it for its escapist mysticism, preferring *Tierra* ("Critical Approaches"). The German Marxist Dieter Herms agrees with Sommers, but his preference for the canon would be *Bracero* (Eugene Nelson, 1972), a novel not even written by a Chicano (Herms 167). Of course, Raymund Paredes ended his essay with a curious statement. His final point is introduced by a rhetorical question: "Can a sense of Chicano ethnicity be acquired by a person who is not of Mexican heritage?" (74). He offers the example of Chester Seltzer, an Anglo newspaper reporter who published stories about Mexican/Chicano characters under the pseudonym Amado Muro. Paredes mentions what to him must be the relevant rites of passage into Chicano ethnicity: Seltzer "married a Chicano . . . and settled in El Paso . . . immersed himself in Chicano culture and finally wrote about it with great understanding." Thus the door is opened for those exceptional outsiders to become Chicano writers, a possibility that Paredes accepts "happily" (75)—that is, after rejecting the likes of Acosta and excluding John Rechy's major novels. Of course, if we apply Paredes's criteria for admitting Amado Muro, Daniel James, who wrote *Famous All over Town* under the name Danny Santiago, would almost pass—if he had divorced his Anglo wife and remarried a Chicana.

The first attempt to systematize this particular facet of Chicano canon was Francisco Lomelí and Donaldo Urioste's coining of the term and category of the Chicanesque writings for their annotated bibliography in 1976. It was to include literature about Chicanos written by non-Chicanos. This approach, of course, has not really resolved the problem, rather only served to focus attention more acutely on the unresolved nature of Chicano ethnicity. And Antonio Márquez, in his article on Chicanesque literature, would like to grant John Nichols's *Milagro Beanfield War* Chicano status but painfully admits that Nichols just does not have the right blood (Leal et al.). Previously I responded to this position by pointing out that, although Márquez would like us to believe in the existence of thematic and cultural criteria through which real Chicano works can be distinguished from Chicanesque ones, in his own discussion of Nichols Márquez can eliminate him only on grounds of not having been born of Mexican parents. Perhaps this argues in favor of Raymund Paredes's stand on learned ethnicity, but then we would be faced with another situation, intolerable for many Chicanos, in which our best novelist might be John Nichols. As I suggested rather sarcastically in my review of Leal's *Decade of Chicano Literature* and the Márquez essay, maybe what we need is yet another category of "casi-casis," or "almost-almosts," for those authors who cannot pass the blood test but whose writing is culturally and ethnically Chicano (Bruce-Novoa 13).

Our inability to submit authors to a *prueba de sangre* before nominating them for canonization can lead to embarrassing faux pas. La Casa de las Américas thought it was honoring another Chicano when it granted an award to Jaime Sagel (sah HELL), aka Jim Sagel (SAY guell), an Anglo-American who has performed the Amado Muro rites of passage and then some—he actually has an advanced degree in Spanish and writes in an interlingual mixture of Spanish and English. So we see that the canon would expand or contract according to the whims or deeply felt concerns of the critic, if critics were the only ones in control.

Such pressures are not all negative. They help ensure that the canon, as it grows, represents the differing views within the community. And despite the appearance of total chaos, there does seem to be some agreed-upon criteria. Although critics generally consider the Chicano novel to be a product of the post-1959 publication of Villarreal's *Pocho*, hardly anyone would deny that before that date some novels were written in the United States by authors of Mexican heritage. These novels are considered precursors to the Chicano novel as such, but the titles begin to appear alongside the others in Chicano bibliographies. Examples of entries added later are Eusebio Chacón's *Hijo de la tempestad: Tras la tormenta la calma* (1892) and Aurelio Macedonio Espinosa's *Conchita Argüello: Historia y novela californiana* (1938). These novels and others have been found in archives and libraries, where perhaps many more will turn up. Research has also revealed that the Chicano community had access to novels in the major newspapers, some of which were written by authors living in the United States. The classification of these works is still to be resolved. Because the opening of the canon into the past has sensitized critics to the historical presence of our literature before the contemporary period, we can expect more discoveries and research into the nature of that writing. Such findings may shed a different light on the canon as we conceive of it. Yet it must be noted that the extremely limited availability of these older texts prevents them from being more widely read or used in classes; thus their active influence on the canon is minuscule.

When referring to the contemporary period, most critics would recommend, and teachers require, the reading of the Big Three plus Villarreal. *Chicano* has largely gone by the wayside, its sociological stereotypes wearing thin over the years. Since works by non-Chicanos have been relegated to the questionable status of Chicanesque, *The Plum Plum Pickers* has been retroactively placed in the position of sometimes in, sometimes out, depending on how much one knows or cares about Barrio's background and how liberally one decides to extend the ethnic circle. Miguel Méndez, while respected by the critics, receives less attention, probably because his highly creative and poetic use of Spanish is difficult for many readers, even those who have no problems with other novelists, like Hinojosa, who write in a more accessible idiom. Most critics tacitly agree to the existence of a category of important works that probably should be read but that, once again, are not considered entirely Chicano because they do not directly address ethnic issues. Examples are *The Road to Tamazunchale*, by Ron Arias, and the Rechy novels.

Novels by women, the few we have, are most often referred to in a similar vein: works that should be read to see what women have written about, but not as essential components of the canon. It may be that until recently even the most generous reader was hard-pressed to overlook the faults in these novels. Yet certainly Sandra Cisneros's *House on Mango Street* can be read as a novel, in a similar fashion as *Tierra*, and it merits inclusion in the inner circle. And although neither author deals directly with Chicano subjects per se, Cecile Pineda and Sheila Ortiz Taylor are novelists of the first order, surpassing in craft many of the previously published Chicano writers.

This last point brings us to another concern. The breakup of Quinto Sol in 1975 has left a void not yet filled by any of the publishers who have taken its place. Both Arte Público Press and Bilingual Press have established excellent records, having published to date more creative literature than Quinto Sol did, but their publications have not come to signify the same thing to Chicano readers. That is to say, these works do not reach us with an a priori status of canonized texts as the Quinto Sol prizewinners managed to do. The reason, of course, lies partly in the realm of merchandising: Quinto Sol carried out a canonizing strategy at a time when the Chicano consumer would accept almost anything offered and was naively prepared to believe almost anything claimed about the books. Octavio Romano, one of the originators of Quinto Sol, attempted to continue this strategy when he began a publishing house, Tonatiuh, in the mid-1970s. The Tonatiuh prize, unlike the Quinto Sol prize—which was an almost strictly in-house operation—was set up with a national selection committee, of which I was a member. The effort was undermined by a lack of cooperation among the judges, and eventually a winner was picked without the judges having read all the manuscripts. The fate of the winning novel, Abelardo Delgado's *Letters to Louise*, can serve as an example of the disintegration of the hegemonic control of Quinto Sol. *Letters to Louise* was never published as a book but only as numbers of *Grito del Sol*, Octavio Romano's journal. It has received almost no critical attention and is never mentioned in the company of the three Quinto Sol prizes. By the time it reached the public, confidence in the Berkeley group—which had split into Tonatiuh and Justa Publications—had so diminished that the prize was no longer respected.

A similar canonization effort has not been attempted, so far, by either Arte Público or Bilingual Press, although the former has now established a literary prize in memory of Tomás Rivera and the latter has begun publishing a series called Chicano Classics. The Arte Público contest has not yet awarded its first prize, so how it will function is still to be seen. Bilingual Press defines the purpose of its Chicano Classics series as the reissuing of significant texts that have gone out of print. However, the fact that the first title in the series, José Antonio Villarreal's *Fifth Horseman*, was never central to the Chicano canon nor a legitimate classic suggests that the series may be more of a merchandising strategy than a real effort to save "classics." Certainly there are some novels we could consider classics that need reissuing—the Oscar Zeta Acosta books come to mind—but to republish a novel like *The Fifth Horseman* is not the act of salvaging a classic but rather an attempt to create a market for a book that never established one in the first place. In that sense, Bilingual Press is repeating the canonization strategy of Quinto Sol. However, the marketing plan did not work with the first title. Perhaps that is why the press chose Raymund Barrio's *Plum Plum Pickers* for the second in the series.

Most likely the kind of hegemony sought by and granted to Quinto Sol from 1969 to 1974 cannot be duplicated, but not because the literature being published is inferior. Some Chicano works of fiction have garnered awards outside the Chicano establishment. Rolando Hinojosa's second book, *Klail City y sus alrededores*, won the Casa de las Américas prize in 1976, cementing his reputation, established through the Quinto Sol prize, as a leading Chicano writer. More recently, Cisneros (*Mango Street*), Gary Soto (*Living up the Street*), and Ana Castillo (*The Mixquiahuala Letters*) have won American Book awards for fiction, yet none of these works has been received as an instant Chicano classic.

More than a matter of the literary merit of new texts, the inability to create a priori Chicano classics results from a change in the critical and reading public. It has more to do with an erosion of the centralizing energy of the cultural awakening released in the mid-1960s and that crystallized in what we called the movement. Just as the criteria began breaking down once the bond of ethnicity was called into question, there has been fragmentation, or perhaps decentralization, in the production of Chicano literature. And decentralization raises the issue of the relativity of values; for instance, the ethnic standard for merit may be replaced by the newer criterion of craft. In short, the reception of a text is no longer guaranteed by the mere fact that it comes from a Chicano source. And finally, when the applicability of the term *Chicano* is under severe attack, not only in the community but also among writers, we can expect that there will be a questioning of the value of ethnicity in a text, or even an assessment of which values are the most authentic. Novels such as those by Nash Candelaria, Arturo Islas, and Alejandro Morales challenge assumptions about the Chicano community and in so doing expand the definition of the culture—one more erosion of the cultural hegemony that allowed canonization to be a much simpler matter in the early 1960s.

Even more disconcerting is the relative absence of critical vehicles—journals, literary magazines, newsletters—in which the literature is reviewed, evaluated, and, yes, canonized. Not that there has ever been a wealth of such outlets in the Chicano community, but the canonization power of Quinto Sol made the process of validification unnecessary. In the mid-1970s, when Quinto Sol began to founder, a series of novels appeared that still have attracted relatively little attention when compared to that given the Quinto Sol group. Francisco Lomelí has called such writers as Morales, Arias, Isabella Rios, Candelaria, and Aristeo Brito members of a lost, or ignored, generation. In fact, this list could be extended up to the present. Little has been published about *The Rain God*, an excellent novel by Islas, or *Muerte en una estrella*, Sergio Elizondo's experimental novel, both published in 1984. More print has been dedicated to the questionable effort to keep Richard Rodríguez out of the Chicano canon than in assuring a place for some deserving authors. If we do not revitalize the canon with new material, books meriting attention will be ignored. Even Juan Rodríguez's tendentious and openly biased *Carta Abierta* was better than the *abulia cerrada* that predominates now. (Since I first wrote that last sentence, Rodríguez has begun to publish *Carta Abierta* once again, necessitating a caveat to my statement: while it is better than nothing, practically any serious critical vehicle would be superior to the arbitrary, gossip-style opinions voiced in the *Carta*).

If we fail to discuss novels by authors we know about, it should be no surprise that little is done to discover others. Our incestuous focus has prevented us from looking beyond the circle of recognized or recognizable Chicano writers to find new and possibly important authors. Some have gone unnoticed. Laurence Gonzales came to our attention only when, in his third novel, *El vago*, he addressed the theme of the Mexican Revolution. Yet Gonzales is a fine writer with years of experience, and a long list of publications in prestigious magazines. Another novelist who escaped even the eye of Roberto Trujillo in *Literatura Chicana*, the most recent Chicano bibliography, is Ernest Brawley, who has three novels to his credit, each with protagonists who can claim at least a distant Chicano link. His second novel, *Selena*, narrates the life of a farmer-worker activist, and his third, *The Alamo Tree*, could be compared to Villarreal's *Fifth Horseman* in its examination of the Mexican backgrounds of what is today the Chicano. The two women I consider the best of the published fiction writers, Ortiz Taylor and Pineda, have not figured in any of the Chicana collections, nor to my knowledge were they written about, discussed, or even mentioned in the Chicano context until I did so in 1985. Yet Pineda's *Face* (1985) is a fine novel, and her second, *Frieze* (1986), surpasses it; Ortiz Taylor's *Faultline* (1982), in my opinion, not only is the best-written novel by a Chicana but can bear comparison with the best in the canon, period.

But now I am practicing canonization, not criticizing the process, and though it is a legitimate and perhaps unavoidable function of criticism, any further indulgence is better left for another forum.

Puerto Rican Literature in the United States: Stages and Perspectives

Juan Flores

Can anyone name the great Puerto Rican novel? It is *La charca* by Manuel Zeno Gandía, published in 1894 and first available to American readers in English translation in 1984. The lapse, of course, is symptomatic. After nearly a century of intense economic and political association, endless official pledges of cultural kinship, and the wholesale importation of nearly half the Puerto Rican people to the United States, Puerto Rican literature still draws a blank among American readers and students of literature. Major writers and authors are unknown and, with a handful of exceptions, untranslated; English-language and bilingual anthologies are few and unsystematic; and there is still not a single introduction to the literature's history available in English. Even the writing of Puerto Ricans living in the United States, mostly in English and all expressive of life in this country, has remained marginal to any literary canon, mainstream or otherwise: among the "ethnic" or "minority" literatures it has probably drawn the least critical interest and the fewest readers.

Yet, as a young Puerto Rican friend once put it, "Puerto Rico is this country's 'jacket.'" In no other national history are twentieth-century American social values and priorities more visibly imprinted than in Puerto Rico's. Puerto Rico, in fact, or at least its treatment at the hands of the United States, is part of American history. Its occupation in 1898 after four centuries of Spanish colonialism, the decades of imposition of English, the unilateral decreeing of American citizenship in 1917, economic and social crisis during the Depression years, externally controlled industrialization, unprecedented migration of the work force and sterilization of the women, ecological depletion and contamination, relentless cultural saturation—all these events pertain not only to Puerto Rican historical reality but to the recent American past as well. And in no foreign national literature is this seamy, repressed side of the "American century" captured at closer range than in the novels of Zeno Gandía and Enrique Laguerre, the stories of José Luis González and Pedro Juan Soto, the poetry of Luis Palés Matos and Julia de Burgos, or the plays of René Marqués and Jaime Carrero. Understandably, Puerto Rican literature in the twentieth century has been obsessed with the United States, whose presence not only lurks, allegorically, as the awesome colossus to the north but is manifest in every aspect of national life. Those intent on reworking literary curricula and boundaries would thus do well to heed this telling record of United States politics and culture as they bear on neighboring peoples and nationalities.

Closer still, of course, and more directly pertinent to a "new" American literary history, is the Puerto Rican literature produced in the United States. Not until the late 1960s, when distinctly "Nuyorican" voices emerged on the American literary landscape, did it occur to anyone to speak of a Puerto Rican literature emanating from life in this country. How, indeed, could such an uprooted and downtrodden community even be expected to produce a literature? Such relative newcomers, many lacking in basic literacy skills in either English or Spanish, were assumed to be still caught up in the immigrant syndrome or, worse, to be languishing in what Oscar Lewis termed the "culture of poverty." But in books like Piri Thomas's *Down These Mean Streets* and Pedro Pietri's *Puerto Rican Obituary*, there was suddenly a literature by Puerto Ricans, in English and decidedly in—and against—the American grain.

This initial impetus has since grown into a varied but coherent literary movement, and since the 1970s the Nuyoricans have come to make up an identifiable current in North American literature. That this movement also retains its association to Puerto Rico's national literature and, by extension, to Latin American literary concerns is a crucial though more complex matter. In fact, it is Nuyorican literature's position straddling two national literatures and hemispheric perspectives that most significantly distinguishes it among the American minority literatures. In any case, those years of cultural and political awakening in the late 1960s generated an active literary practice among Puerto Ricans born and raised in the United States, who have managed to expound a distinctive problematic and language with a bare minimum of institutional or infrastructural support.

Critical and historical interest in this new literature has also grown. Journal articles and introductions to books and anthologies, though scattered, have helped provide some context and approaches. Along with critics like Edna Acosta-Belén, Efraín Barradas, and John Miller, Wolfgang Binder, professor of American studies at the University of Erlangen, deserves special mention. His substantial work on contemporary Puerto Rican literature is based on an ample knowledge of the material and close familiarity with many of the authors. Further study of this kind has ascertained with increasing clarity that Puerto Rican literature in the United States was not born, sui generis, in the late 1960s and that its scope, like that of other emerging literatures, cannot be properly accounted for if analysis is limited by the reigning norms of genre, fictionality, language, or national demarcation.

In 1982 there appeared the first, and still the only, book on Puerto Rican literature in the United States, Eugene Mohr's *The Nuyorican Experience*. Mohr, professor of English at the University of Puerto Rico, offers a helpful overview of many of the works and authors and suggests some lines of historical periodization. I will therefore refer to Mohr's book, and especially to some of its omissions, in reviewing briefly the contours of Puerto Rican literature in the United States. How far back does it go, and what were the major stages leading to the present Nuyorican style and sensibility? To what extent does its very existence challenge the notion of literary and cultural canons, and how does this literature relate to other noncanonical and anticanonical literatures in the United States?

The first Puerto Ricans to write about life in the United States were political exiles from the independence struggle against Spain, who came to New York in the late decades of the nineteenth century to escape the clutches of the colonial authorities. Some of Puerto Rico's most prominent intellectual and revolutionary leaders, such as Eugenio María de Hostos, Ramón Emeterio Betances, Lola Rodríguez de Tío, and Sotero Figueroa, spent more or less extended periods in New York, where along with fellow exiles from Cuba they charted further steps to free their countries from Spanish rule. The lofty ideals of "Antillean unity" found concrete expression in the establishment of the Cuban and Puerto Rican Revolutionary Party, under the leadership of the eminent Cuban patriot Jose Martí. This early community was largely composed of the radical patriotic elite, but there was already a solid base of artisans and laborers who lent support to the many organizational activities. It should also be mentioned that one of these first settlers from Puerto Rico was Arturo Alfonso Schomburg, a founder of the Club Dos Antillas and, in later years, a scholar of the African experience.

The writings that give testimonial accounts and impressions of those years in New York are scattered in diaries, correspondences, and the often short-lived revolutionary newspapers and still await compilation and perusal. Perhaps the most extended and revealing text to have been uncovered thus far is a personal article by the Puerto Rican poet and revolutionary martyr Francisco Gonzalo Marín. "Pachín" Marín, a typesetter by trade who died in combat in the mountains of Cuba, figures significantly in the history of Puerto Rican poetry because of his emphatic break with the airy clichés of romantic verse and his introduction of an ironic, conversational tone and language. In "Nueva York por dentro: Una faz de su vida bohemia," he offers a pointed critical reflection on New York City as experienced by the hopeful but destitute Puerto Rican immigrant.

In *The Nuyorican Experience* Eugene Mohr makes no mention of Pachín Marín or of these first, nineteenth-century samples of Puerto Rican writing in New York, though the Cuban critic Emilio Jorge Rodríguez has drawn proper attention to them. The sources are of course still scarce, and that period of political exile was clearly distinct in character from the later stages, which were conditioned by the labor immigration under direct colonial supervision. Nevertheless, writings like that of Pachín Marín and some of the diary entries and letters of Hostos and others carry immense prognostic power in view of subsequent historical and literary developments. In a history of Puerto Rican literature in the United States they provide an invaluable antecedent perspective, a prelude of foreboding, even before the fateful events of 1898. When read along with the essays and sketches of Jose Martí on New York and the United States, these materials offer the earliest "inside" view of American society by Caribbean writers and intellectuals.

Mohr dates the origins of "the Nuyorican experience" from Bernardo Vega's arrival in New York in 1916, as recounted in the opening chapter of Vega's memoirs. While the *Memorias de Bernardo Vega* (*Memoirs of Bernardo Vega*) is a logical starting point, since it chronicles the Puerto Rican community from the earliest period, the book was actually written in the late 1940s and was not published until 1977. (An English translation appeared in 1984.) Despite the book's belated appearance, though, Bernardo Vega was definitely one of the "pioneers." He and his work belong to and stand for that period from the First through the Second World Wars (1917–45), which saw the growth and consolidation of the immigrant community following the Jones Act, which decreed citizenship (1917), and preceding the mass migration after 1945. In contrast to the political exiles and other temporary or occasional sojourners to New York, Bernardo Vega was also, in Mohr's terms, a "proto-Nuyorican": though he eventually returned to Puerto Rico late in life (he lived there in the late 1950s and the 1960s), Vega was among the first Puerto Ricans to write about New York as one who was here to stay.

Puerto Rican literature of this first stage showed many of the signs of an immigrant literature, just as the community itself, still relatively modest in size, resembled that of earlier immigrant groups in social status, hopes for advancement, and civic participation. The published writing was overwhelmingly of a journalistic and autobiographical kind: personal sketches and anecdotes, jokes and *relatos* printed in the scores of Spanish-language newspapers and magazines that cropped up and died out over the years. It is a first-person testimonial literature: the recent arrivals capturing, in the home language, the jarring changes and first adjustments as they undergo them.

Yet the analogy to European immigrant experience was elusive even then, long before the momentous changes of midcentury made it clear that something other than upward mobility and eventual assimilation awaited Puerto Ricans on the mainland. The most important difference, which has conditioned the entire migration and settlement, is the abiding colonial relationship between Puerto Rico and the United States. Puerto Ricans came here as foreign nationals, a fact that American citizenship and accommodationist ideology tend to obscure; but they also arrived as a subject people. The testimonial and journalistic literature of the early period illustrate that Puerto Ricans entering this country, even those most blinded by illusions of success and fortune, tended to be aware of this discrepant, disadvantageous status.

For that reason, concern for the home country and attachment to national cultural traditions remained highly active, as did the sense of particular social vulnerability in the United States. The discrimination met by the newcomers was compounded by racial and cultural prejudice, as the black Puerto Rican writer and political leader Jesús Colón portrays so poignantly in his book of autobiographical sketches set in those earlier decades, *A Puerto Rican in New York*. In both of these senses—the strong base in a distinct and maligned cultural heritage and the attentiveness and resistance to social inequality—Puerto Rican writing in the United States, even in this initial testimonial stage, needs to be read as a colonial literature. Its deeper problematic makes it more akin to the minority literatures of oppressed groups than to the literary practice and purposes of ethnic immigrants.

Another sign of this kinship, and of the direct colonial context, has to do with the boundaries of literary expression established by the norms of print culture. For in spite of the abundant periodical literature, with its wealth of narrative and poetic samples, in that period and in subsequent periods of Puerto Rican immigrant life surely the most widespread and influential form of verbal culture has been transmitted not through publication but through oral testimony and through the music. The work of oral historians in gathering the reminiscences of surviving pioneers will be indispensable in supplementing the study of printed texts. Also of foremost importance in this regard is the collection and analysis of the popular songs of the migration, the hundreds of boleros, plenas and examples of *jíbaro* or peasant music dealing with Puerto Rican life in the United States, which enjoyed immense popularity throughout the emigrant community. Starting in the 1920s, when many folk musicians joined the migration from the Island to New York, the popular song has played a central role in the cultural life of Puerto

Ricans in this country. It needs to be recognized as an integral part of the people's "literary" production. Only in recent years, and mainly in reference to the salsa style of the present generation, have there been any attempts to cull these sources for broader cultural and theoretical meanings (see Duany). But it was in those earlier decades, when favorites like Rafael Hernández, Pedro Flores, Ramito, Mon Rivera, Cortijo, and Tito Rodríguez were in New York composing and performing songs about Puerto Rican life here, that this tradition of the popular song began.

A turning point in Puerto Rican literature, before the advent of the Nuyoricans in the late 1960s, came around 1950. This second stage covers the years 1945–65. Those two decades after World War II saw the rapid industrialization of Puerto Rico under Operation Bootstrap, and hundreds of thousands of Puerto Rican workers migrated to New York and other United States cities. This avalanche of newly arriving families, a significant part of the country's displaced agricultural proletariat, drastically changed the character of the Puerto Rican immigrant community, distancing it still further from the familiar immigrant experience. The "Puerto Rican problem" became more urgent than ever for official and mainstream America, as did the infusion of drugs, criminality, and the forces of incrimination into the crowded Puerto Rican neighborhoods. It should be remembered that *West Side Story*, written and first performed in the mid-1950s, was intended to ease this explosive situation, though it actually has had the long-term effect of reinforcing some of the very stereotypes, so rampant in the dominant culture, that it sought to dispel. The same must be said of Oscar Lewis's book *La vida* and its infamous notion of the "culture of poverty."

It was in this period and because of these conditions that the migration and the emigrant community in the United States became major themes in Puerto Rican national literature. In prior decades some authors from the Island had of course shown an interest in their uprooted compatriots, setting their works in New York and choosing immigrants as their protagonists: parts of *El negocio* and *Los redentores*, the later novels of Manuel Zeno Gandía, take place in the United States, and frequent bibliographical reference is made to still another unpublished novel by Zeno Gandía entitled *Hubo un escándalo (or En Nueva York)*, though it has not yet been possible to study that manuscript. José de Diego Padró, an interesting but neglected writer active between 1910 and 1930, set much of his long, bizarre novel *En Babia* in New York, as did the dramatist Fernando Sierra Berdecía in his comedy *Esta noche juega el jóker*. But these are random and rare exceptions and still do not indicate any inclusion of emigrant experience in the thematic preoccupations of the national literature.

By midcentury, though, accompanying the more general shift in the literature from a rural to an urban focus, the attention of Island authors turned decisively to the reality of mass migration and the emigrant barrio. Many writers, such as René Marqués, Enrique Laguerre, José Luis González, and Emilio Díaz Valcárcel, came here in those years to witness it directly, while a writer like Pedro Juan Soto, later identified more with the Island literature, actually lived through the emigration firsthand. The result was a flurry of narrative and theatrical works, all appearing in the 1950s and early 1960s, some of which still stand today as the most powerful fictional renditions of Puerto Rican life in the United States. In contrast to the primarily testimonial writings of the previous period, this was the first "literature," in the narrow sense, about the community here, in which imaginative invention, dramatic structure, and stylistic technique are used to heighten the impact of historical and autobiographical experience.

Despite the undeniable artistic merit of some of this work—I would single out the stories of José Luis González, Soto's *Spiks*, and, for historical reasons, René Marqués's *La carreta*—it is also clearly a literature *about* Puerto Ricans in the United States rather than *of* that community. Mohr aptly entitles his second chapter "Views from an Island." That these are the "views" of visiting or temporary sojourners is evident in various ways but is not necessarily a detriment to their literary value. The tendency is to present the arrival and settlement experience in strict existential and instantaneous terms; instead of process and interaction there is above all culture shock and intense personal dislocation. What these glimpses and miniatures gain in emotional intensity they often lose in their reduction of a complex, collective, and unfolding reality to a snapshot of individual behavior. Another sign of the unfamiliarity and distance between the writer and the New York community is the language: though an occasional English or Spanglish usage appears for authenticating purposes, there is a general reliance on standard literary Spanish or, as in *La carreta*, a naturalistic transcription of Puerto Rican dialect. What is missing is any resonance of the community's own language practice, which even then, in the 1950s, was already tending toward the intricate mixing and code switching characteristic of Puerto Rican speech in the United States.

But despite such problems, these "views from an island" rightly remain some of the best-known works of Puerto Rican literature in the United States, their literary impact generally strengthened by the critical, anticolonial standpoint of the authors. The pitiable condition of the authors' compatriots in United States cities is attributed and linked to the status of Puerto Rico as a direct colony. This perspective, and the constant focus on working-class characters, helps dispel the tone of naive optimism and accommodationism that had characterized the writings of such earlier petit bourgeois observers of the emigrant community as Juan B. Huyke and Pedro Juan Labarthe. The writings of Soto, González, and others, because of their quality and the authors' grounding in the national literature of the Island, form an important link to Latin American literature. A story like González's "La noche que volvimos a ser gente," for example, is clearly a work of contemporary Latin American fiction, even though it is set in New York and its attention focuses on the subways and streets of the urban United States. The same is true of Díaz Valcárcel's novel *Harlem todos los días* and many more of these works.

It should be emphasized that during the 1950s there was also a "view from within" the Puerto Rican community, a far less-known literature by Puerto Ricans who had been here all along and who, lovingly or not, considered the barrio home. Here again Bernardo Vega and Jesús Colón come to mind, for although the *Memorias* and *A Puerto Rican in New York* chronicle the arrival and settlement over the decades, they were not written until the late 1940s and 1950s. There were also a number of Puerto Rican poets who had been living in New York for decades and who by the 1950s began to see themselves as a distinctive voice within the national poetry; among them were Juan Aviles, Emilio Delgado, Clemente Soto Vélez, Pedro Carrasquillo, Jorge Brandon, and José Dávila Semprit. Back in the 1940s this group had included as well Puerto Rico's foremost woman poet, Julia de Burgos. What little is available of this material shows it to be largely conventional Spanish-language verse making little reference to the migration or to life in New York, much less anticipating in any way the complex bilingual situation of the generation to come. But much more of interest may still be found with further study, and it is important to refer to Pedro Carrasquillo for his popular *décimas* about a *jíbaro* in New York, to Dávila Semprit for his forceful political poetry, and to Soto Vélez and Brandon for the examples they set for many of the younger poets.

Perhaps the best example of literature from within the community at midcentury is the novel *Trópico en Manhattan* by Guillermo Cotto-Thorner. The contrast with the Island authors' treatment of the emigrant experience is striking: the shock of arrival and first transitions is extended and lent historical depth; individual traumas and tribulations are woven into a more elaborate interpersonal and social context. Most interesting of all as a sign of the author's proximity to and involvement in the community is, once again, the language. The Spanish of *Trópico en Manhattan*, especially in certain dialogue passages, is at times interspersed with bilingual neologisms of various kinds. And at the end of the book there is a lengthy glossary of what Cotto-Thorner calls "Neorkismos."

The contrast between the observers' and the participants' views in Puerto Rican literature of this period does not reflect so much the literary quality as the relation of the writers to the literature's historical development. A novel like *Trópico en Manhattan* may not surpass the stories of José Luis González and Pedro Juan Soto, but it does more extensively reveal the social contradictions internal to the community and give them a sense of epic duration and process. With regard to literary history, that relatively unknown and forgotten novel, with its early sensitivity to "Neorkismos," may more directly prefigure the voice and vantage point of the Nuyoricans than does *La carreta*, or even *Spiks*.

Another such transitional author of the period 1945–65 is Jaime Carrero, who also works to clarify that the "outsider-insider" contrast refers not only to place of residence but to cultural perspective. Carrero, whose bilingual poetry volume *Jet neorriqueño: Neo-Rican Jet Liner* directly foreshadowed the onset of Nuyorican literature in New York, is from the Island, having been to New York for college and other visits. As Eugene Mohr points out, what distinguishes Carrero from those other Island-based writers is "the persistence of his interest in the *colonia* and his sympathy with the Nuyorican viewpoint" (116). His attempts at bilingual verse and especially his plays, from *Pipo subway no sabe reir* to *El lucky seven*, give vivid literary expression to this internal, participants' perspective. Carrero has also written a novel (*Raquelo tiene un mensaje*) about the trauma of Nuyorican return migration to the Island, but Pedro Juan Soto's *Ardiente suelo, fría estación* is as yet unequaled in its treatment of that experience.

The third, Nuyorican stage in emigrant Puerto Rican literature arose with no direct reference to or evident knowledge of the writings of either earlier period. Yet despite this apparent disconnection, Nuyorican creative expression effectively draws together the firsthand testimonial stance of the pioneer stage and the fictional, imaginative approach of writers of the 1950s and 1960s. This combining of autobiographical and imaginative modes of community portrayal is clearest perhaps in the prose fiction: *Down These Mean Streets*, Nicholasa Mohr's *Nilda*, and Edward Rivera's *Family Installments* are all closer to the testimonial novel than to any of the narrative works of previous years.

This sense of a culmination and synthesis of the earlier phases indicates that with the Nuyoricans the Puerto Rican community in the United States has arrived at a modality of literary expression corresponding to its position as a nonassimilating colonial minority. The most obvious mark of this new literature emanating from the community is the language—the switch from Spanish to English and bilingual writing. This language transfer should not be mistaken for assimilation in a wide cultural sense; as the content of the literature indicates, using English is a sign of being here, not necessarily of liking it here or of belonging.

By now, the Nuyorican period of United States–based Puerto Rican literature is already unfolding a history of its own. The sensationalist tenor of the initial outburst has given way to a greater concern for the everyday lives of Puerto Rican working people. The growing diversity and sophistication of the movement is evident in the emergence of women writers and female perspectives, as in books like Sandra María Esteves's *Yerba buena* and Nicholasa Mohr's *Rituals of Survival*, and in the appearance of writers in other parts of the United States. Also of key importance is the ongoing use of an actively bilingual literary field. For it becomes clear that, in the literature as in the community, the switch from Spanish to English is by no means complete or smooth, and it certainly is not a sign of cultural accommodation. For all the young writers Spanish remains a key language-culture of reference even when not used, and some, like Tato Laviera, demonstrate full bilingual capacity in their writing. There also continues to be a Spanish-language literature by Puerto Ricans living here, some of which hovers between Nuyorican concerns and styles and those of contemporary Island literature. Such writers as Iván Silén and Victor Fernandes Fragoso, like Jaime Carrero and Guillermo Cotto-Turner before them, have served as important bridges between the two language poles of present-day Puerto Rican writing.

Thus, rather than abandoning one language in favor of another, contemporary Puerto Rican literature in the United States actually exhibits the full range of bilingual and interlingual use. Like Mexican American and other minority literatures, it cannot be understood and assessed on the basis of a strict English-language conceptualization of "American" literature, or of literary practice in general. Some of the best Nuyorican texts require knowledge of Spanish and English, which does not make them any less a part of American, or Puerto Rican, literature. And the choice and inclusiveness of a literary language is but one aspect of a broader process of cultural interaction between Puerto Ricans and the various nationalities they encounter in the United States.

By its Nuyorican stage Puerto Rican literature in the United States comes to share the features of "minority" or noncanonical literatures of the United States. Like them it is a literature of recovery and collective affirmation, and it is a literature of "mingling and sharing," of interaction and exchange with neighboring, complementary cultures (see Gelfant). What stronger source, after all, for the emergence of Nuyorican literature than African American literature and political culture? What more comparable a context of literary expression than Chicano writing of the same period?

Perhaps most distinctly among these literatures, though, Puerto Rican writing today is a literature of straddling, a literature operative within and between two national literatures and marginal in both. In this respect Nuyorican writing may well come to serve as a model or paradigm for emerging literatures by other Caribbean groups in the United States, such as Dominicans, Haitians, and Jamaicans. Despite the sharp disconnections between Island– and United States–based traditions, and between stages of the literary history here, it is still necessary to talk about modern Puerto Rican literature as a whole and of the emigrant literature—including the Nuyorican—as an extension or manifestation of that national literature. This inclusion within, or integral association with, a different and in some ways opposing national culture stretches the notion of a pluralist American canon to the limit. Ethnic, religious, and racial diversity is one thing, but a plurality of nations and national languages within the American canon—that is a different and more serious issue. After all, if Tato Laviera and Nicholasa Mohr are eligible for canonical status, why not José Luis González or Julia de Burgos, or, for that matter, Manuel Zeno Gandía, the author of the great Puerto Rican novel *La charca*?

Yes, what about *La charca*? It's a fine novel; in fact, if it had been written by an author from a "big" country, say France or Russia, or even Argentina or Mexico, it would probably be more widely admired and even held up as an example of late nineteenth-century realism. It was published in 1894, before the United States acquired the Island, and its plot is set several decades earlier, long before any significant relations had developed between the two countries. And yet, though it does not mention or refer to the United States, *La charca* is still, somehow, about America, a literary presentiment of what contact with North American society had in store for Puerto Rico. The isolated mountain coffee plantation issues into the wider world of commerce and international dealings, represented in Puerto Rican history, and in Zeno Gandía's later novels, by the United States. Like Jose Martí, Pachín Marín, and other Latin American intellectuals of the time, Zeno Gandía anticipated the coming of the United States' values and power. Even at such a remove, with America's presence still but a metaphor, *La charca* touches the American canon and contributes impressively to the larger task of American literature.

Chinese American Women Writers: The Tradition behind Maxine Hong Kingston

Amy Ling

Writing is an act of self-assertion, self-revelation, and self-preservation. One writes out of a delight in one's storytelling powers, out of a need to reveal and explain oneself, or from the desire to record and preserve experience. However, for women brought up in the old Chinese tradition that for eighteen hundred years codified their obedience and submission to the men in their lives—father, husband, son—a tradition that stressed female chastity, modesty, and restraint; that broke girls' toes and bound their feet as an ideal of beauty; that sold daughters into slavery in times of hardship; that encouraged and honored widow suicides—any writing at all was unusual, even an act of rebellion. Working-class women did not have the education or leisure, and upper-class women were taught that writing was "an unwomanly occupation, destructive of one's moral character, like acting" (Han Suyin, *Destination* 8; 1969). Furthermore, since it was the Chinese custom to leave the women at home when the men first immigrated, temporarily they thought, to the Gold Mountain to make their fortunes, the number of Chinese women in America was small. In 1852, for example, of the 11,794 Chinese in California, only 7 were women, and most of these were prostitutes. By the 1880s the ratio had risen to 1 woman for every 20 men (Hirata 226–28). Moreover, from 1924 to 1930, a law specifically prohibited Chinese women, including wives of American-born Chinese, from immigrating to this country. In 1930, the act was revised, and, for the next ten years, an average of 60 Chinese women entered the United States each year. The 1882 Chinese Exclusion Act was not repealed until 1943, and the numbers of Chinese women in the United States did not approach equality with Chinese men until 1954. Thus it is not surprising that we have so little writing by Chinese American women; it is notable that we have so much.

With the exception of Maxine Hong Kingston, most scholars of American literature are at a loss to name Chinese American women writers. Yet Kingston is not an isolated Athena (or Hua Mulan) springing full grown from Zeus's (or Buddha's) forehead. A line of Chinese American women writers dating back nearly a century preceded her. My term *Chinese American* is broadly inclusive, embracing people of full or half Chinese ancestry; American-born or naturalized immigrants; citizens and sojourners, who have published in the United States. Obviously, books written in Chinese by United States residents are also Chinese American, but since the Chinese language is accessible to so few Americans, this study will be limited to works in English and specifically to full-length works of prose. My definition will be stretched to include international figures like Han Suyin, now residing in Lausanne, Switzerland, and Lin Tai-yi, who lived in Hong Kong for many years, who may not consider themselves American and, in the case of the former, who may not even have lived any appreciable length of time in the United States. However, since they write in English and since their books are regularly published in this country, they certainly are addressing an American audience, and their voices, particularly Han Suyin's, have been heard here and have had an impact. Finally, as Vladimir Nabokov is considered "American" enough to be included in American literature anthologies, so Han Suyin and Lin Tai-yi are included here.

Using this definition, we find that the majority of Chinese American works are by immigrants and sojourners, daughters of diplomats and scholars, and those who have had contact with the West through missionaries or mission schools. For the immigrant, the very act of choosing to write in English, a second language, and thereby addressing a predominantly Caucasian audience is significant and colors the purpose and nature of the work. Though generalizations are always riddled with exceptions, we may say that immigrant and sojourner Chinese American writers, like Helena Kuo and Lin Tai-yi, seek primarily to explain and justify China and Chinese ways to the Western world. As their sensibilities were shaped in their homeland, they have what seems a stable, single center. Their upbringing, as Francis Hsu pointed out in his comparative study *Americans and Chinese*, gives them a strong group orientation, a concern for the good of the whole. Transplanted after their formative years, they see their role in the West as interpreters and ambassadors of good will and understanding for China; to borrow David Riesman's term, they are "other-directed."

American-born Chinese American writers, like Kingston, however, tend to be more individualistic and to have an inward focus. Because they have grown up as a racial minority, imbibing the customs of two cultures, their centers are not stable and single. Their consciousness, as W. E. B. Du Bois pointed out for African Americans, is double; their vision bifocal and fluctuating. Therefore, they look inward with an urgency to comprehend and balance the bicultural clashes they have known and must reconcile. That they write and publish is of course indicative of an awareness of an external world and a desire to communicate, but their initial impetus is primarily introspective. Their purpose is to explain themselves to themselves.

Eurasians and Amerasians may be said to combine the characteristics of immigrants and American-born Chinese Americans. They may, as in the case of Han Suyin and Edith Eaton, identify so strongly with the Chinese side of their ancestry that they have all the fervor, and sometimes more, of the Chinese-formed immigrant instructing and explaining her homeland to outsiders. And yet, at times, like the American-born Chinese American, they also look within and express the conflicts of the two cultures, in their cases particularly poignant, when warring factions are represented by the two heritages that are their own.

Apart from the sociological and psychological effects of birth and upbringing on the sense of self, and purpose in writing in relation to self or other, the highly diverse fifteen writers in this study may be roughly placed into three thematic or formal categories:

delight in storytelling often mingled with nostalgia, protest against racial and sexual injustice, and experiment in language or structure. Many of the writers, depending on the time in their lives and on the individual work in question, move from one category to another, and often even a single work crosses categorical boundaries.

II

Chinese American literary history begins with two Eurasian sisters who responded to racism in divergent ways in their writing. Because they created paradigms followed by their successors, we shall examine them in some detail. Edith (1865–1914) and Winnifred (1875–1954) Eaton were two of fourteen surviving children born to an English landscape painter, Edward Eaton, and his Chinese wife, Grace Trefusis. The Eatons immigrated from England to America, living first in the United States and then settling in Montreal. Both sisters, as adults, moved to the United States—Edith lived briefly in the Midwest and for more than ten years in San Francisco and Seattle; Winnifred, in Chicago, New York, and Los Angeles.

Though initially shocked by the first Chinese workers she saw on her arrival in the United States, "uncouth specimens of their race, drest in working blouses and panta-loons with queues hanging down their backs" ("Leaves" 126), Edith Eaton later iden-tified strongly with her mother's people, assumed a Cantonese pen name, Sui Sin Far (Narcissus), and wrote short stories and articles "to fight their battles in the papers" ("Leaves" 128).

At that time the Chinese had many battles to fight, for throughout the late nine-teenth century and the early decades of the twentieth, anti-Chinese sentiment raced across the United States. Imported by the thousands for the construction of the rail-roads, Chinese workers remaining here were seen as a threat to white labor and became targets of mass vilification campaigns, physical abuse, and even murder. From 1882 until 1943, the Chinese Exclusion Act prohibited United States entry to all Chinese except teachers, students, merchants, and diplomats. Japan, by contrast—having won a war against China in 1895 and against Russia in 1904–05, and with few nationals in the United States to be a threat—was highly respected. A dialogue recounted by Edith Eaton in her autobiographical essay "Leaves from the Mental Portfolio of an Eurasian" demonstrates clearly the contrasting attitudes toward Chinese and Japanese in the Unit-ed States at the turn of the century:

> "Somehow or other . . . I cannot reconcile myself to the thought that the Chinese are humans like ourselves." [Mr. K., her new employer]
> "A Chinaman is, in my eyes, more repulsive than a nigger." [the town clerk]
> "Now the Japanese are different altogether. There is something bright and likeable about those men." [Mr. K.] (129)

Though her facial features did not betray her racial background, Edith's response to this conversation was the courageous one of asserting her Chinese ethnicity at the expense of her job with Mr. K.

Winnifred, perhaps reasoning that few could tell the difference between Japanese and Chinese, decided to be the favored "Oriental." Exploiting the prejudices of her day, she invented a Japanese pen name, Onoto Watanna, claimed a Japanese noblewoman for a mother and Nagasaki for a birthplace, and concocted tender romances set in Japan coupling charming Japanese or Eurasian heroines with American or English heroes. Winnifred's works were highly successful, exquisitely published with full-color illustrations by real Japanese artists, the text printed on decorated paper. They went through repeated printings, were translated into European languages, and were adapted for the stage. Winnifred went on to an exclusive contract with Hearst Publications and later became scriptwriter and editor for Universal Studios and MGM before retiring to an elegant home in Calgary, Alberta.

Assertion of her Chinese ethnicity was not easy for Edith Eaton, for initially the Chinese themselves did not recognize her as one of their own and were almost as ignorant and rude as her brief employer, Mr. K.:

> . . . save for a few phrases, I am unacquainted with my mother tongue. How, then, can I expect these people to accept me as their own countrywoman? The Americanized Chinamen actually laugh in my face when I tell them that I am one of their race. ("Leaves" 131)

Nonetheless, after a lifetime of stories and articles in defense of the Chinese, published in the leading magazines of the time, Sui Sin Far received the recognition and appreciation of the Chinese community in the form of an engraved memorial stone erected on her tomb in the Protestant Cemetery in Montreal.

Edith Eaton's collected stories, published under the title *Mrs. Spring Fragrance* (1912), are divided into tales for adults and those for children. They are simply told. Some are marked by a sentiment fashionable in her day. Others introduce themes and perspectives new to American literature. The following passage from the title story gives a sample of the irony Eaton employs in the cause of sexual and racial protest. Lively, independent Mrs. Spring Fragrance, on a visit to San Francisco, writes a letter in Chinese-flavored English to her husband in Seattle, about a lecture a Caucasian woman had taken her to, entitled "America the Protector of China":

> It was most exhilarating, and the effect of so much expression of benevolence leads me to beg of you to forget to remember that the barber charges you one dollar for a shave while he humbly submits to the American man a bill of fifteen cents. And murmur no more because your honored elder brother, on a visit to this country, is detained under the rooftree of this great Government instead of under your own humble roof. Console him with the reflection that he is protected under the wing of the Eagle, the Emblem of Liberty. What is the loss of ten hundred years or ten thousand times ten dollars compared with the happiness of knowing oneself so securely sheltered? All of this I have learned from Mrs. Samuel Smith, who is as brilliant and great of mind as one of your own superior sex. (8–9)

In Edith Eaton's stories the Chinese in America are presented sympathetically, not as one-dimensional heathens but as multidimensional humans, capable of suffering pain and of inflicting it, of loving and being lovable, of being loyal as well as deceiving. Compared with most of the contemporaneous writing about Chinese by white authors, analyzed and discussed comprehensively by William Wu in *The Yellow Peril* (1982), or the writing by Christian missionaries, as represented by *The Lady of the Lily Feet*, by Helen Clark (1900), stressing the sensational, "heathenish" Chinese practices, Edith

Eaton's stories give a balanced view, attempting to portray psychologically realistic conditions. She is most successful in presenting the inner condition of the Eurasian in a society hostile to one part of her heritage. In "Its Wavering Image," and particularly in "Story of One White Woman Who Married a Chinese," she examines the interracial anguish she personally knew. Though the white wife of a Chinese is despised by society for her marriage, she ignores others' opinions until the birth of her son:

> . . . as he stands between his father and myself, like yet unlike us both, so will he stand in after years between his father's and his mother's people. And if there is no kindliness nor understanding between them, what will my boy's fate be? (132)

Edith Eaton compared her own Eurasian identity with bearing a cross and hoped that by giving her right hand to the Occidentals and her left hand to the Orientals, she herself, "the insignificant connecting link," would not be "utterly" destroyed ("Leaves" 132). One has the impression that she felt the anti-Chinese sentiment of her day so strongly and so personally that in a sense (dying at forty-nine, unmarried) she was destroyed early by the strain of attempting to be a bridge.

Winnifred Eaton, in her "Japanese" novels, flourished. With her first book, *Miss Numé of Japan*, she discovered a formula that worked and used it in romance after romance filled with such exotic elements as showers of cherry blossoms, moonlit assignations in bamboo groves, childlike women in colorful kimonos, fragile shoji screens. The formula includes the following elements: the work is short and easily read in one sitting; the setting is exotic; the potential lovers are introduced, then estranged through an initial obstacle (a difference in class, religion, or party, a previous engagement, opposing families); that obstacle is overcome, only to be followed by another one (war, meddling third parties, misunderstanding, duty elsewhere); during the prolonged separation the lovers each suffer mental anguish or physical hardship and illness; finally, by chance or fate or the kind offices of a friend, the lovers are reunited.

Winnifred Eaton's women are nearly always in an inferior, powerless position: social outcasts (*A Japanese Nightingale, The Wooing of Wisteria*), orphans (*Sunny-San* and *The Heart of Hyacinth*), an unwanted stepdaughter (*Love of Azalea*), a blind, homeless wood sprite (*Tama*), a geisha in bondage (*The Honorable Miss Moonlight*). Her men, in clear contrast, are invariably in positions of power and influence: princes, ministers, architects, and professors. The plot, reiterated in book after book, of the helpless, childlike, charming Japanese female looking up to the powerful white male, could not but appeal to the white audience's sense of superiority and generosity, supporting as it did the prevailing stereotypes and prejudices.

However—to give credit where it is due—despite their powerless positions, her heroines are also vivid, witty, spirited. Their seductive powers are quite real, as are Winnifred Eaton's storytelling powers. Though the plots may be a touch melodramatic or may hinge on a coincidence, they are nearly always engrossing, appealing; there is a certain magic that draws the reader into their spell of delicate emotions, of poignant twists and turns. Winnifred Eaton is particularly skilled at depicting tremulous, protractedly unconsummated virgin love. Even as sophisticated a reader as William Dean Howells praised *A Japanese Nightingale* in the *North American Review*: "There is a quite indescribable freshness in the art of this pretty novelette . . . which is like no other art except in the simplicity which is native to the best art everywhere." In an extraliterary way, he was particularly taken with the heroine: "Yuki herself is of a surpassing lovableness. Nothing but the irresistible charm of the American girl could, I should think, keep the young men who read Mrs. Watana's [sic] book from going out and marrying Japanese girls" (881). Even Japanese readers, though recognizing that Winnifred Eaton was not a writer of the first magnitude, nonetheless praised her work and found it worthy of study alongside the books of Lafcadio Hearn and Pierre Loti for playing "an important role in introducing things Japanese to the American public." They ranked her even higher than Hearn and Loti in that "her descriptions of human feelings are more delicate than those of both famous writers" (Swann and Takeda 58). If the Japanese themselves found that their culture was "properly introduced to the West" through Winnifred Eaton's books, her credibility and accomplishment were even further enhanced.

The paradigms presented by the Eaton sisters are what Shirley Lim in a talk at the 1982 MLA Annual Convention called "exotics" and "existentials." The former, "other-directed," like Winnifred Eaton, are keenly aware of the economic, political, and social climate around them and respond by producing work that conforms to or upholds prevalent stereotypes. The latter, "inner-directed," like Edith Eaton, are more concerned with definition of self and exploration of being. The other-directed may perpetuate untruths in an effort to preserve physical well-being and achieve social approval, while the inner-directed seek to clarify truths in an attempt to maintain psychological health.

Throughout her career, Edith Eaton used her pen to protest injustice and prejudice, whether racial or sexual. In addition to fighting battles for the Chinese, she also fought for women, particularly working-class women. Her feminism comes through in a number of stories. In the ironically titled "The Inferior Woman" she shows a woman earning her own living to be superior to one whose family has wealth and status. In "The Heart's Desire," nothing—fancy foods, clothes, doting father, mother, brother—can make a princess happy but the friendship of a poor girl.

Winnifred's writing was more a barometer of the status quo than a protest against it. Her storytelling powers shone through her ethnic camouflage, making her a successful professional writer. She evaded thorny issues and never dealt with her own ethnicity in her books, except for Chinese cooks, minor characters on the Alberta ranches of her last two novels. However, in one of the last novels, *Cattle*, she abandoned the romantic mode for a naturalist one and voiced a feminist protest. Orphaned at fifteen, Nettie Day is purchased, along with her parents' furniture, by Bull Langdon, a ruthless cattle baron, who later rapes her and inadvertently kills their child. Another woman helps Nettie stand up to Bull and eventually marry the man she loves.

Though Winnifred Eaton did not write of bicultural conflicts, her career and the contortions and distortions she went through to become acceptable—hence able to make a living—testify to the existence of such conflicts. At age forty she published, anonymously, an autobiographical work, *Me*, in which, to some extent, she clears her conscience. Although *A Japanese Nightingale* had been in lights on Broadway, she was clearsighted enough to realize how far she was from her youthful dreams:

What then I ardently believed to be the divine sparks of genius, I now perceived to be nothing but a mediocre talent that could never carry me far. My success was founded upon a cheap and popular device, and that jumble of sentimental moonshine that they called my play seemed to me the pathetic stamp of my inefficiency. Oh, I had sold my birthright for a mess of potage. (153–54)

III

Shortly before and particularly after Pearl Harbor, American opinion of the Chinese and Japanese underwent an about-face. The Japanese were now the enemy; the long-suffering Chinese—who had lost Formosa and Korea to Japan in 1895, Manchuria in 1905, Beijing and all the coastal cities by 1938—became a friend and ally. Books by American-born and Chinese-born Chinese Americans suddenly mushroomed. The former were encouraged to write by an American public eager to distinguish friend from foe; the latter were impelled by personal experiences of the horrors of war. *Our Family*, by Adet and Anor Lin, and *Dawn over Chungking*, by Adet, Anor, and Meimei Lin; *Destination Chungking*, by Han Suyin; *Flame from the Rock*, by Adet Lin (under the pseudonym Tan Yun); *War Tide*, by Anor Lin (under the pseudonym Lin Tai-yi); *I've Come a Long Way*, *Peach Path*, and *Westward to Chungking*, by Helena Kuo; *Fifth Chinese Daughter*, by Jade Snow Wong; and *Echo of a Cry*, by Mai-mai Sze—all appeared within a few years of each other. Though published years later, Janet Lim's *Sold for Silver* and Anna Chennault's *A Thousand Springs* and *Education of Anna* are primarily concerned with the same period.

The novels and autobiographies by the Chinese-born writers are moving accounts of women's firsthand experience of war. They describe the refugees waiting day and night outdoors for trains to take them from threatened cities; boats so crammed that people perished in the crush or were drowned trying to get aboard; the devastation of Japanese incendiary bombs flattening buildings, creating giant craters and walls of flame, leaving bloody corpses and charred bones. But these books are filled as well with a glowing nationalism, with a deep pride in China's spiritual resistance, its patient, persistent rebuilding, its survival and endurance.

Dawn over Chungking is an unusual book because of its authors' ages: Adet was seventeen, Anor fourteen, and Meimei ten. The three are daughters of Lin Yutang, well-known novelist, essayist, and explainer of China to the West. Their book describes a return visit to China after a four-year stay in the United States. Through their individual chapters, we see that Meimei is the most Americanized, for she misses American foods; Anor has the strongest sense of humor, for when the bombs destroy their house, she finds her checkers, which the rats had stolen, and concludes impishly that "the Japs were not only trying to gain our love by bombing us, but trying very hard to help us kill rats too!" (120); Adet is the most romantic, ardently patriotic and Chinese. Despite the horrifying sights of rotting corpses, burning buildings, cratered streets, air raids that kept them underground six hours at a stretch, Adet sees the war as a leveler, pulling rich and poor together for a common cause, and she is moved by the beauty of that bond. *Dawn over Chungking* has the poignant appeal, though not the tragic outcome, of *The Diary of Anne Frank*, for it too is an account of tender, idealistic youth confronted with the most brutal human behavior yet still believing in humanity's inherent goodness and still nurturing hope for the future.

The theme of wartime love pervades both *Destination Chungking* and *Flame from the Rock*. The first is a beautifully written, fictionalized autobiography recounting the relationship between Han Suyin, a Chinese-Belgian Eurasian originally named Rosalie Chou, and her first husband, Tang Paohuang, an officer in the Kuomintang army. As children they played together in Beijing; as young adults Pao refuses an arranged marriage with Suyin sight unseen; as Chinese students in London, ironically, they meet and fall in love; as patriots they return to China; despite the interruption of an air raid, Suyin and Pao are married by a missionary in Hankow; despite a yearlong separation (after only two weeks of marriage) while he serves at the front and she works in a hospital, they are finally able to set up housekeeping—only to have their house leveled by a bomb. Ostensibly a love story between a man and a woman, *Destination Chungking* is actually about the love of one's country. Though Han Suyin, in a foreword to the 1953 edition, acknowledged an insecurity about her English, a third language for her, *Destination Chungking*, her first book, reads fluently and well. Its language is vivid and its details are sharp, giving promise of the brilliant and prolific writing career that Han Suyin has since fulfilled, relinquishing a medical career to do so. Han Suyin, like Edith Eaton, identifies most strongly with her Chinese half. *Destination Chungking* stresses the humor of the Chinese, their resilience, their courage, and their staying power.

Adet Lin's *Flame from the Rock*, in contrast, focuses on the romantic and tragic. In this novel, lively young Kuanpo Shen, niece of a professor, is wounded by a bomb and receives a lifesaving blood transfusion from a taciturn soldier. Though her family disapproves because of his peasant background, the young people are drawn to each other. He is killed in battle, however, and she eventually dies of grief. This work may be read as Adet Lin's disavowal of her professor father's retreat from the war to the safety of the United States, for the uncle's snobbery is presented in a highly unfavorable light, and the soldier, for his dogged strength and ultimate sacrifice, is shown as worthy of admiration and love. Skillfully written, *Flame from the Rock* seems much influenced by traditional Chinese novels in being unabashedly romantic; yet its assertion of the importance of an ordinary peasant soldier is extremely modern.

War Tide, by Lin Tai-yi (Anor Lin), and *Westward to Chungking*, by Helena Kuo, are both novels about the effects of war on family. Kuo's book focuses on the father, Lee Tien-men, the head of a multigenerational family, who not only gives away the stock of his shop so that it will not fall into Japanese hands but who also gives his five children to the war effort. With the help of an American friend, Sam Hupper, Lee Tien-men retreats inland from Soochow to a small mountain village near Chungking, where he helps the villagers build air-raid shelters and grows tomatoes. Though a few breaks in the narrative mar the novel's coherence, the variety of character and incident creates an interesting and vivid panorama. Multiply these people several million times, Kuo implies, and you will have a picture of China at war, of the heroism of ordinary men and women.

In *War Tide*, a fuller, richer book, Anor Lin, initiating her pen name Lin Tai-yi, displays her precocious talent and a vigorous, original mind, which would later produce four more novels. This book is peopled with a variety of believable characters but centers on the capable eighteen-year-old daughter. The dialogue is often witty and convincing, the inventive incidents organized around the principle of yin-yang, counterbalancing opposite forces: good fortune follows hard upon disaster, birth upon death, beauty upon ugliness. Although war deprives the Tai family of their livelihood, their home beside the beautiful West Lake, and their father's life, they remain undaunted. Lo-Yin has discovered inner resources strong enough to sustain her extended family.

The most remarkable element in *War Tide* is the experimental quality of its language. At moments of crisis, the writing becomes heightened, almost surreal, exaggerated, sometimes horrifying, a literary counterpart to expressionistic painting. Here, for example, suggesting the misanthropy of a Bosch canvas, is Lin Tai-yi's description of the Japanese invaders of Hangchow:

> They hobbled their way like monkeys hopping among trees, and their long, hairy hands were claws, and they let out monstrous sizzlings or shrieks; they opened their mouths wide and let out shrieks into the open purple winter air, shrieks into the white sky, and their bloody claws scratched over everything they saw, and their eyes were lit by some evil green fire, evil, bitter fire. They scratched the winter sky and broke it like a crust, and from behind the sky rain had poured—black rain, blacker than blood, and the sky was bleeding. . . . When the devils were tired of scratching . . . they sought something warm, something warm and human because they were so afraid, and they sought and found the sight and touch of warm, pale, soft female flesh, and their dirty claws tore the flesh apart, screeching as they did—and the warmth in the flesh had gone with the tearing, and that was how they went. . . . And the city lay rotting, red, wasted, smelling and burning, and on the streets hungry devils and stray dogs hunted; the devils sought among both living and dead to shame them, but the dogs sought for a bone to gnaw from the dead only. (96–97)

The insistent repetition of "shrieks," "fire," "something warm," and "devils," the harsh animal imagery, the devastating final indictment, in which dogs are portrayed as superior to humans—this is powerful writing at any time, but extraordinary for a seventeen-year-old.

In these war books, we find an ulterior purpose: demonstration to the United States, a country superior in arms and supplies, that China was a worthy ally. The character of the adventurer Sam Hupper is an embodiment of United States aid to China as well as a winsome addition to make more palatable to Americans a tale of Chinese suffering. Lin Tai-yi, however, did not sugarcoat her material for her audience. With boldness and sarcasm, she attacks Americans for supplying Japan with materials used to bomb China and protests racism and greed in scathing terms:

> "I'll tell you why I look sad, Mother!" Lo-Yin said. "Wipe the dust off your skin, for did you ever hear of the inferior yellow race, or white superiority, or race prejudice, or empire or trade relations or petty politics, Mother? Did you know of oil? Don't you know oil makes good trade, good profit? Ha! Ha, weak China, polite China, bully the four hundred million people, for they have no feelings, their skins are yellow, how can they feel the difference between life and death, or love of mother and son? Scrap iron, Mother, iron waste, iron—they can be turned into profit. Profit, Mother, profit—don't you know that's the most important thing in the world. . . . Don't you know, Mother, that the white man rules and governs by divine right? Heaven sent the Japs to us, but they forgot white men must make a profit. . . . Burn, burn! . . . Chinese blood is yellow, it is not red. Oh no! But it is good enough to sacrifice to fill the bellies of the red-blooded with gold and silver! So sing out the praises of democracy and equality, but who will pay for all these lives and this torture?" (*War Tide* 121)

With the fervor of Edith Eaton defending her Chinese heritage, with the bitterness of disillusioned idealism and the outspokenness of youth, Lin Tai-yi lashes out against injustice. It is to white America's credit that such words were printed in this country.

More popular by far, however, was homegrown "exotic" Jade Snow Wong's *Fifth Chinese Daughter*, for as Elaine Kim points out in her ground-breaking study *Asian American Literature*: "Bitterness against Asian cultures and values, and Asian American values and life styles, were far better tolerated by publishers and a predominantly white readership, which has been traditionally more receptive to expressions of self-contempt and self-negation on the part of members of racial minority people than to criticism of problems in American society" (59). Resentment of the Asian American community and low self-esteem among its members are very much part of *Fifth Chinese Daughter*, though the surface message, at least by the end of the book, seems to be pride in accomplishment and reconciliation with the author's past. In its day the work was a best-seller, and, under the auspices of the State Department, it was translated into Chinese, Japanese, Thai, German, Urdu, Burmese, and Indonesian (Chun-Hoon 125) and Jade Snow Wong was sent to Asia as a cultural ambassador. A documentary film was made about her as late as 1976, and, until the appearance of Kingston, Jade Snow Wong was the best-known Chinese American spokeswoman. Yet for contemporary readers the book is a stilted, emotionally strangled work, recounting rather spiritlessly and totally without humor Wong's strict, traditional upbringing in San Francisco's Chinatown, and her efforts to achieve self-determination. Overt expressions of resentment and anger are stifled but seethe under the surface of her girlhood memories of unjust parental punishment. As she mingles more with the mainstream community, Wong takes pride in her Chinese background, mainly by cooking Chinese dinners for friends and the dean with whom she lives as a servant. Having learned humility, as Kim points out, she seems unaware of the abnegation of coupling herself with her employer's pets: "All who lived in that home, including a pair of cocker spaniels named Pupuli and Papaia, a black cat named Bessie and Jade Snow, were recipients of the dean's kindness and consideration" (156). The book emphasizes the hurdles that her family set up on her road to self-fulfillment and downplays those erected by the larger society. Thus Wong's success may be attributable in large part to the same characteristics that made Winnifred Eaton's romances so popular: she caters to the stereotypes and myths of the majority about itself. *Fifth Chinese Daughter* is an ethnic Horatio Alger story bearing witness to the achievement of the American dream, in which even the poorest and most unlikely (that is, nonwhite) Cinderella may find her way to the palace of the prince—in this case, gain recognition from the mainstream world by setting up a pottery business in Chinatown in San Francisco.

Contrary to Lowell Chun-Hoon's conclusion that Wong reconciled the conflicts between the Chinese values of her parents and the values of the larger society around her, it is actually her parents who come to accept "their peculiar fifth daughter" and admire her success in making a living through her ceramic business. At the end of the book, only Caucasians flock to see her work; "the Chinese did not come to buy one piece from her." Jade Snow Wong is as much a curiosity in Chinatown as she was at Mills College. In the introduction to her second book, *No Chinese Stranger*, she admits to feeling more at home in the People's Republic than she ever felt in the land of her birth:

> During four weeks of travel in a land physically new to me, it was remarkable how very much I felt at home. Because of a radiance which enveloped me as I moved among the Chinese in the People's Republic of China, I discovered my comfortable bonds as one of

them. Yet when I walk two familiar blocks between home and studio, in the freedom of the U.S., I am conscious of being a minority in a "white" or Western world. (xii)

Though she testified abroad that racism was no barrier to individual accomplishment in the United States, American intolerance of the Chinese caused Wong to feel a divided loyalty and a split sense of self-awareness.

Autobiographical works of this period that did not cater to stereotypes were neglected, despite the fact that some are livelier and better written. Perhaps because the authors were born abroad, the American audience found their experiences too foreign for popular consumption. At the same time, however, Janet Lim's *Sold for Silver* appealed to Americans precisely because of the sensational aspects of her life story. Abandoned at age eight by her mother, sold for $250 to a wealthy Singapore family, Lim had to defend herself against the sexual advances of her master. Rescued by Anglican missionaries, educated and trained as a nurse, she was later shipwrecked and imprisoned by Japanese soldiers. The most striking characteristic of the book is the matter-of-fact manner in which the most repellent events are narrated.

More substantial is the work of Helena Kuo, a journalist, feminist, and self-appointed cultural ambassador from China, as she put it, "a fragment of old China come West." She was an embodiment of the new Chinese woman, a result of the Revolution of 1911, which overthrew the three-hundred-year-old Manchu dynasty, stopped footbinding, gave women the vote and equal education with men, and turned China's face toward Western progress. Kuo's first book, *Peach Path*, commissioned by Methuen, announces its feminist stance from the outset:

This is a woman's book, written by a woman for women. To misquote St. Paul, and thus take revenge on the numerous well-meaning but unworthy translators of Confucius, when I became a woman I thought as a woman, I spoke as a woman, and I understand as a woman. So I write as a woman. (1)

The book is an uneven collage introducing to British and American readers the stories, legends, and maxims of old China—including the legend of Fa Mulan, the woman warrior who provides the central image of Kingston's book—as well as prescriptions for happiness from a young woman, sometimes preachy, sometimes whimsical and humorous, always confident and outspoken. Kuo's autobiography, *I've Come a Long Way*, is the story of an independent woman whose combination of good looks, fortunate contacts, personal integrity, and ingenuity did indeed bring her a long way, from war-torn China to a visit with Eleanor Roosevelt at the White House. Like Edith Eaton, Kuo used her skills and patriotic fervor to lecture on China's behalf, to write newspaper and magazine articles making the Chinese less strange to Westerners. Though her sensibilities were completely formed in China, Kuo confessed, after a few years in the United States, to an internal split:

I live now in a happy if sometimes puzzling state of divided mind: the old Chinese mind and the new mind of the West. I am educated and progressive to the point of being aggressive, but always with me is my happy heritage of Chinese civilization which gives me a heaven-sent balance, and I believe I shall never be wholly westernized, even if sometimes I seem to be walking on the edge of a dangerous chasm. (4)

Since 1939, the United States has been her home; her occasional writing is devoted to books and articles about the work of her husband, the painter Dong Kingman.

By far the most introspective autobiography, delightfully illustrated by the author, is *Echo of a Cry* by Mai-mai Sze. Daughter of Alfred Sze, who was China's "Envoy Extraordinary and Minister Plenipotentiary to the Court of St. James" (16) and a 1902 graduate of Cornell, Sze recounts with humor her Anglicization as a young child, her summer with a religious Quaker family who punished any misbehavior or accident by forcing her to put her pennies into the China Inland Mission box decorated with a picture of a Chinese girl who looked like her. For high school and college, Sze came to the United States. At Wellesley College she encounters racism when white girls refuse to sit next to a black student at a lunch counter. After a conversation with the young black woman, Sze realizes that "we're cause people whether we like it or not" (165). While visiting France she is regarded as a Chinese, but when she visits China finds herself awkward and un-Chinese. Although one of the most privileged of the authors, Sze acknowledges "a funny mixed feeling of being given so much, yet feeling I've lost something" (164). The fragmentation of self resulting from the multiple "reshufflings," as she calls them, leads her to conclude poignantly:

> Fervently we have wanted to belong somewhere at the same time that we have often wanted to run away. We reached out for something, and when by chance we grasped it, we often found that it wasn't what we wanted at all. There is one part of us that is always lost and searching. It is an echo of a cry that was a longing for warmth and safety. And through our adolescent fantasies, and however our adult reasoning may disguise it, the search continues. (202)

As though in belated reaction to the Holocaust, Sze published *Silent Children*, the haunting allegory of a band of homeless children, orphaned by war, eking out a living by stealing. A surreal dimness permeates this book, set in an unnamed land, whose characters bear the unrecognizable names Cruzz, Jolo, Worro, Toor, Lal. One of the boys steals a large trunk that contains not food but velvet gowns, lace parasols, and gold coins. Around the bonfire of their muddy camp, the half-starved children dress up and parade in a grotesque mockery of worldly splendor. Adult strangers intrude, and their greed and ineptness lead to several deaths and to the eventual scattering of the band of children. Sze is protesting the dehumanizing effects of war on the most innocent and powerless of society.

IV

With the repeal of the Chinese Exclusion Act, in 1943, the number of Chinese in America increased and, consequently, the number of Chinese American women writers. Yet, the literary scene through the next three decades was dominated by immigrant Chinese writers, and the traditions continued: explanation of China to the West; protest against discrimination; storytelling and experimentation.

Beijing-born Hazel Lin, who was one-quarter French, came to the United States to study medicine in 1939 and lived here until her death. She juggled a dual career, a primary one as obstetrician-gynecologist and a secondary one as writer. She wrote four novels, all nostalgically set in China. Her best work, *The Physicians*, set in Beijing, recounts a young woman's determination to study Western medicine; eventually she wins the approval of her grandfather, who practices Chinese medicine. *The Moon Vow* is a somewhat sensational story of a young woman who cannot consummate her marriage because of a vow of celibacy to a secret lesbian society. In *House of Orchids* a young girl from a destitute family is sold into prostitution and falls in love with a student from a respectable family. Another novel, *Rachel Weeping for Her Children, Uncomforted*, tells of a Chinese medical student who has an affair with a much older American surgeon-missionary. Dreams, nightmares, and fears are interwoven into the narrative in an experimental fashion, but the book is overwritten in places and underdeveloped as a whole. *Weeping May Tarry* is a brief, moving diary of Lin's battle with cancer. She died of a sudden stroke at age 73 in 1986.

Anor Lin, author of *War Tide*, lived extensively in the United States in her youth, as noted, was for many years a resident of Hong Hong, and has recently moved to the Washington, D.C., area. Her later novels deal with serious, complex themes. *The Golden Coin* pits faith against cynicism in the intriguing story of a mismatched couple: a coldly scheming biology professor and an illiterate girl from the Shanghai slums. Although the author seems to sympathize with the heroine's faith in miracles, her joie de vivre, and capacity to love, Lin Tai-yi shows how misplaced such faith is and how it is ultimately destroyed. *The Eavesdropper* explores the tension between passivity and activity; the central character, a Chinese writer, moves back and forth between the United States and China, unattached to either world but in love with his older brother's tubercular wife. Class conflicts are dramatized in *The Lilacs Overgrow* and, in *Kampoon Street*, the effects of poverty. Though Lin Tai-yi does not discuss social issues directly, the Chinese political scene serves as the background for all the novels, and the events in the foreground parallel contemporaneous historical struggles in China. In *The Lilacs Overgrow*, for example, the marriages of the two nieces of a Nationalist Chinese official may represent the two forces that struggled for control of the country; the work, indeed, may well be a veiled criticism of both Nationalist and Communist excesses. One niece marries a wealthy man who turns out to be spoiled and spineless; the other weds a Communist, who is portrayed at first sympathetically and later as a fanatic. *Kampoon Street*, which has been translated and published in Brazil, Finland, Sweden, Denmark, and China, seems to indicate a leftward shift in the author's politics. The work suggests that not only opportunities but even morality can be severely limited by poverty.

In these novels, particularly in *Kampoon Street*, Lin Tai-yi continues the expressionist strain she used to good purpose in *War Tide*. Here we find a character called Female One, who has a "frog-like face," and "holes . . . which served as eyes . . . so deep they were like tunnels" (98) and who does not know who she is because she has no identity card. Lin Tai-yi is a highly skilled writer, intelligent and observant, sympathetic as well as humorous, poetic as well as pointed, and deserving of much wider recognition.

V

By far the most versatile explainer of China to the West is Han Suyin, whose *Destination Chungking* is discussed above. Autobiographer, biographer, novelist, political analyst, chronicler and traveloguer, and medical doctor as well, she vies with Winnifred

Eaton in being the most productive woman writer of Chinese ancestry with nearly twenty titles to her name. She received her higher education in Belgium and England, practiced medicine in Hong Kong and Singapore, and has lectured frequently in the United States.

Han Suyin is most widely known for *A Many-Splendored Thing* because of the popular movie based on her novel, and most controversial for her strong support for Mao Zedong and the Communist revolution, fully documented in *The Morning Deluge* and *Wind in the Tower*, almost a hagiography. Han Suyin's best work is *The Crippled Tree*, the first book of her four-volume autobiography. Like Kingston's *Woman Warrior*, this work is a mixed genre, combining history (in this case, China's from 1885 to 1928), reconstructed family history, and Han Suyin's personal memories presented in a novelistic mode. Often poetic and deeply felt, it recounts her parents' storybook courtship in Belgium and disillusioned marriage in China, intertwined with and paralleled by the history of a feudal, weak China, represented as a woman struggling to free herself from the economic stranglehold of imperialistic (male) Western powers. Also like *The Woman Warrior*, on a personal level, *The Crippled Tree* is a working out of a painful relationship, from initial rejection by the mother through resentment, anguish, and finally understanding by the daughter. The other volumes of the autobiography, *A Mortal Flower*, *Birdless Summer*, and *My House Has Two Doors*, seem gradually to lose power.

In its attitudes toward the Chinese, white society has apparently changed little since the time of the Eaton sisters; in a 1982 newspaper interview, Han Suyin made the following remark:

> As a Eurasian, I was always fighting. I am still fighting race prejudice today. I was told by people in the sphere of my young life that I was only good enough to be a prostitute. This situation made me strong. It was either show strength or go under. . . . A very important Swiss surgeon once said to me, "All Eurasians are degenerate, syphilitic." I said: "Me, degenerate? Me?" He said that I am the exception. When he was speaking these words, he was hitting the table with his thumb. I told him: "It is not necessary to hit the table." That got him! I was commenting on his bad manners. (Christy)

Han Suyin is more a citizen of the world than of any single nation. Her nonfiction works passionately depict China in English, a language she loves and calls "that rich and inexhaustible treasure of moods and music, feeling and thought, endless ambrosia, a firm enchantment, lifelong" (Wakeman 613). In her novels, the couples are often interracial: the doomed lovers in *A Many-Splendored Thing*, set in Hong Kong, are a Eurasian doctor, a widow, and a married English journalist; a happy ending is allowed an Englishwoman, a writer, and a dark-skinned Indian engineer in *The Mountain Is Young*, set in Nepal. Communist China is the setting of *Till Morning Comes*, in which a Texan journalist, daughter of a millionaire, marries a patriotic Chinese doctor, who is ultimately destroyed by his countrymen. In this novel, Han Suyin again interweaves a moving story of individuals trapped by historical and political forces over which they have no control. She manages to present the Communist revolution sympathetically and yet be critical of the excesses of the cultural revolution and of political fanaticism. China has few advocates more eloquent or passionate than Han Suyin. As a novelist, at her best, she creates engrossing characters whose passions and agonies are deeply moving.

VI

Two Chinese American women novelists born in the United States and educated here are Virginia Lee and Diana Chang. Lee's *House That Tai Ming Built* emphasizes the favorable aspects of the Chinese as a superior ancient culture, symbolized by exquisite artifacts, while gently protesting racial discrimination. Bo Lin, a third-generation Chinese American brought up in San Francisco's Chinatown, falls in love with Scott Hayes; however, the miscegenation laws of California, enforced in the early 1940s, the time of this story—and on the books until 1967 (Kim 97)—forbade marriages between Asians and Caucasians. Scott dies at the front in Europe.

With two exceptions, Diana Chang's books have nothing to do with Chinese or Chinese Americans. Her first work, *Frontiers of Love*, a rich, full novel set in Shanghai at the close of World War II, is the story of three young Eurasians, representing the spectrum of possibilities in the struggle to determine their identities. At one end of the spectrum is Mimi Lambert, who rejects the Asian part of herself, chooses a Caucasian lover, and, when he refuses to marry her, throws herself at any American who can offer what she thinks of as a lifeline: passage out of China. At the other end is Feng Huang, who rejects the European in him and joins the Communists, becoming so committed to their cause that he rationalizes the murder of his fiancée's cousin, in which he inadvertently takes part, as an unfortunate means to a desirable end. In the middle position is Sylvia Chen, who, after much agonizing, realizes that she is "an entity composed of both her parents, but ready to act and not merely react, for one individual—herself" (237). Chang, who is three-quarters Chinese and one-quarter Irish but by upbringing an American, also acts for herself instead of reacting and goes her own way in her other novels.

Chang chooses in her later books to focus on modern varieties of love: love after divorce, in *A Woman of Thirty*; love for an unborn child, even if it is the result of rape, in *A Passion for Life*; interracial love between a Caucasian Peace Corps volunteer and a Chinese Communist dancer, in the minor, farcical *The Only Game in Town*; love as a manifestation of neurosis, in the clever *Eye to Eye*, in which a married white Protestant artist falls in love with a Jewish writer and seeks the help of a psychiatrist; extramarital love between an older woman and a younger man, in *A Perfect Love*. She writes with great skill of Ivy League graduates, artists, writers, publishers, who inhabit the world of New York City, Long Island, Massachusetts. Her characters tend to be blue-eyed Anglo-Saxons; the outsiders are Jews. "Fitness, in evolutionary biology," says the biologist Lewis Thomas, "means fitting in with the rest of life. If a species is good at this, it tends to survive" (32). Like Winnifred Eaton, Diana Chang is conscious of her audience and wants to fit in, to survive; she "subsumes aspects of her background in the interests of other truths" (qtd. in Ling, "Writer" 75), truths she believes will have a broader appeal in the society in which she lives.

A work that incorporates all aspects of its author's background and blends them in a highly sophisticated way is *Crossings*, by Chuang Hua. In theme and style a forerunner of Kingston's *Woman Warrior*, *Crossings* is an experimental novel that requires and rewards the reader's closest concentration. The narrative thread traces the growth and decline of a love affair between a Chinese American woman and a European journalist, but the story is constantly interrupted by memories of childhood and family, by dreams, nightmares, images arresting and resonant. Fourth Jane is the middle child of seven in a well-to-do family that transplanted her, when a child, from China to England and then to the United States. Jane herself, as an adult, spends time in Paris but makes return visits to New York. In all, there are seven crossings of the ocean and four cultural adjustments; as in *Echo of a Cry*, though these travels may be enriching, they increase the protagonist's sense of fragmentation and her difficulty in determining her identity.

As *The Woman Warrior* is infused by the tension between the narrator and her mother, *Crossings* is dominated by the presence of the father, a surgeon in China, a stockbroker in New York, a strong man who is as tyrannical as he is loving. Central to the book is the anguish Jane experiences when, for her own psychological well-being, she must take a stand against him; her pain is intense when she remembers the joy he gave to her childhood. Magnifying the familial tension is the conflict between her two countries—China and America—during the Korean War:

> I saw with dread my two lives ebbing. Each additional day of estrangement increased the difficulty of eventual reconciliation, knowing the inflexibility of Chinese pride. In that paralysis I lived in no man's land, having also lost America since the loss of one entailed the loss of the other. Moments I thought of giving up one for the other, I had such longings to make a rumble in the silence. But both parts equally strong canceled out choice. (122)

Crossings abounds with images interwoven throughout the text, intricately echoing and reechoing one another. Some obviously advance the action, while others that at first seem to arrest the action also, on closer inspection, inform the narration. An example of the second type occurs in the middle of a conversation between the journalist and Jane on his initial visit to her apartment. He speaks first:

> Writers belong in the kitchen. Cooking is an essential part of their imaginative environment.
> Oh. You can put in the steak now.
> A bird plunged like dead weight ten stories from the roof. Two stories from the pavement, with a single flap of wings, it skimmed above the quivering treetops and took off in a sweeping spiral till it disappeared behind the rooftops.
> We can eat now. (24)

In the midst of preparations of an intimate meal, the bird falling "like dead weight" for eight stories is jarring. Then we realize that it is a willful fall, for the bird has wings it prefers not to use until the last minute, when it swoops up and takes off in a display of its flying prowess. Jane is like the bird, falling into a dead-end affair with a married man, trusting that her strength will enable her, when she so decides, to escape relatively unscathed.

Chuang Hua is not afraid to see all sides of life, and, like Lin Tai-yi, she does not shrink from horrifying images: "And in the spring bloated corpses flowed in the current of the yellow river, bobbing among torn roots and bits of watermelon rinds gnawed to the skin" (48). These corpses float past the sugarcane plot where Jane's Chinese nurse cuts the reddest and sweetest stalks for the children. The juxtaposition of negative and positive images recurs often in *Crossings* and indicates a worldview that unflinchingly encompasses both good and bad. By coercing opposite-tending fragments into a whole, Chuang Hua creates an artistic coherence.

In *Crossings*, Chuang Hua has created a highly original expression of the Chinese American hyphenated condition. She has explored her past and made it central, plumbed the depths of her ethnic confusion, mixed memory with fantasy, with reality, with matter-of-fact detail, stretched the language of the novel in the direction of poetry, fragmented the narrative for a kaleidoscopic effect—in short, written what may well be a small masterpiece.

VII

Maxine Hong Kingston's *Woman Warrior* was deservedly recognized for its boldness, power, and beauty, its fullness of voice in expressing the hyphenated condition, but this work did not spring full blown from the empyrean. Most of the writers we have examined, despite the Chinese tradition of repression of women, were also outspoken and individualistic. Nearly all their works have been ignored—in many cases, as I hope to have shown, undeservedly so. Looking back, we find that the works that received accolades in their time—Winnifred Eaton's romantic confections, Jade Snow Wong's autobiography—reflected more their audience and its taste than the quality of the books themselves. The frail Japanese or Eurasian heroines romantically involved with dominant Caucasian men in high positions, the Chinese American success story at a time when the United States was at war with Japan, satisfied a public that sought to confirm its own myths, in stories about its superiority, generosity, and openness. It was not particularly interested in learning about the Chinese themselves or in dispelling stereotypes. In fact, to a large extent, it still finds them "inscrutable."

In "Cultural Mis-Readings by American Reviewers," Kingston expresses her frustration that two-thirds of the critics who praised her book could not see beyond their own stereotyped thinking; she cites examples of the painful "exotic-inscrutable-mysterious-oriental reviewing." Here is one example, from the *Chattanooga News-Free Press*:

> At her most obscure, though, as when telling about her dream of becoming a fabled "woman warrior" the author becomes as inscrutable as the East always seems to the West. In fact, this book seems to reinforce the feeling that "East is East and West is West and never the twain shall meet," or at any rate it will probably take more than one generation away from China. (63)

The inscrutableness, it seems to Kingston and to me, is in the eyes of the beholder, and the unbridgeable gulf as well. Chinese Americans have been explaining themselves for nearly a century, but their voices are either ignored or misunderstood.

A major theme in Kingston's *Woman Warrior* is the importance of articulateness. Finding one's voice and telling one's stories represents power, just as having one's stories buried is powerlessness. From the first episode, "No Name Woman," in which Kingston disobeys her mother's injunction and tells the story of the prodigal aunt whom she calls her "forerunner," through the accounts of her own childhood (her belief that her mother had cut her frenum, her silence in Caucasian school, her terrible bullying of a Chinese American classmate in an effort to make her speak—an act of self-hatred), to the last episode, "A Song for a Barbarian Reed Pipe," Kingston elaborates on this theme. Instead of the confusion and humiliation about her Chinese background that she felt as a child, she now finds, in the stories and customs that set her apart from her Caucasian classmates, her heritage and treasure, her strength and identity. Kingston's work combines the traits of the Chinese American writers who preceded her—protest, storytelling, nostalgia, and experimentation. The effect is one of surprising power and startling beauty.

Despite the tradition of repression and devaluation—as Kingston's mother put it, "It's better to feed geese than girls"—Chinese American women writers have demonstrated their talents, have expressed their concerns and their creativity, and have contributed to American literature. As a nation of immigrants, the United States has the opportunity to become acquainted with the peoples of the world within its own borders and in its own language. In their books, the immigrants and their children are speaking, singing. Together they make up the great American chorus, and it is our special privilege, as teachers and students of literature, to listen.

Twelve Asian American Writers:
In Search of Self-Definition

Shirley Geok-lin Lim

As part of the macrocosm, Asian American writing exhibits the variety of voices, forms, and genres that marks mainstream American literature.[1] At the same time, one finds in it certain inextricably Asian psychological and philosophical perspectives. A strong Confucian patriarchal orientation is a dominant element and with that the corollary of female inferiority, themes that are overtly or unconsciously struck in narratives as disparate as Jade Snow Wong's *Fifth Chinese Daughter*, Jeanne Wakatsuki Houston and James D. Houston's *Farewell to Manzanar*, and Maxine Hong Kingston's *Woman Warrior*. Another major motif is the urge to find a usable past—specifically, for writers to come to terms with the immigrant experiences of their race.

Asian American writing, from its earliest expressions in the first decade of the twentieth century to the most recent plays by David Henry Hwang, shows a strong concern with its immigrant history. Not surprisingly, therefore, it draws heavily on the resources of autobiography, biography, and history, provinces in which writing more faithfully reflects personal experiences, social observations, and memory. Works as varied as Pardee Lowe's, Monica Sone's and the Houstons' autobiographies, Toshio Mori's short stories, John Okada's and Louis Chu's novels, and Kingston's histories share a concern with sociological texture in their attempts to rewrite the past; as such, they exhibit in different degrees a burden of referentiality in which the texts demand to be read for their relevance to historical meaning.

Recent studies on the genres of biography and autobiography claim that "the patterns of modern fiction and contemporary biography have close connections. . . . For a fact to exist in a biography it needs an imaginative as well as referential dimension which the process of writing provides" (Nadel 9–10); "the modernist movement is away from representational discourse towards self-enacting, self-reflexive verbal structures and the critical theories that have been devised to explain this movement conspire to make the very idea of literary modernism seem synonymous with that of autobiography" (Spengemann xiii). Still, it is clear that, despite overlapping boundaries, the genres of life stories and fiction are separate. Alan Shelston reminds us that "the biographer, by implication, is not free but inhibited by the demands of accuracy and attention to detail which, paradoxically, militate against the achievement of a higher form of truth" (1). In particular, biography inspired by motives of commendation "by its nature . . . embodies a preconceived attitude to its subject: the biographer will have clearly in his mind the image of the subject which he wishes to project" (52). "A literary device, however admirable in itself, which thrusts biographical materials outside the dimension of life-writing, ruptures truth more seriously, because less obviously, than outright errors" (P. M. Kendall 9). For the purposes of this article, I assume that "the secret of the novelist's success lies in his unrestricted imagination," while "the biographer is bound by what he has. . . . [T]he sources must be there, and all the relevant sources must be considered" (Garraty 24–25).

In Asian American writing, insofar as works appear composed to meet external referentiality, be it of explanation of ethnic identity to an unknowledgeable audience or of fidelity to sociological and historical-based memory, they are less powerfully literary constructions. Moreover, they are liable to those reductions of authorial self and text that form stereotypes of exoticism—that is, to ancient commonplaces that constitute images presented as conventionally foreign. For an ethnic minority, living as it does always a stranger in the eyes of the majority, the consciousness that "utilizes for its own profit the ontological duality of myself and myself in the eyes of the Other," the "lie consciousness," may be inescapable.[2] The danger inherent in the reduction of text to stereotype is the presentation of self that is not and not of self that is.

It is possible to read all of Asian American writing along a plane of expression of authentic and inauthentic or exotic selves. Authors such as Frank Chin, Jeffery Paul Chan, and Kingston, sensitive to their own themes and voices, like the existentialist philosopher, recognize that "it is necessary that we *make ourselves* what we are" (255). These writers have become self-conscious; they have begun to deal with problems of textuality instead of with racial stereotypes. When imaginings of self occur together with awareness of functions of text, Asian American writers liberate themselves from commonplace notions of the exotic. Moving away from sociological documentation, much contemporary Asian American writing now aspires to the power of the literary artifact.

As artifacts of the imagination, there is little to differentiate between *Fifth Chinese Daughter*, the autobiography of Wong, who was born in the United States, and *Chinatown Family*, the novel by Lin Yutang, born in China. Both books, published around the same period, treat the myth of the cultural drive to success in immigrant Asian society, derived from the dogma of the patriarchal network in which the individual finds value through contributive work. In fact, Lin Yutang's novel remains throughout at the level of social stereotyping. It depicts, with no surprises, the fortunes of a Chinese family in the United States, struggling first with a small laundry, then rising to the restaurant business, fortunes presided over by wise, industrious parents and supported by filial, hardworking children. The novel abounds with those positive stereotypes that have accumulated concerning Asian American culture: its emphasis on education, family obligations, and work; its colorful celebrations of rituals, holidays, and ceremonies. Insofar as writers insist on presenting the various elements of Asian culture to a foreigner in the manner most acceptable to society, they manipulate their materials to suit predisposed interpretations. *Chinatown Family* is less a literary work than a programmatic piece written to a certain coda. Exactness of detail, social realism, and fidelity to experience that the writer seems to adhere to are only pseudo in nature; Lin's true purpose is to reduce action and character to a system of references related directly to those conventions of social behavior and values positively accepted as Asian.

Wong's book, written in the third person, makes for more powerful literature. While, like Lin Yutang, she has deliberately manipulated the structure of the book so as to create opportunities to trot out all the phenomenology that forms the common opinion of Asian experience (Chinese cooking, foods, celebrations, familial duties, and so on), *Fifth Chinese Daughter* has an element of the unpredictable that challenges these stereotypes and promises every now and again to expose these racial myths. The father, a domineering patriarch, is also an ambiguous figure infected by his new country's vision of equality. The underlying drama of the daughter's challenge to her father contradicts and exceeds the given ideas of Chinese familial relationships. In confronting the limitations of popular perceptions of Chinese traits, Wong appears in some danger of offering only a reversal of attitudes. The pieties associated with Asian Americans (based on the primacy of the patriarchal family units, on obedience, and on formality of behavior) observed in conflict with white American countervalues (the importance of individuality, freedom of speech and action, and spontaneity) are unsympathetically portrayed through the point of view of the author's persona, the socially and professionally ambitious daughter.[3]

This book, however, is more than a neat, hostile overturning of Asian pieties. Its power rests on the unconscious paradox that holds together in a larger frame the simpler narration of conflict as the daughter becomes assimilated into white American culture and therefore apparently less filial. While Chinese attitudes frustrate and demean the protagonist in her daily life, her purpose as she develops is to prove worthy of approval from her father who symbolizes Chinese patriarchal society. Unlike conventional fictions of conflict and identity, *Fifth Chinese Daughter*, although it presents the ambivalence of living in two cultures seemingly inimical to each other, does not clearly set up opposing points of view. The narrative does not contain a rejection of or an attempt to integrate the Asian paradigm to a white American model.

Finally, the author subverts her own endeavor and reveals her hidden agenda: not to rebel against her family but to compel her family to recognize and accept her. Actions lead to a reintegration of the individual *into* the Asian paradigm; the latter part of the book is a series of individual accomplishments seen as significant only insofar as they impress the patriarchal structure. The narrator-persona felt triumph at winning an essay competition run by the War Department, for example, because "this was the first occasion when the entire Wong family was assembled in pride of their fifth daughter" (198). In the book's conclusion, the father tells his daughter of a letter he had written to a cousin long ago: "I am hoping that someday I may be able to claim that by my stand I have washed away the former disgraces suffered by the women of our family." As readers we are shocked by his self-ignorant and arrogant assertion—that he was the agent in the daughter's push for her rights—when his past actions had shown him to be reactionary. But it is even more distressing to discover that the author-narrator is herself taken in by his hypocrisy. "For the first time in her life," Wong tells us at this supreme point of paternal approval, "she felt contentment" (246). The absence of irony where it seems to be most pertinent makes *Fifth Chinese Daughter* a peculiarly Asian document. Despite the detailed expressions of conflict between the protagonist and her Chinese milieu, in her incapacity for irony Wong demonstrates the single vision in her autobiography—a vision that is unswervingly Chinese and only incidentally occidental.

Between the 1940s and 1970s, some Asian American writers continued to exploit the fascination of the majority culture with those Asian images perceived as most foreign. For such writers, their minority status was not only uncritically accepted but actively supported through a pseudoliterary tradition. Virginia Lee, in her novel *The House That Tai Ming Built*, frankly adopts the most positive of Chinese stereotypes, a reverse racism that robs her fiction of reality and inherent significance as surely as negative prejudices do. Her description of Lin's family is composed of sentimental clichés: the grandfather is warm, serene, diligently playful, while the father embodies "all the virtues expected of a man" (4). The novel's first section gives a simpering portrait of the grandfather; the second and third sections deal halfheartedly with the increasing conflicts between the children and parents. When, finally, Lin has an affair with Scott, the white hero, the dramatic denouement, in which she wishes she "had been born an O'Malley or a Smith" (191), is lost in the welter of conventional romancing. Triteness of plot (girl meets boy, girl loses boy) is not as damaging as the triteness of language. The influence of racist and sexist ideology on Lee's choice of language is all too apparent, for example, in her use of jade images to represent Chinese identity.[4] Female characters are described by words and images such as *sweet, perfumed, lilacs, lavender, fragrance, graceful, lovely, exquisite, luminous,* and so on.

The novel makes no attempt to plumb the characters' motivation. Many pages are given over to describing Chinese porcelain, old bronzes, and jade carvings (see 135–42; 144–46; 153–55, for example). The opening page sets the tone: "The indoors of the Tai Ming Company displayed the works of the skilled craftsmen of China: potteries, porcelains, lacquerware, enamelware, and ivories. Silk, satin and brocade had a place to themselves and a corner of the red silk, undone from its roll, touched a *blanc-de-chine* Goddess of Mercy." Coincidence replaces psychological and causal relationships; for example, Lin's brother is reported killed in action on her wedding day. The plot proper, the obstacle-strewn path of true love between Asian American heroine and white male hero, does not begin until the book is two-thirds over. Instead, pages padded with enumerations of Chinese artifacts lead one to conclude that the novel is actually an exercise to appeal to a white audience looking for an introduction to an exotic culture. This apparent goal explains the awkwardness of the novel's form and the arbitrary insertion of secondary narratives of various lengths and indeterminate relevance (for example, the retelling of Yang Kwei Fei's tragedy or the explanation of why Chinese men wore queues before 1911). These anecdotes exist, as do the numerous descriptions of Chinese foods, customs, dress, and art objects, for their extraliterary value, as items in a catalog in which the fiction is the pretext.

Writers such as Jade Snow Wong and, to a lesser degree, Virginia Lee are motivated by the desire to balance those base generalizations of the Asian American that Betty Lee Sung has deplored "as insignificant, as handicapped, discriminated against" (3). Their emphasis on ethnocentric objects is governed by a sentimental strategy that relies on and perpetuates the oldest stereotypes and is itself the expression of bigotry, albeit perhaps unconscious and well-meaning. Such sentimentality degrades the literary attempt and the Asian American group for which these writers claim to speak by reducing its vitality to that of mere artistic paraphernalia.

In the 1950s a second group of Asian American writers, equally though differently ethnocentric, became more articulate, prefiguring in their choice of themes and social concerns the protest literature of the 1960s. Monica Sone's autobiography, *Nisei Daughter*, shows the same pressure to explain to a foreigner those features of the author's Asian world that we find in Wong's book; similarly, this necessity is in danger of being corrupted by nostalgia and elegiac sentiment. Explanation comes close to exploitation of the past for its exotic elements.[5] Sone's protagonist, however, is much further on in the process of assimilation. The narrator begins with an American point of view and discovers only later, through the pressures of her cross-cultural position, that she is also an alien. Her loyalties and identity as American are never in doubt (119; Little, 1953), although her entry into the public school system rouses a latent distinction of race (131). It took the war and the family's internment to bring about the recognition of her status as "a despised, pathetic two-headed freak, a Japanese and an American, neither of which seemed to be doing me any good" (159). The conflict between a discarded East and a rejecting West, the theme of doubleness that runs so deep in Asian American writing, concludes happily in Sone's book when, after the protagonist's release from camp and acceptance into a midwestern college (life imitating symbol), "The Japanese and the American parts of me were now blended into one" (238).

Unlike *Nisei Daughter*, John Okada's novel, *No-No Boy*, refuses to make any concessions to a white audience. The two books originate in rage at a shared history of racial oppression. But Okada's work, a more complex and ambiguous creation of Japanese American experiences of detention and discrimination during the Second World War, expresses a more difficult affirmation of American identity. It begins with Ichiro's return to Seattle after two years in camp and two years in prison for refusing the draft. An "intruder in a world to which he had no claim" (17; Tuttle, 1957), Ichiro is intensely, if not irreparably, wounded by his position as alien. Unlike sentimentalists such as Wong and Sone, who assert that their dual identities qualify them to belong to two cultures, Okada portrays the bleak negatives that damn a character who is unable to claim either culture and who has not made an internal reality for himself. Ichiro is doubly damned. Refusing to be drafted, he is rejecting the means by which he can be made acceptable to white America. At the same time, although raised by a fanatically Japanese mother, he cannot identify with Japan.[6] Unable to affirm either the Japanese or American aspects of his identity, he is filled with self-contempt, hatred for his Japanese parents, loathing for the Japanese Americans who revile him, and conflicting emotions toward white America, which he recognizes has shaped him without accepting him as a native son. He is tormented by irresolution. Other characters who embrace a single racial definition of self are not free of pain either and are also divided and violent, if not severely disturbed. Ichiro's mother, with her suicidal fanaticism, represents his Japanese half; his brother, Taro, his American half. Taro rejects his family, drops out of high school to enlist in the army, and beats up his brother. Both mother and brother are sullen, bitter, isolated, and rejecting characters. Significantly, the only character who appears psychologically whole is Kenji, a war hero who has lost both legs in combat. Ken's physical wound results in sexual impotence, but his friendship has a fructifying effect on Ichiro's psychic wound and psychological impotence.

Although Okada's defenders read his novel as a politically motivated attack on white supremacists, the novel's point of view is never so clear. There is as much contempt for Japanese Americans who hang onto a dead cultural definition of self as for those who deny their Japanese identities. In the character of Emi, deserted by her Japanese American husband, ironically, for the United States army, Okada depicts a sympathetic observer who sees Ichiro's torment as caused by his one mistake in denying his American self. Like Ken, she urges him to a reconciliation with his country; after all, "your mistake was no bigger than the mistake your country made" (130). Ichiro's renewal of hope begins when he meets Mr. Carrick, a white American whose willingness to employ him even after he learns of Ichiro's prison term demonstrates the possibility for forgiveness on both sides. The novel concludes in a crescendo of violence and deaths: the mother of suicide, Ken of his wound, Freddie, another draft refuser, in a car accident during a fight. These tragedies, the working out of self-destructiveness in the Japanese American community, lead to Ichiro's return to American society.

The impulse toward raw psychological realism, the turning away from exoticism to an examination of states of existence in which characters no longer conform to racially defined norms and in which the sense of self responds to a universe of random incident, is first marked in Asian American literature through the experiences of detention during the Second World War. Sone's and Okada's books were among the first to examine the deep wound suffered by the outsider. Consciousness of the psychic wound is itself wounding. Divisions between races and cultures give rise to divisions within the individual. Authorial consciousness of the divided self leads to an increasing interiority of narrative style and to irony, the literary mode by which split or opposed points of view are yoked together. The antinostalgia books of Okada, Louis Chu, and the Houstons exhibit this hurt consciousness. In these works, as well as in Kingston's *China Men* and in the shorter fiction of Frank Chin and Jeffery Chan, the hidden psychological wound finds overt expression in the threatening themes of emasculation of self and resulting impotence.

The Houstons' autobiographical history resembles Sone's autobiography in its narration of Japanese American experiences in detention camps on the West Coast and in the Midwest but differs radically in its expressive contours and its preoccupation with the father-daughter relationship. In *Farewell to Manzanar*, the division between Japanese and American selves is unbridgeable. The protagonist is implacably the tormented and the tormenter, victim and assistant to the white oppressor: the wound is deep within the condition of existence as Japanese American. As the narrator explains it, "I lived with this double impulse: the urge to disappear and the desperate desire to be acceptable" (138). Still, the Houstons lay the blame for the evacuation of 110,000 Japanese American citizens, in part, on their acquiescence, their absence of self-esteem (137).

The destruction of the integrity of identity is most clearly delineated in the character of the father. We see him in the first chapter as a successful fisherman directing his own boat. After Pearl Harbor, Papa is arrested by two FBI men; he has become "suddenly a man with no rights who looked exactly like the enemy" (7). At Manzanar camp, "things finished for him there" (41); he becomes alcoholic, withdrawn, given to rages and wife beating. In his daughter's eyes, he has become emasculated: "worst of all, I had lost my respect for Papa" (142). The Houstons draw a convincing picture of the protagonist's growing rejection of her father because he is Japanese—that is, of her hardening racism as she assimilates into white America and learns to want to be white. She describes her shame during an awards ceremony when the father gives a deep Japanese bow: "He was unforgivably a foreigner, then, foreign to them, foreign to me" (145). She was ashamed of him "in a deeper way, for being what had led to our imprisonment, that is, for being so unalterably Japanese" (144).

The father's tragedy is prelude to the daughter's, the disintegration of her identity together with the humiliations suffered by a self resolved to extinguish its ethnicity in favor of white homogeneity. She becomes the lead majorette in a Boy Scout parade, for at an early age she had begun to recognize that racial barriers could be crossed by exploiting her sexuality: "At this age I was too young to consciously use my sexiness or to understand how an oriental female can fascinate Caucasian men, and of course far too young to see that even this is usually just another form of invisibility" (141). The complex ironies in the autobiography rise from the honest yet dual and conflicting perceptions of the destruction of the persona's psyche and the daughter's share in white supremacists' attitudes that lead to that destruction.

Chinese American writers do not share the history of internment that gave Sone, Okada, and the Houstons ready-made material for profoundly moving drama, but they do share a concern with the male, patriarchal worlds of Asian ethnics in the United States, a concern that enlarges into an exploration of power and powerlessness in white America. In their introduction to the anthology *AIIIEEEEE!* Frank Chin, Jeffery Paul Chan, Lawson Inada, and Shawn Wong attack the white stereotype of the Asian as one "utterly without manhood. . . . At worst, the Asian American is contemptible because he is womanly, effeminate, devoid of all traditionally masculine qualities of originality, daring, physical courage, and creativity" (xxx; 1974). Their reaction to the Asian stereotype of effeminacy has been to hold up as models works such as Okada's *No-No Boy* and Chu's *Eat a Bowl of Tea*, which overtly express anxiety over male potency. In Chu's novel the central dramatic device is the sexual and psychological impotence of the protagonist, Ben Loy. Consequently, also, the tendency in Chin's and Chan's writing has been to depict male characters who are sexually potent or who express their manhood in violent and traditionally American ways. Chu's novel, like Okada's, has an antiromantic perspective on parent-child relationships. In Okada's novel, the mad mother is dominant, the sane father passive and helpless; in Chu's novel, parents are remote figures who control their adult children's lives for their own ends, that of maintaining face in their society.

These two authors mark the beginning of the tradition of realism in Asian American writing. Chu exposes a sleazier side of Chinese sojourner life than most Asian American writers have been willing to show. Many early Chinese immigrants, intending to return to China once they had made their fortunes, saw themselves as sojourners and thus did not attempt to assimilate into American culture. The depictions of Chinese men without women, spending their days in endless rounds of mah-jongg, the absence of communication between generations, the tyranny of the older over the younger, the oppressive presence of judgmental relatives, provide a corrective perspective to the conventional glowing picture of close kinship in the Chinese community and convey without exaggeration and with an insider's understanding the contradictions within the family. In this Chinatown drama there is hardly any intrusion of the white, English-speaking world; the characters are all Chinese immigrants operating in the framework of the parent society. The arranged marriage, the approved assault of the aggrieved father-in-law on the marriage breaker, the couple's isolation amid Chinatown gossips, and the political arrangements through which the Tong, the informal communal association, takes over the criminal justice system occur in a relentlessly closed-off Chinese society.

The novel is by no means a successful work. Chu's writing is stilted, full of clichés and clumsy constructions, pointing to the difficulties of a writer to whom English is still a second language. More important, the novel suffers from a lack of credible motivation. Nothing in Mei Oi's character prepares us for the older man's easy seduction of her, and Ben Loy's eagerness to please her even after she has become pregnant by Ah Song does not ring true. Occasionally, from incident to incident, the author forgets the motivation he had previously drawn. When Mei Oi finds herself pregnant, we are told, "her meetings with Ah Song did not hold any significant meaning for her." But sixty-five pages later, without any explanation, she is desperately writing to him, "Please telephone me any evening except Wednesday. I love you" (105, 170). Nonetheless, Chu's novel deserves to be read as the first Chinese American fiction to observe its sojourner society with a realistic eye.

Jeffery Paul Chan's fiction is more sophisticated than Chu's and stylistically superior. Many of his short stories, like Hemingway's, focus on male figures, male activities such as fishing and hunting, and themes of male bonding and the code of manhood. In "The Chinese in Haifa" the protagonist, Bill Weng, in divorcing his Chinese wife, is losing his old cultural world. His Jewish neighbors, Herb and Ethel, are solicitous; however, it soon becomes apparent that Bill, always in control, is the dominant male in this cross-cultural drama. When he goes fishing with Herb, it is Bill who catches the fish, a symbolic act foreshadowing Bill's seduction of Ethel in the second half of the story. Chan's descriptions are suffused with a male sensibility that endows even minor observations with the suggestiveness of sexual encounter.

In "Jackrabbit," the male bonding between a surrogate father, Pete, an old immigrant Chinese, and Frankie, an abandoned second-generation Chinese American youth, is sensitively portrayed. The pathos of the two characters, the older a member of an alien race and the younger a deracinated outsider, in no way detracts from the power of their interactions. Chan deftly uses pidgin English and broken Chinese, coarse language, and descriptions of horseplay to express male affection. When Frankie confides to Pete, "I am fucked up good" (224), Pete responds with a parent's moral concern: "Don't talk like that. Your ma and papa still hear you." During a tussle, Pete "pinned [Frankie's] arms and pulled his shirt over his head. He set his knee firmly on the boy's chest. 'Your problems is you eat too much rabbit and no rice,' he lectured. 'Eat too muchee horse shit, huh?'" (232).

The story forms a coherent and dramatic entity. The resources of fiction, such as foreshadowing (Frankie cuts his finger, an omen of his violent death), symbolism (the wild jackrabbit as a figure of Frankie's condition of rank outsider), surprise, and so on, effectively create a world of overpowering and random violence. Frankie and Pete live in a physical and moral wilderness, like the rank flesh of the jackrabbit that Pete tries to "civilize" in his stew. A stranger, a mechanic, enters this world and fatally wounds Frankie. In the story's conclusion, a series of ironies draw together the themes of American wilderness and loss of identity. As Pete drives Frankie to the hospital, he swerves to avoid some jackrabbits and Frankie's body falls off the truck. A truckdriver, seeing the body, wonders if it were "some injun," while the gas station attendant thinks he may have seen a jackrabbit instead. Although Frankie was born in America, even in death his identity is unknown. Without a racial memory, Frankie is like the jackrabbit, a product of the American wilderness.[7]

Similarly, Frank Chin's short story "Food for All His Dead" treats the theme of male bonding—this time, the failure of the father-son relationship. Set in San Francisco's Chinatown, the story dramatizes the conflict between a Chinese father who insists that his son maintain a Chinese identity and the son, who rejects his father's imposition of identity. Chin movingly portrays the ambiguities in Johnny's feelings for his dying father. His love is inextricably tied up with his rejection, for Johnny "was not waiting for the man to die but waiting for the time after death when he could relax" (49). The patriarch is hated as well as loved; while he lives, the son is compelled to play the role defined by the father. However, when he tells Johnny that he wishes him to stay in Chinatown, Johnny explodes and reveals his true feelings: "most of the people I don't like are Chinese. They even *laugh* with accents, Christ!" (53). Johnny's confession that he dislikes his ethnic background is deeply unfilial, for he is implicitly saying that he will not pay his father those ancestral honors due him after his death. The father's violent rejection of his son is thus a reaction to Johnny's prior rejection of him. As the title of the story suggests, the narrative focuses on the break in cultural and racial continuity; Johnny, no longer Chinese, cannot pay homage to his ancestors and his past.

Using Johnny's point of view, the author implies that Chinese Americans who accept ethnicity are actually exploiting a racial stereotype in order to be accepted in a racist society:

> And they saw that there was a big kick about Chinatown, so they braided their hair into queues and opened up laundries and restaurants and started reading Margaret Mead and Confucius and Pearl Buck and became respectable Chinamen and gained some self-respect. (58)

Chin's contempt for Asian Americans who play the game of inauthentic identity is palpable in this passage and in many of his critical articles. His scorn is fueled by his own wounding in white America, represented in the braiding of queues, for centuries the symbol of the emasculation of Chinese males.[8]

Realism shades almost imperceptibly into protest literature in Okada's, Chan's, and Chin's fiction. The rejection of stereotypes in their work is related to the rejection of conventional literary forms in the work of a later Asian American writer, Kingston; those writers who seek to discover identity rather than to exploit ethnicity pursue an elusive literary form capable of expressing alternative self-images. Open representations of Chinese American identity unfold with the openness of form in *The Woman Warrior* and *China Men*. In these works Kingston eschews conventional narrative structure; instead she brings together collective tales (for example, the stories of fantastic eaters, Kao Chung, Chau Yi-han, Chen Luan-feng, and Wei Pang, in *The Woman Warrior* 88–90); racial myths (the feminist tale of Fa Mulan, in the same work, 20–53; or the legend of Ch'u Yuan in *China Men* 256–60); and autobiographical (her childhood is described in *The Woman Warrior* 164–206), biographical (her parents' life stories appear in that work, 57–87, and in *China Men* 15–73), and historical materials (for example, the chapter on anti-Asian legislation in the United States, in *China Men* 152–59). These diverse subjects form a pastiche made coherent and persuasive through a narrative voice that is at turns puzzled, enraged, fearful, reportorial; it is consistently honest. In what is only the appearance of memoir, the images move from legendary past to childhood past to narrative present to family past, and so on, creating a surreal sense of identity in which myths, history, and invented and biographical narratives exist on the same plane of truth or imagination. The commingling of reality and unreality is organized by a self-conscious narrator who sometimes uses a personal, subjective voice and at other times assumes the impersonal viewpoint of the mythopoeic historian.

Kingston's books are marked by intertextuality—that is, by layers of reinterpretations of earlier literatures and, consequently, by a stylistic inventiveness. The various stories on which the books are built are written in a variety of modes: realistic, satirical, allegorical, heroic, comic, tragicomic, journalistic, and fabled. Fluidity replaces conventional form, and juxtaposition remains the only consistent narrative device. The range of materials and styles, quirky unpredictability of narrative movement, and disturbing juxtapositions imply an authorial mind at work, arranging, organizing, and arriving at a form that reflects an indeterminate cultural content. Paradoxically, Kingston's works are largely self-referential, appealing not to external historical and sociological validations but to insights that come from the confrontation of invented, historical, and biographical selves.

The stories in *The Woman Warrior*, many of them based in a mythic or historic China, are strained through the sensibility of an Asian American narrator who is fascinated and repelled by aspects of the culture that she explores. The idiosyncratic author reads her Chinese mother's tales for significance and operates in the dual role of narrator and interpreter, with herself as audience, agent, and participant. The legend of Fa Mulan, the woman warrior, for example, is retold in a feminist light, as an expression of and a means to the author's understanding of her female position in a male chauvinist society.

Kingston is also out to discover the meaning of her ethnicity; the tone is intelligent, ironic, and angry. Ethnicity is a puzzle: "Mother would pour Seagram's 7 into the cups and, after a while, pour it back into the bottle. Never explaining. How can Chinese keep any tradition at all? They don't even make you pay any attention . . ." (185). And it can be barbarously oppressive. "I looked at their ink drawings of poor people snagging their neighbors' flotage with long flood hooks and pushing the girl babies on down the river. And I had to get out of hating range" (52). Beginning with the familiar position of authorial alienation, Kingston assumes the role of storyteller, which, shamanlike, is also the role of meaning maker. Re-creating and responding to family and racial stories, Kingston does not so much reflect ethnicity as make her own realities. After all, the narrator tells us, "maybe everyone makes [meaning] up as they go along" (185).

In *China Men*, Kingston includes examinations of Chinese males in her continued attempt to remake—that is, to understand—her past and her self. While the mother is the central biographical and fictional figure in *The Woman Warrior*, the father is the protagonist and antagonist in *China Men*. Both books, as befitting a Chinese American writer, are about ancestors. *China Men* is more heavily interlarded with history and biography and has a more explicit political slant. For example, "The Laws," a chapter in the middle of the book, a straightforward documentation of United States legislation aimed at Chinese immigrants, is also an explicit condemnation of American racism. Seven biographical chapters on various Chinese men—father, uncles, grandfathers, brothers, and strangers, whose lives manifest a pioneering heroism, solitary, crazy, rejected, failed—are also on the overarching theme of Chinese immigration in the United States; in the final three chapters, Kingston considers Chinese immigration throughout the world.

Kingston's thematic preoccupation is struck in the opening chapter, on Tang Ao, and is reiterated throughout in the forms of myth, commentary, and invention. Tang Ao, "looking for the Gold Mountain, crossed an ocean" and, coming to the Land of Women, is enslaved and feminized, to become a waitress (3). He symbolizes all those Chinese men who ended up in America in servitude in restaurants and laundries, in traditionally female occupations. Although not explicitly stated, this theme of political, social, and sexual emasculation underlies most of Kingston's depictions of Chinese men in New York, California, Hawaii, and Alaska. Beginning with her father, she observes the complexity of a man who is able to dominate his natural environment but cannot master his American world. "You were twice tricked by gypsies" (12), she remembers. The narrator knows the father's impotence as meaning maker and so actively takes over his past, inventing it for clues to her predicament as an Asian American. In place of his silence she gives us two versions of his voyage to the Gold Mountain: a fanciful version of an illegal journey as a stowaway and a historical version of an entry through Angel Island.

Six chapters are wholly the stuff of imagination: myths, legends, and popular narratives retold almost as if translated through the emotional filter of the narrator's consciousness. Kingston tinkers so heavily with some of these stories as to make them almost her own. The tales possess a similar theme of promise in a quest and eventual emasculation or loss. "The Ghostmate," for example, tells of a young man who is seduced by a beautiful woman, lives with her in a luxurious house, and discovers, near death, that he has been cohabiting with a ghost. The story's actual subject is the sojourner who abandons his home, although "the hero's home has its own magic" (81), for an insubstantial illusion of wealth.

Still, all Kingston's protagonists are survivors. Her sinoized version of Robinson Crusoe (Lo Bun Sun) indicates her fascination with the economic condition of the Chinese American immigrant who undergoes isolation, dangers, hardships, and survives them all. Her narrative on the Grandfather of the Sandalwood Mountain, Bak Goong, is an account of a sojourner lured by the false promises of a recruiter to labor in the Hawaiian sugar plantations. Bak Goong survives by shouting his feelings of homesickness into a hole in the ground. With this chapter the book moves to affirmation. In Kingston's world, the ability to talk (that is, to express and create self) can save the individual. Shouting into the hole symbolizes the desperation of self-expression through which identity is forged. As Bak Goong claims, "We can make up customs because we are the founding ancestors of this place" (118).

Like Bak Goong's boldness, Kingston's authorial daring springs from her desire to create a totality of imaginative impressions of the immigrant experience. Her methods in this work of nonfiction are those of the fiction writer who uses imagination, invention, and linguistic and stylistic resources to make experience vivid. While freely inventing, she stuffs her accounts with concrete details. The juxtaposition of the historical with the imagined corresponds to and satisfies the narrator's intention: "I want to compare China, a country I made up, with what country is really out there" (87). The later chapters are factual and journalistic, reflecting the formation of an American identity, and the chapter "The American Father," the dialectical pole to the early chapter "The Chinese Father," concludes with a paean to the father's success as an immigrant in the United States. But the concluding chapters describe lives of uncertain assimilation; one of the characters is a brother in the Vietnam War, whose nightmare is that of slicing an enemy who turns out to be his own family, with Chinese eyes and cheekbones. In all, the patterning of chapters and styles shows a literary consciousness working on an improvisation of form to contain an Asian past and an American present.

There remains a group of Asian American writers whose works show a shift from ethnoconsciousness to literary consciousness. Their bicultural status is less haunted by the angst of stereotype, nor do they find their materials in their immigrant past. The question of identity is no longer seen in racial or ethnic terms but in an epistemological and metaphysical light.

Toshio Mori's stories stringently emphasize the here and now of Japanese American experience. The opening and concluding stories of *Yokohama, California* are titled, significantly, "Tomorrow Is Coming" and "Tomorrow and Today." Mori seldom focuses on conflicts of dual identity but affirms instead the enfolding of Japanese identity in the American. In the first story, even the Pacific war is seen positively by the grandmother, because it has given her the opportunity "to find where her heart lay." About the United States, she tells her grandchildren, "This is your world" (20; Caxton, 1949). In story after story, in fact, Mori observes the humdrum lives of Americans who happen to be Japanese in origin. The concluding story, a character study of an ugly woman whose consolations in a life full of disappointments are going to the movies and daydreaming of Clark Gable, affirms the value of all human experience because "it is her day that is present and the day that is tomorrow, which is hers and which will not be" (166).

For Mori, interest in character is all; and character is perceived as extraordinary under the mantle of the ordinary. He plumbs his characters to express the ineffable mysteries of their humanity as seen in quirks of daily behavior. "Lil' Yokohama" captures the magic of the ordinary, as the comings and goings of Japanese Americans are gently depicted in American terms. On one level, the sketch of small-town life is almost a cliché, but the ethnic particularity of the community gives the descriptions a poignancy that dispels racial myths and makes an ironic affirmation of the American identity of these Japanese American citizens. Although Mori's catalogs of American scenes are sometimes turgid, insisting too much on the grandeur of his common subjects, the writer comes close to prose poetry in, for instance, his hymns to a laundry truck driver "or an equivalent to such who is living and coming in and out of parks, the homes, the alleys, the dives, the offices" (126). His idealization of the everyday is most lyrically expressed in "The Woman Who Makes Swell Doughnuts," which celebrates the democratic spirit: "I sing gratefully that such a simple and common experience becomes an event, an event of necessity and growth" (23).

Many of the stories, however, in their morbid sensibility and recognition of grotesqueries of characters, offer a pessimistic theme that comes closer to Mori's expressed position of artists as suffering because they perceive the moral incongruities of their world. In "The Seventh Street Philosopher," "Akira Yano," and "The Eggs of the World," the characters are obsessed by unattainable dreams; often the pathos is balanced by a compassionate narrator or by a focusing on the heroic element. "Toshio Mori," an autobiographical piece written in the third person, is the expression of melancholic, brooding self-consciousness. The story concludes with Mori alone in his room at night, "aware that no one knew him as he knew himself . . . that no one in the world could see, and if seeing would not understand and share his state of feeling that was accumulating and has been accumulating since birth" (45). In this, as in other stories, conflicts of ethnicity have been displaced by the anguish of individuals who must come to terms with the human condition, burdened by self-consciousness and hungering for connection.

Mori thus exploits the irrational as a means to power. In "Akira Yano" we find a character who turns to art as a way of celebrating his humanity. Although Mori's stories are filled with vivid social observations, it is the visionary experience he expresses that draws us into his work. His fiction exceeds reporting or ethnocentric boundaries, for it is the intensity of his thoughts that offers an image of his world. His fiction is symbolistic, faithful to a vision within, and the purpose of his art, like that of the symbolists, was to seize and condense experience into its literary analogy.

The theme of being in the world can be seen not solely as a search for identity but as a quest for selfness. It is a theme that has resonated in American literature from the opening line in *Moby-Dick*, "Call me Ishmael," to Ralph Ellison's "I am the invisible man." To a writer such as Diana Chang, plot and characterization, no longer mere devices to explore ethnicity or to protest political trauma, become the means by which characters' selves evolve or are examined.[9] In Chang's novels, the questions of stereotypes, ethnicity, duality, and the forging of a new identity fall under a larger existentialist theme.[10] In most of the works of the Asian American writers discussed so far, authorial identity is indistinguishable from the author's ethnic identity; but Chang is a protean author, a master of disguises whose authorial identity cannot be fixed by ethnicity. In *Eye to Eye*, her fifth novel, for example, the narrator and main character is a white Anglo-Saxon American male married to a long-legged blonde and infatuated with a Jewish woman. What frees Chang to explore the broader oceans of consciousness is her ability to construct alternative points of view. Obviously influenced by Ford Madox Ford, her secular, urban fictions express an intense consciousness of self through this manipulation.

Her first novel, *The Frontiers of Love*, shows her early, abiding attachment to a form of controlling mask and masking control. Begun as an inchoate personal narrative, it was reworked into fiction through the creation of five characters caught in the inertia and anarchy of wartime Shanghai. Through their points of view, Chang examines the inadequacy of racial identity in providing us with a sense of self. Through the tragedies of two young Eurasians, Mimi and Feng Huang, we learn that the alienated and unreflecting self, in its desperation to escape the terrors of freedom (that is, absence of racial belonging), destroys itself. Sylvia, the third Eurasian, alone knows that "if one did not hold on carefully to one's sense of self, one might wake up some morning looking for one's face, so easily lost" (87). Sylvia escapes self-destruction, for in her absence of narrow commitment to race is her capacity for insight. Aware of her dual racial origins, she is unwilling to sacrifice one for the other; aware of the individual's vulnerability in search of self-definition, she is capable of objectivity. Her search for point of view is finally more authentic than "a single comforting bias" (18). The novel ends with Liyi's, Sylvia's father's, vision that "life was not to be resolved, but to be lived—a constant improvisation" (245). The spontaneous creation of self in its encounters with the world, a brave existentialist answer to the question of identity, is Chang's special contribution to Asian American literature.

According to Irving Howe, "what usually shapes a new literary movement is less a common future than a common rejection of the recently dominant past." It is clear in Asian American writing that those literary works that most exploit the dominant stereotypes of their racial history are less powerfully works of imagination. When Asian American writers reject the "recently dominant past," choosing instead, like Kingston and Chang, to construct the fiction of a memory that never took place, their work becomes empowered with the consciousness of literary text. It is not so much conventional form that invests the writing with power as the authorial presence that manipulates and invents form; an unremitting focus on conventional aspects of life, while useful for ethnographers and apologists of Chinese culture, yields fewer insights than author-controlled narratives. The strongest Asian American writing offers alternative self-images to the ethnic commonplaces that substitute for phenomenological texture and is thus modernist in stance.

Notes

[1] See Elaine H. Kim, *Asian American Literature*, for an excellent overview of the genres, forms, and voices in Asian American writing. Kim discusses autobiographies, biographies, political and sociological documents, essays, short stories, novels, dramas, and poetry produced by three generations of Asian American ethnics.

[2] Sartre 49. While Sartre uses the concept of the "lie consciousness" in an abstractly ontological sense, the concept can be read concretely in the condition of the Asian Americans whose "orientalism" is foisted on them by their position in a predominantly Caucasian society.

[3] According to Wong, her early experiences were limited to those of "a dutiful little girl taught to act with propriety" (4) in a world where a brother "because he was a brother was more important to Mamma and Daddy than dear baby Precious Stone, who was only a girl" (27). When scarcely a teen she learns to be a housewife, shopping and cooking for the entire family and suffering from an arbitrary whipping from her father because "Daddy believed that severe whipping was the most effective means of bringing up creditable daughters and illustrious sons" (60).

[4] The Chinese female characters are described repeatedly as speaking in "jade tones" (123); Uncle Fook wears a jade piece tied to his belt; and Lin gives Scott a similar jade piece, a carving of a carp, that is returned to her after his death in World War II.

[5] Whole chapters of *Nisei Daughter* are composed of descriptions of Japanese foods and customs, and the reader is presented with a series of Japanese terms and their meanings. The issue is not whether these descriptions of unique cultural features are interesting but whether they are necessary to define Japanese American experience and, if so, whether there are better ways to integrate them into the narrative flow.

[6] Okada describes Ichiro's internal conflict in a passage of interior monologue: "There was a time when I was your son. . . . I was the boy in the peach and you were the old woman and we were Japanese with Japanese feelings and Japanese pride and Japanese thoughts because it was all right then to be Japanese and feel and think all the things that Japanese do even if we lived in America. Then there came a time when I was only half Japanese because one is not born in America and taught in America and one does not speak and swear and drink and smoke and play and fight and see and hear in America among Americans in American streets and houses without becoming American and loving it" (34–35).

[7] Jeffery Paul Chan has not yet published a book of short stories; he is represented in a number of anthologies, among them *Yardbird Lives!* ed. Ishmael Reed and Al Young; *Yardbird Reader Vol. III*, ed. Frank Chin and Shawn Wong; *Asian-American Authors*, ed. Kai-yu Hsu and Helen Palubinskas; and *AIIIEEEEE!* ed. Frank Chin et al. 12–29.

[8] Frank Chin's fiction and drama appear in various anthologies, including *Asian-American Authors*. His play *The Chickencoop Chinaman* was produced at the American Place Theater in New York in 1972.

[9] Diana Chang is a prolific writer of novels (see Selected Bibliographies) as well as poems and short stories, in numerous magazines such as *Virginia Quarterly Review, Nation, American Scholar, New York Quarterly,* and *New Letters.*

[10] In a talk at Westchester Community College (19 March 1982), Chang said she had read the existentialist philosophers at college and was particularly affected by Kierkegaard's *Fear and Trembling.*

Three Nineteenth-Century American Indian Autobiographers

A. LaVonne Brown Ruoff

Since the early nineteenth century, American Indians have written personal narratives and autobiographies more consistently than any other form of prose.[1] The structure of these personal narratives reflects a diverse range of influences, from Western European forms of spiritual autobiography and slave narratives to the oral traditions of Native America. The full-length confessions or autobiographies of Western European literature are not part of Indian oral tradition. As Barre Toelken points out, in many tribes "one is not to speak of himself in any full way until after he has become someone—such as having had many children or an illustrious life."[2] Nevertheless, as H. David Brumble III makes clear in *American Indian Autobiography*, there were at least six forms of American Indian preliterate autobiographical narratives: coup tales, which described feats of bravery; less formal and usually more detailed stories of warfare and hunting; self-examinations, such as confessions required for participation in rituals or accounts of misfortunes and illnesses; self-vindications; educational narratives; and tales of the acquisition of powers (22–23). Although some Indian authors of personal narratives consciously adopted literary forms popular among white readers, they often blended these with tribal narrative in which personal history was expressed within the contexts of the myths, stories, and histories of their tribes or bands, clans, and families. These narratives also incorporated forceful commentary on whites' treatment of Indians.

This essay will trace the evolution of American Indian written autobiographies in the nineteenth century through the personal narratives of three authors, from the East, Midwest, and West: William Apes (Pequot), George Copway (Ojibwa), and Sarah Winnemucca (Paiute).[3] It will also examine the relation of these works to the history and literature of the age and the influence of such forms as spiritual confessions, missionary reminiscences, and slave narratives; it will discuss, as well, the influence of American Indian oral traditions.

When Indian authors first began to write personal narratives, the word *autobiography* was not in general use. Coined by Robert Southey in 1809, the term did not appear in the titles of books published in the United States until the 1830s. During the first half of the century, American Indian authors were more influenced in their choice of autobiographical form by spiritual confessions, which describe the subject's private or inner life, than by memoirs, which chronicle the subject's public career. As Christian converts, the earliest Indian autobiographers consciously modeled their works on religious narratives, especially on spiritual confessions and missionary reminiscences. Perhaps less consciously, some Indian authors, or their editors or publishers, also incorporated aspects of the slave narratives, which themselves were influenced by religious narratives.

The spiritual confessions were logical models both for religious and ideological reasons. They linked Indian autobiographers to Protestant literary traditions and identified the authors as civilized Christians whose experiences were as legitimate subjects of written analysis as were those of other Christians. As G. A. Starr points out, writing any kind of autobiography assumes both one's own importance and the appropriateness of writing about one's experiences. Implicit in these assumptions is the Protestant principle that only an individual's exertions can influence his or her soul. Consequently each person must examine carefully the events in the development of the soul. Also implicit is the belief that because spiritual life varies little from person to person, individuals can measure their spiritual state by that of others. The double value of spiritual autobiographies was that at the same time that they chronicled the author's spiritual development, they enabled readers to repeat the process by identifying with the writer's spiritual pilgrimages (Starr 5, 14, 19, 27). Although early Indian autobiographers used the structural pattern of the spiritual confession, later writers combined this form with descriptions of their missionary activities as they spread the word of God and of their own salvation.

The task of achieving credibility for their personal narratives was as formidable to American Indians as it was to former slaves. On the one hand, the narrators had to convince their readers that they were members of the human race whose experiences were legitimate subjects of autobiography and whose accounts of these experiences were accurate. On the other hand, they had the moral obligation to portray the harsh injustices they and their fellows suffered at the hands of Christian whites. While chronicling their struggles either to achieve or maintain a sense of individual identity, these narrators had to avoid antagonizing their white audiences. They also had the dual task of describing experiences common to slaves or Indians and those unique to themselves. However, these narrators were not typical of the groups they characterized because they could read and write. In addition, fugitive slaves who wrote were different from other slaves by having escaped bondage, and Christian Indians differed from others by having rejected native for white religion (Butterfield 15–18; F. S. Foster 67–70).

When the first personal narratives by American Indians were published in the late 1820s, the tide of popular taste and of Indian-white relations ensured a ready audience for Indian authors. During this decade, increased literacy and cheaper methods of book production resulted in an expanded market for all kinds of books. Religious, slave, and captivity narratives as well as works about the West were popular during the 1820s and 1830s. The image of the Indians in captivity narratives as unfeeling savages competed with their representation as the "noble-but-doomed redmen" in Cooper's *Leather-Stocking Tales*, widely read during this period (Pearce, "Red Gifts" 196–236; Berkhofer 86–95). The success of these narratives and the public's continuing interest in Indians stimulated the Indians to publish their own autobiographies.

Indian-white relations also influenced the content and popularity of Indian autobiographies. The death knell of Indian hopes for retaining tribal lands east of the Mississippi was sounded in 1830 with the passage of the Indian Removal Act, which authorized the federal government to resettle Indians from these areas to Indian Territory, now Oklahoma, and other locations deemed suitable. As Indian presence became less threatening, whites increasingly wanted to read about vanished red men or assimilated Indian converts to Christianity.

II

The first published, full-life history written by an Indian is William Apes's *Son of the Forest: The Experience of William Apes, a Native of the Forest* (1829).[4] Published in the midst of the controversy over removal, Apes's autobiography, which appeared in a revised and expanded edition in 1831, is a testimony both to the essential humanity of Indian people and to their potential for adapting to white concepts of civilization.[5] *A Son of the Forest* follows the basic structure of the spiritual confession. Because Apes (b. 1798) was not raised in a traditional Indian culture, he does not include the description of tribal life and history that characterizes the autobiographies of Copway and Winnemucca. Physically abused by his alcoholic grandparents, four-year-old Apes was taken from them, nursed for a year by a white couple, and then bound out at age five to a series of white families. He ran off at age fourteen to join the army during the War of 1812. Later he became a Methodist minister.

Like the slave narrators, Apes recognizes the necessity of establishing the authenticity of his autobiography.[6] Early in the second edition, Apes assures his readers that he has told the truth because he must answer to God for every word written. He also authenticates his background by describing his ancestry. Apes's mother was a full-blood Pequot, although his father was half white. His paternal grandmother was a full-blood member of the Pequot tribe. In both editions of *A Son of the Forest*, Apes states that she was descended from King Philip (Wampanoag).[7]

Apes's account of his experiences is especially interesting because he was raised among Indians only until he was four years old. Apes's parents separated when he was around three, leaving their children in the care of the maternal grandparents. Apes movingly describes how his intoxicated grandmother beat him unmercifully with a club, breaking his arm in three places. Lest his audience attribute such abuse to cruelty inherent in the Indian character, Apes emphasizes that only when drunk did his maternal grandparents abuse the children. He also stresses that his paternal grandparents were gentle Christians. Blaming whites, rather than his maternal grandparents, for the abuse, Apes uses the episode to introduce one of the dominant themes of nineteenth-century autobiographies—the destructive impact of white-introduced alcohol on Indian life:

[Whites] introduced among my countrymen, that bane of comfort and happiness, ardent spirits—seduced them into a love of it, and when under its unhappy influence, wronged them out of their lawful possessions—that land, where reposed the ashes of their sires; and not only so, but they committed violence of the most revolting kind upon the persons of the female portion of the tribe, who previous to the introduction among them of the arts, and vices, and debaucheries of the whites, were as unoffending and happy as they roamed over their goodly possessions, as any people on whom the sun of heaven ever shown. (14)

Like the authors of spiritual confessions and slave narratives, Apes gives little information about his personal life, devoting his autobiography primarily to his journey toward salvation.[8] Apes couples the description of his spiritual journey with that of his progress toward racial and individual identity, another characteristic of slave narratives. The book follows the structure of contemporary religious confessions in which the narrator moves through specific stages: growing awareness of God's power, conversion, questioning of faith, fall from grace, and recovery. Like many writers about religious conversion, Apes was converted after a vivid dream revealed to him the horrors of hell. In 1813, fifteen-year-old Apes converted to Christianity and became a Methodist. What determined Apes's conversion was a sermon on Christ's death as the atonement for the world's sins: "I felt convinced that Christ died for all mankind—that age, sect, colour, country, or situation made no difference. I felt an assurance that I was included in the plan of redemption with all my brethren" (41).

A Son of the Forest bears a strong relationship to slave narratives in its emphasis on white injustice. Apes introduces this theme at the beginning of the second edition when he describes how whites stole the land and ravished the daughters of the Pequots, who welcomed whites to their land "in that spirit of kindness, so peculiar to the redmen of the woods" (8). He objects to the word "Indian," which whites frequently used as an epithet, and substitutes "natives" as a more appropriate term. As an Indian raised among whites, Apes experienced the terror that stereotypical stories about savage Indians aroused in children. Such stories made Apes so afraid of his fellow natives that threats to send the young boy to live with Indians effectively controlled his behavior. Especially dramatic is his account of how, while gathering berries in the woods, Apes was frightened by some white females with dark complexions: "I broke from the party with my utmost speed, and I could not master courage enough to look behind until I had reached home. By this time my imagination had pictured out a tale of blood, and as soon as I regained breath sufficient to answer the questions which my master asked, I informed him that we had met a body of the natives in the woods . . ." (22).

Only later did Apes realize that although whites filled him with stories of Indian cruelty, they never told him how cruelly whites had treated Indians. As a bound servant who could be sold at the whim of his masters until age twenty-one, Apes endured experiences similar to those of the slave narrators. He protests the unfeeling manner in which these sales occurred: "If my consent had been solicited as a matter of form, I should not have felt so bad. But to be sold to, and treated unkindly, by those who had got our father's lands for nothing, was too much to bear" (35).

In *A Son of the Forest*, Apes uses a simple, straightforward style to chronicle the events in his life. His own particular style is evident both in his use of "now" as a transition between parts of an episode or between his narration and commentary and in his choice of a first-person narrative voice. Although he does not embellish his autobiography with re-creations of scenes enlivened with direct quotations or detailed descriptions, Apes focuses occasionally on experiences that reveal his state of mind.

Apes departs from this plain style in his account of his conversion, in which he uses the rhapsodic language conventional in spiritual autobiographies to describe his emotional responses. While working in a garden, Apes found that his "heart melted into tenderness—my soul was filled with love—love to God, and love to all mankind. Oh how my poor heart swelled with joy" (45). Apes then saw God in everything. He was so filled with love for people that he would have "pressed them to my bosom, as they were more precious to me than gold" (45). Both in these passages and in his commentaries on white injustice to Indians, Apes adopts the oratorical style that characterizes so much of his later writing.

In his brief autobiography in *The Experiences of Five Christian Indians of the Pequod Tribe* (1833; revised and republished in 1837 as *Experience of Five Christian Indians, of the Pequod Tribe*), Apes is far more critical of whites than he was in *A Son of the Forest*. Later Indian authors also expressed more disillusionment with whites in their second autobiographies than they did in their first. Twenty of the forty-seven pages of the 1833 edition of *The Experiences of Five Christian Indians* are devoted to Apes's autobiography, which emphasizes his religious progress. Apes also speaks out against whites' unjust treatment of him as a child and adolescent. Describing his conflicts with one master over his desire to attend religious meetings after his conversion, Apes comments:

> How hard it is to be robbed of all our earthly rights and deprived of the means of grace, merely because the skin is of a different color; such has been the case with us poor colored people. I would ask the white man, if he thinks that he can be justified in making just such a being as I am, or any other person in the world unhappy; and although the white man finds so much fault because God had made us thus, yet if I have any vanity about it, I choose to remain as I am, and praise my Maker while I live, that Indians he has made. (17; 1833)

Apes's last two books grew out of his commitment to the fight for Indian rights. He describes the Mashpee struggle to retain self-government in *Indian Nullification of the Unconstitutional Laws of Massachusetts, Relative to the Marshpee Tribe* (1835), one of the most powerful pieces of Indian protest literature of the first half of the nineteenth century.[9] His efforts helped the Mashpees regain their rights, one of the few such Indian victories in the 1830s. Apes's final work is the eloquent *Eulogy on King Philip* (1836), originally delivered as a series of lectures at the Odeon in Boston. Apes disappeared from public view after this work has published, and the details of his later life are unknown.

III

The publication of Apes's autobiographies did not immediately inspire other Indian authors to publish theirs. Not until 1847 was another full autobiography published by an Indian writer. Educated Indians had little leisure to write personal narratives, because they devoted their energies to helping their people retain tribal lands, obtain just compensation for land cessions, or gain civil rights. No sooner was removal implemented than whites violated it by migrating westward into Indian territories. What began as a stream of settlers in the 1830s became a flood by the 1850s.

During removal, white authors lamented the passing of the "noble savage" doomed to extinction by the necessity of "Manifest Destiny." Cooper's *Leather-Stocking Tales* vividly portray this stereotype, as do the narratives about famous Indians and their tribes. In 1833, the narrated Indian autobiography, a major literary form in the late nineteenth and twentieth centuries, was introduced, with the publication of *Life of Ma-ka-tai-me-she-kia-kiak, or Black Hawk*. Narrated by Black Hawk (Sauk) to translator Antoine Le Claire and revised for publication by John B. Patterson, this popular book went through five editions by 1847. Biographical dictionaries of famous Indians were also published during this period (Berkhofer 88–89; Pearce, "The Zero of Human Society" 118; Krupat, *For Those* 34–35, 45–47).

Paralleling the interest in the "noble-but-doomed" Indian were scientific studies of the Indian published in the late 1830s (Bieder 309–12). One of the most influential was Henry Rowe Schoolcraft's *Algic Researches*, a study of Ojibwa and Ottawa cultures. Longfellow's popular *Song of Hiawatha*, published after the enthusiasm for the noble savage had waned, strongly reflects Schoolcraft's influence.

The success of books about Indians in the 1830s created a literary climate favorable to the appearance of the Ojibwa writer George Copway (1818–69). To an American public imbued with the belief that the noble red man must assimilate or perish, this Ojibwa convert to Methodism from the woodlands of midwestern Canada seemed to represent what the Indian must become in order to survive—the embodiment of both the noble virtues from the savage past and the Western European culture from the civilized present. The public eagerly embraced Copway, who cast himself in this image in his *The Life, History, and Travels of Kah-ge-ga-gah-bowh (George Copway)* (1847). Enthusiasm for this autobiography was so great that it was reprinted in six editions in one year. A slightly revised edition, to which Copway added speeches and published letters, appeared in 1850 under two different titles: *The Life, Letters and Speeches of Kah-ge-ga-gah-bowh: Or, G. Copway* (New York) and *Recollections of a Forest Life: Or, The Life and Travels of Kah-ge-ga-gah-bowh* (London).[10]

Copway was born near the mouth of the Trent River, in Upper Canada, and was raised as a traditional Ojibwa until 1827, when his parents converted to Christianity. Following the death of his mother in 1830, Copway became a convert and later occasionally attended the Methodist Mission School at Rice Lake, Ontario. During 1834–36, he helped Methodist missionaries spread the gospel among the Lake Superior Ojibwa. In 1838, he entered Ebenezer Manual Labor School at Jacksonville, Illinois, where he received his only formal education. After he left school, Copway traveled in the East before returning to Rice Lake, where he met and married Elizabeth Howell, a white woman. Until 1842, the Copways served as missionaries to the Indian tribes of Wisconsin and Minnesota. Accepted as a preacher by the Wesleyan Methodist Canadian Conference, Copway also was briefly a missionary in Upper Canada. The high point of his career in Canada was his election, in 1845, as vice president of the Grand Council of Methodist Ojibwas of Upper Canada. Later that year, both the Saugeen and Rice Lake bands accused him of embezzlement. After being imprisoned briefly in the summer of 1846, Copway was expelled from the Canadian Conference and went to the United States. Befriended by American Methodists, Copway launched a new career as a lecturer and writer on Indian affairs.

Copway's *Life, Letters and Speeches* incorporates traditions from earlier written personal histories and from American Indian oral narratives. It reflects the influence of the slave narratives in its emphasis on documentation. Like the slave narrators and like Apes, Copway felt he must prove that he was an educated man capable of writing an autobiography. In a prefatory "Word to the Reader," Copway acknowledges that he has had only three years of school and has spoken English only a few years.[11] However, he assures his readers that although a friend corrected all serious grammatical errors, Copway himself both planned and wrote the volume.[12] To substantiate his literacy and status in the world, he buttresses his volume with literary quotations and documentation, particularly in the second edition, to which he added speeches and published letters.

The structure of Copway's autobiography is far more complex than that of Apes's. The first part is an ethnographic account of Ojibwa culture, in which Copway balances general descriptions with specific examples from personal experience. The second part is devoted to the conversions of his band, family, and himself; the third, to his role as mediator between Indians and whites; and the fourth, to a history of Ojibwa-white relations in the recent past. Copway's blending of myth, history, and recent events, and his combining of tribal ethnohistory and personal experience create a structure of personal narrative that later American Indian autobiographers followed. This mixed form, which differs from the more linear, personal confession or life history found in non-Indian autobiographies, was congenial to Indian narrators accustomed to viewing their lives within the history of their tribe or band, clan, and family. Julie Cruikshank makes clear the distinction between Indian and non-Indian concepts of autobiography in the introduction to *Life Lived like a Story*. As Cruikshank compiled the personal narratives of three Yukon women, she found that they responded to her questions about secular events by telling traditional stories. Each explained that "these narratives were important to record *as part of* her life story." According to Cruikshank, the women's accounts included not only reminiscences of the kind we associate with autobiography but also detailed narratives on mythological themes. Cruikshank also notes that these women embedded songs in their chronicles, which they framed with genealogies and with long lists of personal and place names that appear to have both metaphoric and mnemonic value: the women "talk about their lives using an oral tradition grounded in local idiom and a mutually shared body of knowledge" (ms. 2–5). Copway's autobiography reflects this perspective—of narrating one's life within a tribal context—as do numerous other American Indian oral and written personal histories. Copway, like the Yukon women Cruikshank interviewed, incorporates myths, stories, and songs into his personal narrative. In *The Traditional History and Characteristic Sketches of the Ojibway Nation*, Copway emphasized the importance of storytelling to him and his people:

> There is not a lake or mountain that has not connected with it some story of delight or wonder, and nearly every beast and bird is the subject of the story-teller, being said to have transformed itself at some prior time into some mysterious formation—of men going to live in the stars, and of imaginary beings in the air, whose rushing passage roars in the distant whirlwinds. (95–96)

By beginning his narrative with the description of his life as an Ojibwa, Copway demonstrates his strong identification with his tribal culture. In its nostalgia for the tribal past, Copway's autobiography bears a stronger relationship to the narratives published by African slaves in the late eighteenth century than to those by African American slaves in the nineteenth. For example, *The Interesting Narrative of the Life of Olaudah Equiano, or Gustavus Vassa, the African* (1789) begins with accounts of the geography and culture of his native land, Benin (now part of Nigeria), his family, and childhood (F. S. Foster 47). Like the Africans captured on their native continent and transported to North America, Copway and many of the nineteenth-century Native American writers who followed him retained vivid memories of the free tribal life. Copway and other Christian Indian writers, like the African slave writers, undertook the dual task of demonstrating to their audiences both the virtues of traditional tribal life and the capacity of their race to adapt to white civilization after conversion and education in Western European traditions (F. S. Foster 11–13, 44–47). Copway's goal is not to give an exhaustive account of his life and thoughts but rather to present himself as a typical Indian who, after conversion, exemplifies the ability of his tribe to become worthy members of mainstream society. Reticence to discuss one's personal life is characteristic of spiritual confessions and slave narratives as well as many American Indian personal histories.

In the ethnographic sections on Ojibwa life, Copway adopts an overwhelmingly romantic and nostalgic tone. He unabashedly appeals to American affection for the stereotype of the Indian as a child of nature at the same time that he uses himself as an example of the Indian's adaptability to white civilization: "I loved the woods, and the chase. I had the nature for it, and gloried in nothing else. The mind for letters was in me, *but was asleep* until the dawn of Christianity arose, and awoke the slumbers of my soul into energy and action" (11). The ethnographic sections are designed to persuade his audience of the value of tribal culture and of the essential humanity of Indian people, goals adopted by later Indian autobiographers as well. For example, he stresses that the Ojibwa moral code, which embodies universal human values, links Indian and white cultures. Quoting maxims that emphasize kindness, generosity, and respect for parents, the aged, and the indigent, the author concludes that adherence to these precepts brought Indians peace and happiness until they were weaned away by the white man's whiskey. His descriptions of visions also suggest a common ground between Indian and white cultures. Visions and dreams played an important role in the Christian conversion literature of the period and were the subject of Indian oral autobiographies. Throughout this work, Copway stresses that the differences between whites and Indians consist of language and custom rather than humanity.

Copway uses his own experiences to personalize his generalizations about tribal worldviews and customs. Particularly effective are the sketches of his life with his parents. In one of the most moving episodes, the family almost starves after being imprisoned in their birchbark wigwam for eleven days by heavy snow, with only boiled birchbark, beaver skins, and old moccasins for food. By the tenth day, most of the family was too weak to walk: "Oh how distressing to see the starving Indians lying about the wigwam with hungry and eager looks; the children would cry for something to eat. My poor mother would heave *bitter sighs of despair*, the tears falling from her cheeks profusely as she kissed us. Wood, though plenty, could not be obtained, on account of the feebleness of our limbs" (35). The family was saved when a vision led Copway's father to beaver swimming under the ice of a nearby river. The poignancy of such hardships tempers the idyllic scenes of Indian life amid the gentle beauty of nature.

Just as his boyhood experiences illuminate Ojibwa life in general, Copway's descriptions of their conversion and of his own exemplify the power of Christianity to uplift Indians from the darkness of tribal religions and the degradation inflicted on them by whites luring Indians into alcoholism. The account of his spiritual awakening follows the literary conventions of confessions. While attending a church service to hear a powerful preacher, Copway tried to pray but could not. Suddenly, he saw a torch: "The small brilliant light came near to me, and fell upon my head, and then ran all over and through me. . . . I arose; and O! how happy I was! I felt light as a feather. I clapped my hands, and exclaimed in English, "*Glory to Jesus*" (62).

Although Copway expresses the feelings of unworthiness traditional to confessional literature, he casts these in distinctly racial terms. Like Apes, Copway felt God was "*too great* to listen to the words of a poor Indian boy" (62). The appeal of Christianity is the same as it was for Apes—equality with whites. As Copway reminds his audience, "the Great Spirit is no respector of persons; He had made of one blood all the nations of the earth; He loves all his children alike; and his highest attributes are *love, mercy, and justice*. If this be so—and who dare doubt it?—will He not stretch out his hand and help them, and avenge their wrongs?" (157).

The sections of the book that deal with the author's missionary work replace the conventional fall from grace and subsequent recapture of faith found in confessional narratives. Leaving the safety of his home, Copway journeys into the wilds, where his spiritual and physical courage is tested. His harrowing adventures among the Great Lakes Ojibwas appealed to his audience's taste for the sensational and are comparable to those in the Indian captivity, slave, and missionary narratives of the period.

Indian-white relations are a focus of the autobiography, especially white treatment of Indians in the wilderness and the author's impressions of white civilization during his travels; specific recommendations are made for improved relations. Copway strongly criticizes whites for introducing alcohol, which undermined Ojibwa values and family life, and for failing to send missionaries to the Indians. Christianity and education, Copway argues, are what Indians needed to achieve advancement in religion, literature, the arts and sciences.

The work incorporates a variety of styles. In the narrative portions, Copway adopts a plain, journalistic style, while in his discussions of government policy, he employs an oratorical one. In the philosophical sections, Copway unfortunately uses a rhapsodic tone that undercuts the realism of the autobiography, although it undoubtedly appealed to the taste of the average reader. The influence of Byron's *Childe Harold's Pilgrimage* is evident both in Copway's comment that he views his life "like the mariner on the wide ocean, without a compass, in the dark night, as he watches the heavens for the north star" and in subsequent stanzas, which have a distinctly Byronic flavor (13).

After the publication of *The Life, History and Travels*, Copway lectured in the East, South, and Midwest on his plan for a separate Indian state, advocated in his pamphlet *Organization of a New Indian Territory, East of the Missouri River*. The lectures in the East enabled Copway to meet the well-known scholars Henry Rowe Schoolcraft and Francis Parkman, as well as Longfellow, Irving, and Cooper, who provided moral and financial encouragement for his later publishing projects. Copway's second book, *The Traditional History and Characteristic Sketches of the Ojibway Nation*, was the first published book-length history of that tribe written by an Indian; it later appeared under the title *Indian Life and Indian History*. In it, Copway is far more critical of whites than he was in his autobiography. The author reached the zenith of his career in the years 1850–51, when he represented the Christian Indians at the World Peace Congress held in Germany. Copway visited Britain and the Continent before attending the congress, where he created a stir by delivering a lengthy antiwar speech while garbed in his Ojibwa finery. Returning from Europe in December 1850, Copway hurriedly stitched together *Running Sketches of Men and Places, in England, France, Germany, Belgium, and Scotland.*[13] Unfortunately, this travel book, one of the first by an Indian, is padded with newspaper accounts of his triumphal lecture tours in Britain and descriptions taken from other travel books. Between July and October 1851, he established the short-lived journal *Copway's American Indian.*[14] The year 1851 marked the end of his successful career as a writer and of his close relations with eastern intellectuals, now impatient with his too frequent appeals for money.

Little is known of Copway's later life. He recruited Canadian Indians to serve in the American Civil War and surfaced again in 1867, when, in the *Detroit Free Press,* he advertised himself as a healer. The following year, after apparently abandoning his wife and daughter, Copway arrived alone at Lac-des-deux-Montagnes, a large Algonquian and Iroquois mission about thirty miles northwest of Montreal. Describing himself as a pagan, Copway announced his intention to convert to Catholicism. On 17 January 1869, he was baptized Joseph-Antoine. Several days later he died on the evening of his first communion.

IV

Few Indians published during the three decades following the publication of Copway's works. From the 1850s to the 1890s, most of the works by Indian authors were histories of woodland tribes from the East and Midwest.[15] The history of literature written by American Indians parallels the history of white migration across the country. After pressure from white settlement forced Indians onto reservations and pressure from the federal government forced Indian children to be sent to white-run schools, Indians from the Plains and Far West educated in these schools began, at the turn of the century, to publish their autobiographies.

Hostile government policies and public attitudes created a climate generally unfavorable to the development of Indian literature. White audiences were far more interested in the accounts of explorers, settlers, and gold miners than in those of Indians who suffered as a result of the western conquest.

The stereotypes of the "noble savage" and "red devil" persisted, however. Authors like Bret Harte and Mark Twain adopted popular prejudices against the Indian, vividly illustrated in the latter's description of the Gosiute in *Roughing It.* The public's earlier interest in the "noble-but-doomed redman" from the East and Midwest was replaced by its antagonism to the fighting tribes of the West. Among the few authors adopting a romantic treatment of the Indian was Joaquin Miller, who revived the "noble savage" in his *Life among the Modocs.* Helen Hunt Jackson in *A Century of Dishonor* (1881) gave a realistic assessment of Indians and of the injustice of American policies toward them (Berkhofer 104–06).

The decline of the public's fascination with the Indian as a subject for serious literature paralleled the erosion of its fascination with the ex-slave. After abolition, slavery was a subject to be forgotten and the existence of racial prejudice one to be ignored (Cooley 8; Hart 113–14; F. S. Foster 60). While public interest was beginning to wane in the late 1850s, however, slave narrators were altering their life histories in ways later reflected in those by American Indians. Increasingly conscious of their own sense of individual and racial identity, slave narrators resisted the demands of white abolitionists that they simply retell their stories according to accepted formulas. Abandoning the Christian structure and tone of earlier nineteenth-century narratives, they focused less narrowly on the flight from slavery and forthrightly criticized the prejudice they encountered in the North.[16]

One of the few Indian autobiographies published during the last half of the nineteenth century was Sarah Winnemucca's *Life among the Piutes*. The fiery Winnemucca (Thocmetony; Paiute; 1844–91) was the first Indian woman writer of personal and tribal history. Like the slave narrators of the second half of the century, Winnemucca abandons the strongly Christian flavor of earlier personal narratives; unlike Apes and Copway, she does not pattern her narrative after spiritual confessions and missionary reminiscences. Her emphasis on personal experience as part of the ethnohistory of her tribe owes more to tribal narrative traditions than to religious ones. Further, her life history is considerably more militant than theirs.

Winnemucca's *Life among the Piutes* also differs from typical women's autobiographies. In *A Poetics of Women's Autobiography*, Sidonie Smith comments that women autobiographers deal with two stories. On the one hand, the woman autobiographer "engages in the fiction of selfhood that constitutes the discourse of man and that conveys by the way a vision of the fabricating power of male subjectivity." On the other hand, because the story of man is not exactly her story, woman's "relationship to the empowering figure of male selfhood is inevitably problematic." Matters are further complicated by the fact that she must also "engage the fictions of selfhood that constitute the idea of woman and that specify the parameters of female subjectivity, including woman's problematic relationship to language, desire, power, and meaning." This leads Smith to conclude that because the ideology of gender makes woman's life history a nonstory, the ideal woman is "self-effacing rather than self-promoting" and her "natural" story shapes itself "not around the public, heroic life but around the fluid, circumstantial, contingent responsiveness to others that, according to patriarchal ideology, characterizes the life of women but not autobiography" (50).

Smith notes that when the autobiographer is a woman of color or of the working class, she faces even more complex imbroglios of male-female figures:

> Here identities of race and class, sometimes even of nationality, intersect and confound those of gender. As a result, she is doubly or triply the subject of other people's representations, turned again and again in stories that reflect and promote certain forms of selfhood identified with class, race, and nationality as well as with sex. In every case, moreover, she remains marginalized in that she finds herself resident on the margins of discourse, always removed from the center of power within the culture she inhabits. (51)[17]

Although marginalized within the dominant society because of her racial heritage, Winnemucca played a central role in her tribe. Born near the sink of the Humboldt River in Nevada, she was the granddaughter of Truckee, who, Winnemucca claimed, was chief of all the Paiutes, and the daughter of Old Winnemucca, who succeeded his father as chief. Because she and her family followed Truckee's policy of peaceful coexistence with whites, Winnemucca spent much of her life as a liaison between Paiutes and whites.[18] As such she became a courageous and eloquent spokeswoman for her people, pleading the Paiute cause before government officials and the general public. Far from being marginalized, Winnemucca's role as advocate made her the mightiest word warrior of her tribe. In "Indian Women's Personal Narrative," Kathleen Mullen Sands concludes that Winnemucca portrays herself in opposing roles in her autobiography: male and female, private and public: "She not only presents herself as a warrior for Indian justice, but she also develops a portrait of a child terrified by white power who, toward the end of her narrative, has become a dedicated teacher of Indian pupils—a version of motherhood" (ms. 19). In *American Indian Autobiography*, Brumble percep- tively argues that *Life among the Piutes* is a kind of coup tale in which Winnemucca records her deeds in order to establish how she ought to be regarded, as have such Indian men as Two Leggings and White Bull (65–66).

Life among the Piutes covers the period from Winnemucca's birth to 1883, four decades that roughly encompass the first contacts between whites and Paiutes, through their many conflicts with whites, resettlements, and negotiations to receive justice from the federal government. After the discovery of gold in California, in 1849, pressures increased on the tribe as hordes of emigrants passed through Paiute territory on their way to the California goldfields, Idaho ore deposits, or Oregon timber. Winnemucca's disillusionment with federal Indian policy and with its agents aroused her to take the Paiute cause to the public. Encouraged by the success of her first lecture in San Francis- co in 1879, she toured the East, delivering more than three hundred speeches. In Boston, she was befriended by Elizabeth Palmer Peabody, well known for her support of kindergarten education, and by her sister Mary Tyler Mann, widow of Horace. Through their intercession, Winnemucca was invited to speak in the homes of such distinguished Bostonians as Ralph Waldo Emerson, John Greenleaf Whittier, and Sena- tor Henry L. Dawes. Enthusiastic response to her lectures and support from Mary Mann led Winnemucca to write *Life among the Piutes*, a blend of autobiography, ethnography, and history of Paiute-white relations between 1844 and 1883. Both in her lectures and in her book, Winnemucca staunchly supported the General Allotment Act, sponsored by Senator Dawes, under which Indians would be allotted tribal lands in severalty.[19]

In the book, Winnemucca combines the authenticating devices and narrative tech- niques of earlier Indian autobiographies with dramatic re-creations of episodes from her own and her family's personal experiences, a combination that makes the book one of the most colorful personal and tribal histories of the nineteenth century. Like Apes and Copway, Winnemucca is careful to validate her narrative. Her editor, Mary Mann, emphatically states in the "Editor's Preface" that her own "editing has consisted in copying the original manuscript in correct orthography and punctuation, with occasion- al emendations by the author" (ii). Winnemucca appends many documents attesting to her high moral character and to her services as an interpreter and intermediary for the government. In fact, such documents were necessary not only to establish her credibility as someone capable of writing a true account of her own life and history of her tribe but also to defend herself against scurrilous attacks on her virtue and honesty. For example, *The Council Fire and Arbitrator*, a monthly journal supposedly devoted to "civilization" and the "rights of American Indians," publicized accusations that Major William V. Rinehart, an agent whom Winnemucca harshly criticized, had sent to prejudice officials against her on her first trip to Washington: "She is notorious for her untruthfulness as to be wholly unreliable. She is known . . . to have been a common camp follower, consorting with common soldiers" (qtd. in Canfield 204). To combat such libels, Win- nemucca published tributes from Brevet Major General Oliver Howard and other high- ranking officers with whom she served. Although such authenticating devices are common in slave narratives, Brumble also links her use of them to the oral traditions of self-vindication in American Indian personal narratives (*Autobiography* 69).

Unlike Apes and Copway, Winnemucca does not make the spiritual journey a central element in her narrative. She also departs from their example by being much more critical of white hypocrisy; her critical tone parallels that of post–Civil War slave narrators. In fact, her central theme is Indian-white relations, a secondary theme in the narratives by Apes and Copway. The emphasis is clear in the organization of the narrative. Part 1 consists of a single chapter on the background of her family and on the impact of white migration on Paiute life after 1844. Part 2, also composed of only one chapter, describes the domestic and social moralities of the Paiutes and provides ethnographic information about the tribe. The six chapters of part 3 are devoted to the conflicts between the Paiutes and whites from 1860 to 1883, as the Indians struggled to retain their native land, were moved from one reservation to another, and attempted to gain allotments on the Malheur agency in Oregon.

Life among the Piutes is more personalized than the autobiographies of Apes and Copway, a trend in slave narratives after the 1850s as well. The work contains a detailed account of Winnemucca's childhood, stressing, in particular, her strong attachment to her grandfather, Truckee, and her intense fear of white men, who reminded her of owls. Although she provides little information about herself as an adolescent and adult, Winnemucca reveals far more of her adult personality than Apes and Copway. The sensitive side of her nature is illustrated in her anguish when she must tell the Paiutes that they will be forced to move in midwinter to the Yakima agency—despite government assurances at the end of the Bannock War that the tribe would not be relocated. Her anguish is deepened by her realization that the Paiutes will say that she lied. Wishing that this were her last day in "this cruel world," Winnemucca questions the motives of a president who would force the weakened Paiutes to travel through freezing cold and deep snows to Yakima: "Oh what can the President be thinking about? Oh, tell me, what is he? Is he man or beast? Yes, he must be a beast; if he has no feeling for my people, surely he ought to have some for the soldiers" (204, 205).

The personal characteristics Winnemucca most consistently demonstrates are courage and stamina, particularly in her account of her role in the Bannock War. Her exploits rival those of the western adventure tales and recall the harrowing experiences of the heroines of captivity and slave narratives. Between 13 and 15 June 1878, Winnemucca rode 223 miles, on horseback and by wagon, between the Indian and army lines, in danger both from the warring Bannocks and from whites eager to kill her for helping the Paiutes.

Winnemucca is acutely conscious that the role she played in Paiute-white relations was unusual for a woman. In addition to the dangers encountered by any emissary passing between enemy lines, Winnemucca and her sister Mattie, who often accompanied her, faced the threat of rape. Warned by her cousin that whites had been lassoing Paiute women and doing "fearful" things to them, Winnemucca asserted: "If such an outrageous thing is to happen to me, it will not be done by one man or two, while there are two women with knives, for I know what an Indian can do. She can never be outraged by one man; but she may by two" (228). That Winnemucca was prepared to defend herself is illustrated by the incident in which she and her sister were forced by circumstances to share one room overnight with eight cowboys. Touched by one of them during the night, Winnemucca jumped up, punched the offender in the face, and warned: "Go away, or I will cut you to pieces, you mean man!" The startled culprit fled before she could carry out her threat (231).

Winnemucca's narrow escapes titillated the reading public's taste for both the imminence of sexuality and the triumph of virtue. The literary descendants of Pamela were expected to die rather than face dishonor, a fate they usually managed to escape. Sexual violence was a staple of both captivity and slave narratives. The women in captivity narratives trusted to their God to deliver them from the danger of rape or servitude as the captive wives of "heathen savages." If such narratives convinced whites of the innate cruelty of nonwhites, the slave narratives reminded whites of their own brutality. The degradation of slave women at the hands of masters provided the writers of slave narratives with the opportunity to demonstrate how the slave system destroyed the morality of blacks and whites.[20] Unlike the heroines of sentimental literature or of captivity and slave narratives, Winnemucca is not a victim but rather an independent woman determined to fight off her attackers. Her strength of character, as well as a fast horse and sharp knife, enable her to achieve victories denied to her literary sisters. They also distinguish her life history from the less dramatic accounts by other women autobiographers.

The description of the impact of white migration into Paiute territory provides a dramatic backdrop for Winnemucca's discussions of tribal beliefs and customs, which reflect the oral tradition of linking personal narrative to a family, clan, and tribal context. Her detailed accounts of the roles played by girls and women represent a subject receiving little emphasis in nineteenth-century autobiographies and ethnographies. Her description of the Paiute councils is an eloquent reminder that Indian women in traditional cultures had political power that was denied to white women in the "civilized" society: "The women know as much as the men do and their advice is often asked. We have a republic as well as you. The council-tent is our Congress, and anybody can speak who has anything to say, women and all. . . . If women would go into your Congress, I think justice would soon be done to the Indians" (53). Like Copway, Winnemucca stresses the importance of dreams in tribal culture. She vividly illustrates the Paiutes' belief in the truth of dreams when she describes how her father gathered his people to tell them that his vision foretold their destruction by whites. The incident also demonstrates the tribe's process of making decisions by consensus, when its members agree to follow his advice to retreat to the mountains.

In the longest section of *Life among the Piutes*, chronicling the tribe's relations with whites in the 1860s and 1870s, Indian agents got rich, Winnemucca charges, by starting their own stores and then bringing in cattlemen to pay them a dollar a head to graze their cattle on reservation land. Winnemucca bitterly attacks Major Rinehart, the agent at the Malheur reservation, and the Rev. James H. Wilbur, agent of the Yakima reservation in Washington, to which the Paiutes were sent.

Stylistically, *Life among the Piutes* is the most interesting of the three autobiographies, primarily because its author effectively dramatizes key episodes. Carolyn S. Fowler suggests that Winnemucca's re-creation of dialogue derives from the quotative style of Northern Paiute narratives (40). Dramatizing scenes and reproducing dialogue enable Winnemucca to strengthen her attacks against her adversaries by including the testimony of witnesses. The technique emphasizes, as well, the influence of the performance aspects of storytelling in native oral traditions. Examples of her narrative skill occur in the scene in which her grandfather calls his people together to retell the Paiute origin myth (6–7) and in her dramatization of Truckee's death, in 1859, in which she weaves together the threads of autobiography, ethnography, and Indian-white relations that dominate the book. Truckee's final speeches express his love for his family, his wish that his granddaughters be sent to a convent school, and his concern for good relations between Paiutes and whites. The author eloquently describes her grief at his passing: "I could not speak. I felt the world growing cold; everything seemed dark. The great light had gone out. I had father, mother, brothers, and sisters; it seemed I would rather lose all of them than my poor grandpa" (69). Her grief was shared by the Paiutes, who gathered from near and far for his deathwatch and funeral.

Like Apes and Copway, Winnemucca uses oratorical power to great effect in arousing the sympathy of her audience. One of the best examples of this style is her final exhortation:

> For shame! for shame! You dare to cry out Liberty, when you hold us in places against our will, driving us from place to place as if we were beasts. Ah, there is one thing you cannot say of the Indian. You call him savage, and everything that is bad, but one; but, thanks be to God, I am so proud to say that my people have never outraged your women, or have even insulted them by looks or words. . . . Oh, my dear readers, talk for us, and if the white people will treat us like human beings, we will behave like a people; but if we are treated by white savages as if we are savages, we are relentless and desperate; yet no more so than any other badly treated people. Oh, dear friends, I am pleading for God and for humanity. (243–44)

Life among the Piutes is the only book Winnemucca ever published. In 1882, the year before her book appeared, she published an article on Paiute ethnography, "The Pah-Utes," in *The Californian*. Despite her acute observations of Paiute life, her skillful storytelling, and her often eloquent style, Winnemucca did not continue her career as a writer. In 1884, she returned to her brother Naches's farm near Lovelock, Nevada, to establish a school for Paiute children. Ill health, despondence over marital difficulties, and lack of money forced her to abandon the school in 1887. Four years later she died.

V

Over the course of the nineteenth century, both the form and content of American Indian autobiographies changed substantially, reflecting the authors' increasing emphasis on personal accounts of tribal cultures and Indian-white relations, as well as shifts in popular taste. Although Apes's *Son of the Forest* follows the traditions of the spiritual confession, Copway combines this form with the missionary reminiscence and with tribal ethnohistory in his *Life, History, and Travels of Kah-ge-ga-gah-bowh*. The circumstances of Apes's upbringing and the acculturation of the Pequots precluded a detailed discussion of Pequot society. From the publication of Copway's and Winnemucca's autobiographies to the present, Indian authors have made tribal culture and history important parts of their life stories, reflecting their continuing perception of themselves as part of a tribal community, even after conversion and entry into a predominantly Western society. Stress, too, is placed on the art of storytelling. The plain chronicling of events that characterizes much of Apes's book gives way to the dramatization of scenes in Winnemucca's narrative. The result is greater realism and immediacy. Furthermore, Indian authors' movement away from the restrictive religious narrative and toward evocation of personal experiences parallels a similar trend among African American authors. It reflects the influence of the performances of oral narratives that Copway and Winnemucca observed during childhood.

Childhood memories play a significant part in the personal narratives of American Indians. Apes focuses on his spiritual experiences as a boy in order to illustrate his early religious devotion, a theme common to spiritual confessions, and to demonstrate the destruction of Indian family life resulting from the whites' introduction of alcohol and the indenturing of Indian children to whites. Copway devotes even more attention to his childhood than Apes does, in order to illustrate both the mutual bonds of affection that held Indian families together and the methods used to educate Ojibwa children in tribal customs and worldviews. Neither Apes, Copway, nor Winnemucca, however, examines the psychological influences of childhood on adult personality, as do early nineteenth-century European autobiographers.

Both Apes and Copway depict themselves as Christian Indians; Copway also presents himself as an Indian man of letters. Their common goal is to represent themselves as examples of what Indians can become if whites give them the opportunity to be converted and to be educated in white culture. The life histories of Indians, as well as of former slaves, were vehicles for demonstrating the potential of their races to become part of "civilized" society. The autobiographies were intended to educate white audiences about the injustice of their race to nonwhites. Like many of the slave narrators, Apes, Copway, and Winnemucca were eloquent orators in the cause of their people before they became authors. Although the theme of white injustice to Indians runs through the personal narratives of Apes and Copway, it is dominant in that of Winnemucca and in slave narratives as well.

The increasingly strong criticism of white injustice reflects the desperate plight of Indians by the end of the century and also parallels the growing militancy in the slave narratives published after the mid-1850s. By educating white audiences about the value of Indian culture and by advocating an Indian state west of the Missouri River, Copway hoped to ensure a tranquil life for Woodland Indians. By the time that white migration reached the Paiutes of the Far West, however, no such hope remained. Writers like Copway and Winnemucca put their faith in a policy of individual land allotments. All three authors appealed to their Christian audience's humanity. Winnemucca, however, realized that recitations of the value of tribal culture were not enough; she attacked those individuals responsible for the treatment of her people. In their oratorical styles, Apes and Copway undoubtedly reflected the influence of the evangelical tradition, although Native Americans have a heritage of oratory in rituals, council meetings, announcements of victory, formal petitions, addresses of welcome, and expressions of personal feeling. Growing up as they did in tribal societies, Copway and Winnemucca certainly drew on their mastery of traditional oratory. Whatever their approach to writing autobiography, all three authors recognized the importance of the English language in their resistance to white encroachment. For them, the written word became a new weapon in the Indian's battle for survival.

Notes

[1] Research for this essay was done under a grant from the Research Division, NEH.

[2] "Cultural Bilingualism and Composition" 29–30. Toelken emphasizes that Indian students at the University of Oregon who held such an attitude toward the self would simply not write autobiographical theme assignments. Because narrated autobiographies are oral literature, they are not included in this study. Brumble provides a general study of the subject. For bibliographic information about American Indian autobiographies, see his *Annotated Bibliography of American Indian and Eskimo Autobiographies* and "The Autobiographies," supplement to the former appended to *American Indian Autobiography*.

[3] For general information on the Pequot and Ojibwa tribes, see Trigger. For material on the northern Paiutes, see Steward and Wheeler-Voegelin.

[4] The first written autobiographical narrative to be published is Hendrick Aupaumut's (Mohegan) *Narrative of an Embassy to the Western Indians* (1827). However, it is a journal rather than a full-life narrative. In 1791 Aupaumut recorded his experiences as he traveled for eleven months among the Miamis, Senecas, Ottawas, Shawnees, Onondagas, Wyandots, and others. See Brumble, "Autobiographies" in *American Indian Autobiography* 214–15.

[5] Unless otherwise indicated, all quotations are from the 1831 edition. For an account of Apes's career, see McQuaid.

[6] For a discussion of the methods slaves used to authenticate their autobiographies, see Stepto, *From behind the Veil* (ch. 1). F. S. Foster notes that antebellum slave narratives usually begin with what is known about the former slave's birth and childhood (55).

[7] Chief sachem of the Wampanoag Indians and son of Massasoit (d. 1662), Metacomet (c. 1639–76) was given the name King Philip by the English. Because Philip was a Wampanoag, Apes's paternal grandmother would have to be part Wampanoag if she were a blood relative to Philip. However, the relationship could have existed through adoption or membership in the same clan. The Pequots may have originally traced descent through the female line (Salwen 167). Both the Pequots and Wampanoags suffered grave losses because of the Puritans' conquest of their lands during the Pequot War (1637) and King Philip's War (1672–76). Jennings refers to these as the First and Second Puritan Conquests. A strong supporter of the English until pushed beyond endurance, Philip united many New England tribes against the whites. However, the Pequots, who shared with the Wampanoags a long enmity against their neighbors the Narragansetts, sided with the English. For a brief account of these conflicts, see Washburn, "Seventeenth-Century Indian Wars." For fuller accounts see Jennings; D. E. Leach.

[8] Pascal comments that the autobiographer relates experiences rather than facts—that is, the interaction of a person and events (16). According to Starr, spiritual autobiographies placed little emphasis on the actual recording of experience. Undertaken as religious exercises, these works used facts purely as grounds for reflection (27). Shea notes that in the spiritual autobiographies of early America, the autobiographical act is reduced to testifying that one has conformed to certain patterns of feeling and behavior (91). F. S. Foster indicates that slave narratives did not include positive information unless it could directly be used to contrast with a negative experience or to document slave customs: "Courtships and marriages, for example, occur between the lines or are briefly and impersonally mentioned" (112).

[9] Although Joseph Sabin notes that "the real author of this work is said to be William J. Snelling," I find no evidence to support this claim (1: 229).

[10] All citations are to the 1850 edition. For biographical information, see D. B. Smith, "Kahgegagahbowh" and "Life of George Copway." See also Knobel.

[11] D. B. Smith indicates that Copway's accounts of his formal education vary. In his *Life* Copway indicates that James Evans instructed him in the alphabet (1830) and that between 1832 and 1834 he attended school at Rice Lake as "often as possible." He declares (in his *History*) that "twenty months passed in a school in Illinois has been the sum-total of my schooling. . . ." In

Running Sketches, Copway contradicts both versions by claiming that he "was just learning" his English alphabet in 1839 (personal correspondence).

[12] Elizabeth Howell Copway is probably the "friend" who helped her husband prepare his autobiography. Copway was traveling much of the time that it was being prepared. Her letters indicate that she wrote well and she probably suggested the literary quotations Copway included in his works (Smith, "The Life of George Copway" 13–14, 17).

[13] Only one year later, William Wells Brown published the first travel book by an African-American writer, *Three Years in Europe* (Andrews, "1850s" 45 and n.).

[14] Three years earlier, in 1848, Maungwudaus (Ojibwa) had published a brief work entitled *An Account of the Chippewa Indians.* Knobel argues that Copway's autobiography, plan for a separate Indian territory, history of the Ojibwas, and newspaper were his responses to the efforts of the Lake Superior Ojibwa to resist removal. In 1847, Commissioner of Indian Affairs William Medill attempted to secure removal of the Ojibwa to central Minnesota from lands ceded them in 1842. Strongly opposed to this proposal, the Lake Superior bands sent a delegation to Washington in 1849 to persuade the president and Congress to allow them to retain land in Wisconsin and Upper Michigan. In 1850, however, President Zachary Taylor authorized immediate and complete removal of the Ojibwas from the lands ceded in 1842 (174–82).

[15] See, for example, Jones [Kahkewaquonaby] (Ojibwa), *Life* and *History,* both published by Jones's wife after his death; Clarke (Wyandot), *Origin;* Elias Johnson (Tuscarora), *Legends;* Warren, *History;* and Blackbird [Mackawdebenessy] (Ottawa) *History.*

[16] This change is exemplified in two of Frederick Douglass's autobiographies. Although, in his *Narrative,* Douglass examines his life as a slave and gives little information about his life as a freeman, he is optimistic about the future. In *My Bondage* Douglass reassesses his life from twenty-one years of slavery through seventeen years of freedom. Clearly restive under abolitionist demands that he simply tell his story, Douglass was no longer content merely to narrate wrongs; he now wanted to denounce them (Andrews, "1850s" 43, 55–60; Butterfield, ch. 4).

[17] S. Smith gives an excellent summary of the theoretical approaches to autobiography in her chapter "Autobiography Criticism and the Problematics of Gender" (*Poetics* 3–43). See also Jelinek, "Introduction: Women's Autobiography and the Male Tradition" in *Women's Autobiography* (1–20). As Sands points out, in "Indian Women's Personal Narrative," books on women's autobiography have not dealt with American Indian life histories. One of the few books to treat this topic is Bataille and Sands.

[18] For a full-length biography, see Canfield. Additional biographical information is contained in articles by Brimlow; C. Fowler; P. Stewart.

[19] The General Allotment Act of 1887 was designed to end the reservation system. Under the act, supported by both reformers and opportunists, Indians who took their land in severalty became citizens of the United States and were subject to all its obligations. Although the act was passed to enable Indians to become prosperous landowners, the measure instead ushered in an era in which Indians lost their land by fraud and force. By 1934, sixty percent of the land owned by Indians in 1887 had passed from their control. See Washburn, *The Indian in America* 242–43. For an Indian view of the impact of allotment, see D'Arcy McNickle (Cree-Salish), *Native American Tribalism* 80–85, 91–92, an excellent source for the history of Indian-white relations in the twentieth century.

[20] F. S. Foster 132, 58. Harriet A. Brent Jacobs (Linda Brent) treats the theme of sexual harassment in *Incidents in the Life of a Slave Girl* (1861). Elizabeth Keckley's *Behind the Scenes* (1868) treats this theme briefly.

In *American Indian Autobiography,* Brumble concludes that *Life among the Piutes* was probably not influenced by written captivity or slave narratives. Brumble, whose comments are based on a draft of my essay, asserts that "we should not simply *assume* the degree of literacy and breadth of reading which Ruoff's argument would require of Winnemucca" (61, 63, 69). He believes that the elements of sexual violence and daring adventures in Winnemucca's autobiography that I point out as present in captivity and slave narratives "tell us more about Winnemucca's audience than about what might have influenced Winnemucca in writing her autobiography" (61).

Brumble misinterprets the thrust of my argument, which is that Winnemucca's and Copway's autobiographies in particular reflect a complex blend of influences: Native American oral traditions and popular literary forms. This does not suggest that Apes, Copway, or Winnemucca, all of whom had very little education, read widely in the genres whose forms and themes may be reflected in their work. We simply do not know what or how much they read. Such parallels may well reflect other kinds of influences. All three were skilled and experienced platform speakers who developed dramatic presentations of their life histories to convince their audiences of the virtues and values of their native cultures and to horrify their listeners with vivid descriptions of the suffering that whites inflicted on American Indians. To gain the attention of their audiences, they structured their narratives to reflect not only native oral traditions but also the forms and themes to which their readers would respond. The presence of aspects of popular literature in their autobiographies may reflect the narrators' responses to their non-Indian audiences, spouses, friends, and editors. Consequently, these parallels may well mirror the taste of the age rather than the literary background of the narrators.

African American Progress-Report Autobiographies

Frances Smith Foster

From its beginnings, African American autobiography has included a significant number of texts by individuals who have published accounts of their pursuits of life, liberty, and happiness despite their acknowledged failures to accomplish these goals to the extent and in the manners they may have desired. By their own testimonies, they have sought and they have sacrificed. They have survived, but they have not yet succeeded. Nonetheless, they judge their accomplishments to be sufficient to merit documentation and to instruct and motivate others. They recount their adversities as testimonies to the power of faith and the necessity of action. Though their pride is mitigated by the elusiveness of their prize, their struggle has been valiant and their commitment unabated. This essay will focus on three such autobiographies: George Henry's *Life of George Henry*, published in 1894; Jane Edna Hunter's *Nickel and a Prayer* (1940); and Harry Edwards's *Struggle That Must Be* (1980). Since the elements of the genre that these texts exemplify are found in our earliest personal narratives and continue into the present, a brief consideration of the autobiographical tradition within which they wrote will aid our appreciation of the achievements of Henry, Hunter, Edwards, and those other writers whom they represent.

The earliest extant African American autobiography is *A Narrative of the Uncommon Sufferings, and Surprizing Deliverance of Briton Hammon, a Negro Man*. This work concentrates on Hammon's trials and triumphs from 1747 until 1760, the year of its publication. It was intended not as a complete history of Hammon's life but, rather, as a parable. In showing the reader that despite grievous afflictions, Hammon has not only survived but has progressed, the work would encourage and guide others in their efforts to prosper. Hammon states that he offers his personal history to show "the great things the Lord has done for me" and to persuade other Christians to unite with him in praise. The author acknowledges that he has omitted many things from his account, but he assures us that he has "not deviated from truth in any particular of this my narrative" (528). Such verification is helpful, for his adventures were indeed unusual. Since leaving his master on Christmas Day 1747, Briton Hammon had been shipwrecked in Florida and imprisoned in Havana. He survived Indian captivity, two debilitating illnesses, and a stint in the British navy. After his discharge he was employed as a cook aboard various commercial ships. While working on a ship en route from England to the colonies, he was discovered by "his good old Master." Thus, at the time of his writing, Briton Hammon was no longer a free man. Though his story did not end with freedom, his progress was deemed sufficient to offer an instructive and inspiring life history.

Two hundred and twenty five years later, another freedom seeker, James Farmer, published the history of his personal odyssey. Like Briton Hammon, Farmer had experienced "uncommon sufferings and surprizing deliverances," but he, too, had not achieved his desired freedom. In *Lay Bare the Heart* Farmer describes his role in the civil rights movement and shows the changes that involvement wrought. As one of the first Freedom Riders and the founder of the Congress on Racial Equality, Farmer had developed political strategies with Martin Luther King, Jr., Roy Wilkins, and Presidents John F. Kennedy and Lyndon B. Johnson. But when he wrote his autobiography, Farmer was impecunious, politically impotent, and nearly blind. He was, in his own words, "a lonely, aging man" (350). Though his story did not end in freedom, he, too, determined that his published life history would teach and motivate others. Moreover, the process of writing the autobiography was, in itself, another attempt at self-realization. In his closing, Farmer says: "Doing this book has been a kind of catharsis. . . . it placed that which has gone before in perspective, bringing me to terms with the present, and I now face a future full of beckoning sounds of battle" (350).

The stories of Briton Hammon and James Farmer are the stories of many African Americans who wrote themselves into history. Their struggle is spiritual, material, and uniquely American. The literary forms by which that struggle is presented are equally complex and unique. African American autobiographies derive their literary forms, in part, from the prototypal models of Augustine's *Confessions* and Franklin's *Autobiography*. As William Spengemann has noted, *The Confessions* dramatizes a soul's search for rest. Its first section, which became the model for historical autobiography, makes sharp contrast between earlier ignorance and subsequent enlightenment. Like Augustine, African American autobiographers consider their lives from the perspective of changed individuals, who try to understand the meanings of their experiences even as they present those experiences as testimonies to the redemptive power of faith. While Augustine offers a model of the spiritual quest, Franklin illustrates the secular search. As Brian Barbour puts it, Franklin's life story "codified the sense of the opportunity offered by the new American experience in predominantly economic terms" while at the same time posited "the social, public reality" as most important (1). *The Autobiography* affirms the American dream—that is, it confirms the possibility of ascent from humble origins to social esteem by practicing integrity, industry, thrift, and charity.

Like Augustine and Franklin, African American autobiographers assume that the single life is simultaneously distinctive and representative, and they maintain a profound faith in the efficacy of exemplary literature. Some, such as John Marrant, in *A Narrative of the Lord's Wonderful Dealings* . . . (1785), and Jarena Lee, in *The Life and Religious Experiences* . . . (1836), are more Augustinian in their concentration on conversion experiences and spiritual development. Others, such as Mary Church Terrell, who records her life as *A Colored Woman in a White World* (1940), and E. Frederic Morrow, who reviews his *Forty Years a Guinea Pig: A Black Man's View from the Top* (1980), offer versions of the Franklin rise to public service.

Though African American autobiographers participate in the British and American literary traditions, the peculiar experiences of blacks in America generally require form and substance beyond these models. Increasingly, scholars have attempted to describe the particularly African American autobiography cognates. For my discussion here, three are especially important. In *Witnesses for Freedom*, Rebecca Chalmers Barton clarified the centrality of racial consciousness in African American autobiography. In *Where I'm Bound*, Sidonie Smith examined the slave narrator's movement from an enslaving society into a more democratic community as a prototypical pattern in black autobiography. Elizabeth Schultz has asserted African American autobiography as a "blues genre" in which "the voice of the single individual retains the tone of the tribe" (82). In addition, one of the most telling characteristics of African American autobiography is the quest for an ideal freedom and justice. The unique experience of having been slaves in a land that proclaims allegiance to liberty and justice for all has created a preoccupation with freedom that Arnold Rampersad characterizes as having "almost hallucinatory power" (13). From their beginnings, African American autobiographies may be seen as amalgams of the spiritual pilgrimage, the American quest, and the victim's perdurable pursuit of freedom and justice.

Hammon's account resembles the British travel tales, the American Indian captivity narratives, and the New England conversion testimonies. More significant, although his narrative seems to some modern readers disappointingly complacent, close reading reveals Hammon's narrative as a bold affirmation of self and a precursor to the slave narratives. His emphasis on race, his elaborate descriptions of situations that authenticate his account, coupled with his mysterious silences and ambiguities concerning other details, all find their equivalent in later African American autobiography.

Slave narratives are even more obvious examples of the amalgam that constitutes the African American autobiographical tradition. These stories of lives in bondage and efforts to achieve freedom manifest a tripartite structure. They modify the Augustinian pattern as interpreted by spiritual autobiographies. Instead of the stages of "the soul's progress from a sinful indifference to God, through an awakened desire for redemption, to the realization that wisdom and salvation lie in faith alone" (Spengemann 2), the slave narratives chronicle the spirit's progress from an imposed self-realization to the recognition that self-knowledge and spiritual fulfillment begin with physical freedom.

The slave narratives surpass the Franklin model of the self-made man. The ex-slaves' claims to lowly origin are patently greater than those of the runaway apprentice. Denied identification as a human being and officially designated three-fifths of a person, the slave was a thing, a piece of property. By rejecting this chattel status and asserting their humanity, by showing, as Frederick Douglass proclaimed, "how a slave was made a man" (*Narrative* 68; 1982), these narratives present the ultimate definitions of self-made men and women.

The personal achievement theme is necessarily muted. Explicit celebration of the individual's rise from humble origins to social prominence was antithetical to abolitionist philosophy, which designated slavery, and not the slave, as the source of degradation. Moreover, such rises were hardly true to the realities of African American life. No matter how industrious, frugal, or sanctified a black individual might have become, American society simply was not offering unconditional acceptance. In order to be the limited success stories that they were, most slave narratives ended shortly after arrival in the free states. The writers may have failed in their quests for the ideal freedom and justice, but through irony and ambiguity as well as increasingly direct identification of the obstacles to their achievement, they affirm the possibility of such a state. To emphasize their exemplary intentions, African American authors usually followed their names with assertions of group identity. Just as Briton Hammon defined himself as "a Negro Man," so Frederick Douglass is "an American Slave," William Wells Brown is "a Fugitive Slave," and Harriet Jacobs is "a Slave Girl."

The slave narrative is the prototype for black American autobiography, but the compulsion to advertise one's ineffable self and one's triumphs, no matter how qualified, could not be long contained within that form. Even before slavery's demise, writings such as Douglass's *My Bondage and My Freedom* (1855), William Wells Brown's *Memoir* (1859), and Maria W. Stewart's *Productions* (1835) show increased emphasis on individual initiative. With abolition, the constitutional amendments, and the beginnings of urban migration, the ex-slave monolith gave way to a multitude of self-made models. Booker T. Washington's *Up from Slavery* (1901) is the most famous example of the host of success stories that contrasted humble origins with the satisfying status of social leadership, educational achievement, and, in a few cases, economic prosperity. Works such as Elizabeth Keckly's *Behind the Scenes: Or, Thirty Years a Slave and Four Years in the White House* (1868), J. H. Magee's *Night of Affliction and the Morning of Recovery* (1873), Peter Randolph's *From Slave Cabin to the Pulpit* (1893), and James Mercer Langston's *From the Virginia Plantation to the National Capitol* (1894) demonstrate that the new emphasis in black autobiographical writings predated Washington's opus.

Not only did African American autobiography expand to allow increasingly diversified and complex protagonists, but it did so in a variety of literary forms. For example, Harriet Jacobs took language and structures from the novel of seduction to tell her personal history in *Incidents in the Life of a Slave Girl*, and William Wells Brown employed personal experience and elements of the slave narrative to create his historical novel, *Clotel*. By the end of the nineteenth century, African American autobiography had emerged as a genre of multiple significations.

One of the more interesting innovations is the series of texts I am calling *progress-report autobiographies*. As in most African American autobiographies, race is a central concern, the movement is from slavery to freedom, and the protagonist represents on some level other members of the group. But these works have additional similarities. Beginning life in slavery, servitude, or abject poverty, the protagonist sets out from a restrictive environment in conscious search of fame, fortune, or at least a more self-directed life. Like Briton Hammon, the protagonist experiences, if only briefly, the exhilaration of feeling in charge of one's fate. The protagonists are risk takers, preferring to trust industry, integrity, and instinct over the dictates and definitions of the larger society. Some return to the places from which they began their journeys, then reconstruct their experiences for the edification of themselves and their readers. Others, such as James Farmer, use their narratives to continue their struggles. None has found freedom or justice in the form they had envisioned, but each is convinced that progress has been made and that its recitation is as interesting and informative to others as it is to the writer.

These progress-report autobiographies maintain vestiges of the Augustinian confessions but are even more clearly related to their American ancestor, the Franklin advertisements. Though previewed by antebellum works such as *The Rev. J. W. Loguen, as a Slave and as a Freeman* in 1859 and by group autobiographies such as William Wells

Brown's 1874 publication of *The Rising Son: Or, The Antecedents and Advancement of the Colored Race*, it was after 1890 that the progress-report works are clearly evident. The turn of the century encouraged such literary endeavors because it was itself a period of peaks and valleys. The failure of Reconstruction in the South and the increasing discrimination in the North were tempered by the opportunities promised by expansion of the United States economy and international power. Few African Americans were truly well-off, but the black middle class was increasing enough to make African Americans believe that the way would be steep and hard but was, after all, a mountain that could be scaled. "Walk together, Children," "Lifting as we climb," and "Self-help" were more than mottoes; they were maps. The historian John Hope Franklin explains the mood of the 1890s in these words: ". . . in many ways the Negro was attempting to take his fate into his own hands and solve his problems as best he could. His techniques were those commonly known to Americans of all races. They were the use of agencies already in existence, such as the school and the church, and the establishment of new agencies, such as mutual aid societies and business leagues" (300). As autobiographies such as *Life and Times of Frederick Douglass* (1892), Henry Ossian Flipper's *Colored Cadet at West Point* (1878), and *Up from Slavery* reveal, the literature of the period mirrored and motivated such attitudes.

Progress-report autobiographies specifically propose to inspire black people toward increased participation in American society and to assure them and others that their dreams of life, liberty, and the pursuit of happiness were obtainable within the theory, if not the practice, of the United States Constitution. They are personal histories by individuals who could describe their actions as did W. E. B. Du Bois when he said that he "flew round and round with Zeitgeist waving [his] pen and lifting faint voices to explain, expound and exhort; to see, foresee and prophesy, to the few who could or would listen" (*Dusk* 3–4). Though few autobiographers achieved Du Bois's prominence or his publication record, their life histories have commonalities. The circumstances of their lives necessitated a *break from* an oppressive situation, they have managed to *break into* a less restrictive environment, and such moves did not require repudiation of their racial loyalties or rejection of white society. Racial consciousness is at the center of their identities, but they embrace the values and behaviors of middle-class Americans. Their politics range from ultraconservatism to radical liberalism; but, in general, these writers consider themselves more societal trailblazers than political leaders. As the twentieth century advances, they are increasingly individualistic and sometimes sharply critical of perceived weaknesses among those of their own race. They become less examples of a group than exemplars for that group. They supplement their testimonial functions with candid and aesthetic demonstrations of their personal pain and contradictions, as they write to learn, as well as to teach, the significance of their lives. In short, they present themselves as historical figures whose quests have led them further than many, and, though the apex has not been reached, they have a broader view.

George Henry, Jane Edna Hunter, and Harry Edwards are progress reporters. Henry was born a slave in Virginia in 1819. After various jobs including hostler, cook, and sea captain, Henry escaped from slavery. He eventually settled in Providence, Rhode Island, and became a leader of his community. Active in church, education, and civic groups, he served as a juror on the Providence Supreme Court and, with other black citizens, successfully campaigned to desegregate the Providence schools and to abolish the state law against interracial marriage.

Hunter was born in 1882 to former slaves in rural South Carolina. With help from white and black philanthropists, she worked her way through Ferguson and Williams College in Abbeville, South Carolina, and the Cannon Street Hospital and Training School for Nurses in Charleston. Hunter later studied at Hampton Institute and Western Reserve University. Fifteen years before she wrote her life story, she had received her LLB from Baldwin-Wallace Law School and passed the Ohio bar exams. Hunter's work centers on what she considered her largest achievement, her role as founder and president of the Phillis Wheatley Association. At the time of her narrative, she had raised money to build an eleven-story building that housed over one hundred young women and was a national model for black social service agencies.

Edwards was born in 1942 in East St. Louis, Illinois. Though his parents had middle-class aspirations, they were defeated. Edwards's indomitable spirit was aided by exceptional athletic ability. Thus he was able to attend college in California, establish himself as a leader during the student protests of the 1960s, organize the famous Black Power Salute to expose the political basis of the Olympic Games, earn his PhD, and become one of the founders of the discipline now known as sports sociology.

The three autobiographies span the century and the country. Their writers were successful in the primary avenues of African American professional achievement: business, college athletics, and social service. Though they are clearly products of their time and their circumstances, the lives they document and the attitudes they demonstrate are similar. They present individuals of great personal ambition and strong racial integrity who began their quests with little more than a change of clothes and the conviction that they could improve their condition. The same resolve that motivated their initial flights sustained their forays against oppression. Their struggles develop and declare their basic worth and the possibilities of success. These individuals refused to accept racial injustices, and they promote formal education and social organization as tools for building democracy. Their stories proclaim the right and responsibility to participate fully in American society. In both characterization and structure, the three autobiographies exemplify this genre.

Progress-report autobiographies feature protagonists whose innate sense of self-worth compels an assertive stand, disciplined by intelligence and common sense but irrevocably grounded in optimism and faith. They are latter-day Pilgrims determined to progress through the wilderness toward a city built on the hill. They are romantic heroes who must leave their groups, withstand tests of courage and skill, and return to claim more exalted status from their community.

George Henry says that even as a slave child, "I was determined to do none of their mean, low, occupations around houses. I aspired to something higher" (8). When ordered to perform domestic services such as waiting tables or caring for children, he "studied how to get out of it" (7) and always succeeded. One of his goals was to travel because, as he explains, "I longed to visit the cities, to see the great men, hear them talk, and inform myself thoroughly of the peculiar features of civilization" (9). Though few nineteenth-century persons, free or enslaved, enjoyed such privileges, Henry set out to realize his dream. He wrangled assignments first as a hostler, then as a sailor. Ultimately, Henry convinced his owner to build—to Henry's specifications—a schooner and to make him its captain. Validated by his maritime success and inspired by a voyage to Philadelphia, Henry found his chattel status galling, for, as he relates, "I was determined to let them see that though black I was a man in every sense of the word" (23).

Two insults precipitated his escape from slavery. First, his wife was forced to stop preparing his dinner because her mistress wanted something. Then the ship's owner, Sally Griffin, knocked his hat from his head and berated him. Henry decided that despite his considerable achievements, he could not be a slave and a "man." Henry fled the slave South to seek his fortune in the free North.

Like a young Frederick Douglass or Benjamin Franklin, George Henry arrived in his new community, high in ambition but low in status. Says Henry, "I found prejudice so great in the North that I was forced to come down from my high position as captain, and take my whitewash brush and wheelbarrow and get my living in that way" (62). Like Douglass, he became a leader in the struggle for civil rights; like Franklin, he was an entrepreneur. Among Henry's enterprises were cooperative grocery stores, real estate ventures, catering services, and street-cleaning businesses. Like Douglass and Franklin, he writes his history as an experienced and relatively successful individual whose actions others might deem "fit to be imitated, should any of them find themselves in similar circumstances" (Franklin 1).

Unlike Frederick Douglass, whose expanded *Life and Times* preceded Henry's volume by two years, or Booker T. Washington, whose saga followed that work by seven years, Henry did not achieve national prominence. He did, however, move from being the property of a man to being a man of property, a rise that outdoes Franklin's in being the quintessence of the self-made man. Moreover, Henry fought unceasingly for the rights of citizenship for himself and for his people and in so doing discovered himself to be a historical figure. His *Life . . . Together with a Brief History* is an attempt to share that vision and its implications.

Jane Edna Hunter also characterizes herself as an ambitious and resourceful individual. Since she was born free, Hunter's quest began at a different level from Henry's. Nevertheless, like George Henry, she seemed fated to a future of domestic servitude. At age ten she became nurse, cook, laundress, and maid for a family of six but did not long remain in that situation. By the time she was fourteen, her "earnestness and desire to please" had convinced visiting missionaries to arrange for her admission as a work-study student at a nearby college (37). Thus Hunter's pilgrimage began with her adolescence. She gives lavish praise to those who helped her along the way. Her self-depiction was undoubtedly influenced by her need to reassure the post-Depression philanthropists on whom so much of her work depended. But it was also created by her belief that it was not money but well-placed contacts that allowed one to succeed. At the same time, however, she makes clear that she was quite active in soliciting such beneficence. Her image, moreover, is not one of servility or begging. She reveals that at times her "hot temper" made things difficult, and she freely admits "the joy of success and the satisfaction of making my small will prevail in some measure against the buffets of chance" (51).

Hunter's story is an example of the problems particular to poor female immigrants. For example, when she arrived in Cleveland, she did not have the resources to identify a suitable place to live. The first room she tried to rent was in a brothel. Although she did find other, safer, but only slightly more respectable lodging, this experience was only the first in a series of lessons about the "dangers and hardships that beset the Negro woman who is a stranger in a large city" (70). Though she prevailed, Hunter was acutely conscious of those who did not. She made it her life's work to help those less able than herself.

In her struggles and in her decision to use her personal experiences to encourage others, Hunter's story resembles those of earlier African American writers, such as Nancy Prince, Frances E. W. Harper, and Elizabeth Keckley, who also left their homes, survived the perils that beset young women, established impeccable reputations, then wrote to teach and to inspire. However, as a freeborn, college-educated woman of the early twentieth century, Hunter expected and demanded greater changes than the nine-teenth-century women. Like those of her contemporaries Mary Church Terrell, Alice Dunbar-Nelson, and Ida B. Wells, Hunter's story documents her efforts to organize black women for social service, to cultivate white philanthropists, and to serve as a liaison between groups of white women and groups of black women. Though she was successful in her efforts, Hunter recognized the racism that differentiated her achieve-ments from those of white reformers such as Elizabeth Cady Stanton, Jane Addams, and Jane Hull. Hunter was angered but not defeated, for instance, when the Cleveland Board of Education supported the Jane Addams School for white girls but refused to consider the same for blacks. She believed that "if the recital of my humble efforts to be of service to Negro girls and women encourages in another a like spirit, . . . no more fitting reward can come to me" (9).

Harry Edwards's book, like those of Jane Edna Hunter and George Henry, presents its narrator as both running from and running to situations. *The Struggle That Must Be: An Autobiography* chronicles Edwards's rise from obscurity to national prominence through a combination of talent, integrity, and industry. The writer describes East St. Louis, Illinois, as a community pervaded by "turmoil, . . . criminality, . . . filth and . . . hopelessness" (23). Many residents, of course, dreamed of upward mobility; few had been successful. His parents and others could do little more than urge ambitious youth to "go where you can grow and develop" (99).

Instead of the underground railroad, this runner rode an overland train from St. Louis to Fresno, California. Arriving "with one suitcase and a shopping bag" ready to make himself a new life, Edwards went directly to the campus of Fresno City College (101). It was not his academic performance at City College but his athletic ability that won him a scholarship to San Jose State College. Still, the young man was astonished to discover that exercising his mind did not bring the social approval that exercising his muscles had. Nonetheless, Edwards was encouraged by the writings and activities of others whose quests for self-identity resembled his own. For Frederick Douglass it had been *The Liberator* and his association with such intellectuals as David Ruggles. For George Henry it had been Douglass's newspaper, *North Star*, and the proclamations of William Penn. For Edwards it was an unidentified history textbook and the teachings of Louis Lomax and Malcolm X; but he, too discovered that "the very process of learning was self-redemptive" (106). Like Douglass, he suffered from traumatic confrontations with white mentors who urged him to stifle his criticisms and show team spirit. Increas-ingly he devoted less time to playing sports and more time to promulgating his analyses of racism in sports. At the time of his writing, Edwards held a PhD from Cornell and had become a controversial, but tenured, professor at the University of California and a nationally known political activist.

"Most people want to believe that their lives have been meaningful," says Harry Edwards, " . . . I am no different." Though he has neither the optimism of George Henry nor the tangible achievements of Jane Edna Hunter, Edwards, too, considered the story of his struggle to be important: "I also believe that in knowledge there is hope, that understanding is self-redemptive, that there is something to be said for the struggle to live more fully rather than settling for mere existence at the whim of circumstances" (3). To Harry Edwards, the recording of his life history is particularly important because black men have been led to believe that the military and athletics are their only avenues to freedom. "Mine," he says, "is a sports story" (5).

These progress reporters were aware of the African American autobiographical tradition that they were entering, and they acknowledged the expectations for that genre. George Henry, for example, often interrupts his narrative to apologize for the lack of dates or more specific details, telling readers that the circumstances of his life made it impossible to offer more than "history from memory" (6). Hunter states that she would prefer to offer more information about the roles of others who aided her in her venture but that "the publisher has insisted that this is my autobiography and that I must not fill this volume with the names and beneficences" of others (9).

At the same time, these writers did not adhere rigidly to autobiographical formulas. As did the slave narrators and their other literary ancestors, they assumed the prerogatives of creating forms that best suited their intentions. In some ways, every literary artist has this option, but African American autobiographers had to invent particular solutions to their particularly complex situation. Writing about the development of the African American autobiographical form in *To Tell a Free Story*, William Andrews puts it this way: "Self-realization for black autobiographers involved the finding of one's voice, the reclaiming of language from the mouth of the white other, and the initiation of the arduous process of fitting language to voice instead of the other way around" (290).

Moreover, they had to speak in language true to their experiences but not unnecessarily troublesome to their readers. Progress-report autobiographers wrote to a mixed audience that included liberal whites, whose benevolence or right actions were to be encouraged, and blacks, particularly young African Americans, whose ideas of past, present, and future the writers wished to shape and sustain by their testimonies. They wanted especially to encourage the latter's appropriation of the text. In other words, the writers wanted to write in such a way that readers would admire the protagonists and would realize that they themselves could well be or become that same kind of protagonist. The problem could not be solved simply by emphasizing the heroism of their struggles. The writers had to adapt literary forms that would facilitate their ends.

Henry employs a series of characteristic structural devices. First of all, he creates a protagonist who is at once personal and symbolic, establishing an I-we connection through a merging of the participant and the observer. This relationship begins with the first sentences of chapter 1: "George Henry, the author of this work, was born in the state of Virginia, in the year 1819. As my parents died when I was quite young, and there were no records kept in those days, I am compelled to rely upon the testimony of others" (5). Henry initially places a distance between himself as narrator and as subject by using the third person, to make it easier to see him as an exemplar. His subsequent movement to the first person is balanced by his confession that he can document the specific facts of his ancestry only by the testimony of those in his community. Thus his history begins as a story that is at once individual and communal—a solo with the tone of the tribe.

The narrator is both actor and chorus. Chapter transitions help accomplish this duality. For example, chapter 12 concludes with Henry's quitting a job because he had learned as much as he could from his employer. Chapter 13 begins with the following verse:

Come forth, historian of our race,
And with the pen of truth,
Bring to our claim, to manhood's rights
The strength of written proof. . . . (55)

The first sentence of chapter 13 picks up Henry's adventures where chapter 12 left off and relates his next several voyages, his marriage, and the birth of his children. In response to the direct invocation, the "historian of our race" relates further experience of the individual, George Henry. In so doing, he is evidencing the basic structure of slave narratives that makes no consistent distinction between private and public history.

Although the title of Henry's book, *Life of George Henry. Together with a Brief History of the Colored People of America,* implies two separate subjects, reading makes it clear that the emphasis should be on the *Together.* The first part of the book is, essentially, a chronological recitation of the events of his life. But, within this narration, Henry oscillates between his personal experiences and those of his race. For example, a statement that he sailed past Mt. Vernon begets a dissertation on the failure of the Revolutionary War to free the slaves, the settling of Portsmouth, Virginia, the advent of blacks into Plymouth, Massachusetts (noting that once black people arrived, there was no more starvation in that colony), and Hannibal's crossing the Alps. In another chapter Henry describes his tenure as an elected juror on the state Supreme Court and gives particular details of a case that revealed community attitudes toward marriage. He then discusses his involvement in a suit to repeal the law against interracial marriage—a suit he pursued not because he favored such alliances but because a principle was at stake:

When we looked *over history,* and found that law placed on the Statute Book of 1784, by such men as Capts. Gibbs, Scott, and Townsend and other slaveholders of Rhode Island, we had a bitter contest against it. . . . it wasn't the color line or marriage question that had aroused the people, but it was the abuse in the House that we had received from some of our Republicans. (74–75)

By chapter 17, Henry abandons the personal narrative structure altogether. The last two chapters of his "Life" and the entire portion that he labels "History" are as much an account of important events in his community as they are of Henry himself. For example, chapter 17, "Papers and Societies," stresses the achievements of local organizations such as the Young Men's Friendly Assistance Society, the Burnside National Guard, the Rising Daughters of Zion, and the Franklin Lyceum; Henry was a member, or a founder, of them all. He is especially proud of the thirty-four year history of the Henry and Brown Society, which, until the desegregation of public schools, provided funds to send black boys and girls abroad to study and to return to teach in the community.

The "History" section begins with the reprinting of a pamphlet Henry wrote to persuade the General Assembly to repeal the state's interracial-marriage ban. The section includes letters that Henry had published in newspapers and excerpts from articles about his activities as well as essays on slavery, black achievements, and even listings of bequests made for the education of freedom in the South. The final item is a note to his executors instructing them as to the distribution of his autobiography.

Clearly George Henry wanted his story to be an example of a larger story—that of the achievements of many such individuals. In this he is like the slave narrators whose individual stories are representatives of others who, if given the opportunity, would have achieved similar status. Written during the era of self-help and optimism, Henry's documents might cause imitation of his largesse as well as of his progress. His narrative is as much a confession of faith as an advertisement for himself.

Just as the title of Edwards's book, *The Struggle That Must Be*, is more aggressive than that of George Henry's work, so too is Edwards's tone more vociferous than Henry's. The reasons are fairly obvious. During the 1890s, postbellum optimism had been tempered by the failures of Reconstruction, but the war, most blacks felt, was behind them. Though he published his work in 1980, Edwards came of age during the 1960s and 1970s. At the time of his writing, it was not clear that the war for equality would ever be over, but it did seem as if the warriors were abandoning the struggle. Edwards's tone is charged with disappointment and determination. It is more strident and less idealistic but still visionary.

As different in tone as they are, both Henry and Edwards write what Robert Stepto calls "authenticating narratives"—that is, they become "editor[s] of disparate texts for authentication purposes, far more than the goal of recounting personal history" (26). As noted, Henry sprinkles his text with pamphlets, letters, and articles. Edwards begins his book with Claude McKay's defiant, patriotic sonnet "America," which reaffirms his love for "this cultured hell that tests my youth." This epigram not only establishes Edwards's theme but, as a poem written fifty years earlier by a black man, it places Edwards's story in a historical context and supports an allegorical reading of the subtitle, *An Autobiography*. Edwards's prologue begins with six lengthy quotes from a variety of sources, including *Crusader for Justice: The Autobiography of Ida B. Wells* and a news account of the 1917 East St. Louis race riot. The final quote is from an FBI file that records official bafflement that "Edwards with his athletic ability, education and background would be so angry, militant and outspoken" (2). His prologue makes it clear that the writer is angry, militant, and outspoken because his athletic ability, education, and background had revealed to him the extent to which his family, "like so many other families," had been excluded from participation in what he considers "the most modern and technologically sophisticated society on the face of the earth" (4).

Harry Edwards, like George Henry, mixes individual and communal history. He begins his autobiography by describing the thwarted dreams of his grandmother and of his parents. The childhood experiences he relates are usually those involving his siblings or his neighbors. After he leaves home, the experiences are primarily those that other black students or athletes or others in his position might also have encountered. Thus Edwards makes his narrative personal but not private. His sufferings and his successes are to be seen in relation to those with whom he lived and has been identified.

Edwards's work is primarily a chronological narrative until he reaches his college experiences. Then he increasingly interrupts his account to explain the nature of oppression, particularly as it affects the student athlete. He inserts documents, such as newspaper articles, letters, and memoranda from FBI files, to authenticate his conclusions. As George Henry before him, Edwards consciously shifts his emphasis from participant to observer in chapters such as "The Olympic Project for Human Rights,"

"Illumination of Sports behind the Veil," and "From Crises to Catastrophe or Community." Although, like Henry, he has been directly involved in the events he describes, the narrative focus is as much on the social and political impact of organizations and activities as on his participation in them.

In depicting his experiences as culturally influenced, Edwards does not picture himself, as did antebellum slave narrators, as a heroic fugitive and the others as equally heroic but less fortunate. Some of the people in the book serve as foils to contrast, enhance, or underscore Edwards's own sacrifices and achievements. Edwards's characterization of his work as "a sports story" is calculated to expose the myth that a black man's only human value is "practically coextensive with his utility as a purely physical entity" (5). Unlike Archie Moore, the subject of another sports story, Edwards does not suggest that *Any Boy Can* move from an environment of poverty and failure to prosperity and success. With a cynicism born of a waning revolution, Edwards asserts that many blacks have lost "the commitment to struggle, that sense of purpose and collective destiny, that vision of who we are and what we are about, that determined drive for fulfillment and self-realization that has enabled us to survive for four hundred years" (337).

As a sociologist, he interjects analyses of class and race to explain his experiences. For example, Edwards acknowledges that his scholarship and his athletic prowess contributed to his success; he does not attribute it to extraordinary intelligence, talent, or diligence. He argues that such traits "are so mitigated by society and biography as to be virtually meaningless as socially relevant considerations" (99). He credits, instead, the love, persistence, and guidance of family, friends, and a few black professionals. He praises those teachers who lectured their students about the achievements of blacks. He recognizes his great fortune in having mentors, such as the East St. Louis lawyer Frank Summers, who, having traveled a little further along the path, reached back to help individuals like Edwards.

By alluding to other autobiographical writings by blacks, Edwards demonstrates their value as educational and inspirational documents and places his own volume in that context. The title "Illumination of Sports behind the Veil," for instance, echoes a chapter in Du Bois's *Souls of Black Folk.* Elsewhere he is more explicit in depicting his developing self-awareness as part of a larger historical experience. In the chapter on Paul Robeson, an earlier black student, athlete, and activist, Edwards says:

> Robeson taught me that conscientious struggle demands a disciplined fusing of personal life, profession, and politics, a unity that can only be created and perpetuated through development of a broad, analytical perspective on oneself and one's work in relation to events and circumstances in this society and the world. (214)

He offers his book as a continuation of that legacy. In mixing individual and communal history and sublimating the details of individual quest to a more general narration, Edwards, like George Henry and others, wrote "to explain, expound and exhort" (Du Bois, *Dusk* 3).

Coming between George Henry's work and that of Harry Edwards, Jane Edna Hunter's autobiography uses many of the structural elements of both. She, too, depicts her protagonist within the context of the racial community. Her tone is less complacent than Henry's, but the two writers share the sense of significant progress toward realization of the American dream. Hunter's descriptions of her efforts to keep the Phillis Wheatley Association separate from the YWCA shows that she understood more about the politics of power and race than Henry's more limited experiences with integration had revealed to him. Her tone is less boisterous than that of Harry Edwards. Though she writes with a passion nurtured by political activism, hers is of the New Deal and not the Black Nationalism that influenced Edwards.

Hunter, too, uses her protagonist as both example and exemplar. She begins her story by declaring that her parents and maternal grandparents were sharecroppers and then contrasts sharecropping in the past with that of the present; she also compares her personal observations with those published by others. Hunter qualifies her statements with phrases like "as I knew them on Woodburn Farm in South Carolina where I spent my childhood" and "it is true, still. . . " (11). She juxtaposes her personal experiences with the published critiques of writers such as Erskine Caldwell and Margaret Bourke-White, simultaneously underlining her points and establishing her authority as both personal and academic. From the first page she invites the reader to view her familial history within a larger context.

Like George Henry, Hunter merges personal and organizational history. Her last five chapters are primarily reports, lists, and other documentation of the Phillis Wheatley Association and the general condition of black women in urban society. Not only does Hunter provide case histories in the chapter "Types of Girls Given a Chance," she also devotes chapters to such purposes as discussion of educational curriculum and pedagogy and lists of important benefactors. Her authenticating devices include letters and memos, the complete roster of the 1940 Board of Trustees for the Phillis Wheatley Association, and pictures of her birthplace, the new Wheatley buildings, and herself.

Like Harry Edwards, Hunter employs sociological analysis and what may even be considered psychoanalytic conjecture. For example, after observing that as a child, she generally sided with her father against her mother, she suggests that this division may have stemmed from "cultural reasons," since, unlike her mother, she and her father were light-complexioned, with "fine" features and "soft and wavy" hair (15). The Freudian view is suggested in her statements "I have never doubted that my life was shaped by this initial pattern of conflict with mother and unswerving loyalty to father" (12) and "Mother, too, must have been conscious of father's predominant traits in me; and perhaps it was one of the causes of alienation between us" (16).

George Henry, Jane Edna Hunter, and Harry Edwards are but three examples of the scores of blacks who wrote versions of the Discovery of Ourselves in America. Like Augustine, they viewed their early lives from altered perspectives, and, in reciting the experiences that led to their discoveries, they were continuing their quests for understanding. Their works end not with success but with what they realize may be more appropriate—affirmation.

At the same time, such works, like the *Autobiography* of Benjamin Franklin, are consciously presented as how-to-succeed-in-America books. The writers of these inspirational histories have attained some degree of social status and material ease. By the time he wrote his life story, at age thirty-five, Harry Edwards had achieved what he calls "affluence, . . . middle-class integrated life-style, . . . college degrees and Ivy League credentials" (305). Jane Edna Hunter, Esquire, had served on numerous local and state committees and had been awarded two honorary degrees. And former slave George Henry bequeathed more than his legend as a self-made man. To Livingstone College he willed oil paintings, furnishings, and his library of "choice and rare books" (1). Although the writers are clearly proud of their gains, they see them as byproducts of lives dedicated to human service and warn that possessions can never insulate blacks from the injustices that beset black Americans. These beliefs may be seen in the kinds of material possessions they seem to value most. The art collection that Henry left to the black students of Livingstone College featured portraits of himself and other freedom fighters, including John Brown, Charles Sumner, and Toussaint-Louverture. His bequest also included many "valuable books on the history of the race" and at least six copies of his own *Life* (1).

The African American preoccupation with freedom and justice is equally obvious. Some writers, like Henry, who won his legal suits, seek to bring about change within the political system. Others, such as Harry Edwards, who had been the victim of legal and social harassment, advocate radical reforms. But all demonstrate an unerring pursuit of freedom and ideal justice, arguing, like Edwards, that "there can only be American solutions to American problems and they must be developed by all Americans working together" (334).

Autobiographies of black Americans, like self-portraits of any Americans, are as varied as the lives and circumstances of their creators. Modern African American autobiographers continue to challenge the boundaries of literary form and content. They include such structural variations as James Baldwin's essays, *Notes of a Native Son*; Richard Wright's fictionalized *Black Boy*; Ralph Ellison's allegorical *Invisible Man*; the culinary history *Vibration Cooking*, by Verta Mae (Grosvenor); Alex Haley's romanticized *Roots*; and Ntozake Shange's choreopoem *For Colored Girls*. . . . Their political and social statements vary from Donald Reeves's *Notes of a Processed Brother* to Leslie Alexander Lacy's *Rise and Fall of a Proper Negro* (1970); from Eldridge Cleaver's *Soul on Ice* (1968) to Roy Wilkins's *Standing Fast* (1982). They range from the carefully crafted volumes of Maya Angelou and Chester Himes to the ghost-written revelations of Althea Gibson, Billie Holiday, and Sammy Davis, Jr.

Nevertheless, elements of the African American text and social context thus far have been consistent, including the intention of a large number of writers to document their lives not to celebrate themselves but because they believe, like Delilah L. Beasley, that "the most treasured possessions of a people are the records of their activities." Finding the literature of American history bereft of the contributions of blacks, they write what Beasley describes as "labor[s] of love . . . with no effort to flatter" but simply to tell "the facts of their willingness to spend their entire time and their energy to help" the progress of African Americans (1).

IV

Selected
Bibliographies

Minority and Multicultural Literature, Including Hispanic Literature

Compiled by A. LaVonne Brown Ruoff,
Edna Acosta-Belén, Nicolás Kanellos,
and Teresa McKenna

Works referring to authors from more than one Hispanic culture are included here rather than in the Chicano and Puerto Rican bibliographies. Works by or about either Chicano or Puerto Rican authors are found in those bibliographies. Primary works by African American, American Indian, Asian American, and Latino authors are listed in the bibliographies and not in the Works Cited section.

1. Bibliographies and Aids to Research

Etulain, Richard W., comp. *A Bibliographical Guide to the Study of Western American Literature.* Lincoln: U of Nebraska P, 1982. Includes secondary works about minority writers and sections on American Indian and Mexican American literature and the images of these groups in literature of the West.

Foster, David William, ed. *Sourcebook of Hispanic Culture in the United States.* Chicago: American Library Association, 1982. Includes material on Mexican American, Puerto Rican, and Cuban writers.

Kanellos, Nicolás. *Biographical Dictionary of Hispanic Literature in the United States.* Westport: Greenwood, 1989.

Miller, Wayne C., ed. *Handbook of American Minorities.* 2 vols. New York: New York UP, 1976.

2. Anthologies

Blicksilver, Edith, ed. *The Ethnic American Woman: Problems, Protests, Lifestyle.* Dubuque: Kendall, 1978.

Bornstein-Somoza, Miriam, Maya Islas, Inés Hernández Tovar, Eliana Rivero, Margarita Cota Cárdenas, Mireya Robles, and Lucía Sol, eds. *Siete poetas.* Tucson: Scorpion, 1978. Poems, predominantly in Spanish, by seven Latina poets.

A Decade of Hispanic Literature. Spec. issue of *Revista Chicano-Riqueña* 10.1–2 (Winter-Spring 1982). Poems and short stories by some of the better-known Chicano and Nuyorican writers.

Fernández, José B., and Nasario García, eds. *Nuevos horizontes: Cuentos Chicanos, Puertorriqueños y Cubanos.* Boston: Heath, 1982. Short fiction by Chicano, Puerto Rican, and Cuban writers. Spanish-language text, arranged by level of difficulty, and exercises.

Fisher, Dexter, ed. *The Third Woman: Minority Women Writers of the United States.* Boston: Houghton, 1980. Poetry and short stories by African American, American Indian, Asian American, and Chicana writers, with introductions to each writer and bibliography.

Gómez, Alma, Cherríe Moraga, and Mariana Romo-Cardona, eds. *Cuentos: Stories by Latinas.* New York: Kitchen Table, 1983.

Horno-Delgado, Asunción, Eliana Ortega, Nina M. Scott, and Nancy Saporta Sternbach, eds. *Breaking Boundaries: Latina Writings and Critical Readings.* Amherst: U of Massachusetts P, 1989. Includes *testimonios,* critical essays, and a selected bibliography. The collection is divided into writings by Chicanas, Puertorriquenas, and Cubanas.

Kanellos, Nicolás, ed. *Hispanic Theatre in the United States.* Houston: Arte Público, 1985.

Kanellos, Nicolás, and Jorge Huerta, eds. *Nuevos pasos: Chicano and Puerto Rican Drama.* 1985. 2nd ed. Houston: Arte Público, 1989.

Keller, Gary, and Francisco Jiménez, eds. *Hispanics in the United States: An Anthology of Creative Literature.* 2 vols. Ypsilanti: Bilingual, 1980, 1981. Extensive selection of poetry and short stories by Hispanic writers from the major groups, illustrating in the choice of texts the patterns that bind Hispanic life.

Latino Short Fiction. Spec. issue of *Revista Chicano-Riqueña* 8 (1980). A collection of the journal's prizewinning short fiction by Latino authors in the United States.

Mirikitani, Janice, ed. *Third World Women.* San Francisco: Third World Communications, 1972.

Moraga, Cherrie, and Gloria Anzaldúa, eds. *This Bridge Called My Back: Writing by Radical Women of Color.* Introd. Toni Cade Bambara. Watertown: Persephone, 1981. Latham: Kitchen Table, 1983. Autobiographies, poetry, and short fiction.

Nosotros Anthology. Spec. issue of *Revista Chicano-Riqueña* 5 (1977). Latino poetry and graphics by Chicago-based writers and artists.

Reyes Rivera, Louis, ed. *Poets in Motion.* New York: Shamal, 1976. Anthology of works by rising black poets, including those of the editor.

———. *Woman Rise.* New York: Shamal, 1978. Works by emerging minority women poets.

Vigil, Evangelina, ed. *Women of Her Word: Hispanic Women Write.* Houston: Arte Público, 1983. A selection of poetry, fiction, criticism, and art by Hispanic women writers and artists in the United States.

3. Criticism

Baker, Houston A., Jr., ed. *Three American Literatures: Essays in Chicano, Native American, and Asian-American Literature for Teachers of American Literature.* Introd. Walter J. Ong. New York: MLA, 1982. Includes two essays on American Indian, three on Asian American, and two on Chicano literature.

Boelhower, William. *Through a Glass Darkly: Ethnic Semiosis in American Literature.* New York: Oxford UP, 1987. The author applies semiotics to the study of American ethnicity and challenges distinctions between mainstream and ethnic writing.

Bruce-Novoa, Juan. *Retrospace: Collected Essays on Chicano Literature.* Houston: Arte Público, 1990. Includes essays on Chicano, Puerto Rican, and Hispanic literatures.

Dearborn, Mary. *Pocahontas's Daughters: Gender and Ethnicity in American Culture.* New York: Oxford UP, 1986. Discusses American Indian and African American women writers as well as miscegenation as a theme in American literature. Addresses the issue of how gender affects the sense of "otherness" among ethnic writers.

Ethnicity and Literature. Ed. Jules Chametzky. Spec. issue of *Massachusetts Review* 27.2 (1986). Essays on ethnic experience and ethnicity in literature, with particular emphasis on African Americans, American Indians, and Italians.

Fisher, Dexter, ed. *Minority Language and Literature: Retrospective and Perspective.* New York: MLA, 1977. Essays on African American, Chicano, and Puerto Rican literature; the American literary canon; language; orality; and writing and literacy programs.

Kanellos, Nicolás. "La literatura hispana de los Estados Unidos y el género autobiográfico." *Hispanos en los Estados Unidos.* Ed. Rodolfo J. Cortina and Alberto Moncada. Madrid: Inst. de Cultura Iberoamericana, 1988. 219–30.

Multi-Cultural American Autobiography. Ed. James Robert Payne. Spec. issue of *Auto/Biography Studies* 3.2 (1987). Includes essays on African American, American Indian, Chicano, Chinese, and Jewish American autobiographies as well as the image of multicultural America in the personal narratives of Hamlin Garland.

The Nature and Context of Minority Discourse II. Ed. Abdul R. JanMohamed and David Lloyd. Spec. issue of *Cultural Critique* 7 (Fall 1987). Includes essays on minority discourse, African American, American Indian, Bengali, Arabic, and Hebraic literatures.

Payne, James R., ed. *American Lives: Multicultural Autobiography.* Knoxville: U of Tennessee P, 1991. Includes essays on African American, American Indian, Asian American, Chicano, European American, Italian, and Jewish autobiographies.

Simonson, Rick, and Scott Walker, eds. *Multicultural Literacy: Opening the American Mind.* Graywolf Annual Five. St. Paul: Graywolf, 1988. Emphasizing multicultural, ethnic, and feminist perspectives, the volume was designed as a response to Allan Bloom's *Closing of the American Mind* and E. D. Hirsch's *Cultural Literacy.*

Sollors, Werner. *Beyond Ethnicity: Consent and Descent in American Culture.* New York: Oxford UP, 1986. Focuses on the tension between the concern for racial, ethnic, and familial heritage and the conflicting desire to go against one's heritage. Includes discussions of minority literature and the image of minorities in the context of American literature.

———, ed. *Inventing and Re-Inventing Ethnicity.* New York: Oxford UP, 1989. A collection of essays by various authors exploring issues of ethnicity in American literature.

African American Literature

Compiled by

A. LaVonne Brown Ruoff, Jerry W. Ward, Jr.,
Richard Yarborough, Frances Smith Foster,
Paul Lauter, and John W. Roberts

1. Bibliographies and Aids to Research

Abrahams, Roger, and John Szwed. *Afro-American Folk Culture*. 2 vols. Philadelphia: Inst. for the Study of Human Issues, 1978. The most comprehensive bibliography of African American folklore.

Brignano, Russell C. *Black Americans in Autobiography: An Annotated Bibliography of Autobiographies and Autobiographical Books Written since the Civil War*. 1974. Rev. and expanded. Durham: Duke UP, 1984. Includes an unannotated checklist of autobiographies and autobiographical works before 1865.

Carr, Crystal. *Ebony Jewels: A Selected Bibliography of Books by and about Black Women*. Inglewood: Crenshaw-Imperial Branch Library, 1975.

Davis, Thadious M., and Trudier Harris, eds. *Afro-American Fiction Writers after 1955*. Vol. 33 of *Dictionary of Literary Biography*. Detroit: Gale, 1984.

———. *Afro-American Writers after 1955: Dramatists and Prose Writers*. Vol. 38 of *Dictionary of Literary Biography*. Detroit: Gale, 1985. These two volumes provide comprehensive biographical, critical, and bibliographic information about contemporary black writers.

Deodene, Frank, and William P. French. *Black American Fiction since 1952: A Preliminary Checklist*. Chatham: Chatham, 1970.

Fabre, Genevieve. *Afro-American Poetry and Drama, 1760–1975: A Guide to Information Sources*. Detroit: Gale, 1979.

———"Afro-American Theatre: A Bibliographic Survey." *American Quarterly* 30 (1980): 358–73. Critical bibliographic essay.

Fairbanks, Carol, and Eugene A. Engeldinger. *Black American Fiction: A Bibliography*. Metuchen: Scarecrow, 1978. A useful guide to primary sources, biographical and critical articles, and reviews.

Foster, M. Marie Booth. *Southern Black Creative Writers, 1829–1953*. New York: Greenwood, 1988. A biobibliographical guide to writers who have received little critical attention.

Fowler, Carolyn. *Black Arts and Black Aesthetics*. Atlanta: First World Foundation, 1981. An excellent bibliography of material on culture theory, dance, drama, music, negritude, plastic arts, poetry, and fiction that includes a fine introductory essay on black literary tradition and aesthetics.

French, William P., et al. *Afro-American Poetry and Drama, 1760–1975: A Guide to Information Sources*. Detroit: Gale, 1979. The poetry section lists general studies, bibliographies, reference works, critical studies, and anthologies. Primary sources, biographies, and criticism are listed for individual poets. The drama section includes bibliographies, periodicals, play collections, critical studies, and an annotated bibliography of plays by individual dramatists.

Fuller, Juanita B. "An Annotated Bibliography of Biography and Autobiography of Negroes: 1939–1961." Association of College and Research Libraries Microcard. New York: U of Rochester P, 1964.

Gubert, Betty Kaplan. *Early Black Bibliographies, 1863–1918*. New York: Garland, 1982. A collection of bibliographies of African Americana published during the period covered.

Harris, Trudier, ed. *Afro-American Writers, 1940–1955*. Vol. 76 of *Dictionary of Literary Biography*. Detroit: Gale, 1988. This volume and the following three provide comprehensive biographical, critical, and bibliographic information about black writers.

Harris, Trudier, and Thadious M. Davis, eds. *Afro-American Poets since 1955*. Vol. 41 of *Dictionary of Literary Biography*. Detroit: Gale, 1985.

———, eds. *Afro-American Writers Before the Harlem Renaissance*. Vol. 50 of *Dictionary of Literary Biography*. Detroit: Gale, 1986.

———, eds. *Afro-American Writers from the Harlem Renaissance to 1940*. Vol. 51 of *Dictionary of Literary Biography*. Detroit: Gale, 1987.

Hatch, James V., and Omanii Abdullah. *Black Playwrights, 1823–1977: An Annotated Bibliography of Plays*. New York: Bowker, 1977. Identifies and describes more than 2,700 plays written by black Americans between 1823 and 1977. Includes a bibliography of anthologies containing scripts, a list of books and sources on black drama and theater, a bibliography of dissertations, and a list of taped interviews with black theater figures.

Houston, Helen R. *The Afro-American Novel, 1965–75: A Descriptive Bibliography of Primary and Secondary Material*. Troy: Whitson, 1977. Includes works by African American writers who have been mentioned in at least two major black periodicals. Provides biographical statement, description of works between 1965 and 1975, and a list of criticism.

Howard, Sharon M. *African American Women Fiction Writers, 1859–1986: An Annotated Bio-Bibliography*. New York: Garland, 1989. This biobibliography contains books, articles, films, dissertations, unpublished manuscripts, and selected reviews.

Inge, M. Thomas, et al., eds. *Black American Writers: Bibliographic Essays I. The Beginnings through the Harlem Renaissance and Langston Hughes*. New York: St. Martin's, 1978.

———. *Black American Writers: Bibliographic Essays II. Richard Wright, Ralph Ellison, James Baldwin, and Amiri Baraka*. New York: St. Martin's, 1978. These comprehensive companion volumes cover scholarship on the major writers in the African American tradition.

Josey, E. J., and Ann Allen Shockley, eds. *Handbook of Black Librarianship*. Littleton: Libraries Unlimited, 1977.

Kellner, Bruce, ed. *The Harlem Renaissance: A Historical Dictionary for the Era*. 1984. New York: Methuen, 1987.

Margolies, Edward, and David Bakish. *Afro-American Fiction, 1853–1976: A Guide to Information Sources*. Detroit: Gale, 1979. Contains a checklist of novels, a short-story-collection guide, a list of secondary sources for fifteen major authors, bibliographies, and general studies. It is partially annotated.

Matthews, Geraldine O. *Black American Writers, 1773–1949: A Bibliography and Union List*. Boston: Hall, 1975. Lists over 1,600 writers of monographs. Useful for identifying early writers. Since it is organized by subject, the work does not give complete bibliographies for each writer. About half the entries provide library locations.

McPherson, James M., et al. *Blacks in America: Bibliographical Essays.* Garden City: Doubleday, 1971. Useful volume of discussions of African American culture and history from 1500 to 1970.

Miller, R. Baxter. *Langston Hughes and Gwendolyn Brooks: A Reference Guide.* Boston: Hall, 1978. A useful guide to early scholarship.

New York Public Library. *Dictionary Catalog of the Schomburg Collection of Negro Literature and History.* Boston: Hall, 1967.

Page, James A., comp. *Selected Black American, African, and Caribbean Authors: A Bio-Bibliography.* Littleton: Libraries Unlimited, 1985. Most of the 632 writers are African American. Intended for a range of readers, from middle-school students to adult scholars.

Peavy, Charles D. *Afro-American Literature and Culture since World War II: A Guide to Information Sources.* American Studies Information Guide 6. Detroit: Gale, 1979. Part 1 is a good guide to sources on such subjects as the black aesthetic, drama, folklore, religion, music, poetry, prison writing, and politics. Part 2 contains brief bibliographies for fifty-six writers. Most of the entries are annotated.

Perry, Margaret. *The Harlem Renaissance: An Annotated Bibliography.* New York: Garland, 1982. A convenient guide to the primary and secondary literature of the period.

Peterson, Bernard L., Jr. *Contemporary Black American Playwrights and Their Plays: A Biographical Directory and Dramatic Index.* Foreword James Hatch. New York: Greenwood, 1988. Includes an introductory essay on the history of contemporary black American drama; a bibliography of anthologies, books, and periodicals; and title and subject indexes.

Rollock, Barbara. *Black Authors and Illustrators of Children's Books: A Biographical Dictionary.* New York: Garland, 1988.

Rush, Theressa Gunnels, Esther Spring Arata, and Carol Fairbanks Myers. *Black American Writers Past and Present: A Biographical and Bibliographical Dictionary.* Metuchen: Scarecrow, 1975. A useful guide to writers and works up to the early 1970s.

The Schomburg Clipping File, 1925–1974. Teaneck: Chadwyck-Healy, 1985. Microfiche reproduction of newspaper and magazine clippings collected by the New York Public Library Schomburg Center for Research in Black Culture.

Shockley, Ann Allen, and Sue P. Chandler. *Living Black American Authors: A Biographical Directory.* New York: Bowker, 1973. A biobibliographical directory.

Sims, Janet L. *The Progress of Afro-American Women: A Selected Bibliography and Resource Guide.* Foreword Bettye Thomas. Westport: Greenwood, 1980. Selective but fairly comprehensive listing of nineteenth- and twentieth-century sources. Includes black publications, theses, and dissertations. Uses subject headings.

Taft, Michael, comp. *Blues Lyric Poetry: A Concordance.* New York: Garland, 1984. Analyzes the formulas, themes, and linguistic structures of over two thousand blues lyrics recorded from 1920 to 1942.

Turner, Darwin. *Afro-American Writers.* New York: Appleton, 1970. A useful guide to scholarship on drama, fiction, and poetry up to 1969.

Whiteman, Maxwell. *A Century of Fiction by American Negroes, 1853–1952: A Descriptive Bibliography.* 1955. Philadelphia: Saifer, 1968.

Williams, Ora. *American Black Women in the Arts and Social Sciences: A Bibliographic Survey.* 1973. Rev. ed. Metuchen: Scarecrow, 1978. Although the book has few annotations, it gives valuable information about literary works by women.

2. Anthologies and Collections

General

Anthologies and collections of oral literature and autobiographies and slave narratives are listed in separate sections.

Adoff, Arnold, ed. *I Am the Darker Brother: An Anthology of Modern Poems by Negro Americans.* New York: Macmillan, 1968.

Baker, Houston A., Jr., ed. *Black Literature in America.* New York: McGraw, 1971. A chronological survey from the oral prototypes to the 1960s, this anthology has good introductory and biographical notes.

Baraka, Imamu Amiri, and Amina Baraka, eds. *Confirmation: An Anthology of AfricanAmerican Women.* New York: Quill, 1983.

Barksdale, Richard, and Keneth Kinnamon, eds. *Black Writers of America.* New York: Macmillan, 1972. The bibliography included in this book is a good supplement to the material in Turner's *Afro-American Writers* in section 1.

Beam, Joseph, ed. *In the Life: A Black Gay Anthology.* Boston: Alyson, 1986. The first anthology devoted to fiction, nonfiction, and poetry by black gay male writers.

Bontemps, Arna, ed. *American Negro Poetry.* 1964. Rev. ed. New York: Hill, 1974.

Bontemps, Arna, and Langston Hughes, eds. *The Poetry of the Negro, 1746–1949.* Rev. as *The Poetry of the Negro, 1746–1970.* New York: Doubleday, 1970.

Bremen, Paul, ed. *You Better Believe It: Black Verse in English from Africa, the West Indies, and the United States.* Baltimore: Penguin, 1973.

Brooks, Gwendolyn, ed. *A Broadside Treasury.* Detroit: Broadside, 1971.

Brotz, Howard, ed. *Negro Social and Political Thought, 1850–1920: Representative Texts.* New York: Basic, 1966.

Brown, Sterling A., Arthur P. Davis, and Ulysses Lee, eds. *The Negro Caravan: Writings by American Negroes.* 1941. Salem: Ayer, 1987. Now regarded as a classic of its kind, this anthology is still valuable as a text for specialized courses or as corollary reading for a survey course.

Bullins, Ed, ed. *New Plays from the Black Theater.* New York: Bantam, 1969. Eleven plays by Kingsley Bass, Ed Bullins, Ben Caldwell, N. R. Davidson, Charles H. Fuller, Jr., LeRoi Jones [Imamu Amiri Baraka], Salimu, Sonia Sanchez, Herbert Stokes, and Marvin X.

Cade, Toni. *The Black Woman: An Anthology.* New York: NAL, 1970.

Chapman, Abraham, ed. *Black Voices: An Anthology of Afro-American Literature.* New York: NAL, 1968.

———. *New Black Voices: An Anthology of Contemporary Afro-American Literature.* New York: NAL, 1972. Unlike the usual anthologies, these companion volumes include generous selections of literary criticism.

Clarke, John Henrik, ed. *American Negro Short Stories.* New York: Hill, 1966.

Cornwell, Anita, ed. *Black Lesbian in White America: Fiction, Autobiography, Essays.* Tallahassee: Naiad, 1983.

Cunard, Nancy, ed. *Negro Anthology, Made by Nancy Cunard, 1931–33.* 1934. New York: Ungar, 1970. Creative literature and essays on African American culture in the United States, West Indies, South America, Europe, and Africa.

Dann, Martin E., ed. *The Black Press, 1827–1890.* New York: Putnam's, 1971.

Davis, Arthur P., and Michael W. Peplow, eds. *The New Negro Renaissance: An Anthology.* New York: Holt, 1975.

Davis, Arthur P., and Saunders Redding, eds. *Cavalcade: Negro American Writing from 1760 to the Present.* Boston: Houghton, 1971. Contains useful introductory essays for the five periods represented.

DeCosta-Willis, Miriam, and Fannie M. Delk, eds. *Homespun Images: An Anthology of Black Memphis Writers and Artists.* Memphis: LeMoyne-Owen College, 1989. A representative sampling of literature and art that underscores "the importance of community and of tradition" in preserving Memphis's black culture.

Emanuel, James A., and Theodore L. Gross, eds. *Dark Symphony: Negro Literature in America.* New York: Free, 1968. Contains poetry, short stories, and essays by thirty-four writers. The background information on authors and literary periods is good.

Foner, Philip S., ed. *The Voice of Black America: Major Speeches by Negroes in the United States, 1797–1973.* 2 vols. New York: Capricorn, 1975.

Franklin, John Hope, ed. *Three Negro Classics.* New York: Avon, 1965. Includes Booker T. Washington, *Up From Slavery*; W. E. B. Du Bois, *The Souls of Black Folk*; and James Weldon Johnson, *The Autobiography of an Ex-Colored Man.*

Harper, Michael S., and Robert B. Stepto, eds. *Chant of Saints: A Gathering of Afro-American Literature, Art, and Scholarship.* Urbana: U of Illinois P, 1979.

Hatch, James V., ed. *Black Theater, USA: Forty-five Plays by Black Americans, 1847–1974.* New York: Free, 1974.

Hayden, Robert, ed. *Kaleidoscope: Poems by American Negro Poets.* New York: Harcourt, 1967.

Henderson, Stephen, ed. *Understanding the New Black Poetry: Black Speech and Black Music as Poetic References.* New York: Morrow, 1973. Good collection with excellent introductory material. See also list of secondary works, section 4.

Huggins, Nathan Irvin, ed. *Voices from the Harlem Renaissance.* New York: Oxford UP, 1976.

Hughes, Langston, ed. *The Best Short Stories by Negro Writers: An Anthology from 1899 to the Present.* Boston: Little, 1967.

Jones, LeRoi, and Larry Neal, eds. *Black Fire: An Anthology of Afro-American Writing.* New York: Morrow, 1968.

King, Woodie, Jr., ed. *Black Spirits: A Festival of New Black Poets in America.* Foreword Nikki Giovanni. Introd. Don L. Lee. New York: Random, 1972.

———. *The Forerunners: Black Poets in America.* Washington: Howard UP, 1975.

King, Woodie, Jr., and Ronald Milner, eds. *Black Drama Anthology.* 1971. New York: NAL, 1986. With new foreword by King.

Locke, Alain, ed. *The New Negro: An Interpretation.* 1925. New York: Atheneum, 1968. This anthology provides valuable clues about the literary, historical, and sociological ideas that informed the Negro Renaissance.

Loewenberg, Bert James, and Ruth Bogin, eds. *Black Women in Nineteenth-Century American Life: Their Words, Their Thoughts, Their Feelings.* University Park: Pennsylvania State UP, 1976.

Long, Richard A., and Eugenia W. Collier, eds. *Afro-American Writing: An Anthology of Prose and Poetry.* 2 vols. 1972. 2nd ed., enl. University Park: Pennsylvania State UP, 1985.

Major, Clarence, ed. *The New Black Poetry.* New York: International, 1969.

Miller, Ruth, ed. *Blackamerican Literature: 1760–Present.* Foreword John Hope Franklin. Encino: Glencoe, 1971. This anthology contains three fine examples of the folk sermon, work by writers seldom anthologized, and a useful bibliography on individual writers.

Oliver, Clinton, and Stephanie Sills, eds. *Contemporary Black Drama.* New York: Scribner's, 1971.

Parks, Carole A., ed. *NOMMO: A Literary Legacy of Black Chicago (1967–1987).* Chicago: OBAhouse, 1987. An important collection of essays, drama, poetry, and fiction by members of the Organization of Black American Culture (OBAC), one of the most influential of writers' workshops during the Black Arts–Black Aesthetic period.

Patterson, Lindsay, ed. *Black Theatre*. New York: Dodd, 1971.

Porter, Dorothy, ed. *Early Negro Writing, 1760–1837*. Boston: Beacon, 1971. Selected works published between 1760 and 1837. Includes constitutions, bylaws and reports of African American organizations, speeches and sermons, letters, essays, and personal narratives.

Randall, Dudley, ed. *The Black Poets: A New Anthology*. 1971. New York: Bantam, 1983.

Robinson, William H., ed. *Early Black American Poets: Selections with Biographical and Critical Introductions*. Dubuque: Brown, 1969.

Sherman, Joan R., ed. *Collected Black Women's Poetry*. 4 vols. Schomburg Library of Nineteenth-Century Black Women Writers. New York: Oxford UP, 1988. Poetry of eleven nineteenth-and twentieth-century women writers.

Shockley, Ann Allen, ed. *Afro-American Women Writers, 1746–1933: An Anthology and Critical Guide*. Boston: Hall, 1988. Documents the lives and presents selected works of forty African American women writers; provides helpful overviews of the writers, annotations, and bibliography.

Smith, Barbara, ed. *Home Girls: A Black Feminist Anthology*. New York: Kitchen Table, 1983.

Stetson, Erlene, ed. *Black Sister: Poetry by Black American Women, 1746–1980*. Bloomington: Indiana UP, 1981. Introduction to feminist literary tradition via representative writers.

Takaki, Ronald T., ed. *Violence in the Black Imagination: Essays and Documents*. New York: Capricorn, 1972. Includes Frederick Douglass, "The Heroic Slave"; Martin R. Delany, *Blake: Or, The Huts of America*, pt. 1; and William Wells Brown, *Clotelle: A Tale of the Southern States*.

Washington, Mary Helen, ed. *Black-Eyed Susans: Classic Stories by and about Black Women*. Garden City: Anchor-Doubleday, 1975.

———, ed. *Invented Lives: Narratives of Black Women, 1860–1960*. Garden City: Anchor-Doubleday, 1987. Novel excerpts and short stories from ten writers. Includes comprehensive bibliographies and critical essays about the authors and their eras.

———, ed. *Midnight Birds: Stories of Contemporary Black Women Writers*. Garden City: Anchor-Doubleday, 1980.

Wilkerson, Margaret B., ed. *Nine Plays by Black Women*. New York: NAL, 1986. Includes works by Beah Richards, Alice Childress, Lorraine Hansberry, and others.

Oral Literature

Abrahams, Roger D., ed. *Afro-American Folktales: Stories from Black Traditions in the New World*. New York: Pantheon, 1985. A collection of 107 folktales collected from people of African descent throughout the New World. Contains a lengthy introduction.

———. *Deep Down in the Jungle: Negro Narrative Folklore from the Streets of Philadelphia*. 1964. Rev. ed. Chicago: Aldine, 1970. An analytical study of the "dozens," toasts, and jokes as representative examples of black urban folklore.

Adams, Edward C. L. *Tales of the Congaree*. Ed. with introd. Robert G. O'Meally. Chapel Hill: U of North Carolina P, 1987. Includes *Congaree Sketches* (1927) and *Nigger to Nigger* (1928). Together, these volumes present an array of tales dealing with life in the Congaree area of South Carolina. Also includes conversations in dialect.

Botkin, Benjamin A. *Lay My Burden Down: A Folk History of Slavery*. 1945. Chicago: U of Chicago P, 1969. Based on material collected for the Federal Writers' Project in 1938, it includes slave autobiographies, recollections of slavery and its aftermath, and tales about John and Old Master, animals, and religion.

Brewer, J. Mason, ed. *American Negro Folklore*. Chicago: Quadrangle, 1968. An anthology that includes tales, sermons, prayers, and personal narratives.

————, ed. *Worser Days and Better Times: The Folklore of the North Carolina Negro*. Preface and notes by Warren E. Roberts. New York: Quadrangle, 1965. A collection of folktales on religious and secular themes.

Courlander, Harold. *A Treasury of Afro-American Folklore: The Oral Literature, Traditions, Recollections, Legends, Tales, Songs, Religious Beliefs, Customs, Sayings, and Humor of Peoples of African Descent in the Americas*. New York: Crown, 1976. Provides examples of African American folklore from various New World cultures.

Dance, Daryl C. *Shuckin' and Jivin': Folklore from Contemporary Black Americans*. Bloomington: Indiana UP, 1978. This folklore collection, which emphasizes folk narratives, was gathered primarily from black Virginians. Contains commentary.

Dorson, Richard M. *American Negro Folktales*. Bloomington: Indiana UP, 1967. Greenwich: Fawcett, 1967. A compilation of previously published folktales collected by the author in Arkansas and Michigan.

Edet, Edna Smith. *The Griot Sings: Songs from the Black World*. New York: Medgar Evers College P, 1978. Songs collected and adapted by Smith.

Hamilton, Virginia. *The People Could Fly: American Black Folktales*. New York: Knopf, 1985. A collection of folktales told by the author.

Harris, Joel Chandler. *Uncle Remus and His Friends: Old Plantation Stories, Songs and Ballads, with Sketches of Negro Character*. 1892. Philadelphia: West, 1982. Contains stories of animals, as well as songs and ballads.

————. *Uncle Remus, His Songs and His Sayings*. 1880. Ed. Robert Hemenway. New York: Penguin, 1982. A collection of animal tales, songs, and proverbs, with the author's original preface and a new introduction by Hemenway.

Hughes, Langston, and Arna Bontemps, eds. *Book of Negro Folklore*. 1958. New York: Dodd, 1983. An anthology of African American folklore designed for a popular audience.

Hurston, Zora Neale. *Mules and Men*. Introd. Robert E. Hemenway. Bloomington: Indiana UP, 1978. Contains tales of John and Old Master, descriptions of life in the Florida turpentine woods, and supernatural lore from New Orleans.

Jackson, Bruce. *Get Your Ass in the Water and Swim like Me: Narrative Poetry from Black Oral Tradition*. Cambridge: Harvard UP, 1974. A collection of toasts with a lengthy introductory essay dealing with the form, function, and meaning of this poetic form.

————. *Wake Up Dead Man: Afro-American Worksongs from Texas Prisons*. Cambridge: Harvard UP, 1972. A collection and study of the work songs of Texas prisoners.

Johnson, James Weldon, and J. Rosamond Johnson, eds. *The Book of American Negro Spirituals*. 1925. New York: Da Capo, 1977. An anthology of spirituals compiled by the authors from various sources. Contains an introductory essay.

Lester, Julius. *Black Folktales*. 1969. New York: Grove, 1970. African American folktales rewritten by the author for a popular audience.

Odum, Howard W., and Guy B. Johnson. *The Negro and His Songs*. 1925. Nattboro: Folklore Associates, 1964. An examination of black religious and secular songs, containing over two hundred representative examples.

————. *Negro Workaday Songs*. 1926. New York: Negro UP, 1969. A compilation of black songs that includes a discussion of their social settings and examines the blues and the commercial recording industry.

Puckett, Newbell Niles. *Folk Beliefs of the Southern Negro*. 1926. New York: Negro UP, 1968. A study of African American non-Christian beliefs, including superstitions, voodoo, and conjuration.

Sackheim, Eric, comp. *The Blues Line: A Collection of Blues Lyrics*. 1969. New York: Schirmer, 1975. An anthology of blues lyrics emphasizing the historical development of the form and including songs performed by both male and female blues singers.

Taft, Michael, comp. *Blues Lyric Poetry: An Anthology*. New York: Garland, 1983. A fine research tool for comparative studies of varieties of lyric in black culture.

Wepman, Dennis, Ronald B. Newman, and Murray B. Binderman, comps. *The Life: The Lore and Folk Poetry of the Black Hustler*. Folklore and Folklife. Philadelphia: U of Pennsylvania P, 1976. A collection of toasts, with an introduction that emphasizes the relationship between toast performances and participation in the "life."

Autobiographies, Slave Narratives, and Letters

Andrews, William L., ed. *Sisters of the Spirit: Three Black Women's Autobiographies of the Nineteenth Century*. Bloomington: Indiana UP, 1986. Spiritual autobiographies of Jarena Lee, Zilpha Elaw, and Julia Foote.

Barton, Rebecca Chalmers. *Witnesses for Freedom: Negro Americans in Autobiography*. Foreword Alain Locke. 1948. Oakdale: Dowling College P, 1969. Using twenty-three autobiographies, from Frederick Douglass to Richard Wright, the author summarizes life experiences and racial attitudes to create four categories of African American autobiography.

Blassingame, John W. *Slave Testimony: Two Centuries of Letters, Speeches, Interviews, and Autobiographies*. Baton Rouge: Louisiana State UP, 1977.

Bontemps, Arna, ed. *Five Black Lives: The Autobiographies of Venture Smith, James Mars, William Grimes, The Reverend G. W. Offley, and James L. Smith*. Middletown: Wesleyan UP, 1971. Reprints five of the six known slave narratives by Connecticut residents published between 1798 and 1881.

———, ed. *Great Slave Narratives*. New York: Macmillan, 1969. Boston: Beacon, 1969. Reprints narratives of Olaudah Equiano, James W. C. Pennington, and William and Ellen Craft. Autobiography.

Collected Black Women's Narratives. Introd. Anthony G. Barthelemy. Schomburg Library of Nineteenth-Century Black Women Writers. New York: Oxford UP, 1988. Covering the years 1853–1902, these four autobiographies describe the lives of Nancy Prince, Susie King Taylor, Bethany Veney, and Louisa Picquet.

Gates, Henry Louis, Jr., ed. *The Classic Slave Narratives*. New York: NAL, 1987. Includes narratives of Olaudah Equiano, Mary Prince, Frederick Douglass, and Harriet Jacobs.

Katz, William L., ed. *Five Slave Narratives: A Compendium*. New York: Arno, 1969; Ayer, 1970. Reprints the narratives of Lunsford Lane, James W. C. Pennington, William Wells Brown, Jacob Stroyer, and Moses Grandy.

Osofsky, Gilbert, ed. *Puttin' on Ole Massa*. New York: Harper, 1969. Reprints narratives by Henry Bibb, William Wells Brown, and Solomon Northup.

Rawick, George P. *The American Slave: A Composite Autobiography*. 19 vols. Westport: Greenwood, 1972.

———. *The American Slave: A Composite Autobiography*. Supp. Ser. 1. 12 vols. Westport: Greenwood, 1977.

———. *The American Slave: A Composite Autobiography*. Supp. Ser. 2. 10 vols. Westport: Greenwood, 1979. The Rawick series consists of interviews collected by the Federal Writers Project (1936–38) of the WPA collection, plus others. It is probably the most important single collection of oral narratives.

Six Women's Slave Narratives. Introd. William L. Andrews. Schomburg Library of Nineteenth-Century Black Women Writers. New York: Oxford UP, 1988. Includes *The History of Mary Prince, a West Indian Slave* (1831); *The Story of Mattie J. Jackson* (1866); *Memoir of Old Elizabeth, a Coloured Woman* (1863); Lucy A. Delaney's *From the Darkness Cometh the*

Light: Or, Struggles for Freedom (c. 1891); and the stories of Kate Drumgoold and Annie L. Burton.

Slave Narratives. Washington: Federal Writers Project, 1941.

Spiritual Narratives. Introd. Sue E. Houchins. Schomburg Library of Nineteenth-Century Black Women Writers. New York: Oxford UP, 1988. Reprints narratives of Virginia Broughton, Julia A. J. Foote, Jarena Lee, and Maria Stewart.

Starobin, Robert S. *Blacks in Bondage: Letters of American Slaves.* New York: Viewpoints, 1974.

Vincent, Theodore G., ed. *Voices of a Black Nation: Political Journalism in the Harlem Renaissance.* Foreword Robert Chrisman. San Francisco: Ramparts, 1973.

Wiley, Bell I., ed. *Slaves No More: Letters from Liberia, 1833–1869.* Lexington: U of Kentucky P, 1980.

Woodson, Carter G. *The Mind of the Negro as Reflected in Letters Written during the Crisis: 1800–1860.* 1926. New York: Negro UP, 1969.

3. Primary Works

Albert, Octavia V. Rogers. *The House of Bondage: Or, Charlotte Brooks and Other Slaves.* 1890. Introd. Frances Smith Foster. Schomburg Library of Nineteenth-Century Black Women Writers. New York: Oxford UP, 1988. Fiction.

Andrews, Raymond. *Appalachee Red.* 1978. Athens: U of Georgia P, 1987. Fiction.

———. *Baby Sweet's.* 1983. Athens: U of Georgia P, 1988. Fiction.

———. *Rosiebelle Lee Wildcat Tennessee.* 1980. Athens: U of Georgia P, 1988. Fiction.

Angelou, Maya. *All God's Children Need Traveling Shoes.* New York: Random, 1986. Autobiography.

———. *Gather Together in My Name.* New York: Random, 1974. Autobiography.

———. *The Heart of a Woman.* New York: Random, 1981; Bantam, 1984. Autobiography.

———. *I Know Why the Caged Bird Sings.* New York: Random, 1969; Bantam, 1971. Autobiography.

———. *Singin' and Swingin' and Gettin' Merry like Christmas.* 1976. New York: Bantam, 1985. Autobiography.

Attaway, William. *Blood on the Forge.* 1941. Afterword Richard Yarborough. Voices of Resistance. New York: Monthly Review, 1987. Fiction.

———. *Let Me Breathe Thunder.* 1939. Chatham: Chatham, 1969. Fiction.

Aubert, Alvin. *South Louisiana: New and Selected Poems.* Grosse Point Farms: Lunchroom, 1985.

Baldwin, James. *Another Country.* 1962. New York: Dell, 1985. Fiction.

———. *The Fire Next Time.* 1963. New York: Dell, 1985. Nonfiction.

———. *Giovanni's Room.* 1956. New York: Dell, 1988. Fiction.

———. *Go Tell It on the Mountain.* 1953. New York: Dell, 1985. Fiction.

———. *If Beale Street Could Talk.* 1974. New York: Dell, 1986. Fiction.

———. *Just above My Head.* 1979. New York: Dell, 1980. Fiction.

———. *Nobody Knows My Name.* 1961. New York: Dell, 1978. Nonfiction.

———. *Notes of a Native Son.* 1955. Boston: Beacon, 1984. Nonfiction.

———. *The Price of the Ticket: Collected Nonfiction, 1948–1985.* New York: St. Martin's–Marek, 1985.

———. *Tell Me How Long the Train's Been Gone.* 1968. New York: Dell, 1986. Fiction.

Bambara, Toni Cade. *Gorilla, My Love.* 1972. New York: Vintage, 1981. Short fiction.

———. *The Salt Eaters.* New York: Random, 1980. New York: Vintage, 1981. Fiction.

———. *The Sea Birds Are Still Alive.* 1977. New York: Random, 1982. Short fiction.

Baraka, Imamu Amiri (LeRoi Jones). *The Autobiography of LeRoi Jones/Amiri Baraka.* New York: Freundlich, 1984.

————. *Black Magic: Sabotage, Target Study, Black Art: Collected Poetry, 1961–67.* Indianapolis: Bobbs, 1969. Poetry.

————. *Blues People: Negro Music in White America.* 1963. Westport: Greenwood, 1980. Nonfiction.

————. *Daggers and Javelins: Essays, 1974–1979.* New York: Morrow, 1984.

————. *Dutchman and* The Slave. New York: Morrow, 1964; Faber, 1964. Drama.

————. *Four Black Revolutionary Plays: All Praises to the Black Man.* Indianapolis: Bobbs, 1969.

————. *Preface to a Twenty-Volume Suicide Note.* New York: Corinth, 1961. Poetry.

————. *Selected Plays and Prose of Amiri Baraka/LeRoi Jones.* New York: Morrow, 1979. Drama, fiction, and nonfiction.

————. *The System of Dante's Hell.* New York: Grove, 1965. Fiction.

————. *Tales.* New York: Grove, 1967. Short fiction.

Beckham, Barry. *Runner Mack.* 1972. Washington: Howard UP, 1983. Fiction.

Bennett, Hal. *A Wilderness of Vines.* 1966. Washington: Howard UP, 1987. Fiction.

Bibb, Henry. *Narrative of the Life and Adventures of Henry Bibb, an American Slave.* 1849. Miami: Mnemosyne, 1969. Introd. Lucius E. Matlock. New York: Negro UP, 1969. Osofsky, *Puttin' on Ole Massa* 51–171. Autobiography.

Bonner, Marita. *Frye Street & Environs: The Collected Works of Marita Bonner.* Ed. and introd. Joyce Flynn and Joyce Occomy Stricklin. Boston: Beacon, 1987. Mixed genres.

Bontemps, Arna. *Black Thunder.* 1936. Boston: Beacon, 1968. Fiction.

Bradley, David. *The Chaneysville Incident.* New York: Harper, 1981; Avon, 1982. Fiction.

————. *South Street.* 1975. New York: Scribner's, 1986. Fiction.

Brent, Linda, pseud. See Jacobs, Harriet A.

Brooks, Gwendolyn. *Blacks.* Chicago: David, 1987. Poetry, fiction, and nonfiction.

————. *Maud Martha.* 1953. New York: AMS, 1974. Rpt. in Brooks, *Blacks* 141–322. Fiction.

————. *Report from Part One.* Prefaces Don L. Lee and George E. Kent. Detroit: Broadside, 1972. Autobiography.

————. *Selected Poems.* New York: Harper, 1963.

————. *The World of Gwendolyn Brooks.* New York: Harper, 1971. Poetry and fiction.

Brown, Claude. *The Children of Ham.* New York: Stein, 1976. Fiction.

————. *Manchild in the Promised Land.* 1965. New York: NAL, 1966. Autobiography.

Brown, Hallie Q. *Homespun Heroines and Other Women of Distinction.* 1926. Introd. Randall K. Burkett. Schomburg Library of Nineteenth-Century Black Women Writers. New York: Oxford UP, 1988. Biography.

Brown, Sterling A. *The Collected Poems of Sterling A. Brown.* Ed. Michael S. Harper. New York: Harper, 1980.

Brown, William Wells. *Clotel: Or, The President's Daughter.* 1853. New York: Arno, 1969. Salem: Ayer, 1984. Fiction.

————. *Clotelle: Or, The Colored Heroine.* 1867. Miami: Mnemosyne, 1969. Fiction; rev. ed. of *Clotel.*

————. *Memoir of William Wells Brown, an American Bondman.* Boston: Anti-Slavery Office, 1859. Autobiography.

————. *Narrative of William Wells Brown, a Fugitive Slave.* 1847. New York: Johnson, 1970. Osofsky, *Puttin' on Ole Massa* 172–223. Autobiography.

————. *The Rising Son: Or, The Antecedents and Advancement of the Colored Race.* 1873. New York: Johnson, 1970. Nonfiction.

————. *Three Years in Europe: Or, Places I Have Seen and People I Have Met.* 1852. London: Gilpin, 1852. Autobiography.

Bullins, Ed. *Five Plays.* New York: Bobbs, 1968. Includes *Goin' a Buffalo; In the Wine Time; A Son, Come Home; The Electronic Nigger;* and *Clara's Ole Man.*

Butler, Octavia E. *Clay's Ark.* New York: St. Martin's, 1984. Fiction.

————. *Dawn.* New York: Warner, 1987. Fiction.

————. *Kindred.* 1979. Introd. Robert Crossley. Boston: Beacon, 1988. Fiction.

————. *Mind of My Mind.* Garden City: Doubleday, 1977. Fiction.

————. *Patternmaster.* Garden City: Doubleday, 1976. New York: Avon, 1979. Fiction.

————. *Survivor.* Garden City: Doubleday, 1978. Fiction.

————. *Wild Seed.* 1980. New York: Warner, 1988. Fiction.

Cain, George. *Blueschild Baby.* 1970. New York: Ecco, 1987. Fiction.

Campbell, Israel. *An Autobiography.* Philadelphia, 1861.

Chase-Riboud, Barbara. *Sally Hemings.* New York: Viking, 1979; Avon, 1980. Fiction.

Cheatwood, Kiarri T.-H. *Bloodstorm: Five Books of Poems and Docupoems.* Detroit: Lotus, 1986.

————. *Elegies for Patrice: A Lyrical Historical Remembrance.* Detroit: Lotus, 1984. Poetry.

Chesnutt, Charles W. *The Conjure Woman.* 1899. Introd. Robert M. Farnsworth. Ann Arbor: U of Michigan P, 1969. Short fiction.

————. *The House behind the Cedars.* 1900. Foreword William L. Andrews. Athens: U of Georgia P, 1988. Fiction.

————. *The Marrow of Tradition.* 1901. Introd. Robert Farnsworth. Ann Arbor: U of Michigan P, 1969. Fiction.

————. *The Short Fiction of Charles W. Chesnutt.* Ed. Sylvia Lyons Render. Washington: Howard UP, 1974.

————. *The Wife of His Youth and Other Stories of the Color Line.* 1899. Ann Arbor: U of Michigan P, 1968.

Childress, Alice. *A Hero Ain't Nothin' but a Sandwich.* 1973. New York: Avon, 1977. Fiction.

————. *Like One of the Family . . . Conversations from a Domestic's Life.* 1956. Introd. Trudier Harris. Boston: Beacon, 1986. Fiction.

————. *A Short Walk.* New York: Coward, 1979. New York: Avon, 1981. Fiction.

Cleaver, Eldridge. *Soul on Ice.* Foreword Maxwell Geismar. New York: McGraw, 1968; Dell, 1968. Autobiography.

Clifton, Lucille. *An Ordinary Woman.* New York: Random, 1974. Poetry.

————. *Two-Headed Woman.* Amherst: U of Massachusetts P, 1980. Poetry.

Coleman, Wanda. *Heavy Daughter Blues: Poems and Stories, 1968–1986.* Santa Rosa: Black Sparrow, 1987.

————. *Imagoes.* Santa Barbara: Black Sparrow, 1983. Poetry.

————. *Mad Dog Black Lady.* Santa Barbara: Black Sparrow, 1979. Poetry.

Colter, Cyrus. *The Amoralists & Other Tales.* New York: Thunder's Mouth, 1988. Short fiction.

————. *The Beach Umbrella.* Iowa City: U of Iowa P, 1970. Athens: Swallow–Ohio UP, 1971. Short fiction.

————. *A Chocolate Soldier.* New York: Thunder's Mouth, 1988. Fiction.

————. *The Hippodrome.* Athens: Swallow–Ohio UP, 1973. Fiction.

————. *Night Studies.* Athens: Swallow–Ohio UP, 1979. Fiction.

————. *The Rivers of Eros.* Athens: Swallow–Ohio UP, 1972. Fiction.

Cooper, Anna Julia. *A Voice from the South.* 1892. Introd. Mary Helen Washington. Schomburg Library of Nineteenth-Century Black Women Writers. New York: Oxford UP, 1988. Nonfiction.

Cortez, Jayne. *Coagulations: New and Selected Poems.* New York: Thunder's Mouth, 1984.

————. *Mouth on Paper.* New York: Bola, 1977. Poetry.

Cullen, Countee. *One Way to Heaven.* 1932. New York: AMS, 1975. Fiction.

————. *On These I Stand: An Anthology of the Best Poems of Countee Cullen.* New York: Harper, 1947.

Danner, Margaret. *Iron Lace.* Millbrook: Kriya, 1968. Poetry.

Davis, Angela. *Angela Davis: An Autobiography.* New York: Random, 1974; Bantam, 1974.

Davis, George. *Coming Home.* 1971. Washington: Howard UP, 1984. Fiction.

Davis, Ossie. *Purlie Victorious: A Comedy in Three Acts.* New York: Samuel French, 1961. Drama.

Davis, Sammy, Jr., with Jane Boyar and Burt Boyar. *Yes, I Can: The Story of Sammy Davis, Jr.* New York: Farrar, 1965.

Delany, Martin R. *Blake: Or, The Huts of America.* 1859–61. Introd. Floyd J. Miller. Boston: Beacon, 1970. Fiction.

Delaney, Samuel R. *Dhalgren.* New York: Bantam, 1975. Introd. Jean Mark Gawron. Boston: Gregg, 1977. Fiction.

———. *Driftglass.* 1971. New York: NAL, 1986. Fiction.

———. *The Motion of Light in Water: Sex and Science Fiction Writing in the East Village, 1957–1964.* New York: Arbor, 1988; NAL, 1989. Autobiography.

———. *Neveryona: Or, The Tale of Signs and Cities.* New York: Bantam, 1983. Fiction.

———. *Nova.* 1968. New York: Bantam, 1986. Fiction.

———. *Stars in My Pocket like Grains of Sand.* New York: Bantam, 1984. Fiction.

———. *The Tales of Neveryon.* New York: Bantam, 1979. Fiction.

———. *Triton.* 1976. New York: Bantam, 1986. Fiction.

Demby, William. *Beetlecreek.* 1950. Chatham: Chatham, 1972. Fiction.

———. *The Catacombs.* 1965. New York: Harper, 1970. Fiction.

———. *Love Story Black.* 1978. New York: Dutton, 1986. Fiction.

Dent, Tom. *Blue Lights and River Songs.* Detroit: Lotus, 1982. Poetry.

Dodson, Owen. *The Confession Stone: Song Cycles.* London: Paul Bremen, 1970. Poetry.

Douglass, Frederick. *Life and Times of Frederick Douglass: Written by Himself.* 1881. Expanded ed. 1892. Introd. Rayford W. Logan. New York: Macmillan, 1962. Autobiography.

———. *The Life and Writings of Frederick Douglass.* Ed. Philip S. Foner. 5 vols. New York: International, 1950– . Fiction and nonfiction (essays and speeches).

———. *My Bondage and My Freedom.* 1855. New York: Arno, 1968. Introd. Philip S. Foner. Black Rediscovery. New York: Dover, 1969. Ed. William L. Andrews. Urbana: U of Illinois P, 1988. Autobiography.

———. *The Narrative and Selected Writings.* Ed. Michael Meyer. New York: Modern Library, 1983. Fiction and nonfiction.

———. *Narrative of the Life of Frederick Douglass, an American Slave.* 1845. Ed. Benjamin Quarles. Cambridge: Harvard UP, 1960. Ed. Houston A. Baker, Jr. American Library. New York: Penguin, 1982. Gates, *The Classic Slave Narratives* 243–331. Autobiography.

Dove, Rita. *Fifth Sunday.* 1985. Callaloo Fiction. Lexington: U of Kentucky P, 1988.

———. *Museum. Poems.* Pittsburgh: Carnegie Mellon UP, 1983.

———. *Thomas and Beulah.* Poetry Ser. Pittsburgh: Carnegie Mellon UP, 1986.

———. *The Yellow House on the Corner.* Poetry Ser. Pittsburgh: Carnegie Mellon UP, 1980.

Du Bois, W. E. B. [William Edward Burghardt]. *Black Folk Then and Now: An Essay in the History and Sociology of the Negro Race.* 1939. Introd. Herbert Aptheker. Millwood: Kraus, 1975. Nonfiction.

———. *Black Reconstruction in America.* 1935. Introd. Herbert Aptheker. Millwood: Kraus, 1976. Studies in American Life. New York: Atheneum, 1983. Nonfiction.

———. *The Complete Published Works of W. E. B. Du Bois.* Ed. Herbert Aptheker. Millwood: Kraus, 1973– .

———. *Dark Princess.* 1928. Introd. Herbert Aptheker. Millwood: Kraus, 1974. Fiction.

———. *Darkwater: Voices from Within the Veil.* 1920. Introd. Herbert Aptheker. Millwood: Kraus, 1975. Mixed genres.

———. *Dusk of Dawn: An Essay toward an Autobiography of a Race Concept.* 1940. Introd. Herbert Aptheker. Millwood: Kraus, 1975. Nonfiction.

———. *The Quest of the Silver Fleece.* 1911. Introd. Herbert Aptheker. Millwood: Kraus, 1974. Introd. Arnold Rampersad. Boston: Northeastern UP, 1989. Fiction.

———. *The Souls of Black Folk: Essays and Sketches.* 1903. Ed. John Hope Franklin. New York: Avon, 1965. Introd. Saunders Redding. Greenwich: Fawcett, 1969. Introd. Herbert Aptheker. Millwood: Kraus, 1973. Introd. Nathan Hare and Alvin F. Poussaint. New York: NAL, 1982. Cutchogue: Buccaneer, 1986. Franklin, *Three Negro Classics* 207–389. Fiction and nonfiction.

———. *W. E. B. Du Bois Speaks: Speeches and Addresses, 1890–1919.* Ed. Philip S. Foner. New York: Pathfinder, 1970.

Dumas, Henry. *Ark of Bones and Other Stories.* 1970. Ed. Hale Chatfield and Eugene H. Redmond. New York: Random, 1974.

———. *Goodbye Sweetwater: New and Selected Stories.* Ed. with introd. Eugene B. Redmond. New York: Thunder's Mouth, 1988.

———. *Jonah and the Green Stone.* Ed. Eugene B. Redmond. New York: Random, 1976. Fiction.

———. *Play Ebony Play Ivory.* Ed. Eugene B. Redmond. New York: Random, 1974. Poetry.

———. *Rope of Wind and Other Stories.* Ed. and introd. Eugene B. Redmond. New York: Random, 1979.

Dunbar, Paul Laurence. *The Complete Poems of Paul Laurence Dunbar.* 1913. New York: Dodd, 1980.

———. *The Sport of the Gods.* 1902. Miami: Mnemosyne, 1969. Introd. Charles Nilon. New York: Collier, 1970. Introd. Kenny J. Williams. New York: Dodd, 1981. Salem: Ayer, 1984. Fiction.

———. *The Strength of Gideon and Other Stories.* The American Negro, His History and Literature. New York: Arno, 1969.

Dunbar-Nelson, Alice. *An Alice Dunbar-Nelson Reader.* Ed. R. Ora Williams. Comment by Agnes Moreland Jackson. Washington: UP of America, 1979. Poetry and prose.

———. *Give Us Each Day: The Diary of Alice Dunbar-Nelson.* Ed., introd., and annot. Gloria T. Hull. New York: Norton, 1984.

———. *The Works of Alice Dunbar-Nelson.* Ed. Gloria T. Hull. 3 vols. Schomburg Library of Nineteenth-Century Black Women Writers. New York: Oxford UP, 1988. Fiction, nonfiction, poetry, drama.

Edwards, Harry. *The Struggle That Must Be: An Autobiography.* New York: Macmillan, 1980.

Edwards, Junius. *If We Must Die.* 1963. Washington: Howard UP, 1984. Fiction.

Elder, Lonne, III. *Ceremonies in Dark Old Men.* New York: Farrar, 1969; Samuel French, 1969. Drama.

Ellison, Ralph. *Going to the Territory.* New York: Random, 1986; Vintage, 1987. Nonfiction.

———. *Invisible Man.* 1952. New York: Modern Library, 1972; Random, 1982. Fiction.

———. *Shadow and Act.* New York: NAL, 1964. New York: Vintage, 1972. Nonfiction.

Equiano, Olaudah. *The Interesting Narrative of the Life of Olaudah Equiano, or Gustavus Vassa, the African.* 1789. Repub. as *The Life of Olaudah Equiano, or Gustavus Vassa, the African.* Bontemps, *Great Slave Narratives* 1–192. Gates, *The Classic Slave Narratives* 1–182. Autobiography.

Evans, Mari. *I Am a Black Woman.* New York: Morrow, 1970. Poetry.

———. *Nightstar, 1973–1978.* Foreword Romey T. Keys. Los Angeles: UCLA Center for Afro-American Studies, 1981. Poetry.

Everett, Percival L. *Suder.* New York: Viking, 1983. Fiction.

———. *The Weather and Women Treat Me Fair.* Little Rock: August House, 1987. Fiction.

Fabio, Sarah Webster. *A Mirror: A Soul.* San Francisco: Richardson, 1969. Poetry.

———. *Rainbow Signs.* 7 vols. Privately printed, 1974. Poetry.

Farmer, James. *Lay Bare the Heart: An Autobiography of the Civil Rights Movement.* New York: Arbor, 1985; NAL, 1986.

Fauset, Jessie Redmon. *Plum Bun: A Novel without a Moral.* 1929. Introd. Deborah E. McDowell. Boston: Pandora, 1985. Fiction.

———. *There is Confusion.* 1924. New York: AMS, 1974. Introd. Thadious Davis. Boston: Northeastern UP, 1989. Fiction.

Fields, Mamie Garvin, with Karen Fields. *Lemon Swamp and Other Places: A Carolina Memoir.* New York: Free, 1983. Autobiography.

Fisher, Rudolph. *The Walls of Jericho.* 1928. New York: Arno, 1969. Fiction.

Flipper, Henry Ossian. *The Colored Cadet at West Point.* 1878. New York: Arno, 1969. Autobiography.

Forrest, Leon. *The Bloodworth Orphans.* 1977. Introd. John G. Cawelti. Chicago: Another Chicago, 1987. Fiction.

———. *There Is a Tree More Ancient Than Eden.* 1973. Preface Ralph Ellison. Chicago: Another Chicago, 1988. Fiction.

———. *Two Wings to Veil My Face.* 1983. Preface Toni Morrison. Chicago: Another Chicago, 1988. Fiction.

Forten, Charlotte. *See* Grimke, Charlotte Forten.

Fuller, Charles. *A Soldier's Play.* New York: Samuel French, 1981. Drama.

Gaines, Ernest J. *The Autobiography of Miss Jane Pittman.* 1971. New York: Bantam, 1972. Garden City: Doubleday, 1987. Fiction.

———. *Bloodline.* 1968. New York: Norton, 1976. Short fiction.

———. *Catherine Carmier.* 1964. San Francisco: North Point, 1981. Fiction.

———. *A Gathering of Old Men.* New York: Knopf, 1983; Vintage, 1984. Fiction.

———. *In My Father's House.* 1978. New York: Norton, 1983. Fiction.

———. *Of Love and Dust.* 1967. New York: Norton, 1979. Fiction.

Gibson, Althea. *I Always Wanted to Be Somebody.* Ed. Edward E. Fitzgerald. New York: Harper, 1958. Autobiography.

Giovanni, Nikki. *Black Feeling, Black Talk.* 1968. Detroit: Broadside, 1970. Poetry.

———. *Gemini: An Extended Autobiographical Statement on My First Twenty-five Years of Being a Black Poet.* 1971. New York: Penguin, 1976.

Gordone, Charles. *No Place to Be Somebody: A Black Comedy in Three Acts.* New York: Samuel French, 1969. Introd. Joseph Papp. Indianapolis: Bobbs, 1969. Drama.

Greenlee, Sam. *The Spook Who Sat by the Door.* 1969. New York: Schocken, 1985. Fiction.

Griggs, Sutton E. *Imperium in Imperio.* 1899. Miami: Mnemosyne, 1969. New York: AMS, 1975. Fiction.

Grimke, Charlotte Forten. *The Journal of Charlotte Forten: A Free Negro in the Slave Era.* 1953. Ed. Ray Allen Billington. New York: Norton, 1981. Autobiography.

———. *The Journals of Charlotte Forten Grimke.* Ed. Brenda Stevenson. Schomburg Library of Nineteenth-Century Black Women Writers. New York: Oxford UP, 1988. Autobiography.

[Grosvenor], Verta Mae. *Vibration Cooking: Or, The Travel Notes of a Geechee Girl.* New York: Doubleday, 1970. Autobiography-cookbook.

Guy, Rosa. *Bird at My Window.* 1966. New York: Schocken, 1985. Fiction.

———. *The Disappearance.* 1979. New York: Dell, 1986. Fiction.

———. *Edith Jackson.* New York: Viking, 1978. Fiction.

———. *The Friends.* 1973. New York: Bantam, 1983. Fiction.

———. *A Measure of Time.* New York: Holt, 1983; Bantam, 1986. Fiction.

———. *My Love, My Love: Or, The Peasant Girl.* New York: Holt, 1985. Fiction.

———. *Ruby.* New York: Viking, 1976; Bantam, 1979. Fiction.

Haley, Alex. *Roots.* New York: Doubleday, 1976; Dell, 1980. Autobiography-fiction.

Hammon, Briton. *A Narrative of the Uncommon Sufferings and Surprizing Deliverance of Briton Hammon, a Negro Man.* 1760. New York: Garland, 1978. Porter, *Early Negro Writing* 522–28. Autobiography.

Hansberry, Lorraine. *The Collected Last Plays*. Ed. Robert Nemiroff. Foreword and afterword Julius Lester. Introd. Margaret Wilkerson. New York: NAL, 1983. Includes *Les Blancs, The Drinking Gourd*, and *What Use Are Flowers?*

———. *A Raisin in the Sun*. 1959. New York: Samuel French, 1984; NAL, 1987. Drama.

Harper, Frances Ellen Watkins. *Complete Poems*. Ed. Maryemma Graham. Schomburg Library of Nineteenth-Century Black Women Writers. New York: Oxford UP, 1988.

———. *Iola Leroy: Or, Shadows Uplifted*. 1892. Introd. Hazel V. Carby. Boston: Beacon, 1987. Introd. Frances Smith Foster. Schomburg Library of Nineteenth-Century Black Women Writers. New York: Oxford UP, 1988. Fiction.

Harper, Michael S. *Dear John, Dear Coltrane*. 1970. Urbana: U of Illinois P, 1985. Poetry.

———. *Healing Song for the Inner Ear*. Urbana: U of Illinois P, 1984. Poetry.

———. *Images of Kin: New and Selected Poems*. Urbana: U of Illinois P, 1977.

Hayden, Robert E. *Collected Poems*. Ed. Frederick Glaysher. New York: Liveright, 1985.

———. *Selected Poems*. New York: October, 1966.

Henderson, George Wylie. *Ollie Miss*. 1935. Introd. Blyden Jackson. Tuscaloosa: U of Alabama P, 1987. Fiction.

Henry, George. *Life of George Henry. Together with a Brief History of the Colored People in America*. 1894. Freeport: Books for Libraries, 1971.

Herndon, Angelo. *Let Me Live*. 1937. New York: Arno, 1969. Autobiography.

Himes, Chester. *Cotton Comes to Harlem*. 1965. New York: Schocken, 1984. Fiction.

———. *If He Hollers Let Him Go*. 1945. Classic Reprint. New York: Thunder's Mouth, 1986. Fiction.

———. *Lonely Crusade*. 1947. Classic Reprint. New York: Thunder's Mouth, 1986. Fiction.

———. *My Life of Absurdity*. Garden City: Doubleday, 1976. Autobiography.

———. *The Quality of Hurt*. Garden City: Doubleday, 1972. Autobiography.

Holiday, [Eleonore] Billie, with William Dufty. *Lady Sings the Blues*. 1956. New York: Penguin, 1984. Autobiography.

Hopkins, Pauline E. *Contending Forces: A Romance Illustrative of Negro Life North and South*. 1900. Afterword Gwendolyn Brooks. Carbondale: Southern Illinois UP, 1978. Introd. Richard Yarborough. Schomburg Library of Nineteenth-Century Black Women Writers. New York: Oxford UP, 1988. Fiction.

———. *The Magazine Novels of Pauline Hopkins*. Introd. Hazel V. Carby. Schomburg Library of Nineteenth-Century Black Women Writers. New York: Oxford UP, 1988. Includes *Hagar's Daughter; Winona;* and *Of One Blood*. The novels appeared in the *Colored American Magazine* between 1901 and 1903.

Hughes, Langston. *The Best of Simple*. 1961. New York: Hill, 1965. Short fiction.

———. *The Big Sea*. 1940. American Century. New York: Hill, 1963. Foreword Imamu Amiri Baraka. Classic Reprint. New York: Thunder's Mouth, 1986. Autobiography.

———. *Five Plays*. Ed. Webster Smalley. 1963. Bloomington: U of Indiana P, 1968.

———. *Good Morning, Revolution: Uncollected Social Protest Writings*. Ed. and introd. Faith Berry. Foreword Saunders Redding. New York: Hill, 1973.

———. *I Wonder as I Wander: An Autobiographical Journey*. 1956. New York: Hill, 1964. Foreword Margaret Walker. Classic Reprint. New York: Thunder's Mouth, 1986. Autobiography.

———. *The Langston Hughes Reader*. 1958. New York: Braziller, 1965. Poetry, fiction, and nonfiction.

———. *Not without Laughter*. 1930. Introd. Arna Bontemps. New York: Collier, 1974. Fiction.

———. *The Selected Poems of Langston Hughes*. 1959. New York: Vintage, 1974; Knopf, 1981.

———. *Simple Speaks His Mind*. 1950. Mattituck: Aeonian, 1976. Short fiction.

———. *Simple's Uncle Sam*. New York: Hill, 1965. Short fiction.

———. *Something in Common and Other Stories*. New York: Hill, 1963.

——. *The Ways of White Folks*. 1934. New York: Vintage, 1971; Knopf, 1979. Short fiction.

Hunter, Jane Edna. *A Nickel and a Prayer*. Cleveland: Kani, 1940. Autobiography.

Hunter, Kristin. *God Bless the Child*. 1964. Washington: Howard UP, 1986. Fiction.

Hurston, Zora Neale. *Dust Tracks on a Road: An Autobiography*. 1942. Introd. Larry Neal. Philadelphia: Lippincott, 1971. Ed. and introd. Robert Hemenway. Urbana: U of Illinois P, 1984. Includes three chapters omitted from the 1942 edition.

——. *I Love Myself When I Am Laughing. . . : A Zora Neale Hurston Reader*. Ed. Alice Walker. Old Westbury: Feminist, 1979. Autobiography, fiction, nonfiction.

——. *Jonah's Gourd Vine*. 1934. Introd. Larry Neal. Philadelphia: Lippincott, 1971. Fiction.

——. *Moses, Man of the Mountain*. 1939. Introd. Blyden Jackson. Urbana: U of Illinois P, 1984. Fiction.

——. *The Sanctified Church*. Berkeley: Turtle Island, 1981. Nonfiction.

——. *Spunk: The Selected Short Stories of Zora Neale Hurston*. Berkeley: Turtle Island, 1985.

——. *Tell My Horse*. 1938. Berkeley: Turtle Island, 1981. Nonfiction.

——. *Their Eyes Were Watching God*. 1937. Foreword Sherley Anne Williams. Urbana: U of Illinois P, 1978. Fiction.

Jackson, Angela. *Solo in the Boxcar Third Floor E*. 1981. Chicago: OBAhouse, 1985. Poetry.

——. *VooDoo/Love Magic*. Chicago: Third World, 1974. Poetry.

Jackson, George. *Soledad Brother: The Prison Letters of George Jackson*. Introd. Jean Genet. 1970. New York: Bantam, 1972.

Jacobs, Harriet A. Brent [Linda Brent]. *Incidents in the Life of a Slave Girl, Written by Herself (Linda Brent)*. Ed. L. Maria Child. 1861. New York: AMS, 1973. Ed. and introd. Jean Fagan Yellin. Cambridge: Harvard, 1987. Introd. Valerie Smith. Schomburg Library of Nineteenth-Century Black Women Writers. New York: Oxford UP, 1988. Gates, *The Classic Slave Narratives* 333–515. Autobiography.

Jeffers, Lance. *My Blackness Is the Beauty of This Land*. Detroit: Broadside, 1970. Poetry.

——. *O Africa, Where I Baked My Bread*. Detroit: Lotus, 1977. Poetry.

——. *Witherspoon*. Atlanta: Flippin, 1983. Fiction.

Johnson, Amelia. E. *Clarence and Corinne: Or, God's Way*. 1890. Introd. Hortense J. Spillers. Schomburg Library of Nineteenth-Century Black Women Writers. New York: Oxford UP, 1988. Fiction.

——. *The Hazley Family*. 1894. Introd. Barbara Christian. Schomburg Library of Nineteenth-Century Black Women Writers. New York: Oxford UP, 1988. Fiction.

Johnson, Charles R. *Faith and the Good Thing*. 1974. New York: Atheneum, 1987. Fiction.

——. *Oxherding Tale*. 1982. New York: Grove, 1984. Fiction.

——. *The Sorcerer's Apprentice: Tales and Conjurations*. New York: Atheneum, 1986; Penguin, 1987. Short fiction.

Johnson, James Weldon. *Along This Way: The Autobiography of James Weldon Johnson*. 1933. New York: Viking, 1973.

——. *The Autobiography of an Ex-Coloured Man*. 1912. New York: Hill, 1960; Knopf, 1970. Franklin, *Three Negro Classics* 391–511. Fiction.

——. *Black Manhattan*. Introd. Allan H. Spear. New York: Atheneum, 1972. Nonfiction.

——. *God's Trombones: Seven Negro Sermons in Verse*. New York: Viking, 1927; Penguin, 1976.

Jones, Gayl. *Corregidora*. 1975. Boston: Beacon, 1986. Fiction.

——. *Eva's Man*. 1976. Boston: Beacon, 1987. Fiction.

——. *Song for Anninho*. Detroit: Lotus, 1981. Poetry.

——. *White Rat*. New York: Random, 1977. Short fiction.

——. *Xarque and Other Poems*. Detroit: Lotus, 1985.

Jordan, Barbara, and Shelby Hearon. *Barbara Jordan: A Self-Portrait*. Garden City: Doubleday, 1979. Autobiography.

Jordan, June. *Civil Wars.* Boston: Beacon, 1981. Nonfiction.

———. *His Own Where.* New York: Crowell, 1971. Fiction.

———. *Living Room: New Poems.* New York: Thunder's Mouth, 1985.

———. *On Call: Poetical Essays.* Boston: South End, 1985. Nonfiction.

———. *Passion: New Poems, 1977–1980.* Boston: Beacon, 1980.

———. *Things That I Do in the Dark: Selected Poetry.* 1977. Boston: Beacon, 1981.

Kaufman, Bob. *The Ancient Rain: Poems 1956–78.* New York: New Directions, 1981.

———. *Golden Sardine.* Pocket Poets 21. San Francisco: City Lights, 1967.

———. *Solitudes Crowded with Loneliness.* New York: New Directions, 1965. Poetry.

Keckley, Elizabeth. *Behind the Scenes: Or, Thirty Years a Slave and Four Years in the White House.* 1868. New York: Arno, 1968. Introd. James Olney. Schomburg Library of Nineteenth-Century Black Women Writers. New York: Oxford UP, 1988. Autobiography.

Kelley, William Melvin. *Dancers on the Shore.* 1964. Washington: Howard UP, 1984. Fiction.

———. *dem.* Garden City: Doubleday, 1967. Fiction.

Kelley-Hawkins, Emma D. *Four Girls at Cottage City.* 1898. Introd. Deborah E. McDowell. Schomburg Library of Nineteenth-Century Black Women Writers. New York: Oxford UP, 1988. Fiction.

———. *Megda.* 1891. Introd. Molly Hite. Schomburg Library of Nineteenth-Century Black Women Writers. New York: Oxford UP, 1988. Fiction.

Kennedy, Adrienne. *Adrienne Kennedy in One Act.* Minneapolis: U of Minnesota P, 1988. Drama.

Killens, John O. *And Then We Heard the Thunder.* 1963. Introd. Mel Watkins. Washington: Howard UP, 1984. Fiction.

———. *The Cotillian: Or, One Good Bull Is Half the Herd.* 1971. New York: Ballantine, 1988. Fiction.

———. *'Sippi.* 1967. Classic Reprint. New York: Thunder's Mouth, 1988. Fiction.

———. *Youngblood.* 1954. Foreword Addison Gayle. Athens: U of Georgia P, 1982. Fiction.

King, Coretta Scott. *My Life with Martin Luther King, Jr.* New York: Holt, 1969. Autobiography.

King, Martin Luther, Jr. *Strength to Love.* 1963. New York: Pocket, 1968. Philadelphia: Fortress, 1981. Nonfiction.

———. *Stride toward Freedom: The Montgomery Story.* 1958. New York: Harper, 1964. Nonfiction.

———. *Why We Can't Wait.* New York: Harper, 1964; NAL, 1964. Nonfiction.

———. *The Words of Martin Luther King, Jr.* Selected by Coretta Scott King. New York: Newmarket, 1983. Nonfiction.

Knight, Etheridge. *Born of a Woman: New and Selected Poems.* Boston: Houghton, 1980.

———. *The Essential Etheridge Knight.* Pittsburgh: U of Pittsburgh P, 1986. Poetry.

Komunyakaa, Yusef. *Copacetic.* Middletown: Wesleyan UP, 1984. Poetry.

———. *Dien Cai Dau.* Middletown: Wesleyan UP, 1988. Poetry.

Lacy, Leslie Alexander. *The Rise and Fall of a Proper Negro.* New York: Macmillan, 1970. Autobiography.

Lane, Lunsford. *Narrative of Lunsford Lane, Published by Himself.* 1842. Katz, *Five Slave Narratives* 1–54.

Lane, Pinkie Gordon. *I Never Scream: New and Selected Poems.* Detroit: Lotus, 1985.

Langston, John Mercer. *From the Virginia Plantation to the National Capitol: Or, The First and Only Negro Representative in Congress from the Old Dominion.* 1894. New York: Bergman, 1969. Autobiography.

Larison, Cornelius W. *Silvia Dubois: A Biografy of the Slav Who Whipt Her Mistres and Gand Her Fredom.* 1883. Ed., trans., and introd. Jared C. Lobdell. 1980. Schomburg Library of Nineteenth-Century Black Women Writers. New York: Oxford UP, 1988. Autobiography.

Larsen, Nella. *Passing*. 1929. New York: Negro UP, 1969. Fiction.

———. *Quicksand*. 1928. New York: Negro UP, 1969. Fiction.

———. Quicksand *and* Passing. Ed. and introd. Deborah E. McDowell. American Women Writers. New Brunswick: Rutgers UP, 1986. Fiction.

Lee, Andrea. *Russian Journal*. 1981. New York: Vintage, 1984. Autobiography.

———. *Sarah Phillips*. New York: Random, 1984; Penguin, 1985. Fiction.

Lee, Don L. *See* Madhubuti, Haki.

Lee, Jarena. *The Life and Religious Experiences of Jarena Lee, a Coloured Lady*. 1836. *The Female Autograph*. Ed. Donna Stanton. Chicago: U of Chicago P, 1987. Andrews, *Sisters of the Spirit* 25–48. *Spiritual Narratives* 1–97.

Lester, Julius. *Do Lord Remember Me*. New York: Holt, 1984; Pocket, 1986. Fiction.

Lincoln, C. Eric. *The Avenue, Clayton City*. New York: Morrow, 1988. Fiction.

Locke, Alain. *The Critical Temper of Alain Locke: A Selection of His Essays on Art and Culture*. Ed. Jeffrey C. Stewart. New York: Garland, 1983. Nonfiction.

Loguen, Jermain W. *The Rev. J. W. Loguen, as a Slave and as a Freeman*. 1859. New York: Negro UP, 1968. Autobiography.

Lorde, Audre. *The Black Unicorn*. New York: Norton, 1978. Poetry.

———. *A Burst of Light: Essays*. Ithaca: Firebrand, 1988. Nonfiction.

———. *The Cancer Journals*. Argyle: Spinster's, 1980. Autobiography.

———. *Chosen Poems, Old and New*. New York: Norton, 1982.

———. *Sister Outsider: Essays and Speeches*. Trumansburg: Crossing, 1984. Nonfiction.

———. *Zami: A New Spelling of My Name*. Watertown: Persephone, 1982. Feminist Ser. Trumansburg: Crossing, 1983. Autobiography.

Madhubuti, Haki (Don L. Lee). *Black Pride*. Introd. Dudley Randall. Detroit: Broadside, 1968. Poetry.

———. *Directionscore: Selected and New Poems*. Detroit: Broadside, 1971.

———. *Don't Cry, Scream*. Introd. Gwendolyn Brooks. Detroit: Broadside, 1969. Poetry.

———. *Earthquakes and Sunrise Missions*. Afterword Darwin T. Turner. Chicago: Third World, 1984. Nonfiction and poetry.

———. *Killing Memory: Seeking Ancestors*. Detroit: Lotus, 1987. Poetry.

———. *We Walk the Way of the New World*. Detroit: Broadside, 1970. Poetry.

Magee, J. H. *The Night of Affliction and the Morning of Recovery: An Autobiography*. Cincinnati, 1873.

Major, Clarence. *All-Night Visitors*. New York: Olympia, 1969. Fiction.

———. *My Amputations*. New York: Fiction Collective, 1986. Fiction.

———. *No*. New York: Emerson Hall, 1973. Fiction.

———. *Reflex and Bone Structure*. New York: Fiction Collective, 1975. Fiction.

———. *Such Was the Season*. San Francisco: Mercury, 1987. Fiction.

———. *The Syncopated Cakewalk*. New York: Barlenmir, 1974. Poetry.

Malcolm X, with Alex Haley. *The Autobiography of Malcolm X*. 1965. New York: Ballantine, 1973.

Marrant, John. *A Narrative of the Lord's Wonderful Dealings with John Marrant, a Black*. 1785. New York: Garland, 1978. Porter, *Early Negro Writing* 427–47. Autobiography.

Marshall, Paule. *Brown Girl, Brownstones*. 1959. Afterword Mary Helen Washington. Old Westbury: Feminist, 1981. Fiction.

———. *The Chosen Place, the Timeless People*. 1969. New York: Vintage, 1984. Fiction.

———. *Praisesong for the Widow*. New York: Putnam, 1983; Dutton, 1984. Fiction.

———. *Reena and Other Stories*. Old Westbury: Feminist, 1984.

———. *Soul Clap Hands and Sing*. 1961. Library of Contemporary Literature. Washington: Howard UP, 1988. Short fiction.

Mayfield, Julian. *The Hit.* 1957. Introd. Phillip Richards. Boston: Northeastern UP, 1989. Fiction.

————. *The Long Night.* 1958. Introd. Phillip Richards. Boston: Northeastern UP, 1989. Fiction.

McKay, Claude. *Banana Bottom.* 1933. New York: Harcourt, 1974. Fiction.

————. *Banjo: A Story without a Plot.* 1929. New York: Harcourt, 1970. Fiction.

————. *Home to Harlem.* 1928. Foreword Wayne F. Cooper. Boston: Northeastern UP, 1987. Fiction.

————. *A Long Way from Home.* 1937. Introd. St. Clair Drake. New York: Harcourt, 1970. Autobiography.

————. *The Passion of Claude McKay: Selected Poetry and Prose, 1912-1948.* Ed. and introd. Wayne F. Cooper. Source Books in Negro History. New York: Schocken, 1973.

————. *Selected Poems.* 1953. New York: Harcourt, 1969.

McPherson, James A. *Elbow Room.* 1977. New York: Scribner's, 1987. Short fiction.

————. *Hue and Cry.* 1969. New York: Fawcett, 1979. Short fiction.

Meriwether, Louise. *Daddy Was a Number Runner.* 1970. Foreword James Baldwin. Afterword Nellie Y. McKay. New York: Feminist, 1986. Fiction.

Miller, E. Ethelbert. *Season of Hunger/Cry of Rain: Poems, 1975-1980.* Introd. June Jordan. Detroit: Lotus, 1982.

————. *Where Are the Love Poems for Dictators?* Washington: Open Hand, 1986. Poetry.

Millican, Arthenia Bates. *Seeds beneath the Snow: Vignettes from the South.* 1969. Washington: Howard UP, 1975. Short fiction.

Moody, Anne. *Coming of Age in Mississippi.* 1968. New York: Dell, 1976. Autobiography.

Moore, Archie, and Leonard B. Pearl. *Any Boy Can: The Archie Moore Story.* Englewood Cliffs: Prentice, 1971.

Morrison, Toni. *Beloved.* New York: Knopf, 1987; NAL, 1988. Fiction.

————. *The Bluest Eye.* 1970. New York: Washington Square, 1972. Fiction.

————. *Song of Solomon.* 1977. New York: NAL, 1988. Fiction.

————. *Sula.* 1973. New York: NAL, 1987. Fiction.

————. *Tar Baby.* New York: Knopf, 1981; NAL, 1983. Fiction.

Morrow, E. Frederic. *Forty Years a Guinea Pig: A Black Man's View from the Top.* New York: Pilgrim, 1980. Autobiography.

Mossell, Gertrude E. H. Bustill (Mrs. N. F.). *The Work of the Afro-American Woman.* 1894. Introd. Joanne Braxton. Schomburg Library of Nineteenth-Century Black Women Writers. New York: Oxford UP, 1988. Nonfiction.

Murray, Albert. *Train Whistle Guitar.* 1974. Foreword Robert O'Meally. Boston: Northeastern UP, 1989. Fiction.

Naylor, Gloria. *Linden Hills.* 1985. New York: Penguin, 1986. Fiction.

————. *Mama Day.* New York: Ticknor, 1988. Fiction.

————. *The Women of Brewster Place.* New York: Viking, 1982; Penguin, 1983. Fiction.

Neal, Larry. *Hoodoo Hollerin' Bebop Ghosts.* Washington: Howard UP, 1974. Poetry.

Northup, Solomon. *Twelve Years a Slave.* 1853. Introd. Philip S. Foner. New York: Dover, 1970. Osofsky, *Puttin' on Ole Massa* 225–406. Autobiography.

Osbey, Brenda Marie. *Ceremony for Minneconjoux: Poems.* Callaloo Poetry. Charlottesville: UP of Virginia, 1983.

————. *In These Houses.* Middletown: Wesleyan UP, 1987. Poetry.

Parks, Gordon. *The Learning Tree.* New York: Harper, 1963; Fawcett, 1963. Fiction.

Pennington, James W. C. *The Fugitive Blacksmith: Or, Events in the History of James W. C. Pennington.* 1850. New York: Negro UP, 1971. Bontemps, *Great Slave Narratives* 193–267. Autobiography.

Perry, Richard. *Montgomery's Children*. San Diego: Harcourt, 1984. New York: NAL, 1985. Fiction.

Petry, Ann. *Miss Muriel and Other Stories*. 1971. Introd. Barbara Smith. Boston: Beacon, 1989.

———. *The Narrows*. 1953. Introd. Nellie McKay. Boston: Beacon, 1988. Fiction.

———. *The Street*. 1946. Boston: Beacon, 1985. Fiction.

Phillips, Jane J. *Mojo Hand: An Orphic Tale*. 1966. Berkeley: City Miner, 1985. Fiction.

Plato, Ann. *Essays, Including Biographies and Miscellaneous Pieces, in Prose and Poetry*. 1841. Introd. Kenny J. Williams. Schomburg Library of Nineteenth-Century Black Women Writers. New York: Oxford UP, 1988.

Plumpp, Sterling D. *Black Rituals*. Chicago: Third World, 1972. Nonfiction.

———. *Blues: The Story Always Untold*. Chicago: Another Chicago, 1989. Poetry.

———. *Clinton*. Detroit: Broadside, 1976. Poetry.

———. *The Mojo Hands Call, I Must Go*. New York: Thunder's Mouth, 1982. Poetry.

———. *Steps to Break the Circle*. Introd. Keorapetse Kgositsile. Chicago: Third World, 1974. Poetry.

Polite, Carlene Hatcher. *The Flagellants*. 1967. Introd. Claudia Tate. Boston: Beacon, 1987. Fiction.

Prince, Mary. *The History of Mary Prince*. 1831. Gates, *Classic Slave Narratives* 183–242. *Six Women's Slave Narratives* 1–40. Autobiography.

Prince, Nancy Gardener. *A Narrative of the Life and Travels of Mrs. Nancy Prince*. Boston: privately printed, 1850.

Randall, Dudley. *Cities Burning*. Detroit: Broadside, 1968. Poetry.

———. *More to Remember: Poems of Four Decades*. Chicago: Third World, 1971.

Randolph, Peter. *From Slave Cabin to the Pulpit: The Autobiography of Rev. Peter Randolph, the Southern Question Illustrated and Sketches of Slave Life*. Boston: Earle, 1893.

Redding, J. Saunders. *No Day of Triumph*. 1942. Introd. Richard Wright. New York: Harper, 1968. Autobiography.

———. *Stranger and Alone*. 1950. Introd. Pancho Savery. Boston: Northeastern UP, 1989. Fiction.

Reed, Ishmael. *Flight to Canada*. New York: Random, 1976; Avon, 1977. Fiction.

———. *The Freelance Pallbearers*. 1967. New York: Avon, 1985. Fiction.

———. *God Made Alaska for the Indians: Selected Essays*. New York: Garland, 1982. Nonfiction.

———. *The Last Days of Louisiana Red*. 1974. New York: Avon, 1982. Fiction.

———. *Mumbo Jumbo*. 1972. New York: Atheneum, 1989. Fiction.

———. *New and Collected Poems*. New York: Atheneum, 1988.

———. *Reckless Eyeballing*. New York: St. Martin's, 1986; Atheneum, 1988. Fiction.

———. *Shrovetide in Old New Orleans*. Garden City: Doubleday, 1978. Nonfiction.

———. *The Terrible Threes*. New York: Atheneum, 1989. Fiction.

———. *The Terrible Twos*. 1982. New York: Avon, 1983. Fiction.

———. *Writin' Is Fightin': Thirty-Seven Years of Boxing on Paper*. New York: Atheneum, 1988. Nonfiction.

———. *Yellow Back Radio Broke-Down*. 1969. New York: Avon, 1985. Fiction.

Reeves, Donald. *Notes of a Processed Brother*. New York: Pantheon, 1971. Autobiography.

Rodgers, Carolyn. *The Heart as Ever Green: Poems*. Garden City: Doubleday, 1978.

———. *How I Got Ovah: New and Selected Poems*. Garden City: Anchor-Doubleday, 1975.

Sanchez, Sonia. *Home Coming: Poems*. Introd. Don L. Lee. Detroit: Broadside, 1969.

———. *Homegirls and Handgrenades*. New York: Thunder's Mouth, 1984. Nonfiction and poetry.

———. *It's a New Day: Poems for Young Brothas and Sistuhs*. Detroit: Broadside, 1971.

———. *I've Been a Woman: New and Selected Poems*. 1978. Chicago: Third World, 1985.

———. *We a BaddDDD People*. Introd. Dudley Randall. Detroit: Broadside, 1970. Poetry.

Schuyler, George. *Black No More.* 1931. Introd. James Miller. Boston: Northeastern UP, 1989. Fiction.

Seacole, Mary. *Wonderful Adventures of Mrs. Seacole in Many Lands.* 1857. Introd. William L. Andrews. Schomburg Library of Nineteenth-Century Black Women Writers. New York: Oxford UP, 1988. Autobiography.

Shange, Ntozake. *Betsey Brown.* New York: St. Martin's, 1985. Fiction.

———. *For Colored Girls Who Have Considered Suicide When the Rainbow Is Enuf: A Choreopoem.* 1977. New York: Bantam, 1980. Drama.

———. *Nappy Edges.* New York: St. Martin's, 1978. Poetry.

———. *Ridin' the Moon in Texas: Word Paintings.* New York: St. Martin's, 1987. Mixed genres.

———. *Sassafrass, Cypress and Indigo.* 1976. New York: St. Martin's, 1982. Fiction.

Smith, Amanda. *An Autobiography: The Story of the Lord's Dealings with Mrs. Amanda Smith the Colored Evangaelist.* 1893. Introd. Jualynne E. Dodson. Schomburg Library of Nineteenth-Century Black Women Writers. New York: Oxford UP, 1988.

Smith, William Gardner. *Last of the Conquerors.* 1948. Washington: Howard UP, 1987. Fiction.

Stewart, Maria W. *Maria W. Stewart, America's First Black Woman Political Writer: Essays and Speeches.* Ed. and introd. Marilyn Richardson. Bloomington: Indiana UP, 1987. Nonfiction.

———. *Productions of Mrs. Maria W. Stewart.* Boston, 1835. *Spiritual Narratives* 1–82. Autobiography.

Terrell, Mary Church. *A Colored Woman in a White World.* 1940. Salem: Ayer, 1986. Autobiography.

Thomas, Lorenzo. *The Bathers.* New York: I. Reed, 1981. Poetry.

———. *Chances Are Few.* Berkeley: Blue Wind, 1979. Poetry.

Thurman, Wallace. *The Blacker the Berry.* 1929. Introd. Therman B. O'Daniel. New York: Collier, 1970. Fiction.

———. *Infants of the Spring.* 1932. Afterword John A. Williams. Carbondale: Southern Illinois UP, 1979. Fiction.

Tolson, Melvin B. *A Gallery of Harlem Portraits.* Ed. and afterword Robert M. Farnsworth. Columbia: U of Missouri P, 1979. Poetry.

———. *Harlem Gallery.* Introd. Karl Shapiro. New York: Twayne, 1965; Collier, 1969. Poetry.

Toomer, Jean. *Cane.* 1923. Introd. Darwin T. Turner. New York: Liveright, 1975; Norton, 1988. Fiction, poetry.

———. *The Collected Poems of Jean Toomer.* Ed. Robert B. Jones and Margery Toomer Latimer. Introd. Robert B. Jones. Chapel Hill: U of North Carolina P, 1988. Poetry.

———. *The Wayward and the Seeking: A Collection of Writings by Jean Toomer.* Ed. Darwin T. Turner. Washington: Howard UP, 1980. Mixed genres.

Van Dyke, Henry. *Ladies of the Rachmaninoff Eyes.* 1965. Washington: Howard UP, 1987. Fiction.

Vassa, Gustavus. *See* Equiano, Olaudah.

Walker, Alice. *The Color Purple.* New York: Harcourt, 1982; Pocket, 1985. Fiction.

———. *Good Night, Willie Lee, I'll See You in the Morning: Poems.* 1979. New York: Harcourt, 1984.

———. *Horses Make a Landscape More Beautiful: Poems.* New York: Harcourt, 1984.

———. *In Love and Trouble: Stories of Black Women.* 1967. New York: Harcourt, 1974. Short fiction.

———. *In Search of Our Mothers' Gardens: Womanist Prose.* New York: Harcourt, 1983. Nonfiction.

———. *Living by the Word: Selected Writings, 1973-1987.* San Diego: Harcourt, 1988. Mixed genres.

———. *Meridian.* 1976. New York: Pocket, 1988. Fiction.

———. *Once: Poems.* 1968. New York: Harcourt, 1976.

———. *Revolutionary Petunias and Other Poems*. New York: Harcourt, 1973.

———. *The Temple of My Familiar*. New York: Harcourt, 1989. Fiction.

———. *The Third Life of Grange Copeland*. 1970. New York: Harcourt, 1977. Fiction.

———. *You Can't Keep a Good Woman Down: Stories*. New York: Harcourt, 1981.

Walker, Margaret. *For My People*. 1942. New Haven: Yale UP, 1968. Poetry.

———. *"How I Wrote* Jubilee*" and Other Essays on Life and Literature*. Ed. Maryemma Graham. New York: Feminist, 1989. Autobiography and nonfiction.

———. *Jubilee*. 1966. New York: Bantam, 1975. Fiction.

———. *Prophets for a New Day*. Detroit: Broadside, 1970. Poetry.

Washington, Booker T. *Up from Slavery: An Autobiography*. 1901. Introd. Louis Lomax. New York: Dell, 1968; Penguin, 1986. Franklin, *Three Negro Classics* 23–205.

Wells, Ida B. *Crusade for Justice: The Autobiography of Ida B. Wells*. Ed. Alfreda M. Duster. Chicago: U of Chicago P, 1970.

West, Dorothy. *The Living Is Easy*. 1948. Afterword Adelaide Cromwell Gulliver. Old Westbury: Feminist, 1982. Fiction.

Wheatley, Phillis. *Complete Works of Phillis Wheatley*. Ed. John C. Shields. Schomburg Library of Nineteenth-Century Black Women Writers. New York: Oxford UP, 1988. Poetry and nonfiction.

———. *The Poems of Phillis Wheatley*. 1966. Ed. and introd. Julian D. Mason, Jr. Rev. ed. Chapel Hill: U of North Carolina P, 1989.

Wideman, John E. *Brothers and Keepers*. New York: Holt, 1984; Penguin, 1985. Autobiography.

———. *Fever: Twelve Stories*. New York: Holt, 1989.

———. *A Glance Away*. 1967. New York: Holt, 1985. Fiction.

———. *The Homewood Trilogy*. New York: Avon, 1985. Includes *Damballah* (1981); *Hiding Place* (1981); and *Sent for You Yesterday* (1983). Fiction.

———. *Hurry Home*. 1970. New York: Holt, 1986. Fiction.

———. *The Lynchers*. 1973. New York: Holt, 1986. Fiction.

———. *Reuben*. New York: Holt, 1987; Penguin, 1988. Fiction.

Wilkins, Roy, with Tom Mathews. *Standing Fast: The Autobiography of Roy Wilkins*. New York: Viking, 1982.

Williams, John A. *Captain Blackman*. 1972. Classic Reprint. New York: Thunder's Mouth, 1988. Fiction.

———. *!Click Song*. 1982. Foreword Ishmael Reed. Contemporary Fiction. New York: Thunder's Mouth, 1987. Fiction.

———. *Jacob's Ladder*. Contemporary Fiction. New York: Thunder's Mouth, 1987. Fiction.

———. *The Junior Bachelor Society*. Garden City: Doubleday, 1976. Fiction.

———. *The King God Didn't Save: Reflections on the Life of Martin Luther King, Jr*. New York: Coward, 1970. Nonfiction.

———. *The Man Who Cried I Am*. 1967. Classic Reprint. New York: Thunder's Mouth, 1985. Fiction.

———. *Mothersill and the Foxes*. Garden City: Doubleday, 1975. Fiction.

———. *Sissie*. 1963. Classic Reprint. New York: Thunder's Mouth, 1988. Fiction.

Williams, Sherley Anne. *Dessa Rose*. New York: Morrow, 1986; New York: Berkley, 1987. Fiction.

———. *The Peacock Poems*. Wesleyan Poetry Program 79. Middletown: Wesleyan UP, 1975.

———. *Some One Sweet Angel Chile*. New York: Morrow, 1982. Poetry.

Wilson, August. *Fences*. Introd. Lloyd Richards. New York: NAL, 1986. Drama.

———. *Joe Turner's Come and Gone*. New York: NAL, 1988. Drama.

———. *Ma Rainey's Black Bottom*. New York: NAL, 1985. Drama.

Wilson, Harriet E. *Our Nig: Or, Sketches from the Life of a Free Black*. 1859. Ed. and introd. Henry Louis Gates, Jr. New York: Random, 1983; Vintage, 1983. Fiction.

Wright, Jay. *Death as History.* Millbrook: Kriya, 1967. Poetry.

———. *Dimensions of History.* Santa Cruz: Kayak, 1976. Poetry.

———. *The Double Invention of Komo.* Poetry 5. Austin: U of Texas P, 1980.

———. *Elaine's Book.* Callaloo Poetry. Charlottesville: U of Virginia P, 1988.

———. *The Homecoming Singer.* New York: Corinth, 1971. Poetry.

———. *Selected Poems of Jay Wright.* Ed. and introd. Robert B. Stepto. Princeton: Princeton UP, 1987.

———. *Soothsayers and Omens.* New York: Seven Woods, 1976.

Wright, Richard. *American Hunger.* 1977. Afterword Michel Fabre. New York: Harper, 1983. Autobiography.

———. *Black Boy: A Record of Childhood and Youth.* 1945. New York: Harper, 1969. Autobiography.

———. *Eight Men.* 1961. Foreword David Bradley. Classic Reprint. New York: Thunder's Mouth, 1987. Short fiction.

———. *Lawd Today.* 1963. Foreword Arnold Rampersad. Boston: Northeastern UP, 1986. Fiction.

———. *The Long Dream.* 1958. New York: Harper, 1987. Fiction.

———. *Native Son.* 1940. Afterword John Reilly. New York: Harper, 1986. Fiction.

———. *The Outsider.* 1953. New York: Harper, 1965. Fiction.

———. *Richard Wright Reader.* Ed. Ellen Wright and Michel Fabre. New York: Harper, 1978. Mixed genres.

———. *Savage Holiday.* 1954. Madison: Chatham, 1975. Fiction.

———. *Twelve Million Black Voices: A Folk History of the Negro in the United States.* Photo dir. Edwin Rosskam. 1941. Foreword David Bradley. Classic Reprint. New York: Thunder's Mouth, 1988. Nonfiction.

———. *Uncle Tom's Children.* 1938. New York: Harper, 1965. Short fiction.

Wright, Sarah E. *This Child's Gonna Live.* 1969. New York: Feminist, 1986. Fiction.

ya Salaam, Kalamu. *Revolutionary Love: Poems and Essays.* New Orleans: Ahidiana-Habari, 1978.

Young, Al. *Ask Me Now.* New York: McGraw, 1980. Fiction.

———. *The Blues Don't Change: New and Selected Poems.* Baton Rouge: Louisiana State UP, 1982.

———. *Bodies and Soul: Musical Memoirs.* Berkeley: Creative Arts, 1981. Nonfiction.

———. *Seduction by Light.* New York: Delta, 1988. Fiction.

———. *Sitting Pretty.* 1976. Berkeley: Creative Arts, 1986. Fiction.

———. *Snakes.* 1970. Berkeley: Creative Arts, 1981. Fiction.

———. *Who Is Angelina?* New York: Holt, 1975. Fiction.

4. Secondary Works

General

Abramson, Doris E. *Negro Playwrights in the American Theatre, 1925–1959.* New York: Columbia UP, 1969.

Andrews, William L. *To Tell a Free Story: The First Century of African American Autobiography, 1760–1865.* Urbana: U of Illinois P, 1986. Using various forms of poststructuralist theory, Andrews sheds light on black autobiography in the struggle for literacy, freedom, and self-determination. Includes discussions of Nat Turner, Frederick Douglass, Harriet Jacobs, and other authors.

Baker, Houston A., Jr. *Blues, Ideology, and Afro-American Literature: A Vernacular Theory.* Chicago: U of Chicago P, 1984. Using blues as a literary matrix and metaphor, Baker constructs a vernacular theory of African American literature and illustrates how the theory functions in literary historical discourse, recent theory and criticism, and works by Paul Laurence Dunbar, Richard Wright, and Ralph Ellison.

———. *The Journey Back: Issues in Black Literature and Criticism.* Chicago: U of Chicago P, 1980. Challenging essays on the study of literature in its cultural context.

———. *Long Black Song: Essays in Black American Literature and Culture.* Charlottesville: U of Virginia P, 1972.

———. *Modernism and the Harlem Renaissance.* Chicago: U of Chicago P, 1987. An extended essay on the process by which an African American modernism is constructed.

———. *Singers of Daybreak: Studies in Black American Literature.* Washington: Howard UP, 1974. Essays on themes and techniques in African American literature as exemplified in the work of James Weldon Johnson, Ralph Ellison, Paul Laurence Dunbar, Gwendolyn Brooks, Jean Toomer, George Cain, and others.

Barthold, Bonnie J. *Black Time: Fiction of Africa, the Caribbean, and the United States.* New Haven: Yale UP, 1981. Argues that a non-Western conception of time is a distinguishing feature of black fiction.

Bastin, Bruce. *Red River Blues: The Blues Tradition in the Southeast.* Urbana: U of Illinois P, 1986. Examines the origins and evolution of the black American blues tradition.

Bell, Bernard W. *The Afro-American Novel and Its Tradition.* Amherst: U of Massachusetts P, 1987. Comprehensive, interpretative history of the African American novel from 1853 to 1983. Describes novels by one hundred writers and examines those by forty-one.

Bell, Roseann, et al., eds. *Sturdy Black Bridges: Visions of Black Women in Literature.* Garden City: Doubleday, 1979. Illuminating essays on the image of black women in American, African, and Caribbean literatures.

Berzon, Judith R. *Neither White nor Black: The Mulatto Character in American Fiction.* New York: New York UP, 1978. A historical review of the topic, including a discussion of racial ideals and the mulatto in works by African American and non–African American writers.

Bethel, Lorraine, and Barbara Smith, eds. *Conditions Five: The Black Women's Issue.* 1979. New York: Women of Color, 1988.

Bigsby, C. W. E., ed. *The Black American Writer.* 1969. 2 vols. Baltimore: Pelican, 1971. Vol. 1 contains essays on fiction; vol. 2, essays on poetry and drama.

Bluestein, Gene. *The Voice of the Folk: Folklore and American Literary Theory.* Amherst: U of Massachusetts P, 1972. The essays pertinent to African American literature are "The Sources of American Folksong" and "The Blues as a Literary Theme."

Bone, Robert A. *Down Home: A History of Afro-American Short Fiction from Its Beginnings to the End of the Harlem Renaissance.* 1975. With new preface. New York: Columbia UP, 1988. Explores how pastoral and antipastoral "deep structures" of black short fiction evolve from Paul Laurence Dunbar to Arna Bontemps.

———. *The Negro Novel in America.* 1958. Rev. ed. New Haven: Yale UP, 1965. Though controversial in its treatment of black novelists as integrationists and nationalists, this book was one of the first to study the literary traditions of black fiction.

Bontemps, Arna, ed. *The Harlem Renaissance Remembered.* New York: Dodd, 1972.

Brown, Lloyd, ed. *The Black Writer in Africa and the Americas.* Los Angeles: Hennessey and Ingalls, 1973. These nine papers from the University of Southern California's Fourth Annual Conference on Comparative Literature (1970) represent diverse strategies for using aesthetic criteria in interpretation and evaluation.

Brown, Sterling. *Negro Poetry and Drama and The Negro in American Fiction.* 1937. Preface Robert Bone. Studies in Negro Life. New York: Atheneum, 1969.

Brown-Guillory, Elizabeth. *Their Place on Stage: Black Women Playwrights in America.* Foreword Margaret Walker Alexander. Afterword Gloria T. Hull. New York: Greenwood, 1988. An examination of works by twentieth-century black women playwrights in the context of African American theatrical tradition.

Butterfield, Stephen. *Black Autobiography in America.* Amherst: U of Massachusetts P, 1974. Examines African American autobiographies of literary or historical merit published between 1830 and 1972.

Callahan, John F. *In the African-American Grain: The Pursuit of Voice in Twentieth-Century Black Fiction.* Urbana: U of Illinois P, 1988.

Campbell, Jane. *Mythic Black Fiction: The Transformation of History.* Knoxville: U of Tennessee P, 1986. Explores the ways romance has served as the predominant mode of black historical fiction writers. Includes discussions of William Wells Brown, Ralph Ellison, James Baldwin, Leon Forrest, and Alice Walker.

Carby, Hazel V. *Reconstructing Womanhood: The Emergence of the Afro-American Woman Novelist.* New York: Oxford UP, 1987. A cultural and social history of the activities of black women from the mid-nineteenth to the early twentieth centuries. Places the work of writers like Frances Ellen Watkins Harper and Pauline Hopkins in the contexts provided by the intense political activism of black women of the period.

Charters, Samuel B. *The Country Blues.* 1959. With new introd. by author. New York: Da Capo, 1975. A study of the early blues tradition, with biographical sketches of many of the pioneering blues musicians.

———. *The Poetry of the Blues.* 1963. New York: Avon, 1970. Examines the background, contents, and poetic conventions of the blues.

Christian, Barbara. *Black Feminist Criticism: Perspectives on Black Women Writers.* Athene. New York: Pergamon, 1985. Examples of black feminist theory, these essays provide fresh perspectives on the works of Toni Morrison, Alice Walker, Paule Marshall, Gwendolyn Brooks, Audre Lorde, and Frances Harper, and on the theme of lesbianism.

———. *Black Women Novelists: The Development of a Tradition, 1892-1976.* Westport: Greenwood, 1980. A pioneering study of the development of a black female literary tradition. The opening chapters describe the parameters of the tradition, while the final three chapters focus on the works of Paule Marshall, Toni Morrison, and Alice Walker.

Cooke, Michael G. *Afro-American Literature in the Twentieth Century: The Achievement of Intimacy.* New Haven: Yale UP, 1984. Treats four major modes and stages in black American literature: self-veiling, solitude, kinship, and intimacy.

———, ed. *Modern Black Novelists: A Collection of Critical Essays.* Englewood Cliffs: Prentice, 1971. Essays on black novelists in the United States, Africa, and the West Indies.

Crowley, Daniel J., ed. *African Folklore in the New World.* Austin: U of Texas P, 1977. Essays discussing the African origins of African American folklore.

Cruse, Harold. *The Crisis of the Negro Intellectual.* 1967. New York: Quill, 1984. A classic critique of movements and ideas often reflected in African American literature.

Davis, Arthur P. *From the Dark Tower: Afro-American Writers, 1900–1960.* 1974. Washington: Howard UP, 1981. This survey contains a valuable selected bibliography of general works as well as those by and about the authors discussed in the volume.

Davis, Charles T. *Black Is the Color of the Cosmos: Essays on Afro-American Literature and Culture, 1942-1981.* Ed. Henry Louis Gates, Jr. Critical Studies on Black Life and Culture 1. New York: Garland, 1982. Posthumous collection of Davis's writings on theory; the structure of literary tradition; and Richard Wright, Ralph Ellison, and James Baldwin.

Davis, Charles T., and Henry Louis Gates, Jr., eds. *The Slave's Narrative.* New York: Oxford UP, 1985. Contemporary reviews and modern essays illustrating the complementariness of interpreting slave narratives as history and literature.

Davis, Gerald L. *"I Got the Word in Me and I Can Sing It, You Know": A Study of the Performed African-American Sermon.* Philadelphia: U of Pennsylvania P, 1985. Using performance theory as a basic approach, Davis examines the content of African American sermons.

Dixon, Melvin. *Ride Out the Wilderness: Geography and Identity in Afro-American Literature.* Urbana: U of Illinois P, 1987. Suggests that the images of spiritual and physical landscapes and African American literature reveal a changing topography in black American quests for selfhood.

Dundes, Alan, comp. *Mother Wit from the Laughing Barrel: Readings in the Interpretation of Afro-American Folklore.* 1972. New York: Garland, 1981. Essays that shed light on the folkloric aspects of literature and culture.

Edwards, Jay D. *The Afro-American Trickster Tale: A Structural Analysis.* Bloomington: Folklore Publications Group, 1978.

Elder, Arlene A. *The "Hindered Hand": Cultural Implications of Early African-American Fiction.* Westport: Greenwood, 1978. Discusses literary and cultural backgrounds for early African American fiction. Focuses on works of Sutton Griggs, Paul Laurence Dunbar, and Charles Chesnutt.

Epstein, Dena. *Sinful Tunes and Spirituals: Black Folk Music to the Civil War.* Urbana: U of Illinois P, 1977. Using a hemispheric perspective, Epstein examines the development of African American folk song.

Evans, Mari, ed. *Black Women Writers, 1950–1980: A Critical Evaluation.* Garden City: Anchor-Doubleday, 1984. A collection of essays, biographies and bibliographies, and statements by the authors considered.

Foster, Frances Smith. *Witnessing Slavery: The Development of Ante-bellum Slave Narratives.* Contributions in Afro-American and African Studies 46. Westport: Greenwood, 1979. Comprehensive analytical survey of early slave narratives which examines the literary conventions and themes that evolved in this genre.

Gates, Henry Louis, Jr., ed. *Black Literature and Literary Theory.* New York: Methuen, 1984. Theoretical and practical essays, many of which apply recent critical strategies to African American texts and their connections to African materials.

———. *Figures in Black: Words, Signs, and the "Racial" Self.* New York: Oxford UP, 1987. Gates argues against evaluating African American literature as a reflection of the black experience. Instead, he suggests that critics should turn to the language of the text and analyze it in terms of modern literary theory. In his analyses, he covers a broad range of authors, from Phillis Wheatley to Ishmael Reed and Alice Walker.

———. *"Race," Writing, and Difference.* Chicago: U of Chicago P, 1986. This important collection of essays provides models of how race functions as a master trope in contemporary theory and criticism.

———. *The Signifying Monkey: A Theory of Afro-American Literary Criticism.* New York: Oxford UP, 1988. In essays that focus on African and African American vernacular traditions, Gates explores the traditions from within and evolves a new critical approach.

Gayle, Addison, ed. *The Black Aesthetic.* Garden City: Anchor-Doubleday, 1971. Essays on black literature, music, and art that reflect a nationalist critical approach.

———, ed. *Black Expression: Essays by and about Black Americans in the Creative Arts.* New York: Weybright, 1969. Essays on folk culture and literature.

———. *The Black Situation.* New York: Horizon, 1970. Essays on the relations of society, nationalist vision, and literature during the 1960s.

———. *The Way of the New World: The Black Novel in America.* Garden City: Anchor-Doubleday, 1975. A provocative study of the ideological dimensions of black fiction.

Gibson, Donald B., ed. *Five Black Writers.* New York: New York UP, 1970. A collection of essays on the work of Richard Wright, Ralph Ellison, James Baldwin, Langston Hughes, and LeRoi Jones (Imamu Amiri Baraka).

———, ed. *Modern Black Poets: A Collection of Critical Essays.* Englewood Cliffs: Prentice, 1973. Essays on the significant poets from the 1920s to the 1960s.

———. *The Politics of Literary Expression: A Study of Major Black Writers.* Westport: Greenwood, 1981. Explores the political implications of African American literary and cultural expression. Chapters on Richard Wright, Ralph Ellison, James Baldwin, Charles W. Chesnutt, and Jean Toomer.

Gloster, Hugh M. *Negro Voices in American Fiction*. 1948. New York: Russell, 1965. A pioneering study of African American fiction in its historical and social contexts.

Harris, Trudier. *Exorcising Blackness: Historical and Literary Lynching and Burning Rituals*. Bloomington: Indiana UP, 1984. An important study combining anthropology, folklore, history, and literary criticism.

————. *From Mammies to Militants: Domestics in Black American Literature*. Philadelphia: Temple UP, 1982. Discusses the portrayal of the domestic servant in the literature of more than thirty writers, by combining folkloristic, sociological, historical, and psychological analyses with literary ones.

Heilbut, Anthony. *The Gospel Sound: Good News and Bad Times*. 1971. Rev. ed. New York: Limelight, 1985. A study of the development of gospel song as a commercial enterprise.

Hemenway, Robert, ed. *The Black Novelist*. Columbus: Merrill, 1970. Essays on black fiction from the turn of the century through the 1960s.

Henderson, Stephen, ed. *Understanding the New Black Poetry: Black Speech and Black Music as Poetic References*. New York: Morrow, 1973. Contains a lengthy and excellent introduction, a major contribution to ethnopoetics. See also its list of anthologies, section 2.

Hernton, Calvin C. *The Sexual Mountain and Black Women Writers: Adventures in Sex, Literature, and Real Life*. New York: Anchor-Doubleday, 1987. Essays on Alice Walker, Ann Petry, and other black women writers and poets. Also includes a chapter on women in the works of Langston Hughes.

Hill, Errol, ed. *The Theater of Black Americans: A Collection of Critical Essays*. 2 vols. 1980. New York: Applause, 1987. A good collection of essays on the history of African American drama.

Hill, Herbert, ed. *Anger and Beyond: The Negro Writer in the United States*. New York: Harper, 1966. Essays, interviews, discussions.

Hogue, W. Lawrence. *Discourse and the Other: The Production of the Afro-American Text*. Durham: Duke UP, 1986. Examines the influence of literary production, mainstream values, and other sources of political and economic power on African American literature.

Huggins, Nathan. *The Harlem Renaissance*. New York: Oxford UP, 1971. Discusses the literature in its historical context.

Hull, Gloria T. *Color, Sex, and Poetry: Three Women Writers of the Harlem Renaissance*. Bloomington: Indiana UP, 1987. Discusses roles of women during the literary movement of the 1920s, with emphasis on Angelina Weld Grimke, Alice Dunbar-Nelson, and Georgia Douglas Johnson.

Hull, Gloria T., et al., eds. *All the Women Are White, All the Blacks Are Men, But Some of Us Are Brave: Black Women's Studies*. Old Westbury: Feminist, 1982. The bibliographies and bibliographic essays in section 6 and the selected course syllabi in section 7 make this collection especially valuable for curriculum planning.

Johnson, Abby Arthur, and Ronald Maberry Johnson. *Propaganda and Aesthetics: The Literary Politics of Afro-American Magazines in the Twentieth Century*. Amherst: U of Massachusetts P, 1979.

Johnson, Charles. *Being and Race: Black Writing since 1970*. Bloomington: Indiana UP, 1988. Focuses on the problem of the black writer coming to grips with received literary tradition and the black experience. Analyzes works of the major contemporary black writers.

Joyce, Donald. *Gatekeepers of Black Culture: Black-Owned Book Publishing in the United States, 1817–1981*. Westport: Greenwood, 1983.

Joyner, Charles. *Down by the Riverside: A South Carolina Slave Community*. Blacks in the New World. Urbana: U of Illinois P, 1984. Study of the folklore of a community in the Sea Islands off South Carolina.

Keil, Charles. *Urban Blues*. Chicago: U of Chicago P, 1966. Focuses on the relation between blues and other expressive forms.

Kent, George E. *Blackness and the Adventure of Western Culture*. Chicago: Third World, 1972. Essays on the black aesthetic as reflected in the writers from the Harlem Renaissance to the present. Also includes an essay on Faulkner.

Klotman, Phyllis R. *Another Man Gone: The Black Runner in Contemporary Afro-American Literature*. Port Washington: Kennikat, 1977. A study of the flight motif in contemporary black literature.

Kochman, Thomas, ed. *Rappin' and Stylin' Out: Communication in Urban Black America*. Urbana: U of Illinois P, 1972. Collection of essays focusing on black expressive forms.

Kramer, Victor A. *The Harlem Renaissance Re-examined*. New York: AMS, 1987. Essays focusing both on black writers of the Harlem Renaissance—such as Du Bois, Toomer, Hurston, Hughes, Larsen, and Cullen—and on the impact of the Renaissance on Eugene O'Neill, Du Bose Heyward, and other nonblack authors.

Kutzinski, Vera M. *Against the American Grain: Myth and History in William Carlos Williams, Jay Wright, and Nicolas Guillen*. Baltimore: Johns Hopkins UP, 1987. Argues that Wright, like Williams and Guillen, creates within a tradition of "New World" writing.

Lee, A. Robert, ed. *Black Fiction: New Studies in the Afro-American Novel since 1945*. New York: Barnes, 1980. Fresh evaluations of black writers from Richard Wright to Toni Morrison, John Wideman, and Leon Forrest.

Levine, Lawrence W. *Black Culture and Black Consciousness: Afro-American Folk Thought from Slavery to Freedom*. New York: Oxford UP, 1977. Historical study of the development of African American folklore and thought.

Lewis, David Levering. *When Harlem Was in Vogue*. 1981. New York: Oxford UP, 1989. Excellent historical and cultural survey of the Harlem Renaissance.

Loggins, Vernon. *The Negro Author: His Development in America to 1900*. 1931. Port Washington: Kennikat, 1964. One of the first comprehensive studies of African American writing.

Lovell, John. *Black Song: The Forge and the Flame: The Story of How the Afro-American Spiritual Was Hammered Out*. 1972. New York: Paragon House, 1986. A study of the spirituals as social and poetic expression.

Major, Clarence. *The Dark and Feeling: Black American Writers and Their Work*. New York: Third World, 1974. Discusses the achievements of black writers in a racist society.

Martin, Tony. *Literary Garveyism: Garvey, Black Arts and the Harlem Renaissance*. Dover: Majority, 1983.

McDowell, Deborah E., and Arnold Rampersad, eds. *Slavery and the Literary Imagination*. Baltimore: Johns Hopkins UP, 1989. Includes essays by William Andrews, Hazel Carby, Carolyn Karcher, Deborah McDowell, James Olney, Arnold Rampersad, Hortense Spillers.

Miller, R. Baxter, ed. *Black American Literature and Humanism*. Lexington: UP of Kentucky. 1981. Essays designed to expand understanding of the humanism implicit in the African American literary tradition.

————, ed. *Black American Poets between Worlds, 1940–1960*. Knoxville: U of Tennessee P, 1986. A collection of essays assessing the work of distinguished poets from the post–Harlem Renaissance period through the Black Arts movement.

Mitchell, Loften. *Black Drama: The Story of the American Negro in the Theatre*. New York: Hawthorn, 1967.

Moses, Wilson J. *Black Messiahs and Uncle Toms: Social and Literary Manipulations of a Religious Myth*. University Park: Pennsylvania State UP, 1982. In addition to examining the prevalence of these motifs in African American culture and literature in general, the author discusses their relevance to the work of W. E. B. Du Bois and Ralph Ellison.

Nichols, Charles H. *Many Thousand Gone: The Ex-Slaves' Account of Their Bondage and Freedom.* 1963. Bloomington: Indiana UP, 1969. An excellent discussion of slave narratives as historical documents.

O'Brien, John, ed. *Interviews with Black Writers.* New York: Liveright, 1973. Interviews with seventeen writers, revealing their thoughts about literature and the creative process.

Pryse, Marjorie, and Hortense J. Spillers, eds. *Conjuring: Black Women, Fiction, and Literary Tradition.* Bloomington: Indiana UP, 1985. A collection of essays on black women's narrative writings, from nineteenth-century autobiography to contemporary fiction.

Redding, J. Saunders. *To Make a Poet Black.* 1939. Introd. Henry Louis Gates, Jr. Ithaca: Cornell UP, 1988.

Redmond, Eugene B. *Drumvoices: The Mission of Afro-American Poetry.* Garden City: Anchor-Doubleday, 1976. An ambitious attempt to provide a critical introduction to the development of black poetry.

Richmond, Merle A. *Bid the Vassal Soar: Interpretive Essays on the Life and Poetry of Phillis Wheatley and George Moses Horton.* Washington: Howard UP, 1974.

Roberts, John W. *From Trickster to Badman: The Black Folk Hero in Slavery and Freedom.* Philadelphia: U of Pennsylvania P, 1989. Roberts analyzes African American folk heroic creations during the slavery and postemancipation eras, emphasizing the relation between African and African American cultures and oral traditions.

Sekora, John, and Darwin T. Turner, eds. *The Art of Slave Narrative: Original Essays in Criticism and Theory.* Macomb: Western Illinois UP, 1982. Essays emphasizing literary aspects of slave narratives. Designed for both scholars and teachers, the work includes appendixes on the use of narratives in classrooms and a checklist of criticism.

Sherman, Joan. *Invisible Poets: Afro-Americans in the Nineteenth Century.* 1974. 2nd ed. Urbana: U of Illinois P, 1989. Examines the works of twenty-six nineteenth-century poets. Includes bibliographies of their works and a bibliographic essay on available research materials.

Singh, Amritjit, Stanley Brodwin, and William S. Shiver, eds. *Harlem Renaissance: Revaluations.* New York: Garland, 1989. Includes essays by Bruce Kellner, Arnold Rampersad, Robert Stepto, Richard Barksdale, Charles Nichols, Thadious Davis, and others.

Smith, Sidonie. *Where I'm Bound: Patterns of Slavery and Freedom in Black American Autobiography.* Westport: Greenwood, 1974. Discusses autobiography as derived in both theme and structure from prototypes established by the slave narratives.

Smith, Valerie. *Self-Discovery and Authority in Afro-American Narrative.* Cambridge: Harvard UP, 1987. An innovative study of issues in African American narratology.

Starke, Catherine Juanita. *Black Portraiture in American Fiction: Stock Characters, Archetypes and Individuals.* New York: Basic, 1971.

Starling, Marion Wilson. *The Slave Narrative: Its Place in American History.* 1946. 2nd ed. Washington: Howard UP, 1988.

Stepto, Robert B. *From behind the Veil: A Study of Afro-American Narratives.* Urbana: U of Illinois P, 1979. A pioneering work in the formulation of African American narrative theory.

Sundquist, Eric J., ed. *New Essays on Uncle Tom's Cabin.* New York: Cambridge UP, 1986. Includes essays on African American writers and Stowe's work by Robert Stepto and Richard Yarborough.

Tate, Claudia, ed. *Black Women Writers at Work.* New York: Continuum, 1983. Interviews fourteen major black women writers regarding their personal experiences and critical assumptions.

Titon, Jeff T. *Early Downhome Blues: A Musical and Cultural Analysis.* Urbana: U of Illinois P, 1977. Describes the origins of blues in the plantation setting of the Mississippi Delta.

Toop, David. *The Rap Attack: African Jive to New York Hip Hop.* Boston: South End, 1984. Discusses the origins and growth of the rap music that grew out of the New York City gangs and demonstrates its relationship to other forms of African American folklore.

Turner, Darwin T. *In a Minor Chord: Three Afro-American Writers and Their Search for Identity.* Carbondale: Southern Illinois UP, 1971. Three essays on the work of Countee Cullen, Zora Neale Hurston, and Jean Toomer as Harlem Renaissance writers.

Wade-Gayles, Gloria. *No Crystal Stair: Visions of Race and Sex in Black Women's Fiction.* New York: Pilgrim, 1984. An interdisciplinary study of black women's lives as depicted in twelve novels by African American women writers between 1946 and 1976.

Wagner, Jean. *Black Poets of the United States: From Paul Laurence Dunbar to Langston Hughes.* Trans. Kenneth Douglas. Urbana: U of Illinois P, 1973. A study of major poets.

Watson, Carole McAlpine. *Prologue: The Novels of Black American Women, 1891–1965.* Westport: Greenwood, 1985. Thematic study of fifty-eight novels by African American women published between 1891 and 1965. Focuses in depth on the literary and aesthetic characteristics of ten novels during the periods 1891–1920, 1921–45, 1946–65 and includes an annotated bibliography of the novels on which the study is based.

Weixlmann, Joe, and Houston A. Baker, Jr., eds. *Black Feminist Criticism and Critical Theory.* Vol. 3 of *Studies in Black American Literature.* Greenwood: Penkevill, 1988. These essays show how feminist concerns can transform the nature of theory.

Weixlmann, Joe, and Chester J. Fontenot, eds. *Black American Prose Theory.* Vol. 1 of *Studies in Black American Literature.* Greenwood: Penkevill, 1984. Eight essays dealing with critical and theoretical approaches to prose fiction and nonfiction.

———. *Belief vs. Theory in Black American Literary Criticism.* Vol. 2 of *Studies in Black American Literature.* Greenwood: Penkevill, 1986. Essays exploring the tensions in African American literary criticism between various beliefs and theoretical postulates.

Whitlow, Roger. *Black American Literature: A Critical History.* 1973. Totowa: Littlefield, 1974. Rev. ed. Chicago: Nelson-Hall, 1976.

Williams, Kenny J. *They Also Spoke: An Essay on Negro Literature in America, 1787–1930.* Nashville: Townsend, 1970. Emphasizes that "Negro literature" is really American literature.

Williams, Sherley Anne. *Give Birth to Brightness: A Thematic Study in Neo-Black Literature.* New York: Dial, 1972. Discusses the heroic traditions in black fiction and drama.

Willis, Susan. *Specifying: Black Women Writing the American Experience.* Madison: U of Wisconsin P, 1987. Willis uses Marxist approaches to place works of Zora Neale Hurston, Toni Morrison, Alice Walker, and Paule Marshall in critical and cultural contexts.

Yellin, Jean Fagan. *The Intricate Knot: Black Figures in American Literature, 1776–1863.* New York: New York UP, 1972. Examines views of black people in selected examples of American prose, from the Declaration of Independence to emancipation.

Young, James O. *Black Writers of the Thirties.* Baton Rouge: Louisiana State UP, 1973. A comprehensive examination of the ideas of black writers in a variety of political, economic, and sociocultural contexts during the Depression.

Teaching African American Literature

Fisher, Dexter, and Robert B. Stepto, eds. *Afro-American Literature: The Reconstruction of Instruction.* New York: MLA, 1979. Indispensable for curriculum planning. The essays on African American literary history, language, literature and folklore, theory, and course design are model guides for pedagogy.

MacCann, Donnarae, and Gloria Woodard, eds. *The Black American in Books for Children: Readings in Racism.* 1972. 2nd ed. Metuchen: Scarecrow, 1985. Essays by writers, teachers, and critics concerning racism in literature by or about African Americans.

Sims, Rudine. *Shadow and Substance: Afro-American Experience in Contemporary Children's Fiction.* Urbana: NCTE, 1982. An analysis of changes in depictions of blacks in literature for children, based on a survey of 150 books of realistic fiction published from 1965 to 1979.

Stanford, Barbara Dodds, and Karima Amin. *Black Literature for High School Students.* Urbana: NCTE, 1978. Update of the Turner-Stanford book below. Introduces works by black writers and discusses the impact of cultural preconceptions on literary criticism.

Turner, Darwin T., and Barbara Dodds Stanford. *Theory and Practice in the Teaching of Literature by Afro-Americans.* Urbana: NCTE, 1971. Turner's section on theory foregrounds the problem of periodicity; Stanford's discussion of practice, directed at high school teachers, is stimulating.

Works on Individual Authors

Baldwin, James

Harris, Trudier. *Black Women in the Fiction of James Baldwin.* Knoxville: U of Tennessee P, 1985. Analyzes Baldwin's development of female characters over a thirty-year period.

Kinnamon, Keneth. *James Baldwin: A Collection of Critical Essays.* Englewood Cliffs: Prentice, 1974.

O'Daniel, Therman B., ed. *James Baldwin: A Critical Evaluation.* Washington: Howard UP, 1977. Provides evaluations of Baldwin as a novelist, essayist, short-story writer, playwright, and screenwriter. Includes a bibliography of primary and secondary sources.

Porter, Horace A. *Stealing the Fire: The Art and Protest of James Baldwin.* Middletown: Wesleyan UP, 1989. Focuses on elements of ambivalence in Baldwin's artistic and personal identity.

Pratt, Louis. *James Baldwin.* Boston: Twayne, 1978. An introductory survey of Baldwin's life and work.

Standley, Fred L., and Nancy V. [Burt] Standley, eds. *Critical Essays on James Baldwin.* Boston: Hall, 1988. Contains thirty-six essays and reviews of Baldwin's work since 1953.

———, eds. *James Baldwin: A Reference Guide.* Boston: Hall, 1980.

Troupe, Quincy, ed. *James Baldwin: The Legacy.* New York: Simon, 1989. Includes photographs, interviews with Baldwin, and essays by Wole Soyinka, Maya Angelou, Toni Morrison, Amiri Baraka, and others.

Baraka, Imamu Amiri (LeRoi Jones)

Benston, Kimberly W. *Baraka: The Renegade and the Mask.* New Haven: Yale UP, 1976.

Brown, Lloyd W. *Amiri Baraka.* United States Authors 383. Boston: Twayne, 1980.

Harris, William J. *The Poetry and Poetics of Amiri Baraka.* Columbia: U of Missouri P, 1985. Examines Baraka's transformation of avant-garde poetics and his use of the jazz aesthetic.

Lacey, Henry C. *To Raise, Destroy, and Create: The Poetry, Drama, and Fiction of Imamu Amiri Baraka.* Troy: Whitston, 1981.

Brooks, Gwendolyn

Kent, George E. *A Life of Gwendolyn Brooks*. Lexington: UP of Kentucky, 1989. This biography surveys the author's life and work to 1978.

Melhem, D. H. *Gwendolyn Brooks: Poetry and the Heroic Voice*. Lexington: UP of Kentucky, 1987.

Mootry, Maria K., and Gary Smith, eds. *A Life Distilled: Gwendolyn Brooks, Her Poetry and Fiction*. Urbana: U of Illinois P, 1987. Collection of essays on Brooks's works.

Brown, Sterling A.

Gabbin, Joanne V. *Sterling A. Brown: Building the Black Aesthetic Tradition*. Contributions in Afro-American and African Studies 86. Westport: Greenwood, 1985. This first full-length study of Brown's life and works includes an extensive bibliography.

Brown, William Wells

Farrison, William Edward. *William Wells Brown: Author and Reformer*. Chicago: U of Chicago P, 1969.

Chesnutt, Charles W.

Andrews, William L. *The Literary Career of Charles W. Chesnutt*. Southern Literature. Baton Rouge: Louisiana State UP, 1980. Examines Chesnutt's canon and assesses his role in the evolution of black literature.

Cullen, Countee

Baker, Houston A., Jr. *A Many-Colored Coat of Dreams: The Poetry of Countee Cullen*. Detroit: Broadside, 1974.

Perry, Margaret. *A Bio-Bibliography of Countee P. Cullen, 1903-1946*. Foreword Don M. Wolfe. Westport: Greenwood, 1971.

Shucard, Alan R. *Countee Cullen*. United States Authors 470. Boston: Twayne, 1984. An introductory survey of Cullen's life and work.

Douglass, Frederick

Martin, Waldo E., Jr. *The Mind of Frederick Douglass*. Chapel Hill: U of North Carolina P, 1985.

Du Bois, W. E. B. [William Edward Burghardt]

Lester, Julius. Introduction. *The Seventh Son: The Thought and Writings of W. E. B. Du Bois*. Ed. Julius Lester. New York: Random, 1971. 3-152.

Rampersad, Arnold. *The Art and Imagination of W. E. B. Du Bois*. 1976. New York: Schocken, 1990. A comprehensive study of how Du Bois's poetic vision shaped his career as a writer.

Dunbar, Paul Laurence

Brawley, Benjamin. *Paul Laurence Dunbar: Poet of His People*. 1936. Port Washington: Kennikat, 1967.

Gayle, Addison. *Oak and Ivy: A Biography of Paul Laurence Dunbar*. Garden City: Doubleday, 1971.

Martin, Jay, ed. *A Singer in the Dawn: Reinterpretations of Paul Laurence Dunbar*. New York: Dodd, 1975.

Revell, Peter. *Paul Laurence Dunbar*. United States Authors 298. Boston: Twayne, 1979. An introduction to Dunbar's life and work.

Ellison, Ralph

Benston, Kimberly W., ed. *Speaking for You: The Vision of Ralph Ellison*. Washington: Howard UP, 1987. A representative sampling of critical responses to Ellison's craft, philosophy, and ideology. Includes Robert O'Meally's extensive bibliography of Ellison's works.

Hersey, John, ed. *Ralph Ellison: A Collection of Critical Essays*. Englewood Cliffs: Prentice, 1974.

List, Robert N. *Dedalus in Harlem: The Joyce-Ellison Connection*. Washington: UP of America, 1982. A study of James Joyce's influence on Ellison's fiction.

Nadel, Alan. *Invisible Criticism: Ralph Ellison and the American Canon*. Iowa City: U of Iowa P, 1988. A critical analysis of *Invisible Man*, focusing on its relation to the American literary canon.

O'Meally, Robert G. *The Craft of Ralph Ellison*. Cambridge: Harvard UP, 1980. Examines the forces that shaped Ellison's writing from 1937 to 1979.

————, ed. *New Essays on* Invisible Man. New York: Cambridge UP, 1988.

Reilly, John M., ed. *Twentieth-Century Interpretations of* Invisible Man. Englewood Cliffs: Prentice, 1970.

Equiano, Olaudah [Gustavus Vassa]

Costanzo, Angelo. *Surprizing Narrative: Olaudah Equiano and the Beginnings of Black Autobiography*. New York: Greenwood, 1987. Examines the literary devices used by the first black writers, with emphasis on Equiano's autobiography.

Gaines, Ernest J.

Ernest J. Gaines. Spec. issue of *Callaloo* 3.1 (1978): 1–133.

Hicks, Jack. *In the Singer's Temple: Prose Fictions of Barthelme, Gaines, Brautigan, Piercy, Kesey and Kosinski*. Chapel Hill: U of North Carolina P, 1981. One chapter contains an extensive discussion of Gaines's work from *Catherine Carmier* to *In My Father's House*.

Hansberry, Lorraine

Cheney, Anne. *Lorraine Hansberry*. United States Authors 430. Boston: Twayne, 1984. A general survey of her life and work.

Hayden, Robert

Hatcher, John. *From the Auroral Darkness: The Life and Poetry of Robert Hayden.* Oxford: George Ronald, 1984. Discusses the variety in Hayden's poetry and the link between the poet and the Baha'i faith.

Williams, Pontheolla Taylor. *Robert Hayden: A Critical Analysis of His Poetry.* Urbana: U of Illinois P, 1987.

Himes, Chester

Lundquist, James. *Chester Himes.* New York: Ungar, 1976. An introduction to the author's life and work.

Milliken, Stephen F. *Chester Himes: A Critical Appraisal.* Columbia: U of Missouri P, 1976.

Hughes, Langston

Berry, Faith. *Langston Hughes: Before and Beyond Harlem.* Westport: Hill, 1983. A full-length critical and biographical study.

Emanuel, James A. *Langston Hughes.* United States Authors 123. New York: Twayne, 1967.

Fontenot, Chester J., ed. *Langston Hughes.* Spec. issue of *Black American Literature Forum* 15 (1981): 82–119.

Jemie, Onwuchekwa. *Langston Hughes: An Introduction to the Poetry.* 1976. Columbia Introductions to Twentieth-Century American Poetry. New York: Columbia, 1985. Considers Hughes's poetics and aesthetic and his use of the blues and jazz.

O'Daniel, Therman B., ed. *Langston Hughes, Black Genius: A Critical Evaluation.* New York: Morrow, 1971.

Rampersad, Arnold. *The Life of Langston Hughes.* 2 vols. New York: Oxford UP, 1986–88. The definitive biography.

Hurston, Zora Neale

Hemenway, Robert. *Zora Neale Hurston.* Foreword Alice Walker. Urbana: U of Illinois P, 1977. A definitive literary biography of a pathbreaking black woman writer.

Holloway, Karla F. *The Character of the Word: The Texts of Zora Neale Hurston.* New York: Greenwood, 1987. A study of Hurston's works in literary and political contexts.

Newson, Adele S. *Zora Neale Hurston: A Reference Guide.* Boston: Hall, 1987. The first guide to scholarship on Hurston.

Johnson, James Weldon

Levy, Eugene. *James Weldon Johnson: Black Leader, Black Voice.* Negro American Biographies and Autobiographies. Chicago: U of Chicago P, 1973.

Locke, Alain

Stewart, Jeffrey C. *Alain Locke: A Research Guide*. New York: Garland, 1989. Annotated bibliography of works by and about Locke.

McKay, Claude

Cooper, Wayne F. *Claude McKay: Rebel Sojourner in the Harlem Renaissance*. Baton Rouge: Louisiana State UP, 1987. This perceptive biography casts new light on the life and work of a complex artist.

Morrison, Toni

Holloway, Karla F., and Stephanie Demetrakopoulos. *New Dimensions of Spirituality: A Bi-Racial and Bi-Cultural Reading of the Novels of Toni Morrison*. Contributions in Women's Studies. New York: Greenwood, 1987. Focuses on survival as a germinal force in Morrison's literary production.
McKay, Nellie Y., ed. *Critical Essays on Toni Morrison*. Boston: Hall, 1988. First collection of critical articles on Morrison's contributions to the black literary tradition.
Middleton, David L. *Toni Morrison: An Annotated Bibliography*. New York: Garland, 1987.

Reed, Ishmael

Settle, Elizabeth A., and Thomas A. Settle. *Ishmael Reed: A Primary and Secondary Bibliography*. Boston: Hall, 1982.

Toomer, Jean

Kerman, Cynthia Earl, and Richard Eldridge. *The Lives of Jean Toomer: A Hunger for Wholeness*. Baton Rouge: Louisiana State UP, 1987. The most complete biography of Toomer to date.
McKay, Nellie Y. *Jean Toomer, Artist: A Study of His Literary Life and Work, 1894–1936*. Chapel Hill: U of North Carolina P, 1984. Explores Toomer's growth, development, and decline by interpreting the intersection of his published works and life.
O'Daniel, Therman B. *Jean Toomer: A Critical Evaluation*. Washington: Howard UP, 1988.

Walker, Alice

Banks, Erma Davis, and Keith Byerman. *Alice Walker: An Annotated Bibliography*. New York: Garland, 1989.

Wheatley, Phillis

Richmond, Merle A. *Bid the Vassal Soar: Interpretive Essays on the Life and Poetry of Phillis Wheatley and George Moses Horton*. Washington: Howard UP, 1974. Critical assessments of two early African American poets.

Robinson, William H. *Phillis Wheatley and Her Writings*. New York: Garland, 1984. Includes all extant poems, many letters, and a facsimile of the 1773 *Poems of Various Subjects*. Also provides originals of poems Wheatley translated and an essay describing her life in the context of the Boston colony.

Wideman, John Edgar

Coleman, James W. *Blackness and Modernism: The Literary Career of John Edgar Wideman*. Jackson: UP of Mississippi, 1989. Explores the use of modernist and postmodernist strategies in Wideman's fiction.

Wright, Richard

Avery, Evelyn Gross. *Rebels and Victims: The Fiction of Richard Wright and Bernard Malamud*. National University Publications in Literary Criticism. Port Washington: Kennikat, 1979. A comparative thematic study of Wright and Malamud.

Baker, Houston A., Jr., ed. *Twentieth-Century Interpretations of* Native Son. Englewood Cliffs: Prentice, 1972. Essays on the themes, style, genre, structural elements, artistic influences, and historical background of the novel.

Bakish, David. *Richard Wright*. New York: Ungar, 1973. In this chronological study, Bakish seeks to explain how Wright's life and works illuminate one another.

Bloom, Harold, ed. *Richard Wright*. Modern Critical Views: Modern American. New York: Chelsea, 1987.

Davis, Charles T., and Michel Fabre. *Richard Wright: A Primary Bibliography*. Boston: Hall, 1982. A descriptive bibliography of Wright's published and unpublished works. Includes appendixes on translations and materials on Wright's published works in the James Weldon Johnson Collection, Yale University.

Fabre, Michel. *The Unfinished Quest of Richard Wright*. Trans. Isabel Barzun. New York: Morrow, 1973. A scholarly biographical study of Wright's centrality in African American letters.

———. *The World of Richard Wright*. Center for the Study of Southern Culture. Jackson: UP of Mississippi, 1985. Essays from a bibliographical study of Wright's first personal library to an examination of his interest in negritude and African writing.

Felgar, Robert. *Richard Wright*. United States Authors 386. Boston: Twayne, 1980. A chronological study of Wright's themes, ideas, and techniques.

Fishburn, Katherine. *Richard Wright's Hero: The Faces of the Rebel-Victim*. Metuchen: Scarecrow, 1977. Examines heroic types in Wright's works, from the innocent victim to the metaphysical rebel.

Gayle, Addison. *Richard Wright: Ordeal of a Native Son*. Garden City: Anchor-Doubleday, 1980. Using material obtained under the Freedom of Information Act, Gayle reassesses the literary and political dimensions of Wright's life.

Hakutani, Yoshinobu, ed. *Critical Essays on Richard Wright*. Boston: Hall, 1982. Includes general essays and articles on Wright's fiction, nonfiction, and poetry.

Joyce, Joyce Ann. *Richard Wright's Art of Tragedy*. Iowa City: U of Iowa P, 1986. An interpretation of *Native Son* as an example of classical tragedy.

Kinnamon, Keneth. *The Emergence of Richard Wright*. Urbana: U of Illinois P, 1972. Considers Wright's early work in its black, proletarian, and American contexts.

———, ed. *New Essays on* Native Son. New York: Cambridge UP, 1990. Contains Kinnamon's introductory essay on the manuscript and printed version of *Native Son* and four scholarly essays on the politics of narrative, the portrayal of women, the dynamics of place, and the articulation of African American modernism in the novel.

————, comp. *A Richard Wright Bibliography: Fifty Years of Criticism and Commentary, 1933–1982*. New York: Greenwood, 1988.

Macksey, Richard, and Frank E. Moorer, eds. *Richard Wright: A Collection of Critical Essays*. Englewood Cliffs: Prentice, 1984. Essays on Wright's southern background, *Native Son*, and his use of existentialism.

Reilly, John M., ed. *Richard Wright: The Critical Reception*. New York: Franklin, 1978. A comprehensive collection of reviews of Wright's work up to 1977.

Trotman, C. James, ed. *Richard Wright: Myths and Realities*. New York: Garland, 1988. Essays from the 1985 Richard Wright Literary Symposium at West Chester University.

Walker, Margaret. *Richard Wright: Daemonic Genius. A Portrait of the Man, a Critical Look at His Work*. New York: Warner, 1988. A biographical study of Wright and his literature.

American Indian Literature

Compiled by
A. LaVonne Brown Ruoff

The following bibliography pertains primarily to American Indian and Alaska Native tribes and authors from the United States. Because many tribes and cultures spread across international boundaries, works and authors representing tribes outside the United States are included when they are important to an understanding of the history and development of American Indian literatures as a whole.

1. Bibliographies and Aids to Research

Bataille, Gretchen M., and Charles L. P. Silet. *Images of American Indians on Film: An Annotated Bibliography*. New York: Garland, 1987. Comprehensive bibliography containing an annotated list of books and articles tracing the image of the American Indian in film. It also contains sections on the evolution of images from the early seventeenth century to the present, essays on the development of film stereotypes, reviews of individual films about American Indians, and a list of available sound films.

Beidler, Peter G., and Marion F. Egge. *The American Indian in Short Fiction: An Annotated Bibliography*. Metuchen: Scarecrow, 1979. Careful survey of the image of the Indian in short fiction.

Brumble, H. David, III, comp. *An Annotated Bibliography of American Indian and Eskimo Autobiographies*. Lincoln: U of Nebraska P, 1981. An excellent guide with suggestions for further reading.

——, comp. "A Supplement to *An Annotated Bibliography of American Indian and Eskimo Autobiographies*." *Western American Literature* 17 (1982): 243–60. Expanded in his *American Indian Autobiography*. Berkeley: U of California P, 1988. 211–57.

Clements, William M., and Frances M. Malpezzi, comps. *Native American Folklore, 1879–1979: An Annotated Bibliography*. Athens: Swallow–Ohio UP, 1984. Indispensable guide to American Indian oral literatures.

Colonnese, Tom, and Louise Owens (Cherokee), comps. *American Indian Novelists: An Annotated Critical Bibliography*. New York: Garland, 1985. The compilers give brief summaries of novels and include primary and selected secondary works.

Green, Rayna (Cherokee), comp. *Native American Women: A Contextual Bibliography*. Newberry Library Center for the History of the American Indian. Bibliography. Bloomington: Indiana UP, 1983. The only full guide to the subject.

Handbook of American Indians North of Mexico. Ed. Frederick W. Hodge. 2 vols. Washington: GPO, 1907–10. New York: Rowan, 1970. St. Clair Shores: Scholarly, 1971. Westport: Greenwood, 1971. Though long out of date, this book contains essays and helpful bibliographies to early works.

Handbook of North American Indians. Ed. William C. Sturtevant. Rev. ed. Washington: Smithsonian Inst. 20 vols., in progress. Essential guide to the field that contains essays on a variety of topics and extensive bibliography. *Arctic*. Ed. David Damas. Vol. 5, 1984. *California*. Ed. Robert F. Heizer. Vol. 8, 1978. *Great Basin*. Ed. Warren D'Azevedo. Vol. 11, 1986. *Northeast*. Ed. Bruce G. Trigger. Vol. 15, 1978. *Subarctic*. Ed. June Helm. Vol. 6, 1981. *Southwest*. Ed. Alfonso Ortiz. Vol. 9 (Pueblo), 1979; Vol. 10 (non-Pueblo), 1983.

Heard, Norman, comp. *The Southeastern Woodlands*. Vol. 1 of *Handbook of the American Frontier: Four Centuries of Indian-White Relationships*. Native American Resources 1. Metuchen: Scarecrow, 1987. First of a projected five-volume series: Vol. 2—Northeast; Vol. 3—Plains; Vol. 4—Southwest; Vol. 5—index, chronology, bibliography. Presents articles on individuals, events, and ethnohistory. Brief lists of sources conclude each short article.

Hirschfelder, Arlene B., Mary Gloyne Byler (Cherokee), and Michael A. Dorris (Modoc), comps. *Guide to Research on North American Indians*. Chicago: American Library, 1983. A useful general guide; emphasizes history rather than literature.

Littlefield, Daniel L., Jr. (Cherokee), and James W. Parins, comps. *American Indian and Alaska Native Newspapers and Periodicals, 1826–1924*. Westport: Greenwood, 1984. Extensive guide to newspapers and periodicals edited or published by Native Americans and other periodicals focusing on their contemporary affairs. Contains a brief history of the newspapers and periodicals included.

———. *A Biobibliography of Native American Writers, 1772–1924*. Native American Bibliography 1. Metuchen: Scarecrow, 1981. Comprehensive guide with brief biographies of the authors. Includes literature, political essays and addresses, published letters, historical works, myths and legends. Also lists authors known only by pen names. This series publishes bibliographies of many Indian tribes and on many topics pertaining to American Indians.

———. *A Biobibliography of Native American Writers, 1772-1924: A Supplement*. Native American Bibliography 5. Metuchen: Scarecrow, 1985. Supplements volume above and adds annotation.

Marken, Jack, comp. *The American Indian: Language and Literature*. Arlington Heights: Harlan Davidson, 1978. Though not complete and not annotated, this is a good listing of traditional literatures and anthropological or linguistic studies.

Martin, M. Marlene, and Timothy J. O'Leary, comps. *Ethnographic Bibliography of North America: Supplement to the 1975 Edition*. 3 vols. New Haven: Human Relations Area Files, 1990. Essential guide covers over 20,000 new citations to publications from 1973 through 1987. Includes subject, ethnic group, and author indexes.

Murdock, George P., comp. *Ethnographic Bibliography of North America*. 4th ed. Rev. Timothy J. O'Leary. 5 vols. New Haven: Human Relations Area Files, 1975. An important guide to American Indian ethnography and ethnohistory.

Prucha, Francis P., comp. *A Bibliographical Guide to the History of Indian-White Relations in the United States*. Chicago: U of Chicago P, 1977. Standard guide to the field; contains a section on literature.

———, comp. *Indian-White Relations in the United States: A Bibliography of Works Published 1975-1980*. Lincoln: U of Nebraska P, 1982. Updates the volume above.

Ruoff, A. LaVonne Brown. *American Indian Literatures: An Introduction, Bibliographic Review, and Selected Bibliography*. New York: MLA, 1990. An introduction to the oral and written literatures of Native America, an analysis of scholarship in the field, and extensive bibliography.

Slapin, Beverly, and Doris Seale, comps. *Books without Bias: Through Indian Eyes.* 2nd ed., enl. Berkeley: Oyate, 1988. Reviews existing children's literature on American Indian subjects and gives recommended reading levels. Includes reprinted essays by Mary Gloyne Byler (Cherokee), Michael Dorris (Modoc), and Joseph Bruchac (Abenaki) and a checklist of criteria for evaluating children's books about American Indians.

Stensland, Anna, comp. *Literature by and about the American Indian: An Annotated Bibliography.* Urbana: NCTE, 1973. Focuses on books appropriate to high- and middle-school readers.

———, comp. *Literature by and about the American Indian: An Annotated Bibliography.* 2nd ed., with Aune M. Fadum. Urbana: NCTE, 1979. Stresses books published since 1973, appropriate to high-, middle-, and elementary-school readers.

Thompson, Stith. *Motif-Index of Folk-Literature: A Classification of Narrative Elements in Folktales, Ballads, Myths, Fables, Medieval Romances, Exempla, Fabliaux, Jest-Books and Local Legends.* 2nd ed. 6 vols. Bloomington: Indiana UP, 1955–58. Contains much information about American Indian oral narratives.

Wiget, Andrew O. "Native American Literature: A Bibliographic Survey of American Indian Literary Traditions." *Choice* June 1986: 1503–12.

2. Anthologies and Collections

The following are anthologies of oral and written literatures. As yet no authoritative classroom anthology of both oral and written literatures exists. In selecting oral texts, teachers should look for those that reproduce as much as possible of the original ritual, song, or narrative as performed and that include commentary and notes on ethnographic backgrounds.

General

Allen, Paula Gunn (Laguna/Sioux), ed. *Spider Woman's Granddaughters: Traditional Tales and Contemporary Writing by Native American Women.* Boston: Beacon, 1989. This varied collection demonstrates the relation between traditional myths about women and stories written by American Indian women writers.

Bartlett, Mary Dougherty, ed. *The New Native American Novel: Works in Progress.* Albuquerque: U of New Mexico P, 1986. Interesting selection of works by contemporary authors.

Brandt, Beth (Mohawk), ed. *A Gathering of the Spirit: North American Indian Women's Issue.* Spec. issue of *Sinister Wisdom* 22–23 (1983): 1–223. Collection of contemporary writing by Native American women.

Bruchac, Joseph (Abenaki), ed. *Songs from This Earth on Turtle's Back: Contemporary American Indian Poetry.* Greenfield Center: Greenfield Review, 1983. An important recent collection.

Dauenhauer, Nora (Tlingit), Richard Dauenhauer, and Gary Holthaus, eds. *Alaska Native Writers, Storytellers and Orators.* Spec. issue of *Alaska Quarterly Review* 4.3–4 (1986). Collection of oral and written literature by Alaskan natives. Also available is Patricia H. Partnow, *Teacher's Guide.* Anchorage: Alaska Humanities Forum, 1988.

Day, David, and Marilyn Bowering, eds. *Many Voices: An Anthology of Contemporary Canadian Indian Poetry.* Vancouver: Douglas, 1977. An early, useful collection.

Evers, Larry, ed. *The South Corner of Time: Hopi, Navajo, Papago, and Yaqui Tribal Literature.* Tucson: U of Arizona P, 1980. Though it contains written literature, this exemplary southwestern anthology emphasizes oral literatures.

Gedalof, Robin [McGrath], ed. *Paper Stays Put: A Collection of Inuit Writing*. Edmonton: Hurtig, 1980. A valuable collection.

Green, Rayna (Cherokee), ed. *That's What She Said: Contemporary Poetry and Fiction by Native American Women*. Bloomington: Indiana UP, 1984. A fine collection that includes glossary and bibliography of works by and about American Indian women.

Highwater, Jamake, ed. *Words in the Blood: Contemporary Indian Writers of North and South America*. New York: NAL, 1984. Although it includes a few oral selections, it is primarily a collection of twentieth-century written literature.

Hobson, Geary (Cherokee), ed. *The Remembered Earth*. 1979. Albuquerque: U of New Mexico P, 1981. A good collection of contemporary poetry and prose.

Hogan, Linda (Chickasaw), ed. *Native American Women*. Spec. issue of *Frontiers* 6 (1981): 1–133. Creative works and articles by and about Indian women; includes bibliography.

Katz, Jane B., ed. *I Am the Fire of Time: The Voices of Native American Women*. New York: Dutton, 1977. Essays, statements, and short autobiographies.

King, Thomas (Cherokee), ed. *An Anthology of Canadian Native Fiction*. Spec. issue of *Canadian Fiction Magazine* 60 (1987). A valuable collection.

Nabokov, Peter, comp. *Native American Testimony. An Anthology of Indian and White Relations: First Encounter to Dispossession*. Preface Vine Deloria, Jr. (Sioux). New York: Crowell, 1978; Harper, 1978. Thematic collection of excerpts from speeches, statements, and writings, including some by non-Indians.

Niatum, Duane (Klallam), ed. *Carriers of the Dream Wheel*. New York: Harper, 1975. A good contemporary poetry anthology by a fine poet.

———, ed. *Harper's Anthology of 20th Century Native American Poetry*. Introd. Brian Swann. San Francisco: Harper, 1988. The best anthology of contemporary American Indian poetry, containing the work of thirty-six writers. An informative introduction discusses themes common to American Indian literature that are present in the selections.

Ortiz, Simon J. (Acoma), ed. *Earth Power Coming: Short Fiction in Native American Literature*. Tsaile: Navajo Community College P, 1983. Includes a wide selection of authors.

Petrone, Penny, ed. *First People, First Voices*. Toronto: U of Toronto P, 1983. Collection of oral and written literature by Canadian Native Americans.

———, ed. *Northern Voices: Inuit Writing in English*. Toronto: U of Toronto P, 1988. Important collection of writing by Canadian Inuit.

Peyer, Bernd. *The Singing Spirit: Early Short Stories by North American Indians*. Tucson: U of Arizona P, 1989. Short stories written between 1881 and 1936.

Rosen, Kenneth, ed. *The Man to Send Rainclouds: Contemporary Stories by American Indians*. New York: Viking, 1974. One of the earliest and finest anthologies of contemporary short fiction.

———. *Voices of the Rainbow: Contemporary Poetry by American Indians*. New York: Viking, 1975. An early, good collection.

Velie, Alan, ed. *American Indian Literature: An Anthology*. Norman: U of Oklahoma P, 1979. Contains some oral literature, including creation and trickster myths; the emphasis is on contemporary literature by Oklahoma males.

Oral Literatures

Oral songs and narratives constitute the largest body of collected American Indian literature. Songs are frequently designated as "poems" by non-Indians. The anthologies and collections listed below represent a variety of Indian cultures, including most of those from which the American Indian writers listed under "Primary Works" are descended. The texts include material collected by anthropologists (Indian and non-Indian), tribes, and individuals, as well as those reinterpreted by writers.

Important sources for collections of oral literature recorded from the late nineteenth century to the present are the bulletins and annual reports of the American Museum of Natural History and publications of the American Ethnological Society, the American Folklore Society, and the Canadian Museum of Man. Additional resources can be found in the anthropological series published by several universities, notably Columbia and California, Berkeley. The Native American Tribal Religions series of the University of Nebraska Press and the Sun Tracks series of the University of Arizona Press publish twentieth-century collections of oral literature. For fuller listings, consult the "Bibliographies and Aids to Research" section. See particularly the bibliographies by Clements and Malpezzi, Marken, and Ruoff.

Armstrong, Virginia, comp. *I Have Spoken*. Introd. Frederick W. Turner III. Chicago: Swallow–Ohio UP, 1971. Oral and written speeches.

Astrov, Margot, ed. *American Indian Prose and Poetry*. New York: Capricorn: 1962. Prev. pub. as *The Winged Serpent: An Anthology of American Indian Poetry* (1946). Miscellaneous collection of oral literature organized by culture areas. Stories are brief excerpts. Contains an introduction and some notes.

Bahr, Donald. *Pima and Papago Ritual Oratory: A Study of Three Texts*. San Francisco: Indian Historian, 1975. An excellent bilingual text with a valuable introduction and notes.

Barnouw, Victor. *Wisconsin Chippewa Myths and Tales and Their Relation to Chippewa Life*. Madison: U of Wisconsin P, 1977. A good collection of stories from Lac de Flambeau Ojibwa Indians, including several trickster cycles. Contains full introduction, careful notes, Jungian commentary, and bibliography.

Beavert, Virginia, project dir. (Yakima). *The Way It Was, Inaku Iwacha: Yakima Legends*. Yakima: Franklin, 1974. Tribally prepared collection.

Benedict, Ruth F. *Tales of the Cochiti Indians*. 1931. Foreword Alfonso Ortiz (San Juan). Albuquerque: U of New Mexico P, 1981.

———. *Zuni Mythology*. Columbia University Contributions to Anthropology 21 (1935). Rpt. 2 vols. New York: AMS, 1969.

Bierhorst, John, ed. *Four Masterworks of American Indian Literature*. 1974. Tucson: U of Arizona P, 1984. Offers opportunity for study of individual long works, which Bierhorst abbreviates or constructs from several sources. Includes the "Iroquois Ritual of Condolence" and "Navajo Night Chant."

———, ed. *The Red Swan: Myths and Tales of the American Indians*. New York: Farrar, 1976. A broad and representative sampling of narratives.

———, ed. *The Sacred Path: Spells, Prayers and Power Songs of the American Indians*. New York: Morrow, 1983. A varied collection of prayers and songs, some excerpted from ceremonies.

Bingham, Sam, and Janet Bingham, eds. *Between Sacred Mountains: Navajo Stories and Lessons from the Land*. Tucson: U of Arizona P, 1984. A collection of accounts of oral history and personal experiences pertaining to the Navajos' concepts of the importance of the land.

Boas, Franz, ed. *Keresan Texts*. 2 vols. Publications of the American Ethnological Soc. 8 (1928). New York: AMS, 1974.

———, ed. *Kwakiutl Culture as Reflected in Mythology*. Memoirs of the American Folklore Soc. 28 (1935). Millwood: Kraus, 1970.

———, ed. *Kwakiutl Tales*. Columbia University Contributions to Anthropology 2 (1910). New York: AMS, 1969.

————, ed. *Tsimshian Texts.* Bulletin of the Bureau of American Ethnology 27 (1902). St. Claire Shores: Scholarly, 1977.

Boyd, Maurice. *Kiowa Voices.* Vol. 1. *Ceremonial Dance, Ritual and Song.* Vol. 2. *Myths, Legends and Folktales.* Fort Worth: Texas Christian UP, 1981–83.

Bullchild, Percy (Blackfeet). *The Sun Came Down: The History of the World as My Blackfeet Elders Told It.* Native American Ser. San Francisco: Harper, 1985. A contemporary, full retelling of the basic Blackfeet myths and tales.

Bunzel, Ruth L., ed. "Zuni Origin Myths." Annual Report of the Bureau of American Ethnology 47 (1929–30). Washington: GPO, 1932. 545–609.

————, ed. "Zuni Ritual Poetry." Annual Report of the Bureau of American Ethnology 47 (1929–30). Washington: GPO, 1932. 611–835.

————, ed. *Zuni Texts.* Publications of the American Ethnological Soc. 15 (1933). New York: AMS, 1974.

Clutesi, George (Tlingit). *Son of Raven, Son of Deer: Fables of the Tse-Shat People.* Illus. by author. Sidney: Gray's, 1975.

Cornplanter, Jesse (Seneca). *Legends of the Longhouse.* 1938. Iroquois Reprints. Ohswehen: Irografts, 1986.

Courlander, Harold, ed. *Hopi Voices: Recollections, Traditions, and Narratives of the Hopi Indians.* Albuquerque: U of New Mexico P, 1982.

Cronyn, George W., ed. *The Path on the Rainbow: An Anthology of Songs and Chants from the Indians of North America.* Introd. Mary Austin. New York: Liveright, 1918. Repub. and enl. as *American Indian Poetry: The Standard Anthology of Songs and Chants.* New York: Liveright, 1934, 1970. Unannotated songs from various culture areas. Includes part of Alice Fletcher's version of the Pawnee Hako ceremony.

Curtin, Jeremiah, ed. *Creation Myths of Primitive America in Relation to the Religious History and Mental Development of Mankind.* 1898. New York: Bloom, 1969. Salem: Ayer, 1980. Primarily myths from California.

Curtin, Jeremiah, and J. N. B. Hewitt (Tuscarora), eds. *Seneca Fiction, Legends, and Myths.* Annual Report of the Bureau of American Ethnology 32 (1910–11). Washington: GPO, 1918. 37–813.

Curtis, Nathalie Burlin, ed. *The Indians' Book: Songs and Legends of the American Indians.* 1907. 2nd ed. 1923. New York: Dover, 1968. Reasonably reliable anthology of songs.

Day, A. Grove, ed. *The Sky Clears: Poetry of the American Indians.* 1951. Lincoln: U of Nebraska P, 1964. Arranged by culture areas (including Arctic and Mexico). Contains a useful introduction, brief interpretations, and a bibliography that gives the sources for the songs.

Deloria, Ella C. (Sioux). *Dakota Texts.* Publications of the American Ethnological Soc. 14 (1932). New York: AMS, 1974. Ed. with notes by Anes Picotte and Paul N. Pavich. Vermillion: Dakota, 1978. The latter edition excludes the Sioux texts.

Densmore, Frances. *Chippewa Music.* Bulletin of the Bureau of American Ethnology 45 (1910). Millwood: Kraus, n.d. Densmore was one of the first to collect Indian songs, which she discusses in their cultural contexts.

————. *Chippewa Music 2.* Bulletin of the Bureau of American Ethnology 53 (1913). Millwood: Kraus, n.d.

————. *Chippewa Music.* 2 vols in 1. Rpt. of Bulletin of the Bureau of American Ethnology 45, 53. Music Reprint Ser. Jersey City: Da Capo, 1972.

————. *Menominee Music.* Bulletin of the Bureau of American Ethnology 10 (1932). Music Reprint Ser. Jersey City: Da Capo, 1972.

————. *Teton Sioux Music.* Bulletin of the Bureau of American Ethnology 61 (1918). Music Reprint Ser. Jersey City: Da Capo, 1972. St. Claire Shores: Scholarly, 1977.

Dorsey, G.A. *The Pawnee Mythology.* Pub. of the Carnegie Inst. (1906). New York: AMS, 1974.

Eastman, Charles A. (Sioux), and Elaine Goodale Eastman. *Wigwam Evenings: Sioux Folktales Retold.* Boston: Little, 1909. Repub. as *Smokey Day's Wigwam Evenings: Indian Stories Retold.* Boston: Little, 1910. Originally written for children.

Erdoes, Richard, and Alfonso Ortiz (San Juan), eds. *American Indian Myths and Legends.* Albuquerque: U of New Mexico P, 1984. Thematically organized anthology containing both previously published and new versions collected by the authors. Includes brief introductions.

Evers, Larry, and Felipe S. Molina (Yaqui). *Yaqui Deer Songs / Maso Bwikam: A Native American Poetry.* Sun Tracks 14. Tucson: U of Arizona P, 1986. Exemplary bilingual collection that includes full introductions and notes explaining cultural contexts and interpretations of songs, backgrounds of singers. Also includes bibliography.

Fletcher, Alice F. "The Hako: A Pawnee Ceremony." Annual Report of the Bureau of American Ethnology 22.2 (1900–01). Washington: GPO, 1904. 5–368.

Goddard, Pliney E. "Myths and Tales from the San Carlos Apache." Anthropological Papers of the American Museum of Natural History 24.1 (1918). New York: AMS, 1980.

Grinnell, George B. *Blackfoot Lodge Tales.* 1892. Lincoln: U of Nebraska P, 1962. One of several tribal collections by a skilled storyteller.

———. *By Cheyenne Campfires.* 1926. Lincoln: U of Nebraska P. 1971.

———. *Pawnee Hero Stories and Folk Tales.* 1889. Introd. Maurice Frink. Lincoln: U of Nebraska P, 1961.

———. *The Punishment of Stingy and Other Indian Stories.* 1901. Introd. Jarold Ramsey. Lincoln: U of Nebraska P, 1982.

Haile, Berard, O.F.M., ed. *Navajo Coyote Tales: The Curly Tó Aheedliinii Version.* Ed. with introd. Karl W. Luckert. American Tribal Religions 8. Lincoln: U of Nebraska P, 1984.

———, ed. *Origin Legend of the Navaho Flintway.* Publications in Anthropology and Linguistics 38. Chicago: U of Chicago P, 1943. New York: AMS, 1978.

———, ed. *The Upward Moving and Emergence Way: The Gishin Biye Version.* American Tribal Religions 7. Lincoln: U of Nebraska P, 1981.

Hewitt, John N. B. (Tuscarora). *Iroquoian Cosmology.* 2 pts. in 1. Rpt. of Annual Report of the Bureau of American Ethnology 21, 43. New York: AMS, 1974.

———. "Iroquoian Cosmology, Part One." Annual Report of the Bureau of American Ethnology 21 (1899–1900). Washington: GPO, 1903. 127–339.

———. "Iroquoian Cosmology: With Introduction and Notes, Part Two." Annual Report of the Bureau of American Ethnology 43 (1925–26). Washington: GPO, 1928. 449–819.

Hilbert, Vi (Lushootseed), trans. and ed. *Haboo: Native American Stories from Puget Sound.* Foreword and introd. Thom Hess. Seattle: U of Washington P, 1985. A varied selection of stories told by members of Skagit tribe of the Puget Sound region; contains a bibliography.

Hinton, Leanne, and Lucille Watahomigie (Yuma), eds. *Spirit Mountain: An Anthology of Yuman Story and Song.* Sun Tracks 10. Tucson: U of Arizona P, 1984. A good collection with introduction, notes, and bibliography.

Jacobs, Melville. *The Content and Style of an Oral Literature: Clackamas Chinook Myths and Tales.* Chicago: U of Chicago P, 1959. Important work by a pioneer in the field of the expressive content of oral narrative.

———. *The People Are Coming Soon: Analyses of Clackamas Chinook Myths and Tales.* Seattle: U of Washington P, 1960.

Johnson, Elias (Tuscarora). *Legends, Traditions and Laws of the Iroquois, or Six Nations, and History of the Tuscarora Indians.* 1881. New York: AMS, 1977.

Jones, William (Fox), ed. *Fox Texts.* Ed. Franz Boas. Publications of the American Ethnological Soc. 1 (1907). New York: AMS, 1978.

———, ed. *Ojibwa Texts.* Ed. Truman Michelson. Publications of the American Ethnological Soc. 7.1 (1917); 2 (1919). New York: AMS, 1974.

Kilpatrick, Jack Frederick, and Anna Gritts Kilpatrick (Cherokee), eds. *Friends of Thunder: Folktales of the Oklahoma Cherokees.* Dallas: Southern Methodist UP, 1964.

Klah, Hosteen (Navajo), and Mary C. Wheelwright. *Navaho Creation Myth: The Story of Emergence.* 1942. New York: AMS, 1977.

Kroeber, A. L., ed. "Gros Ventre Myths and Tales." *Anthropological Papers of the Museum of Natural History* 1.3 (1907): 59–139.

———, ed. *Yoruk Myths.* Berkeley: U of California P, 1976.

Kroeber, Theodora. *The Inland Whale: Nine Stories Retold from California Indian Legends.* Foreword Oliver La Farge. Bloomington: Indiana UP, 1959. Sensitive interpretations of California Indian myths about nine heroines.

La Flesche, Francis (Omaha), ed. "The Osage Tribe." Annual Report of the Bureau of American Ethnology. Washington: GPO, 1921, 1925, 1928, 1930. "Rites of the Chiefs," 36 (1914–15): 37–597. New York: Johnson, 1970. "Rite of Vigil," 39 (1917–18): 31–330. "Two Versions of the Child-Naming Rite," 43 (1925–26): 23–164. "Rite of Wa-x'be," 45 (1927–28): 523–833.

La Flesche, Francis (Omaha), and Alice Fletcher, eds. "The Omaha Tribe." Annual Report of the Bureau of American Ethnology 27 (1905–06). Washington: GPO, 1911. 17–642. Rpt. as 2 vols. New York: Johnson, 1970. Lincoln: U of Nebraska P, 1972.

Lankford, George E., comp. and ed. *Native American Legends: Southeastern Legends: Tales from the Natchez, Caddo, Biloxi, Chickasaw, and Other Nations.* Introd. W. K. McNeil. American Folklore. Little Rock: August House, 1987. One of the few collections of oral literature from Southeastern tribes.

La Pointe, James (Sioux). *Legends of the Lakota.* San Francisco: Indian Historian, 1976. Contemporary versions by a Sioux writer.

Lewis, Richard, ed. *I Breathed New Song: Poems of the Eskimo.* Introd. Edmund Carpenter. New York: Simon, 1971.

Lowenstein, Tom, trans. *Eskimo Poems from Canada and Greenland.* Poetry Ser. Pittsburgh: U of Pittsburgh P, 1973. One of the few such collections available.

Lowie, Robert H., ed. "Myths and Traditions of the Crow Indians." Anthropological Papers of the American Museum of Natural History 25.1 (1918). New York: AMS, 1974.

Luckert, Karl, ed. *Coyoteway: A Navajo Healing Ceremony.* Tucson: U of Arizona P, 1979.

Malotki, Ekkehart, and Michael Lomatuway'ma (Hopi). *Hopi Coyote Tales/Istutuwutsi.* 1978. American Tribal Religions 9. Lincoln: U of Nebraska P, 1984.

———. *Stories of Maasaw, a Hopi God.* American Tribal Religions 10. Lincoln: U of Nebraska P, 1987. Both this book and that above provide bilingual texts, with introductions and notes that explain the cultural contexts of the stories. They contain full bibliographies.

Malotki, Ekkehart, and Herschel Talashoma (Hopi). *Hopitutuwututsi: Hopi Tales.* Sun Tracks 9. Tucson: U of Arizona P, 1983.

Marriott, Alice, and Carol Rachlin, eds. *American Indian Mythology.* New York: Crowell, 1968. Thematically arranged excerpts of stories from a variety of tribes.

Matthews, Washington, ed. "The Mountain Chant: A Navajo Ceremony." Annual Report of the Bureau of American Ethnology 5 (1883–84). Washington: GPO, 1897. 379–467. Glorietta: Rio Grande, 1971.

———, ed. *Navaho Legends,* Memoirs of the American Folklore Soc. 5 (1897). Millwood: Kraus, 1969.

———, ed. "The Night Chant, a Navajo Ceremony." Anthropological Papers of the American Museum of Natural History 6 (1902). New York: AMS, 1974.

Mattina, Anthony, and Madeline de Sautel (Colville), trans. *The Golden Woman: The Colville Narrative of Peter J. Seymour.* Tucson: U of Arizona P, 1985. A carefully annotated edition of Seymour's version of a European tale.

McClintock, Walter. *The Old North Trail: Or, Life, Legends and Religion of the Blackfeet Indians.* 1910. Lincoln: U of Nebraska P, 1965. Traditional stories retold by a skilled narrator.

Mooney, James, ed. "Myths of the Cherokees." Annual Report of the Bureau of American Ethnology 19.1 (1897–98): 3–575. St. Claire Shores: Scholarly, 1970.

Morriseau, Norval (Ojibwa). *Legends of My People, the Great Ojibway.* Ed. Selwyn H. Dewdney. Toronto: Ryerson, 1965.

Mourning Dove [Christine Quintasket] (Colville). *Coyote Stories.* Notes by Lucullus Virgil McWhorter. Foreword Chief Standing Bear. Ed. Heister Dean Guie. 1933. New York: AMS, 1977.

———. *The Tales of the Okanogans.* Ed. Donald M. Hines. Fairfield: Ye Galleon, 1976.

Nelson, Edward W. *The Eskimo about Bering Strait.* Annual Report of the Bureau of American Ethnology 18 (1896–97): 3–518. New York: Johnson, 1971.

Nequatewa, Edmund (Hopi). *Truth of a Hopi: Stories Relating to the Origin, Myths, and Clan Histories of the Hopi.* 1936. Flagstaff: Northland, 1967.

O'Bryan, Aileen, ed. *The Diné Origin Myths of the Navaho Indians.* Bulletin of the Bureau of American Ethnology 163 (1956). Washington: GPO, 1956.

Oman, Lela Kiana (Putu-Noorvik). *Eskimo Legends.* 2nd ed. Anchorage: Alaska Methodist UP, 1975.

Parker, Arthur C. (Seneca), ed. *Seneca Myths and Folktales* 27. Buffalo Historical Soc. (1923). New York: AMS, 1978.

Phinney, Archie (Nez Perce), ed. *Nez Percé Texts.* Columbia University Contributions to Anthropology 25 (1934).

Radin, Paul. *The Trickster: A Study in American Indian Mythology.* Commentaries by Karl Kerenyi and Carl Jung. New introd. Stanley Diamond. 1956. New York: Schocken, 1972. Widely taught Winnebago trickster cycle, with introductions and notes explaining ethnohistory of the tribe and the work.

Ramsey, Jarold, ed. *Coyote Was Going There: Indian Literature of the Oregon Country.* Seattle: U of Washington P, 1977. Diverse collection emphasizing oral narratives and containing useful annotation.

Sapir, Edward, and Jeremiah Curtin, eds. *Wishram Texts, Together with Wasco Tales and Myths.* Publications of the American Ethnological Soc. 2 (1909). New York: AMS, 1974.

Saxton, Dean, and Lucille Saxton, eds. *O'otham Hoho'ok Aagitha: Legends of the Papago and Pima Indians.* Tucson: U of Arizona P, 1973. Bilingual edition with good notes.

Schultz, James Willard. *Why Gone Those Times? Blackfoot Tales.* Ed. Eugene Lee Silliman. Civilization of the American Indian 127. Norman: U of Oklahoma P, 1974. Tales retold by a fine storyteller.

Slickpoo, Allen P., Sr. (Nez Perce), et al. *Nu Mee Poom Tit Wah Tit (Nez Perce Stories).* Lawai: Nez Perce Tribe, 1972.

Standing Bear, Luther (Sioux). *Stories of the Sioux.* 1934. Lincoln: U of Nebraska P, 1988.

Tedlock, Dennis, trans. *Finding the Center: Narrative Poetry of the Zuni Indians.* 1972. Rev. ed. Lincoln: U of Nebraska P, 1978. A collection based on tape-recorded performances. Tedlock uses special typography to approximate the changes in pitch and length of the original performances. The introduction and notes explain the cultural contexts of the narratives.

Theisz, R. D., ed. *Buckskin Tokens: Contemporary Oral Narratives of the Lakota.* Rosebud: Sinte Gleska College, 1975. Contemporary tape-recorded versions, with careful introduction, notes, and bibliography.

Thompson, Stith, ed. *Tales of the North American Indians.* 1929. Bloomington: Indiana UP, 1966. Varied collection of short oral narratives, with notes indicating locations of similar stories.

Underhill, Ruth M., ed. *Singing for Power: The Song Magic of the Papago Indians of Southern Arizona.* 1938. Berkeley: U of California P, 1976. Translations of Papago songs, with sensitive, informative discussions of cultural context.

Underhill, Ruth Murray, et al., eds. *Rainhouse and Ocean: Speeches for the Papago Year.* 1979. American Tribal Religions 4. Lincoln: U of Nebraska P, 1981.

Vanderwerth, W. C., ed. *Indian Oratory: Famous Speeches by Noted Indian Chieftains.* Foreword William R. Carmack. Civilization of the American Indian 110. Norman: U of Oklahoma P, 1971.

Vaudrin, Bill (Ojibwa), ed. *Tanaina Tales from Alaska.* Introd. Joan B. Townsend. Norman: U of Oklahoma P, 1969. One of the few collections of Alaskan narratives.

Vizenor, Gerald. *Summer in the Spring: Ojibwa Lyric Poems and Tribal Stories.* Minneapolis: Nodin, 1981. Reprints *Anishinabe Adisokan: Tales of the People* (Minneapolis: Nodin, 1970) and *Anishinabe Nagamon: Songs of the People* (Minneapolis: Nodin, 1965; rev. 1970). Includes Vizenor's recreations of Densmore's translations of Ojibwa songs and oral narratives originally printed in *The Progress,* a weekly newspaper published on the White Earth Reservation.

Walker, James R. *Lakota Myth.* Ed. Elaine A. Jahner. Lincoln: U of Nebraska P, 1983. An important anthology of Sioux narratives collected by Walker at the turn of the century. Contains detailed introduction, notes, and bibliography.

Welsch, Roger, ed. *Omaha Tribal Myths and Trickster Tales.* Athens: Ohio UP, 1981.

White, Leslie A., ed. "The Acoma Indians." Annual Report of the Bureau of American Ethnology 47 (1929–30). Washington: GPO, 1932. 17–192. Pub. separately. Washington: GPO, 1932. New preface. New foreword by the author. Glorietta: Rio Grande, 1973.

Wissler, Clark, and D. C. Duvall (Blackfeet), eds. "Mythology of the Blackfoot Indians." Anthropological Papers of the American Museum of Natural History 2.1 (1908). New York: AMS, 1975.

Wyman, Leland, ed. *The Blessingway.* Tucson: U of Arizona P, 1970.

———, ed. *The Red Antway of the Navaho.* Navajo Religion 5. Santa Fe: Museum of Navajo Ceremonial Art, 1965.

Yazzie, Ethelou (Navajo), ed. *Navajo History.* 1 vol. Many Farms: Navajo Community College P, 1971. Tribal collection and history.

Zepeda, Ofelia (Papago), ed. *Mat Hekid O Ju: O'odham Ha-Cegitodag / When It Rains: Papago and Pima Poetry.* Sun Tracks 7. Tucson: U of Arizona P, 1982. Bilingual edition with introduction, notes and bibliography.

Zitkala-Ša [Gertrude Bonnin] (Sioux). *Old Indian Legends, Retold by Zitkala-Ša.* 1901. Introd. Agnes Picotte (Sioux). Lincoln: U of Nebraska P, 1985.

Zolbrod, Paul G. *Diné bahane': The Navajo Creation Story.* Albuquerque: U of New Mexico P, 1984. A scholarly re-creation that compiles many versions of this story. Contains careful annotations.

Autobiography

Cruikshank, Julie, Angela Sidney, Kitty Smith, and Annie Ned. *Life Lived like a Story: Life Stories of Three Yukon Elders.* American Indian Lives. Lincoln: U of Nebraska P, 1991. An exemplary collection of life histories that contains a detailed introduction to the cultural backgrounds to the women's stories and discusses the ways anthropologists use and interpret autobiography.

Johnson, Broderick H., ed. *Stories of Traditional Navajo Life and Culture.* Tsaile: Navajo Community College Press, 1977. Oral life histories.

Kelley, Jane Holden. *Yaqui Women: Contemporary Life Histories.* Lincoln: U of Nebraska P, 1978.

Quam, Alvina, ed. and trans. *The Zunis: Self-Portrayals.* Albuquerque: U of New Mexico P, 1972. New York: NAL, 1974.

Roessel, Ruth H., ed. *Navajo Stories of the Long Walk Period.* Tsaile: Navajo Community College, 1973.

Swann, Brian, and Arnold Krupat, comps. *I Tell You Now: Autobiographical Essays by Native American Writers*. American Indian Lives. Lincoln: U of Nebraska P, 1987. A moving collection of autobiographies that includes selections by Paula Gunn Allen (Laguna/Sioux), Jim Barnes (Choctaw), Joseph Bruchac (Abenaki), Barney Bush (Shawnee/Cayuga), Elizabeth Cook-Lynn (Sioux), Jimmy Durham (Cherokee), Jack D. Forbes (Powhatan), Diane Glancy (Cherokee), Joy Harjo (Creek), Linda Hogan (Chickasaw), Maurice Kenny (Mohawk), Duane Niatum (Klallam), Simon J. Ortiz (Acoma), Carter Revard (Osage), Ralph Salisbury (Cherokee), Wendy Rose (Hopi/Miwok), Mary Tall Mountain (Athapaskan) and Gerald Vizenor (Ojibwa).

3. Primary Works

Works both written and narrated by American Indians are included below. Before 1969, more personal histories and autobiographies were published than any other genre. "As-told-to" personal narratives are a transitional form of oral literature in which Indian authors narrate their life histories to translators, collaborators, or editors. Occasionally the authors wrote such narratives in their tribal languages, which others then prepared for publication. As-told-to life narratives are designated by *; for these narratives, the name of the author is given first, followed by the name(s) of the collaborator(s).

Since 1969, Indian writers have published more fiction and poetry than autobiography. Chapbooks that have been incorporated into collected books of poetry are not listed separately.

Allen, Paula Gunn (Laguna/Sioux). *Shadow Country*. Native American. Los Angeles: U of California P, 1982. Collected poems.

———. *Skins and Bones: Poems 1979–87*. Albuquerque: West End, 1988.

———. *The Woman Who Owned the Shadows*. San Francisco: Spinster's, 1983. Fiction.

———. *Wyrds*. San Francisco: Taurean Horn, 1987. Poetry.

Apes, William (Pequot). *Eulogy on King Philip, as Pronounced at the Odeon, in Federal Street, Boston, by the Rev. William Apes, an Indian*. Boston: Author, 1836. Nonfiction prose.

———. *The Experiences of Five Christian Indians of the Pequod Tribe*. Boston: Dow, 1833. Rev. and repub. as *Experience of Five Christian Indians, of the Pequod Tribe*. Boston: Printed for the Publisher, 1837. Nonfiction.

———. *Indian Nullification of the Unconstitutional Laws of Massachusetts, Relative to the Marshpee Tribe: Or, The Pretended Riot Explained*. 1835. Foreword Jack Campisi. Stanfordville: Coleman, 1979. Nonfiction.

———. *A Son of the Forest: The Experience of William Apes, a Native of the Forest, Comprising a Notice of the Pequod Tribe of Indians*. New York: Author, 1829. Repub. as *A Son of the Forest. The Experience of William Apes, a Native of the Forest*. 2nd ed. rev. and cor. New York: Author, 1831. Autobiography.

Arnett, Caroll [Gogisgi] (Cherokee). *Tsalagi*. New Rochelle: Elizabeth, 1976. Poetry.

Aupaumut, Hendrick (Mohegan). *A Narrative of an Embassy to the Western Indians, from the Original Manuscript of Hendrick Aupaumut, with Prefatory Remarks by Dr. B. H. Coates*. *Pennsylvania Historical Soc. Memoirs* 2.1 (1827): 61-131. Autobiography.

Barnes, Jim (Choctaw). *The American Book of the Dead*. Urbana: U of Illinois P, 1982. Poetry.

———. *La Plata Cantata: Poems*. West Lafayette: Purdue UP, 1989.

———. *A Season of Loss*. West Lafayette: Purdue UP, 1985. Poetry.

*Betzinez, Jason (Apache). Wilbur Sturtevant Nye. *I Fought with Geronimo*. 1959. Lincoln: U of Nebraska P, 1987. Autobiography.

Blackbird, Andrew J. [Mackawdebenessy] (Ottawa). *History of the Ottawa and Chippewa Indians of Michigan; a Grammar of Theirr [sic] Languages, and Personal and Family History of the Author*. 1887. Petosky: Little Traverse Regional History Soc., 1977. Nonfiction.

*Black Elk (Sioux). John G. Neihardt. *Black Elk Speaks*. 1932. Introd. Vine Deloria, Jr. (Sioux). Lincoln: U of Nebraska P, 1979. Autobiography.

*Black Hawk (Sauk). Antoine Le Claire and John B. Patterson. *Black Hawk, an Autobiography*. Orig. pub. as *Life of Ma-ka-tai-me-she-kia-kiha, or Black Hawk*. 1833. Ed. with new introd. Donald Jackson. Urbana: U of Illinois P, 1955. Autobiography.

*Blowsnake, Sam [Crashing Thunder] (Winnebago). Paul Radin. *The Autobiography of a Winnebago Indian*. 1926. Foreword and app. Arnold Krupat. Lincoln: U of Nebraska P, 1983.

Blue Cloud, Peter (Mohawk). *Elderberry Flute Song: Contemporary Coyote Tales*. Trumansburg: Crossing, 1982. Poetry and short stories.

———. *Turtle, Bear and Wolf*. Pref. Gary Snyder. Mohawk Nation via Rooseveltown: Akwesasne Notes, 1976. Poetry.

———. *White Corn Sister*. New York: Strawberry, 1971. 2nd ed., 1981. Poetry.

Brown, Emily Ivanoff [Ticasuk] (Inupiat). *The Roots of Ticasuk: An Eskimo Woman's Family Story*. 1974. Rev. ed. Anchorage: Alaska Northwest, 1981. Autobiography.

Bruchac, Joseph J. (Abenaki). *Ancestry*. Lewiston: Great Raven, 1980. Poetry.

———. *The Dreams of Jesse Brown*. Austin: Cold Mountain, 1977. Fiction.

———. *Entering Onondaga*. Austin: Cold Mountain, 1978. Poetry.

———. *No Telephone to Heaven*. Merrick: Cross-Cultural Communications, 1984. Fiction.

———. *There Are No Trees inside the Prison*. Southharpswell: Blackberry, 1979. Fiction.

———. *This Earth Is a Drum*. Austin: Cold Mountain, 1977. Poetry.

———. *Translator's Son*. Merrick: Cross-Cultural Communications, 1981. Poetry.

Burns, Diane (Ojibwa-Chemehuevi). *Riding the One-Eyed Ford*. New York: Contact II, 1981. Poetry.

Bush, Barney (Shawnee/Cayuga). *Inherit the Blood*. New York: Thunder's Mouth, 1985. Poetry and fiction.

———. *My Horse and a Jukebox*. Native American 4. Los Angeles: U of California P, 1979. Poetry.

———. *Petroglyphs*. Greenfield Center: Greenfield, 1982. Poetry.

Carter, Forrest Asa (Cherokee). *The Education of Little Tree*. 1976. Foreword Rennard Strickland (Cherokee). Albuquerque: U of New Mexico P, 1986. Fiction.

———. *Gone to Texas: The Rebel Outlaw Josey Wales*. 1973. New York: Buccaneer Books, 1985.

———. *Josey Wales: Two Westerns by Forrest Carter*. Afterword Lawrence Clayton. Albuquerque: U of New Mexico P, 1989. Fiction. Includes *Gone to Texas* (1973) and *The Vengeance Trail of Josey Wales* (1976).

———. *The Outlaw Josey Wales*. 1973. New York: Dell, 1976. Original title of the book above. Fiction.

———. *The Vengeance Trail of Josey Wales*. 1976. New York: Dell, 1977. Fiction.

———. *Watch for Me on the Mountain*. New York: Delacorte, 1978. Fiction.

*Chona, Maria (Papago). Ruth M. Underhill. *The Autobiography of a Papago Woman*. 1936. New York: Holt, 1979.

Clarke, Peter Dooyentate (Wyandot). *Origin and Traditional History of the Wyandotts, and Sketches of Other Indian Tribes of North America: True Traditional Stories of Tecumseh and His League, in the Years 1811 and 1812*. Toronto: Hunter, 1870.

Conley, Robert J. (Cherokee). *The Rattlesnake Bank and Other Poems*. Muskogee: Indian UP, 1984.

————. *The Witch of Goingsnake and Other Stories*. Foreword Wilma P. Mankiller (Cherokee). Norman: U of Oklahoma P, 1988.

Cook-Lynn, Elizabeth (Sioux). *Seek the House of Relatives*. Marvin: Blue Cloud, 1983. Poetry.

————. *Then Badger Said This*. New York: Vantage, 1977. Poetry, narratives, history.

Copway, George (Ojibwa). *The Life, History, and Travels of Kah-ge-ga-gah-bowh (George Copway . . .)*. Albany: Weed, 1847. Rev. ed. *The Life, Letters and Speeches of Kah-ge-ga-gah-bowh: Or, G. Copway. . . .* New York: Benedict, 1850.

————. *Organization of a New Indian Territory, East of the Missouri River. Arguments and Reasons Submitted to the Honorable Members of the Senate and House of Representatives to the 31st Congress of the United States; by the Indian Chief Kah-ge-ga-gah-bouh [sic], or Geo. Copway*. New York: Benedict, 1850. Nonfiction.

————. *Running Sketches of Men and Places, in England, France, Germany, Belgium, and Scotland*. New York: Riker, 1851. Nonfiction prose.

————. *The Traditional History and Characteristic Sketches of the Ojibway Nation*. London: Gilpin, 1850. Repub. as *Indian Life and Indian History, by an Indian Author, Embracing the Traditions of the North American Indian Tribes Regarding Themselves, Particularly of That Most Important of All the Tribes, the Ojibways*. 1858. New York: AMS, 1977.

Deloria, Ella C. *Waterlily*. Biography Agnes Picotte (Sioux). Afterword Raymond J. De Mallie. Lincoln: U of Nebraska P, 1988. Fiction; completed by 1944.

Deloria, Vine, Jr. (Sioux). *Custer Died for Your Sins: An Indian Manifesto*. 1969. Norman: U of Oklahoma P, 1988. Nonfiction.

————. *We Talk, You Listen: New Tribes, New Turf*. New York: Macmillan, 1970. Nonfiction.

Dorris, Michael (Modoc). *The Broken Cord: A Family's On-Going Struggle with Fetal Alcohol Syndrome*. Foreword Louise Erdrich (Ojibwa). New York: Harper, 1989. Nonfiction.

————. *A Yellow Raft on Blue Water*. New York: Holt, 1987; Warner, 1988. Fiction.

Downing, [George] Todd (Choctaw). *The Case of the Unconquered Sisters*. Garden City: Doubleday, 1936. Fiction.

————. *The Cat Screams*. Garden City: Doubleday, 1934. Fiction.

————. *The Last Trumpet; Murder in a Mexican Bull Ring*. Garden City: Doubleday, 1937. Fiction.

————. *The Lazy Lawrence Murders*. New York: Doubleday, 1941. Fiction.

————. *The Mexican Earth*. New York: Doubleday, 1940. Fiction.

————. *Murder on the Tropic*. Garden City: Doubleday, 1935. Fiction.

————. *Murder on Tour*. New York: Putnam's, 1933. Fiction.

————. *Vultures in the Sky*. Garden City: Doubleday, 1935.

Eastman, Charles A. (Sioux). *From the Deep Woods to Civilization: Chapters in the Autobiography of an Indian*. 1916. Introd. Raymond Wilson. Lincoln: U of Nebraska P, 1977.

————. *Indian Boyhood*. 1902. New York: Dover, 1971. Autobiography.

————. *Indian Heroes and Great Chieftains*. Boston: Little, 1918. Nonfiction.

————. *The Indian To-day: The Past and Future of the First Americans*. 1915. New York: AMS, 1975. Nonfiction.

————. *Old Indian Days*. 1907. Rapid City: Fenwyn, 1970. Fiction.

————. *Red Hunters and the Animal People*. 1904. New York: AMS, 1976. Fiction.

————. *The Soul of the Indian: An Interpretation*. 1911. Lincoln: U of Nebraska P, 1980. Nonfiction.

Erdrich, Louise (Ojibwa). *Baptism of Desire: Poems*. New York: Harper, 1989.

————. *Beet Queen*. New York: Holt, 1986. Fiction.

————. *Jacklight: Poems*. New York: Holt, 1984. Poetry.

————. *Love Medicine*. New York: Holt, 1984. Fiction.

————. *Tracks*. New York: Holt, 1988. Fiction.

Fire, John [Lame Deer] (Sioux). Richard Erdoes. *Lame Deer: Seeker of Visions*. New York: Simon, 1972. Autobiography.

Geigogamah, Hanay (Kiowa/Delaware). *New Native American Drama: Three Plays.* Introd. Jeffrey Huntsman. Norman: U of Oklahoma P, 1980.

Glancy, Diane (Cherokee). *Offering: Poetry and Prose.* Duluth: Holy Cow! 1988. Poetry.

———. *One Age in a Dream.* Minneapolis: Milkweed, 1986. Poetry.

Grayson, G. W. (Creek). *A Creek Warrior for the Confederacy: The Autobiography of Chief G. W. Grayson.* Ed. with introd. W. David Baird. Civilization of the American Indian 189. Norman: U of Oklahoma P, 1988.

Hale, Janet Campbell (Coeur D'Alene/Kootenai). *Custer Lives in Humboldt County.* Greenfield Center: Greenfield, 1978. Poetry.

———. *The Jailing of Cecelia Capture.* 1985. Albuquerque: U of New Mexico P, 1987. Fiction.

———. *Owl Song.* 1974. New York: Avon, 1976. Fiction.

Harjo, Joy (Creek). *In Mad Love and War.* Middletown: Wesleyan UP, 1990. Poetry.

———. *She Had Some Horses.* New York: Thunder's Mouth, 1983. Poetry.

———. *What Moon Drove Me to This?* New York: I. Reed, 1979. Poetry.

Henson, Lance (Cheyenne). *Selected Poems: 1970–1983.* Greenfield Center: Greenfield, 1985.

Hogan, Linda (Chickasaw). *Eclipse.* Foreword Kenneth Lincoln. Native American Ser. 6. Los Angeles: U of California P, 1983. Poetry.

———. *Mean Spirit.* New York: Atheneum, 1990. Fiction.

———. *Savings.* Minneapolis: Coffee House, 1988. Poetry.

———. *Seeing through the Sun.* Amherst, U of Massachusetts P, 1985. Poetry.

Hogan, Linda (Chicasaw), and Charles C. Henderson. *That Horse.* Acoma: Pueblo of Acoma, 1985. Short fiction.

Johnson, Emily Pauline (Mohawk). *Canadian Born.* Toronto: Morang, 1903. Poetry.

———. *Flint and Feather.* Toronto: Musson, 1912. Markam: PaperJacks, 1973. Poetry.

———. *The Moccasin Maker.* 1913. Ed., annot., and introd. A. LaVonne Brown Ruoff. Tucson: U of Arizona P, 1987. Fiction and nonfiction.

———. *The Shagganappi.* Introd. Ernest Thompson Seton. Vancouver: Briggs, 1913. Short fiction.

———. *The White Wampum.* London: Bodley Head, 1895. Poetry.

Jones, Peter [Kahkewaquonaby] (Ojibwa). *History of the Ojebway Indians: With Especial Reference to Their Conversion to Christianity.* 1861. Freeport: Books for Libraries, 1970. Nonfiction.

———. *Life and Journals of Kah-ke-wa-quo-na-by (Rev. Peter Jones), Wesleyan Missionary.* Pub. under the direction of the Missionary Comm., Canada Conference. Toronto: Green, 1860. Nonfiction.

Kenny, Maurice (Mohawk). *Between Two Rivers: Selected Poems, 1956–84.* Fredonia: White Pine, 1987.

———. *Humors and/or Not So Humorous.* Buffalo: Swift Kick, 1988. Poetry.

King, Thomas (Cherokee). *Medicine River.* Toronto: Penguin, 1990. Fiction.

La Flesche, Francis (Omaha). *The Middle Five: Indian School Boys of the Omaha Tribe.* 1900. Foreword David A. Baeris. Lincoln: U of Nebraska P, 1978. Autobiography.

Least-Heat Moon, William [William L. Trogden] (Osage). *Blue Highways: A Journey into America.* Boston: Little, 1982.

Long, Sylvester [Long Lance] (Lumbee). *Long Lance: The Autobiography of a Blackfoot Indian Chief.* New York: Cosmopolitan, 1928. Fiction.

Markoosie (Eskimo). *Harpoon of the Hunter.* Montreal: McGill-Queens UP, 1970. Fiction.

Mathews, John Joseph (Osage). *Sundown.* Introd. Virginia H. Mathews. Norman: U of Oklahoma P, 1988. Fiction.

———. *Talking to the Moon.* 1945. Foreword Elizabeth Mathews. Norman: U of Oklahoma P, 1981. Autobiography.

———. *Wah'Kon-Tah: The Osage and the White Man's Road.* Civilization of the American Indian 3. Norman: U of Oklahoma P, 1932, 1968. Fiction.

Maungwudaus [George Henry] (Chippewa). *An Account of the Chippewa Indians, Who Have Been Travelling among the Whites, in the United States, England, Ireland, Scotland, France and Belgium.* Boston: Author, 1848. Autobiography.

McNickle, D'Arcy (Cree/Salish). *The Runner in the Sun: A Story of Indian Maize.* 1954. Afterword Alfonso Ortiz (San Juan). Albuquerque: U of New Mexico P, 1987. Fiction.

———. *The Surrounded.* 1936. Introd. William Towner. Albuquerque: U of New Mexico P, 1978. Fiction.

———. *Wind from an Enemy Sky.* 1978. Afterword Louis Owens (Cherokee). Albuquerque: U of New Mexico P, 1988. Fiction.

*Mitchell, Frank (Navajo). Charlotte Johnson Frisbie and David P. McAllester. *Navajo Blessingway Singer: The Autobiography of Frank Mitchell, 1881-1967.* Tucson: U of Arizona P, 1978. Autobiography.

Momaday, N. Scott (Kiowa). *The Ancient Child.* New York: Doubleday, 1989. Fiction.

———. *Angle of Geese and Other Poems.* Boston: Godine, 1974.

———. *The Gourd Dancer: Poems.* New York: Harper, 1976.

———. *The House Made of Dawn.* New York: Harper, 1968, 1989. Fiction.

———. *The Names: A Memoir.* New York: Harper, 1976. Autobiography.

———. *The Way to Rainy Mountain.* Albuquerque: U of New Mexico P, 1969. Myth, history, autobiography.

*Mountain Wolf Woman (Winnebago). Nancy Oestreich Lurie. *Mountain Wolf Woman, Sister of Crashing Thunder: The Autobiography of a Winnebago Indian.* Ann Arbor: U of Michigan P, 1961.

Mourning Dove [Christine Quintasket] (Colville). *Co-ge-we-a, the Half-Blood: A Depiction of the Great Montana Cattle Range.* Notes and biographical sketch by Lucullus Virgil McWhorter. 1927. Introd. Dexter Fisher. Lincoln: U of Nebraska P, 1981. Fiction.

———. *Mourning Dove: A Salishan Autobiography.* Ed. Jay Miller. American Indian Lives. Lincoln: U of Nebraska P, 1990.

Niatum, Duane (Klallam). *Ascending Red Cedar Moon.* Native American. New York: Harper, 1969. Poetry.

———. *Digging Out the Roots.* Native American. New York: Harper, 1977. Poetry.

———. *Drawings of the Song Animals: New and Selected Poems.* Duluth: Holy Cow! 1990. Poetry.

———. *Songs for the Harvester of Dreams.* Seattle: U of Washington P, 1981. Poetry.

Oandasan, William (Yuki). *A Branch of California Redwood.* Native American 4. Los Angeles: U of California P, 1980. Poetry.

———. *Round Valley Songs.* Minneapolis: West End, 1984. Poetry.

Occom, Samson (Mohegan). *A Choice Collection of Hymns and Spiritual Songs Intended [sic] for the Edification of Sincere Christians of All Denominations.* London: Timothy Green, 1774.

———. *A Sermon Preached at the Execution of Moses Paul, an Indian Who Was Executed at New-Haven, on the 2d of September 1772.* Bennington: William Watson, 1772.

Ortiz, Simon J. (Acoma). *Fight Back: For the Sake of the People, for the Sake of the Land. INAD Literary Journal.* 1.1 (1980). Inst. for Native American Development, Univ. of New Mexico. Poetry and nonfiction.

———. *Fightin'.* New York: Thunder's Mouth, 1983. Short fiction.

———. *From Sand Creek.* New York: Thunder's Mouth, 1981. Poetry.

———. *Going for the Rain.* New York: Harper, 1976. Poetry.

———. *A Good Journey.* 1977. Sun Tracks 12. Tucson: U of Arizona P, 1986. Poetry.

———. *Howbah Indians.* Tucson: Blue Moon–U of Arizona P, 1978. Short fiction.

Oskison, John Milton (Cherokee). *Black Jack Davy.* New York: Appleton, 1926. Fiction.

———. *Brother's Three.* New York: Macmillan, 1935. Fiction.

———. *Wild Harvest: A Novel of Transition Days in Oklahoma.* New York: Appleton, 1925. Fiction.

Pokagon, Simon (Potawatomi). *O-gî-mäw-kwe Mit-i-gwä-kî (Queen of the Woods). Also Brief Sketch of the Algaic Language*. 1899. Berrien Springs: Hardscrabble, 1972. Fiction; Pokagon's authorship is questionable.

Posey, Alexander (Creek). *The Poems of Alexander Lawrence Posey*. Ed. Mrs. Minnie H. Posey. Memoir by William Elsey Connelly. Topeka: Crane, 1910. Poetry.

Revard, Carter (Osage). *Ponca War Dancers*. Norman: Pointer Riders, 1980. Poetry.

Ridge, John Rollin (Cherokee). *The Life and Adventures of Joaquín Murieta, the Celebrated California Bandit, by Yellow Bird*. 1854. Introd. Joseph Henry Jackson. Norman: U of Oklahoma P, 1977. Fiction.

———. *Poems*. San Francisco: Payot, 1868.

———. *A Trumpet of Our Own: Yellow Bird's Essays on the North American Indian*. Comp. and ed. David Farmer and Rennard Strickland. San Francisco: Book Club, 1981. Essays, biography, bibliography.

Riggs, [Rolla] Lynn (Cherokee). Russet Mantle *and* The Cherokee Night. New York: Samuel French, 1936. Drama.

———. *Green Grow the Lilacs*. New York: Samuel French, 1931. Folk drama that was the basis for the musical *Oklahoma!*

———. *The Iron Dish*. Garden City: Doubleday, 1930. Poetry.

———. *This Book, This Hill, These People: Poems by Lynn Riggs*. Tulsa: Lynn Chase, 1982.

Rogers, Will (Cherokee). *Complete Works*. Ed. Joseph A. Stout, Jr. The Writings of Will Rogers. Stillwater: Oklahoma State UP. Nonfiction.

Rose, Wendy (Hopi/Miwok). *The Halfbreed Chronicles*. Los Angeles: West End, 1985. Poetry.

———. *Lost Copper*. Introd. N. Scott Momaday (Kiowa). Banning: Malki Museum, 1980. Poetry.

———. *What Happened When the Hopi Hit New York*. New York: Contact II, 1982. Poetry.

Salisbury, Ralph (Cherokee). *Spirit Beast Chant*. Marvin: Blue Cloud, 1982. Poetry.

Sanchez, Carol Lee (Laguna/Sioux). *Message Bringer Woman*. San Francisco: Taurean Horn, 1976. Poetry.

Savala, Refugio (Yaqui). Kathleen Mullen Sands. *The Autobiography of a Yaqui Poet*. Tucson: U of Arizona P, 1980.

*Sekaquaptewa, Helen (Hopi). Louise Udall. *Me and Mine: The Life Story of Helen Sekaquaptewa*. Tucson: U of Arizona P, 1969.

*Sewid, James (Kwakiutl). James P. Spradley. *Guests Never Leave Hungry: The Autobiography of James Sewid, a Kwakiutl Indian*. New Haven: Yale UP, 1969. Autobiography.

Shaw, Anna Moore (Pima). *A Pima Past*. Foreword Edward H. Spicer. Tucson: U of Arizona P, 1974. Autobiography.

Silko, Leslie Marmon (Laguna). *Almanac of the Dead*. Forthcoming

———. *Ceremony*. New York: Viking, 1977; NAL, 1978; Viking-Penguin, 1986. Fiction.

———. *Storyteller*. New York: Seaver, 1981. Short fiction, poetry, and autobiographical commentary.

Smith, Martin Cruz (Senecu del Sur/Yaqui). *The Analog Bullet*. New York: Leisure, 1977, 1981. Fiction. Under name of Martin William Smith.

———. *Gorky Park*. New York: Random, 1981; Ballantine, 1982. Fiction.

———. *Gypsy in Amber*. 1971. New York: Ballantine, 1982. Fiction.

———. *Gypsy in Amber; Canto for a Gypsy*. Garden City: Doubleday, 1971. Fiction.

———. *The Indians Won*. 1970. New York: Leisure, 1981. Fiction. Under name of Martin William Smith.

———. *Nightwing*. New York: Norton, 1977. Fiction.

———. *Polar Star*. New York: Random, 1989. Fiction.

———. *Stallion Gate*. New York: Random, 1986; Ballantine, 1987. Fiction.

*Standing Bear, Luther [Ota K'te] (Sioux). E. A. Brininstool. *Land of the Spotted Eagle*. 1933. Foreword Richard Ellis. Lincoln: U of Nebraska P, 1978. Autobiography.

————. *My Indian Boyhood, by Chief Luther Standing Bear, Who Was the Boy Ota K'te (Plenty Kill)*. 1931. Lincoln: U of Nebraska P, 1988.

*————. E. A. Brininstool. *My People, the Sioux*. 1928. Introd. Richard N. Ellis. Lincoln: U of Nebraska P, 1975. Autobiography.

*Stands in Timber, John (Cheyenne). Margot Liberty. *Cheyenne Memories*. 1967. Lincoln: U of Nebraska P, 1972. Autobiography.

Storm, Hyemeyohsts (Cheyenne). *Seven Arrows*. New York: Harper, 1972. Fiction.

————. *Song of Heyoehkah*. New York: Harper, 1981. Fiction.

Strete, Craig Kee (Cherokee). *Death Chants*. New York: Doubleday, 1988. Short fiction.

————. *To Make Death Love Us*. New York: Doubleday, 1987. Fiction.

Talayesva, Don C. (Hopi). Leo W. Simmons. *Sun Chief: The Autobiography of a Hopi Indian*. 1942. New Haven: Yale UP, 1974.

Tapahonso, Luci (Navajo). *A Breeze Swept Through*. Albuquerque: West End, 1987. Poetry.

————. *One More Shiprock Night*. San Antonio: Tejas Art, 1981. Poetry.

————. *Seasonal Woman*. Santa Fe: Tooth of Time, 1982. Poetry.

Vizenor, Gerald (Ojibwa). *Darkness in St. Louis Bearheart*. St. Paul: Truck, 1978. Repub. as *Bearheart*. Minneapolis: U of Minnesota P, 1990. Fiction.

————. *Earthdivers: Tribal Narratives on Mixed Descent*. Minneapolis: U of Minnesota P, 1981. Fiction and nonfiction.

————. *The Everlasting Sky: New Voices from the People Named the Chippewa*. New York: Macmillan, 1972. Nonfiction.

————. *Griever: An American Monkey King in China*. Normal: Illinois State; New York: Fiction Collective, 1987. Minneapolis: U of Minnesota P, 1990. Fiction.

————. *Matsushima: Pine Islands*. Minneapolis: Nodin, 1984. Poetry.

————. *The People Named the Chippewa: Narrative Histories*. Minneapolis: U of Minnesota P, 1984. Fiction and nonfiction.

————. *Tribal Scenes and Ceremonies*. 1976. With new essays. Minneapolis: U of Minnesota P, 1990. Nonfiction.

————. *The Trickster of Liberty: Tribal Heirs to a Wild Baronage at Petronia*. Emergent Literatures. Minneapolis: U of Minnesota P, 1988. Fiction.

————. *Wordarrows: Indians and Whites in the New Fur Trade*. Minneapolis: U of Minnesota P, 1978. Short fiction and nonfiction.

Walker, Bertrand N. O. [Hen-Toh] (Wyandot). *Yon-Doo-Shah-We-Ah (Nubbins)*. Oklahoma City: Harlow, 1924. Poetry.

Walsh, Marnie (Sioux). *A Taste of the Knife*. Boise: Ahsahta, 1976. Poetry.

Walters, Anna Lee (Pawnee/Otoe). *Ghost Singer*. Flagstaff: Northland, 1988. Fiction.

————. *The Sun Is Not Merciful*. Ithaca: Firebrand, 1985. Short fiction.

Warren, William Whipple (Ojibwa). *History of the Ojibway, Based upon Traditions and Oral Statements*. Collections of the Minnesota Historical Soc. 5. 1885. Minneapolis: Ross, 1957. Introd. W. Roger Buffalohead (Ponca). Minneapolis: Minnesota Historical Soc., 1984.

Welch, James (Blackfeet/Gros Ventre). *The Death of Jim Loney*. New York: Harper, 1979; Viking-Penguin, 1987. Fiction.

————. *Fools Crow*. New York: Viking, 1986. Fiction.

————. *Riding the Earthboy 40*. Native American. New York: Harper, 1971. Rev. ed. 1976. Poetry.

————. *Winter in the Blood*. New York: Harper, 1974; Viking-Penguin, 1986. Fiction.

*White Bull, Chief Joseph (Sioux). James H. Howard. *The Warrior Who Killed Custer: The Personal Narrative of Chief Joseph White Bull*. Lincoln: U of Nebraska P, 1968. Autobiography.

Whiteman, Roberta Hill (Oneida). *Star Quilt*. Foreword Carolyn Forche. Minneapolis: Holy Cow! 1984. Poetry.

Williams, Ted (Tuscarora). *The Reservation*. Syracuse: Syracuse UP, 1976. Autobiography.

Winnemucca, Sarah [Hopkins] (Thocmetony; Paiute). *Life among the Piutes: Their Wrongs and Claims*. Ed. Mrs. Horace Mann. 1883. Bishop: Chalfant, 1969. Autobiography.

*Yava, Albert (Tewa/Hopi). Harold Courlander. *Big Falling Snow: A Tewa-Hopi Indian's Life and Times and the History and Traditions of His People*. New York: Crown, 1978. Autobiography.

Young Bear, Ray (Mesquakie). *The Invisible Musician*. Duluth: Holy Cow! 1990. Poetry.

——. *Winter of the Salamander: The Keeper of Importance*. Native American 10. New York: Harper, 1980. Poetry.

Zitkala-Ša [Gertrude Bonnin] (Sioux). *American Indian Stories*. 1921. Introd. Dexter Fisher. Lincoln: U of Nebraska P, 1986. Autobiography, fiction, nonfiction.

4. Secondary Works

General

Allen, Paula Gunn (Laguna/Sioux). *The Sacred Hoop: Recovering the Feminine in American Indian Traditions*. Boston: Beacon, 1986. A collection of essays examining the role of women in Indian culture and literature.

——, ed. *Studies in American Indian Literature*. New York: MLA, 1983. Indispensable guide to the field; emphasis on written literature. Includes essays, course designs, review of scholarship, and extensive bibliography.

——. "'Whose Dream Is This, Anyway?' Remythologizing and Self-Redefinitions of Contemporary American Indian Fiction." *Literature and the Visual Arts in Contemporary Society*. Ed. Suzanne Ferguson and Barbara Groselclose. Columbus: Ohio State UP, 1985. 95–122.

Bataille, Gretchen M., and Kathleen Mullen Sands. *American Indian Women: Telling Their Lives*. Lincoln: U of Nebraska P, 1984. Excellent analysis of as-told-to and written autobiographies of American Indian women; examines the methods by which editors collected and recorded these works.

Bright, William. *American Indian Linguistics and Literature*. Berlin: Mouton, 1984. Good introduction to Native American linguistics and oral literatures.

Bruchac, Joseph (Abenaki). *Survival This Way: Interviews with American Indian Poets*. Tucson: U of Arizona P, 1987. Interviews with Paula Gunn Allen (Laguna/Sioux), Peter Blue Cloud (Mohawk), Diane Burns (Ojibwa/Chemehuevi), Elizabeth Cook-Lynn (Sioux), Louise Erdrich (Ojibwa), Joy Harjo (Creek), Lance Henson (Cheyenne), Linda Hogan (Chickasaw), Karoniaktatie (Mohawk), Maurice Kenny (Mohawk), Harold Littlebird (Laguna/Santo Domingo), N. Scott Momaday (Kiowa), Duane Niatum (Klallam), Simon Ortiz (Acoma), Carter Revard (Osage), Wendy Rose (Hopi/Miwok), Luci Tapahonso (Navajo), Gerald Vizenor (Ojibwa), James Welch (Blackfeet/Gros Ventre), Roberta Hill Whiteman (Oneida), Ray Young Bear (Mesquakie).

Brumble, H. David, III. *American Indian Autobiography*. Berkeley: U of California P, 1988. Historical and theoretical analysis of the genre. Includes a supplement to his *American Indian and Eskimo Autobiographies*.

Castro, Michael. *Interpreting the Indian*. Albuquerque: U of New Mexico P, 1983. Examines the influence of American Indians in Anglo literature as well as Indian literature. Includes a discussion John G. Neihardt's relationship to Black Elk.

Chapman, Abraham, ed. *Literature of the American Indians: Views and Interpretations*. New York: NAL, 1975. Literature and criticism, including essays by several Indian writers.

Coltelli, Laura, ed. *Native American Literature*. Pisa: U of Pisa P, 1989. Essays on oral and written literature.

————, ed. *Winged Words: Native American Writers Speak*. American Indian Lives. Lincoln: U of Nebraska P, 1990. Interviews with Paula Gunn Allen (Laguna/Sioux), Michael Dorris (Modoc), Louise Erdrich (Ojibwa), Joy Harjo (Creek), Linda Hogan (Chickasaw), N. Scott Momaday (Kiowa), Simon Ortiz (Acoma), Wendy Rose (Hopi/Miwok), Leslie Marmon Silko (Laguna), Gerald Vizenor (Ojibwa), and James Welch (Blackfeet/Gros Ventre).

Densmore, Frances. *The American Indians and Their Music*. 1926. New York: Johnson, n.d.

Dundes, Alan. *The Morphology of North American Folktales*. Folklore Fellows Communications 195. Helsinki: Suomalainen Tiedeakatemia, 1964.

Foster, Michael K. *From the Earth to Beyond the Sky: An Ethnograpahic Approach to Four Longhouse Iroquois Speech Events*. National Museum of Man, Mercury Ser., Canadian Ethnology Service Paper 20. Ottawa: National Museums of Canada, 1974.

Frisbie, Charlotte Johnson. *Music and Dance Research of Southwestern United States: Past Trends, Present Activities, and Suggestions for Future Research*. Detroit Studies in Music Bibliography 36. Detroit: Information Coordinators, 1977. A fine overview of the subject.

————, ed. *Southwestern Indian Ritual Drama*. Albuquerque: U of New Mexico P, 1980. Essays providing an excellent introduction to the ceremonies of southwestern Indian tribes.

Herndon, Marcia (Cherokee). *Native American Music*. Norwood: Norwood, 1980. A helpful introduction to the subject.

Hultkrantz, Åke. *The North American Indian Orpheus Tradition*. Stockholm: Statens Ethnografiska, 1957. A detailed, comparative study of this theme in Indian literature.

Hymes, Dell. *"In Vain I Tried to Tell You": Essays in Native American Ethnopoetics*. Studies in Native American Literature 1. Philadelphia: U of Pennsylvania P, 1981. An essential work on ethnopoetic and structural approaches to American Indian oral literatures.

Jaskoski, Helen. "From the Time Immemorial: Native American Traditions in Contemporary Short Fiction." Loren Logsdon and Charles W. Mayer, eds. *Since Flannery O'Connor: Essays on the Contemporary American Short Story*. Essays in Literature. Macomb: Western Illinois UP, 1987. 54–71. Jaskoski examines how Louise Erdrich (Ojibwa), Leslie Marmon Silko (Laguna), and Gerald Vizenor (Ojibwa) use the short-story form and incorporate traditional American Indian material in their fiction.

————. "'My Heat Will Go Out': Healing Songs of Native American Women." *International Journal of Women's Studies* 4.4 (1981): 118–34. In her analysis of the healing songs of American Indian women, Jaskoski focuses on those of Owl Woman (Papago), Pretty-Shield (Crow), Djun (Tlingit), and Sanapia (Comanche) and examines the Chiricahua Apache girl's puberty ritual.

Kroeber, Karl, comp. and ed. *Traditional Literatures of the American Indian: Texts and Interpretations*. Lincoln: U of Nebraska P, 1981. Excellent starting point for the study of narratives. Includes texts and critical essays.

Krupat, Arnold. *For Those Who Come After: A Study of Native American Autobiography*. Los Angeles: U of California P, 1985. Study of narrated autobiographies and analysis of those by Geronimo, Crashing Thunder (Sam Blowsnake), Yellow Wolf, and Black Elk.

Larson, Charles R. *American Indian Fiction*. Albuquerque: U of New Mexico P, 1978. The first book-length study of Indian novelists, 1899–1978. Stronger on plot summary than on criticism.

Lincoln, Kenneth. *Native American Renaissance*. Los Angeles: U of California P, 1983. 2nd ed. expanded, 1985. Perceptive book that includes some material on oral literatures, although the emphasis is on close reading of works by contemporary American Indian authors.

Lyon, Thomas, and J. Golden Taylor, eds. *Literary History of the American West*. Dallas: Texas Christian UP, 1989. Contains essays by Larry Evers and Paul Pavich on oral literature, A. LaVonne Brown Ruoff on written literature to 1969, and Paula Gunn Allen (Laguna/Sioux) and Patricia Smith on literature since that date.

Merriam, Alan P., ed. *Ethnomusicology of the Flathead Indians*. Viking Fund Pub. in Anthropology 44. New York: Werner Gren Foundation, 1967. Books Demand UMI. Collection of Salish music, carefully analyzed and annotated. Few lyrics included.

Native American Literature. Spec. issue of *MELUS* 12.1 (1985). Contains essays on oral and written literature and an interview with N. Scott Momaday.

Radin, Paul. *Literary Aspects of North American Mythology*. Canada Dept. of Mines. Museum Bulletin 16. Anthropological Ser. 6. Ottawa: Government Printing Bureau, 1915. An early, general introduction to themes and motifs in American Indian oral literatures.

Ramsey, Jarold. *Reading the Fire: Essays in the Traditional Indian Literatures of the Far West*. Lincoln: U of Nebraska P, 1983. Perceptive essays on the interpretation of oral literature. Includes discussions of the influence of the Bible and on tradition in modern Indian writing.

Rothenberg, Jerome, and Diana Rothenberg, eds. *Symposium of the Whole: A Range of Discourse toward an Ethnopoetics*. Berkeley: U of California P, 1983. Contains several essays on American Indian oral literatures.

Ruoff, A. LaVonne Brown. *American Indian Literatures*. See section 1 above.

———. "The Survival of Tradition: American Indian Oral and Written Narratives." *Ethnicity and Literature*. Spec. issue of *Massachusetts Review* 27.2 (1986): 274–93. Surveys types and themes in oral narratives and discusses use of the culture hero quest in modern novels dealing with war veterans (Mathews, *Sundown*; Momaday, *House Made of Dawn*; and Silko, *Ceremony*). Also examines Vizenor's use of the trickster figure.

Ruppert, James. "Mediation and Multiple Narrative in Contemporary Native American Fiction." *Texas Studies in Literature and Language* 28.2 (1986): 209–25. Suggests that American Indian authors, as mediators between oral and written literature and between Indian and non-Indian cultures, create unique artistic structures. Focuses on Momaday (Kiowa), Silko (Laguna), and Vizenor (Ojibwa).

———. "Paula Gunn Allen and Joy Harjo: Closing the Distance between Person and Mythic Space." *American Indian Quarterly* 7 (1983): 27–40.

———. "The Uses of Oral Tradition in Six Contemporary Native American Poets." *American Indian Culture and Research Journal* 4 (1980): 87–100. Maurice Kenny (Mohawk), Peter Blue Cloud (Mohawk), Wendy Rose (Hopi/Miwok), Liz Sohappy Bahe (Yakima), Ray Young Bear (Mesquakie), and Elizabeth Cook-Lynn (Sioux).

Scholer, Bö, ed. *Coyote Was Here: Essays on Contemporary Native American Literary and Political Mobilization*. Spec. issue of *Dolphin* 9 (1984). *Seklos*. Dept. of English. U of Aarhus, 800 Aarhus C., Denmark. Essays and an interview on contemporary American Indian writers, most by Indian authors.

Sherzer, Joel, and Anthony Woodbury, eds. *Native American Discourse: Poetics and Politics*. Studies in Oral and Literate Culture 13. New York: Cambridge UP, 1987. Essays by the editors, Dell and Virginia Hymes, and Dennis Tedlock on the discourse of the natives of North and Central America.

Swann, Brian, ed. *Smoothing the Ground: Essays on Native American Oral Literature*. Berkeley: U of California P, 1983. Essays by a variety of critics.

Swann, Brian, and Arnold Krupat, eds. *Recovering the Word: Essays on Native American Literature*. Berkeley: U of California P, 1987. Interdisciplinary essays on American Indian literature; contributors include work of literary critics, anthropologists, folklorists, poets, and social scientists.

Tedlock, Dennis. *The Spoken Word and the Work of Interpretation*. Conduct and Communication. Philadelphia: U of Pennsylvania P, 1983. Significant study of Indian oral literatures. Tedlock emphasizes the importance of tape-recorded oral performance as a guide to the structure of narratives.

Velie, Alan R. *Four American Indian Literary Masters: N. Scott Momaday, James Welch, Leslie Marmon Silko, and Gerald Vizenor*. Norman: U of Oklahoma P, 1982. One of the first books on contemporary American Indian literature.

Vizenor, Gerald (Ojibwa), ed. *Narrative Chance: Postmodern Discourse on Native American Indian Literatures.* Albuquerque: U of New Mexico P, 1989. Essays examining American Indian literature from postmodernist perspectives, with emphasis on works by Erdrich (Ojibwa), Momaday (Kiowa), Silko (Laguna), and Vizenor (Ojibwa).

Wiget, Andrew, ed. *Critical Essays on Native American Literature.* Boston: Hall, 1985. Essays by various authors on historical and methodological perspectives as well as on traditional and written literatures.

—————. *Native American Literature.* United States Authors 467. Boston: Twayne, 1985. Excellent introduction to oral and written literatures; contains a good bibliography.

Works on Individual Authors

Allen, Paula Gunn (Laguna/Sioux)

Jahner, Elaine. "A Laddered, Rain-Bearing Rug: Paula Gunn Allen's Poetry." *Women and Western American Literature.* Ed. Helen Winter Stauffer and Susan J. Rosnowski. Troy: Whitston, 1982. 311–26.

Black Elk (Sioux)

Castro, Michael. "Translating Indian Consciousness: Lew Sarret and John G. Neihardt." *Interpreting the Indian: Twentieth-Century Poets and the Native American.* By Castro. Albuquerque: U of New Mexico P, 1983. 71–97. Examines Neihardt's revisions of Black Elk's narrative.

Couser, G. Thomas. "*Black Elk Speaks* with Forked Tongue." *Studies in Autobiography.* Ed. James Olney. New York: Oxford UP, 1988. 73–88. Argues that *Black Elk Speaks* is not genuine autobiography.

Deloria, Vine, Jr. (Sioux). *A Sender of Words: Essays in Memory of John G. Neihardt.* Salt Lake City: Howe, 1984. Essays on Neihardt and on *Black Elk Speaks.*

DeMallie, Raymond, ed. *The Sixth Grandfather: Black Elk's Teachings Given to John G. Neihardt.* Foreword Hilda Neihardt Petri. Lincoln: U of Nebraska P, 1984. Indispensable to understanding *Black Elk Speaks.* Transcripts of Neihardt's interviews with Black Elk in 1931 and 1944. Contains lengthy introduction and detailed notes that include comparisons of the interviews with the published book.

Rice, Julian. "*Akicita* of the Thunder: Horses in Black Elk's Vision." *MELUS* 12.1 (1985): 5–23. Examines the Sioux backgrounds of *Black Elk Speaks.*

Sayre, Robert. "Vision and Experience in *Black Elk Speaks.*" *College English* 32 (1971): 509–35.

Blowsnake, Sam (Winnebago)

Brumble, H. David, III. "Sam Blowsnake's Confessions: *Crashing Thunder* and the History of American Indian Autobiography." *Canadian Review of American Studies* 16.3 (1985): 271–82. Rpt. in Swann and Krupat, *Recovering the Word* 537–51.

Carter, Forrest [Asa] (Cherokee)

Clayton, Lawrence. "Forrest Carter/Asa Carter and Politics." *WAL* 21.1 (1986): 19–26. Traces Carter's political activism as a supporter of segregation and examines the antigovernment theme in Carter's works.

Copway, George (Ojibwa)

Knobel, Dale T. "Know-Nothings and Indians: Strange Bedfellows?" *Western Historical Quarterly* 15 (1984): 175–98. Traces the involvement of American Indians, especially George Copway, in this political group.

Ruoff, A. LaVonne Brown. "George Copway: Nineteenth-Century American-Indian Autobiographer." *Auto/Biography Studies* 3.2 (1987): 6–17.

Smith, Donald B. "The Life of George Copway or Kah-ge-ga-gah-bowh (1818–1869)—and a Review of His Writings." *Journal of Canadian Studies* 23.3 (1988): 5–38.

Deloria, Ella C. (Sioux)

Medicine, Bea (Sioux). "Ella C. Deloria: The Emic Voice." *MELUS* 7.4 (1980): 23–30. A discussion of Deloria's life and work by her niece.

Eastman, Charles A. (Sioux)

Wilson, Raymond. *Ohiyesa: Charles Eastman, Santee Sioux*. Urbana: U of Illinois P, 1983. The standard biography.

Erdrich, Louise (Ojibwa)

Brewington, Lillian, Normie Bullard, and Robert W. Reising, comps. "Writing in Love: An Annotated Bibliography of Critical Responses to the Poetry and Novels of Louise Erdrich and Michael Dorris. *American Indian Culture and Research Journal* 10.4 (1986): 81–86.

Gleason, William. "'Her Laugh an Ace': The Function of Humor in Louise Erdrich's *Love Medicine*." *American Indian Culture and Research Journal* 11.2 (1987): 51–73. Argues that Erdrich's vision in the book is one of redemption accomplished through an expert and caring use of humor.

McKenzie, James. "Lipsha's Good Road Home: The Revival of Chippewa Culture in *Love Medicine*." *American Indian Culture and Research Journal* 10.3 (1986): 53–63. Arguing that many critics mistakenly read the book as an anthropological document, McKenzie emphasizes the homage it pays to the tenacity of a small, minority culture pitted against the juggernaut of contemporary American life.

Johnson, Emily Pauline (Mohawk)

Keller, Betty. *Pauline: A Biography of Pauline Johnson*. Vancouver: Douglas, 1981. The standard biography.

Long, Sylvester [Long Lance] (Lumbee)

Smith, Donald B. *Long Lance, the True Story of an Impostor*. Toronto: Macmillan, 1982.

Mathews, John Joseph (Osage)

Hunter, Carol (Osage). "The Historical Context in John Joseph Mathews' *Sundown*." *MELUS* 9 (1982): 61–72.

———. "The Protagonist as a Mixed-Blood in John Joseph Mathews's Novel: *Sundown*." *American Indian Quarterly* 6 (1982): 319–37.

Ruoff, A. LaVonne Brown. "John Joseph Mathews's *Talking to the Moon*: Literary and Osage Contexts." *Essays in Multicultural Autobiography*. Ed. James Robert Payne. Knoxville: U of Tennessee P, 1991. Analyzes the influences of Thoreau's *Walden* and Muir's works as well as Osage oral traditions on *Talking to the Moon*.

Wilson, Terry P. (Potawatomi). "Osage Oxonian: The Heritage of John Joseph Mathews." *Chronicles of Oklahoma* 59 (1981): 264–91.

McNickle, D'Arcy (Cree-Salish)

Owens, Louis (Cherokee). "The 'Map of the Mind': D'Arcy McNickle and the American Indian Novel." *Western American Literature* 19.4 (1985): 275–83.

Ruppert, James. *D'Arcy McNickle*. Western Writers 85. Boise: Boise State UP, 1988. An introduction to McNickle's life and works.

———. "Politics and Culture in the Fiction of D'Arcy McNickle." *Rocky Mountain Review of Language and Literature* 42.4 (1988): 185–95.

Momaday, N. Scott (Kiowa)

Evers, Larry. "Words and Place: A Reading of *House Made of Dawn*." *Western American Literature* 11 (1977): 297–320. Rpt. in Wiget, *Critical Essays on Native American Literature* 211–30. Excellent article on this complex novel.

Lincoln, Kenneth. "Tai-Me to Rainy Mountain: The Makings of American Indian Literature." *American Indian Quarterly* 10.2 (1986): 101–17. Discusses Momaday's tribulations with his publisher and manuscript readers as *Journey of Tai-Me* was expanded into *The Way to Rainy Mountain*.

Roemer, Kenneth, ed. *Approaches to Teaching Momaday's* The Way to Rainy Mountain. New York: MLA, 1988. Essays on materials and the following contexts: biographical, cultural, and general; critical; and pedagogical. Includes an epilogue by Gary Kodaseet (Kiowa).

Scarberry-Garcia, Susan. *Landmarks of Healing: A Study of* House Made of Dawn. Albuquerque: U of New Mexico P, 1990. Scarberry-Garcia examines Momaday's incorporation of Pueblo stories and Navajo chantways. She particularly focuses on his use of the Twins motif, animal transformers (especially the bear), and Navajo concepts of healing.

Schubnell, Matthias. *N. Scott Momaday: The Cultural and Literary Background*. Norman: U of Oklahoma P, 1985. Literary biography with extensive bibliography of Momaday's works.

Watkins, Floyd. "Culture versus Anonymity in *House Made of Dawn*." *Time and Place: Some Origins of American Fiction*. By Watkins. Athens: U of Georgia P, 1977. 133–71. Discusses the influence of Jemez culture and Momaday's life there on the novel.

Woodard, Charles L. *Ancestral Voice: Conversations with N. Scott Momaday*. Lincoln: U of Nebraska P, 1989. The interviews in 1986–87 cover the author's philosophy, individual and tribal identity, literary and artistic theories. Illustrated with Momaday's own paintings and drawings.

Mourning Dove [Christine Quintasket] (Colville)

Brown, Alanna. "Mourning Dove's Voice in *Cogewea*." *Wicazo Sa Review* 4.2 (1988): 2–15. Distinguishes between Mourning Dove's and Lucullus Virgil McWhorter's contributions.
Dearborn, Mary. *Pocahontas's Daughters: Gender and Ethnicity in American Culture*. New York: Oxford UP, 1986. Includes a discussion of Mourning Dove and McWhorter.
Miller, Jay. "Mourning Dove: The Author as Cultural Mediator." *Being and Becoming Indian: Biographical Studies of North American Frontiers*. Ed. James A. Clifton. Chicago: Dorsey, 1989. 169–82. The only biographical study.

Occom, Samson (Mohegan)

Blodgett, Harold. *Samson Occom*. Dartmouth Coll. Manuscript Ser. 3. Hanover: Dartmouth College P, 1935. Standard biography.
Love, W. DeLoss. *Samson Occom and the Christian Indians of New England*. Boston: Pilgrim, 1899. Discusses Occom's life in the context of the history of the Christian Indians of the Northeast. Includes citations of letters and works, some of which are not available in other printed sources.

Ortiz, Simon (Acoma)

Gingerich, Willard. "The Old Voices of Acoma: Simon Ortiz's Mythic Indigenism." *Southwest Review* 64 (1979): 18–30.
Smith Patricia. "Coyote Ortiz: *Canis latrans latrans* in the Poetry of Simon Ortiz." *Minority Voices* 3 (1979): 1–17. Discusses Ortiz's use of the coyote or trickster tale.
Wiget, Andrew O. *Simon Ortiz*. Western Writers 74. Boise: Idaho State UP, 1986. Best general introduction.

Pokagon, Simon (Potawatomi)

Buechner, Cecilia Bain. *The Pokagons*. 1933. Berrien Springs: Hardscrabble, 1976.
Clifton, James. *The Pokagons, 1683–1983: Catholic Potawatomi of the St. Joseph River Valley*. Washington: Potawatomi Nation and UP of America, 1984. Both here and in the article below, Clifton, a specialist in Potawatomi history, contends that Pokagon did not write *Queen of the Woods*.
———. "Simon Pokagon and the Sand-Bar Case: Michigan Potawatomi Indians Sue for Chicago's Lake Front." *Michigan History* 71.5 (1987): 12–17.
Dickason, David H. "Chief Simon Pokagon: 'The Indian Longfellow.'" *Indiana Magazine of History* 57 (1971): 127–40.

Posey, Alexander L. (Creek)

Barnett, Leona G. (Creek) "*Este Cate Emunkv*. Red Man Always." *Chronicles of Oklahoma* 46 (1968): 20–40. Discussion of Posey's life and work.
Dale, Edward Everett. "Journal of Alexander Lawrence Posey with Annotations. *Chronicles of Oklahoma* 45 (1967–68): 393–432.

Ridge, John Rollin (Cherokee)

Debo, Angie. "John Rollin Ridge." *Southwest Review* 17 (1932): 59–71.
Foreman, Carolyn Thomas. "Edward W. Bushyhead and John Rollin Ridge, Cherokee Editors in California." *Chronicles of Oklahoma* (1936): 195–30.
Parins, James L. *John Rollin Ridge*. American Indian Lives. Lincoln: U of Nebraska P, 1991. A scholarly and literary biography.
Walker, Franklin. *San Francisco's Literary Frontier*. 1939. Seattle: U of Washington P, 1969.

Riggs, [Rolla] Lynn (Cherokee)

Braunlich, Phyllis Cole. *Haunted by Home: The Life and Letters of Lynn Riggs*. Norman: U of Oklahoma P, 1988. An authoritative biography that traces Riggs's life and career and quotes copiously from his letters.
Erhard, Thomas. *Lynn Riggs: Southwest Playwright*. Austin: Steck-Vaughn, 1970. An appreciative biography.

Rogers, Will (Cherokee)

Alworth, E. Paul. *Will Rogers*. United States Authors 236. Boston: Twayne, 1974. Best general introduction.
Day, Donald. *Will Rogers: A Biography*. New York: McKay, 1962. A full but popular biography.
Gibson, Arrell M., ed. *Will Rogers: A Centennial Tribute*. Oklahoma Ser. 12. Oklahoma City: Oklahoma Historical Soc., 1979. Also pub. as *Chronicles of Oklahoma* 57.3 (1979). See especially Blue Clark (Creek), "The Literary Will Rogers" (385–94), and bibliography.

Silko, Leslie Marmon (Laguna)

Danielson, Linda L. "*Storyteller*: Grandmother Spider's Web." *Journal of the Southwest* 30:3 (1988): 325–55.
Krupat, Arnold. "The Dialogic of Silko's *Storyteller*." Vizenor, *Narrative Chance*. 55–68.
Nelson, Robert. "Place and Vision: The Function of Landscape in *Ceremony*." *Journal of the Southwest* 30.3 (1988): 281–316.
Ruoff, A. LaVonne Brown. "Ritual and Renewal: Keres Traditions in the Short Fiction of Leslie Silko." *MELUS* 5 (1978): 3–17.
Ruppert, James. "The Reader's Lessons in *Ceremony*." *Arizona Quarterly* 44.1 (1988): 78–85. Discusses Silko's blending of poetry and prose, a reflection of the epistemological unity of Laguna narrative aesthetic and worldview.
Sands, Kathleen Mullen, ed. *Leslie Marmon Silko's Ceremony*. Spec. issue of *American Indian Quarterly* 5 (1979): 1–75.

Seyersted, Per. *Leslie Marmon Silko*. Western Writers 45. Boise: Boise State UP, 1980. Brief but excellent survey of her work.

Swann, Edith. "Healing via the Sunwise Cycle in Silko's *Ceremony*." *American Indian Quarterly* 12.4 (1988): 313–28. Argues that the novel's circular structure replicates the sunwise cycle invented by Spider Woman.

———. "Laguna Symbolic Geography and Silko's *Ceremony*." *American Indian Quarterly* 12.3 (1988): 229–49. Suggests that the Laguna symbolic geography serves as a guide for understanding the protagonist's spiritual journey toward healing.

Vizenor, Gerald (Ojibwa)

Owens, Louis (Cherokee). "Estatic Strategies": Gerald Vizenor's *Darkness in Saint Louis Bearheart*. Vizenor, *Narrative Chance* 141–53. Analyzing the book as a trickster novel whose principal target is the sign "Indian," Owens argues that central to its thrust is the identification of the author with the trickster.

Ruoff, A. LaVonne Brown. "Woodland Word Warrior: An Introduction to the Works of Gerald Vizenor." *MELUS* 13.1 and 2 (1986): 13–43. An analysis of the genres, motifs, and themes in Vizenor's major works and selected bibliography of his publications.

Velie, Alan. "The Trickster Novel." Vizenor, *Narrative Chance* 121–37. Applying the theories of M. M. Bakhtin, Velie analyzes Vizenor's treatment of the trickster figure in *Darkness in Saint Louis Bearheart*.

Wilson, Terry P. (Potawatomi), and Robert Black, eds. *Gerald Vizenor Issue*. *American Indian Quarterly* 9.1 (1985): 1–78. New and reprinted essays and selected bibliography of Vizenor's work.

Welch, James (Blackfeet/Gros Ventre)

Beidler, Peter, ed. *James Welch's* Winter in the Blood. Spec. issue of *American Indian Quarterly* 4 (1978): 93–172.

McFarland, Ron, ed. *James Welch*. American Authors 1. Ed. James R. Hepworth. Lewiston: Confluence, 1986. Interview, new and reprinted essays on Welch's work, selection from *Fools Crow*, and bibliography of Welch's publications.

Ruoff, A. LaVonne Brown. "The Influence of Emilio Vittorini's *In Sicily* on James Welch's *Winter in the Blood*." Coltelli, *Native American Literature* 141–50.

Sands, Kathleen Mullen. "Closing the Distance: Critic, Reader and the Works of James Welch." *MELUS* 14.2 (1987): 73–85. Sands examines how Welch closes the distance between the reader and the landscape out of which he writes, one "haunted by loneliness, tensions, and a sense of loss."

Wild, Peter. *James Welch*. Western Writers 57. Boise: Boise State UP, 1983. An overview of Welch's work.

Winnemucca, Sarah (Paiute)

Canfield, Gae Whitney. *Sarah Winnemucca of the Northern Paiutes*. Norman: U of Oklahoma P, 1983. Definitive life of this fascinating woman, author of the first written autobiography by an Indian woman.

Asian American Literature

Compiled by Amy Ling

1. Bibliographies and Aids to Research

Cheung, King-Kok, and Stan Yogi. *Asian American Literature: An Annotated Bibliography*. New York: MLA, 1988. An extensive bibliography of primary and secondary works, including interviews and profiles. It also contains selected literature for children and young adults, works by non-Asians about Asians and Asian Americans, and background sources.

Kim, Elaine H. "Asian American Writers: A Bibliographical Review." *American Studies International* 22.2 (1984): 41–78.

Ling, Amy. "Asian American Literature: A Brief Introduction and Selected Bibliography." *ADE Bulletin* 80 (1985): 29–33. Discusses the definitions of Asian American used in the first three anthologies of Asian American literature. Includes an overview of the history and major writers of Asian American literature.

Yung, Judy, et al. "Asian American Women: A Bibliography." *Bridge* 6 (1978–79): 49–53.

2. Anthologies and Collections

Asian American: North and South. Ed. Laureen Mar and Alan Chong Lau. Spec. issue of *Contact/II* 7.38–40 (1986): 1–99. Poetry, art, and reviews from Canada, the United States, and South America.

Asian-American Writers. Spec. issue of *Greenfield Review* 6 (1977): 1–112.

Asian Women. Berkeley: Asian Women's Journal Workshop, 1971.

Bruchac, Joseph J., ed. *Breaking Silence: An Anthology of Contemporary Asian American Poets*. Greenfield Center: Greenfield, 1983.

Cachapero, Emily, et al., eds. *Liwanag: Literary and Graphic Expressions by Filipinos in America*. San Francisco: Liwanag, 1975.

Chiang, Fay, et al. *American Born and Foreign Born: An Anthology of Asian American Poetry*. New York: Sunbury 3.1, 2 (1979).

Chin, Frank, Jeffery Chan, Lawson Inada, and Shawn Wong, eds. *AIIIEEEEE! An Anthology of Asian-American Writers*. Washington: Howard UP, 1974, 1983.

————. *Yardbird Reader.* Vol. 3. Berkeley: Yardbird, 1974.

Chock, Eric, and Darrell H. Y. Lum, eds. *The Best of Bamboo Ridge: The Hawaii Writer's Quarterly.* Spec. issue of *Bamboo Ridge.* Honolulu: Bamboo Ridge, 1986.

Chock, Eric, et al., eds. *Talk Story: An Anthology of Hawaii's Local Writers.* Honolulu: Petronium, 1978.

Echoes from Gold Mountain. 2 vols. Asian American Student Assn., California State Univ., Long Beach. Los Angeles: Peace, 1978, 1979.

Gee, Emma, ed. *Counterpoint: Perspectives on Asian America.* Los Angeles: UCLA Asian American Studies Center, 1976.

Graham, Judith. *Hawaiian Voices.* Honolulu: Bess, 1982.

Higa, Lori, et al., eds. *Rising Waters.* Santa Cruz: U of California, Asian American Studies Planning Group, 1975.

Hongo, Garrett Kaoru, Alan Chong Lau, and Lawson Fusao Inada. *The Buddha Bandits down Highway 99.* Mountain View: Buddhahead, 1978. Poetry by two Japanese Americans and a Chinese American.

Hsu, Kai-yu, and Helen Palubinskas, eds. *Asian-American Authors.* Boston: Houghton, 1972.

Leong, George. *A Lone Bamboo Doesn't Come from Jackson Street.* San Francisco: Isthmus, 1977.

————. *Time to Greez! Incantations from the Third World.* San Francisco: Glide–Third World Communications, 1975.

Lim, Shirley Geok-lin, Mayumi Tsutakawa, and Margarita Donnelly, eds. *The Forbidden Stitch: An Asian American Women's Anthology.* Corvallis: Calyx, 1989.

Miyasaki, Gail. *Montage: An Ethnic History of Women in Hawaii.* Honolulu: U of Hawaii P, 1977.

Planas, Alvin, and Diana Chow, eds. *Winter Blossoms.* Berkeley: Univ. of California, Asian American Studies Dept., 1978.

Planas, Alvin, et al., eds. *Hanai: An Anthology of Asian American Writings.* Berkeley: Univ. of California, Asian American Studies Dept., 1980.

Reed, Ishmael, and Al Young, eds. *Yardbird Lives!* New York: Grove, 1978.

Wand, David Hsin-Fu, ed. *Asian-American Heritage: An Anthology of Prose and Poetry.* New York: Washington Square, 1974.

Without Ceremony: An Anthology of Work by Asian and Asian American Women. Comp. Asian Women United. Spec. issue of *Ikon* 9. New York: Ikon, 1988. Poems, essays, interviews, photographs, and art.

Yee, Carl, ed. *Dwell among Our People.* Berkeley: Univ. of California, Asian American Studies Dept., 1977.

3. Criticism

Chan, Jeffery Paul, Frank Chin, Lawson Inada, and Shawn Wong. "Resources for Chinese and Japanese American Literary Traditions." *Amerasia* 8 (1981): 19–31.

Kim, Elaine H. *Asian American Literature: An Introduction to the Writings and Their Social Contexts.* Philadelphia: Temple UP, 1982.

Ling, Amy. "Asian American Literature: A Brief Introduction and Selected Bibliography." *ADE Bulletin* 80 (1985): 29–33.

Newman, Katharine. "Hawaiian-American Literature: The Cultivation of Mangoes." *MELUS* 6 (1979): 46–77.

4. Chinese American Literature

Anthologies

Hom, Marlon K. *Songs of Gold Mountain: Cantonese Rhymes from San Francisco Chinatown.* Berkeley: U of California P, 1987. Poetry.

Lai, Him Mark, Genny Lim, and Judy Yung, eds. and trans. *Island: Poetry and History of Chinese Immigrants on Angel Island, 1910-1940.* San Francisco: Hoc Doi, 1980. Poetry.

Primary Works

Berssenbrugge, Mei-Mei. *Fish Souls.* San Francisco: Greenwood, 1972. Poetry.

———. *Heat Bird.* Providence: Burning Deck, 1983. Poetry.

———. *Random Possession.* New York: I. Reed, 1979. Poetry.

———. *Summits Move with the Tide.* Greenfield Center: Greenfield, 1974. Poetry.

Chan, Jeffery Paul. "The Chinese in Haifa." Chin et al., *AIIIEEEEE!* 12-29. Short story.

———. "Jackrabbit." *Yardbird Reader* 3 (1974): 217-38. Short story.

Chang, Diana. *Eye to Eye.* New York: Harper, 1974. Fiction.

———. *The Frontiers of Love.* New York: Random, 1956. Fiction.

———. *The Horizon Is Definitely Speaking.* Port Jefferson: Backstreet Editions, 1982. Poetry.

———. *The Only Game in Town.* New York: Signet, 1963.

———. *A Passion for Life.* New York: Random, 1961. Fiction.

———. *A Perfect Love.* New York: Jove, 1978. Fiction.

———. *A Woman of Thirty.* New York: Random, 1959. Fiction.

Chang, Eileen. *Naked Earth.* Hong Kong: Union, 1956. Fiction.

———. *The Rice Sprout Song.* New York: Scribner's, 1955. Fiction.

———. *The Rouge of the North.* London: Cassell, 1967. Fiction.

Chang, Hsin-hai. *The Fabulous Concubine.* New York: Simon, 1956. Fiction.

Chao, Evelina. *Gates of Grace.* New York: Warner, 1985. Fiction.

Chen, Su Hua Ling. *Ancient Melodies.* Introd. V. Sackville-West, 1953. New York: Universe, 1988.

Chen, Yuan-tsung. *The Dragon's Village.* New York: Pantheon, 1980. Fiction.

Cheng, Nien. *Life and Death in Shanghai.* New York: Grove, 1986. Autobiography.

Chennault, Anna. *The Education of Anna.* New York: Times, 1980. Autobiography.

———. *A Thousand Springs: The Biography of a Marriage.* New York: Eriksson, 1962. Autobiography.

Chia, Cheng Sait. *Turned Clay.* Fredericton, NB: Fiddlehead, 1982. Poetry.

Chiang, Fay. *In the City of Contradictions.* New York: Sunbury, 1979. Poetry.

———. *Miwa's Song.* New York: Sunbury, 1982. Poetry.

Chiang, Monlin. *Tides from the West.* New Haven, Yale UP, 1947. Autobiography.

Chin, Frank. *The Chickencoop Chinaman and the Year of the Dragon.* Seattle: U of Washington P, 1981. Drama.

———. *The Chinaman Pacific and Frisco R.R. Co.* Minneapolis: Coffee House, 1988. Short fiction.

———. "Food for All His Dead." Hsu and Palubinskas, *Asian-American Authors* 48-61. Short story.

Chin, Marilyn. *Dwarf Bamboo.* Greenfield Center: Greenfield, 1987. Poetry.

Ching, Frank. *Ancestors: Nine Hundred Years in the Life of a Chinese Family.* New York: Morrow, 1988. Nonfiction.

Chiu, Tony. *Port Arthur Chicken*. New York: Morrow, 1979. Fiction.

Chu, Louis N. *Eat a Bowl of Tea*. 1961. Seattle: U of Washington P, 1979. Fiction.

Chuang Hua. *Crossings*. 1968. Introd. Amy Ling. Boston: Northeastern UP, 1986. Fiction.

Eaton, Edith [Sui Sin Far]. *Mrs. Spring Fragrance*. Chicago: McClurg, 1912. Short fiction.

Eaton, Winnifred [Onoto Watanna]. *Cattle*. London: Hutchinson, 1924. Fiction.

———. *The Diary of Delia*. New York: Doubleday, 1907. Fiction.

———. *The Heart of Hyacinth*. New York: Harper, 1903. Fiction.

———. *The Honorable Miss Moonlight*. New York: Harper, 1912. Fiction.

———. *A Japanese Nightingale*. New York: Harper, 1901. Fiction.

———. *Love of Azalea*. New York: Dodd, 1904. Fiction.

———. *Me. A Book of Remembrance*. New York: Century, 1915. Autobiography.

———. *Miss Numé of Japan: A Japanese-American Romance*. Chicago: Rand, 1899. Fiction.

———. *Sunny-San*. New York: Doran, 1922. Fiction.

———. *Tama*. New York: Harper, 1910. Fiction.

———. *The Wooing of Wisteria*. New York: Harper, 1902. Fiction.

Han Suyin. [pseud. of Rosalie Chou]. *Birdless Summer*. New York: Putnam, 1968. Autobiography.

———. *The Crippled Tree*. New York: Putnam, 1965. Nonfiction.

———. *Destination Chungking*. 1942. London: Jonathan Cape, 1956; Mayflower, 1969. Fiction.

———. *The Enchantress*. New York: Bantam, 1985. Fiction.

———. *The Four Faces*. New York: Putnam, 1963. Fiction.

———. *A Many-Splendored Thing*. Boston: Little, 1952. Fiction.

———. *The Morning Deluge: Mao Tsetung and the Chinese Revolution, 1893-1954*. Boston: Little, 1972. History and biography.

———. *A Mortal Flower*. New York: Putnam, 1966. Autobiography.

———. *The Mountain Is Young*. New York: Putnam, 1958. Fiction.

———. *My House Has Two Doors*. New York: Putnam, 1980. Autobiography.

———. *Till Morning Comes*. New York: Bantam, 1982. Fiction.

———. *Wind in the Tower: Mao Tsetung and the Chinese Revolution, 1940-1975*. Boston: Little, 1976. History and biography.

Hwang, David Henry. *Broken Promises: Four Plays*. New York: Avon, 1983. Includes *FOB*; *The Dance and the Railroad*; *Family Devotions*; and *The House of Sleeping Beauties*.

———. "M. Butterfly." *American Theatre* July–August 1988: 1–16.

Joe, Jeanne. *Ying-Ying: Pieces of a Childhood*. San Francisco: East/West, 1982. Autobiography.

Kingston, Maxine Hong. *China Men*. New York: Knopf, 1980. Biography, history, and fiction.

———. *Tripmaster Monkey*. New York: Knopf, 1989. Fiction.

———. *The Woman Warrior: Memoirs of a Girlhood among Ghosts*. New York: Knopf, 1976. Autobiography and fiction.

Kuo, Alexander. *New Letters from Hiroshima and Other Poems*. Greenfield Center: Greenfield, 1974.

———. *The Window Tree*. Peterborough: Windy Row, 1971. Poetry.

Kuo, Helena. *I've Come a Long Way*. New York: Appleton, 1942. Autobiography.

———. *Peach Path*. London: Methuen, 1940. Nonfiction.

———. *Westward to Chungking*. New York: Appleton, 1944. Fiction.

Lau, Alan Chong. *Songs for Jadina*. Greenfield Center: Greenfield, 1980. Poetry.

Lee, Chin-yang. *Flower Drum Song*. New York: Farrar, 1957. Fiction.

———. *Lover's Point*. New York: Stratford, 1958. Fiction.

Lee, Virginia. *The House That Tai Ming Built*. New York: Macmillan, 1963. Fiction.

Lem, Carol. *Don't Ask Why*. Los Angeles: Peddler, 1982. Poetry.

Leong, Monfoon. *Number One Son*. San Francisco: East/West, 1975. Short fiction.

Lim, Janet. *Sold for Silver*. Cleveland: World, 1958. Autobiography.

Lim, Shirley Geok-lin. *Crossing the Peninsula*. Kuala Lumpur: Heinemann, 1980. Poetry.

———. *Modern Secrets*. Sydney: Dangaroo, 1989. Poetry.

———. *No Man's Grove*. Dept. of English Lang. and Lit., National Univ. of Singapore, 1985. Poetry.

Lin, Adet, and Anor Lin. *Our Family*. New York: Day, 1939. Autobiography.

Lin, Adet, Anor Lin, and Meimei Lin. *Dawn over Chungking*. New York: Day, 1941. Autobiography.

Lin, Alice. *Grandmother Had No Name*. San Francisco: China, 1988. Autobiography.

Lin, Hazel Ai Chun. *House of Orchids*. New York: Citadel, 1960. Fiction.

———. *The Moon Vow*. New York: Pageant, 1958. Fiction.

———. *The Physicians*. New York: Day, 1951. Fiction.

———. *Rachel Weeping for Her Children, Uncomforted*. Boston: Branden, 1976. Fiction.

———. *Weeping May Tarry*. Boston: Branden, 1980. Autobiography.

Ling, Amy. *Chinamerican Reflections*. Lewiston: Great Raven, 1984. Poetry.

Lin Tai-yi. *The Eavesdropper*. Cleveland: World, 1959. Fiction.

———, trans. *Flowers in the Mirror*. By Li Ju-chen. Berkeley: U of California P, 1965. Fiction.

———. *The Golden Coin*. New York: Day, 1946. Fiction.

———. *Kampoon Street*. Cleveland: World, 1964. Fiction.

———. *The Lilacs Overgrow*. Cleveland: World, 1960. Fiction.

———. *War Tide*. New York: Day, 1943. Fiction.

Lin Yutang. *Chinatown Family*. New York: Day, 1948. Fiction.

———. *Moment in Peking*. New York: Day, 1939. Fiction.

Liu, Stephen. *Dream Journeys to China*. Beijing: New World, 1982. Poetry.

Lord, Bette Bao. *Eighth Moon*. New York: Harper, 1964. Biography of her sister, Sansen.

———. *Spring Moon*. New York: Harper, 1981. Fiction.

Lowe, Pardee. *Father and Glorious Descendant*. Boston: Little, 1943. Autobiography.

McCunn, Ruthanne Lum. *Sole Survivor*. San Francisco: Design Enterprises, 1985. Fictionalized biography of Poon Lim who holds Guinness World Record for survival at sea (133 days).

———. *Thousand Pieces of Gold*. San Francisco: Design Enterprises, 1981. Fictionalized biography of Lalu Nathoy, pioneer Chinese American woman.

Phou, Lee Yan. *When I Was a Boy in China*. Boston: Lothrop, 1887. Autobiography.

Sledge, Linda Ching. *Empire of Heaven*. New York: Bantam, 1990. Fiction.

Sze, Arthur. *Dazzled*. Pt. Reyes Station: Floating Island, 1982. Poetry.

———. *Two Ravens*. Santa Fe: Tooth of Time, 1976. Poetry.

———. *The Willow Wind*. Santa Fe: Tooth of Time, 1981. Poetry.

Sze, Mai-Mai. *China*. Cleveland: Western Reserve UP, 1944. Nonfiction.

———. *Echo of a Cry: A Story Which Began in China*. New York: Harcourt, 1945. Autobiography.

———. *Silent Children*. New York: Harcourt, 1948. Fiction.

Telemaque, Eleanor Wong. *It's Crazy to Stay Chinese in Minnesota*. New York: Nelson, 1978. Fiction.

Tsui, Kitty. *Words of a Woman Who Breathes Fire: Poetry and Prose*. San Francisco: Spinster's, 1983. Poetry.

Wang, David Rafael. *The Goblet Moon*. Lunenburg: Stinehaur, 1955. Poetry.

———. *The Intercourse*. Greenfield Center: Greenfield, 1974. Poetry.

———. *Rivers on Fire*. Dunkirk: Basilisk, 1974–75. Poetry.

Wei, Katherine, and Terry Quinn. *Second Daughter*. Boston: Little, 1984. Autobiography.

Wing, Yung. *My Life in China and America*. New York: Holt, 1909. Autobiography.

Wong, Jade Snow. *Fifth Chinese Daughter*. New York: Harper, 1945. Autobiography.

———. *No Chinese Stranger*. New York: Harper, 1975. Autobiography.

Wong, May. *Reports*. New York: Harcourt, 1970. Poetry.

————. *Superstitions*. New York: Harcourt, 1978. Poetry.

Wong, Nellie. *The Death of the Long Steam Lady*. Los Angeles: West End, 1986. Poetry.

————. *Dreams in Harrison Railroad Park*. Berkeley: Kelsey St., 1977. Poetry.

Wong, Shawn. *Homebase*. New York: I. Reed, 1979. Fiction.

Wong, Su-ling, and Earl Herbert Cressy. *Daughter of Confucius*. New York: Farrar, 1952. Autobiography.

Wu, K. C. *The Lane of Eternal Stability*. New York: Crown, 1962. Fiction.

Yau, John. *Broken Off by the Music*. Providence: Burning Deck, 1981. Poetry.

————. *Corpse and Mirror*. New York: Holt, 1983. Poetry.

————. *Sometimes*. New York: Sheep Meadow, 1979.

Yee, Chiang. *A Chinese Childhood*. New York: Day, 1952. Autobiography.

————. *The Silent Traveller in Boston*. New York: Norton, 1959. Nonfiction, with paintings.

————. *The Silent Traveller in New York*. New York: Norton, 1950. Nonfiction, with paintings.

————. *The Silent Traveller in San Francisco*. New York: Norton, 1964. Nonfiction, with paintings.

Yeh, Chun-chan. *Mountain Village*. New York: Putnam, 1947. Fiction.

Yen, Liang. *Daughter of the Khans*. New York: Norton, 1955. Autobiography.

Yun, Tan [Adet Lin]. *Flame from the Rock*. New York: Day, 1943. Fiction.

Secondary Works

General

Hom, Marlon K., trans. "Chinatown Literature during the Last Ten Years (1939–49)." By Wenquan. *Amerasia* 9 (1982): 75–100.

Ling, Amy. *Between Worlds: Women Writers of Chinese Ancestry*. New York: Pergamon, 1990. A history and critical study of prose works written in English by women of Chinese ancestry and published in the United States. Among the writers discussed are Eileen Chang, Edith and Winnifred Eaton, Maxine Hong Kingston, Helena Kuo, Lin Tai-yi, and Amy Tan.

————. "A Perspective on Chinamerican Literature." *MELUS* 8.2 (1981): 76–81.

————. "A Rumble in the Silence: *Crossings* by Chuang Hua." *MELUS* 9.3 (1982): 29–37.

————. "Writer in the Hyphenated Condition: Diana Chang." *MELUS* 7.4 (1980): 69–83.

McDonald, Dorothy Ritsuko. "An Introduction to Frank Chin's *The Chickencoop Chinaman* and *The Year of the Dragon*." *Three American Literatures: Essays in Chicano, Native American, and Asian-American Literature for Teachers of American Literature*. Ed. Houston A. Baker, Jr. New York: MLA, 1982. 229–53.

Works on Individual Authors

Eaton, Edith and Winnifred

Ling, Amy. "Edith Eaton: Pioneer Chinamerican Writer and Feminist." *American Literary Realism* 16 (1983): 287–98.

————. "Revelation and Mask: Autobiographies of the Eaton Sisters." *Multi-Cultural American Autobiography*. Ed. James R. Payne. Spec. issue of *Auto/Biography Studies* 3.2 (1987): 46–52.

————. "Winnifred Eaton: Ethnic Chameleon and Popular Success." *MELUS* 11.3 (1984): 5–15.

————. "Writers with a Cause: Sui Sin Far and Han Suyin." *Women's Studies International Forum* 9.4 (1986): 411–19.

Kingston, Maxine Hong

Blinde, Patricia Lin. "Icicle in the Desert: Form and Perspective in the Works of Two Chinese-American Women Writers." *MELUS* 6.3 (1979): 51–71. Comparative analysis of work of Jade Snow Wong and Kingston.

Cheung, King-kok. "'Don't Tell': Imposed Silences in *The Color Purple* and *The Woman Warrior*." *PMLA* 103 (1988): 162–74.

Holaday, Woon-Ping Chin. "From Ezra Pound and Maxine Hong Kingston: Expressions of Chinese Thought." *MELUS* 5.2 (1978): 15–24.

Homsher, Deborah. "*The Woman Warrior*, by Maxine Hong Kingston: A Bridging of Autobiography and Fiction." *Iowa Review* 10.4 (1979): 93–98.

Juhasz, Suzanne. "Towards a Theory of Form in Feminist Autobiography: Kate Millet's *Flying* and *Sita*; Maxine Hong Kingston's *The Woman Warrior*." *International Journal of Women's Studies* 2 (1979): 62–75.

Ling, Amy. "Thematic Threads in Maxine Hong Kingston's *The Woman Warrior*." *Tamkang Review* 14 (1983–84): 155–64.

Neubauer, Carol E. "Developing Ties to the Past: Photography and Other Sources of Information in Maxine Hong Kingston's *China Men*." *MELUS* 10.4 (1983): 17–36.

Sledge, Linda Ching. "Maxine Hong Kingston's *China Men*: The Family Historian as Epic Poet." *MELUS* 7.4 (1980): 3–22.

Smith, Sidonie. "Maxine Hong Kingston's *Woman Warrior*: Filiality and Woman's Autobiographical Storytelling." Smith, *A Poetics of Women's Autobiography: Marginality and the Fictions of Self-Representation*. Bloomington: Indiana UP, 1987. 150–73.

5. Japanese American Literature

Anthologies

Okutsu, Jim, ed. *Fusion '83: A Japanese American Anthology*. San Francisco: San Francisco State UP, 1984.

————. *Fusion Too: A Japanese American Anthology*. San Francisco: San Francisco State UP, 1985.

Mirikitani, Janice, ed. *Ayumi: The Japanese American Anthology*. San Francisco: Japanese American Anthology Committee, 1979.

Primary Works

Ai. *Cruelty*. Boston: Houghton, 1973. Poetry.

————. *Killing Floor*. Boston: Houghton, 1979. Poetry.

Fujita, June. *Poems in Exile*. Chicago: Covic, c. 1923. Poetry.

Harada, Margaret N. *The Sun Shines on the Immigrant*. New York: n.p., 1960. Autobiography.

Hartmann, Sadakichi. *Buddha, Confucius, Christ: The Prophetic Plays*. Ed. Harry M. Lawton and George Knox. New York: Herder, c. 1971.

————. *Drifting Flowers of the Sea and Other Poems to Elizabeth Walsh*. N.p.: n.p., 1904.

————. *My Rubaiyat*. St. Louis: Mangan, 1913. Poetry.

————. *Tanka and Haikai: Fourteen Japanese Rhythms.* New York: Gruno, 1915.

————. *White Chrysanthemums, Literary Fragments and Pronouncements.* New York: Herder, 1971. Poetry.

Hatsumi, Reiko. *Rain and the Feast of the Stars.* Boston: Houghton, 1959. Autobiography.

Hongo, Garrett K. *Yellow Light.* Middletown: Wesleyan UP, 1982. Poetry.

————. *The River of Heaven.* New York: Knopf, 1988. Poetry.

Houston, Jeanne Wakatsuki. *Beyond Manzanar: View of Asian-American Womanhood.* Santa Barbara: Capra, 1985. Nonfiction, and two chapters from a forthcoming novel.

Houston, Jeanne Wakatsuki, and James D. Houston. *Farewell to Manzanar.* San Francisco: San Francisco Book–Houghton, 1973. Autobiography.

Ikeda, Patricia. *House of Wood, House of Salt.* Cleveland: Cleveland State U Poetry Center, 1978. Poetry.

Inada, Lawson F. *Before the War: Poems as They Happened.* New York: Morrow, 1971.

Inouye, Daniel K. *Journey to Washington.* Englewood Cliffs: Prentice, 1967. Autobiography.

Ishimoto, Shizue. *Facing Two Ways: The Story of My Life.* New York: Farrar, 1935. Autobiography.

Itani, Frances. *No Other Lodgings.* Fredericton, NB: Fiddlehead, 1978. Poetry.

Kaneko, Hizakazu. *Manjiro, the Man Who Discovered America.* Boston: Houghton, 1956. Biography.

Kikuchi, Charles. *The Kikuchi Diary: Chronicle from an American Concentration Camp.* Urbana: U of Illinois P, 1973. Autobiography.

Kikumura, Akemi. *Through Harsh Winters: The Life of a Japanese Immigrant Woman.* Novato: Chandler, 1981. Biography.

Kogawa, Joy. *A Choice of Dreams.* Toronto: McClelland, 1974. Canadian Japanese poetry.

————. *Jericho Road.* Toronto: McClelland, 1977. Canadian Japanese poetry.

————. *Obasan.* 1981. New York: Penguin, 1983. Canadian Japanese fiction.

Kudaka, Geraldine. *Numerous Avalanches at the Point of Intersection.* Greenfield: Greenfield, 1979. Poetry.

Matsui, Haru [Ayako Ishigaki]. *Restless Wave.* New York: Modern Age, 1940. Autobiography.

Michina, Sumie Seo. *My Narrow Isle.* New York: Day, 1941. Autobiography.

Mirikatani, Janice. *Awake in the River.* San Francisco: Isthmus, 1978. Poetry.

Miyamoto, Kazuo. *Hawaii, End of the Rainbow.* Rutland: Tuttle, 1964. Fiction.

Mori, Toshio. *The Chauvinist and Other Stories.* Los Angeles: Asian-American Studies Center, Univ. of California, 1979.

————. *Yokohama, California.* Caldwell: Caxton, 1949. Introd. Lawson Fusao Inada. Seattle: U of Washington P, 1985. Short fiction.

Murayama, Milton. *All I Asking for Is My Body.* San Francisco: Supa, 1975. Fiction.

Noda, Barbara. *Strawberries.* San Francisco: Shameless Hussy, 1979. Poetry.

Noguchi, Yone. *From the Eastern Sea.* New York: Kennerley, 1910. Poetry.

————. *The Story of Yone Noguchi Told by Himself.* London: Chatto, 1914.

Oka, Francis Naohiko. *Poems: Memorial Edition.* San Francisco: City Lights, 1970.

Okada, John. *No-No Boy.* Rutland: Tuttle, 1957. Seattle: U of Washington P, 1979. Fiction.

Okimoto, Daniel. *American in Disguise.* New York: Walker, 1971. Autobiography.

Okubo, Mine. *Citizen 13660.* New York: Columbia UP, 1946. Drawings of camp life, with captions.

Ota, Shelley Ayame Nishimura. *Upon Their Shoulders: A Novel.* New York: Exposition, 1951. Fiction.

Saiki, Patsy Sumi. *Sachi, A Daughter of Hawaii.* Honolulu: Kisaku, 1977. Autobiography.

Shirota, Jon. *Lucky Come Hawaii.* New York: Bantam, 1965. Fiction.

————. *Pineapple White.* Los Angeles: Ohara, 1972. Fiction.

Sone, Monica. *Nisei Daughter*. Boston: Little, 1953. Seattle: U of Washington P, 1979. Autobiography.

Sugimoto, Etsu Inaki. *A Daughter of the Narikin*. New York: Doubleday, 1932. Fiction.

——. *A Daughter of the Nohfu*. New York: Doubleday, 1935. Fiction.

——. *A Daughter of the Samurai*. New York: Doubleday, 1925. Fiction.

——. *Grandmother O Kyo*. New York: Doubleday, 1940. Fiction.

Takashima, Shizuyu. *A Child in Prison Camp*. New York: Morrow, 1974. Fiction.

Tamagawa, Kathleen. *Holy Prayers in a Horse's Ear*. New York: Long & Smith, 1932. Autobiography.

Tanaka, Ronald. *The Shino Suite: Sansei Poetry, Opus 2*. Greenfield Center: Greenfield, 1981.

Tasaki, Hanama. *Long the Imperial Way*. 1949. Westport: Greenwood, 1970. Fiction.

Uchida, Yoshiko. *Desert Exile: The Uprooting of a Japanese American Family*. Seattle: U of Washington P, 1982. Autobiography.

Yamada, Mitsuye. *Camp Notes*. Lorenzo: Shameless Hussy, 1976. Poetry.

——. *Desert Run*. Latham: Women of Color, 1989. Poetry.

Yamamoto, Hisaye. *Seventeen Syllables*. Introd. King-Kok Cheung. Latham: Kitchen Table–Women of Color, 1989. Short stories.

Yoshida, Jim, and Bill Hosokawa. *The Two Worlds of Jim Yoshida*. New York: Morrow, 1972. Autobiography.

6. Korean American Literature

Primary Works

Cha, Theresa Hak Kyung. *Dictée*. New York: Tanam, 1982. Experimental poetry, prose.

Kang, Younghill. *East Goes West: The Making of an Oriental Yankee*. New York: Scribner's, 1937. Autobiography.

——. *The Grass Roof*. New York: Scribner's, 1931. Autobiography.

——. *The Happy Grove*. New York: Scribner's, 1933. Autobiography.

Kim, Richard. *The Innocent*. Boston: Houghton, 1968. Fiction.

——. *Lost Names: Scenes from a Korean Boyhood*. New York: Praeger, 1970. Short fiction.

——. *The Martyred*. New York: Braziller, 1964. Fiction.

Kim, Ronyoung. *Clay Walls*. New York: Permanent, 1986. Fiction.

Kim, Yong Ik. *Blue in the Seed*. Boston: Little, 1964. Fiction.

——. *The Diving Gourd*. New York: Knopf, 1962. Fiction.

——. *The Happy Days*. Boston: Little, 1960. Fiction.

——. *The Shoes from Yan San Valley*. New York: Doubleday, 1970. Short fiction.

New, Il-Han. *When I Was a Boy in Korea*. Boston: Lothrop, 1928. Autobiography.

Pahk, Induk. *September Monkey*. New York: Harper, 1954. Fiction.

Pak, Ty. *Guilt Payment*. Honolulu: Bamboo Ridge, 1983. Fiction.

Song, Cathy. *Picture Bride*. New Haven: Yale UP, 1983. Poetry.

7. Philippine American Literature

Primary Works

Alvarez, Emigdio Enrique. *The Devil Flower*. New York: Hill, 1959. Fiction.

Bulosan, Carlos. *America Is in the Heart*. 1943. Seattle: U of Washington P, 1973. Autobiography.

———. *The Laughter of My Father*. New York: Harcourt, 1944. Short fiction.

———. *The Voice of Bataan*. New York: Coward, McCann, 1943. Short fiction.

Carunungan, Celso Al. *Like a Big Brave Man: A Novel*. New York: Farrar, 1960. Fiction.

Chock, Eric. *Ten Thousand Wishes*. Honolulu: Bamboo Ridge, 1978. Poetry.

Francia, Luis. *Her Beauty Likes Me Well*. New York: Petrarch, 1979. Poetry.

Gonzalez, Nestor Vicente M. *The Bamboo Dancers*. Denver: Swallow, 1964. Fiction.

———. *Children of the Ash-Covered Loam and Other Stories*. Manila: Benipayo, 1954.

———. *Look, Stranger, on This Island Now*. Manila: Benipayo, 1963. Short fiction.

———. *Seven Hills Away*. Denver: Swallow, 1947. Short fiction.

Hagedorn, Jessica Tarahata. *Dangerous Music*. San Francisco: Momo's, 1975. Poetry.

———. *Petfood and Tropical Apparitions*. San Francisco: Momo's, 1981. Fiction.

Javellana, Steven. *Without Seeing the Dawn*. Boston: Little, 1947. Fiction.

Santos, Bienvenido N. *The Man Who (Thought He) Looked like Robert Taylor*. Quezon City: New Day, 1983. Fiction.

———. *Scent of Apples*. Seattle: U of Washington P, 1979. Short fiction.

———. *What the Hell for You Left Your Heart in San Francisco*. Quezon City: New Day, 1987. Fiction.

Villa, Jose Garcia. *Appassionata: Poems in Praise of Love*. New York: King, 1979.

———. *Footnote to Youth: Tales of the Philippines and Others*. New York: Scribner's, 1933.

———. *Have Come, Am Here*. New York: Viking, 1942. Poetry.

———. *Seven Poems*. Cambridge: Wake, 1948.

———. *Volume Two*. New York: New Directions, 1949. Poetry.

8. Southeast Asian American Literature

Primary Works

Haing Ngor. *A Cambodian Odyssey*. With Roger Warner. New York: Macmillan, 1987. Autobiography.

Larson, Wendy, and Tran Thi Nga. *Shallow Graves: Two Women and Viet Nam*. New York: Random, 1986. Poetry.

Law-Yone, Wendy. *The Coffin Tree*. New York: Knopf, 1983. Burmese fiction.

Mukherjee, Bharati. *Darkness*. New York: Penguin, 1985. East Indian American Short Fiction.

———. *The Tiger's Daughter*. Boston: Houghton, 1971. Fiction.

Tran Van Dinh. *Blue Dragon, White Tiger: A Tet Story*. Philadelphia: Tri Am, 1983. Vietnamese fiction.

Chicano Literature

Compiled by Teresa McKenna

1. Bibliographies and Aids to Research

Eger, Ernestina N., comp. *A Bibliography of Criticism of Contemporary Chicano Literature*. Monograph 5. Berkeley: Chicano Studies Library, 1982. A comprehensive listing of references in Chicano literature and literary criticism. The subject areas analyzed include collections, bibliography, Chicanas, linguistics, poetry, theater, prose fiction, anthologies, and reviews.

————, comp. "A Selected Bibliography of Chicano Criticism." Jiménez, *The Identification and Analysis of Chicano Literature* 389–403. A compilation of references on texts useful for an introduction to the literature, covering bibliography, la Chicana, criticism, poetry, fiction, and theater.

Foster, Virginia Ramos, comp. "Literature." *Sourcebook of Hispanic Culture in the United States.* Ed. David William Foster. Chicago: American Library Assn., 1982. 86–111. A brief review of literature by Mexican American authors.

Heisley, Michael, comp. *An Annotated Bibliography of Chicano Folklife from the Southwestern United States.* Los Angeles: Center for the Study of Comparative Folklore and Mythology. U of California P, 1977. A useful guide that covers bibliographies, narrative traditions, drama, theater, games, art, architecture, technology, customs, rituals and healing practices, among others.

Keller, Gary, ed. *Chicano Cinema: Research, Reviews and Resources.* New York: Bilingual, 1985. Includes research and criticism as well as reviews of films. Accompanied by a directory of Chicano/Latino films and distributors, prepared by Héctor Garza.

Lomelí, Francisco A., and Donaldo W. Urioste, comps. *Chicano Perspectives in Literature: A Critical and Annotated Bibliography.* Albuquerque: Pajarito, 1976. One of the first comprehensive, annotated bibliographies in the field. Noted for its inclusion of little-known, small-press works.

Martínez, Julio A., and Francisco A. Lomelí. *Chicano Literature: A Reference Guide.* Westport: Greenwood, 1985. Alphabetically arranged short biographical-critical articles that contain bibliographies, chronology of Chicano literature, and brief general bibliography.

Najera-Ramirez, Olga. "Greater Mexican Folklore in the U.S.: An Annotated Bibliography." *Ethnic Affairs* 1 (1987): 63–115. A badly needed, updated, annotated bibliography of scholarly work since the 1977 publication of the Heisley bibliography above.

Trujillo, Roberto G., and Andrés Rodríguez, comps. *Literatura Chicana: Creative and Critical Writings through 1984*. Stanford: Stanford Univ. Libraries, 1985. Comprehensive list of major texts by genre. Includes separate sections on oral tradition, unpublished dissertations, literary periodicals, and video and sound recordings.

2. Anthologies and Collections

General

Adame, Leonard, Luis Omar Salinas, Gary Soto, and Ernesto Trejo. *Entrance: Four Chicano Poets*. New York: Greenfield, 1975. This chapbook contains some of the early poetry of four productive Chicano poets.

Aguilar, Ricardo, Armando Armegol, and Oscar U. Somoza. *Palabra nueva: Cuentos chicanos*. El Paso: Texas Western, U of Texas P, 1984. Previously unpublished short stories written in Spanish by such authors as Rolando Hinojosa, Lucha Corpi, Salvador Rodríguez del Pino, Miguel Méndez, and Rosaura Sánchez.

Alarcón, Norma, ed. *Third Woman: Texas and More*. Spec. issue of *Third Woman* 3.1–2. Bloomington: Third Woman, 1986. Includes poetry, narrative, essays, interviews, and reviews as well as selections from the visual arts.

Alarcón, Norma, Ana Castillo, and Cherríe Moraga, eds. *Third Woman: The Sexuality of Latinas*. Vol. 4. Berkeley: Third Woman Press, 1989. Includes poetry, prose, drama, and critical reviews on literature and the arts, as well as a bibliography.

Alurista, et al., eds. *Festival de Flor y Canto: An Anthology of Chicano Literature*. Los Angeles: U of Southern California P, 1976. Commemorates the first annual Festival de Flor y Canto, held in 1973 at the University of Southern California. Containing much of the early work of contemporary Chicano writers, the collection includes selections from a variety of genres.

———. *Literatura fronteriza: Antología del primer festival San Diego–Tijuana, mayo 1981*. San Diego: Maíze, 1982. Poetry and short fiction commemorating the first literary festival on border literature held in May 1981.

Anaya, Rudolfo A., ed. *Voces: An Anthology of New Mexico Writers*. Albuquerque: El Norte, 1987.

Anaya, Rudolfo A., and José Griego y Maestas, eds. *Cuentos: Tales from the Hispanic Southwest*. Santa Fe: Museum of New Mexico, 1980. Bilingual collection of oral tales, from stories originally collected by Juan B. Rael and adapted in Spanish by Griego y Maestas.

Anaya, Rudolfo A., and Antonio Márquez, eds. *Cuentos chicanos*. Spec. issue of *New America* 4.1. Albuquerque: New America, 1980.

Anzaldúa, Gloria. *Borderlands / La Frontera: The New Mextiza*. San Francisco: Spinsters–Aunt Lute, 1987. Poetry and prose.

Binder, Wolfgang, ed. *Contemporary Chicano Poetry*. Erlangen: Palm & Enke, 1986.

Cárdenas de Dwyer, Carlota, ed. *Chicano Voices*. Boston: Houghton, 1975.

Carrillo, Leonardo, Antonio Martínez, Carol Molina, and Marie Wood, eds. *Canto al Pueblo: An Anthology of Experiences*. San Antonio: Penca, 1978. Primarily a collection of poetry, with some short fiction as well. Includes early works of such writers as Lorna Dee Cervantes, Evangelina Vigil, and Carmen Tafolla.

Castañeda Shular, Antonia, Tomás Ybarra-Frausto, and Joseph Sommers, eds. *Literatura Chicana texto y contexto / Chicano Literature Text and Context*. Englewood Cliffs: Prentice, 1972. One of the first anthologies of Chicano literature that includes a variety of genres. Each section is preceded by contextual statements and/or short historical sketches. The international perspective of the anthology is of particular interest and has rarely been duplicated.

García, Nestor, ed. *Recuerdos de los viejitos / Tales of the Rio Puerco*. Albuquerque: U of New Mexico P, 1987.

Garza, Robert J., ed. *Contemporary Chicano Theatre*. Notre Dame: U of Notre Dame P, 1976. Eight plays.

Gomez, Alma, Cherrie Moraga, and Mariana Romo-Cardona. *Cuentos: Stories by Latinas*. New York: Kitchen Table–Women of Color, 1983.

Harth, Dorothy E., and Lewis M. Baldwin, eds. *Voices of Aztlán: Chicano Literature of Today*. New York: NAL, 1974.

Herrera-Sobek, María, and Helena María Viramontes, eds. *Chicana Creativity and Criticism: Charting New Frontiers in American Literature*. Houston: Arte Público, 1988. Poetry, short stories, drama, and literary criticism by and about Chicana feminist writers.

Huerta, Jorge A., ed. *The Necessary Anthology: Plays of the Chicano Experience*. Houston: Arte Público, 1989. Includes works by Luis Valdez, Milcha Sánchez-Scott, Arthur Girón, Teatro de la Esperanza, Servo Pérez, and others.

————, ed. *El Teatro de la Esperanza: An Anthology of Chicano Drama*. Goleta: Teatro de la Esperanza, 1973. Plays written and performed by this Southern California theater troupe.

Ortego, Philip D., ed. *We Are Chicanos: An Anthology of Mexican American Literature*. New York: Washington Square, 1973.

Paredes, Américo, and Raymund A. Paredes, eds. *Mexican American Authors*. Boston: Houghton, 1972. Primarily an anthology of short fiction and some poetry, the volume also includes folklore. Questions follow each selection to assist students in understanding the literature.

Rodríguez, Armando Rafael, ed. *The Gypsy Wagon: Un sancocho de cuentos sobre la experiencia chicana*. Los Angeles: Aztlán, 1974. Short fiction by a variety of writers, including Yolanda García, David González, Irene McKenna, Francisco Martínez, René Martínez, Roberto Sifuentes, Antonio Salazar, and Mario Suárez. Illustrated by Carmen Lomás Garza.

Romano-V., Octavio, and Herminio Rios-C., eds. *El espejo / The Mirror: Selected Mexican American Literature*. Berkeley: Quinto Sol, 1969.

Simmen, Edward, ed. *The Chicano: From Caricature to Self-Portrait*. New York: NAL, 1971. A collection of short fiction emphasizing the portrayal of Mexican Americans in American literature. Mexican Americans' view of themselves is the least emphasized of the sections.

Valdez, Luis, and El Teatro Compesino. *Actos*. Fresno: Cucaracha, 1971. Seminal collection of Chicano drama containing plays written and performed by El Teatro Compesino Collective under Valdez's direction.

Valdez, Luis, and Stan Steiner, eds. *Aztlán: An Anthology of Mexican American Literature*. New York: Knopf, 1972.

Vento, Arnold C., Alurista, and José Flores Peregrino, eds. *Festival de Flor y Canto II: An Anthology of Chicano Literature*. Albuquerque: Pajarito, 1976. Commemorates the second annual Festival de Flor y Canto, held in Austin, Texas, on 12–16 March 1975. Includes poetry, short fiction, and literary criticism.

Vigil, Evangelina, ed. *Woman of Her Word: Hispanic Women Write*. Houston: Arte Público, 1983. Poetry, prose, literary criticism, and art.

Oral Literature

Hernández, Guillermo. *Canciones de la Raza: Songs of the Chicano Experience*. Berkeley: El Fuego de Aztlán, 1978. Bilingual texts of songs as well as music for some songs.

Miller, Elaine K. *Mexican Folk Narrative from the Los Angeles Area*. Austin: U of Texas P, 1973. Derived primarily from information provided by women, this important work illustrates the presence of oral literature in a major metropolitan area in the 1960s. It contains short introductions for each generic section and is well annotated.

Paredes, Américo. *A Texas-Mexican Cancionero: Folksongs of the Lower Border*. Urbana: U of Illinois P, 1976. A compilation, including text and musical score, of major folk songs and ballads of the Texas-Mexican border. Paredes's commentary about the evolution of the form out of the *romance* is particularly important.

Sifuentes, Roberto, ed. *Antología del saber popular*. Los Angeles: Aztlán, 1971. Folklore from the United States and Mexico, including folktales, jests and anecdotes, legends, beliefs, popular medicine, prayers, verses, children's games, lullabies, riddles, proverbs, and customs. Prepared by Stanley L. Robe.

3. Primary Works

Acosta, Oscar Zeta. *The Autobiography of a Brown Buffalo*. San Francisco: Straight Arrow, 1972. Fiction.

———. *The Revolt of the Cockroach People*. San Francisco: Straight Arrow, 1973. Fiction.

Alurista. *Floricanto en Aztlán*. Los Angeles: Chicano Studies Center, 1971. Poetry.

———. *Nationchild Plumaroja: Poems 1969–1972*. San Diego: Toltecas en Aztlán Centro Cultural de la Raza, 1972.

———. *Spik in Glyph?* Houston: Arte Público, 1981. Poetry.

———. *Timespace Huracán*. Albuquerque: Pajarito, 1976. Poetry.

Alvarado, Arturo Roca. *Crónica de Aztlán / A Migrant's Tale*. Berkeley: Quinto Sol, 1977. Autobiography.

Anaya, Rudolfo A. *The Adventures of Juan Chicaspatas*. Houston: Arte Público, 1985. Poetry.

———. *Bless Me, Ultima*. Berkeley: Quinto Sol, 1972. Fiction.

———. *Heart of Aztlán*. Berkeley: Justa, 1976. Fiction.

———. *Lord of the Dawn: The Legend of Quetzalcoatl*. Albuquerque: U of New Mexico P, 1987. Fiction.

———. *The Silence of the Llano: Short Stories*. Berkeley: Tonatiuh–Quinto Sol, 1982.

———. *Tortuga*. Berkeley: Justa, 1979. Fiction.

Arias, Ron. *The Road to Tamazunchale*. Reno: West Coast Poetry Review, 1975, 1978. Ypsilanti: Bilingual, 1987. Fiction.

Baca, Jimmy Santiago. *Immigrants in Our Own Land*. Baton Rouge: Louisiana State UP, 1979. Poetry.

———. *Swords of Darkness*. Chicano Chapbook 9. Ed. Gary Soto. San Jose: Mango, 1981. Poetry.

Barrio, Raymond. *The Plum Plum Pickers*. Sunnyvale: Ventura, 1969, 1977. Fiction.

Brawley, Ernest. *The Alamo Tree*. New York: Simon, 1984. Fiction.

———. *Selena*. New York: Atheneum, 1979. Fiction.

Brito, Aristeo. *El diablo en Texas*. Tucson: Editorial Peregrinos, 1976. Fiction.

Bruce-Novoa, Juan D. *Inocencia perversa / Perverse Innocence*. Phoenix: Baleen, 1977. Poetry.

Candelaria, Nash. *Inheritance of Strangers*. Binghamton: Bilingual, 1986. Fiction.

———. *Memories of the Alhambra*. Palo Alto: Cibola, 1977. Fiction.

———. *Not by the Sword*. Ypsilanti: Bilingual, 1982. Fiction.

Castillo, Ana. *The Mixquiahuala Letters*. Binghamton: Bilingual, 1986. Fiction.

———. *My Father Was a Toltec*. Albuquerque: West End, 1988. Poetry.

———. *Otro canto*. Chicago: Alternativa, 1975, 1978. Poetry.

———. *Women Are Not Roses*. Houston: Arte Público, 1984. Poetry.

Cervantes, Lorna Dee. *Emplumada*. Poetry Ser. Pittsburgh: U of Pittsburgh P, 1981.

Chacón, Eusebio. *El hijo de la tempestad: Tras la tormenta la calma.* Santa Fe: Tipografía de *El boletín popular*, 1892. Fiction.

Chávez, Denise. *The Last of the Menu Girls.* Houston: Arte Público, 1986. Fiction.

Chávez, Fray Angélico. *Clothed with the Sun.* Santa Fe: Winter's Editions, 1939. Poetry.

———. *La Conquistadora: The Autobiography of an Ancient Statue.* Paterson: St. Anthony Guild, 1954. Fiction.

———. *The Short Stories of Fray Angélico Chávez.* Ed. Genaro M. Padilla. Albuquerque: U of New Mexico P, 1987.

Chávez, Mario. *When It Rains in Cloves.* Chicano Chapbook 5. Ed. Gary Soto. San Jose: Mango, n.d.

Cisneros, Sandra. *Bad Boys.* Chicano Chapbook 8. Ed. Gary Soto. San Jose: Mango, 1980.

———. *The House on Mango Street.* Houston: Arte Público, 1983. Short fiction.

———. *My Wicked Wicked Ways.* Bloomington: Third Woman, 1986. Poetry.

Corpi, Lucha. *Delia's Song.* Houston: Arte Público, 1988. Fiction.

———. *Palabras de mediodía: Noon Words.* Trans. Catherine Rodríguez-Nieto. Berkeley: El Fuego de Aztlán, 1980. Poetry.

Cota-Cárdenas, Margarita. *Noches despertando inconciencias.* Tucson: Scorpion, 1977. Poetry.

de Hoyos, Angela. *Arise, Chicano! and Other Poems.* Trans. Mireya Robles. San Antonio: M&A Editions, 1975. Poetry written in English and accompanied by a Spanish translation.

———. *Woman, Woman.* Introd. Rolando Hinojosa. Houston: Arte Público, 1985.

De León, Nephtalí. *5 Plays.* Denver: Totinem, 1972. Drama.

Delgado, Abelardo. *Chicano: 25 Pieces of a Chicano Mind.* Denver: Barrio, 1969. Poetry.

———. *Letters to Louise.* Spec. issue of *Grito del Sol.* Berkeley: Tonatiuh–Quinto Sol, 1979. Fiction.

Elizondo, Sergio. *Muerte en una estrella.* México: Tinta Negra, 1984. Fiction.

———. *Perros y antiperros.* Trans. Gustavo Segade. Berkeley: Quinto Sol, 1972. Poetry. Bilingual edition.

Espinosa, Aurelio Macedonio. *Conchita Argüello: Historia y novela californiana.* New York: Macmillan, 1938. Fiction.

Galarza, Ernesto. *Barrio Boy: The Story of a Boy's Acculturation.* Notre Dame: U of Notre Dame P, 1971. Fictionalized autobiography.

García, Lionel G. *Leaving Home.* Houston: Arte Público, 1985. Fiction.

———. *A Shroud in the Family.* Houston: Arte Público, 1987. Fiction.

García, Richard. *Selected Poetry.* Berkeley: Quinto Sol, 1973.

Gómez-Quiñones, Juan. *5th and Grande Vista: Poems 1960–1973.* New York: Colección Mensaje, 1974.

Gonzales, Laurence. *El vago.* New York: Atheneum, 1983. Fiction.

González, César A. *Unwinding the Silence.* La Jolla: Lalo, 1987. Poetry.

González, Genaro. *Rainbow's End.* Houston: Arte Público, 1988. Fiction.

González, Ray. *From These Restless Roots.* Houston: Arte Público, 1986. Poetry.

Herrera, Juan Felipe. *Exiles of Desire.* 1983. Houston: Arte Público, 1985. Poetry.

———. *Rebozos of Love / We Have Woven / Sudor de Pueblos / On Our Backs.* San Diego: Toltecas en Aztlán, 1974. Poetry.

Hinojosa, Rolando. *Claros varones de Belken / Fair Gentlemen of Belken.* Tempe: Bilingual, 1986. Fiction.

———. *Dear Rafe.* Houston: Arte Público, 1985. Hinojosa's translation of his *Mi querido Rafa.*

———. *Estampas del valle y otras obras: Sketches of the Valley and Other Works.* Berkeley: Quinto Sol, 1973; Justa, 1977, 1980. Fiction.

———. *Generaciones y semblanzas.* Trans. Rosaura Sánchez. Berkeley: Justa, 1977. Fiction.

———. *Klail City.* Trans. Hinojosa. Houston: Arte Público, 1987. Fiction. Hinojosa's translation of his *Klail City y sus alrededores.*

————. *Klail City y sus alrededores.* Havana: Casa de las Américas, 1976. Fiction.

————. *Korean Love Songs.* Berkeley: Justa, 1978, 1980. Poetry.

————. *Mi querido Rafa.* Houston: Arte Público, 1981. Fiction.

————. *Partners in Crime.* Houston: Arte Público, 1985. Fiction.

————. *Rites and Witnesses.* Houston: Arte Público, 1982. Fiction.

————, ed. *This Migrant Earth.* By Tomás Rivera. Houston: Arte Público, 1987. Fiction. Hinojosa's reconstruction of Rivera's *. . . y no se lo tragó la tierra / And the Earth Did Not Part,* according to Rivera's intention before the Quinto Sol editing that preceded the novel's initial publication. See also Rivera.

————. *The Valley.* Ypsilanti: Bilingual, 1983. Fiction.

Huerta, Jorge A. *Chicano Theatre: Themes and Forms.* Ypsilanti: Bilingual, 1982.

Islas, Arturo. *Migrant Souls.* New York: Morrow, 1990. Fiction.

————. *The Rain God: A Desert Tale.* Palo Alto: Alexandrian, 1984. Fiction.

Keller, Gary. *Tales of Huitlacoche.* Introd. Rosaura Sánchez. Colorado Springs: Maíze, 1984.

Luera, Yolanda. *Solitaria J.* La Jolla: Lalo, 1986. Poetry.

Martínez, Max. *The Adventures of the Chicano Kid and Other Stories.* Houston: Arte Público, 1982. Short fiction.

————. *Schooland.* Houston: Arte Público, 1988. Fiction.

Martínez-Serros, Hugo. *The Last Laugh and Other Stories.* Houston: Arte Público, 1988.

Méndez, Miguel. *Cuentos para niños traviesos / Stories for Mischievous Children.* Trans. Eva Price. Berkeley: Justa, 1979.

————. *Peregrinos de Aztlán.* Tucson: Peregrinos, 1975. Fiction. Multilingual—predominantly Spanish.

————. *El sueño de Santa María de las Pietras.* Guadalajara: U of Guadalajara P, 1986. Fiction.

————. *Tata Casehua y otros cuentos.* Berkeley: Justa, 1980. Short fiction.

Mora, Pat. *Borders.* Houston: Arte Público, 1986. Poetry.

————. *Chants.* Houston: Arte Público, 1984. Poetry.

Moraga, Cherríe. *Loving in the War Years: Lo que nunca pasó por sus labios.* Boston: South End, 1983. Mixed genre.

Morales, Alejandro. *The Brick People.* Houston: Arte Público, 1988. Fiction.

————. *Caras viejas y vino nuevo.* Spanish—México: Mortiz, 1975. English—Colorado Springs: Maíze, 1975. Fiction.

————. *Reto en el paraíso.* Ypsilanti: Bilingual, 1983. Fiction. Bilingual text.

————. *La verdad sin voz.* México: Mortiz, 1979. Fiction. Spanish-language text.

Morton, Carlos. *The Many Deaths of Danny Rosales and Other Plays.* Houston: Arte Público, 1983.

Navarro, J. L. *Blue Day on Main Street.* Berkeley: Quinto Sol, 1973. Short fiction.

Niggli, Josephina. *Mexican Village.* Chapel Hill: U of North Carolina P, 1945. Fiction.

————. *Step Down, Elder Brother: A Novel.* New York: Rinehart, 1947.

Ortega, Adolfo. *A Turn of Hands.* Chicano Chapbook 10. Ed. Gary Soto. San Jose: Mango, 1981. Poetry.

Otero, Miguel Antonio. *My Life on the Frontier.* 2 vols. New York: Press of the Pioneers, 1935, 1939. Autobiography.

————. *Otero: An Autobiographical Trilogy.* New York: Arno, 1974.

Palomares, José Francisco. *Memoirs.* Trans. Thomas Workman Temple II. Los Angeles: Glen Dawson, 1955. Autobiography.

Pineda, Cecile. *Face.* New York: Viking, 1985. Fiction.

————. *Frieze.* New York: Viking, 1986. Fiction.

Portillo-Trambley, Estela. *Rain of Scorpions and Other Writings.* Berkeley: Tonatiuh International, 1975. Short fiction.

————. *Sor Juana and Other Plays.* Ypsilanti: Bilingual, 1983.

Quiñones, Naomi. *Sueño de colibrí: Hummingbird Dream*. Los Angeles: West End, 1985. Poetry.

Rechy, John. *City of Night*. New York: Grove, 1963, 1984; Ballantine, 1964, 1973. Fiction.

———. *The Fourth Angel*. New York: Viking, 1972; Grove, 1983. Fiction.

———. *Numbers*. New York: Grove, 1967. Fiction.

Ríos, Alberto. *Elk Heads on the Wall*. Chicano Chapbook 4. Ed. Gary Soto. San Jose: Mango, 1979. Poetry.

———. *Whispering to Fool the Wind*. New York: Sheep Meadows, 1982. Poetry.

Rios, Isabella (Diane López). *Victuum*. Ventura: Diana-Etna, 1976. Fiction.

Rivera, Tomás. *The Harvest Stories by Tomás Rivera*. Ed. Julian Olivares. Houston: Arte Público, 1989. Short fiction. Bilingual edition.

———. *This Migrant Earth*. Ed. Rolando Hinojosa. Houston: Arte Público, 1986. Hinojosa's reconstruction of Rivera's . . . *y no se lo tragó la tierra / And the Earth Did Not Part*, in which he rearranges and adds chapters according to Rivera's intention before the Quinto Sol editing.

———. *. . . y no se lo tragó la tierra / And the Earth Did Not Part*. Trans. Herminio Rios. Berkeley: Quinto Sol, 1971. Trans. Evangelina Vigil-Piñon. Houston: Arte Público, 1987.

Robles, Margarita Luna, and Juan Felipe Herrera. *A Night in Tunisia*. Foreword Victor Hernández Cruz. Menlo Park: Diseños Literarios, 1985. Poetry.

Rodríguez, Joe. *Oddsplayer*. Houston: Arte Público, 1988. Fiction.

Rodríguez, Richard. *Hunger of Memory: The Education of Richard Rodríguez*. Boston: Godine, 1982. Autobiography.

Romero, Orlando. *Nambe-Year One*. Berkeley: Tonatiuh International, 1976. Fiction.

Salas, Floyd. *Tattoo the Wicked Cross*. New York: Grove, 1967. Sag Harbor: Second Chance, 1981. Fiction.

———. *What Now My Love*. New York: Grove, 1969. Fiction.

Salinas, Luis Omar. *Afternoon of the Unreal*. Fresno: Abramas, 1980. Poetry.

———. *Crazy Gypsy*. Fresno: La Raza Studies, Fresno State Coll., 1970. Poetry.

———. *I Go Dreaming Serenades*. Chicano Chapbook 2. Ed. Gary Soto. San Jose: Mango, 1979.

———. *The Sadness of Days*. Houston: Arte Público, 1987. Poetry.

Salinas, Raúl R. *Un Trip through the Mind Jail y Otras Excursions*. San Francisco: Pocho-Che, 1980. Poetry.

Sánchez, Ricardo. *Canto y grito mi liberación*. El Paso: Mictla, 1971. Garden City: Doubleday, 1973. Poetry.

———. *Hechizospells*. Los Angeles: Chicano Studies Center, 1976. Poetry. Illustrated by Willie Hérron.

———. *Selected Poems*. Houston: Arte Público, 1986.

Sapia, Yvonne. *Valentino's Hair*. Boston: Northeastern UP, 1987. Poetry.

Sierra, Michael. *In Their Father's Time*. Chicano Chapbook 7. Ed. Gary Soto. San Jose: Mango, n.d.

Somoza, Joseph. *Backyard Poems*. El Paso: Cinco Puntos, 1986.

Soto, Gary. *Como arbustos de niebla*. Chicano Chapbook 6. Ed. Gary Soto. San Jose: Mango, 1980. Trans. Ernesto Trejo. México: Latitudes, 1980.

———. *The Elements of San Joaquin*. Poetry Ser. Pittsburgh: U of Pittsburgh P, 1977.

———. *Father Is a Pillow Tied to a Broom*. Slow Loris Poetry. Pittsburgh: Slow Loris, 1980. Poetry.

———. *Lesser Evils: Ten Quartets*. Houston: Arte Público, 1988. Autobiography.

———. *Living up the Street: Narrative Recollections*. San Francisco: Strawberry Hill, 1985. Autobiography.

———. *Small Faces*. Houston: Arte Público, 1986. Autobiography.

———. *The Tale of Sunlight*. Poetry Ser. Pittsburgh: U of Pittsburgh P, 1978. Poetry.

Tafolla, Carmen. *Curandera*. San Antonio: M&A, 1983. Poetry.

Taylor, Sheila Ortiz. *Faultline*. Tallahassee: Naiad, 1982. Fiction.

Topete, Eutimio, and Jerry Gonzales. *Recordar es vivir*. Berkeley: Justa, 1978. Autobiography. Bilingual selections of recollections of Mexican Americans.

Trejo, Ernesto. *El día entre las hojas*. México: Fondo de Cultura Económica, 1984. Poetry.

Ulibarri, Sabine R. *El Condor and Other Stories*. Houston: Arte Público, 1988. Short fiction. Bilingual text.

———. *Mi abuela fumaba puros y otros cuentos de Tierra Amarilla / My Grandmother Smoked Cigars and Other Stories*. Berkeley: Quinto Sol, 1977.

Vásquez, Richard. *Chicano*. Garden City: Doubleday, 1970. New York: Avon, 1971. Fiction.

Vigil, Evangelina. *The Computer Is Down*. Houston: Arte Público, 1988. Poetry.

———. *Thirty an' Seen a Lot*. Houston: Arte Público, 1982. Poetry.

Villanueva, Alma. *Bloodroot*. Austin: Place of Herons, 1977. Poetry.

———. *Crónica de mis años peores*. La Jolla: Lalo, 1987. Poetry.

———. *Mother, May I?* Pittsburgh: Motheroot, 1978. Poetry.

Villanueva, Tino. *Hay otra voz: Poems (1968–1971)*. Staten Island: Coleccíon Mensaje, 1972, 1979. Poetry in Spanish and English.

———. *Shaking Off the Dark*. Houston: Arte Público, 1984. Poetry.

Villarreal, José Antonio. *Clemente Chacón*. Binghamton: Bilingual, 1984. Fiction.

———. *The Fifth Horseman*. Garden City: Doubleday, 1974. Introd. Luis Leal. Chicano Classics. Binghamton: Bilingual, 1984. Fiction.

———. *Pocho*. Garden City: Doubleday, 1959, 1970. Fiction.

Viramontes, Helena Maria. *The Moths and Other Stories*. Introd. Yvonne Yarbro-Bejarano. Houston: Arte Público, 1986.

Zamora, Bernice, and José Antonio Burciaga. *Restless Serpents*. Menlo Park: Diseños Literarios, 1976. Poetry.

4. Secondary Works

Anaya, Rudolfo A., and Francisco Lomelí, eds. *Aztlán: Essays on the Chicano Homeland*. Albuquerque: Academia–El Norte, 1989.

Bruce-Novoa, Juan D., ed. *Chicano Authors: Inquiry by Interview*. Austin: U of Texas P, 1980. In-depth interviews with major Chicano authors.

———. *Chicano Poetry: A Response to Chaos*. Austin: U of Texas P, 1982. Critical reappraisal of such major Chicano writers as José Montoya, Sergio Elizondo, Alurista, Bernice Zamora, Ricardo Sánchez, and Gary Soto.

Córdova, Teresa, Norma Cantú, Gilberto Cárdenas, Juan García, and Christine M. Sierra. *Chicana Voices: Intersections of Class, Race, and Gender*. Austin: Center for Mexican American Studies, 1986. Proceedings of the National Assn. of Chicano Studies Annual Meeting, Austin, Texas, 1984. "Language, Literature and the Theatre" section is notable for its collection of five articles on Chicana literary criticism.

Espinosa, Aurelio M. *Hispanic Folklore of the Southwest*. Norman: U of Oklahoma P, 1985.

"Fiesta of the Living: A Chicano Symposium." *Books Abroad* 49.3 (1975). Includes critical articles on Chicano literature by several scholars.

Gómez-Quiñones, Juan. *On Culture*. Popular Ser. 1. Los Angeles: Chicano Studies Center, 1977. This essay analyzes the importance of culture and the significance of the arts in the intellectual and political resistance against domination.

Herrera-Sobek, Maria. *The Bracero Experience*. Introd. James W. Wilkie. Los Angeles: U of California P, 1978. Study of the personal narratives and folk songs of Mexican braceros.

Jiménez, Francisco, ed. *The Identification and Analysis of Chicano Literature*. Ypsilanti: Bilingual, 1979. Essays on origins, background, development, critical trends, and practical criticism. Contains a selected bibliography by Ernestina Eger.

Kanellos, Nicolás. *Mexican American Theatre: Legacy and Reality*. Pittsburgh: Latin American Literary Review, 1987.

———. *Mexican American Theater: Then and Now*. Houston: Arte Público, 1983.

Leal, Luis, and Pepe Barrón. "Chicano Literature: An Overview." *Three American Literatures: Essays on Chicano, Native American, and Asian-American Literature for Teachers of American Literature*. Ed. Houston A. Baker, Jr. New York: MLA, 1982. 9–32.

Leal, Luis, et al., eds. *Aztlán y México: Pérfiles literarios e históricos*. Binghamton: Bilingual, 1984.

———. *A Decade of Chicano Literature (1969–79): Critical Essays and Bibliography*. Santa Barbara: La Causa, 1982. Contains analysis of genres of Chicano literature along with selected bibliography.

Limón, José E. "Mexican Ballads, Chicano Epic: History, Social Dramas and Poetic Persuasions." Working Paper 14. Stanford: Stanford Center for Chicano Research, 1986. Argues for the importance of the social drama and Bloom's *Anxiety of Influence* as critical vehicles for addressing Chicano poetry, particularly Rodolfo "Corky" Gonzalez's poem "I Am Joaquin."

———. "Return of the Mexican Ballad: Américo Paredes and His Anthropological Text as Persuasive Political Performance." Working Paper 16. Stanford: Stanford Center for Chicano Research, 1986. An interpretation of Américo Paredes's seminal *"With His Pistol in His Hand"* as an analogue to the folk performance of the border ballad.

Madrid-Barela, Arturo. "In Search of the Authentic Pachuco." *Aztlán* 4 (1973): 31–60. Analysis of several literary representations of the pachuco and a critical assessment of the importance of the image of the pachuco in Chicano literature.

McKenna, Teresa. "Immigrants in Our Own Land: A Chicano Literature Review and Pedagogical Assessment." *ADE Bulletin* 91 (1988): 30–38.

Olivares, Julián, ed. *International Studies in Honor of Tomás Rivera*. Houston: Arte Público, 1986. Critical articles divided into two sections: "Tomás Rivera: Recollections and Essays" and "Chicano and Hispanic Literature of the United States."

Paredes, Américo. *The Folktales of Mexico*. Chicago: U of Chicago P, 1970. The best existing collection of folktales of greater Mexico, including narratives collected in the Republic of Mexico and in the United States among Mexican Americans.

———. *"With His Pistol in His Hand": A Border Ballad and Its Hero*. Austin: U of Texas P, 1958. Seminal study of the border ballad "Gregorio Cortez." This book is a major critical reference for Chicano literary study.

Paredes, Raymund. "Autobiography and Ethnic Politics: Richard Rodríguez's *Hunger of Memory*." *Multi-Cultural American Autobiography*. Ed. James R. Payne. Spec. issue of *Auto/Biography* 3.2 (1987): 18–25.

———. "The Evolution of Chicano Literature." *Three American Literatures: Essays on Chicano, Native American, and Asian-American Literature for Teachers of American Literature*. Ed. Houston A. Baker, Jr. New York: MLA, 1982. 33–79.

Rodríguez Del Pino, Salvador. *La novela chicana escrita en Español: Cinco autores comprometidos*. Ypsilanti: Bilingual, 1982. Analysis of the works of five Chicano authors who write in Spanish: Tomás Rivera, Rolando Hinojosa, Miguel Méndez, Alejandro Morales, and Aristeo Brito.

Romano-V., Octavio I. "Goodbye Revolution–Hello Slum." *El espejo / The Mirror: Selected Mexican American Literature*. Ed. Octavio I. Romano-V. and Herminio Rios-C. Berkeley: Quinto Sol, 1969. An early essay on the importance of politics in generating creative production and social change for Chicanos.

Romo, Ricardo, and Raymund Paredes, eds. *New Directions in Chicano Scholarship*. La Jolla: Univ. of California Chicano Studies, 1978. Includes some essays on literature.

Saldívar, José David, ed. *The Rolando Hinojosa Reader: Essays Historical and Critical*. Houston: Arte Público, 1984. First collection of critical essays on Rolando Hinojosa. A major study of this significant Chicano writer.

Sánchez, Marta. *Contemporary Chicana Poetry: An Approach to an Emerging Literature*. Berkeley: U of California P, 1985. Critical volume analyzing four Chicana poets: Alma Villanueva, Lorna Dee Cervantes, Lucha Corpi, and Bernice Zamora.

Sommers, Joseph, and Tomás Ybarra-Frausto, eds. *Modern Chicano Writers: A Collection of Critical Essays*. Englewood Cliffs: Prentice, 1979. Important volume of critical essays that focus on theory and applied analysis.

Tatum, Charles. *Chicano Literature*. Boston: Twayne, 1982. A critical analysis using historical and genre studies. Includes selected bibliography.

Van Bardeleben, Renate, Dietrick Briesmeister, and Juan Bruce-Novoa, eds. *Missions in Conflict: Essays on U.S.-Mexican Relations and Chicano Culture*. Tübingen: Gunternarr, 1986. Essays on Chicano literature and theater by European and American critics.

Ybarra-Frausto, Tomás. "The Chicano Movement and the Emergence of a Chicano Poetic Consciousness." *New Scholar* 6 (1977): 81–109.

Puerto Rican Literature in the United States

Compiled by Edna Acosta-Belén

Most of this bibliography is devoted to the literature produced by Puerto Rican writers born or raised in the United States, commonly referred to as *Nuyorican* literature. These writers express themselves primarily in English or bilingually. The first two sections of this bibliography include most of the creative works published in anthologies and works by individual authors. A few works originally written in English by first-generation Puerto Rican migrants are also listed.

The many facets of the literature of the Puerto Rican migration would be incomplete without some consideration of the works produced by Puerto Rican writers from the Island who have visited or lived in the United States at some point in their lives, and written primarily in Spanish about the immigrant experience. Their work is generally studied within the context of Puerto Rican insular literature. The final section of the bibliography includes a selection of the most representative works of this group.

1. Anthologies and Collections

Algarín, Miguel, and Miguel Piñero, eds. *Nuyorican Poetry: An Anthology of Puerto Rican Words and Feelings*. New York: Morrow, 1975. The first attempt to collect the poetic work of emerging New York Puerto Rican writers. Algarín's introduction was intended as a Nuyorican manifesto that postulates the emergence of what he considers a new poetry with its own creative and ideological principles.

Babín, María Teresa, and Stan Steiner, eds. *Borinquen: An Anthology of Puerto Rican Literature*. New York: Knopf, 1974. The only anthology of Puerto Rican literature in translation that includes poetry, fiction, and essays. Selections are by Island authors and New York–based Puerto Rican writers, and emerging Nuyorican writers and community leaders.

Barradas, Efraín, and Rafael Rodríguez. *Herejes y mitificadores: Muestra de poesía puertorriqueña en los Estados Unidos*. Río Piedras: Huracán, 1981. A bilingual collection of Puerto Rican poetry in the United States. Barradas's excellent introduction is a pioneering effort to characterize Puerto Rican poetry in the United States.

Marzán, Julio, ed. *Inventing a Word: An Anthology of Twentieth-Century Puerto Rican Poetry*. New York: Columbia UP, 1980. A bilingual anthology of poetry by Island authors, New York-based writers, and Nuyorican writers.

Matilla, Alfredo, and Iván Silén, eds. *The Puerto Rican Poets*. New York: Bantam, 1972. A mixture of well-known Island writers and emerging Nuyorican writers.

Ramos, Juanita, ed. *Compañeras: Latina Lesbians*. New York: Latina Lesbian History Project, 1987.

Silén, Iván. *Los paraguas amarillos: Los poetas latinos en Nueva York*. Binghamton: Bilingual, 1984. Includes poetry texts by Latino writers who live in New York and write in Spanish, as well as a few poems by the Nuyorican writer Pedro Pietri.

2. Primary Works

Algarín, Miguel. *Body Bee Calling from the Twenty-first Century*. Houston: Arte Público, 1982. Poetry.

———. *Mongo Affair*. New York: Nuyorican, 1978. Poetry.

———. *On Call*. Houston: Arte Público, 1980. Poetry.

———. *Time's Now / Ya es tiempo*. Houston: Arte Público, 1985. Poetry.

Algarín, Miguel, and Tato Laviera. *Olú Clemente*. Kanellos and Huerta 151–71. Drama.

Barreto, Lefty. *Nobody's Hero*. New York: NAL, 1976. Fiction.

Carrero, Jaime. *Jet neorriqueño: Neo-Rican Jet Liner*. San Germán: Univ. Interamericana, 1964. Poetry.

———. *Noo Jork*. In *Revista Chicano-Riqueña* 2.4 (Fall 1974): 3–31. Drama.

Cintrón, Humberto. *Frankie Cristo*. New York: Taino, 1972. Fiction.

Colón, Jesús. *A Puerto Rican in New York and Other Sketches*. New York: Mainstream, 1961. Memoirs.

Cruz, Nicky. *The Lonely Now*. Plainfield: Logos, 1971. Fiction.

———. *Run Baby Run*. Plainfield: Logos, 1968. Fiction.

Espada, Martin. *Trumpets from the Island of Their Eviction*. Tempe: Bilingual, 1988. Poetry.

Esteves, Sandra María. *Tropical Rains*. New York: African Caribbean Poetry Theater, 1984. Poetry.

———. *Yerba buena*. Greenfield: Greenfield, 1980. Poetry.

Figueroa, José A. *East 100th Street*. Detroit: Broadside, 1973. Poetry.

———. *Noo Jork*. Trans. Víctor Fernández Fragoso. San Juan: Inst. de Cultura Puertorriqueña, 1981. Poetry.

———. *Unknown Poets from the Full-Time Jungle*. New York: Noo Jork, 1975. Poetry.

Hernández Cruz, Víctor. *By Lingual Wholes*. San Francisco: Momo's Place, 1982. Poetry.

———. *Mainland*. New York: Random, 1973. Poetry.

———. *Rhythm, Content and Flavor: Poems, Selected and New*. Houston: Arte Público, 1988. Poetry.

———. *Snaps*. New York: Random, 1968. Poetry.

———. *Tropicalization*. New York: Canon, 1976. Poetry.

Kanellos, Nicolás, and Jorge A. Huerta, eds. *Nuevos Pasos: Chicano and Puerto Rican Drama*. Spec. issue of *Revista Chicano-Riqueña* 7.1 (Winter 1979).

Labarthe, Pedro Juan. *The Son of Two Nations: The Private Life of a Columbia Student*. New York: Carranza, 1931. Fiction.

Laviera, Tato. *AmeRican*. Houston: Arte Público, 1985. Poetry.

———. *La Carreta Made a U-Turn*. Gary: Arte Público, 1979. Poetry.

———. *Enclave*. Houston: Arte Público, 1981. Poetry.

———. *Mainstream Ethics*. Houston: Arte Público, 1988. Poetry.

Levins Morales, Aurora, and Rosario Morales. *Getting Home Alive*. Ithaca: Firebrand, 1986. Poetry.

Manrique, Manuel. *Island in Harlem*. New York: Day, 1966. Fiction.

Marzán, Julio. *Translations without Originals*. Berkeley: I. Reed, 1986. Poetry.

Meléndez, Jesús Papoleto. *Street Poetry and Other Poems*. New York: Barlenmir, 1972. Poetry.

Miraflores, Carmen de. *Cantando bajito: Singing Softly*. San Francisco: Spinsters–Aunt Lute, 1989. Fiction.

Mohr, Nicholasa. *El Bronx Remembered*. 1975. Houston: Arte Público, 1986. Fiction.

———. *Going Home*. New York: Dial, 1986. Fiction.

———. *In Nueva York*. 1977. Houston: Arte Público, 1987. Fiction.

———. *Nilda*. 1973. Houston: Arte Público, 1986. Fiction.

———. *Rituals of Survival: A Woman's Portfolio*. Houston: Arte Público, 1985. Fiction.

Ortiz Cofer, Judith. *The Line of the Sun*. Atlanta: U of Georgia P, 1988. Fiction.

———. *Searching for the Mainland*. In *Triple Crown: Chicano, Puerto Rican, and Cuban American Poetry*. By Robert Duran, Ortiz, and Gustavo Perez Firmat. Tempe: Bilingual, 1987. Poetry.

———. *Terms of Survival*. Houston: Arte Público, 1987. Poetry.

Pietri, Pedro. *Lost in the Museum of Natural History / Perdido en el Museo de Historia Natural*. Río Piedras: Huracán, 1981. Fiction.

———. *The Masses Are Asses*. Maplewood: Waterfront, 1984. Drama.

———. *Puerto Rican Obituary*. New York: Monthly Review, 1973. *Obituario puertorriqueño*. Trans. Alfredo Matilla. San Juan: Inst. de Cultura Puertorriqueña, 1981. Poetry.

———. *Traffic Violations*. Maplewood: Waterfront, 1983. Poetry.

Piñero, Miguel. *La Bodega Sold Dreams*. Houston: Arte Público, 1980. Poetry.

———. *Outrageous One-Act Plays*. Houston: Arte Público, 1986.

———. *Short Eyes*. New York: Hill, 1975. Drama.

———. *The Sun Always Shines for the Cool; Midnight Moon at the Greasy Spoon; Eulogy for a Small-Time Thief*. Houston: Arte Público, 1984. Drama.

Rivera, Edward. *Family Installments*. New York: Morrow, 1982; Penguin, 1983. Fiction.

Ruiz, Richard. *The Hungry American*. Bend: Maverick, 1978. Fiction.

Thomas, Piri. *Down These Mean Streets*. New York: Knopf, 1967. Fiction.

———. *Savior, Savior, Hold My Hand*. New York: Doubleday, 1972. Fiction.

———. *Seven Long Times*. New York: Mentor, 1975. Fiction.

———. *Stories from El Barrio*. New York: Knopf, 1978.

Torres, Edwin. *After Hours*. New York: Dial, 1979. Fiction.

———. *Carlito's Way*. New York: Dutton, 1975. Fiction.

Vega, Ed. *The Comeback*. Houston: Arte Público, 1985. Fiction.

———. *Mendoza's Dreams*. Houston: Arte Público, 1987. Fiction.

3. Secondary Works

Acosta-Belén, Edna. "Conversations with Nicholasa Mohr." *Revista Chicano-Riqueña* 8.2 (1980): 35–41.

———. "The Literature of the Puerto Rican Minority in the United States." *Bilingual Review / Revista Bilingüe* 5.1–2 (1978): 107–16.

Alarcón, Norma. "An Interview with Miguel Piñero." *Revista Chicano-Riqueña* 2.4 (1984): 55–57.

Algarín, Miguel. "Nuyorican Language." Algarín and Piñero, *Nuyorican Poetry* 9–27.

———. "Nuyorican Literature." *MELUS* 8.2 (1981): 89–92.

Aparicio, Frances. "Tato Laviera y Alurista: Hacia una poética bilingüe." *Centro* 2.3 (1988): 7–13.

———. "La vida es un Spanglish disparatero." *European Perspectives on Hispanic Literature in the United States.* Ed. Genevieve Fabré. Houston: Arte Público, 1988. 147–60.

Azize, Yamila. "A Commentary on the Works of Three Puerto Rican Women Poets in New York." Horno-Delgado et al. 146–65.

Babín, María Teresa. "The Path and the Voice." Babín and Steiner, *Borinquen* 11–26.

Barradas, Efraín. "Conciencia femenina, conciencia social: La voz poética de Sandra María Esteves." *Third Woman* 1.2 (1982): 31–34.

———. "De lejos en sueños verla . . . : Visión mítica de Puerto Rico en la poesía neoyorrican." *Revista Chicano-Riqueña* 7.3 (1979): 46–56.

———. "Puerto Rico acá, Puerto Rico allá." *Revista Chicano-Riqueña* 8.2 (1980): 43–49.

Binder, Wolfgang. "An Interview with Piri Thomas." *Minority Voices* 4.1 (1980): 63–78.

Carrero, Jaime. "Notes of Neorican Seminar." San Germán: Univ. Interamericana, 1972.

Cortés, Félix, Angel Falcón, and Juan Flores. "The Cultural Expression of Puerto Ricans in New York City: A Theoretical Perspective and Critical Review." *Latin American Perspectives* 3.3 (1976): 117–50.

Daydí-Tolson, Santiago. "The Right to Belong: A Critic's View of Puerto Rican Poetry in the United States." *Bilingual Review / Revista Bilingüe* 10.1 (1983): 81–86.

———. "*Tropicalization*: In Search of Poetic Language." *Bilingual Review / Revista Bilingüe* 7.1 (1979): 94–96.

Fernández-Olmos, Margarite. "From the Metropolis: Puerto Rican Women Poets and the Immigration Experience." *Third Woman* 1.2 (1982): 40–51.

———. *Sobre la literatura puertorriqueña de aquí y de allá: Aproximaciones feministas.* Santo Domingo: Alfa & Omega, 1989.

Flores, Juan. "Back Down These Mean Streets: Introducing Nicholasa Mohr and Louis Reyes Rivera." *Revista Chicano-Riqueña* 8.2 (1980): 51–56.

———. "Que assimilated, brother, yo soy asimilao: la estructuración de la identidad puertorriqueña en los Estados Unidos." *Casa de las Américas* 26:152 (1985): 54–63.

Flores, Juan, Juan Attinasi, and Pedro Pedraza. "'La Carreta Made a U-Turn': Puerto Rican Language and Culture in the United States." *Daedalus* 110.2 (1982): 193–213.

Gavin, Larry. "The World of Piri Thomas." *Crisis* 82.6 (1975): 196–203.

Kanellos, Nicolás. "Canto y declamación en la poesía nuyoriqueña." *Confluencia* 1.1 (1985): 102–06.

———. "Puerto Rican Literature from the Diaspora to the Mainstream." *American Book Review* 7.1 (1984): 16–17.

———. "Víctor Hernández Cruz and *la salsa de Dios.*" Milwaukee: Institute Paper, Spanish-Speaking Outreach Institute, Univ. of Wisconsin, 1979.

Laguardia, Gari. "The Canon and the Air-Conditioner: Modern Puerto Rican Poetry." *Bilingual Review / Revista Bilingüe* 9.2 (1982): 178–181.

Lane, James B. "Beating the Barrio: Piri Thomas and *Down These Mean Streets.*" *English Journal* 61.6 (1972): 814–23.

Matilla, Alfredo. "The Broken English Dream: Poesía puertorriqueña en Nueva York." *Libertad y crítica en el ensayo político puertorriqueño.* Iris Zavala and Rafael Rodríguez, eds. Río Piedras: Puerto, 1975. 427–43. Trans. "The Broken English Dream: Puerto Rican Poetry in New York." *The Intellectual Roots of Independence: An Anthology of Puerto Rican Political Essays.* Iris Zavala and Rafael Rodríguez, eds. New York: Monthly Review, 1980. 295–310.

Miller, John. "The Emigrant and the City: Four Puerto Rican Writers." *MELUS* 5.3 (1978): 82–99.

————. "Hispanic Theatre in New York, 1965–1977." *Revista Chicano-Riqueña* 6.1 (1977): 40–59.

————. "Nicholasa Mohr: Neorican Writing in Progress." *Revista / Review Interamericana* 9.4 (1979/80): 543–49.

Mohr, Eugene. "Lives from El Barrio." *Revista Chicano-Riqueña* 7.4 (1980): 60–68.

————. *The Nuyorican Experience: Literature of the Puerto Rican Minority.* Westport: Greenwood, 1982.

————. "Piri Thomas: Author and Persona." *Caribbean Studies* 20.2 (1980): 61–74.

Mohr, Nicholasa. "Puerto Rican Writers in the U.S., Puerto Rican Writers in Puerto Rico: A Separation Beyond Language." Horno-Delgado 111–16.

Morton, Carlos. "Social Realism on Astor Place: The Latest Piñero Play." *Revista Chicano-Riqueña* 2.4 (1974): 33–34.

Ortega, Eliana. "Poetic Discourse of the Puerto Rican Woman in the U.S.: New Voices of Anacaonian Liberation." Horno-Delgado 122–35.

Ortega, Eliana, and Nancy Saporta Sternback. "At the Threshold of the Unnamed: Latina Literary Discourse in the Eighties." Horno-Delgado 2–23.

Pacífico, Patricia. "Piri Thomas Talks at the Inter American University." *Revista / Review Interamericana* 7.4 (1977–78): 666–73.

Reyes Rivera, Louis. "Within the Context of a Nuyorican Element: Sandra María Esteves." *Centro* 2.3 (1988): 50–55.

Rivero, Eliana. "Nota sobre las voces femeninas en *Herejes y mitificadores: Muestra de poesía puertorriqueña en los Estados Unidos.*" *Third Woman* 1.2 (1982): 91–93.

Rodríguez de Laguna, Asela, ed. *Imágenes e identidades: El puertorriqueño en la literatura.* Río Piedras: Huracán, 1985.

————. *Images and Identities: The Puerto Rican in Literature.* New Brunswick: Transaction, 1987.

Rojas, Lourdes. "Latinas at the Crossroads: An Affirmation of Life in Rosario Morales and Aurora Levins Morales' *Getting Home Alive.*" Horno-Delgado 166–77.

Rosa, Víctor. "Interview with Víctor Hernández Cruz." *Bilingual Review / Revista Bilingüe* 2.3 (1975): 281–87.

Turner, Faythe. "Puerto Rican Writers on the Mainland: The Neoricans." Diss. U of Massachusetts, Amherst, 1978.

Umpierre, Luz María. "La ansiedad de la influencia en Sandra María Esteves y Marjorie Agosín." *Revista Chicano-Riqueña* 11.3–4 (1983): 139–47.

Wallenstein, Barry. "The Poet in New York: Víctor Hernández Cruz." *Bilingual Review / Revista Bilingüe* 1.3 (1974): 312–19.

4. Puerto Rican Literature, Originally Written in Spanish, Dealing with the Immigrant Experience

Andreu Iglesias, César, ed. *Memorias de Bernardo Vega.* Río Piedras: Huracán, 1977. *Memoirs of Bernardo Vega.* Trans. Juan Flores. New York: Monthly Review, 1984. Autobiography.

Carrero, Jaime. *Pipo subway no sabe reir.* Río Piedras: Puerto, 1973. Drama.

————. *Raquelo tiene un mensaje.* San Juan: Pareja, 1970. Fiction.

Cotto-Thorner, Guillermo. *Trópico en Manhattan.* New York: Las Americas, 1959. Fiction.

Díaz Valcárcel, Emilio. *Harlem todos los días.* Río Piedras: Huracán, 1979. Fiction.

González, José Luis. *En Nueva York y otras desgracias.* México: Siglo XXI, 1973. Fiction.

————. *Paisa.* New York: n.p., 1950. Fiction.

Laguerre, Enrique. *El laberinto*. New York: Las Americas, 1959. *The Labyrinth*. Trans. William Rose. New York: Las Americas, 1960. Fiction.

Marqués, René. *La carreta*. Río Piedras: Cultural, 1955. *The Oxcart*. Trans. Charles Pildich. New York: Scribner's, 1972. Drama.

Méndez Ballester, Manuel. *Encrucijada*. San Juan: n.p., 1958. Drama.

Sierra Berdecía, Fernando. *Esta noche juega el jóker*. San Juan: Biblioteca de Autores Puertorriqueños, 1939. San Juan: Inst. de Cultura Puertorriqueña, 1960. Drama.

Soto, Pedro Juan. *Ardiente suelo, fría estación*. México: Veracruzana, 1961. *Hot Land, Cold Season*. Trans. Helen R. Lane. New York: Dell, 1973. Fiction.

———. *Spiks*. México: Los Presentes, 1956. *Spiks*. Trans. Victoria Ortiz. New York: Monthly Review, 1973. Fiction.

Vivas, José Luis. *A vellón las esperanzas o Melania*. New York: Las Americas, 1971. Fiction.

Zeno Gandía, Manuel. *La charca*. 1894. Trans. Kal Wagenheim. Maplewood: Waterfront, 1984. Fiction.

———. *El negocio*. Río Piedras: Edil, 1973. Fiction.

———. *Los redentores*. Vol. 2 of *Obras completas*. Río Piedras: Inst. de Cultura Puertorriqueña, 1973. Fiction.

V

Selected Journals
and Presses

Journals

1. General

The following journals frequently publish works by African American, American Indian, Asian American, Chicano, and Puerto Rican authors and criticism of these literatures.

Contact II. P.O. Box 451, Bowling Green Sta., New York, NY 10004.

Dispatch. Newsletter of the Center for American Culture Studies, Columbia Univ., 603 Lewisohn Hall, New York, NY 10027.

Journal of American Folklore. 1703 New Hampshire Ave., NW, Washington, DC 20009.

Journal of Ethnic Studies. Univ. of Western Washington, Bellingham, WA 98225.

Journal of the Southwest. Univ. of Arizona, Tucson, AZ 85719.

MELUS (Multi-Ethnic Literatures of the United States). Dept. of English, Univ. of Massachusetts, Amherst, MA 01003.

NAIES. Ethnic Studies Dept., California State Polytechnic Univ., Pomona, CA 91768. Newsletter of the National Assn. of Interdisciplinary Ethnic Studies.

Puerto del Sol. Box 3E, New Mexico State Univ., Las Cruces, NM 88003. Southwestern literary magazine that often publishes Chicano and American Indian authors.

Sinister Wisdom. P.O. Box 186, Montague, MA 01251. Devoted to women's writing. Often publishes work by Third World women.

Third Woman. Ethnic Studies Dept., Univ. of California, Berkeley, CA 94720. First published in 1982, this journal focuses on scholarship and creative writing by Hispanic women in the United States.

Yardbird Reader. Yardbird Publications, Inc., Box 2370, Sta. A., Berkeley, CA 94702. Literary magazine of Third World poetry.

Selected Journals and Presses

2. African American

Black American Literature Forum. Formerly *Negro American Literature Forum.* PH 237, Indiana State Univ., Terre Haute, IN 47809.

Black Scholar: Journal of Black Studies and Research. Black Scholar Press, P.O. Box 2869, Oakland, CA 94609.

Callaloo: A Black South Journal of Arts and Letters. Dept. of English, Univ. of Virginia, Charlottesville, VA 22903.

CLA Journal. Morehouse Coll., Atlanta, GA 30314.

Journal of Black Studies. Sage Publications, 275 South Beverly Dr., Beverly Hills, CA 90212.

Langston Hughes Review. Afro-American Studies Program, Brown Univ., Providence, RI 01912.

Literary Griot: International Journal of Black Oral and Literary Studies. Dept. of English, Indiana Univ. of Pennsylvania, Indiana, PA 15705.

Obsidian II: Black Literature in Review (formerly *Obsidian: Black Literature in Review*). Dept. of English, Box 8105, North Carolina State Univ., Raleigh, NC 27695–8105.

Phylon. Atlanta Univ., Atlanta, GA 30314.

Sage: A Scholarly Journal on Black Women. P.O. Box 4271, Atlanta, GA 30311-0741.

Western Journal of Black Studies. Black Studies Program, Washington State Univ., Pullman, WA 99164.

3. American Indian

American Indian Culture and Research Journal. American Indian Studies Center, 3220 Campbell Hall, Univ. of California, Los Angeles, CA 90024.

American Indian Quarterly. Native American Studies Program, Univ. of California, Berkeley, CA 94720.

ASAIL Notes. Dept. of English, Central Oregon Community Coll., 2600 N.W. College Way, Bend, OR 97701.

Studies in American Indian Literatures. Dept. of English, Univ. of Richmond, Richmond, VA 23173. Editorial Office: Dept. of English, California State Univ., Fullerton, CA 92734. Formerly published at Columbia Univ. and briefly absorbed into *Dispatch*, this journal has been reactivated.

Wicazo Sa Review. Indian Studies, Eastern Washington Univ., Cheney, WA 99004.

4. Asian American

Amerasia. Asian American Studies Center, Univ. of California, Los Angeles, CA 90024.

5. Hispanic

Americas Review (formerly *Revista Chicano-Riqueña*). Arte Público, Univ. of Houston, University Park, Houston, TX 77004-2090.

Bilingual Review / Revista Bilingüe. Hispanic Research Center, Arizona State Univ., Tempe, AZ 85287.

Latin America Literary Review. 2300 Palmer Street, Pittsburgh, PA 15218.

Revista Chicano-Riqueña. See *Americas Review* above.

6. Chicano

Atzlán: International Journal of Chicano Studies Research. Univ. of California, 405 Hilgard Ave., Los Angeles, CA 90024.

Campo Libre. Chicano Studies Dept., California State Univ., Los Angeles, CA 90024.

De Colores–Journal of Emerging Raza Philosophies. Pajarito Publications, 2633 Granite St., NW, Albuquerque, NM 87104.

IMAGINE–International Chicano Poetry Journal. Imagine Press, Suite 7, 645 Beacon St., Boston, MA 02215.

Llueve Tlaloc. Bilingual Bicultural Program, Pima Community Coll., Box 3010, Tucson, AZ 85702.

Tonantzin. Guadalupe Cultural Arts Center, 1300 Guadalupe, San Antonio, TX 78207.

Presses

The following small presses, cited in the selected bibliographies and listed in current directories, publish works by and about American Indian, African American, Asian American, Chicano, and Puerto Rican writers, their literatures, and their cultures. The addresses given here are the most recent listed.

Ahsahta Press, University Bookstore, Boise, ID 83725

Akwesasne Notes, Mohawk Nation, via Rooseveltown, NY 13683

Alexanderian Press, 700 Hansen Way, Palo Alto, CA 94303

American Indian Studies Center, 3220 Campbell Hall, Univ. of California, Los Angeles, CA 90024

Another Chicago Press, P.O. Box 11223, Chicago, IL 60611

Arte Público, Univ. of Houston, University Park, Houston, TX 77004-2090

Asian American Studies Center, Univ. of California, Los Angeles, CA 90024

Asian-American Studies Dept., Univ. of California, Berkeley, CA 94720

Atzlán, Chicano Studies Research Center, Univ. of California, 405 Hilgard Ave., Los Angeles, CA 90024

Ayer, 382 Main St., P.O. Box 958, Salem, NH 03079

Backstreet Editions, Box 555, Port Jefferson, NY 11777

Bamboo Ridge Press, P.O. Box 61781, Honolulu, HI 96822

Barlenmir Press, 413 City Island Ave., Bronx, NY 10464

Barrio Publications, 9892 West 26th St., Apt. 5A, Lakewood, CO 80215

Barron Press, 250 Wireless Blvd., Hauppauge, NY 11788

Basilisk Press, P.O. Box 71, Fredonia, NY 14063

Bess Press, P.O. Box 22388, Honolulu, HI 96822

Bilingual Review/Press, Hispanic Research Center, Arizona State Univ., Tempe, AZ 85287

Blackberry Press, Chimney Farm, R.R. 1, Box 228, Nobleborrow, ME 04555

Black Scholar, P.O. Box 2869, Oakland, CA 94609

Blue Cloud Quarterly, Box 98, Marvin, SD 57251

Blue Wind, Box 7175, Berkeley, CA 94707

Bookslinger Press, 2163 Ford Parkway, St. Paul, MN 55116

Broadside Press, P.O. Box 04257, Northwestern Sta., Detroit, MI 58204

Burning Deck Press, 71 Elmgrove Ave., Providence, RI 02906

Callaloo, Univ. of Virginia Press, Box 3608, Univ. Sta., Charlottesville, VA 11903

Center for Adirondack Studies, North Country Community College Press, 20 Winona Ave., Saranac Lake, NY 12983

Chalatien Press, 5859 Woodleigh Dr., Carmichael, CA 95608

Chalfant Press, P.O. Box 787, Bishop, CA 93514

Chatham, 8 Green Village Rd., Madison, NJ 07940

Chicano Studies Research Center Publications, Univ. of California, 405 Hilgard Ave., Los Angeles, CA 90024

City Lights, 261 Columbus Ave., San Francisco, CA 94133

Contact II, P.O. Box 451, Bowling Green Sta., New York, NY 10004

Crossing Press, 17 West Main St., Trumansburg, NY 14886

Design Enterprises, P.O. Box 14695, San Francisco, CA 94114

East-West Publishing, 2413 South Broadway St., Santa Ana, CA 92707

Editorial Justa Publications, 2831 Seventh St., Berkeley, CA 94710

Elizabeth Press, 103 Van Etten, New Rochelle, NY 10804

Feminist Press, City Univ. of New York, 311 E. 94th St., New York, NY 10128

Fiction Collective, English Dept., Brooklyn Coll., Brooklyn, NY 11210. Distributed by Sun and Moon Press, 6363 Wilshire Blvd., Suite 115, Los Angeles, CA 90048

Fiddlehead Press, Old Arts Bldg., U of New Brunswick, P.O. Box 440, Fredericton, NB E3B 5A3, Canada

Firebrand Press, 141 The Commons, Ithaca, NY 14850

Floating Island, P.O. Box 516, Point Reyes Sta., CA 94956

Graywolf Press, P.O. Box 75006, Saint Paul, MN 55175

Great Raven, Box 858, Lewiston, ME 04240

Greenfield Review Press, 2 Middlegrove Rd., Greenfield Center, NY 12833

Harlen Davidson, 3110 North Arlington Heights Rd., Arlington Heights, IL 60004

Holy Cow! Press, P.O. Box 3170, Mount Royal Sta., Duluth, MN 55803

Imagine Press, 645 Beacon St., Suite 7, Boston, MA 02215

Indian Press, Bacone College, Muskogee, OK 74401

International Publishers, 381 Park Ave., Suite 1301, New York, NY 10016

Irografts Ltd., R.R. 2, Okswehen, ON NOA 1MO Canada

Jove, 200 Madison Ave., New York, NY 10016

Kelsy Street Press, P.O. Box 9235, Berkeley, CA 94709

Kitchen Table—Women of Color Press, Box 2753, New York, NY 10185

La Raza Studies, Fresno State Coll., Fresno, Ca 93740

Selected Journals and Presses

Lawrence Hill, 520 Riverside Ave., Westport, CT 06880. Distributed by Independent Publishers Group, 814 No. Franklin St., Chicago, IL 60610

Limelight Editions, 118 East 30th St., New York, NY 10016

Lotus, P.O. Box 21607, Detroit, MI 48221

Lunchroom, Box 36027, Grosse Point Farms, MI 48236

M&A Editions, Rt. 5, P.O. Box 332, San Antonio, TX 78211

Malki Museum, Morongo Indian Reservation, Banning, CA 92220

Milkweed Editions, P.O. Box 3226, Minneapolis, MN 55403

Momo's Place, P.O. Box 14061, San Francisco, CA 94114

Monthly Review Press, 122 West 27th St., New York, NY 10001

Motheroot, P.O. Box 8306, Pittsburgh, PA 15218

NAIES Publications (National Assn. of Interdisciplinary Ethnic Studies), Ethnic Studies Dept., California State Polytechnic Univ., Pomona, CA 91768

Navajo Community College Press, Many Farms, AZ 86538

Nodin Press, c/o Bookmen, Inc., 519 N. Third St., Minneapolis, MN 55401

Northland Books, P.O. Box N, Flagstaff, AZ 86002

Open Hand Press, Suite 565, 600 E. Pine St., Seattle, WA 98122

Oyate Press, 2702 Mathews St., Berkeley, CA 94707

Paragon House, 90 Fifth Ave., New York, NY 10011

Patterson Smith, 23 Prospect Terr., Montclair, NJ 07042

Permanent Press, c/o Second Chance Press, R.D. 2, Noyac Rd., Sag Harbor, NY 11963

Place of Herons Press, P.O. Box 1952, Austin, TX 78767

Point Riders Press, Box 2731, Norman, OK 73070

I. Reed Books, Suite D, 1446 Sixth St., Berkeley, CA 94704

Sheep Meadow, 5247 Independence Ave., Riverdale-on-Hudson, NY 10471. Distributed by Persea Books, 225 Lafayette St., New York, NY 10012

Slow Lorris Press, 923 Highview St., Pittsburgh, PA 15206

South End Press, 116 St. Botolph St., Boston, MA 02115

Spinster's Inc., P.O. Box 410687, San Francisco, CA 94107

Straight Arrow Books, P.O. Box 1236, San Francisco, CA 94023

Strawberry Hill Press, 2594 15th St., San Francisco, CA 94127

Strawberry Press, P.O. Box 456, Bowling Green Sta., New York, NY 10004

Sun Tracks Press, Dept. of English, Univ. of Arizona, Tucson, AZ 85721

Tanam, 40 White St., New York, NY 10013

Taurean Horn Press, 920 Leavenworth St., #401, San Francisco, CA 94109

Tejas Art Press, 207 Terrell Rd., San Antonio, TX 78209

Third Woman, Ethnic Studies Dept., Univ. of California, Berkeley, CA 94720

Third World Press, 7524 South Cottage Grove Ave., Chicago, IL 60019

Thunder's Mouth Press, 93–99 Greene St., New York, NY 10012

Toltecas en Aztlán Central Cultural de la Raza, Division of Central Cultural de la Raza, P.O. Box 8251, San Diego, CA 92102

Tonatiuh–Quinto Sol International, Box 9275, Berkeley, CA 94709

Tooth of Time, 634 Garcia St., Santa Fe, NM 87501

Turtle Island Foundation, 2845 Buena Vista Way, Berkeley, CA 94708

University Microfilms International, 300 N. Zeeb Rd., Ann Arbor, MI 48106

Richard West, Box 6404, Philadelphia, PA 19145

West End Press, Box 27334, Albuquerque, NM 87125

White Pine Press, 76 Center St., Fredonia, NY 14063

Works Cited

Primary works by African American, Native American, Asian American, and Hispanic writers are listed in the selected bibliographies.

Abrahams, Roger D. "The Complex Relations of Simple Forms." *Genre* 2 (1969): 104–28.

———. *Deep Down in the Jungle: Negro Narrative Folklore from the Streets of Philadelphia.* 1964. New York: Aldine, 1973.

———. "Folklore and Literature as Performance." *Journal of the Folklore Institute* 8 (1972): 75–94.

———. "Some Varieties of Heroes in America." *Journal of the Folklore Institute* 3 (1967): 341–62.

Alcorn, Marshall W., Jr., and Mark Bracher. "Literature, Psychoanalysis, and the Re-Formation of the Self: A New Direction for Reader-Response Theory." *PMLA* 100 (1985): 342–54.

Alcott, Louisa May. "Psyche's Art." *Alternative Alcott.* Ed. Elaine Showalter. New Brunswick: Rutgers UP, 1988. 207–26.

Algarín, Miguel. "Volume and Value of the Breath in Poetry." *Revista Chicano-Riqueña* 6.3 (1978): 52–69.

Algarín, Miguel, and Miguel Piñero, eds. *Nuyorican Poetry: An Anthology of Puerto Rican Words and Feelings.* New York: Morrow, 1975.

Allen, Gay Wilson, et al., eds. *American Poetry.* New York: Harper, 1965.

Allen, Paula Gunn, ed. *Studies in American Indian Literature.* New York: MLA, 1983.

Alurista. "From Tragedy to Caricature . . . and Beyond." *Aztlan* 11 (1980): 89–98.

Ammons, Elizabeth. "Going in Circles: The Female Geography of Jewett's *Country of the Pointed Firs.*" *Studies in the Literary Imagination* 16 (1983): 83–92.

———. "Stowe's Dream of the Mother-Savior: *Uncle Tom's Cabin* and American Women Writers before the 1920s." Sundquist 155–95.

Andrews, William L. "The 1850s: The First Afro-American Literary Renaissance." *Literary Romanticism in America.* Ed. Andrews. Baton Rouge: Louisiana State UP, 1981. 38–60.

———. *To Tell a Free Story: The First Century of Afro-American Autobiography, 1760–1865.* Urbana: U of Illinois P, 1986.

Auerbach, Nina. *Communities of Women: An Idea in Fiction.* Cambridge: Harvard UP, 1978.

Augustinus, Aurelius. *St. Augustine's Confessions.* Trans. William Watts. London: Heinemann, 1912.

Austin, J. L. *How to Do Things with Words.* New York: Oxford UP, 1960.

Babcock-Abrahams, Barbara, ed. Introd. *The Reversible World.* Ithaca: Cornell UP, 1978.

———. "'A Tolerated Margin of Mess': Trickster and His Tales Reconsidered." *Journal of the Folklore Institute* 9 (1975): 147–86. Rpt. in Wiget, *Critical Essays on Native American Literature* 153–85.

Baker, Houston A., Jr. *Blues, Ideology, and Afro-American Literature: A Vernacular Theory.* Chicago: U of Chicago P, 1984.

———, ed. *Three American Literatures: Essays in Chicano, Native American, and Asian-American Literature for Teachers of American Literature.* New York: MLA, 1982.

———. "To Move without Moving: Creativity and Commerce in Ralph Ellison's Trueblood Episode." Gates, *Black Literature and Literary Theory* 221–48.

Barbour, Brian. "Introduction: Franklin, Lawrence, and Tradition." *Benjamin Franklin: A Collection of Critical Essays.* Ed. Barbour. Englewood Cliffs: Prentice, 1979. 1–8.

Barthes, Roland. "Historical Discourse." *Introduction to Structuralism.* Ed. Michael Lane. New York: Basic, 1970. 148–68.

Barton, Rebecca Chalmers. *Witnesses for Freedom: Negro Americans in Autobiography.* New York: Harper, 1948.

Bascom, William. "The Four Functions of Folklore." *Journal of American Folklore* 67 (1954): 333–49.

Basso, Keith. *Portraits of the Whiteman.* London: Cambridge UP, 1979.

Bataille, Gretchen M., and Kathleen Mullen Sands. *American Indian Women: Telling Their Lives.* Lincoln: U of Nebraska P, 1984.

Bataille, Gretchen M., and Charles L. P. Silet, eds. *The Pretend Indians: Images of Native Americans in the Movies.* Foreword Vine Deloria, Jr. Ames: Iowa UP, 1980.

Bauman, Richard. "Conceptions of Folklore in the Development of Literary Semiotics." *Semiotica* 19 (1982): 1–20.

———. "Differential Identity and the Social Base of Folklore." *Journal of American Folklore* 84 (1971): 31–41.

———. "Verbal Art as Performance." *American Anthropologist* 75 (1975): 290–322.

———. *Verbal Art as Performance.* Rowley: Newbury, 1977.

Bauman, Richard, and Roger D. Abrahams, eds. *"And Other Neighborly Names": Social Process and Cultural Image in Texas Folklore.* Austin: U of Texas P, 1981.

Bauman, Richard, and Joel Sherzer. *Explorations in the Ethnography of Speaking.* London: Cambridge UP, 1974.

Bauman, Richard, Roger D. Abrahams, and Susan Kalcik. "American Folklore and American Studies." *American Quarterly* 28 (1976): 360–77.

Baym, Nina. "Melodramas of Beset Manhood: How Theories of American Fiction Exclude Women Authors." *American Quarterly* 33 (1981): 123–39.

———. *Woman's Fiction: A Guide to Novels by and about Women in America, 1820–1870.* Ithaca: Cornell UP, 1984.

Baym, Nina, Ronald Gottesman, Laurence B. Holland, David Kalstone, Francis Murphy, Hershel Parker, and William H. Pritchard, eds. *The Norton Anthology of American Literature.* 2 vols. 2nd ed. New York: Norton, 1985. 3rd ed. New York: Norton, 1989.

Beasley, Delilah L. Preface. *Lifting as They Climb.* Ed. Elizabeth Lindsay Davis. Chicago: n.p., 1933.

Beidelman, T. O. "The Moral Imagination of the Kaguru: Some Thoughts on Trickster, Translation, and Comparative Analysis." *American Ethnologist* 7 (1980): 27–42.

Bell, Michael J. "William Wells Newell and the Foundations of American Folklore Scholarship." *Journal of American Folklore* 10 (1973): 7–21.

Ben-Amos, Dan. "Analytical Categories and Ethnic Genres." *Genre* 2 (1969): 275–301. Rpt. in Ben-Amos, *Folklore Genres* 213–42.

Ben-Amos, Dan, ed. *Folklore Genres*. Austin: U of Texas P, 1976.

Ben-Amos, Dan, and Kenneth Goldstein, eds. *Folklore: Performance and Communication*. The Hague: Mouton, 1975.

Benamou, Michel. "The Concept of Marginality in Ethnopoetics." Fisher, *Minority Language and Literature* 150–60.

Bercovitch, Sacvan. *American Jeremiad*. Madison: U of Wisconsin P, 1978.

———, ed. *Reconstructing American Literary History*. Cambridge: Harvard UP, 1986.

Berkhofer, Robert F., Jr. *The White Man's Indian: Images of the American Indian from Columbus to the Present*. 1978. New York: Vintage, 1979.

Berry, Erlinda Gonzalez. "Perros y Antiperros: The Voice of the Bard." *De colores* 5 (1980): 45–68.

Bevis, William. "American Indian Verse Translations." *College English* 35 (1974): 693–703.

Bieder, Robert. "Anthropology and History of the American Indian." *American Quarterly* 33 (1981): 309–26.

Binder, Wolfgang. *"Anglos Are Weird People for Me": Interviews with Chicanos and Puerto Ricans*. Berlin: John F. Kennedy-Inst. für Nordamerikastudien, Freie Univ., 1979.

———. *Puerto Ricaner in New York: Volk zwischen zwei Kulturen*. Erlangen: Städtische Galerie, 1978.

Birch, Cyril, ed. *Anthology of Chinese Literature*. New York: Grove, 1967.

Blair, Walter, et al., eds. *Literature of the United States*. 2 vols. 3rd ed. Glenview: Scott, 1971.

Blassingame, John W. *The Slave Community*. New York: Oxford UP, 1972.

Bloom, Allan. *The Closing of the American Mind: How Higher Education Has Failed Democracy*. New York: Simon, 1987.

Bloom, Harold. *The Anxiety of Influence: A Theory of Poetry*. New York: Oxford UP, 1973.

———. *The Breaking of the Vessels*. Chicago: U of Chicago P, 1982.

———. *A Map of Misreading*. New York: Oxford UP, 1975.

———. *Poetry and Repression: Revisionism from Blake to Stevens*. New Haven: Yale UP, 1976.

Bloomfield, Leonard. *Plains Cree Texts*. Publications of the American Ethnological Soc. 16. New York: Stechert, 1934.

———. *Sacred Stories of the Sweet Grass Cree*. Bulletin 60. Ottawa: Dept. of Mines, 1930.

Boas, Franz. *Kutenai Tales*. Bulletin of the Bureau of American Ethnology 59. Washington: GPO, 1918.

———. *Tsimshian Mythology*. Annual Report of the Bureau of American Ethnology 31 (1909–10). Washington: GPO, 1916.

Boatright, Mody C., Wilson M. Hudson, and Allen Maxwell, eds. *Madstones and Twisters*. Dallas: Southern Methodist UP, 1958.

Bontemps, Arna, ed. *Great Slave Narratives*. Boston: Beacon, 1969.

Bouchard, Randy, and Dorothy Kennedy, eds. *Shuswap Stories*. Vancouver: CommCept, 1979.

Bowen, Barbara E. "Untroubled Voice: Call and Response in *Cane*." Gates, *Black Literature and Literary Theory* 187–203.

Bradley, Sculley, Richmond Croom Beatty, and E. Hudson Long, eds. *The American Tradition in Literature*. New York: Norton, 1957. 2nd ed. New York: Norton, 1962. 3rd ed. New York: Norton, 1967. 4th ed. New York: Grosset, 1974. 5th ed. Ed. Bradley, Beatty, Long, and George Perkins. New York: Random, 1981. 6th ed. New York: Random, 1985.

Brettville, Shiela de. "A Re-Examination of Some Aspects of the Design Arts from the Perspective of a Woman Designer." *Women and the Arts: Arts in Society* 1 (1974): 117–18.

Bricker, Victoria. "Some Zinancanteco Joking Strategies." *Speech Play*. Ed. Barbara Kirshenblatt-Gimblett. Philadelphia: U of Pennsylvania P, 1976.

Brimlow, George F. "The Life of Sarah Winnemucca: The Formative Years." *Oregon Historical Quarterly* 58 (1952): 103–34.

Brooks, Cleanth, R. W. B. Lewis, and Robert Penn Warren, eds. *American Literature: The Makers and the Making.* 2 vols. New York: St. Martin's, 1973.

Broyles, Yolanda Julia. "Hinojosa's *Klail City y sus alrededores*: Oral Culture and Print Culture." Saldívar, *The Rolando Hinojosa Reader* 109–30.

Bruce-Novoa, Juan D., ed. *Chicano Authors: Inquiry by Interview.* Austin: U of Texas P, 1980.

———. *Chicano Poetry: A Response to Chaos.* Austin: U of Texas P, 1982.

———. "Década literaria chicana." *La communidad: Supplemento domincal de* La opinion 2 Jan. 1983: 12–13.

Brumble, H. David, III. *American Indian Autobiography.* Berkeley: U of California P, 1988.

———, comp. *An Annotated Bibliography of American Indian and Eskimo Autobiographies.* Lincoln: U of Nebraska P, 1981.

Brutus, Dennis. "English and the Dynamics of South African Creative Writing." Fiedler and Baker 1–14.

Burke, Kenneth. "What Are Signs of What?" *Laughing as Symbolic Action.* Berkeley: U of California P, 1966.

Butterfield, Stephen. *Black Autobiography in America.* Amherst: U of Massachusetts P, 1974.

Canfield, Gae Whitney. *Sarah Winnemucca of the Northern Paiutes.* Norman: U of Oklahoma P, 1983.

Cantoni-Harvey, Gina, and M. S. Heiser, eds. *Southwest Languages and Linguistics in Educational Perspective.* San Diego: Inst. for Cultural Pluralism, San Diego State Univ., 1975.

Carby, Hazel. *Reconstructing Womanhood: The Emergence of the Afro-American Woman Novelist.* New York: Oxford UP, 1987.

Cary, Alice. *Clovernook Sketches and Other Stories.* Ed. Judith Fetterley. New Brunswick: Rutgers UP, 1987.

Catalán, Diego, and Teresa Catarella. "El romance tradicional, un sistem abierto." *El romancero en la tradición moderna.* Madrid: U of Madrid, 1972. 181–205.

Catlin, George. *Letters and Notes on the Manners, Customs, and Conditions of the North American Indians.* New York: Dover, 1973. 2 vols.

Chang, H. C. *Chinese Literature.* Edinburgh: Edinburgh UP, 1973.

Channing, William Ellery. *Thoreau, the Poet-Naturalist.* Boston: Roberts, 1873.

Chapman, Abraham. *Literature of the American Indian: Views and Interpretations.* New York: NAL, 1975.

Charrow, Robert P., and Veda R. Charrow. "Making Legal Language Understandable: A Psycholinguistic Study of Jury Instructions." *Columbia Law Review* 79 (1979): 1306–60.

Charters, Samuel. "Sleepy John Estes." *Saturday Review* 10 Nov. 1962: 57–58.

Chesnutt, Charles W. Journal. 8 May 1880. Qtd. in introduction to *The Short Fiction of Charles W. Chesnutt.* Ed. Sylvia Lyons Render. Washington: Howard UP, 1974. 3–56.

Child, Francis J. *The English and Scottish Popular Ballads.* 5 vols. 1882–98. New York: Dover, 1965.

Child, Lydia Marie. *Appeal in Favor of That Class of Americans Called Africans.* 1833. Salem: Ayer, 1968.

Chin, Frank, Jeffery Chan, Lawson Inada, and Shawn Wong, eds. *AIIIEEEEE! An Anthology of Asian-American Writers.* Washington: Howard UP, 1974, 1983.

Christensen, A. H. M. *Afro-American Folklore.* Boston: Cupples, 1892.

Christian, Barbara. *Black Feminist Criticism: Perspectives on Black Women Writers.* New York: Pergamon, 1985.

———. *Black Women Novelists: The Development of a Tradition, 1892–1976.* Westport: Greenwood, 1980.

Christy, Marian. "Doctor-Author Battles to Maintain Independent Spirit." *Los Angeles Times* Syndicate. *Home News* [New Brunswick, NJ] 12 Aug. 1982: 23.

Chun-Hoon, Lowell. "Jade Snow Wong and the Fate of Chinese-American Identity." *Amerasia Journal* 1 (1971): 52–63. Rpt. in *Asian-Americans: Psychological Perspectives*. 2 vols. Ed. Stanley Sue and Nathaniel N. Wagner. Palo Alto: Science and Behavior, 1973. 1: 125–35.

Clark, Helen. *The Lady of the Lily Feet and Other Tales of Chinatown*. Philadelphia: Griffith, 1900.

Coffin, Tristram P., ed. *Our Living Traditions*. New York: Basic, 1968.

Colbert, Edwin H. *Men and Dinosaurs*. New York: Dutton, 1968.

Cooley, Thomas. *Educated Lives: The Rise of Modern Autobiography in America*. Columbus: Ohio State UP, 1976.

Crocker, Christopher. "The Social Function of Rhetorical Forms." *The Social Use of Metaphor*. Ed. Crocker and J. David Sapir. Philadelphia: U of Pennsylvania P, 1977. 33–66.

Crowley, Daniel J., ed. *African Folklore in the New World*. Austin: U of Texas P, 1977.

Curtius, Ernst. *European Literature and the Latin Middle Ages*. Princeton: Princeton UP, 1973.

Dabney, Lewis. *The Indians of Yoknapatawpha*. Baton Rouge: Louisiana State UP, 1974.

Darnell, Regna. "Correlates of Cree Narrative Performance." Bauman and Sherzer, *Explorations in the Ethnography of Speaking* 315–36.

Davidson, Cathy. *Revolution and the Word: The Rise of the Novel in America*. New York: Oxford, 1988.

Davis, Rebecca Harding. *Life in the Iron Mills and Other Stories*. 1861. Ed. Tillie Olsen. New York: Feminist, 1985.

Deloria, Ella C. *Dakota Texts*. Publications of the American Ethnological Soc. 14 (1932). New York: AMS, 1974.

de Man, Paul. "Literary History and Literary Modernity." *Daedalus* 99 (1970): 384–404.

Denham, Robert D., ed. Introd. *Northrop Frye on Culture and Literature*. Chicago: U of Chicago P, 1979. 1–64.

Donovan, Josephine. *New England Local Color Literature: A Women's Tradition*. New York: Ungar, 1983.

Dorson, Richard M. *American Folklore and the Historian*. Chicago: U of Chicago P, 1971.

———. "American Folklore vs. Folklore in America." *Journal of the Folklore Institute* 15 (1978): 97–111.

———. *American Negro Folktales*. Greenwich: Fawcett, 1967.

———. "Davy Crockett and the Heroic Age." *Southern Folklore Quarterly* 6 (1942): 95–102.

———. "A Theory for American Folklore." *Journal of American Folklore* 72 (1959): 197–215.

Dorson, Richard M., Inta Gale Carpenter, Elizabeth Peterson, and Angela Maniak, eds. *Handbook of American Folklore*. Bloomington: Indiana UP, 1983.

Douglas, Mary C. *Natural Symbols*. New York: Pantheon, 1970.

———. *Purity and Danger*. New York: Praeger, 1966.

———. "The Social Control of Cognition: Some Factors in Joke Perception." *Man* 3 (1968): 361–76.

Duany, Jorge. "Popular Music in Puerto Rico: Toward an Anthropology of Salsa." *Latin American Music Review* 5.2 (1984): 186–216.

Dundes, Alan. "The American Concept of Folklore." *Journal of the Folklore Institute* 3 (1966): 226–49.

———. "The Study of Folklore in Literature and Culture: Identification and Interpretation." *Journal of American Folklore* 78 (1965): 136–42.

———. "Text, Texture, and Context." *Southern Folklore Quarterly* 28 (1964): 251–65.

Edwards, Carol L. "The Parry-Lord Theory Meets Operational Structuralism." *Journal of American Folklore* 96 (1983): 151–69.

Edwards, Jay D. *The Afro-American Trickster Tale: A Structural Analysis*. Bloomington: Folklore Publications Group, 1978.

Eliot, T. S. "The Metaphysical Poets." *Selected Essays, 1917–1932*. New York: Harcourt, 1950. 241–50.

Elizondo, Sergio. "Sergio Elizondo." Bruce-Novoa, *Chicano Authors* 67–82.

Eoyang, Eugene. "The Immediate Audience: Oral Narration in Chinese Fiction." *Critical Essays on Chinese Literature*. Ed. William J. Nienhauser, Jr. Hong Kong: Chinese U of Hong Kong P, 1976. 43–57.

Evans, Mari, ed. *Black Women Writers, 1950–1980: A Critical Evaluation*. Garden City: Doubleday, 1984.

Evers, Larry, and Felipe S. Molina. *Yaqui Deer Songs / Maso Bwikam: A Native American Poetry*. Sun Tracks 14. Tucson: U of Arizona P, 1986.

Faber, Eunice. "Overcoming Obstacles to Curriculum Change in Foreign Languages." Fisher, *Minority Language and Literature* 107–14.

Feldmann, Susan. *African Myths and Tales*. New York: Dell, 1963.

Fetterley, Judith, ed. *Provisions: A Reader from Nineteenth-Century American Women*. Bloomington: Indiana UP, 1985.

Fiedler, Leslie. Preface. Fiedler and Baker viii.

Fiedler, Leslie, and Houston A. Baker, Jr., eds. *English Literature: Opening Up the Canon*. Selected Papers from the English Institute, 1979. Baltimore: Johns Hopkins UP, 1981.

Finnegan, Ruth. "Literacy and Literature." *Universals of Human Thought: Some African Evidence*. Ed. Barbara Lloyd and John Gay. Cambridge: Cambridge UP, 1981. 234–55.

Fisher, Dexter, ed. *Minority Language and Literature: Retrospective and Perspective*. New York: MLA, 1977.

———. *The Third Woman: Minority Women Writers of the United States*. Boston: Houghton, 1980.

Fisher, Dexter, and Robert B. Stepto, eds. *Afro-American Literature: The Reconstruction of Instruction*. New York: MLA, 1979.

Flanagan, John T., and Arthur P. Hudson, eds. *Folklore in American Literature*. Evanston: Row, 1958.

Foerster, Norman, ed. *American Prose and Poetry*. Boston: Houghton, 1957.

Foster, Frances Smith. *Witnessing Slavery: The Development of the Antebellum Slave Narratives*. Contributions in Afro-American and African Studies 46. Westport: Greenwood, 1979.

Foster, George R. "What Is Folk Culture?" *American Anthropologist* 55 (1953): 159–73.

Foucault, Michel. *The Archaeology of Knowledge*. Trans. A. M. Sheridan Smith. New York: Harper, 1972.

Fowler, Alastair. "The Selection of Literary Constructs." *New Literary History* 7 (1975): 39–56.

Fowler, Carolyn S. "Sarah Winnemucca, Northern Paiute, 1844–1891." *American Indian Intellectuals*. Ed. Robert F. Spencer. 1976 Proceedings of the American Ethnological Soc. St. Paul: West, 1978. 33–42.

Franklin, Benjamin. *Autobiography and Other Writings*. Ed. Russell B. Nye. Boston: Houghton, 1958.

Franklin, H. Bruce. *The Victim as Criminal and Artist: Literature from the American Prison*. New York: Oxford UP, 1978.

Franklin, John Hope. *From Slavery to Freedom: A History of Negro America*. 4th ed. New York: Knopf, 1974.

Frederickson, George M. *The Black Image in the White Mind*. New York: Harper, 1971.

Freeman, Mary E. Wilkins. "A Church Mouse." "The Revolt of 'Mother.'" 1891. *Selected Stories of Mary E. Wilkins Freeman*. Ed. Marjorie Pryse. New York: Norton, 1983. 273–92; 293–313.

———. "Old Woman Magoun." 1909. *The Norton Anthology of Literature by Women: The Tradition in English.* Ed. Sandra J. Gilbert and Susan Gubar. New York: Norton, 1985. 1103–19.

Frye, Northrop. "Literature and Myth." *Relations of Literary Study: Essays on Interdisciplinary Contributions.* Ed. James Thorpe. New York: MLA, 1967. 27–41.

Garraty, John A. *The Nature of Biography.* London: Cape, 1958.

Garza, Mario. "Duality in Chicano Poetry." *De colores* 3 (1977): 37–45.

Gates, Henry Louis, Jr., ed. *Black Literature and Literary Theory.* New York: Methuen, 1984.

———. "The North Star, Moonbeams, and Magnolia Blossoms." MLA Convention. 27 Dec. 1981.

———. [Response.] *Profession 81.* New York: MLA, 1981. 5–7.

Geertz, Clifford. *The Interpretation of Cultures.* New York: Basic, 1973.

Gelfant, Blanche H. "Mingling and Sharing in American Literature: Teaching Ethnic Fiction." *College English* 43 (1981): 763–72.

Genovese, Eugene. *The Political Economy of Slavery.* New York: Vintage, 1965.

———. *Roll, Jordon, Roll.* New York: Pantheon, 1974.

———. *The World the Slaveholders Made.* New York: Vintage, 1971.

Giglioli, Pier Paolo. *Language and Social Context.* London: Penguin, 1972.

Gilbert, Sandra A., and Susan Gubar, eds. *The Norton Anthology of Literature by Women: The Tradition in English.* New York: Norton, 1985.

Gill, Sam. *Sacred Words: A Study of Navajo Religion and Prayer.* Westport: Greenwood, 1981.

Gilman, Charlotte Perkins. "The Yellow Wallpaper." 1892. Gilbert and Gubar, 1148–61.

Gombrich, E. H. *Ideals and Idols: Essays on Values in History and in Art.* Oxford: Phaidon, 1979.

González, José Luis. "La noche que volvimos a ser gente." *Mambru se fué a la guerra.* México: Mortiz, 1972. 117–34.

Gordon, David. "Form and Feeling." *Yale Review* 62 (1973): 582–93.

Gorman, Margaret, Michael Gorman, and Arthur P. Young. "The 1982–83 Writing and Literature Survey." Unpublished paper. New York: ADE.

Gossen, Gary. *Chamulas in the World of the Sun: Time and Space in a Maya Oral Tradition.* Cambridge: Harvard UP, 1974.

Gottesman, Ronald, Laurence B. Holland, David Kalstone, Francis Murphy, Hershel Parker, and William H. Pritchard, eds. *The Norton Anthology of American Literature.* 2 vols. New York: Norton, 1979. 2nd ed. New York: Norton, 1985.

Grindal, Bruce. "The Sisala Trickster." *Journal of American Folklore* 86 (1973): 173–75.

Gumperz, John J., and Dell Hymes. *Directions in Sociolinguistics: The Ethnography of Communication.* New York: Holt, 1972.

Gura, Philip F. "Thoreau's Maine Woods Indians: More Representative Men." *American Literature* 49 (1977): 366–84.

Habegger, Alfred. *Gender, Fantasy, and Realism in American Literature.* New York: Columbia UP, 1982.

Hampton, Bill R. "On Identification and the Trickster." *Southern Folklore Quarterly* 3 (1967): 55–65.

Hanan, Patrick. *The Chinese Vernacular Story.* Cambridge: Harvard UP, 1981.

Harris, Joel Chandler. *Uncle Remus, His Songs and His Sayings.* 1880. Ed. Robert Hemenway. New York: Penguin, 1982.

Hart, James. *The Popular Book: A History of America's Literary Taste.* New York: Oxford UP, 1950.

Hartman, Geoffrey. *Criticism in the Wilderness.* New Haven: Yale UP, 1980.

Hawkes, Terence. *Structuralism and Semiotics.* Berkeley: U of California P, 1977.

Herms, Dieter. "Chicano Literature: A European Perspective." *International Studies in Honor of Tomás Rivera.* Ed. Julián Olivares. Houston: Arte Público, 1986. 163–72.

Hernández, Guillermo. "On the Theoretical Bases of Chicano Literature." *De colores* 5 (1980): 5–18.

Hieb, Louis. "Meaning and Mismeaning: Toward an Understanding of the Pueblo Clown." Ortiz, *New Perspectives on the Pueblos* 163–96.

Hilgers, Thomas, and Michael Molloy. "An Interview with Maxine Hong Kingston." *Island Interviews: The Humanities in Hawaii.* Interoffice newsletter. Kapiolani Community Coll. and KAIM-FM. Honolulu, June 1980. N. pag.

Hirata, Lucie Chang. "Chinese Immigrant Women in Nineteenth-Century California." *Women of America, a History.* Ed. Carol Ruth Berkin and Mary Beth Norton. Boston: Houghton, 1979. 223–44.

Hirsch, E. D., Jr. "Cultural Literacy." *American Scholar* 52 (1983): 159–69.

———. *Cultural Literacy: What Every American Needs to Know.* Boston: Houghton, 1987.

Hoffman, Daniel G. *Form and Fable in American Fiction.* New York: Oxford UP, 1961.

———. "Notes toward a Theory of Interpretation." *Journal of American Folklore* 70 (1957): 1–24.

Holoka, James P. "Homeric Originality: A Survey." *Classical World* 66 (1973): 257–93.

Homsher, Deborah. "The *Woman Warrior* by Maxine Hong Kingston: A Bridging of Autobiography and Fiction." *Iowa Review* 10.4 (1979): 93–98.

Horton, Rod W., and Herbert W. Edwards, eds. *Backgrounds of American Literary Thought.* 3rd ed. Englewood Cliffs: Prentice, 1974.

Howard, Leon. *Literature and the American Tradition.* New York: Doubleday, 1970.

Howe, Irving. Rev. of *The Poetry Anthology, 1912-1977,* ed. Daryl Hine and Joseph Parisi. *New York Times Book Review* 19 Nov. 1978: 1.

Howells, William D. "A Psychological Counter-Current in Recent Fiction." *North American Review* 173 (1901): 872–88.

Hsu, Francis. *Americans and Chinese.* Honolulu: UP of Hawaii, 1970.

Hsu, Kai-yu, and Helen Palubinskas, eds. *Asian-American Authors.* Boston: Houghton, 1972.

Hubbell, Jay B. *Who Are the Major American Writers?* Durham: Duke UP, 1972.

Hudson, Arthur Palmer. "Folklore." Spiller, *Literary History of the United States.* Rev. ed., 1953. 703–27.

Huizinga, Johan. *Homo Ludens.* Boston: Beacon, 1950.

Hymes, Dell. "Discovering Oral Performance and Measured Verse in American Indian Narrative." *New Literary History* 8 (1977): 433–57. Rpt. in Hymes, *"In Vain I Tried to Tell You"* 309–41.

———. "Folklore's Nature and the Sun's Myth." *Journal of American Folklore* 88 (1975): 345–69.

———. *Foundations in Sociolinguistics.* Philadelphia: U of Pennsylvania P, 1974.

———. "Identification and Interpretation." *Journal of American Folklore* 78 (1965): 136–42.

———. *"In Vain I Tried to Tell You": Essays in Native American Ethnopoetics.* Studies in Native American Literature 1. Philadelphia: U of Pennsylvania P, 1981.

Idema, W. L. "Storytelling and the Short Story in China." *T'oung Pao* 59 (1973). Rpt. in *Chinese Vernacular Fiction: The Formative Period.* By Idema. Sinica Leidensia 13. Leiden: Brill, 1974. 1–67.

Irvine, Judith. "Formality and Informality in Communicative Events." *American Anthropologist* 81 (1979): 773–90.

Iser, Wolfgang. "The Current Situation of Literary Theory: Key Concepts and the Imaginary." *New Literary History* 11 (1979): 1–20.

Jackson, Helen Hunt. *A Century of Dishonor: The Early Crusade for Indian Reform.* 1886. St. Clair Shores: Scholarly, 1973.

Jacobs, Melville. *The Content and Style of an Oral Literature: Clackamas Chinook Myths and Tales.* Chicago: U of Chicago P, 1959.

James, Daniel (Danny Santiago). *Famous All over Town.* New York: Simon, 1983.

James, Henry. "The Art of Fiction." 1888. *Representative Selections.* Ed. Lyon N. Richardson. New York: American, 1941. 75–97.

Jameson, Fredric. *Marxism and Form: Twentieth-Century Dialectical Theories of Literature.* Princeton: Princeton UP, 1971.

———. *The Political Unconscious: Narrative as a Socially Symbolic Act.* Ithaca: Cornell UP, 1981.

———. "The Symbolic Inference: Or, Kenneth Burke and Ideological Analysis." *Critical Inquiry* 4 (1978): 507–23.

Jansen, William H. "Classifying Performance in the Study of Verbal Folklore." *Studies in Folklore: Essays in Honor of Distinguished Service Professor Stith Thompson.* Ed. Edson Richmond. Folklore Series 9. Bloomington: Indiana UP, 1957. 110–18.

Jelinek, Estelle, ed. *Women's Autobiography: Essays in Criticism.* Bloomington: Indiana UP, 1980.

Jennings, Francis. *The Invasion of America: Indians, Colonialism, and the Cant of Conquest.* 1975. New York: Norton, 1976.

Jewett, Sarah Orne. "Aunt Cynthy Dallett." Jewett, *Country of the Pointed Firs* 279–96.

———. *The Country of the Pointed Firs and Other Stories.* Ed. Mary Ellen Chase. New York: Norton, 1981.

———. "The Foreigner." Jewett, *Country of the Pointed Firs* 157–87.

Johnson, Emily Pauline. *The Moccasin Maker.* Ed., annot., and introd. A. LaVonne Brown Ruoff. Tucson: U of Arizona P, 1987.

Keiser, Albert. *The Indian in American Literature.* New York: Oxford UP, 1933.

Kendall, Martha. *Coyote Stories II.* IJAL–Native American Texts. Chicago: U of Chicago P, 1980.

Kendall, Paul Murray. *The Art of Biography.* London: Allen, 1965.

Kennedy, John C. "Bonds of Laughter among the Tarahumara Indians." *The Social Anthropology of Native America: Essays in Honor of Ralph Leon Beals.* Los Angeles: U of California P, 1970. 36–68.

Kim, Elaine. *Asian American Literature: An Introduction to the Writings and Their Social Contexts.* Philadelphia: Temple UP, 1982.

King, Michael J., ed. *The Collected Early Poems of Ezra Pound.* New York: New Directions, 1976.

Kingston, Maxine Hong. "Cultural Mis-Readings by American Reviewers." *Asian and Western Writers in Dialogue: New Cultural Identities.* Ed. Guy Amirthanayagam. London: Macmillan, 1982. 55–65.

Kirkland, Caroline Matilda Stansbury. *A New Home . . . Who'll Follow?* 1839. Ed. William S. Osborne. New Haven: College, 1965.

Knobel, Dale T. "Know-Nothings and Indians: Strange Bedfellows?" *Western Historical Quarterly* 15 (1984): 175–98.

Kolodny, Annette. "The Integrity of Memory: Creating a New Literary History of the United States." *American Literature* 57 (1985): 291–307.

Krieger, Murray. "The Recent Revolution in Theory and the Survival of the Literary Disciplines." *ADE Bulletin* 62 (1979): 27–34.

Kroeber, Karl. "Deconstructionist Criticism and American Indian Literature." *Boundary 2* 7.3 (1978): 73–87.

———. "An Introduction to the Art of Traditional American Indian Narration." Kroeber, *Traditional Literatures* 1–24.

———, ed. *Traditional Literatures of the American Indian: Texts and Interpretation.* Lincoln: U of Nebraska P, 1981.

Krupat, Arnold. "An Approach to Native American Texts." *Critical Inquiry* 9 (1982): 323–38.

———. *For Those Who Come After: A Study of Native American Autobiography.* Los Angeles: U of California P, 1985.

————. "The Indian Autobiography: Origins, Type, and Function." *American Literature* 53 (1981): 22–42. Rpt. in Krupat, *For Those Who Come After* 2–27.

Lai, Him Mark, Genny Lim, and Judy Yung, eds. and trans. *Island: Poetry and History of Chinese Immigrants on Angel Island, 1910–1940.* San Francisco: Hoc Doi, 1980.

Lamming, George. *Season of Adventure.* London: Allison, 1979.

Lanier Seward, Adrienne. "The Legacy of Early Afro-American Folklore Scholarship." Dorson et al., *Handbook* 48–56.

Lattin, Vernon E. "The Quest for Mythic Vision in Contemporary Native American and Chicano Fiction." *American Literature* 50 (1979): 625–40.

Lauter, Paul. "Caste, Class, and Canon." *A Gift of Tongues: Critical Challenges in Contemporary American Poetry.* Athens: U of Georgia P, 1987. 57–82.

————, ed. *Reconstructing American Literature.* Old Westbury: Feminist, 1983.

Lawrence, D. H. *Studies in Classic American Literature.* New York: Seltzer, 1923.

Leach, Douglas Edward. *Flintlock and Tomahawk: New England in King Philip's War.* 1958. New York: Norton, 1966.

Leach, Edmund. *Culture and Communication.* London: Cambridge UP, 1976.

Leach, Maria. *Funk and Wagnalls Standard Dictionary of Folklore, Mythology, and Legend.* 2 vols. New York: Funk, 1949.

Leal, Luis. "Mexican American Literature: A Historical Perspective." Sommers and Ybarra-Frausto, *Modern Chicano Writers* 18–30.

Leal, Luis, Fernando de Necochea, Francisco Lomelí, and Roberto G. Trujillo, eds. *A Decade of Chicano Literature (1970–1979): Critical Essays and Bibliography.* Santa Barbara: La Causa, 1982.

Leavis, Frank R. *Great Tradition: George Eliot, Henry James, Joseph Conrad.* New York: Stewart, 1948.

Lee, Rose Hum. *The Chinese in the United States of America.* Hong Kong: Hong Kong UP, 1960.

Leland, Charles G. *Algonquin Legends of New England.* 1884. Detroit: Rising Sun, 1968.

Lentricchia, Frank. *After the New Criticism.* Chicago: U of Chicago P, 1980.

Leslie Silko's Ceremony. Ed. Kathleen Mullen Sands. Spec. issue of *American Indian Quarterly* 5 (1979).

Le Sueur, Meridel. *The Girl.* Minneapolis: West End, 1978.

Levine, Lawrence W. *Black Culture and Black Consciousness: Afro-American Folk Thought from Slavery to Freedom.* New York: Oxford UP, 1977.

Lévi-Strauss, Claude. "History and Dialectic." *The Structuralists from Marx to Lévi-Strauss.* Ed. Richard DeGeorge and Fernande DeGeorge. New York: Doubleday, 1972. 209–37.

————. *The Savage Mind.* Chicago: U of Chicago P, 1963.

————. "The Structural Study of Myth." *Structural Anthropology.* Garden City: Doubleday, 1967. 202–28.

Lewis, Mary Ellen B. "The Study of Folklore in Literature: An Expanded View." *Southern Folklore Quarterly* 40 (1976): 343–51.

Lewis, Oscar. *La vida: A Puerto Rican Family in the Culture of Poverty.* New York: Random, 1965.

Lewis, Thomas H. "The *heyoka* Cult in Historical and Contemporary Oglala Sioux Society." *Anthropos* 69 (1974): 17–32.

Li Ju-Chen. *Flowers in the Mirror.* Berkeley: U of California P, 1965.

————. "The Women's Kingdom." Chang, *Chinese Literature* 421–61.

Limón, José E. "Américo Paredes: A Man from the Border." *Revista Chicano-Riqueña* 8 (1980): 1–5.

————. "The Folk Performance of *Chicano* and the Cultural Limits of Political Ideology." Bauman and Abrahams, *"And Other Neighborly Names"* 197–225.

————. "The Rise, Fall, and 'Revival' of the Mexican-American Corrido: A Review Essay." *Studies in Latin American Popular Culture* 2 (1983): 202–06.

Ling, Amy. "Writer in the Hyphenated Condition: Diana Chang." *MELUS* 7.4 (1980): 69–83.

Lin Yutang, ed. and trans. *The Wisdom of Confucius*. New York: Modern Library, 1938.

List, George. "The Boundaries of Speech and Song." *Ethnomusicology* 7 (1963): 1–16.

Liu, James J. Y. *Chinese Theories of Literature*. Chicago: U of Chicago P, 1975.

————. *Essentials of Chinese Literary Art*. North Scituate: Duxbury, 1979.

Lomax, Alan. *Folksong Style and Culture*. Washington: American Assn. for the Advancement of Science, 1968.

Lomelí, Francisco A., and Donaldo W. Urioste, comps. *Chicano Perspectives in Literature: A Critical and Annotated Bibliography*. Albuquerque: Pajarito, 1976.

Longfellow, Henry Wadsworth. *The Song of Hiawatha*. 1855. Facs. ed. New York: Crown, 1969.

Lopez, Barry Holstun. *Giving Birth to Thunder, Sleeping with His Daughter*. New York: Avon, 1977.

Lord, Albert B. *The Singer of Tales*. Cambridge: Harvard UP, 1960.

Lu Hsun. *A Brief History of Chinese Fiction*. Peking: Foreign Language, 1959.

Lyman, Stanford M. *Chinese Americans*. New York: Random, 1974.

Ma, Y. W., and Joseph Lau, eds. *Traditional Chinese Stories*. New York: Columbia UP, 1978.

Madhubuti, Haki R. (Don L. Lee) "Black Writers and Critics: Developing a Critical Process without Readers." *The Black Scholar* 10 (1978): 35–40.

Makarius, Laura. "Ritual Clowns and Symbolic Behavior." *Diogenes* 69 (1970): 44–73.

Malinowski, Bronislaw. "Myth in Primitive Psychology." *Magic, Science, and Religion*. Garden City: Doubleday, 1954. 93–148.

Maquet, Jacques. "Introduction to Aesthetic Anthropology." *A McCaleb Module in Anthropology*. Ed. Joseph B. Casagrande, Ward H. Goodenough, and Eugene E. Hammel. Reading: Addison, 1971. 1–38.

Marias, E. J. *African Thought*. Cape Province: Fort Hare UP, 1972.

Marín, Pachín. "Nueva York por dentro: Una faz de su vida bohemia." *La gaceta del pueblo* [1892?].

Márquez, Antonio. "Literatura Chicanesca." Leal et al., *Decade* 73–81.

Marx, Karl. *Capital*. Ed. Friedrich Engels. Chicago: Encyclopaedia Britannica, 1952.

Matthews, Washington. *Navajo Legends*. Memoirs of the American Folklore Soc. 5 (1897). Milwood: Kraus, 1969.

Mattina, Anthony, and Madeline de Sautel, trans. *The Golden Woman: The Colville Narrative of Peter J. Seymour*. Tucson: U of Arizona P, 1985.

Mbiti, John S. *African Religions and Philosophy*. Garden City: Doubleday, 1970.

McDowell, John H. "The Corrido of Greater Mexico as Discourse, Music, and Event." Bauman and Abrahams, *"And Other Neighborly Names"* 44–75.

McMichael, George, ed. *Anthology of American Literature*. 3rd ed. New York: Macmillan, 1985.

McNickle, D'Arcy. *Native American Tribalism: Indian Survivals and Renewals*. New York: Oxford UP, 1973.

McQuade, Donald, et al., eds. *The Harper American Literature*. 2 vols. New York: Harper, 1987.

McQuaid, Kim. "William Apes, Pequot, an Indian Reformer in the Jackson Era." *New England Quarterly* 50 (1977): 605–25.

Mei, J., J. Yip, and R. Leong, trans. "The Bitter Society: *Ku Shehui*, a Translation, Chapters 37–46." *Amerasia Journal* 8 (1981): 33–68.

Melville, Herman. *Moby-Dick*. New York: Modern Library, 1950.

Mendoza, Vicente T. *El corrido mexicano*. México: Fonda de Cultura Economica, 1954.

Miller, J. Hillis. "The Function of Rhetorical Study at the Present Time." *ADE Bulletin* 62 (1979): 10–18.

Miller, Joaquin. *Life among the Modocs: Unwritten History.* 1873. Introd. Alan Rosenus. Eugene: Urion, 1982.

Miller, Perry. *Errand into the Wilderness.* Cambridge: Harvard UP, 1956.

Mohr, Eugene. *The Nuyorican Experience: Literature of the Puerto Rican Minority.* Westport: Greenwood, 1982.

Montejano, David. "A Journey through Mexican Texas, 1900–1930: The Making of a Segregated Society." Diss. Yale U, 1982.

Mooney, James. *Myths of the Cherokees.* Annual Report of the Bureau of American Ethnology 19.1 (1897–98): 3–575. St. Claire Shores: Scholarly, 1970.

Morgan, Lewis Henry. *The League of the Iroquois.* 1851. Secaucus: Lyle Stuart, 1984.

Morrison, Toni. Speech. MLA Convention. Washington, Dec. 1984.

Muro, Amado [Chester Seltzer]. *The Collected Stories of Amado Muro.* Austin: Thorp Springs, 1979.

Nadel, Ira Bruce. *Biography: Fiction, Fact, and Form.* London: Macmillan, 1984.

National Center for Education Statistics. *Digest of Education Statistics: 1972.* Washington: GPO, 1972.

———. *Digest of Education Statistics: 1982.* Washington: GPO, 1982.

Nee, Victor G., and Brett de Bary Nee. *Longtime Californin': A Documentary Study of an American Chinatown.* New York: Pantheon, 1973.

Needler, Howard I. "Sacred Books and Sacral Criticism." *New Literary History* 13 (1962): 393–409.

Nelson, Eugene. *Bracero.* Berkeley: Throp Springs, 1972.

Neruda, Pablo. *Song of Protest.* Trans. Miguel Algarín. New York: Morrow, 1976.

Newell, William Wells. "On the Field and Work of a Journal of American Folklore." *Journal of American Folklore* 1 (1888): 3–7.

Ngal, M. "Literary Creation in Oral Civilization." *New Literary History* 8 (1977): 335–44.

Niatum, Duane. "On Stereotypes." *Parnassus* 7 (1978): 160–66.

Nichols, John. *The Milagro Beanfield War.* New York: Holt, 1978.

Norwood, Vera. "'Thank You for My Bones': Connections between Contemporary Women Artists and the Traditional Arts of Their Foremothers." *New Mexico Historical Review* 58.1 (1983): 57–78.

Ohmann, Richard. "The Shaping of a Canon: U.S. Fiction, 1960–75." *Critical Inquiry* 10 (1983): 199–223.

Oliver, Paul. *The Story of the Blues.* London: Chilton, 1969.

Olsen, Tillie. *Silences.* New York: Delacorte, 1978.

Ong, Walter J. "African Talking Drums and Oral Noetics." Ong, *Interfaces of the Word* 92–110.

———. *Interfaces of the Word: Studies in the Evolution of Consciousness and Culture.* Ithaca: Cornell UP, 1977.

———. "Oral Culture and the Literate Mind." Fisher, *Minority Language and Literature* 134–49.

———. *Orality and Literacy: The Technologizing of the Word.* London: Methuen, 1982.

———. *The Presence of the Word.* New Haven: Yale UP, 1967.

Opland, Jeff. "Imbongi Nezibongo: The Xhosa Tribal Poet and the Contemporary Poetic Tradition." *PMLA* 90 (1975): 185–208.

Ortego, Philip. "The Chicano Renaissance." *Social Casework* 52.5 (1971): 294–307.

Ortego y Gasca, Felipe de. "An Introduction to Chicano Poetry." Sommers and Ybarra-Frausto, *Modern Chicano Writers* 108–16.

Ortiz, Alfonso, ed. *New Perspectives on the Pueblos.* Albuquerque: U of New Mexico P, 1972.

Padró, José de Diego. *En Babia.* México: Manuscripto de un Braquicéfalo, 1961.

Paredes, Américo. "Flute Song." Unpub. poem, 1935.

———. "The Folk Base of Chicano Literature." Sommers and Ybarra-Frausto, *Modern Chicano Writers* 4–17.

———. "Guitarreros (Guitarists)." 1935. *Southwest Review* 19 (1964): 306.

———. "The Mexican Corrido: Its Rise and Fall." Boatright, Hudson, and Maxwell, *Madstones and Twisters* 91–105.

———. "Some Aspects of Folk Poetry." *Texas Studies in Literature and Language* 6 (1964): 213–25.

———. "Tributaries to the Main Stream: The Ethnic Groups." Coffin, *Our Living Traditions* 70–80.

———. *"With His Pistol in His Hand": A Border Ballad and Its Hero.* Austin: U of Texas P, 1958.

Paredes, Raymund. "The Evolution of Chicano Literature." Baker, *Three American Literatures* 33–79.

Park, Robert E. *Race and Culture.* Glencoe: Free, 1950.

Parker, Samuel. *Journal of an Exploring Tour beyond the Rocky Mountains.* Ithaca: Mack, 1838.

Parrington, Vernon Louis. *Main Currents in American Thought.* New York: Harcourt, 1930.

Parry, Milman. *The Making of Homeric Verse: The Collected Papers of Milman Parry.* Ed. Adam Parry. Oxford: Clarendon, 1971.

Parsons, Elsie Crew. *Folk-Lore of the Sea Islands, South Carolina.* New York: American Folklore Soc., 1923.

Pascal, Roy. *Design and Truth in Autobiography.* Cambridge: Harvard UP, 1960.

Pearce, Roy Harvey. "Red Gifts and White: The Image in Fiction." Pearce, *Savagism, Savages of America*, 196–236.

———. *Savagism and Civilization: A Study of the Indian and the American Mind.* 1953. Rpt. as *The Savages of America: A Study of the Indian and the Idea of Civilization.* Baltimore: Johns Hopkins UP, 1965. Rpt. under original title. Introd. Arnold Krupat. Afterword Pearce. Berkeley: U of California P, 1988.

———. "The Zero of Human Society: The Idea of the Savage." Pearce, *Savagism, Savages of America*, 105–34.

Phelps, Elizabeth Stuart. *Dr. Zay.* New York: Feminist, 1987.

———. *The Silent Partner.* New York: Feminist, 1983.

———. *The Story of Avis.* Ed. Carol F. Kessler. New Brunswick: Rutgers UP, 1985.

Piercy, Marge. *Braided Lives.* New York: Fawcett, 1982.

Pochmann, Henry A. "The Mingling of Tongues." Spiller et al., *Literary History of the United States.* Rev. ed., 1953. 676–93.

Porter, Dorothy, ed. *Early Negro Writing: 1760–1837.* Boston: Beacon, 1971.

Postell, William D. *The Health of Slaves on Southern Plantations.* Baton Rouge: Louisiana State UP, 1951.

Pratt, Annis. *Archetypal Patterns in Women's Fiction.* Bloomington: Indiana UP, 1981.

Pratt, Mary Louise. *Toward a Speech Act Theory of Literary Discourse.* Bloomington: Indiana UP, 1977.

Pryse, Marjorie, and Hortense J. Spillers, eds. *Conjuring: Black Women, Fiction, and Literary Tradition.* Bloomington: Indiana UP, 1985.

Purdue, Charles L., Jr., Thomas E. Burden, and Robert K. Phillip, eds. *Weevils in the Wheat.* Bloomington: Indiana UP, 1976.

Radin, Paul. *The Trickster: A Study in American Indian Mythology.* Commentaries by Karl Kerenyi and Carl Jung. New introd. Stanley Diamond. 1956. New York: Schocken, 1972.

———. *The Winnebago Tribe.* Annual Report of the Bureau of American Ethnology 37 (1915–16). Lincoln: U of Nebraska P, 1970, 1990.

Rampersad, Arnold. "Biography, Autobiography, and Afro-American Culture." *Yale Review* 73 (1983): 1–16.

Ramsey, Jarold. "The Bible in Western Indian Mythology." *Journal of American Folklore* 90 (1977): 442–54. Rpt. in Ramsey, *Reading the Fire* 166–80.

———, ed. *Coyote Was Going There: Indian Literature of the Oregon Country.* Seattle: U of Washington P, 1977.

———. *Reading the Fire: Essays in the Traditional Indian Literatures of the Far West.* Lincoln: U of Nebraska P, 1983.

———. "The Teacher of Modern American Indian Writing as Ethnographer and Critic." *College English* 41 (1979): 163–69.

———. "The Wife Who Goes Out Like a Man, Comes Back as a Hero: The Art of Two Oregon Indian Stories." *PMLA* 92 (1977): 9–18. Rev. and expanded in Ramsey, *Reading the Fire* 76–95.

Redfield, Robert. "The Social Organization of Tradition." *Far Eastern Quarterly* 15.1 (Nov. 1955): 13–21.

Reed, Ishmael, and Al Young, eds. *Yardbird Lives!* New York: Grove, 1978.

Ricketts, Mac Linscott. "The North American Indian Trickster." *History of Religions* 5 (1966): 327–50.

Rodríguez, Emilio Jorge. "Apuntes sobre la visión del emigrante en la narrativa puertorriqueña." *Primer seminario sobre la situacion de las comunidades negra, chicana, cubana, india y puertorriqueña en Estados Unidos.* Habana: Política, 1984. 445–85.

Rodriguez, Juan. "El desarollo del cuento Chicano: Del folklore al tenebroso mundo del yo." *The Identification and Analysis of Chicano Literature.* Ed. Francisco Jimenez. New York: Bilingual, 1979. 58–67.

Rogers, Jane. "The Function of the *la llorona* Motif in Rudolfo Anaya's *Bless Me, Ultima.*" *Latin American Literature Review* 5 (1977): 64–69.

Romano-V., Octavio, and Herminio Rios-C., eds. *El espejo / The Mirror: Selected Mexican American Literature.* Berkeley: Quinto Sol, 1969.

Rosenberg, Bruce A. "Literature and Folklore." *Interrelations of Literature.* Ed. Jean-Pierre Barricelli and Joseph Gibaldi. New York: MLA, 1982. 90–106.

Rothenberg, Jerome. *Pre-Faces and Other Writings.* New York: New Directions, 1981.

———. *Shaking the Pumpkin.* Garden City: Doubleday, 1972.

———. *Technicians of the Sacred.* Garden City: Doubleday, 1968.

Ruch, E. A., and K. C. Anyanwu. *African Philosophy.* Rome: Catholic Book Agency, 1984.

Sabin, Joseph. *A Dictionary of Books Relating to America, from Its Discovery to the Present Time.* New York: Sabin, 1868.

Sacco, Nicola, and Bartolomeo Vanzetti. *The Letters of Sacco and Vanzetti.* Ed. Marion D. Frankfurter and Gardner Jackson. New York: Dutton, 1960.

Sagel, Jim. *Tunomás Honey.* Havana: Casa de las Américas, 1981.

Saldívar, José David, ed. *The Rolando Hinojosa Reader: Essays Historical and Critical.* Houston: Arte Público, 1984.

Saldívar, Ramon. "*Korean Love Songs*: A Border Ballad and Its Heroes." J. D. Saldívar, *Rolando Hinojosa Reader* 143–57.

Salwen, Bert. "Indians of Southern New England and Long Island." Trigger, *Northeast* 160–76.

Sands, Kathleen Mullen. "Indian Women's Personal Narrative: Voices Past and Present." *American Women's Autobiography.* Ed. Margot Culley. Madison: U of Wisconsin P, forthcoming.

Santiago, Danny. *See* James, Daniel.

Sartre, Jean-Paul. *Being and Nothingness: An Essay on Phenomenological Ontology.* Trans. Hazel E. Barnes. New York: Philosophical Library, 1956.

Sayre, Robert. *Thoreau and the American Indians.* Princeton: Princeton UP, 1977.

Scholes, Robert, and Robert Kellogg. *The Nature of Narrative.* 1966. London: Oxford UP, 1979.

Schoolcraft, Henry Rowe. *Algic Researches, Comprising Inquiries Respecting the Mental Characteristics of the North American Indian.* 2 vols. New York: Harper, 1839.

———. *The Indian in His Wigwam: Or, Characteristics of the Red Race of America*. New York: Graham, 1848.

———. *Schoolcraft's Indian Legends*. Ed. Mentor C. Williams. East Lansing: Michigan State UP, 1956.

Schultz, Elizabeth. "To Be Black and Blue: The Blues Genre in Black American Autobiography." *Kansas Quarterly* 7 (1975): 81–96.

Searle, John. *Speech Acts*. London: Cambridge UP, 1965.

Selzer, Chester. *See* Muro, Amado.

Shea, Daniel B., Jr. *Spiritual Autobiography in Early America*. Princeton: Princeton UP, 1968.

Shelston, Alan. *Biography*. London: Methuen, 1977.

Sherzer, Joel. *Kuna Ways of Speaking*. Austin: U of Texas P, 1983.

———. "Strategies in Text and Context: Cuna *kaa kwento*." *Journal of American Folklore* 92 (1979): 145–83.

Sherzer, Joel, and Anthony Woodbury, eds. *Native American Discourse*. New York: Cambridge UP, 1987.

Shumaker, Wayne. *Literature and the Irrational: A Study of Anthropological Backgrounds*. Englewood Cliffs: Prentice, 1960.

Sidney, Sir Philip. *A Defense of Poesy*. Ed. Lewis Jones. Lincoln: U of Nebraska P, 1970.

"Slavery in a 'Migrant Stream.'" *Philadelphia Inquirer* 17 Jan. 1982: 1.

Sledge, Linda Ching. "Maxine Hong Kingston's *China Men*: The Family Historian as Epic Poet." *MELUS* 7.4 (1980): 3–22.

Slotkin, Richard. *Regeneration through Violence: The Mythology of the American Frontier, 1600–1860*. Middletown: Wesleyan UP, 1973.

Smith, Barbara Herrnstein. *On the Margins of Discourse*. Chicago: U of Chicago P, 1978.

Smith, Donald B. "Kahgegagahbowh." *Dictionary of Canadian Biography*. Ed. George W. Brown et al. 1961–70 ed. 9: 419–21.

———. "The Life of George Copway or Kah-ge-ga-gah-bowh (1818–1869) and a Review of His Writings." *Journal of Canadian Studies* 23.3 (1988): 5–38.

Smith, Frank. *Understanding Reading: A Psycholinguistic Analysis*. 3rd ed. New York: Holt, 1982.

Smith, Henry Nash. "The Widening of Horizons." Spiller et al., *Literary History of the United States*. Rev. ed., 1953. 639–51.

Smith, Sidonie. *A Poetics of Women's Autobiography: Marginality and the Fictions of Self-Representation*. Bloomington: Indiana UP, 1987.

———. *Where I'm Bound: Patterns of Slavery and Freedom in Black American Autobiography*. Westport: Greenwood, 1974.

Snyder, Gary. "The Incredible Survival of Coyote." *The Old Ways*. San Francisco: City Lights, 1977. 67–93.

Sollors, Werner. *Beyond Ethnicity*. New York: Oxford UP, 1986.

Sommers, Joseph. "Critical Approaches to Chicano Literature." Sommers and Ybarra-Frausto, *Modern Chicano Writers* 51–80.

Sommers, Joseph, and Tomás Ybarra-Frausto, eds. *Modern Chicano Writers: A Collection of Critical Essays*. Englewood Cliffs: Prentice, 1979.

Speck, Frank. "Penobscot Transformer Tales." *International Journal of American Linguistics* 1 (1918): 187–245.

Spencer, Benjamin T. *The Quest for Nationality: An American Literary Campaign*. Syracuse: Syracuse UP, 1957.

Spengemann, William C. *The Forms of Autobiography*. New Haven: Yale UP, 1980.

Spiller, Robert E. "The Cycle and the Roots: National Identity in American Literature." *Toward a New American Literary History*. Ed. Louis J. Budd, Edwin H. Cady, and Carl L. Anderson. Durham: Duke UP, 1980. 3–18.

Spiller, Robert E., et al. *Literary History of the United States*. Rev. ed. New York: Macmillan, 1953. 3rd ed. New York: Macmillan, 1963. 4th rev. ed. New York: Macmillan, 1974.

Stahl, Sandra K. D. "Studying Folklore and American Literature." Dorson et al., *Handbook of American Folklore* 422–533.

Starr, G. A. *Defoe and Spiritual Autobiography*. Princeton: Princeton UP, 1965.

Steiner, George. *After Babel: Aspects of Language and Translation*. London: Oxford UP, 1975.

Stepto, Robert B. *From behind the Veil: A Study of Afro-American Narratives*. Urbana: U of Illinois P, 1979.

——. "Make One Music as Before: Toward a Greater Balance in American Literary Studies." Unpublished essay. Cited by permission.

Stevens, Philips, Jr. "The Bachama Trickster as a Model for Clowning Behavior." *Rice University Studies* 66 (1980): 137–50.

Steward, Julian H., and Erminie Wheeler-Voegelin. *The Northern Paiute Indians*. Vol. 3 of *The Paiute Indians*. New York: Garland, 1974.

Stewart, Patricia. "Sarah Winnemucca." *Nevada Historical Quarterly* 14 (1971): 23–38.

Stewart, Susan. *Nonsense: Aspects of Inter-textuality in Folklore and Literature*. Baltimore: Johns Hopkins UP, 1978.

Stolz, B. A., and R. S. Shannon. *Oral Literature and the Formula*. Ann Arbor: Center for Coordination of Ancient and Modern Studies, Univ. of Michigan, 1976.

Sui Sin Far [pseud. of Edith Eaton]. "Leaves from the Mental Portfolio of an Eurasian." *Independent* 21 Jan. 1909: 125–32.

Sundquist, Eric J., ed. *New Essays on* Uncle Tom's Cabin. New York: Cambridge UP, 1986.

Sung, Betty Lee. *Mountain of Gold*. New York: Macmillan, 1967.

Swann, Brian, ed. *Smoothing the Ground: Essays on Native American Oral Literature*. Berkeley: U of California P, 1983.

Swann, Brian, and Arnold Krupat, eds. *Recovering the Word: Essays on Native American Literature*. Berkeley: U of California P, 1987.

Swann, Thomas E., and Katsuhiko Takeda. *Essays on Japanese Literature*. Tokyo: Waseda-Daigaku-Shuppanbu, 1969.

Tannacito, Dan. "Poetry of the Colorado Miners, 1903–1906." *Radical Teacher* 15 (Mar. 1980): 1–15.

Tax, Sol, et al., eds. *An Appraisal of Anthropology Today*. Chicago: U of Chicago P, 1953.

Tedlock, Dennis, trans. *Finding the Center: Narrative Poetry of the Zuni Indians*. Lincoln: U of Nebraska P, 1972.

——. "On the Translation of Style in Oral Narrative." *Journal of American Folklore* 84 (1971): 114–33. Rpt. in Tedlock, *Spoken Word* 31–61.

——. "Pueblo Literature: Style and Verisimilitude." Ortiz, *New Perspectives on the Pueblos*. Rpt. as "The Poetics of Verisimilitude" in Tedlock, *Spoken Word* 159–77.

——. *The Spoken Word and the Work of Interpretation*. Conduct and Communication. Philadelphia: U of Pennsylvania P, 1983.

——. "Toward an Oral Poetics." *New Literary History* 8 (1977): 507–19.

Thanet, Octave. "Folklore in Arkansas." *Journal of American Folklore* 5 (1892): 121–25.

Thomas, Lewis. "Paradoxes." *The Dial* Jan. 1982: 32–33.

Thompson, Stith. *The Folktale*. New York: Holt, 1946.

——. "The Indian Heritage." Spiller, *Literary History of the United States*. Rev. ed., 1953. 694–702.

——. *Tales of the North American Indians*. 1929. Bloomington: Indiana UP, 1966.

Thoreau, Henry David. *The Maine Woods*. Ed. Joseph J. Moldenhauer. Princeton: Princeton UP, 1972.

Three Thousand Futures: Final Report of the Carnegie Council on Policy Studies in Higher Education. San Francisco: Jossey, 1981.